The Laws of Islam

Āyatullāh Sayyid Muḥammad Taqī al-Mudarrisī al-Ḥusaynī

Table of Contents

Part One: Islamic Doctrines from the Qur'ān and *Sunna*

Introduction

Who am I? Where did I come from? Where am I going? What is my moral responsibility towards myself and others? The human being asks himself these and tens of other crucial questions from time to time, but can find no satisfactory answer unless he listens to the call of revelation. When he does this, his heart responds to the call as a parched tongue responds to drinking cool water.

And the more he becomes aware of the verses of the Qur'ān and the words of the Prophet and his Household ﷺ which explain them, the more open his intellect, the more tranquil his conscience, and the more restful his spirit becomes. In this way, scripture incites the intellect to find the correct beliefs, and awakens the conscience.

Our early jurists followed an excellent practice: before writing a treatise on the laws and practices of Islam, they would first lay out the doctrines and beliefs of Islam. We would like to follow this excellent practice in a concise manner in this book.

We ask Allah, the High and Mighty, to let both the author and reader benefit together from this undertaking and recompense them with the best rewards in this world and the hereafter. Verily He is All-hearing of supplication!

Why do we discuss beliefs?

Why should we study doctrines and believe in them on the basis of knowledge, awareness and insight?

Because beliefs show the human being where he came from, where he is going, and how he will get there in this life and the next. Anyone who does not study his beliefs with insight might think that he is on the path to salvation, while in reality he follows a miserable path in this world and is heading to Hellfire in the next! Someone like this has lost his worldly life as well as his hereafter, and who could be more miserable than someone who has lost both of these things? Allah says in the Qur'ān: '**Say, "Shall we inform you about the**

biggest losers in regard to works? Those whose endeavours go awry in the life of the world, while they suppose they are doing good."'[1]

There are three different approaches to the study of our beliefs:

1. **The philosophical approach:** This relies on Aristotelian logic, Greek philosophy, and Islamic theology that drew inspiration from them. Studying beliefs using the framework of philosophy is problematic, however, because philosophy is contaminated with the ideas of idol-worshippers. Islam, however, provides man with a new, monotheistic beginning that has been revealed to him from the Unseen, along with its own framework that is suited to it. Forcing philosophical concepts, methods and terms into its theoretical structure will invariably taint it, imbalance it, and destroy its own internal unity. The Commander of the Faithful ﷷ described the first person to undertake this erroneous endeavour amongst the Muslims as 'The Zimri (Sāmirī) of this nation'[2] because he replaced the worship of Allah, the One, with the worship of heretical conjecture when he polluted the pure message of Islam with the philosophy of idol-worshipping Greeks.
2. **The mystical approach:** This approach relies on immersing oneself in asceticism. It considers the human being to be essentially evil and fallible, and thinks that the human being annihilating himself in the darkness of non-existence and negation is the correct way to arrive at the truth. We think that this erroneous idea was borrowed from Hindu and other far eastern philosophies, which arrived in the Muslim world at the beginning of the second Islamic century with the emergence of the translation movement amongst the Muslims. This approach denies the role of reason in apprehending the truths of the universe; it calls for the negation of organized religion and a reliance of spiritual purity, which ultimately leads to introversion and detachment. In truth, the distance between this approach and the spirit of Islam is like the distance between Islam from the spirit of pre-Islamic age of ignorance.[3]
3. **The Qur'ānic approach** to studying beliefs is the approach inspired by the wise revelation of the Qur'ān and which rests on the firm principles of human nature, free from the motivations of desire or anger. The distinctive features of the Qur'ānic approach are: Awakening human

---

[1] Sūrat al-Kahf (18):103-104

[2] *Biḥār al-anwār* 42/141, ch. 123, ḥ. 2 – this is an allusion to the *Sāmirī*.

[3] For more on this, you can refer to the author's other works: *al-Fikr al-islāmī muwajihat ḥadāriyya* and *al-'Irfān al-islāmī*.

awareness, kindling the intellect, calling humanity to pondering and reflection, directing people to examine life to know its depths, and to reach its depths and speak to its pure spirit. The methods laid down by the *aḥādīth* in this approach are: Remembrance and awakening, and keeping away completely from hypocrisy, contrarianism, and arrogance towards the truth.

It is the Muslim's duty to follow the last approach in learning about his beliefs, because Islam cannot be understood in any way except that which the Creator has laid down. It is the direct way, plainly delineated, with clear explanations, that accords with human nature and the exigencies of life.

For this reason, our approach here, in concisely discussing the doctrines of Islam is to take inspiration from the noble Qur'ān and the *sunna* which explains it, without trying to interpret the verses of the Qur'ān according to ideas that are alien to it.

First: About Divine Unity (*Tawḥīd*)

Divine Unity in the Qur'ān

We cannot escape the darkness of polytheism if we do not first escape the prison of the soul, which is held captive by the inclinations of the self. If you reflect seriously, you will see that the root of every kind of disbelief, polytheism, and sinfulness is love of the self and its desires. Even those who worshipped idols or false gods only worshipped their own desires in the form of these false gods, and their own lusts in the shape of idols. So when you escape the love of your own self, and leave the darkness of desire, you find yourself in the vastness of Divine Unity by Allah's leave, with no chains and no limitations. Your gateway to understanding Divine Unity is the *sūra* (chapter) of the Qur'an, *al-Ikhlāṣ*, which summarizes all the insights of revelation in knowledge of the divine in a few short sentences:

In the Name of Allah, the All-beneficent, the All-merciful,

Say, 'He is Allah, the One (*aḥad*).

Allah is the All-embracing (*ṣamad*).

He neither begat, nor was begotten,

nor has He any equal.'

Although the Arabic word, *aḥad* (meaning 'one') is derived from *wāhid* (which also means 'one'), it is a more eloquent expression of Allah's oneness (*waḥdāniyya*): namely, that He has no equal and no partner; no limbs and no parts, whether these be real, conceptual, or imagined. The words *aḥad* and *wāḥid* do not mean He is one as opposed to two, or one of a group of entities. Rather, they mean that He is one without number, utterly alone, and without anything similar or comparable.

Allah's absolute oneness (*aḥadiyya*) manifests in recognizing His complete authority over everything; that He does whatever He wills; that it is His right to be worshipped and that whatever is worshipped besides Him is nothing.

Another manifestation of Allah's absolute oneness is that He is the All-embracing (*ṣamad*), which encompasses various realities that can be comprehended with a single insight; namely that Allah has neither limbs, nor parts, nor transient states.

His quality of being All-embracing also manifests in the fact that He neither begat, nor was begotten, in that the act of begetting shows that something has been added to Him that was not previously there, or that something that was previously there has been separated from Him. But because the All-embracing has no parts, we cannot conceive of Him being increased (by being begotten) or decreased (by begetting).

By grasping that Allah is All-embracing, without parts or development, and that He is neither begat nor begotten, we will have lifted the greatest veil separating us from Allah, namely the veil of making Allah similar to His creation (*tashbīh* – anthropomorphism) which emanates from Man's ignorance and lack of education. Because Man sees only himself and his fellow creatures, he compares his Creator to himself sometimes and to his fellow creatures at others, forgetting that such a comparison does away with the very idea of the Creator, in that we read at the end of *Sūrat al-Ikhlāṣ*: **'nor has He any equal.'**

The greatest witness

Allah says: **'Say, "What thing is greatest as witness?" Say, "Allah! [He is] witness between me and you, and this Qur'ān has been revealed to me that I may warn thereby you and whomever it may reach." "Do you indeed bear witness that there are other gods besides Allah?" Say, "I do not bear witness**

[to any such thing]." Say, "Indeed He is the One God, and I indeed disown what you associate [with Him].""[4]

Events flow seamlessly into one another and life is thrown around like a ship upon a stormy sea, but behind this apparent chaos there is finely-tuned order which drives it. Allah is behind this order, controlling it and directing it. Allah is the Unseen of the universe – of whom no place is devoid – and a witness over all things, present with all things. Everything is a sign pointing towards Him because everything is created by Him, with Him, and going towards Him. Therefore, Allah is the greatest witness of all. He guides to His being through His own being, and guides mankind to everything; He gave you hearing, sight and the ability to reflect, and manifested Himself through the festival that is life. You live with Him in every moment and in everything. You still could go away from your Lord (though He never leaves you), but He is very close at hand: all that is between you and Him is a moment of attentiveness. To help you reach Him and elevate your soul to the level of living with your Lord, He has sent prophets to mankind and furnished them with scriptures to warn you, because warning people is the quickest way to reach their hearts.

One God

Allah says: **'And Allah has said, "Do not worship two gods. Indeed He is the One God, so be in awe of Me [alone]." To Him belongs whatever is in the heavens and the earth, and to Him belongs the enduring religion. Will you, then, be wary of other than Allah?'[5]**

A disbeliever (*kāfir*) is someone who submits to that which itself submits to Allah: he submits himself to the Sun, the Moon, the stars; to lights, trees, and stones; to riches, power, and propaganda. But why should Man fear natural phenomena and worship them instead of Allah, and why should he fear false gods and surrender to them?

Most of the time, when people worship things it is out of fear and reverence. So let this fear of things be cast aside, and let us fear their Lord and Creator instead!

Once we have transcended this fear of natural phenomena, and guarded ourselves against their reverence, we will have submitted our countenance to the

---

[4] Sūrat al-Anʿām (6):19
[5] Sūrat al-Naḥl (16):51-52

Lord of the Worlds, and surrendered to His governance and authority alone, and therefore to His pure religion.

Complete belief in Divine Unity

Allah says: **'There is certainly a good exemplar for you in Abraham and those who were with him, when they said to their own people, "Indeed we repudiate you and whatever you worship besides Allah. We disavow you, and between you and us there has appeared enmity and hate for ever, unless you come to have faith in Allah alone," except for Abraham's saying to his father, "I will surely plead forgiveness for you, though I cannot avail you anything against Allah." "Our Lord! In You do we put our trust, and to You do we turn penitently, and toward You is the destination."'**[6]

The belief of a servant of Allah in his Lord is not complete unless he disassociates from everything besides Allah, casts aside the worship of anything other than Allah, and refuses to submit to anyone who disbelieves in Allah. Belief in Allah is completed through rejection of superstitions and false deities.

Abraham ﷺ, for example, was an orphan who needed social and economic protection, but he would not submit to his uncle, Terah, who worshipped idols, in order to obtain that protection. Instead, he embarked on his own monotheistic course by holding fast to his belief in Divine Unity and rejecting everything besides Allah. He did not confront the faithless while relying on his uncle and his people, rather he confronted his own people beginning with his uncle, and challenged every kind of polytheism beginning with that of his own people. In doing so, he became an exemplar for how the faithful can complete their belief in Allah and His Divine Unity by rejecting everything besides Him.

Divine Unity in the *sunna*

The right way to know Allah

How can we achieve knowledge of Allah, and what is the right way to know Him? When is our belief in His Divine Unity free from impurity? Let us heed the words of Allah's Messenger ﷺ when someone asked him: 'What is the head of knowledge?' He said: 'Knowing Allah as He deserves to be known.' The questioner asked: 'And what is the way in which He deserves to be known?' The Prophet ﷺ told him: 'That you know Him without similitude or likeness, and you know of Him as One (*wāḥid*), a Creator (*khāliq*), Powerful (*qādir*), First,

---

[6] Sūrat al-Mumtaḥana (60):4

Last, Manifest (*ẓāhir*) and Hidden (*bāṭin*), without equal or likeness. That is knowing Allah as He deserves to be known.'[7]

'I call to Allah…'

In all the ups and downs of life that affect every aspect of man's existence, are the effects of Allah's power and authority; when man is afflicted by some hardship, he seeks refuge with Allah and invokes Him to remove this hardship from him and senses His infinite power; and when he suffers some distress, he seeks Allah's help to overcome it. This is true in all the vicissitudes of life.

There came to the Prophet ﷺ a man called Abū Umayya from the Tamīm tribe. He asked: 'O Muḥammad, to what do you call people?' Allah's Messenger ﷺ replied: 'I call to Allah upon insight, me and those who follow me; I call to one who when you are afflicted by hardship and invoke Him, He removes it from you, and who helps you when you seek His assistance in distress, and who will enrich you if you ask Him when you are in need.'[8]

By what means did you know your Lord?

When man contemplates on the creation and the Creator, he knows – through his own innate nature – the difference between the two: created things are limited in dimensions and have material forms which can be sensed and touched; they can be near one place and far from another; they produce one another in succession and consume one another, etc. The Creator, however, has no similarity to His creation in any of that; utterly glorified and exalted is He above all of that.

Someone asked Imam ʿAlī ؑ, the Commander of the Faithful: 'By what means did you know your Lord?' He replied: 'He made me know Himself.' The questioner asked: 'How did He make you know Himself?' He replied: 'No form resembles Him; the senses do not perceive Him; He is not comparable to people. He is imminent in transcendence, transcendent in imminence. Above all things and without anything said to be above him. He is in front of everything, without being said to have a front. He is within everything, but not like one thing within another. He is beyond everything, but not like one thing outside another. Glory be to He who is like this; nothing but He is like this. Everything has a beginning.'[9]

---

[7] *Biḥār al-anwār* 3/14
[8] *Tuḥāf al-ʿuqūl* 35
[9] *Uṣūl al-kāfi* 1/67

Negation of attributes

When we ponder over creation, we see that it has attributes of deficiency and weakness, and these transform into attributes of perfection and strength, before again returning to their original deficiency. An ignorant man becomes knowledgeable through learning, only to return to ignorance through forgetfulness and error. One who is weak becomes strong through exercise, only to return to weakness through illness and old age. One who is small grows large, then diminishes again. One who is poor becomes wealthy through earning, but becomes poor again when he loses everything, and so on and so forth. But these attributes and vicissitudes do not apply to the Creator, for Divine Unity means negating all such attributes from Him. For the appearance and disappearance of these attributes demonstrate that such a thing has been created, while Allah is the Creator and not created Himself. Here we should heed the words of the Commander of the Faithful 🕮, for they are an eloquent lesson in Divine Unity:

'The foremost of Allah's worship is knowing Him, and the root of knowing Him is Divine Unity, and the order of Divine Unity is negating attributes from Him. He is beyond having attributes, because reason testifies that everything with attributes is created, and that He is a creator who has not been created. So by Allah's act of creation, we are guided towards Him; by the intellect is knowledge of Him obtained; by pondering is His authority (*hujja*) established. He made creation evidence of Himself and thereby disclosed His lordship (*rubūbiyya*). He is One and Unique in pre-eternity, without partner in divinity, and without equal in lordship.'[10]

The lowest degree of knowledge

What is the lowest degree of knowing Allah? Imam ʿAlī 🕮 answered this question in the narration of al-Fath b. Yazīd, who asked him what the lowest degree of knowledge was. The Imam 🕮 said: 'Affirming that there is no god except He, that He is without likeness or peer, that He is eternal and unchanging, existent without deficiency, and that there is nothing that resembles Him.'[11]

'Do not contemplate Allah's essence...'

Since Allah is our maker and creator, He is greater than us; He encompasses us in knowledge but we do not Him. So why do we contemplate

---

[10] *Bihār al-anwār* 4/253
[11] *Uṣūl al-kāfī* 1/67

Allah's essence when such contemplation only increases man in confusion and error? That is why the *sunna* prohibits it:

Imam al-Bāqir ﵇ said: 'Beware of contemplating Allah's essence! If you wish to see His greatness, then look to the great things He has created.'[12]

Imam al-Ṣādiq ﵇ said: 'Beware of contemplating Allah's essence! Contemplating Allah's essence only increases people in confusion. Allah cannot be apprehended by the sights, nor can He be attributed a quantity.'[13]

Imam al-Bāqir ﵇ said: 'Speak of Allah's creation, but do not speak of Allah's essence, for speaking of Allah's essence only increases one in confusion!'[14]

The value of Divine Unity

If knowing Allah is the foremost way to to worship Him, and Divine Unity is the foundation of knowing Him – as we saw in the aforementioned narration from the Commander of the Faithful ﵇ – then Divine Unity is the basis of everything in life, as it is on this basis, or the lack thereof, that a person earns Paradise of Hellfire. Divine Unity is the gate of Paradise, and associating partners with Allah is a grave sin for which Allah will cast someone into Hellfire. Allah's Messenger ﷺ said: '[Belief in] divine unity is the price of Paradise.'[15]

---

[12] *Uṣūl al-kāfī* 1/73
[13] *Biḥār al-anwār* 3/259
[14] *Uṣūl al-kāfī* 1/72
[15] *Uṣūl al-kāfī* 1/73

Second: Concerning Divine Justice (*ʿAdl*)

Divine Justice in the Qurʾān

One of Allah's greatest attributes is the justice with which He makes flow throughout the Universe, in that He lays down practices (*sunan*) for life which He implements by His power and authority, such that he does not let one side thereof cover another. To mankind alone He gave the gift of freedom, but this freedom is limited by time; after this time expires man will return to his limits by force if he has not already returned to them through guidance. And who better to do justice in life than the Almighty (the powerful) and All-wise (who is aware of everything)? Allah says: **'Allah bears witness that there is no god except Him - and [so do] the angels and those who possess knowledge - maintainer of justice, there is no god but Him, the Almighty, the All-wise.'**[16]

He wrongs no one

Allah says: **'Indeed Allah does not wrong [anyone] [even to the extent of] an atom's weight.'**[17]

One of the most visible manifestations of Allah's justice is that he never wrongs anyone, not even to the extent of an atom's weight. He recompenses people exactly as they deserve: if someone disbelieves to the extent of an atom, He will recompense him only to the extent of his disbelief and not a fraction more. But if someone does good to the extent of an atom's weight, his work will not be wasted: **'So whoever does an atom's weight of good will see it, and whoever does an atom's weight of evil will see it.'**[18]

Allah says: **'Indeed Allah does not wrong people in the least; rather it is people who wrong themselves.'**[19]

Thus, when a person closes his eyes and ears to the waves of divine guidance, he cannot then claim that Allah has wronged him by depriving him of sight and hearing! Allah does not wrong anyone. Rather it is the human being himself that does not benefit from his sight and hearing, and therefore wrongs himself. So people do not benefit from the senses with which Allah has endowed them to be guided with. Perhaps the reason the Qurʾān uses the words 'people' and 'themselves' here, because people wrong one another by leading each other

---

[16] Sūrat Āl ʿImrān (3):18
[17] Sūrat al-Nisāʾ (4):40
[18] Sūrat al-Zalzala (99):7-8
[19] Sūrat Yūnus (10):44

astray from the path of guidance, and therefore they are also responsible for guiding one another.

The scales of justice

Allah says: 'We shall set up the scales of justice on the Day of Resurrection, and no soul will be wronged in the least. Even if it be the weight of a mustard seed We shall produce it and We suffice as reckoners.'[20]

On the Resurrection Day, each person will face his recompense in the form of a precise and difficult accounting; good shall be requited with good, and evil with evil. Allah is exalted above wronging anyone in any matter; even if someone does good to the weight of a mustard seed anywhere on the face of the earth, whether openly or secretly, Allah will bring its record – through His infinite power and knowledge – and display it to its owner on the Resurrection Day, before giving Him his recompense.

Divine Justice in the *Sunna*

He is justice

There is no doubt that Allah has power over all things. In the blink of an eye, He can cause guidance to sprout in the hearts of those who are astray, or lead astray the rightly guided. But never would He use His power to wrong His servants; when guidance is firmly rooted in a person's heart, Allah will not wrong him by tearing it out.

Someone asked Imam al-Ṣādiq 🕮: 'Is it possible for a man to be a believer of firm faith, only for Allah to move him after faith to disbelief?' The Imam 🕮 replied: 'Allah is justice; He only sent messengers to call people to faith in Allah – they do not call anyone to disbelief.'[21]

One who does not know Allah

There are some people in life who shirk responsibility for their evil deeds by putting the burden of their sins upon Allah, and claiming that He intended them to commit those sins. Had it not been such, they would not have sinned! But this view contradicts Allah's divine justice.

---

[20] Sūrat al-Anbiyāʾ (21):47
[21] *Biḥār al-anwār* 11/40

Imam al-Riḍā ﷺ said: 'One who makes Allah similar to His creation does not know Him, nor does one who blames Him for the sins of His servants call Him just.'[22]

Allah is too generous...

Because Allah is just, He does not burden anyone with a duty that he cannot fulfil, as this is another kind of wrongdoing and Allah is glorified above all levels and types of wrongdoing. Imam al-Ṣādiq ﷺ has said: 'Allah is too generous to burden people with what they cannot bear, and Allah is too mighty that anything could happen in His domain save what He wills.'[23]

He tests whomsoever He wills

Why do we find some people rich and others poor? Is it not better that Allah divide people's sustenance equally so that there will be no rich and no poor? No, because equality does not always mean justice. The abode of this world is an abode of trial and tribulation, and one of the ways in which people are tested is through abundance or shortage of sustenance. The Commander of the Faithful, ʿAlī b. Abī Ṭālib ﷺ said: 'He apportioned people's sustenance; to some He gave much and to others less. He divided them in abundance and shortage, and He did justice in sustenance to test whomever He wills with hardship and ease, to discover thereby who amongst the rich and poor would give thanks, and who would be patient...'[24]

---

[22] *Biḥār al-anwār* 5/29
[23] *Biḥār al-anwār* 5/29
[24] *Biḥār al-anwār* 5/148

Third: Concerning Divine Messages and Messengers

The Message in the Qur'ān

Allah says: **'Certainly We sent Our Messengers with manifest proofs, and We sent down with them the Book and the Balance, so that mankind may maintain justice; and We sent down iron, in which there is great might and uses for mankind, and so that Allah may know those who help Him and His Messengers in [their] absence. Indeed Allah is all-strong, all-mighty.'**[25]

Allah sent messengers to guide people to Him and help them know Him; they bear the special responsibility of conveying the message of the Creator to His creation; guiding them to know Him, to believe in Him, and to follow His message to them. Messengers are ambassadors from the Creator to His creation, and the 'Rope of Allah' extended between the heavens and the earth.

But how do we know that someone who claims to have a message from Allah is truly a prophet and not a charlatan? The Qur'ān answers: **'with manifest proofs'** – *bayyināt* – and this word has two meanings, both of which appear to be intended by this verse:

First: Detailed guidance exemplified by insights and approaches that flow from them. The fact that the messages of the prophets contain such guidance demonstrates that they are a revelation sent by Allah. Perhaps a person, through the purity of their soul, could realize some spiritual truths, but when could such a person ever bring a complete way of life comprising such spiritual insights? This shows that he has a direct connection to revelation.

Second: Proofs and signs which overcome people's hearts and minds, such as miracles, freedom from desires or self-interest, and dedication to the truth. This shows us that the divine messages rests, before anything else, upon conviction, because that is what puts faith in someone's heart and drives him to strive more than any other motivation. Likewise, whenever a person of faith fails to respond to the messenger or revelation, this indicates that his conviction is shaky.

Faith in messengers is fruitless unless it leads to an educational, social, economic, political, and cultural program encompassing all aspects of life, and guaranteeing happiness for mankind. Along with these manifest proofs, Allah

---

[25] Sūrat al-Ḥadīd (57):25

sent down a complete code of practice, represented by the Book: '**and We sent down with them the Book.**'

Messengers and man's responsibility

The goal of sending messengers is not to deprive people of responsibility for their own affairs and burden the prophets with this, as some claim. One such group claims that a messenger came only to be responsible in place of the people, or to compel them to be guided, or to practically guarantee them all the means of happiness. But Allah refutes this claim by saying: '**We do not send the Messengers except as bearers of good news and warners. As for those who are faithful and righteous, they will have no fear, nor will they grieve.**'[26]

The purpose of sending messengers is to provide the means of obtaining security in one's heart and in the world. That those who believe in the messengers and follow them shall have no fear in the future shows they enjoy a state of inner peace, and that they will not grieve for the past shows that they will enjoy peace in the world as well. Grief will afflict them either, because they hold fast to the way of the messengers.

The purpose of messengers

The purpose of sending messengers was to give glad tidings of a better life and warn people against destruction, so that no one can say tomorrow: 'Our Lord! Why did you not send messengers to us, so that we would not go astray or perish?' This rational goal is clear evidence that Allah has certainty sent messengers, because Allah is certainly *capable* of sending messengers, and because He is wise; He will not punish people if they have a valid excuse. Allah says: '**Messengers, as bearers of good news and warners, so that mankind may not have any argument against Allah, after the [sending of the] Messengers; and Allah is all-mighty, all-wise.**'[27]

No compulsion

One of the effects of Allah's mercy is that He does not rush to send down punishments on His servants as soon as they go astray from the right path, which puts them on a collision course with the Divine Practice. No, rather Allah only warns them through His messengers.

If you have ever seen a child doing something dangerous, were you not worried that they might hurt themselves, and so rushed to stop them? That is how Allah's messengers try to stop entire nations falling victim to false beliefs.

---

[26] Sūrat al-Anʿām (6):48
[27] Sūrat al-Nisāʾ (4):165

This does not mean that they compel people to be guided. Rather, those who sin are only exposing themselves to their Lord's punishment in the end, whereas it is the right of those who believe in the messengers that Allah help them. Allah says: **'Certainly We sent Messengers to their people before you, and they brought them manifest proofs. Then We took vengeance upon those who were guilty, and it was a must for Us to help the faithful.'**[28]

The Messenger in the Qurʾān

For all mankind

Allah says: **'We did not send you except as a bearer of good news and warner to all mankind, but most people do not know.'**[29]

What distinguishes Allah's Messenger ﷺ from all other prophets عليهم السلام is that he was sent for all mankind; his mission was neither for one group of people but not another, nor for one nation but not another. This in itself demonstrates the truth of his message, because however hard a person tries to detach himself, he will always be a product of his environment, whose cultural traits he reflects just as readily as its physical ones. So when the Messenger comes with a message that transcends national, tribal, or racial affiliations in theory and practice, this demonstrates that it is a divine message.

The Messenger is an exemplar

Allah says: **'In the Messenger of Allah there is certainly for you a good exemplar, for those who look forward to Allah and the Last Day, and remember Allah greatly.'**[30]

Knowing the Messenger and following him is impossible for anyone who does not already know and believe in Allah, because the Messenger has come from Allah; and the more a person knows his Lord, the more he knows his Lord's chosen prophet. In one supplication, we read: 'O Allah! Let me know Your being, for if You do not let me know Your being, I would not know Your prophet. O Allah! Let me know Your prophet, for if You do not let me know Your prophet, I would not know Your authority (*ḥujja*). O Allah! Let me know Your authority, for if you do not let me know Your authority, I would go astray in my religion.'

---

[28] Sūrat al-Rūm (30):47
[29] Sūrat al-Sabaʾ (34):28
[30] Sūrat al-Aḥzāb (33):21

But as for someone whose only goal is to satisfy his desires or enjoy this worldly life, then he will not be able to follow the Messenger ﷺ, who dedicated himself entirely to Allah, and practiced abstinence in all aspects of this lowly world and its false glamour.

To prevail over all religions

Allah says: **'It is He who has sent His Messenger with the guidance and the religion of truth, that He may make it prevail over all religions, though the polytheists should be averse.'**[31]

Allah sent His messenger ﷺ to achieve two fundamental goals:

1. To give all people the opportunity to be guided, so that He could hold them fully accountable. Guidance means to arrive at the truth, and people cannot arrive at the truth save through knowing it and submitting their hearts to it. Knowledge without belief is insufficient, because opposition and negligence remain as barriers between a person and the truth.
2. To establish the true governance: a governance of justice and law, principles and values; as opposed to the governance of power, which is nothing more than the law of the jungle and the logic of tyranny. Clearly, society is governed either by the law of the jungle or the law of the Creator; the law of truth or the law of falsehood. Allah created life and endowed mankind with freedom, but the ultimate victory belongs to truth. And the waves of truth have resonated throughout the world from the moment Allah sent His final and greatest messenger, Muḥammad b. ʿAbd Allah ﷺ, until this very day. Does this not show that Allah's promise has been realized, in that Islam has prevailed over all religions?

Obeying the Messenger

Allah says: **'And obey Allah and the Messenger so that you may be granted [His] mercy.'**[32]

When society emerged from its bondage, it freed itself from the main causes of rebellion and hypocrisy, and prepared itself to follow the Messenger; especially because he had been given authority in all matters of disagreement between the different elements of society. Obedience to the Messenger was a source of mercy, because it eliminated all sources of evil and disagreement. It

---

[31] Sūrat al-Tawba (9):33
[32] Sūrat Āl ʿImrān (3):132

turned the entire *umma* (nation) towards progress because of the burgeoning confidence the Muslims felt knowing that their efforts would not be in vain.

Obedience and development

Allah says: **'Whoever obeys the Messenger certainly obeys Allah; and as for those who turn their backs [on you], We have not sent you to keep watch over them.'**[33]

Obeying the Messenger is the same as obeying Allah; there is neither difference nor contradiction between the two, as the Messenger only explains Allah's revelation. If there was no obedience due to the Messenger, the entire edifice of Divine Unity would collapse. The firmness, harmony, and perfection we find in Islam's principles are further evidence that Islam is from Allah, insofar as any manmade principles will naturally yield contradictions between ideology and legislation, between the points of its essential doctrines and the particular laws that it legislates.

On this basis, the *umma* needs this fundamental guidance more than anything else, in that development, cooperation, confronting its enemies, and building up its infrastructure—all of this is a direct result of obedience. Nations only develop through solidarity, a shared purpose, and a unity of action, and these can only be achieved through obedience.

Divine messages and divine messengers in the *sunna*

Why did Allah send prophets?

This is a question people have asked throughout history, unaware of the urgent need they have for someone to show them the best way to live and warn them of the roads leading to perdition. Someone once asked Imam al-Ṣādiq ﷷ: 'For what reason did Allah send prophets and messengers to mankind?' The Imam ﷷ replied: 'So that people would have no argument against Allah after they were sent messengers, lest they say: "No preacher or warner came to us," and so that Allah will have a decisive argument over them. Have you not heard Allah when He relates how the keepers of Hellfire will argue against its inhabitants by referring to the prophets and messengers? They say: "**'Did there not come to you any warner?' They will say, 'Yes, a warner did come to us, but we impugned [him] and said, 'Allah did not send down anything; you are only in great error.'**"'[34]

[33] Sūrat al-Nisā' (4):80

[34] *Biḥār al-anwār*, 11/39; the verse is Sūrat al-Mulk (67):8-9

In the same vein, Imam ʿAlī ﷺ has said: 'Allah sent Muḥammad ﷺ with the truth, that he might free His servants from worshipping idols to instead worship Him, and [to free them] from obedience to Satan to instead obey Him. [He sent him] with a Qurʾān he had made clear and firm, that the servants might know their Lord when [previously] they knew Him not, acknowledge Him while they had once rejected Him, and bear witness to Him where they had once denied Him. So He revealed Himself to them in His book without their having seen Him, through showing them some of His might and instilling them with fear of His wrath: how He destroyed those whom He destroyed through chastisement, and ruined those whom He ruined through retribution!'[35]

How do we prove that messengers have been sent?

Hishām b. al-Ḥakam narrates that an atheist (*zindīq*) came to Imam al-Ṣādiq ﷺ and asked him: 'From whence do you prove that prophets and messengers [have been sent]?'

Imam al-Ṣādiq ﷺ responded: 'Having established that there is a Creator and Maker who is exalted above us and all that He hath created, and that this Maker is all-wise, and that He can neither be touched nor seen by His creatures, nor can He address them directly nor they Him, nor can He argue with them nor they with Him, then we know that He must have ambassadors amongst His creatures to guide them to that which avails and benefits them, to take hold of that which will sustain them and to relinquish that which will destroy them. In this way, we establish that there must be those who command and prohibit on behalf of the All-wise and All-knowing amongst His creatures, whereat we establish that He has those who speak on His behalf. They are His prophets and the chosen amongst His creation, wise persons who teach wisdom to others, heaven-sent with this wisdom. They share the people's shape and design, but they do not share their [internal] states, [for] they are supported by the wisdom, proofs, arguments and signs that are with the All-wise and All-knowing. They bring the dead back to life, cure the blind and the leper. Allah's earth is never without [such] a divine authority (*ḥujja*), who has the knowledge to demonstrate the veracity of what the messenger has said, and the necessity of his righteousness.'[36][37]

---

[35] *Nahj al-balāgha*, sermon no. 147

[36] *Biḥār al-anwār* 11/30

[37] *Tuḥāf al-ʿuqūl*, 285

A manifest authority

Some claim that our intellects are sufficient to act as Allah's authority over us, and so we do not need messengers or prophets. They forget that people's intellects are hidden authorities, which can be buried beneath heaps of ignorance, neglect, and prejudice; they need something external to support them, namely messengers. Imam ʿAlī (ʿa) says: 'Allah sent messengers by distinguishing them with revelation, and made them an authority over His creatures, so that He would leave them no argument or excuse. He called them to the path of truth with the speech of the veracious.'[38]

Imam al-Kāẓim (ʿa) says: 'Verily Allah has two authorities over mankind; a manifest authority and a hidden one. As for the manifest one, it is the messengers, prophets and imams; and as for the hidden one, it is the intellect.'[39]

The peak of the prophets

The Commander of the Faithful (ʿa) eloquently explained the wisdom of sending messengers in the following points:

First: Allah took a pledge of obedience from the prophets. Consequently, they differ from everyone else by virtue of their moral rectitude and divine protection from error.

Second: Most people forsook Allah's pledge of obedience with them and became followers of Satan, so it was necessary to send prophets in order to guide them.

Third: Because Allah has endowed mankind with an innate belief in His divine unity and taken a pledge from them to uphold it (in *ʿālam al-dharr*, the world of pre-existence), He sent prophets to call on them to fulfil it.

Fourth: Because he endowed them with knowledge of Him but they forgot it, He sent prophets to remind them of this forgotten blessing.

Fifth: Because Allah will recompense people for their disbelief, He sent prophets so that they would be left with no excuse.

Sixth: Because people's intellects have been buried beneath heaps of ignorance, Allah sent prophets to bring them out that they might know the

---

[38] *Nahj al-balāgha*, sermon no. 144

[39] *Tuḥāf al-ʿuqūl*, 285

difference between truth and falsehood, and the means of distinguishing. The messengers show people signs from their Lord on the horizons.

So now let us ponder carefully on the words of the Imam ﷺ:

'He chose prophets from amongst [Adam's] progeny, taking a pledge from them to receive revelation and convey the message with which they were entrusted, for most of His creation had perverted His covenant with them, ignored His due, and taken up compeers beside Him. They had allowed Satan to turn them away from knowing Him and keep them aloof from worshipping Him. So Allah sent messengers amongst them and dispatched a succession of prophets to call on them to fulfil the pledge of human nature and remind them of His forgotten blessings, to conclusively establish Allah's authority over them through preaching, to unearth the hidden treasures of their intellects and show them the signs of His omnipotence.'

Then the Imam ﷺ added, referring to the final messenger, Muḥammad ﷺ:

'Then Allah, may He be glorified, sent Muḥammad ﷺ, His Messenger, to fulfil His promise and complete His prophecy; his pledge had been taken from the prophets, his name was renowned, and his birth was auspicious. On that day, the inhabitants of the earth were disparate, fractious, and divided into parties; between those who likened Allah to His creation, twisted His name or turned to other than Him. Through [Muḥammad], He led them from error, and through his importance, delivered them from ignorance. Then He – may He be glorified – chose that Muḥammad ﷺ should meet Him, selected him for what was with Him, ennobled Him above the abode of this world, and desired that He should endure its hardships no longer. So He took him unto Himself nobly. But he left amongst you what prophets past had left amongst their nations, for they did not leave them untended, without a clear path or a raised banner [to follow.]'[40]

The seal of the prophets

Imam ʿAlī b. Abī Ṭālib ﷺ said:

'Allah deposited [the prophets] in the best repositories and lodged them in the best residences. He continuously moved them from noble loins to chaste

---

[40] *Nahj al-balāgha*, sermon no. 1

wombs; whenever amongst them a predecessor departed, there rose with Allah's religion a successor.

[And so it went] until Allah's nobility – may He be glorified – reached Muḥammad ﷺ, whom He brought forth from the most eminent of origins and the most noble of roots, from the same tree from whence His prophets were cut, and from whence His trustees were chosen. His progeny are the best progeny, his family are the best family, and his tree is the best tree: it grew in sanctity and rose in nobility, it has lengthy boughs and unattainable fruits. It is a leader for him who would be pious, an insight for him who would seek guidance, a radiant lamp, a dazzling comet, a flint with blazing sparks. His conduct is balance, his practice is guidance, his words are decisiveness, and his judgement is justice. He sent him after an interval in messengers, a lapse in righteous conduct, and the foolishness of nations.'[41]

Fourth: Concerning Imamate and Imams

Imamate and Imams in the Qur'ān

Why do we need an Imam?

Just as the message is not complete without a messenger, the religion is not complete without a leader (*imām*). Because human nature always inclines to its base desires, it is insufficient that it has only a divinely-protected religion in its journeys. It also requires religion to be given form in a man who enjoys religious pre-eminence, which in turn gives him the right to implement the teachings of the religion over people. Every law needs someone who will apply it effectively, or else it will remain nothing more than ink on paper.

Allah willed that man should be happy in his life, without compelling him such that it would deny him his nobility and freedom. In the same way, it was befitting Him to provide Man with all the means of attaining happiness, should the latter choose to make use of them. It is for this reason that he laid down religious codes for him and made ready different paths, then sent a messenger to clarify for him, warn him, give him glad tidings, and call him to apply all of that, and take charge of its implementation. Allah could not have left His creation unattended, without someone to implement the religion after His Messenger ﷺ. In fact, it befitted Him to appoint leaders for mankind who enjoyed the same pre-eminence as His Messenger, and would undertake the same duties as him. All of that was to complete His blessing, realize His wisdom,

---

[41] *Nahj al-balāgha*, sermon no. 94

and provide Man with the means to attain happiness. But just as Allah did not desire to compel people to guidance during the era of the messengers, so as not to deprive them of the greatest blessing He had given them—namely the blessing of free-will—so too He did not desire to compel them to follow the Imam by force. In this way, He preserved the final Imam, the Master of the Age (may Allah hasten his return) to complete His authority over His creation, and to provide the greatest opportunity for mankind to attain happiness in this world and the Hereafter.

Those in authority

Allah has bid us to obey those in authority after the Messenger ﷺ, and said: **'O you who have faith! Obey Allah and obey the Messenger and those vested with authority among you...'**[42]

Those in authority are the natural extension of Allah's Messenger ﷺ, and they are his household and his successors: those who know Allah, who are entrusted with knowledge of the lawful and unlawful, who suffice for enacting His command, who are patient and godwary, and who are, therefore, the most obedient of people towards Allah and the nearest of them to the way of Allah's Messenger.

Who appoints the Imam?

Just as it is not possible for people to appoint a divine messenger over themselves, because he is a medium between them and Allah, neither is it possible for anyone to appoint an *imām* except Allah.

In other words, the Imam is someone who must be assisted by the Unseen, who knows Allah, His religion and its disciplines, who is far removed from any materialistic concerns. Allah does not assist the one whom people choose for themselves, only the one He chooses Himself. People have no right to choose in a matter that Allah has decided, because His servants are in His care, and consequently must submit to Allah's absolute authority in all matters. Allah says: '**And when his Lord tested Abraham with certain words, and he fulfilled them, He said, "I am making you the Imam of mankind." Said he, "And from among my descendants?" He said, "My pledge does not extend to the unjust."'**[43] And He says: **'"O David! Indeed We have made you a vicegerent (*khalīfa*) on the earth..."'**[44] And He says: **'"Indeed I am going to set a viceroy**

[42] Sūrat al-Nisā' (4):59
[43] Sūrat al-Baqara (2):124
[44] Sūra Ṣād (38):26

(*khalīfa*) on the earth…"'[45] This verse clearly show that leadership and succession – which are two words for a single reality – are not in anyone's hands except Allah's alone; He has no partner.

Imamate and Allah's grace

Allah has made His prophets and imams successful by granting them knowledge and wisdom from Him, which He has not granted to anyone else. Their knowledge is superior to the knowledge of other people. Allah says: '**…and he who is given wisdom, is certainly given an abundant good.**'[46] And He says of Saul: '**Indeed Allah has chosen him over you, and enhanced him vastly in knowledge and physique, and Allah gives His kingdom to whomever He wishes, and Allah is all-bounteous, all-knowing.**'[47] And He says: '**…great is Allah's grace upon you.**'[48] And Allah says about the Imams of the Prophet's Household: '**Or do they envy the people for what Allah has given them out of His grace? We have certainly given the progeny of Abraham the Book and wisdom, and We have given them a great sovereignty.**'[49]

When Allah chooses one of His servants to hold authority over others, He opens his chest, deposits springs of wisdom in his heart, and inspires him with knowledge.

Who are the Imams?

Allah says: '**And amongst them We appointed imams to guide [the people] by Our command, when they had been patient and had conviction in Our signs.**'[50]

This sacred verse directs us to a number of leading qualities found in a divinely-appointed leader:

1. They guide people to Allah by His command. They do not guide people merely to themselves, their faction, or their nation, or other such banners of ignorance.
2. They are patient and endure difficulties. A divine leader is one whose personality is formed through struggle and sacrifice in Allah's way; he is not someone who rides a wave of popularity or basks in the glory of

---

[45] Sūrat al-Baqara (2):30
[46] Sūrat al-Baqara (2):269
[47] Sūrat al-Baqara (2):247
[48] Sūrat al-Nisā' (4):113
[49] Sūrat al-Nisā' (4):54
[50] Sūrat al-Sajda (32):24

victory without having done any work himself. And perhaps this is why Allah chose his prophets, messengers, and imams from the most difficult circumstances, and after they overcame the greatest of adversities.

3. They possess 'certainty,' meaning they have attained a very high level of faith in Allah, such that they will never falter or doubt the right path, whether they attain victory or suffer setbacks.

Imamate and Imams

ʿAbd al-ʿAzīz b. Muslim said: 'We were with Imam ʿAlī b. Mūsā al-Riḍā ﷺ in Merv, gathered in its central mosque. People began to discuss the issue of Imamate and mentioned the many disagreements about it, so I went to my master, Imam al-Riḍā ﷺ, and told him of what the people had delved into. He ﷺ sighed, then said:

"O ʿAbd al-ʿAzīz! People have grown foolish and been duped out of their religion. Allah did not take His prophet's ﷺ life before perfecting his religion for him, sending down the Qurʾān to him in which is contained the clarification of all things, the explanation of the permitted, the prohibited, the limits and the laws, and everything that people need altogether. He says: '**We have not omitted anything from the Book.**'[51] And during the Farewell Pilgrimage, at the end of [the Prophet's] life ﷺ, He revealed: '**Today I have perfected your religion for you, and I have completed My blessing upon you, and I have approved Islam as your religion.**'[52] And the matter of Imamate is part of perfecting the religion; he ﷺ did not pass away until he had explained the symbols of the religion to his *umma*, made clear to them their ways, left them heading towards the truth, and appointed ʿAlī as a leader and a guide for them. There was nothing that the *umma* needed except that he had explained it. So whoever claims that Allah did not perfect His religion has rejected the Book of Allah, and whoever rejects the Book of Allah has disbelieved. Do they know the rank of Imamate and its position in relation to the *umma*, such that they are allowed to have a say in it?

"Abraham ﷺ, Allah's friend (*khalīl*), was singled out for imamate after prophethood, and friendship (*khulla*) is a third degree, a grace with which Allah honoured and commended him. He says: '**And when his Lord tested Abraham with certain words, and he fulfilled them, He said, "I am making you the Imam of mankind."**' Then Abraham ﷺ said, gladdened: '"**And from among**

---

[51] Sūrat al-Anʿām (6):38
[52] Sūrat al-Māʾida (5):3

my descendants?" He said, "My pledge does not extend to the unjust."'[53] This verse invalidates the governance of every wrongdoer until the Day of Judgement, and restricts it to those whom Allah has chosen. Then Allah ennobled Abraham by placing Imamate amongst the descendants of His pure and chosen ones. He says: '**And We gave him Isaac, and Jacob as well for a grandson, and each of them We made righteous. We made them imams, guiding by Our command, and We revealed to them the performance of good deeds, the maintenance of prayers, and the giving of *zakāt*, and they used to worship Us.**'[54] Their legacy remained amongst his descendants, one after the other, generation after generation, until the Prophet ﷺ inherited it. Allah says: '**Indeed the nearest of all people to Abraham are those who follow him, and this prophet and those who have faith...**'[55] So they had a special position, which the Prophet ﷺ bestowed on ʿAlī, and it passed to his pure descendants who were granted knowledge and faith. That is [the meaning of] Allah's saying: '**But those who were given knowledge and faith will say, "Certainly you remained in Allah's Book until the Day of Resurrection. This is the Day of Resurrection, but you did not know."'**[56] According to the divine plan, which flows, and which Allah has assigned to his offspring until the Day of Resurrection, there is no prophet after Muḥammad ﷺ; so from whence do these fools choose Imamate according to their own whims?

"Imamate is the station of the prophets and the inheritance of the legatees. It is Allah's deputyship and to Allah's Messenger ﷺ, the station of the Commander of the Faithful عليه السلام, and the successorship of Ḥasan and Ḥusayn عليهما السلام.

"To the Imam are entrusted the reins of the religion, the command of the Muslims, the interests of this world, and the honour of the faithful. The Imam is the foundation of the living religion of Islam and its lofty branches. It is through the Imam that prayer, *zakāt*, fasting, *ḥajj*, and *jihād* are completed. [It is through him that] spoils and charity are distributed, the laws and boundaries of Islam are enforced, and the borders and frontiers are secured.

"The Imam permits what Allah has permitted and forbids what He has forbidden. He maintains Allah's bounds and protects His religion. He calls to Allah's way with wisdom, beautiful preaching, and decisive arguments.

---

53 Sūrat al-Baqara (2):124
54 Sūrat al-Anbiyāʾ (21):72-73
55 Sūrat Āl ʿImrān (3):68
56 Sūrat al-Rūm (30):56

"The Imam is like the rising sun, whose light illuminates the world while it is upon the horizon, beyond sight and beyond reach.

"The Imam is the luminous full moon, the bright lamp, the shining light, the star that guides travellers through the dark wilderness, the one who directs people to guidance and saves them from ruin.

"The Imam is a fire upon the hill, a comfort for those who seek warmth, and a guide to those in peril. Whoever leaves him perishes.

"The Imam is a rain cloud, bringing a downpour of relief; [he is] the shaded heavens, the flat expanse of the earth, the natural spring, the valley and the meadow.

"The Imam is a trusted friend, a kind father, a loving brother, a nurturing mother, a refuge for all of Allah's servants.

"The Imam is Allah's trustee upon His earth and amongst His creatures, His authority over His servants, His deputy in His lands, the one who summons mankind to Him and defends His sanctity.

"The Imam purifies mankind of sins and cleanses them of imperfections. He is elect in his knowledge and marked by his good sense. He is what brings order to the religion, the honour of the Muslims, the scourge of the hypocrites, and the ruin of the faithless.

"The Imam is peerless in his era; no one else comes close. No scholar equals him, no substitute exists for him; he has no likeness and no peer. He is distinguished in merit, without having to seek or acquire it, for his distinction is from the Giver and Source of all grace – who can seek the knowledge of the Imam or the essence of his qualities?

"No, never! Intellects go astray, good sense becomes perplexed, and the hearts become heated; the speakers fall short, the poets grow dim, the writers are rendered incapable, the eloquent stutter, and the scholars are dumfounded before they can even begin to articulate his station or merit. And if they cannot describe one aspect of him, how can they describe his entirety, or convey his qualities, or find anyone that could take his place? How, when he is like a star beyond their reach and comprehension? Do they think that they can find this anywhere save in the Household of Allah's Messenger ﷺ? By Allah, they themselves know they cannot! For they have chosen to do something hard—rather, impossible—that will only end in their failure: they have tried to set up an Imam according to their own opinions – how can they choose an Imam? The

Imam is learned without ignorance, protects without scheming; he is the treasury of prophethood without blemish, with a lineage that none of noble descent can rival. He is of the tribe of Quraysh, of the clan of Hāshim, the offspring of Allah's Messenger ﷺ, the most noble of nobles, a branch of the ʿAbd Manāf, whose knowledge lives, whose good sense is complete, who is in charge of all affairs, skilled in politics, entitled to leadership, deserving of obedience, who undertakes Allah's command and advises Allah's servants.'"[57]

Allah's authorities over His creatures

Allah's Messenger ﷺ said: 'O ʿAli! You and the Imams from your progeny are Allah's authorities over His creatures, and His luminaries amongst His beasts. Whoever denies a single one of them has denied me, whoever disobeys a single one of them has disobeyed me, and whoever shows cruelty to a single one of them has shown cruelty to me. [Conversely,] whoever joins you has joined me, whoever obeys you has obeyed me, whoever is loyal to you has been loyal to me, and whoever makes an enemy of you makes an enemy of me; for you are of me, you were made of my clay, and I am of you.'[58]

Whoever is loyal to them … is of me

Imam Muḥammad al-Bāqir ؑ said: 'When the verse was revealed: **"The day We shall summon every group of people with their *imām*,"**[59] the Muslims asked: "O Messenger of Allah, are you not the Imam of everyone altogether?" Allah's Messenger ﷺ replied: "I am the Messenger of Allah to all people, but after me there will be Imams over the people from my Household, [appointed by] Allah. They will stand amongst the people, but [the people] will deny them, and the imams of disbelief and misguidance, along with their followers, will oppress them. Lo! So whoever is loyal to them, follows them, and believes in them, is of me, with me, and shall meet me. Lo! And whoever oppresses them, or helps others to oppress them, and denies them, so he is not of me and I disassociate from him!"'[60]

Knowing the Imam

Allah's Messenger ﷺ said: 'Whoever dies without knowing his Imam, dies the death of [the pre-Islamic age of] ignorance!'[61]

---

[57] *Tuḥāf al-ʿuqūl*, 322-234
[58] *Biḥār al-anwār* 24/266
[59] Sūrat al-Isrāʾ (17):71
[60] *Biḥār al-anwār* 24/266
[61] *Biḥār al-anwār* 23/18

Imam al-Ṣādiq 🕮 said: 'Whoever spends a night, not knowing the Imam of his time, shall die the death of ignorance!'[62]

And he 🕮 said: 'We are those to whom Allah has enjoined obedience. People cannot help but know us, and they have no excuse for remaining ignorant of us. Whoever knows us is faithful, and whoever denies us is faithless, and whoever neither knows us nor denies us is astray until he returns to the guidance upon which Allah has enjoined obedience to us. So if one dies while astray, Allah will do with him as He pleases.'[63]

Be loyal to ʿAlī!

Allah's Messenger 🕮 says: 'Whoever desires to live a life like that of the prophets, die a death like that of the martyrs, and dwell in the gardens which the All-Merciful has planted, then let him be loyal to ʿAlī, support his successor, and follow the Imams after him, for they are my progeny who were created from my clay. O Allah, sustain them with my understanding and knowledge, and woe to those of my *umma* who oppose them. O Allah, grant not my intercession [to those who oppose them]!'[64]

Twelve Imams

Allah's Messenger 🕮 said:

1. 'The Imams after me are twelve, all of whom are from Quraysh.'[65]
2. 'The Imams after me are twelve, so whoever loves and follows them has attained success and salvation, and whoever refrains from them has strayed and erred.'[66]
3. 'Twelve of my household are those to whom Allah has granted my understanding, knowledge, wisdom, and manners, and whom He created from my clay. Woe to those who haughtily reject them after [I am gone], who disconnect [me from] my progeny—what is the matter with them? Allah shall deny them my intercession!'[67]
4. 'O ʿAlī! You are my legatee. To fight you is to fight me, to be at peace with you is to be at peace with me. You are the Imam, and the father of eleven Imams who are purified and protected from sin. Among them is the Mahdī, who shall fill the earth with justice and

---

[62] Ibid., 28
[63] *Uṣūl al-kāfī* 1/144
[64] Ibid., 162
[65] Ṣāfī, *Muntakhab al-athar fī al-imām al-thānī ʿashar*, 24
[66] Ibid., 28
[67] Ibid., 32

fairness. So woe to those who hate them! O ʿAlī! Were a man to love you and your offspring, so Allah would resurrect him with you and your progeny, and you are all with me in the highest levels. You are the divider between Paradise and Hellfire. Those who love you will enter Paradise and those who hate you will enter Hell.'[68]

Our responsibility towards the Imam ﷺ

What is the duty of the people towards the Imam?

This is an obvious question for anyone who believes that the Imam is someone chosen by Allah, and the answer to this question can only come from the Imams themselves – after one has a general belief in them. There are a number of duties imposed on people with regards to the Imams, and we will highlight ten of them, in their own words:

First: Knowing the Imam

Imam Jaʿfar al-Ṣādiq ﷺ narrated from Allah's Messenger ﷺ: 'Whoever dies not knowing his Imam, dies the death of [the age of] ignorance.'[69]

Second: Believing in their authority (walāya)

Imam Jaʿfar al-Ṣādiq ﷺ said: 'The first thing a servant will be asked when he stands before Allah – may He be magnified – is about his obligatory prayers, charity, fasting, pilgrimage and about his allegiance to us, the Prophet's Household ﷺ. Whoever affirms his allegiance to us and dies upon it, his prayer, fasting, almsgiving, and pilgrimage will be accepted. But if he does not affirm his allegiance to us before Allah, then none of his good deeds will be accepted.'[70]

Third: Submitting to them

Imam ʿAlī b. al-Ḥusayn ﷺ said: 'Allah's religion cannot be attained by imperfect intellects, false opinions, or spurious analogies; it cannot be attained except through submission. So whoever submits to us is safe, and whoever seeks our guidance is guided, but whoever takes his religion through analogy and personal opinion perishes. And whoever finds himself averse to anything we have said or any verdict we have given has disbelieved in the One who sent down the seven oft-repeated verses and the Great Qurʾān, while he is unaware!'[71]

---

[68] Ibid., 56

[69] *Biḥār al-anwār* 22/78, tradition no. 1

[70] Ibid. 80/10

[71] *Biḥār al-anwār* 2/303

Fourth: Obeying them

Imam al-Bāqir عليه السلام said: 'The matter's peak, its summit, its key; the gate of the prophets and the satisfaction of the All-Merciful is to obey the Imam after knowing Him... Allah says: **"Whoever obeys the Messenger certainly obeys Allah; and as for those who turn their backs [on you], We have not sent you to keep watch over them."**'[72]

Fifth: Referring all disputes to them

Sudayr said that he told Imam al-Bāqir عليه السلام: 'I left your followers in dispute, with some disassociating from others. He said: "What do you have to do with that? People have only been made responsible for three things: Knowing the Imams, submitting to them in whatever they present to them, and referring to them in whatever they disagree."'[73]

Sixth: Acquiring knowledge from them

Allah's Messenger ﷺ says: 'My *umma* shall split into 73 sects. One will be saved and the others will perish. Those who will be saved shall hold fast to [Ali's] allegiance, acquire your knowledge, and not take knowledge from their own opinions, so no harm shall come to them.'[74]

Seventh: Referring the explanation of the Qur'ān to them

Imam Muḥammad al-Bāqir عليه السلام says: '**"But no one knows its interpretation except Allah and those firmly grounded in knowledge"**[75] – we know its interpretation...'[76]

Eighth: Seeking refuge with them in calamity

Imam ʿAlī b. Mūsā al-Riḍā عليه السلام says: 'The Imam is the trusted friend, kind brother, and refuge of the servants in calamity.'[77]

Ninth: Awaiting them

Imam Muḥammad al-Bāqir عليه السلام says: 'People have only been bid to circumambulate these stones [i.e. the Kaʿba] then to go forth to us, inform us of their allegiance, and offer their support.'[78]

---

[72] Ibid. 23/294 – the verse is Sūrat al-Nisā' (4):80
[73] Ibid. 2/202
[74] Ibid. 36/336
[75] Sūrat Āl ʿImrān (3):7
[76] *Biḥār al-anwār* 92/89
[77] Ibid. 25/123-124
[78] Ibid. 12/90

Tenth: Believing in them

Imam Muḥammad al-Bāqir 🕊 says, explaining the verse '**So have faith in Allah and His Messenger and the light which We have sent down...**'[79]: 'The light, by Allah, refers to the Imams of Muḥammad's 🕊 progeny until the Day of Resurrection.'[80]

Our responsibilities today

These are the general duties with which we have been charged towards the Imam of every age, but there are also a number of major responsibilities towards the Imams 🕊 that are upon our shoulders today in a special way. Namely:

First: To grasp the teachings of the Imams 🕊, which are the true teachings of Islam, in a way that is free from the erroneous tendencies that have crept into the Islamic intellectual milieu. These are three in particular:

The philosophical tendency, which entered the Islamic world in the second century and took on an Islamic hue, while at its core containing materialistic Greek thinking.

The foreign tendency, which continues to penetrate the depths of our societies by way of modern media outlets, which contains a terrible poison with regards to its foundations, its suggestions, and its orientation.

The ignorant tendency, which springs from our distance from the sources that are the infallible Imams 🕊, in that we follow personal inclinations and opinions.

We can only protect ourselves from these tendencies by turning to the primary sources of Islamic knowledge, namely the narrations, without using any of the aforementioned tendencies to help us understand or interpret them. Rather we must rely on thinking deeply upon the meanings of these traditions, as if the Imams 🕊 had addressed them to us directly.

Second: We must shape our intellectual and practical existences according to the directions of the pure Imams 🕊, by making sure that every single facet of them conforms to their teachings.

---

[79] Sūrat al-Taghābun (64):8
[80] *Biḥār al-anwār* 22/308

Third: We must spread the teachings of the rightly-guided Imams ﷺ through all levels of society; spending our time, energy and wealth for that cause.

We ask Allah to grant us success in that, so that we may enjoy happiness in this world and the Hereafter!

Fifth: Concerning the Resurrection and the Afterlife

Resurrection and Afterlife in the Qur'ān

A conscious glance at what happens in the wider world around us calls us to believe in life after death.

There are many people who live with us, who live and die as good people – in their hearts and actions – and who spare no effort in offering humanitarian aid to other people like themselves, without desiring any reward or gratitude in return. They worship their Lord, remember him night and day, and yet you find them oppressed and defeated, their lives harsh, their sorrows many, their difficulties never-ending.

Additionally, you find others who enjoy wealth and power beyond imagination, and yet – contrary to what you might expect – they continue to oppress and exploit others, violating every sacred thing, commit every sin, and most of them dying without ever receiving their just desserts in this world.

Many of the first group are the best people imaginable, like the prophets, the righteous, and the lovers of truth. They number thousands upon thousands.

Many of the second group sink ever deeper into evil deeds; they kill millions and commit crimes against humanity.

But Allah is the All-wise, and we see the effects of His wisdom in the heavens and the earth. He did not create anything without purpose, nor did he need any amusement or diversion – He is exalted above that! Allah is the All-powerful, and we find the signs of His power in us and all around us without limit. How can He not recompense these two groups of people?

Did He create this second group without purpose? Did He create them so that the strong could oppress the weak for no reason? Or did he wish to cause harm to the harmless thereby? Or is He incapable of rewarding the good and punishing the wicked for their deeds? The answer to all of these questions is no.

Allah is the All-wise and the All-needless, who is glorified above creating anything without purpose, glorified above being incapable of recompensing them, or resurrecting them when He created them the first time!

All the signs we see in the universe guide us to the fact that everything in it is at our disposal (or is created for our sake). Whether it is the sun, the moon, or the stars; they work day and night to perpetuate life. Everything the universe contains is at our disposal by virtue of the intellect, power, and freedom with which Allah endowed us. If everything is there for us, then for what are we here? Were we created merely to enjoy this world? Who amongst us can find true happiness in this world, whether they are young or old, master or servant, leader or follower? There is no one in this world who can taste true happiness – so why are we here?

There can only be two possible answers to this question:

The first is that Allah wanted to play, so He made us for His amusement. But this does not accord with the signs of His wisdom that we see throughout the universe, or that to which our intellects guide us regarding our Lord's perfection – He is perfect without flaw!

The second is that we were created for another world, and whatever good we find in this world is meant to guide us to something better and more perfect than it in the Hereafter, while whatever is evil here is supposed to serve as an example of something worse and longer-lasting than itself in the Hereafter. We taste both of these experiences at different times, and then learn from His messengers how we can attain the first and avoid the latter.

This is the reason why everything exists.

It is to this that the verses of the Qurʾān, which we shall mention a selection below, allude, and which themselves constitute an independent proof for the life of the Hereafter. And insofar as rational arguments have conclusively shown that we have a perfect God, and that He sent truthful messengers who warned us on his behalf that whoever does evil shall be requited for it and whoever does good shall be rewarded, we know that beyond this world lies punishment and reward! So let us now turn to these verses:

A day in which there is no doubt

Allah says: '**Say, "It is Allah who gives you life, then He makes you die. Then He will gather you on the Day of Resurrection, in which there is no doubt. But most people do not know."**'[81]

Truly there is no doubt that the Day of Resurrection will come. It is something about which there is no uncertainty, yet most people are not aware of this reality. However, ignorance of a fact does not change anything about it.

---

[81] Sūrat al-Jāthiya (45):26

We may be ignorant of the solar system, for instance, but does this mean that it will cease to exist because of our ignorance? Of course not!

Why will we be resurrected?

One of the reasons we will be resurrected after death is to make the truth clear and reveal the deceit of the faithless. And thusly he whose faith in the Hereafter was firm, and who believed that there were fixed criteria for truth, shall be resurrected with the rest of the people, and judgment shall be made between them concerning that over which they had disagreed. Allah says: '**That He may clarify for them what they differ about, and that the faithless may know that they were liars.**'[82] No one can turn truth into falsehood and convince himself that the falsehood has become truth, for there awaits us a day in which the truth will be made completely clear from falsehood.

The life of the Hereafter

Allah says: '**The life of this world is nothing but diversion and play, but the abode of the Hereafter is indeed Life, had they known!**'[83]

In its usual form, elements, and material dimensions, the life of this world is merely play without purpose. The real goals of life are only purposeful insofar as they are connected to the Hereafter and matters unseen.

In the abode of the Hereafter, all the elements of life for an eternal existence will be present, for abundant joy, and complete and utter contentment. Thus the faithful will be freed from the concerns and distractions of this worldly life.

A day that awaits you

The human being cannot escape the love of this world except by remembering the Hereafter. Whoever seeks Paradise will forget about his lowly desires, and whoever fears Hellfire will see the troubles of this life as trivial by comparison.

Allah says: '**Indeed man is ungrateful to his Lord, and indeed he is [himself] witness to that! He is indeed avid in the love of wealth. Does he not know, when what is in the graves is turned over, and what is in the breasts is divulged, indeed their Lord will be best aware of them on that day?**'[84]

---

[82] Sūrat al-Naḥl (16):39
[83] Sūrat al-ʿAnkabūt (29):64
[84] Sūrat al-ʿĀdiyāt (100):6-11

This day awaits each and every one of us, wherein the graves will be overturned to bring out what they contain, and people will be raised up to be held to account: their own limbs will testify against them and the contents of their hearts will be manifest; their secrets will be divulged and the veils will fall. Then the human being will know how much of his life he squandered by not purifying himself from the love of this world and its trinkets, and all people will know with certainty that Allah encompasses them.

This is how we see faith in the Hereafter, and remembrance of the accounting that awaits us in it curbs mankind's worldly desires.

The hour is bound to come

It is human nature to believe in the Resurrection, but insofar as the whispering of Satan afflicts each person, he will disbelieve in it unless he tries to resist those whispers.

If the human being suffers doubts about the Resurrection, then he should look to his past and see if he can say, 'Allah cannot create me anew!' while Allah has already created him from nothing.

Allah says: **'O people! If you are in doubt about the resurrection, [consider that] We indeed created you from dust, then from a drop of [seminal] fluid, then from a clinging mass, then from a fleshy tissue, partly formed and partly unformed, so that We may manifest [Our power] to you. We establish in the wombs whatever We wish for a specified term, then We bring you forth as infants, then [We rear you] so that you may come of age. [Then] there are some of you who are taken away, and there are some of you who are relegated to the nethermost age, so that he knows nothing after [having possessed] some knowledge. And you see the earth torpid, yet when We send down water upon it, it stirs and swells, and grows every delightful kind [of plant].'**[85]

Allah created man from dust, then from a drop of semen, then He made him a clinging mass, and then a fleshy tissue; and then, after his birth, in a cycle of development: from childhood to youth, then to old age and death. This progression follows a wise order, instituted by the All-wise and All-powerful.

In order to know your future, you need only consider the origin of your creation. After you were weak and vulnerable in your mother's womb, you grew strong, but you shall again be relegated to the nethermost age. Is not the one

---

[85] Sūrat al-Ḥajj (22):5

who shaped you in the darkness of the womb and in your life, with creation upon creation, not able to create you again after your death?

Allah says: 'That is because Allah is the Reality and it is He who revives the dead, and He has power over all things, and the Hour is bound to come, there is no doubt in it, and Allah will resurrect those who are in the graves.'[86]

In short, the above verses call us to two things: First, to believe in Allah's power; second, to believe in the Day of Resurrection. This is because believing in Allah's power is the way in which we can believe in the Day of Resurrection. So whenever we doubt the Resurrection, we must look at the signs of Allah's power, because doubting the resurrection is a result of doubt in Allah's names. As for someone who knows Allah truly, he does not doubt the Resurrection.

Resurrection and the Afterlife in the *Sunna*
Imam Zayn al-ʿĀbidīn ʿAlī b. al-Ḥusayn 🕮 said:

'O people! Beware Allah and know that to Him you will return, and each soul will find whatever good it has done present, and it shall wish there was a great distance between it and whatever evil it has done; Allah warns you of Himself!

'Woe to you, O neglectful son of Adam who is never neglected! Verily your end comes to you fastest of all; advancing toward you rapidly, stalking you, ready to pounce. It is as though you have already met your end, the angel has seized your spirit and taken you alone to your grave, whereat your spirit returned to you and the questioners, Nakīr and Munkar, have entered your presence to question you and test you severely. Lo! And the first question you shall be asked concerns the Lord you used to worship, then the prophet who was sent to you, the religion you followed, the scripture you read, the *imām* to whom you gave your allegiance, your life and how you passed it, and your wealth and how you earned and spent it.

'So be on your guard and look to yourself; prepare your answer before you are tried, tested and measured. If you are a believer who knows his religion, follows the truthful, is an ally to Allah's friends, then Allah will send you your conclusive argument and inspire your tongue to speak right. Then you will have

---

[86] Sūrat al-Ḥajj (22):6-7

answered well, and been guaranteed Paradise and Allah's satisfaction. The angels will welcome you with ease and sweet fragrances.

'But if you are not like this, then you tongue will stutter, your arguments will fail, and you will be unable to answer—whereat you will be guaranteed Hellfire, and the angels will greet you with the punishment of scalding, putrid water, and the blaze of Hell.

'So know, O son of Adam, that beyond this is something more terrible, shocking, and painful to the hearts: the Day of Resurrection. [That is] the day on which mankind will be gather; that is the day Allah shall gather the first and the last; the day on which the trumpet will be blown and the graves will be torn open. That day has drawn near when men's hearts will choke up their throats, a day when no falsehood shall be uttered, nor ransom taken, nor [invalid] excuse accepted, nor opportunity for repentance given. There is only recompense for good deeds and retribution for evil ones. Whoever was faithful in this world and did an atom's weight of good shall see it, and whoever was faithful in this world and did an atom's weight of evil shall see it.'[87]

He shall bring it back as He created it

Hishām b. al-Ḥakam narrated that an atheist asked Imam Jaʿfar b. Muḥammad al-Ṣādiq ﵇: 'How can the spirit be brought back when the body has vanished and the bones have crumbled? One limb may have been eaten by a beast of prey in one land, while another has been torn apart by vermin elsewhere, and yet another was reduced to dust that is now in the clay of a wall!'

The Imam ﵇ replied: 'Verily He who made it from nothing, and fashioned it without an example to work from, is able to bring it back just as He originated it.'

'Explain this to me,' said the atheist.

'The spirit resides in its place—a good person's spirit in a bright expanse, and a wicked person's spirit in dark confines—while the body returns to the dust from which it was created. Whatever parts the predators and vermin devour and tear apart, all of that is in the dust, preserved by He whom not an atom's weight escapes in the darkness of the earth, He who knows the number of all things and their weights. Verily the dust of the godly is like gold in the dust; when the Resurrection comes, the earth will be rained upon and swell up, then it will be churned with the churning of a milkskin, whereat from the dust will emerge

---

[87] *Tuḥāf al-ʿuqūl* 180-181

men just as gold emerges from the dust when it is washed with water, or cream from milk when it is churned. The dust of each container will gather and be taken by Allah's leave to where the spirit resides, and its form will return by the leave of the Fashioner to its original form, and the spirit will enter it. And when the person rises up, he will recognize himself completely.'[88]

You were created for the Hereafter

Man's problem is that he becomes absorbed in the vanities and false glamour of this world, such that he forgets he was not created for this world, but is only passing through it. He forgets that death waits to transport him to the abode of the Hereafter. In his letter to Imam al-Ḥasan عليه السلام, the Commander of the Faithful, Imam ʿAlī b. Abī Ṭālib عليه السلام said: 'Know that you were created for the Hereafter, not for this world; for annihilation, not for perpetuation; for death, not for life. You are like unto a fortress, a gate of sufficiency, and a road to the Hereafter.'[89]

And he عليه السلام also said: 'You were created for the Hereafter, so strive for its sake.'[90]

And he عليه السلام said: 'The goal of the Hereafter is to remain.'[91]

And he عليه السلام said: 'Remember the Hereafter abundantly, and the bliss and painful punishment it contains, for that will make you abstinent in this world and make it seem trivial to you.'[92]

And he عليه السلام said: 'Blessed is the one who remembers the Resurrection and strives for the Reckoning.'[93]

Read your book

Khālid b. Najīḥ narrated that Imam al-Ṣādiq عليه السلام said: 'On the Day of Resurrection, each person will be given their book [of deeds] and told: "Read it!"' Khālid asked: 'Do they know what it contains?' He replied: 'They remember it. There is not a single moment, a single word, or a single footstep save that he remembers it as though it had just occurred. For this reason: **"The Book will be set up. Then you will see the guilty apprehensive of what is in it. They will**

---

[88] *Biḥār al-anwār* 7/37-38
[89] *Tuḥāf al-ʿuqūl*, 57
[90] *Ghurar al-ḥikam*, 288
[91] Ibid., 504
[92] *Tuḥāf al-ʿuqūl*, 57
[93] *Nahj al-balāgha*, maxim no. 44

say, 'Woe to us! What a book is this! It omits nothing, big or small, without enumerating it.'"'[94]

Use this world to secure the next

Those who despise this world are in error for doing so, for in reality this world is the means by which we can secure happiness in the Hereafter. Imam ʿAlī b. Abī Ṭālib ﷺ said: 'With death this world is sealed, and through this world is the next secured. Through resurrection, Paradise is brought near for the godwary, and Hell is brought into view for the perverse.'[95]

The Hereafter is in front of you

A believer must prepare to meet his Lord, and preparation means working positively and doing his utmost to attain the highest levels in the Hereafter. Imam ʿAlī b. Abī Ṭālib ﷺ said: 'Prepare for a day in which gazes will be transfixed, minds driven mad by terror, and thoughts stupefied.'[96]

And he ﷺ said: 'Work for a day, a day for which provisions have been set aside, on which secrets will be revealed.'[97]

And he ﷺ said: 'Beware of a day on which deeds will be weighed, on which there will be much shaking, and in which children will grow old [before their time].'[98]

---

[94] *Tafsīr nūr al-thaqalayn*, 3/267 about Sūrat al-Kahf (18):49
[95] Ibid., 47
[96] *Ghurar al-ḥikam*, 140
[97] Ibid.
[98] Ibid., 146

Part Two: Rulings for Acts of Worship (*ʿIbādāt*)

Following a Jurist (*Taqlīd*) and Legal Maturity (*Bulūgh*)

What is *taqlīd*?

1. Islam is the seal of divine messages. It is a complete way of life that encompasses all dimensions of human existence, including doctrines (*ʿaqīda*), ethics (*akhlāq*), worship (*ʿibāda*), individual and social conduct, and mankind's connection to everything in the universe.
2. Whoever takes Islam as a religion must follow the way of Islam completely in all aspects of one's life, adopting its behaviours and practices according to the divine laws (*aḥkām al-sharīʿa*).
3. This requires every mature (*bāligh*) Muslim to know whatever divine laws he requires and to understand them such that he is able to apply them in his life.
4. There are two ways in which someone can know the divine laws (*aḥkām al-shariʿa*):
    a. Personally deducing the laws from their original sources, namely the Qurʾān, the Sunna, reason (*ʿaql*) and consensus (*ijmāʿ*) – a process known as *ijtihād* in jurisprudence (*fiqh*) – and then acting accordingly. Naturally, however, this is a difficult feat requring more effort and time than most people have to spare.
    b. Following the legal verdicts of someone else whom he trusts, and who can derive and deduce the divine laws from their sources. This practice of emulating a jurist is what we call *taqlīd*.[99] So *taqlīd* is acting in accordance with the opinion of a jurist (*mujtahid*) who possesses the necessary qualifications – which we shall detail below.

---

[99] *Taqlīd* here does not mean blindly following the actions and practices of someone else without any understanding whatsoever; this is something blameworthy in light of reason and religion. Rather, *taqlīd* means following (consciously and with understanding) a scholar who holds the necessary qualifications, as laid down by reason and religion, to derive laws from their sources, and whom the person trusts sufficiently to take him as a guide for his own practice in life.

5. Therefore, most *bāligh* individuals (those who have reached the legal age of maturity) follow jurists in order to know the divine laws. They follow this guidance in their daily affairs, and take the lead from those jurists in various aspects of life. This method, which supports human nature and human reason, allows a Muslim to be confident that he is living his life – in a general sense – in accordance with proper Islamic teachings.

Rules of *taqlīd*

6. If someone acts without recourse to either *ijtihād* or *taqlīd*, his acts are invalid (*bāṭil*) if they are not in accordance with the actual ruling that applies to him, or the opinion of the jurist whom he presently follows.
7. The dominant view amongst jurists, both classical and modern, is that one cannot begin to follow a deceased jurist[100] and this opinion stands in accord with precaution (*iḥtiyāṭ*), especially in those issues where they may have been some developments in jurisprudence, which have expanded the scope of a jurists *ijtihād* compared to that of the deceased jurist.

Pre-eminence in knowledge

8. The strongest opinion[101] is that a person does not have to follow the most-learned jurist. Instead it is more appropriate that they choose the one who is best in piety, learning, and practical competence.
9. The strongest opinion is that a person can switch from doing *taqlīd* of a living jurist to do that of another living one, regardless of whether the latter is more learned than the former or not.
10. If the jurist someone is following does not have a *fatwā*[102] on a particular issue, he can refer to another jurist.

---

[100] In other words, you cannot elect to begin following him after his demise but if you were already following him while he was alive, then you can continue to do so now that he is dead.

[101] Whenever the expression "the strongest opinion" appears, it denotes Grand Āyatullāh al-Mudarrisī's juristic view.

[102] A *fatwā* is a legal opinion which a jurist has obtained from the sources concerning a particular issue.

How can we identify a jurist?

11. Before performing *taqlīd* we must be certain that the jurist we want to follow is qualified. This can be achieved via one of the following ways:
    a. Direct knowledge: if the *muqallid* (one who follows a *marja*ʿ) is an expert in religious matters, such that he is able to identify who is a jurist and distinguish him from others.
    b. The testimony of two just and expert persons.
    c. The apparent ruling[103] is that one can identify a jurist via the testimony a single just and expert person, if this person's testimony yields trust and confidence according to common sense.
    d. Through a jurist's renown, if this yields confidence.

Conditions for being *marja*ʿ *al-taqlīd*

12. The mere ability to deduce law and practice *ijtihād* is insufficient as a basis for others to take religious teachings and laws from a person. Rather, in addition to *ijtihād,* he must be:
    a. At the age of legal maturity (*bulūgh*)
    b. Of sound mind (*ʿaql*)
    c. Of correct belief (*īmān*)[104]
    d. Of just conduct (*ʿadāla*)
    e. Male (*dhukūra*)
    f. Living (*ḥayāt*)
    g. Of pure birth (*ṭahārat al-mawlid*), i.e. that he was not born from fornication or adultery.
13. A jurist does not need to be an expert in all areas of Islamic law; it is permissible to follow a specialist (*mutajazzi*ʾ - someone who is a *mujtahid* in some areas of law, but not all) in those areas where he is capable of deriving laws. However, it is not appropriate for him to occupy the position of a *marja*ʿ as this requires him to derive laws in all areas.
14. Just conduct (*ʿadāla*) means that he displays the spirit of godwariness (*taqwā*) and faith (*īmān*), as demonstrated by his observance of all Allah's limits and laws. This can be identified through good outward conduct that would be typically considered indicative of its reality. Just conduct also implies that a jurist should not be seeking worldly benefits or pursuing its vanities.

---

[103] This also denotes the author's *fatwā*.
[104] Meaning that he is a Twelver Shīʿa.

15. If a jurist lacks any of the aforementioned qualities (such as soundness of mind or just conduct), then the *muqallid* must switch to the *taqlīd* of another jurist who fulfils the necessary conditions.
16. The legal agent (*mukallaf*) must know that he has discharged his duty: that he has fulfilled his religious obligations through knowing all the details of the acts of worship—their parts, conditions, impediments, and preliminaries; and of acts related to transactions and contracts—by following someone who knows these rulings and who can be trusted to perform them correctly; in the same way a *ḥajj* pilgrim who follows the caravan's guide without knowing the detailed practice and obligations of *ḥajj* in advance.
17. *Taqlīd* is obligatory for everyone who is not a *mujtahid* in all prohibited and obligatory matters. As for recommended and disliked acts, it is not necessary to do *taqlīd* for them; it suffices for the believer to know that they are neither obligatory or prohibited, so that if he acts upon them thereafter it suffices him to be anticipating divine reward (or absence of divine punishment). It also suffices him to refer to manuals of supplications and manners (*ādāb*) written by reliable scholars. As for all other day-to-day matters, he must be sure that they do not contravene divine law.
18. In the case of one who follows a jurist, then doubts whether that jurist meets the necessary qualifications: if this doubt concerns whether the jurist *continues* to possess these qualities [after the fact of following him], his prior certainty suffices him. That is, he can assume that these qualities are still present until he becomes certain – through religious evidence – that they are not. But if one doubts whether a jurist possesses all the necessary qualities at all, then he must carry out research to determine whether he can do *taqlīd*. As for his prior deeds [done while following this jurist], they are still valid [and do not need to be repeated], God willing.
19. If some time has passed since he reached legal maturity, only for him to doubt thereafter: were his deeds performed until now based on valid *taqlīd* or not? Then he should assume that his prior deeds are valid, but he must ensure that his *taqlīd* is valid from now on.
20. One can divide their *taqlīd* between different jurists. For example, they can follow one jurist in acts of worship and another in transactions,[105] but in this case the legal agent should ensure his

---

105 His Eminence's definition of division of *taqlīd* also permits for following a number of qualified jurists on any variety of rulings across areas of *fiqh*. This is referred to as *tabʿīḍ*.

intentions are purely for Allah when choosing which jurist to follow, rather than just following his own desires and inclinations.

21. If someone errs in conveying the *fatwā* of a jurist to others, he must inform them of that, just as a jurist who errs in explaining his *fatwā* must do likewise.

Rules of legal maturity (*bulūgh*)

1. Maturity is a natural state of human beings – as with all other living creatures – and regardless of how someone comes to realize that he is legally mature, the relevant laws immediately apply to him.
2. Scripture has explained which signs indicate legal maturity, and usually these indications appear at similar times, but it is possible to rely on only one of them so long as we do not know with certainty that it is inaccurate.
3. The signs of maturity are as follows:
   i. Sexual maturity (*ihtilām*): When someone begins to experience sexual urges – whether awake or asleep – by the emission of semen and its accompanying orgasm, whether this occurs in male or female persons, and whether this is brought about by an external factor (such as masturbation) or an internal factor (such as a dream). It is also not necessary to emit semen; if one knows he or she is ready for marriage, this suffices.
   ii. Hair growth: A sign of sexual maturity for both genders is the growth of pubic hairs.
   iii. Menstruation (in girls): One of the most important signs of a girl's maturity is menstruation. She becomes legally mature by mere virtue of seeing her first menstrual blood, even before she has a regular monthly cycle.
   iv. Pregnancy (in girls): Pregnancy indicates that a girl is already legally mature.
   v. Age: A male child reaches maturity, normally, at fifteen years of age, while a female child reaches maturity at twelve, though a female child can reach maturity as young as nine in some conditions.

   The well-known opinion of our jurists is that males mature at age fifteen and females at age nine. There are narrations supporting both of these ages. However, Qur'ānic verses and traditions from the Prophet ﷺ and his Household عليهم السلام have also provided the aforementioned indicators of maturity and these (i.e., conditions 'i' through 'v') are the fundamental criteria by which any ambiguities must be resolved. However, it is closer to precaution to set the maturity of a girl at nine years, so long as this precaution does not put undue pressure upon her or harm her health, and Allah knows best.[106]

4. If a child matures very late due to illness, and we know that they are still in a state of childhood, then they are not considered mature even if they exceed the stated age (e.g. sixteen years for boys).
5. If a child matures early due to some external factor and the child's development is complete such that he or she displays the aforementioned indicators of maturity, then this maturity is legally effective, with the condition that we know with certainty that this child is mentally mature.

Ritual Purity (*Ṭahāra*)

Introduction

Allah has bid His servants to purity in whatever is connected to the spirit, the body and nature. Our Lord says about purity of the spirit: '**...by the soul and Him who fashioned it and inspired it with [discernment between] its virtues and vices: one who purifies it is felicitous...**'[107] As for avoiding impurities of the body, the religion enjoins this when our Lord says: '**and purify your cloak, and keep away from all impurity!**'[108]

As for purity of nature, Allah has enjoined it by saying: 'And do not cause corruption on the earth after its restoration...'[109]

And He prohibited all vicious things, meaning all manner of impurities, as they contain that which harms human beings. Allah says: '**...he makes lawful to them all the good things and forbids them from all vicious things...**'[110]

---

[106] Precaution (*iḥtiyāṭ*) here means that a girl, from nine lunar years of age until she attains legal maturity according to the criteria we mentioned, must observe the divine laws so long as they do not put her under pressure or cause her harm. For example, she should wear *ḥijāb*, pray and fast so long as fasting is not harmful to her health; if it causes her harm, she must not fast. And if she performs *ḥajj* at this age, then is able to perform it again after reaching full maturity, she should do so out of precaution. And if she marries at this age (as in some cultures happens), her husband should not have intercourse with her.

[107] Sūrat al-Shams (91):7-9

[108] Sūrat al-Mudaththir (74):4-5

[109] Sūrat al-Aʿrāf (7):56, 85

[110] Sūrat al-Aʿrāf (7):157

Turning away from impurity is considered to be mankind's natural state (*fiṭra*). Allah explains that spiritual impurity, like physical impurity, should be avoided, saying: **'Indeed wine, gambling, idols and the divining arrows are abominations of Satan's doing, so avoid them...'**[111]

The religion has specified a group of purifying substances, and explained how to use them to purify oneself (water, dust, and sunlight), but it does not restrict purification to these alone. Rather we are instructed in clear and absolute terms that we must use whatever means necessary to purify ourselves. Allah says: **'...and keep away from all impurity!'**[112]

And Allah says: 'So avoid the abomination of idols...'[113]

When He bids us to purity and cleanliness, He wants us to attain these through whatever means possible. If we know that there is some purifying substance that will remove filth and leave no trace of it, we must use it in obedience of Allah's command to purify ourselves.

For example: if we cannot remove blood which has dried upon our body or clothes except by using soap, then we must use it to that end.

The same is true of any impurity that contaminates a particular place and cannot be removed except through cleaning substances; we must use these to attain the goal of cleanliness.

The religion has instituted the general rule that everything around us in nature is pure until we know definitively that it is otherwise. A tradition from Imam al-Ṣādiq ﷺ said: 'Everything is clean until you know [with certainty] that it is dirty.'[114]

In regards to the importance of cleanliness, the Prophet ﷺ has said: 'Clean yourselves as much as you are able, for verily Allah built Islam upon cleanliness and none shall enter Paradise save he who is clean!'[115]

---

[111] Sūrat al-Mā'ida (5):90
[112] Sūrat al-Mudaththir (74):5
[113] Sūrat al-Ḥajj (22):30
[114] *Wasā'il al-shī'a* 2/1054; *abwāb al-najāsāt*, ch37, tradition no. 4
[115] Mīzān al-ḥikma 10/93

He ﷺ also said: 'Islam is clean, so cleanse yourselves; for none shall enter Paradise save he who is clean!'[116]

And he ﷺ said: 'Allah is pleasant and He loves that which is pleasant; He is clean and He loves cleanliness.'[117]

Islam has bid people to purity and encouraged them to pursue it so that the believer will always be clean, and avoid filth and impurity in body and soul, so that his spirit may be pure and his soul cleansed. The goal behind legislating purity is not limited to the material realm, but includes the spiritual realm as well.

As for spiritual purity, this is attained through *wuḍū'*, *ghusl*, *tayammum,* and embracing Islam. These, in turn, are attained through water, dust, and pronouncing the two testimonies of faith, according to their specific requirements.

Ritual purity in the noble *sunna*

- ʿAlī ؑ said: 'Purification is half of faith.'[118]
- The Prophet ﷺ has said: 'Clean yourselves by any means at your disposal, for Allah Almighty established Islam upon cleanliness, and no will enter Paradise unless clean.'[119]
- And he ﷺ has also said: 'Verily Islam is clean, so clean yourselves; for none will enter Paradise unless clean.'[120]
- And he ﷺ also said: 'Verily Allah is good and loves goodness, [and is] clean and loves cleanliness.'[121]
- And it is reported from him ﷺ: 'Cleanliness comes from faith.'[122]
- And it is narrated from the Prophet ﷺ: 'Cleanliness calls to faith, and faith is with its owner in Paradise.'[123]
- And the Prophet ﷺ said to Anas: 'O Anas, increase in purification and Allah will increase your lifespan. So if you could be in a state of ritual

[116] Mīzān al-ḥikma 10/93
[117] Ibid., 92
[118] *ʿAwālī al-laʾālī*, v. 1, p. 115
[119] *Mīzān al-ḥikma*, v. 10, p. 93
[120] *Mīzān al-ḥikma*, v. 10, p. 93
[121] *Mīzān al-ḥikma*, v. 10, p. 92
[122] *Mustadrak al-wasāʾil*, v. 16, p. 319, ḥ. 9
[123] Mustadrak safīnat al-biḥār, v. 10, p. 93

purity nightly and daily, then do so, then you will be, if you die upon ritual purity, one who dies a martyr.'[124]

Section one: Purifying agents (*muṭahhirāt*)

First: Water
The noble *sunna*:

- ❖ Imam Abū ʿAbd Allah al-Ṣādiq 🕮 has said in a report: 'Verily Allah has made the earth pure just as He made the water pure.'[125]
- ❖ And he also said: 'All water is clean until you know that it is unclean.'[126]
- ❖ And he said in another report: 'Water cleanses but cannot be cleansed.'[127]
- ❖ It has also been narrated from Imam al-Ṣādiq 🕮 that he said: 'Water—all of it—is pure until it becomes known that it is impure.'[128]
- ❖ In a supplication from the Commander of the Believers 🕮 during ritual ablutions, [he said] while looking at the water: 'Praise be to Allah who made water ritually pure, and did not make it ritually impure.'[129]
- ❖ Imam al-Bāqir 🕮 said: 'Break your fast with sweets. If you could not find any, then break your fast with water, for verily water cleanses.'[130]

Rulings:
Water is of two kinds: Unmixed (*muṭlaq*) and mixed (*muḍāf*).

Unmixed water is water in its natural state, or what we would call 'water' without qualifying it with any other adjective, and is the water that rains from the heavens. Unmixed water is ritually pure, and is able to ritually purify other objects. It removes ritually impure substances and removes the condition of ritual impurity.

Mixed water is any other liquid besides unmixed water, such as rose water, vinegar, fruit juice, and tea. It is ritually pure in and of itself, but is incapable of use in ritual purification; it neither removes ritually impure substances nor lifts ritually impure states.

---

[124] Makāram al-akhlāq, p. 40
[125] *Wasāʾil al-shīʿa*, v. 1, p. 99, ḥ. 1
[126] *Wasāʾil al-shīʿa*, v. 1, p. 99, ḥ. 2
[127] *Wasāʾil al-shīʿa*, v. 1, p. 99, ḥ. 3
[128] *Wasāʾil al-shīʿa*, v. 1, p. 200, ḥ. 5
[129] *Wasāʾil al-shīʿa*, v. 1, p. 282, ḥ. 1
[130] *Wasāʾil al-shīʿa*, v. 1, p. 101, ḥ. 10

Unmixed water is divided into five types:

1. Rain water
2. Flowing water
3. Well water
4. Abundant water (*kurr*)
5. Small quantities of water (*qalīl*)

1. Rain water

The noble *sunna*:

- Hishām b. Sālim asked Abū ʿAbd Allah al-Ṣādiq ﷺ about a surface that is urinated upon, so rainwater reaches it, and it stops, and then some touches his garment. So he said: 'There is no problem with it; what reaches it is of water more than [urine].'[131]
- In a report from al-Kāhilī from Imam Abū ʿAbd Allah ﷺ: 'Everything visible that rain has reached has been purified.'[132]
- It has been narrated that Abū al-Ḥasan [al-Kāẓim] ﷺ said, regarding mud puddles: 'There is no problem if the rainwater [from mud] reaches your clothing for three days [after it rains], unless it is known that something made it impure after it rained.'[133]

Rulings:

In order for water falling from the sky to purify other objects, it must be of a sufficient quantity for the name 'rain water' to apply to it. According to precaution (*iḥtiyāṭ*), it should be of such a quantity that it would flow if it fell on hard ground.

1. If rain falls on ground contaminated by agents of impurity (*ʿayn al-najāsa*) like rain, causing some drops of it to splash up, these are pure so long as there has been no change to their colour, odour or taste as a result of the impurity.
2. If rain falls on the terrace of a house where there is urine, blood or some other agent of impurity, then the water flowing from the roof is ritually pure so long as rain continues to fall, even if it flows over the agent of impurity.
3. Just as impure ground is purified by rain falling directly upon it, it is also purified by rainwater flowing over it; for example, if the

---

[131] *Wasāʾil al-shīʿa*, v. 1, p. 108, ḥ. 1
[132] *Wasāʾil al-shīʿa*, v. 1, p. 109, ḥ. 5
[133] *Wasāʾil al-shīʿa*, v. 1, p. 109, ḥ. 6

ground was beneath a roof, or there were two pieces of ground next to one another, and rain falls on one of them then flows to the other.

4. Mud produced by rainwater is ritually pure; if rain falls on *najis* (ritually contaminated) dirt and it turns into mud, then it has been ritually purified by the rain.

2. *Flowing water*

The noble *sunna*:

❖ Dāwud b. Sarḥān said: I asked Abū ʿAbd Allah [al-Ṣādiq] ﷺ: What do you say about bathhouse water? He said: 'It is like flowing water.'[134]

❖ Imam al-Bāqir ﷺ said: 'Bathhouse water is no problem if it has a [continuous] source.'[135]

❖ It is narrated that Ibn Abī Yaʿfūr said to Imam al-Ṣādiq ﷺ: Inform me about bathhouse water, in which those in a state of major ritual impurity, children, Jews, Christians, and Zoroastrians wash themselves? So he said: 'Verily bathhouse water is like the water of a river: a part of it purifies the other.'[136]

Rulings:

Flowing water refers to any kind of water than flows from any water supply, such as springs, channels[137] and rivers. And there are a number of rulings, which we highlight below:

1. Flowing water is not impurified through contact with impurity, whether it is abundant (*kurr*) or small in quantity – so long as it is connected to a source.
2. Springs that do not flow or gush unless water is taken from them follow the same ruling as flowing water even though they do not actually flow, because they are still connected to a water source.
3. Streams and pools connected to flowing water follow the same rules as flowing water so long as they are deemed to be connected to

---

[134] *Wasāʾil al-shīʿa*, v. 1, p. 110, ḥ. 1

[135] *Al-Kāfi*, v. 3, p. 14, ḥ. 2

[136] *Wasāʾil al-shīʿa*, v. 1, p. 112, ḥ. 7

[137] Channels are a collection of wells dug close together, such that they become linked underground, so that water may flow through them from high ground to lower ground, and their waters are treated as underground sources, even though the flow like springs.

flowing water according to common sense (*ʿurf*); it makes no difference whether they are connected above or below ground.

4. A network of water pipes connected to their sources, which are – naturally – abundant water, are considered to be abundant water, rather than flowing water.
5. Flowing water must continue to be connected to its source, even if this takes the form of trickling, or continuous and heavy dripping. But if this connection is broken in any way, such that water no longer reaches it, then this water is treated as stagnant (*rākid*); so if its quantity is less than *kurr*, it follows the same ruling as a small quantity of water.

3. Well water

The noble *sunna*:

❖ Imam al-Riḍā ﷺ said: 'Well water is deep (vast), and nothing contaminates it unless it changes the water.'[138]

❖ It is narrated that Abū Baṣīr asked Imam al-Ṣādiq ﷺ about a well from which people use the water to perform ablutions, wash their garments, and add to flour to make dough; then it is discovered that there is a corpse in it. He said: 'There is no problem, and there is no need to rewash the clothing washed with that water, or repeat prayers consecrated with it.'[139]

❖ It is narrated that Muʿāwiya b. ʿAmmār heard Imam Abū ʿAbd Allah al-Ṣādiq ﷺ saying: 'There is no need to rewash garments or repeat prayers because something [dead] fell into the well, unless it was decomposing. If it was, then rewash the garment, repeat the prayer, and drain the well.'[140]

Rulings:

Well water is protected (*muʿtaṣim*) from becoming ritually impure, and does not become so unless there is a change in its colour, taste, or odour.

1. If some ritual impurity falls into a well, it is strongly recommended (*mustaḥabb mu'akkad*) to drain a quantity of water from the well, appropriate to the bulk of the impurity that fell in it, until common sense no longer deems it filthy. In fact, precaution should not be ignored by [simply] draining several buckets of water from it, if

---

[138] *Wasā'il al-shīʿa*, v. 1, p. 125, ḥ. 1
[139] *Wasā'il al-shīʿa*, v. 1, p. 126, ḥ. 5
[140] *Wasā'il al-shīʿa*, v. 1, p. 127, ḥ. 10

someone wants to drink from it, especially if some wine or disintegrating carcass fell into it.

2. If some impurity is poured into a well, and its colour, odour, or taste change [rendering it ritually impure], and then this change disappears, the well water is treated as ritually pure again, even if nothing has been drained from it.

4. Abundant water (kurr)

The noble *sunna*:

❖ It is narrated from Abū Baṣīr that he asked Imam Abū ʿAbd Allah al-Ṣādiq ﷺ about one *kurr* of water: what is its volume? So he said: 'If the volume of water was three-and-a-half hand spans cubed then it is one *kurr* of water.'[141]

❖ It is also narrated that: 'A *kurr* is three hand spans [of water] cubed.'[142]

❖ Imam al-Ṣādiq ﷺ said: 'If water's volume has reached at least one *kurr*, then nothing can make it ritually impure.'[143]

Rulings:

1. A *kurr* is a measure that was used in ancient times. Historically there has been some disagreement amongst jurists about the precise quantity of a *kurr*—even though it was never really an exact measure, but more of a common-sense estimation. This means that it is sufficient to observe the minimum, even if it is better to observe the maximum. If you wish to know the amount of water in a cylindrical vessel [has reached *kurr*], then all one needs to do is measure its diameter and depth. If both are more than three-and-a-half hand spans, then that is sufficient. If the vessel was not cylindrical (e.g., a square basin), then it is sufficient that the length, width, and depth, are all [at least] three hand spans. And because spans are of different lengths, the criterion here is the average hand-span.[144]
2. Abundant water – namely that which is at least the volume of a *kurr* – is not rendered impure by anything unless there is a change to its colour, taste, or odour as a result of the ritual impurity.
3. If a portion of *kurr* water is rendered impure by an agent of impurity and the rest is less than a *kurr* in volume, then the remainder is also

---

[141] *Wasāʾil al-shīʿa*, v. 1, p. 122, ḥ. 6
[142] *Wasāʾil al-shīʿa*, v. 1, p. 122, ḥ. 2
[143] *Wasāʾil al-shīʿa*, v. 1, p. 117, ḥ. 2
[144] The volume of *kurr* is approximately 384 liters, or 101 gallons of water.

ritually impure. However, it is very likely that the latter remains pure so long as all the water is not changed.

5. Small quantities of water

The noble *sunna*:

❖ ʿAlī b. Jaʿfar asked his brother, Imam Mūsā b. Jaʿfar 🕮, about chickens, pigeons, and the like, which have stepped in dung, and then enter the water: can one perform ablutions for prayer from that water? So he said: 'No, unless the volume of water was so much that it amounted to [at least] one *kurr*.'[145]

❖ Abū Baṣīr narrated from one of the Imams 🕮: 'If you put your hand in the water pitcher before washing it, then it is not a problem unless your hand had been in contact with urine or sexual fluids. If you put your hand in the water and it had been in contact with either of those, then you must throw out that water.'[146]

❖ Samāʿa narrated that he asked Imam Abū ʿAbd Allah al-Ṣādiq 🕮 about the case of a man who has two vessels of water. Something impure fell into one of them, but he does not know which, and no other water is available [to perform ablutions for prayer]. He said: 'He should throw out the contents of both and perform *tayammum*.'[147]

Rulings:

Any water whose volume is less than a *kurr*, or which is not connected to a source (such as a spring) is classed as a small quantity of water (*māʾ qalīl*). And here we mention its subsidiary rulings:

1. If a small quantity of water comes into contact with ritual impurity, it becomes ritually impure.

2. If a small quantity of water is poured over a ritually impure object to remove the source of impurity, and that water comes off of the object, then the used water (*ghasāla*) is ritually impure, even after the source of impurity has been removed, and before the object has been purified.

3. Water which remains in an item of clothing that has been washed and wrung out, and a container after it has been washed and had its used water emptied, is pure according to the strongest opinion.

---

[145] *Wasāʾil al-shīʿa*, v. 1, p. 115, ḥ. 13
[146] *Wasāʾil al-shīʿa*, v. 1, p. 113, ḥ. 4
[147] *Wasāʾil al-shīʿa*, v. 1, p. 113, ḥ. 2

4. When water is used to purify oneself after using the lavatory (whether for urine or faeces), if drops of that water come into contact with the body or clothing, there is no problem and there is no need to cleanse the body or clothing as a result of that. But the water used in this fashion should not be reused for the purposes of cleansing ritual impurity, *wuḍūʾ* or *ghusl*.

Rules pertaining to mixed water

The noble *sunna*:

- Abū Baṣīr asked Abū ʿAbd Allah [al-Ṣādiq] ﷺ about a man who has milk with him: can he perform *wuḍūʾ* with it? He said: 'No, that is only done with water or earth.'[148]
- Al-Sukūnī narrated from Imam Jaʿfar al-Ṣādiq, from his father Imam al-Bāqir ﷺ: 'Verily ʿAlī was asked about a pot that was being used for cooking, and then a mouse fell into it. He said: "Throw out the broth and wash off the meat."'[149]

Rulings:

1. Jurists say that mixed water does not purify any impure thing, though some classical jurists believed that impurity could be removed from mixed water. In and of itself, this is a sound (*ḥasan*) opinion when one is compelled to do so because there is no water, with the condition that a person must be sure that the source of impurity and any trace thereof has been removed, and the average person would conclude that the object has been cleansed. One example of this is using medical sterilizing liquids.
2. Mixed water becomes ritually impure through contact with ritual impurities, and the mixing of these impurities with it according to common sense, such that they make it unclean and dirty. This is included in Allah's saying: '**and keep away from all impurity**'[150] and His saying: '**and [the Prophet] forbids them from all unclean things.**'[151] On the above basis, this ruling does not include the following:
Oil wells and drums, medicine containers, large vats of fruit juice, and large quantities of carbonated liquids. If these come into contact with a ritually impure hand, or a drop of blood falls into them, this impurity

[148] *Wasāʾil al-shīʿa*, v. 1, p. 146, ḥ. 1
[149] *Wasāʾil al-shīʿa*, v. 1, p. 150, ḥ. 3
[150] Sūrat al-Mudaththir (74):5
[151] Sūrat al-Aʿrāf (7):157

does not permeate them according to common sense, so the strongest opinion is that they do not become impure thereby, because they are not included under the general prohibition on impure substances.

3. Ritually impure mixed waters are purified if absorbed completely by a body of protected water (*ma' 'āṣim*), i.e. pure water of volume equal to, or greater than, one *kurr*. Additionally, it retains its ritual purity if returned to its prior (mixed) state. So, if ritually impure oil or fat melts into boiling protected water, then it is purified if it mixes with the water, even if the oil or fat is not completely absorbed by the water.

4. If impure mixed water is vaporized, then its vapour is ritually pure as a result of change (*istiḥāla*).

Changes in water

The noble *sunna*:

❖ Imam al-Ṣādiq ؏ said: 'So long as [a body of] water overcomes the smell of the carcass [in it], then [it is fine to] perform *wuḍū'* with it and drink it. But if the [smell of the] water changes, or its taste is altered, then do not perform *wuḍū'* with it or drink it.'[152]

❖ It is narrated from Muḥammad b. 'Alī b. al-Ḥusayn that Imam al-Ṣādiq ؏ was asked about a pond in which there was a carcass. So he said: 'So long as the water overcomes it, and the smell of the carcass cannot be detected, then one may use [that pond] for *wuḍū'* and washing.'[153]

❖ Al-'Alā' b. al-Fuḍayl said: I asked Abū 'Abd Allah al-Ṣādiq ؏ about a pond in which people or animals urinate. So he said: 'It is no problem [to use its water] so long as the colour of the water is not altered by the colour of urine.'[154]

Rulings:

1. Abundant water is impure if some ritually impure substance, such as blood, urine, or carrion enters it, and one of three of its qualities – taste, odour, or colour – change as a result of this.

2. The change must only be the result of the ritual impurity; abundant water does not become impure if the change has occurred as a result of two factors; the impurity and something else.

3. If the source of impurity loses its characteristics, such as if blood loses its qualities (colour, taste, etc.), or the carrion is sterilized such that its

---

[152] *Wasā'il al-shī'a*, v. 1, p. 102, ḥ. 1
[153] *Wasā'il al-shī'a*, v. 1, p. 105, ḥ. 13
[154] *Wasā'il al-shī'a*, v. 1, p. 104, ḥ. 7

odour does not affect the water, then the apparent ruling is that the abundant water is not impure because no change has really occurred, even though the change may have occurred if there was no impediment. However, precaution requires that such water still be avoided.

4. Water becomes ritually impure even if the change occurs after the source of impurity is removed from it, unless the change is caused by something else.
5. If one doubts whether such a change has in fact occurred, or whether a change has occurred because of an impurity, then the water is judged to still be ritually pure, because the certainty that the water was pure is not invalidated by uncertainty about whether it has become ritually impure.

How can water whose qualities have changed be purified?

The noble *sunna*:

❖ Imam al-Riḍā ﷺ said: 'Well water is deep and nothing can contaminate it unless its smell or taste is altered. [If that happens] then drain the well until the odor leaves and the taste becomes good again, because it has a [continuous] supply.'[155]

Rulings:

1. Water whose qualities have changed is purified if it becomes connected to protected water, such as abundant or flowing water, or if rain falls upon it, and the changes in its qualities disappear.
2. Well water whose qualities have changed because of an impurity is purified when these changes disappear as a result of draining it; so the well should be drained until the changes disappear.
3. Once the change in water has disappeared, the water is purified again simply by becoming connected to protected water, even with the slightest mixing between them.
4. If a change in water disappears by itself, it is obligatory precaution to avoid it until it has been connected to purifying water.

Establishing the ritual impurity or purity of abundant water

The noble *sunna*:

❖ ʿAmmār b. Mūsā al-Sābāṭī asked Imam Abū ʿAbd Allah al-Ṣādiq ﷺ about a man who finds a [dead] mouse in his water jug. He had frequently performed *wuḍū'* from that jug, or *ghusl*, or washed his garments. The mouse was decomposing. So he said: 'If he saw it in the

---

[155] *Wasā'il al-shīʿa*, v. 1, p. 105, ḥ. 12

jug before he performed *ghusl*, *wuḍū'*, or washed his clothes, and he did that [anyway] after seeing it in the jug, then he must wash his clothes, and wash everything that came into contact with the water [from that jug], and repeat his *wuḍū'* and prayers. And if he only saw it after he had finished those things, then do not allow that water to touch anything else; and he does not need to repeat anything since he did not know when it fell in.' Then he said: 'Perhaps it only fell in the very hour he saw it.'[156]

Rulings:

1. If something was impure, establishing whether it is now pure requires either knowledge or confidence (*iṭmi'nān*). This is also the case for establishing the water being of a small quantity after having been abundant.
2. It is also established by evidence, namely the testimony of two just witnesses, or even the testimony of one just witness if it yields relative confidence. If, however, one cannot obtain confidence for whatever reason, he should still observe precaution.
3. It is also established by the testimony of an item's owner, namely someone who is responsible for a thing in such a way that cultural custom says he possesses it.
4. It is also established by any rational means that fall under the rubric of 'clarification' (*istibāna*), about which reason has no doubts to the contrary. Hearing reports that give one confidence (*itmi'nān*), evidence that water has come into contact with some impurity – even if there are some far-fetched explanations for it – and the trusted testimony of experts, etc.: all of these are rational means for uncovering the truth about anything, including ritual purity and impurity.
5. Ritual impurity cannot be established on the basis of suspicion, speculation, or devilish misgivings (*waswās*), even if the one who has them is 'certain' of ritual impurity, because these are irrational and come only from Satan. Observing precaution on such basis is disliked because the suspicious individual is following Satanic *waswās*.

Rulings pertaining to ritually impure water

The noble *sunna*:

❖ 'Alī b. Ja'far narrates that he asked his brother, Imam al-Kāẓim ﷺ about a jug of water containing a thousand *ritl* (less than one *kurr*) in

---

[156] *Wasā'il al-shī'a*, v. 1, p. 106, ḥ. 1

which some urine had fallen: can it be used for drinking or *wuḍūʾ*? So he said: 'It cannot be used.'[157]

- ʿAlī b. Jaʿfar said: I asked him ﷺ about a man who has a nosebleed. While he is performing *wuḍūʾ*, a drop of blood falls into his jug. Can that water still be used for *wuḍūʾ*? So he said: 'No.'[158]
- Saʿīd al-Aʿraj narrates that he asked Abū ʿAbd Allah [al-Ṣādiq] ﷺ about [using] water left over from Jews or Christians. So he said: 'No.'[159]
- Zurāra narrates from Imam al-Bāqir or Imam al-Ṣādiq ﷺ: 'When the Prophet ﷺ performed *wuḍūʾ*, people would take whatever water fell from him, and use it for *wuḍūʾ* themselves.'[160]
- Imam Abū ʿAbd Allah al-Ṣādiq ﷺ was asked about someone in a state of major ritual impurity. While he is performing *ghusl*, some dirt falls into the water jug. So he said: 'There is no problem. To this applies what Allah Almighty has said: "And We did not make any unbearable hardship for you in religion."'[161]

Rulings:

1. It is unlawful to drink ritually impure water, or to give it to children. It is however lawful to sell it or give it to a Muslim so long as you inform him that it is ritually impure. It is lawful to water plants and animals with it.
2. It is lawful to drink ritually impure water in situations of necessity (*ḍurūra*), such as if one fears for his life due to extreme thirst; but one may only consume the minimum amount necessary, and not more.
3. It is unlawful to use ritually impure water for *wuḍūʾ* or *ghusl*. If no pure water is available for these, then the worshipper's duty is to purify himself with *tayammum* (purification with earth).

Water about which there are doubts

The noble *sunna*:

- Imam al-Ṣādiq ﷺ said: 'All water is pure until you know [conclusively] that it is impure.'[162]

---

157 *Wasāʾil al-shīʿa*, v. 1, p. 116, ḥ. 16
158 *Wasāʾil al-shīʿa*, v. 1, p. 112, ḥ. 1
159 *Wasāʾil al-shīʿa*, v. 1, p. 165, ḥ. 1
160 *Wasāʾil al-shīʿa*, v. 1, p. 152, ḥ. 1
161 *Wasāʾil al-shīʿa*, v. 1, p. 153, ḥ. 1
162 *Wasāʾil al-shīʿa*, v. 1, p. 99, ḥ. 2

- Imam al-Ṣādiq ﷺ said: 'Water—all of it—is pure until it is known that it is impure.'[163]
- A man asked Imam al-Ṣādiq ﷺ: I am passing on the road and some water trickles down onto me from a gutter. It is during the time that I know people are performing *wuḍū'*. So he said: 'There is no problem with it; you do not need to ask about it.'[164] The author says in *al-Wasā'il*: The intended meaning of *wuḍū'* [in this report] is *istinjā'*.

Rulings:

1. All water is considered ritually pure until you know it to be contaminated. If you knew some water had become impure, but are presently uncertain as to whether it was later purified, then you must act according to your prior knowledge of its impurity.
2. Water is by nature unmixed. If you realize that it had become mixed water, but later you become uncertain as to whether it is still mixed or has returned to its unmixed state, you must follow your prior certainty and treat it as mixed.
3. If you encounter a liquid and you do not know whether it is water or not, it is unlawful to use it to remove ritual impurities, or to perform *wuḍū'* or *ghusl*, until you know it to be water.

Leftover water

The noble *sunna*:

- It is narrated that ʿAlī b. Jaʿfar asked his brother, Imam Mūsā b. Jaʿfar ﷺ, about a pig that drank from a water container. What do you do with the container? He said: 'It should be washed seven times.'[165]
- Muḥammad b. Muslim asked Imam al-Ṣādiq ﷺ about a dog that drinks from a container. So he said: 'Wash the container.'[166]
- Saʿīd al-Aʿraj narrates that he asked Abū ʿAbd Allah [al-Ṣādiq] ﷺ about [using] water left over from Jews or Christians. So he said: 'No.'[167]
- Muʿāwiya b. ʿAmmār narrates from Abū ʿAbd Allah al-Ṣādiq ﷺ, regarding cats: 'They are from the members of the household, so one

163 *Wasā'il al-shīʿa*, v. 1, p. 100, ḥ. 5
164 *Wasā'il al-shīʿa*, v. 1, p. 161, ḥ. 3
165 *Wasā'il al-shīʿa*, v. 1, p. 162, ḥ. 2
166 *Wasā'il al-shīʿa*, v. 1, p. 162, ḥ. 3
167 *Wasā'il al-shīʿa*, v. 1, p. 165, ḥ. 1

may perform *wuḍūʾ* from its leftover water (that is, water from which the cat drank).'[168]

- It is narrated by ʿAlī b. Jaʿfar in his book that he asked his brother, Imam Mūsā b. Jaʿfar ﷷ, about menstruating women. He said: 'You may drink from their leftover drinking water, but you should not perform *wuḍūʾ* with it.'[169]
- ʿAlī b. Yaqṭīn narrates from Imam al-Kāẓim ﷷ, concerning a man who performs *wuḍūʾ* with water from which a menstruating woman has drank? He said: 'If she is trustworthy [in matters of ritual purity] then it is not a problem.'[170]
- Imam al-Ṣādiq ﷷ said: 'In the believer's leftover drinking water there is a cure for seventy maladies.'[171]

Second: The earth

The noble *sunna*:

- It is narrated from Imam al-Ṣādiq ﷷ, regarding a man who walks over an unclean place, then walks on a clean place after that: 'There is no problem if it was fifteen arm lengths or similar.'[172]
- Muḥammad b. al-Ḥalabī narrates that he said to Imam al-Ṣādiq ﷷ: My route to the mosque passes through an alleyway where people urinate. It is possible that I pass through it, and I am not wearing any shoes, and some of its moisture gets on my foot. So he said: 'Do you not walk upon dry earth after that?' I said: Of course. He said: 'Then there is no problem. Verily the earth purifies itself, one part the other.'[173]
- Jābir b. ʿAbd Allah said of the Messenger of Allah ﷺ: 'Verily Allah Almighty said to him: "I have made for you and your nation the entire earth a place of prostration, and made its soil pure."'[174]

Rulings:

Allah made the earth pure. It purifies the soles of feet, shoes, and car tyres, according to specific criteria that we shall detail as follows:

---

168 *Wasāʾil al-shīʿa*, v. 1, p. 164, ḥ. 1
169 *Wasāʾil al-shīʿa*, v. 1, p. 167, ḥ. 2
170 *Wasāʾil al-shīʿa*, v. 1, p. 170, ḥ. 5
171 *Wasāʾil al-shīʿa*, v. 17, p. 208, ḥ. 1
172 *Wasāʾil al-shīʿa*, v. 2, p. 1046, ḥ. 1
173 *Wasāʾil al-shīʿa*, v. 2, p. 1048, ḥ. 9
174 *Mustadrak al-wasāʾil*, v. 2, p. 529, ḥ. 3

1. The earth's ability to purify is no different whether the ground consists of dirt, sand, or stone; however, asphalt and cement are not included.
2. The aforementioned things are only capable of ritual purification, whether by walking or wiping upon the ground, after the external traces of a ritually impure substance have completely disappeared.
3. The earth purifies things that move upon it, such as a car's tyres, the bottom of a cane, the hands of a crawling child, socks, horseshoes, etc.
4. It makes no difference whether the source of an impurity is from the ground or elsewhere. If you had cut your foot, and then walked upon the earth with it until all trace of the impurity disappeared, your foot would become ritually pure.

Third: The sun

The noble *sunna*:

- Imam Muḥammad al-Bāqir ﵇, addressing Abū Bakr al-Ḥaḍramī, said: 'O Abū Bakr, whatever the sun shines upon has become purified.'[175]
- ʿAlī b. Jaʿfar said: I asked my brother, Imam Mūsā b. Jaʿfar ﵇, about a straw mat that some urine had reached: can it be used for prayer if it dries out [in the sun], without being washed? He said: 'Yes, it is not a problem.'[176]

Rulings:

1. Everything the sun shines upon, causing it to dry (i.e., the impurity evaporates due to sunshine), becomes ritually pure, such as the ground, buildings, doors, windows, and so on, with the condition that the source of ritual impurity and all of its visible traces are removed.
2. The jurists, may Allah be pleased with them, exclude from this ruling anything movable, such as containers that are not fixed in the ground, clothes, beds – but not mats and rugs – and acting on what they say is in accordance with recommended precaution.[177]
3. The sunlight must shine directly on the object, not indirectly by way of a mirror, through a window, or through fog.
4. Floors, woodpiles, pieces of metal, cars, trains, boats, and log piles, etc., are all purified by the sun shining upon them, according to what is indicated by the evidences.

---

[175] *Wasāʾil al-shīʿa*, v. 2, p. 1043, ḥ. 5

[176] *Wasāʾil al-shīʿa*, v. 2, p. 1042, ḥ. 3

[177] This suggests that His Eminence disagrees with the opinion of the jurists, but feels it would be more prudent to act according to their view if one can do so.

Fourth: Change and transformation

The noble *sunna*:

- Al-Ḥasan b. al-Maḥbūb asked Imam Abū al-Ḥasan [al-Kāẓim] عليه السلام about some plaster, which has some dung or bone fragments baked into it, and then it is used in the place of prayer [for the floor]. Can it be prostrated upon? So he wrote back to me the following words: 'Verily water and fire have purified it.' And the author of *Wasāʾil* has said: Fire purifies ritual impurity by changing it to ash or vapor.[178]
- ʿUbayd b. Zurāra said: I asked Abū ʿAbd Allah عليه السلام about a man who takes wine and make it into vinegar. He said: 'There is no problem.'[179]

Rulings:

1. If a source of impurity or a ritually impure object undergoes chemical transformation (*istiḥāla*) into something else entirely, then it becomes ritually pure. For instance, if faeces, a carcass, or blood becomes soil, or is burnt to ash, it becomes ritually pure. Even if ritually impure wood is turned completely into charcoal, then it becomes ritually pure, though precaution should be observed.[180]
2. If wine turns into vinegar, it has transformed from something unlawful into something lawful. It makes no difference, according to this ruling, whether this happens by itself (transformation – *inqilāb*), or through external agency, such as putting vinegar or salt into the wine. If a drop of wine falls into a container of vinegar and transforms into vinegar, the drop becomes ritually pure, and the vinegar does not become ritually impure. But if we were to suppose that it remained wine, then the vinegar would become ritually impure. Additionally, wine's container is purified at the same time as its contents transform into vinegar.

Fifth: Islam

If a disbeliever embraces Islam, he becomes ritually pure, as does any moisture in contact with him and his extremities. As for his clothing, if it had become impure through contact with him or through any other source of impurity, the strongest opinion is that he must not use them until he has purified them. The same applies to an apostate who was not born a Muslim

---

[178] *Wasāʾil al-shīʿa*, v. 2, p. 1099, ḥ. 1

[179] *Wasāʾil al-shīʿa*, v. 2, p. 1098, ḥ. 2

[180] This kind of *iḥtiyāṭ* is recommended, meaning it is recommended to avoid this kind of charcoal, but there is no sin if someone does not avoid it.

(*murtadd millī*) after he has repented; as for an apostate who was born a Muslim (*murtadd fiṭrī*), if his repentance is accepted, then he becomes pure thereafter.

Sixth: Other purifiers

The noble *sunna*:

- Al-Ṣadūq narrates that a mouse or some other small animal fell in a well and died there. Its water was used for making bread, and there was no problem with eating it so long as fire had reached it. And al-Ṣādiq عليه السلام said: 'The fire consumed whatever was in it.'[181]
- Khālid al-Qalānisī has narrated that he said to Imam al-Ṣādiq عليه السلام: What if I meet a *dhimmī* (a *kitābī* living under protection of Islam) and he shakes my hand? He said: 'Wipe it with dust or against a wall.' I said: And what about the *nāṣib* (one who bears enmity towards the holy household or their followers)? He said: 'Wash your hand.'[182]
- Imam al-Ṣādiq عليه السلام was asked about a man who bleeds from his nose: must he wash the inside—meaning its nostrils? So he said: 'He only needs to wash what the outer portion of it.'[183]
- Imam al-Ṣādiq عليه السلام said: If a dog brushes by your garment and the dog is dry, then sprinkle some water on the place it touched. But if it was there was moisture on it, then wash the area it touched.' And the like is narrated about pigs.[184]
- Imam al-Ṣādiq عليه السلام said: 'Do not eat the meat of an animals that consume excrement, and if its sweat touches you then wash the affected area.'[185]
- It is narrated that ʿAlī b. Jaʿfar asked his brother, Imam Mūsā b. Jaʿfar al-Kāẓim عليه السلام, about a wet mouse that fell into some water, then walked upon a garment: can it be prayed in? He said: 'Wash wherever you see a trace of it (i.e., its tracks), and sprinkle wherever you find no trace of it with water.'[186]
- Imam al-Ṣādiq عليه السلام was asked about prayer in the garment of a Zoroastrian, so he said: 'Sprinkle it with water.'[187]

---

[181] Man lā yaḥḍuruh al-faqīh, v. 1, p. 11
[182] *Wasāʾil al-shīʿa*, v. 2, p. 1019, ḥ. 4
[183] *Wasāʾil al-shīʿa*, v. 2, p. 1032, ḥ. 5
[184] *Wasāʾil al-shīʿa*, v. 2, p. 1034, ḥ. 3
[185] *Wasāʾil al-shīʿa*, v. 16, p. 304, ḥ. 1
[186] *Wasāʾil al-shīʿa*, v. 2, p. 1049, ḥ. 2
[187] *Wasāʾil al-shīʿa*, v. 2, p. 1093, ḥ. 3

Rulings:

1. If a source of impurity disappears from the body of a ritually pure animal, the apparent ruling is that the animal becomes ritually pure. So, for instance, if blood disappears from a bird's beak or a cat's mouth or the like, then it is purified thereby, and the same applies to inside the animal.
2. If a source of ritual impurity disappears, or is caused to disappear, from the inside of the human being, then it is purified by the disappearance of this impurity. If someone expels the impure food or blood from the inside of his mouth, then the inside of it becomes ritually pure thereby. Anything that the eyelids and lips close over, or the like thereof, is considered part of the inside.
3. If an animal, whose flesh is lawful for consumption, eats excrement and its flesh grows thereby, and the odour appears in its sweat, then it is known as an excrement-eater (*jallāl*), and becomes unlawful as food and ritually impure. It can only be rendered ritually pure and licit for consumption again by cleansing it, and this is accomplished by preventing it from consuming further excrement, and feeding it clean food, until it is no longer considered an excrement-eater.
4. A camel takes forty days to become clean again, a cow twenty – though some say thirty days, and this is more appropriate – a sheep ten, a duck five – though seven is better – and a chicken three days. This is if it is no longer considered an 'excrement-eater' within this limited time, but if it persists in this state after the aforementioned times, then it must continue to be cleansed until it is no longer considered such.
5. All reasonable people must assume that whatever a Muslim does is religiously correct, and this is the practice of religious persons. If a Muslim departs with some ritual impurity, only to return with the source of impurity and all trace of it having been removed—or if his body, clothes or property are somehow ritually contaminated, and he returns after that—then he, his clothes, and his possessions are all presumed ritually pure. However, if we realized he was unaware of the impurity on his clothes or body, or we are certain that he pays no mind to matters of ritual purity or impurity (whether in anything, or this thing in particular), then ritual purity is no longer presumed. The same applies if we know that, for whatever reason, he could not have purified himself or the property in question.
6. If a tiny amount of blood falls into a boiling pot, the content of the pot is not ritually impure, because according to the transmitted reports of [Prophetic and Imamic] narrations, the fire consumes it. It is closer to precaution, however, to pour it out. In fact, if a drop of wine, urine, or

some other ritual impurity falls in, it contaminates the pot and its contents must be poured out.

Section two: Impurities

Introduction

The verses of the Qur'ān have informed us that we must avoid all uncleanliness: '...and do not be of the mind to give the unclean part of it...'[188] 'He makes lawful to them all the good things and forbids them from all unclean things...'[189] And we have been ordered to turn away from impurities and filth: 'and keep away from all impurity!'[190] and to pursue purity, cleanliness and beauty: '...and Allah loves those who keep pure.'[191]

And the noble *sunna* has been given to us to explain divine revelation and apply it to particular cases, expounding upon the different kinds of impurities, whether spilt blood, animal carcasses, urine, faeces etc.

These examples are well known in that they have been given a firm foundation in the verses of the Qur'ān and further elucidation in the transmitted reports.

Therefore, we must turn away from everything we know to be impure and foul, and seek cleanliness by every possible means.

What is ritual impurity (*najāsa*)?

Linguistically, *najāsa* means filth, but in technical religious terminology it refers to those impurities from which Islam instructs us to cleanse ourselves, our clothes, bodies, and anything else which must be ritually pure when we use it. For example, our clothes and body must be ritually pure when we want to pray or circumambulate the Kaʿba.

The ritual impurities for which the religion has commanded avoidance and separation are ten in number:

1. Urine
2. Faeces
3. Semen
4. Carrion

---

[188] Sūrat al-Baqara (2):267
[189] Sūrat al-Aʿrāf (7):157
[190] Sūrat al-Muddaththir (74):5
[191] Sūrat al-Tawba (9):108

5. Blood
6. Dogs
7. Pigs
8. Disbelievers
9. Intoxicants and beer
10. The sweat of an excrement-eating animal, and the sweat of someone in a state of major ritual impurity due to illicit sexual intercourse.

Each of these has specific rulings that we shall discuss in order:

Urine and faeces

The noble *sunna*:

- Imam Jaʿfar b. Muḥammad al-Ṣādiq ﷺ said: 'Wash your clothing from the urine of any animal that is not eaten.'[192]
- Imam al-Ṣādiq ﷺ said: 'Whatever flies, there is no problem with its urine or faeces.'[193]
- Dāwud al-Raqqī said: I asked Abū ʿAbd Allah al-Ṣādiq ﷺ about the urine of bats: what should one do if it gets on their clothing, but when they look for it, they cannot find it? So he said: 'Wash your garment.'[194]

Rulings:

It is mandatory to keep away from the urine and faeces of human beings, as well as those of animals which are unlawful to eat, but there is no problem with the excrement of insects, such as flies and beetles, which do not have blood that gushes.

As for a person is unsure about whether some urine or faeces is ritually impure because they do not know its source, or because they do not know whether the flesh of the animal in question is impermissible to consume: in this case, the criterion is the presumption of ritual purity (*aṣālat al-ṭahāra*),[195] although if one is able they must first investigate as a precaution.

---

[192] *Wasā'il al-shīʿa*, v. 2, p. 1008, ḥ. 3

[193] *Wasā'il al-shīʿa*, v. 2, p. 1013, ḥ. 1

[194] *Wasā'il al-shīʿa*, v. 2, p. 1013, ḥ. 4

[195] This is a general rule whereby Islam deems everything to be ritually pure until someone knows it with utter certainty to be ritually impure. So everything is assumed to be ritually pure; hence it is called the presumption of ritual purity (*aṣālat al-ṭahāra*).

Semen

The noble *sunna*:

- Samāʿa said: I asked one of the Imams about what to do if semen gets on my clothing. So he answered: 'Wash the entire garment if you are unsure of its location and whether it was little or a lot.'[196]
- Muḥammad b. Muslim said: I asked one of the two Imams, al-Bāqir or al-Ṣādiq عليهما السلام, about what to do if pre-ejaculate gets on a person's clothing. So he said: 'He can sprinkle [the affected area] with water if he wants.'[197]

Rulings:

The texts have stressed the ritual impurity of semen, and consider its ritual impurity to be greater than that of urine. Literally, the word *manī* only applies to human semen. As for that of all other animals, jurists have considered the semen of every animal with blood that gushes (e.g., cows and camels) to be ritually impure, and it is best to avoid it.

Carrion and corpses

The noble *sunna*:

- Ibrāhīm b. Maymūn said: I asked Imam Abū ʿAbd Allah al-Ṣādiq عليه السلام about a man whose clothing touches the corpse of a dead man. He said: 'If the corpse has been washed, so there is no need to wash whatever part of his clothing touched it. If the corpse had not been washed, then wash whatever part of the clothing touched it—meaning if the corpse had already become cold.'[198]
- ʿAmmār al-Sābāṭī said: Imam al-Ṣādiq عليه السلام was asked about beetles, flies, rats, ants, and similar things, which die in a well, or in [cooking] oil or lard, and so on. So he answered: 'Whatever does not have blood is not a problem.'[199]
- Al-Ḥusayn b. Zurāra said: I was with Abū ʿAbd Allah al-Ṣādiq عليه السلام, and my father asked him about milk, eggs, or rennet from a carcass. So he said: 'All of these are lifeless' (meaning even not considered a living part of the animal to begin with, and hence not a problem). ʿAlī b. ʿUqba

---

[196] *Wasāʾil al-shīʿa*, v. 2, p. 1022, ḥ. 5
[197] *Wasāʾil al-shīʿa*, v. 2, p. 1023, ḥ. 1
[198] *Wasāʾil al-shīʿa*, v. 2, p. 1050, ḥ. 1
[199] *Wasāʾil al-shīʿa*, v. 2, p. 1051, ḥ. 1

and ʿAlī b. al-Ḥasan b. Ribāṭ both said he also added: 'And the hair and wool, all of it is lifeless.'[200]

Rulings:

The carrion of an animal that has blood that gushes[201] is ritually impure whether its flesh is usually permitted for consumption or not.

Human corpses are ritually impure until they have been properly washed, as are body parts severed while a person is still alive, such as his forearm, or a chunk of flesh separated from it. Even pustules, hair roots, warts, scabs that form over wounds, and calluses are all ritually impure if they are separated from someone who is living, or a corpse before it is washed. However, if pustules or blisters fall from the body by themselves, they are ritually pure.

Blood

The noble *sunna*:

- ʿAmmār al-Sābāṭī said: I asked Abū ʿAbd Allah [al-Ṣādiq] ﷷ about a man who bleeds from his nose: must he wash the inside—meaning its nostrils? So he said: 'He only needs to wash what the outer portion of it.'[202]
- ʿAlī b. Jaʿfar said: I asked him ﷷ about a man who has a nosebleed. While he is performing *wuḍū'*, a drop of blood falls into his jug. Can that water still be used for *wuḍū'*? So he said: 'No.'[203]
- Saʿīd al-Aʿraj said: I asked Abū ʿAbd Allah [al-Ṣādiq] ﷷ about a pot being used to cook meat, when tiny amount of blood falls into the pot: can its contents still be eaten? He said: Yes, for verily the fire consumes the blood.'[204]

Rulings:

Ritually impure blood is any that is spilt from human beings or animals with blood that gushes whether they are alive or dead. As for blood consumed by fleas, bedbugs and the like, it is ritually pure. As for the blood of fish that does not gush, it is better to avoid it, as is the case with carrion of this variety.

---

[200] *Wasā'il al-shīʿa*, v. 2, p. 1089, ḥ. 2, 3

[201] This refers to an animal whose blood gushes out if its carotid artery is severed.

[202] *Al-Kāfī*, v. 3, p. 59, ḥ. 5

[203] *Wasā'il al-shīʿa*, v. 2, p. 1100, ḥ. 1

[204] *Wasā'il al-shīʿa*, v. 16, p. 376, ḥ. 3

Pus that flows from wounds is ritually pure, unless one knows [with certainty] it has mixed with blood.

According to the available legal indicators, there is no problem with a small quantity of blood that falls into a boiling pot because the fire consumes it. However, it is better to avoid it out of precaution.

Pigs and dogs

The noble *sunna*:

- Muḥammad b. Muslim asked Imam al-Ṣādiq ﷺ about a dog that drinks from a container. So he said: 'Wash the container.'[205]
- In another report, the narrator said: I asked Imam Abū ʿAbd Allah al-Ṣādiq ﷺ about dogs: what should be done if anything from them touches a person? So he answered: 'Wash the place that it touched.'[206]
- Khayrān al-Khādim said: I wrote to the Imam ﷺ, asking him about a garment that has come into contact with wine or pork: can one pray in it? So he wrote back: 'Do not pray in it because it is dirty (ritually impure).'[207]

Rulings:

Pigs and dogs are both ritually impure, though this ruling does not apply to seals (called *kalb baḥrī* – *lit.* 'sea dog' – In Arabic) or dugongs (called *khinzīr baḥrī* – *lit.* 'sea pig' – in Arabic), because these are neither related to the land species, nor are they mentioned in any religious evidences; they simply share a name in Arabic.

Polytheists and disbelievers

The noble *sunna*:

- Regarding the case of someone who shakes a Zoroastrian's hand, Imam Muḥammad al-Bāqir ﷺ said: 'He should wash his hand, but he does not need to perform *wuḍū'*.'[208]
- One of the two Imams, al-Bāqir or al-Ṣādiq ﷺ, was asked about shaking hands with a Jews and Christians. So he said: 'Do it from

---

[205] *Wasā'il al-shīʿa*, v. 2, p. 1015, ḥ. 3
[206] *Wasā'il al-shīʿa*, v. 2, p. 1015, ḥ. 4
[207] *Wasā'il al-shīʿa*, v. 2, p. 1017, ḥ. 2
[208] *Wasā'il al-shīʿa*, v. 2, p. 1018, ḥ. 2

beneath a garment, and if you shook his hand [directly] then wash your hand.'[209]

❖ Sa'īd al-A'raj said: I asked Imam Abū 'Abd Allah al-Ṣādiq ﷺ about the leftover drinking water of Jews and Christians. So he said: 'No (you should not do it).'[210]

Rulings:

In the twenty-eighth verse of *Sūrat al-Tawba*, Allah says: **'O you who have faith! The polytheists are indeed unclean: so let them not approach the Holy Mosque after this year...,'**[211] because polytheism is an impure element which pollutes the human being and takes him far away from his nature.

By polytheists (*mushrikūn*), the Qur'ān means the idol worshippers who were spread throughout the Arabian Peninsula at that time, as well as polytheists, who attribute partners to Allah.

As for those who do not associate any partners with Allah and believe in the Oneness of their Lord, they are included in Allah's saying: **'Today all the good things have been made lawful to you: - the food of those who were given the Book is lawful to you, and your food is lawful to them - and the chaste ones from among faithful women, and chaste women of those who were given the Book before you...'**[212]

In fact, one should avoid associating with them anyway, because they do not avoid those ritual impurities laid down in the *sharī'a* such as wine, pork, dogs, etc.

Intoxicants and beer

The noble *sunna*:

❖ Imam al-Ṣādiq ﷺ said: If wine or intoxicating date wine comes into contact with your garment, then wash [the affected area] if you know the location. If you do not know the location, then wash the entire garment. If you prayed in it, then repeat your prayer.'[213]

---

209 *Wasā'il al-shī'a*, v. 2, p. 1019, ḥ. 5
210 *Wasā'il al-shī'a*, v. 2, p. 1019, ḥ. 8
211 Sūrat al-Tawba (9):28
212 Sūrat al-Mā'ida (5):5
213 *Wasā'il al-shī'a*, v. 2, p. 1055, ḥ. 3

- Hishām b. al-Ḥakam narrates that he asked Imam al-Ṣādiq ﷺ about beer. So he said: 'Do not drink it, for it is [like] wine; and if your garment came into contact with it, then wash [the affected area].'[214]
- Imam al-Ṣādiq ﷺ said: Do not pray in any house that keeps wine or intoxicants, because the angels will not enter it; and do not pray in your garment if any wine or [liquid] intoxicant came into contact with it until you have washed [the affected area].'[215]
- It is narrated from Imam al-Ṣādiq ﷺ that he said: 'Any juice that has been heated by fire is unlawful until two thirds of it has been boiled off and a [only] a third of it remains.'[216]

Rulings:

1. All liquid intoxicants are ritually impure and must be avoided, whether wine (*khamr* and *nabīdh*) or beer (*fuqāʿ*), and whether in large or small quantities.
2. It is better for one to avoid solid intoxicants as well, such as certain intoxicating plants, although the drugs opium or marijuana are not ritually impure because they are not intoxicants in the same manner as wine. However, just because these drugs are not ritually impure does not mean you are allowed to partake of them; taking drugs – as is widespread today – and using them is forbidden because of the great harm they cause, even if we do not consider them ritually impure.
3. Beer – a drink made from fermented grains – is forbidden and ritually impure. But before fermentation or foaming, then there is no problem in consuming it. The criterion for both its prohibition and impurity is that it is intoxicating, and the same applies for any beer or alcoholic beverage made from other sources.

Sweat from excrement-eaters and fornicators

The noble *sunna*:

- Abū Baṣīr said: I asked Imam al-Ṣādiq ﷺ about the case of a shirt. The man wearing it is in a state of major ritual impurity, and sweats in it, and remains in such a state until he removes the shirt. So he said: 'There is no problem, though I would love it if he sprinkled the shirt with water, so he should do that.'[217]

---

[214] *Wasāʾil al-shīʿa*, v. 2, p. 1055, ḥ. 5
[215] *Wasāʾil al-shīʿa*, v. 2, p. 1056, ḥ. 7
[216] *Wasāʾil al-shīʿa*, v. 17, p. 223, ḥ. 1
[217] *Wasāʾil al-shīʿa*, v. 2, p. 1038, ḥ. 8

- Imam al-Hādī about the case of a garment which has been worn by someone in a state of major ritual impurity, and was sweating in it: can he pray in it? He said: 'If his state of major ritual impurity was from a lawful activity, then he should pray in it. But if it was from something unlawful, then he must not pray in it.'[218]
- It is narrated that Imam Abū ʿAbd Allah al-Ṣādiq said: 'Do not eat the meat of an animal that has grown from eating human excrement, and if any of its sweat comes into contact with you, then wash [the affected area].'[219]

Rulings:

1. If someone enters a state of major ritual impurity by illicit means, then the strongest opinion is that one should not pray in clothes that have come into contact with his sweat, rather one should avoid that person entirely.
2. This includes someone who has intercourse with his wife while she is menstruating, fasting, or during a *ẓihār* divorce before he has repented – as a precaution.
3. One must also avoid the sweat of excrement-eating camels and any other animal that eats excrement as a precaution.

General rules

The noble *sunna*:

- Zurāra said: I said to Abū Jaʿfar [al-Bāqir] that my garment came into contact with blood from a nosebleed or some semen. I found its traces so that I could pour water on it. As I went to pour the water, the time for prayer came. I forgot there was still something on my garment, and I prayed in it. Then I remembered afterwards. The Imam said: 'Repeat the prayer and wash it.' I said: What if I had not seen its location, and I merely thought that it had come into contact with my garment, and I searched for it but, finding nothing, I prayed. Then, after praying, I found it? He said: 'Wash it, but you do not need to repeat the prayer.'

  I said: And why is that? He said: 'Because you had been certain of its being clean, and then doubted it; and you should never violate certainty with doubt.'

---

[218] *Wasāʾil al-shīʿa*, v. 2, p. 1039, ḥ. 12
[219] *Wasāʾil al-shīʿa*, v. 2, p. 1021, ḥ. 1

I said: What if I knew that it had come into contact with my garment, but was unsure where. Should I wash it? He said: 'Wash whatever side of your garment you saw had contact with it until you are certain of its purity.'

I said: If I am doubtful that any of it made contact, then am I required to look for it elsewhere [on the garment]? He said: 'No, rather you only want to do that to remove the doubt that has come over you.'

I said: What if I see it on my garment while I am in prayer? He said: 'If you doubted its presence and then saw it on your garment, abort your prayer and repeat it. If you had no doubt, but then saw its moisture, you should wash the garment and re-establish the prayer. If you were not sure whether there might be something [ritually impure] on you, then do not allow your [prior] certainty [about your garment's state of ritual purity] to be violated by doubt.'[220]

❖ 'Alī b. Ja'far said: I asked [my brother] Imam Mūsā al-Kāẓim ☙ about mice, chicken, pigeons, etc., that have stepped in dung, then walked over a garment: must it be washed? He said: 'If something was visible from their tracks, then wash [the affected area], and if not, then there is no problem.'[221]

❖ 'Alī b. Ja'far also said: I asked him ☙ about a man who steps in dried up excrement, and it comes into contact with his garment and legs. Can he enter a mosque and pray without washing the areas it touched? He said: 'If it (the feces) was dry, then there is no harm.'[222]

❖ Imam Abū Ja'far al-Bāqir ☙ said: 'If a mouse fell into some cooking fat and died there, and the fat was semisolid (lard), then throw out the mouse and whatever of the fat it has touched, and you can eat what remains. And if it was liquid fat, then do not eat it—but you can use it as a fuel source for lamps, and the same goes for oil.'[223]

Rulings:

1. Everything is clean until you know that it is dirty, and if you do not know something is dirty there is no problem with you using it.

2. In order for ritual impurity to be transferred or spread from agents of impurity to pure items, the following conditions must be met:

   a. That there must be contact between the impurity and the pure item

---

[220] *Biḥār al-anwār*, v. 77, p. 124, cited in *'Illal al-sharā'i'*, v. 2, p. 49

[221] *Biḥār al-anwār*, v. 77, p. 127, cited in *Qurb al-isnād*, p. 117

[222] *Biḥār al-anwār*, v. 77, p. 128, cited in *Qurb al-isnād*, p. 94

[223] *Wasā'il al-shī'a*, v. 16, p. 374, ḥ. 3

   b. The contact must involve the transference of moisture between them.
3. Solid grease does not become impure through contact with a dry impurity, and one can make use of it.
4. Ritually impure objects can also contaminate others. However, if neither the source of impurity nor its traces are transferred from the contaminated object (either due to multiple intermediaries or because a duration of time has passed in which its traces would usually have disappeared), such that common sense would not say that the other object has come into contact with impurity, then it is not necessary to avoid it, although avoiding it would be in keeping with precaution.
5. One must remove any impurity from one's clothes and body for obligatory or supererogatory prayers and circumambulation, and for anything subsidiary to the obligatory prayers, such as the prayer for precaution, making up for *tashahhud*, forgotten prostrations, and even for the prostrations for error (*sajdatay al-sahw*). It is also obligatory to remove ritual impurities from mosques and shrines.

Section three: Three methods of ritual purification

Introduction

Allah says: **'O you who have faith! Do not approach prayer when you are intoxicated, [not] until you know what you are saying, nor [enter mosques] in the state of ritual impurity - except while passing through - until you have washed yourselves. But if you are sick or on a journey, or any of you has come from the toilet, or you have touched women, and you cannot find water, then make your ablution on clean ground and wipe a part of your faces and your hands. Indeed Allah is all-excusing, all-forgiving.'**[224]

Prayer is a moment in which we turn towards Allah and stand before Him to receive His teachings and purify our souls by reciting the Qur'ān, to seek His mercy through supplication and glorify Him through remembrance (*dhikr*). For this reason, you cannot pray while intoxicated, whether because of wine or because of sleep. One must purify himself after sleeping in preparation for standing before the Lord of the heavens and the earth. Hence we know that one of the wisdoms behind *wuḍū'* is to awaken our minds and prepare our souls for awareness of what the believer says in prayer [in the form] of recitation, remembrance, and supplication.

---

[224] Sūrat al-Nisā' (4):43

Whoever comes from using the lavatory (whether passing urine, faeces, gas, or vomiting), he must purify himself with water if it is available; otherwise he must perform *tayammum*.

It is narrated from Allah's Messenger 🕊 that he said: 'Prayer is opened by ablutions (*wuḍū'*), consecrated by saying *takbīr,* and finished by invoking peace (*taslīm*).'

And Faḍl b. Shādhān narrates from Imam 'Alī b. Mūsā al-Riḍā 🕊, concerning the reason for which Allah enjoined *wuḍū'*: 'He only bid people to perform *wuḍū'* so that the servant would be pure when he stood before the Almighty when supplicating to Him, obedient to Him in what He has commanded, cleansed of filth and impurity. [He also bid it] because it rouses one from laziness and awakens one from drowsiness, and readies the mind to stand before the Almighty.' And he said: 'And [Allah] only allowed people to pray over the deceased without *wuḍū'* because this prayer has no bowing or prostration, and one need only perform *wuḍū'* for prayers in which there is bowing and prostration.

What requires ritual purity

1. A state of ritual purity is mandatory in order to offer prayers, whether these are obligatory or supererogatory (additional recommended prayers). This includes performing the forgotten parts of prayer, though not the prostrations for errors (*sahw*) except if one wishes to observe precaution (*iḥtiyāṭ*).
2. One must perform ritual ablutions for obligatory circumambulations during *ḥajj* or *'umra*. Recommended circumambulations can be performed without ritual purity, but the prayer of circumambulation cannot be established without being in a state of ritual purity.
3. If someone wants to touch the written text of the Qur'ān, or any of Allah's names, requires an individual to be in a state of ritual purity.

First: *Wuḍū'*

The noble *sunna:*

❖ Abū 'Abd Allah 🕊 said: 'Whoever seeks a need without *wuḍū'*, and it is not achieved, he has no one to blame but himself.'[225]

---

[225] *Wasā'il al-shī'a*, v. 1, p. 262, ḥ. 1

- Al-Ṣādiq عليه السلام said: 'Truly I am amazed if someone seeks his need with *wuḍū'* and it is not accomplished.'[226]
- Zurāra said: I said to Abū Jaʿfar عليه السلام: Can a man pray night and day with a single *wuḍū'*? He said: 'Yes, if he did nothing to break it.' I said: What about with a single *tayammum*? He said: 'Yes, all of the prayers, so long as he did nothing to break his state of ritual purity and water remained unavailable.'[227]
- Samāʿa b. Mahrān said: Abū al-Ḥasan Mūsā عليه السلام said: 'Whoever performs *wuḍū'* for the dusk prayer, his *wuḍū'* is expiation for whatever sins he committed during the day, apart from the cardinal sins. Whoever performs *wuḍū'* for the dawn prayer, his *wuḍū'* is expiation for whatever sins he committed in the night, apart from cardinal sins.'[228]
- Imam al-Ṣādiq عليه السلام said: 'Purification upon purification (performing *wuḍū'* when one's previous *wuḍū'* is still valid) earns 10 rewards.'[229]
- Imam al-Riḍā عليه السلام said: 'I swear by Allah that renewing *wuḍū'* for the second evening prayer expunges [sins].'[230]
- Mufaḍḍal b. ʿUmar has narrated that Abū ʿAbd Allah عليه السلام said: 'Whoever renews his *wuḍū'* without having broken it [in the first place], Allah will renew His forgiveness of him without his needing to seek it.'[231]
- And in another narration: '*Wuḍū'* upon *wuḍū'* is a light upon a light.'[232]
- And in another narration: 'The Prophet ﷺ would renew his *wuḍū'* for every obligatory act and every prayer.'[233]
- Muḥammad b. ʿAlī b. al-Ḥasan has narrated that al-Ṣādiq عليه السلام said: 'Whoever ritually purifies himself, then goes to bed for the night, his bed is like his mosque. So if he remembered that he had not performed *wuḍū'*, he can perform *tayammum* from his cushion, and his soul [while he sleeps] will remain in prayer and as Allah has mentioned.'[234]
- Imam al-Ṣādiq عليه السلام said: 'Verily Salmān narrated from the Messenger of Allah ﷺ: "Whoever goes to bed in a state of ritual purity, his spirit will be reinvigorated that night."'[235]

---

226 *Wasā'il al-shīʿa*, v. 1, p. 262, ḥ. 2
227 *Wasā'il al-shīʿa*, v. 1, p. 263, ḥ. 1
228 *Wasā'il al-shīʿa*, v. 1, p. 264, ḥ. 4
229 *Wasā'il al-shīʿa*, v. 1, p. 264, ḥ. 3
230 *Wasā'il al-shīʿa*, v. 1, p. 264, ḥ. 6
231 *Wasā'il al-shīʿa*, v. 1, p. 264, ḥ. 7
232 *Wasā'il al-shīʿa*, v. 1, p. 265, ḥ. 8
233 *Wasā'il al-shīʿa*, v. 1, p. 265, ḥ. 9
234 *Wasā'il al-shīʿa*, v. 1, p. 265, ḥ. 2
235 *Wasā'il al-shīʿa*, v. 1, p. 266, ḥ. 3

Actions of wuḍū'

The noble *sunna*:

❖ It is narrated that Zurāra b. Aʿyan said to Abū Jaʿfar Imam al-Bāqir 🕮: Inform me about the limits of the face, which is necessary to wash when one performs *wuḍū*? So he said: 'The face is that which Allah Almighty has commanded us to wash, to which no one should go beyond, and from which no one should subtract. For if one increased the area, then he would receive no reward for doing so; and if he subtracted from it, then he would have sinned. The face is whatever is passed over between the tip of the middle finger and the tip of the thumb, from the hairline to the chin, and whatever the fingers happen to cover from the cheeks. Anything but that is not from the face.' So Zurāra said to him: Are the temples part of the face? So he said: 'No.'[236]

❖ Muḥammad b. Muslim has narrated from Imam al-Ṣādiq 🕮: 'The ears are not part of the face or the head (i.e., in a legal sense).'[237]

❖ It is narrated that Bukayr and [his brother] Zurāra b. Aʿyan asked Imam al-Bāqir 🕮 about the *wuḍū'* of the Messenger of Allah 🕮. So he 🕮 called for bowl of water and washed his hands. Then he scooped his right palm into the bowl and washed his face with it, and he used the palm of his left hand to wash his face [also]. Then he scooped up some water with his let palm and washed his right arm from the elbow to his fingertips, never washing the water upwards to his elbow. Then he submerged his right hand, scooped up some water with it, and emptied it over his left arm, from the elbow to the fingertips, never washing the water upwards to his elbow—just as he had done with the right—then with his palm he wiped the top of his forehead, and the tops of his feet up to the bump of the arches, without taking new water.[238]

❖ Muʿammar b. ʿUmar has narrated from Imam al-Bāqir 🕮: 'The space of wiping on the head is the area of three fingers [side-by-side], and the same for the [tops of the] feet.'[239]

❖ Mālik b. Aʿyan has narrated from Imam al-Ṣādiq 🕮: 'If someone forgets to wipe their head, and remembers that they did not, can do so with

---

[236] *Wasā'il al-shīʿa*, v. 1, pp. 283-284, ḥ. 1
[237] *Wasā'il al-shīʿa*, v. 1, p. 284, ḥ. 1
[238] *Wasā'il al-shīʿa*, v. 1, p. 275, ḥ. 11
[239] *Wasā'il al-shīʿa*, v. 1, p. 294, ḥ. 5

whatever moisture is still in their beard. If there was no moisture left in their beard, then they should hasten and repeat their *wuḍū'*.'[240]

Rulings:

The first of the three purifications, and most oft performed in a believer's daily life, is *wuḍū'*. It consists of two washings and two wipings: washing the face and forearms, and wiping the head and feet. This is detailed as follows:

One: Washing the face

1. Everyone knows what the face is, but the jurists have defined it according to the traditions as extending lengthways from the hairline to the tip of the chin, and widthways as the distance between the tip of the thumb and middle finger [in an average size hand].
2. When washing the face, this must be done in a way that would typically be understood as 'washing,' either by moving water over the face or covering it with water.
3. Washing must begin from what is commonly considered the top [of the face], and include the face's entire surface. If part of the 'face' (according to its legal definition) is covered by hair, then washing the surface of this hair suffices.
4. Any and all barriers to water [reaching the skin] must be removed from the face, such as thick colourings and caked-on dirt. There is no problem with colour or dirt that does not prevent water from reaching the skin. If one doubts whether there is a barrier or not, he does not need to investigate; it is sufficient that there is no evidence for its existence, so long as the presumption of non-existence applies.

Two: Washing the forearms

1. It is necessary to wash the forearms beginning from the elbow and ending at the fingertips; first the right arm, then the left. It is impermissible to reverse this order, beginning with the fingertips and ending at the elbow. Additionally, it is obligatory to wash the hair that grows on the arms.
2. It is necessary to remove anything that prevents water from reaching the skin. However, anything normally present—such as dirt under the fingernails—does not need to be removed, unless someone

---

[240] *Wasā'il al-shī'a*, v. 1, p. 288, ḥ. 7

trims their nails, in which case he must remove any dirt that is left exposed.

3. It is not necessary to remove any gypsum or lime on the surface of the arm so long as these are not thick enough to act as a barrier to water. The same applies to dirt.
4. It is permitted to wash the face and hands with rainwater, under a faucet, or to submerge them in a stream, or pool of water.

Three: Wiping the head

It is necessary to wipe the front portion of the head with whatever moisture is left on the palm of the hand, without adding any more water to it. The slightest movement that can be called 'wiping' is sufficient, though it is best that its width should be that of three fingers closed together, and that the wiping extends to their length as well. It is permissible to wipe in reverse, and to wipe upon the hair of the forelock. But if this hair originates from another part of the head and merely falls on the area of wiping, one is not permitted to wipe upon it (for the purpose of *wuḍū'*), nor upon long hair growing from the forelock that falls elsewhere.

Four: Wiping the feet

1. It is obligatory to wipe the tops of both feet, up to the arches, with your palms. It is best to wipe until the ankle. Precaution requires that one not wipe with less than three fingers, and it is best to use the entire palm. It is also better to wipe from the toes until the ankles.
   It is permitted to wipe both feet at the same time, but the left foot should not be wiped before the right foot as a matter of precaution. It is best to wipe the right foot before the left, and precaution requires that you wipe your right foot with your right hand, and your left foot with your left hand.
2. It is necessary to remove any barriers to wiping. The hair on the feet does not count as a barrier, and you can wipe over the hair no matter how thick it might be.
3. The wiping must be performed with the moisture left over from *wuḍū'*. If your hand dries out, take from the remaining moisture from any of the limbs you washed in the course of *wuḍū'*. It makes no difference which limb, you can even take the moisture from the beard.
4. It is not necessary to dry the top of your foot before wiping it, even if it is moister than the palm of your hand, though it is nearer to precaution to dry it first.

Conditions of wuḍūʾ

The noble *sunna*:

- Regarding the case of someone who has applied henna dye to their head, then he begins to perform *wuḍūʾ*, Imam al-Ṣādiq ﷺ has said: 'It is impermissible until the water can directly reach his scalp.'[241]
- ʿAlī b. Jaʿfar said: I asked my brother Mūsā b. Jaʿfar ﷺ about a woman who has some bracelets or bangles covering part of her arm, and she is not sure whether water reached under them or not. What should she do if she is trying to perform *wuḍūʾ*? He said: She should move them around until water enters beneath, or take them off.' And regarding a tight ring, such that one does not know if water reached beneath it or not during *wuḍūʾ*: what should the person do? He said: 'If he knew that water would not get under it, then he must take it off to perform *wuḍūʾ*.'[242]
- Zurāra said: One of the two Imams (al-Bāqir or al-Ṣādiq) ﷺ was asked about a man who began *wuḍūʾ* by washing his forearms before washing his face, or by wiping his feet before washing his forearms. He said: 'He should begin with what Allah has commanded him, and he should repeat [his *wuḍūʾ*].'[243]
- ʿAbd Allah b. Sinān has narrated from Abū ʿAbd Allah Imam al-Ṣādiq ﷺ: 'There is no problem if someone performs *wuḍūʾ* with water that was already used for it. [As for] water that was used for washing clothing, or water that was used for *ghusl* by someone in a state of major ritual impurity, and suchlike, it is impermissible to use it for *wuḍūʾ*. As for if a man washes his face and hands from it in something clean, then there is no problem in someone else using that water for *wuḍūʾ*.'[244]

Rulings:

1. *Wuḍūʾ* is only correct when performed with ritually pure, unmixed water.
2. If one of the body parts cleansed in the course of *wuḍūʾ* has been made ritually impure, it is nearer to precaution to purify it [separately] before *wuḍūʾ*.
3. If there is a tight-fitting ring on your hand, you should either twist it around or remove it to ensure that water reaches the area beneath it.

---

[241] *Wasāʾil al-shīʿa*, v. 1, p. 320, ḥ. 1
[242] *Wasāʾil al-shīʿa*, v. 1, p. 329, ḥ. 1
[243] *Wasāʾil al-shīʿa*, v. 1, p. 317, ḥ. 3
[244] *Wasāʾil al-shīʿa*, v. 1, p. 155, ḥ. 13

The same applies to a woman wearing a bracelet, and to any kind of wristwatch: you must ensure that it does not prevent water reaching the skin.

4. The one performing *wuḍūʾ* must begin as Allah ordained it, by washing the face, followed by the right forearm, then the left, followed by wiping the head and then finally wiping the feet. One must never begin any of these stages with the left limb as a matter of precaution.
5. The parts of *wuḍūʾ* must proceed in order from one another because it is a single deed. Thus, it is impermissible separate its constituent actions such that common sense would say they are not continuous.
6. If performing *wuḍūʾ* would cause serious harm to someone, they must perform *tayammum* instead (see below).
7. Because *wuḍūʾ* is part of prayer (*ṣalāt*), such that Allah has commanded us to perform it when we stand up to pray, our jurists have said we must make the intention of performing ritual purifications just as we make our intention to pray. This means a number of things:
    a. That the one performing ritual purifications must be conscious of what he is doing and intending to do it. Thus, if rain falls on him and his limbs are made wet without his intending to perform *wuḍūʾ*, then this is not considered *wuḍūʾ*.
    b. That one's objective in ritual purification must be to enact the command of Allah; not merely to cool himself down or look after his personal hygiene.
    c. That one should dedicate this action entirely to Allah, and not intend to show off or draw attention to oneself thereby.
8. The jurists have mentioned other conditions for *wuḍūʾ* and there is no doubt that observing these is usually in accordance with precaution:
    a. They say that the *wuḍūʾ* must not not be unlawful in and of itself, such as using stolen or usurped (*maghṣūb*) water (water that belongs to someone else and is used without their permission), in a usurped place, with a usurped container, or even pouring water in a usurped place. The criterion here is that the actions of *wuḍūʾ* should in no way, shape, or form, rely on something that has been misappropriated.
    b. In their view, using gold and silver utensils for *wuḍūʾ* is the same as misappropriation because the use of these is unlawful if those utensils are actually used in the *wuḍūʾ* itself (for example, using a gold pitcher to pour the water).
    c. They say that the one performing *wuḍūʾ* must perform the washing himself. If someone else washes his forearm or face for him, then this is considered contrary to Allah's command to

wash and wipe, and he must repeat his ablutions. Of course, if someone else helps him to bring and pour water, there is no problem with this, though it is legally discouraged (*makrūh*).

The etiquettes of wuḍū'

The noble *sunna*:

- The Prophet ﷺ said: 'If not for fear of imposing hardship upon my nation, I would have ordered them to use a toothbrush when performing *wuḍū'* for every prayer.'[245]
- Imam al-Ṣādiq ؑ said: 'Whoever mentions the name of Allah during *wuḍū'*, it is like he has performed *ghusl*.'[246]
- Imam al-Ṣādiq ؑ said: 'Whoever performs *wuḍū'*, then uses a towel, will receive one goodness; but whoever performs *wuḍū'* and does not use a towel until after his *wuḍū'* dries, he will receive thirty goodnesses.'[247]
- Isḥāq b. ʿAmmār has narrated from Imam al-Ṣādiq ؑ about basins, jugs, tubs, and containers that bearing icons or portraits, or made with silver: 'Do not perform *wuḍū'* from it or in it.'[248]
- Al-Sukūnī has narrated from Imam al-Ṣādiq ؑ: 'The Messenger of Allah ﷺ said: "Concerning water which has been warmed by the sun's rays, perform neither *wuḍū'* nor *ghusl* with it, and do not use it for making dough, for it leads to leprosy."'[249]
- Concerning the use of malodorous water for *wuḍū'*, al-Ḥalabī has narrated from Abū ʿAbd Allah [al-Ṣādiq] ؑ: 'If you cannot find other water, then you can use it.'[250]

Rulings:

1. It is recommended (*mustaḥabb*) to use neither more nor less than one measure (*mudd*) of water for *wuḍū'*, which is equal to about 750 grams (a little under 3¼ cups). More than this is considered wasteful (*isrāf*), and less than this is deemed insufficient.
2. It is recommended to brush one's teeth at every *wuḍū'* and to rinse one's mouth afterwards.
3. It is recommended to invoke Allah's name before touching the water, and the best formula is: '*bismillāhi wa billāhi wal-ḥamdu lillāh iladhī jaʿal*

---

245 *Wasā'il al-shīʿa*, v. 1, p. 354, ḥ. 4
246 *Wasā'il al-shīʿa*, v. 1, p. 298, ḥ. 3
247 *Al-Kāfī*, v. 3, p. 70, ḥ. 4
248 *Wasā'il al-shīʿa*, v. 1, p. 344, ḥ. 1
249 *ʿIllal al-sharāʾiʿ*, p. 281, ḥ. 2
250 *Wasā'il al-shīʿa*, v. 1, p. 103, ḥ. 2

al-mā' ṭahūran wa lam yaj'alahu najisan.' (In the name of Allah and by Allah, praise belongs to Allah who made water pure and did not make it impure).

a. When rinsing one's mouth, recite: *'allāhumma laqqinī ḥujjatī ḥīn alqāka wa aṭluq lisānī bi dhikrik wa shukrik.'* (O Allah! Give me my *ḥujja* when I submit to You, and release my tongue with Your remembrance and thanksgiving.)
b. Then rinse out the nose three times by snorting water into it and say: *'allāhumma la taḥrum 'alayya rīh ul-janna waj'alnī mimman yashamm rīhuhā wa rawḥuhā wa ṭayyibuhā.'* (O Allah! Do not deny me the scent of Paradise, but make me amongst those who smell its pleasant fragrance!)
c. When washing the face, it is recommended to recite: *'allāhumma bayyaḍ wajhī yawma tasawwadu fīh il-wujūh wa la tusawwid wajhī yawma tabayyaḍ fīh il-wujūh.'* (O Allah! Brighten my face on a day when faces darken, and do not darken my face on a day when faces brighten!)
d. When washing the right forearm, say: *'allāhumma a'tinī kitābī bi yamīnī wal-khuld fil-jinān bi yasārī wa hāsibnī hisāban yasīrā.'* (O Allah! Give me my record of deeds in my right hand and eternal life in Paradise in my left, and account me an easy accounting.)
e. When washing the left forearm, say: *'allāhumma lā ta'tinī kitābī bi shimālī wa lā min warā' ẓahrī wa lā taj'alhā maghlūla ilā 'anqī wa a'ūdhu bika min muqaṭṭa'āt in-nayrān.'* (O Allah! Give me neither my record of deeds in my left hand, nor from behind my back, nor make it chained to my neck. I seek refuge in you from the blaze of Hell!)
f. When wiping the head, say: *'allāhumma ghashshanī bi raḥmatika wa barakātika wa 'afūk.'* (O Allah! Cover me with Your mercy, blessings and forgiveness!)
g. When wiping the feet, say: *'allāhumma thabbatnī 'alaṣ-ṣirāṭ yawma tazal fīh il-aqdām waj'al sa'iyi fī mā yarḍīka 'annī yā dhāl-jalāli wal-ikrām.'* (O Allah! Steady me upon the Straight Path on a day when feet shall slip, and let me hasten in that which will please You, O Master of Magnificence and Munificence!)

Invalidators of wuḍū'

The noble *sunna*:

- Zakariyya b. Ādam said: I asked al-Riḍā عليه السلام about blood that comes from a kind of hemorrhoid: does it break one's *wuḍū'*? He said: '*Wuḍū'* is only broken by three things: urination, defecation, or passing gas.'[251]
- Imam ʿAlī b. Mūsā al-Riḍā عليه السلام said: '*Wuḍū'* is only broken by defecation, urination, passing gas, sleeping, or a state of major ritual impurity.'[252]
- The Prophet ﷺ said: 'Verily Satan comes to one of you while you are in prayer, saying: "Do something to break your *wuḍū'*, do something to break your *wuḍū'*," and he does not withdraw until he hears a sound or notices a smell (gas).'[253]
- Imam ʿAlī said: 'When sleep afflicts the heart then *wuḍū'* becomes necessary [again].'[254]
- It is narrated that Zurāra said to the Imam عليه السلام: A man dozes while he has *wuḍū'*; if his head droops once or twice, is he obliged to perform *wuḍū'* [again]? So he said: 'O Zurāra, the eyes may sleep while the heart and ears do not. When the eyes, the ears, and the heart all sleep, then *wuḍū'* has become obligatory [again].'[255]
- The Commander of the Believers عليه السلام did not see a need for *wuḍū'* or *ghusl* due pre-ejaculate, but for washing whatever of it had come into contact with one's garment.[256]
- It is narrated that Zurāra said to the Imam عليه السلام: A man dozes while he has *wuḍū'*; if his head droops once or twice, is he obliged to perform *wuḍū'* [again]? So he said: 'O Zurāra, the eyes may sleep while the heart and ears do not. When the eyes, the ears, and the heart all sleep, then *wuḍū'* has become obligatory [again].' Zurāra said: Even if someone shakes his side and he does not notice? He said: 'Not until he is absolutely certain that he slept, not until the issue becomes clear to him, for he was certain of his [prior] *wuḍū'*, and certainty can never be violated by doubt—only by another certainty.'[257]

---

[251] *Al-Kāfī*, v. 3, p. 36, ḥ. 2
[252] *ʿUyūn akhbār al-riḍā*, v. 2, p. 121
[253] *Mustadrak al-wasāʾil*, v. 1, p. 31, ḥ. 5
[254] *Wasāʾil al-shīʿa*, v. 1, p. 175, ḥ. 6
[255] *Wasāʾil al-shīʿa*, v. 1, p. 174, ḥ. 1
[256] *Man lā yaḥḍuruh al-faqīh*, v. 1, p. 39, ḥ. 1
[257] *Wasāʾil al-shīʿa*, v. 1, p. 174, ḥ. 1

- Al-Ḥalabī has narrated from Abū ʿAbd Allah al-Ṣādiq ﷺ: 'If you remembered, while in prayer, that you missed something obligatory in your *wuḍū'*, then you must withdraw, complete what was forgotten of your *wuḍū'*, and repeat your prayer.'[258]
- Muḥammad b. Muslim said: I asked Abū Jaʿfar Imam al-Bāqir ﷺ about someone who is incontinent. He said: 'He establishes his prayer [anyway].'[259]
- Imam al-Bāqir ﷺ said: 'The incontinent person [whose prayer is broken due to that] should renew his *wuḍū'*, return to his prayer, and complete what was left of it.'[260]

Rulings:

1. *Wuḍū'* is invalidated by urination or defecation, whether in large or small amounts.
2. *Wuḍū'* is not invalidated by anything that comes out of the urethra or anus other than urine and faeces, such as worms or stones, or other fluids such as pre-ejaculate that comes out when one is sexually aroused, or the fluid that comes out after urination, ejaculation, or because of illness. The same applies to pus and blood, unless these are mixed with urine or faeces.
3. Flatulence invalidates *wuḍū'* if it comes from the anus, whether it is accompanied by sound or not.
4. Sleeping invalidates *wuḍū'*. The criterion of sleep is that it should overcome the limbs; so if the mind is still in control of the limbs, sleep has not occurred. So drowsiness, dozing, or relaxing do not affect *wuḍū'* so long as one is still conscious and in control of one's limbs.
5. Jurists say that falling unconscious, intoxication, temporary insanity, and anything else that deprives the mind of its control over the body invalidates *wuḍū'* in the same manner as sleep. This is closest to precaution.
6. Spotting (*istiḥāḍa*) in women invalidates *wuḍū'* and requires that they perform *wuḍū'* for each and every prayer for which they do not perform the *ghusl* for spotting. As for if they have performed *ghusl*, then the strongest opinion is that they do not need to perform *wuḍū'* as well, even if this is closer to precaution.

---

258 *Wasā'il al-shīʿa*, v. 1, p. 331, ḥ. 3
259 *Wasā'il al-shīʿa*, v. 1, p. 210, ḥ. 1
260 *Wasā'il al-shīʿa*, v. 1, p. 210, ḥ. 3

Rulings for performing ablutions over bandages

The noble *sunna*:

- It is narrated that Ibn al-Ḥajjāj asked Imam al-Riḍā ﵇ about someone with a cast on a broken limb, or there is wound: how does he perform *wuḍū'*? And what of *ghusl* for major ritual impurity, or for Friday? So he said: 'He should wash what he can reach from whatever is apparent and not covered by the dressing, leave alone what he is unable to reach, and not remove the cast or tamper with the wound.'[261]
- Al-Ḥalabī has narrated from Imam al-Ṣādiq ﵇, who was asked about a man with a sore on his forearm or something similar from the places where *wuḍū'* takes place. He wraps a cloth around it, performs *wuḍū'*, wiping over it in the process. So he said 'If the water would harm him, then he should wipe over the bandage, and if it would not harm him, then he should remove the bandage and wash over it.'[262]

Rulings:

Whoever has a wound, sore, or broken bone by one of the places he must cleanse in *wuḍū'*, and has covered it with something that would prevent water reaching the skin, but opening this dressing would cause harm to him, then he must make the water reach that which is under the covering (called a dressing[263]) if this is possible without causing any harm or difficulty. Otherwise one must wipe over the dressing. There are several issues here:

1. The covering must be ritually pure; otherwise, another ritually pure covering should be placed over it.
2. If the wound is exposed, it suffices to wash the area around it.
3. In places where one would wipe rather than wash, the dressing should be wiped if it is not possible to wipe on any other place.
4. If the use of water itself would cause harm to someone (not because of a wound, broken bone or sore), then they should perform *tayammum* for their prayers.
5. Anyone who has a piece of tar on one of the limbs they must cleanse for *wuḍū'*, or any other obstruction which they cannot remove, or some medicine or complex device which they cannot remove, then it suffices to wipe over it. And if contact with water will harm it, it

---

[261] *Wasā'il al-shī'a*, v. 1, p. 326, ḥ. 1

[262] *Wasā'il al-shī'a*, v. 1, p. 326, ḥ. 2

[263] This includes bandages, splints, plaster casts, and anything else that is used to cover wounds and broken bones.

suffices to wash around it. Precaution requires that *tayammum* be performed *as well* as *wuḍū'* in this case.

6. Dressings that interfere with *ghusl* or *tayammum* follow the same rulings as outlined above.

Second: *Ghusl*

Rules pertaining to post-coital impurity (janāba*)*

The noble *sunna*:

- Imam Mūsā b. Jaʿfar said: '*Ghusl* is obligatory for someone in a state of major ritual impurity.'[264]
- Imam al-Ṣādiq said: 'Whoever intentionally leaves a single hair in a state of major ritual impurity will be in the fire.'[265]
- It is narrated that a woman asked the Messenger of Allah ﷺ about a woman who sees in her dream like what a man sees (i.e., a sexual dream). So he said: 'Did she experience climax?' She said: Yes. So he said: 'She is obliged to do the same as a man (i.e., perform *ghusl*).'[266]
- It is narrated from Isḥāq b. ʿAmmār that he asked Imam al-Ṣādiq ؑ about a man who is traveling with his wife, but is unable to find any water: can he sleep with his wife? He said: 'I wish that he would refrain from it unless he fears for himself.' So Isḥāq said: What if he is seeking pleasure or lusting over women? So he said: 'Experiencing lust is [the same as] fearing for himself.' Isḥāq said: And if he is only seeking pleasure? He said: 'It is [still] lawful.'[267]
- Sulaymān b. Khālid said: I asked Imam al-Ṣādiq ؑ about a man who enters a state of major ritual impurity, so he performs *ghusl* prior to urinating, and [afterwards] something comes out of his genitals. He said: 'He repeats the *ghusl*.' So I said: And what if something comes out of a woman after *ghusl*? He said: 'She does not need to repeat it.' I said: So what is the difference between the two? He said: 'It is because what came out of the woman is only from the semen of the man.'[268]
- ʿAmmār b. Mūsā has narrated from Imam al-Ṣādiq ؑ: 'Someone in a state of major ritual impurity should not touch a single dirham or dinar that bears the name of Allah.'[269]

---

[264] *Wasā'il al-shīʿa*, v. 1, p. 462, ḥ. 1
[265] *Wasā'il al-shīʿa*, v. 1, p. 463, ḥ. 5
[266] *Wasā'il al-shīʿa*, v. 1, p. 476, ḥ. 23
[267] *Wasā'il al-shīʿa*, v. 14, p. 76, ḥ. 1
[268] *Wasā'il al-shīʿa*, v. 1, p. 482, ḥ. 1
[269] *Wasā'il al-shīʿa*, v, 1, p. 491, ḥ. 1

- Zurāra has narrated from Imam al-Bāqir ﷺ: If someone in a state of major ritual impurity wants to eat or drink, then he should wash his hands, gargle water, wash his face, and then proceed to eat and drink.'[270]
- Al-Ḥalabī said: Imam al-Ṣādiq was asked if a man should sleep while he is in a state of major ritual impurity. He said: 'It is disliked for him to do so until he has [at least] performed *wuḍū'*.'[271]

Rulings:

Ghusl must be performed due to post-coital impurity, menstruation, spotting, postpartum bleeding, and touching an unwashed corpse. It is also obligatory to wash a corpse, and we shall mention the rulings for that later.

Post-coital impurity (*janāba*) occurs as a result of ejaculation (i.e. the emission of semen) and penetrative sexual intercourse. Each of these has rulings:

1. If a man or woman experiences a night emission, or a fluid is emitted from the man, which he knows to be semen, then they must perform *ghusl*. In the case that he is not sure whether the fluid that comes out is semen or some other fluid: if he experienced the sensations of ejaculation (namely orgasm) or anything that would indicate that this was semen, then it is judged to be semen. Otherwise it is not treated as semen. If some fluid comes out after ejaculation but before *istibrā'* (i.e., after purity from urination), then it too is considered to be semen. However, if the fluid comes out after *istibrā'*, it is not considered semen.
2. Jurists say that ejaculation must result in the emission of semen; it is not enough for someone to experience an orgasm and feel the movement of semen within the body. However, precaution[272] requires one in such a scenario to assume that they have entered a state of post-coital ritual impurity, especially in the case of women who do not emit semen, for there are narrations which say women experience night emissions just as a man does.
3. A person enters a state of post-coital ritual impurity (*janāba*) by penetrative sexual intercourse. This is when the private parts meet; so if a man's penis or part of it enters the vagina or rectum, then he

---

[270] *Wasā'il al-shī'a*, v. 1, p. 490, ḥ. 1

[271] *Wasā'il al-shī'a*, v. 1, p. 501, ḥ. 1

[272] This is obligatory precaution: If a man or woman experiences an orgasm, even if no semen is emitted, or the man feels the movement of semen within his body but it does not come out, he is said to be in a state of ritual impurity and he must perform *ghusl* as a matter of obligatory precaution.

has become ritually impure, as has his partner. As for someone who penetrates an animal there is uncertainty, but obligatory precaution requires that they perform *ghusl.*

4. Post-coital impurity, like any other phenomenon, is only established by definite knowledge (*yaqīn*) or some indication that gives us customary confidence (*iṭmi'nān 'urfī*). So if someone sees semen on clothing which only he wears—such as would indicate he had experienced a night emission—then he must perform *ghusl.* The same is true if he feels sensations that would indicate ejaculation in his sleep. But if he has sexual relations with his wife, but doubts whether he actually penetrated her [and did not ejaculate], then he need not do anything. If there is any doubt about whether one has entered a state of post-coital impurity, it is not necessary to perform *ghusl.*
5. Penetration with some sort of covering, whether underwear, condoms, etc., requires *ghusl* afterwards.
6. Being purified from post-coital impurity is required for the same things for which *wuḍū'*, such as obligatory prayers and circumambulation, and touching the text of the Qur'ān, as well as fasting in the month of Ramaḍān (which we shall discuss later).
7. It is forbidden for someone in a state of post-coital impurity to enter the Holy Sanctuary in Mecca or the Prophet's Mosque in Medina in any way, shape, or form. As for all other mosques, it is not forbidden to pass through them but it is forbidden to loiter therein. Shrines fall under the same rules.
8. They say that someone in a state of post-coital impurity should not recite the *'azā'im sūras*[273] of the Qur'ān, nor any verse from them. This is nearest to precaution.[274] However, the strongest opinion is that it is only forbidden to recite the verses containing the obligatory prostration.
9. It is disliked (*makrūh*) for one in a state of post-coital impurity to eat or drink before performing *ghusl* or *wuḍū'*, and if he only washes his hands, and rinses his mouth and nose, this reduces the dislike.

---

[273] The *'azā'im* are those four *sūras* which contain obligatory prostrations, namely: i. *Sūrat al-Sajda* (no. 32), ii. *Sūra Fuṣṣilat* (no. 41), iii. *Sūrat al-Najm* (no. 53) and iv. *Sūrat al-'Alaq* (no. 96).

[274] This is recommended precaution (*iḥtiyāt istiḥbābī*), meaning that it is recommended for the legal agent to avoid reciting any *sūra* containing an obligatory prostration while in a state of post-coital impurity; as for what is forbidden: it is only forbidden to recite the verses which require these prostrations.

It is also disliked to sleep before making *wuḍū'*, or to dye or oil one's hair [prior to *wuḍū'*]. And if the reason for the post-coital impurity was a nocturnal emission, then it is disliked to engage in sexual intercourse. They say that it is disliked to recite more than seven verses of the Qur'ān, and it is better to go and perform *ghusl* straight away and if he cannot then he may read whatever he likes from the Qur'ān, and reciting remembrance (*dhikr*) of Allah. It is disliked for someone to hold the Qur'ān against themselves while they are in a state of ritual impurity.

Rules and method of ghusl

The noble *sunna*:

❖ Zurāra asked Imam al-Ṣādiq about the *ghusl* of major ritual impurity. So the Imam 🕮 said to him: 'You begin by washing your hands, then you empty [the water] from your right over your left. Next, you wash your genitals. Then you gargle water and spit it out, snort some into your nostrils and blow it back out, and finally you wash your body.'[275]

❖ Muḥammad b. Muslim asked one of the two Imams (al-Bāqir or al-Ṣādiq) 🕮 about the *ghusl* of someone in a state of major ritual impurity. So he said: 'You begin by washing your hands, followed by your genitals. Then you pour water over your head three times, then over the rest of your body twice. Whatever the water flows upon has been purified.'[276]

❖ 'Alī b. Ja'far said: I asked [my brother, Imam al-Kāẓim 🕮] about a man who enters a state of major ritual impurity, and is unable to find water, but rain falls on him. Will that suffice him, or must he perform *tayammum*? So he said: 'If it washes him then it suffices, otherwise he must perform *tayammum*.'[277]

❖ Al-Ḥalabī said: I heard Abū 'Abd Allah [al-Ṣādiq] 🕮 saying: 'If someone in a state of major ritual impurity submerges himself in water one full submersion, then that suffices him for his *ghusl*.'[278]

❖ Muḥammad b. Muslim has narrated from the Imam 🕮: '*Ghusl* suffices for *wuḍū'*. What *wuḍū'* is more purifying than *ghusl*?'[279]

---

[275] *Wasā'il al-shī'a*, v. 1, p. 499, ḥ. 1
[276] *Wasā'il al-shī'a*, v. 1, p. 502, ḥ. 1
[277] *Wasā'il al-shī'a*, v. 1, p. 504, ḥ. 11
[278] *Wasā'il al-shī'a*, v. 1, p. 504, ḥ. 12
[279] *Wasā'il al-shī'a*, v. 1, p. 513, ḥ. 1

- Al-Ḥalabī has narrated that Abū ʿAbd Allah [al-Ṣādiq] ﷺ was asked about a man who [was in a state of major ritual impurity and] performs *ghusl*, only to discover some moisture [from his genitals] afterwards, though he had urinated prior beforehand. He said: 'He should perform *wuḍū'*, and as for someone who did not urinate beforehand, then he should repeat the *ghusl*.'[280]
- Some of their companions have narrated that one of the two Imams (al-Bāqir or al-Ṣādiq) ﷺ said: If someone in a state of major ritual impurity performs *ghusl* after daybreak, then it suffices him for every [supererogatory] *ghusl* he might need for that day (e.g., *ghusl* for Friday, for *ziyāra*, etc.).'[281]

Rulings:

1. *Ghusl* is a prerequisite (*muqaddima*) for prayer, and Allah has ordered it with the following words: '**O you who have faith! When you stand up for prayer... If you are *junub* [in a state of post-coital impurity], purify yourselves.**'[282] For this reason, *ghusl* must be performed with the intention (*niyya*) of *ghusl*.
2. *Ghusl* is, in and of itself, a religiously recommended (*mustaḥabb*) act, as Allah says: '**Indeed Allah loves the penitent and He loves those who keep clean.**'[283] And *ghusl* in and of itself purifies, as Allah says: '**If you are *junub*, purify yourselves.**'[284] And the reality of *ghusl* is one and the same, regardless of whether it is after sexual intercourse, or after menstruation, or before *iḥrām*. *Ghusl* purifies you from every state of impurity and avails you completely in all situations that require ritual purity like *wuḍū'*; it also suffices you in place of *wuḍū'*, and even if you perform *ghusl* for no particular reason, you are ritually pure and do not need to perform *wuḍū'* afterwards. Likewise, if you perform *ghusl* with no apparent reason, then realize you had actually been in a state of post-coital impurity, it will suffice you too, God-willing.
3. It is not necessary to make any intention when performing *ghusl* except seeking nearness to Allah, because Allah loves those who purify themselves. It is not necessary to specify the cause or occasion for which you are performing *ghusl*, although doing so out of devotion will increase your reward, God-willing.

---

[280] *Wasāʾil al-shīʿa*, v. 1, p. 517, ḥ. 1
[281] *Wasāʾil al-shīʿa*, v. 1, p. 526, ḥ. 2
[282] Sūrat al-Māʾida (5):6
[283] Sūrat al-Baqarah (2):222
[284] Sūrat al-Māʾida (5):6

4. It is necessary to prepare pure water for yourself, which meets all the criteria we have already mentioned for *wuḍū'*, and then wash every external part of your body without exception. It is not necessary to wash any internal parts (such as inside the mouth, the eyes, or the ear canals). It is nearest to precaution that you wash your hair and beard and any other bodily hair you might have.
5. To wash your entire body with the intention of self-purification, you can also submerge yourself in water in a single go, and there is no problem with slowly entering the water until you are submerged entirely. And if your arm remains out of the water or your foot steps in mud and then you wash either of these, it suffices you. What qualifies as submersion is down to common sense.
6. You can also wash your body gradually. Precaution requires that you begin by washing your head and neck, then move on to the rest of your body. It is most appropriate to begin with the right side and then the left, but this order (from left to right) is not obligatory. Although if you forget the order between the head and the body, precaution says you should repeat it.
7. There is no need for continuity when performing *ghusl* for post-coital impurity. If someone washes their head first, then washes the rest of their body an hour later – for example – then his *ghusl* is valid. There is also no need for him to wash his body from top to bottom; if, for example, he washes his feet before his hands, it is correct, and if he realizes he has forgotten to wash a part of his body, or notices that there was some barrier to water there, it suffices him to wash that part. However, precaution requires that if the part he missed was on his head, that he should repeat the washing of the rest of his body, but every part of your body that water touches becomes ritually pure.
8. Some jurists require that the entire body be cleansed of ritual impurities (*najāsa*) before beginning *ghusl*. Others say that each limb should be cleansed [of impurities as needed] before it is washed for *ghusl*. Obligatory precaution only requires the latter, though it is recommended precaution to observe the first.
9. It is allowed to perform *ghusl* in a shower, under a tap, hose, or in the train. So long as water reaches the entire body with the intention of *ghusl*, it suffices. However, it is more appropriate to follow the order of *ghusl* beginning with the head and neck, then the right side of the body, then the left side, although the latter part of this order is not obligatory, as we have mentioned.
10. The famous legal opinion of the jurists is that any water used for *ghusl* must be permitted for use (that is, it must not be stolen, usurped, or

the private property of another used without the owner's permission), as must be the place of *ghusl*, and any implement used to pour water. This is nearest to precaution.

11. It is best for a man who is in a state of post-coital impurity to urinate before making *ghusl*. That way, if he emits some moisture after *ghusl* but is uncertain that it is semen, he need not pay it any heed.
12. It is recommended for a person to supplicate while performing *ghusl* using the words narrated from Imam al-Ṣādiq عليه السلام: 'O Allah! Cleanse my heart, purify my deeds, accept my efforts, and make what is with You best for me!' (*allāhumma ṭahhir qalbī wa zakki ʿamalī wa taqabbal saʿyī, wajʿal mā ʿindaka khayran lī*), and then add: 'O Allah! Make me one of the penitents, and make me one of those who purify themselves!' (*allāhumma ajʿalnī min al-tawwābīn wajʿalnī min al-mutaṭahhirīn*).
13. If there are multiple reasons for performing *ghusl* (for instance, if one is in a state of major ritual impurity *and* it is Friday), one can perform a single *ghusl* with the intention of fulfilling them all, and they will be rewarded for all of them God-willing.
14. Performing *ghusl* – like *wuḍūʾ* – is an act of self-purification, and all acts of self-purification are recommended (*mustaḥabb*) [even when they are not obligatory]. There is an abundance of traditions which encourage people to perform *ghusl* at various special times and places, or for specific acts of worship, and following these traditions (see below) is part of perfecting one's faith as a Muslim.

Recommended *ghusl*

The noble *sunna*:

- Muʿāwiya b. ʿAmmār said: I heard Abū ʿAbd Allah [al-Ṣādiq] عليه السلام saying: '*Ghusl* is for major ritual impurity, and for Friday, and for the two *ʿīd*s, and the state of consecration, and for entering Mecca and Medina, and for the Day of ʿArafa, and for visiting the House of Allah, and entering the Kaʿba, and for the nineteenth, twenty-first, and twenty-third of the month of Ramaḍān, and for washing the dead.'[285]
- Al-Ḥasan b. Khālid said: I asked Abū al-Ḥasan the First [al-Kāẓim] عليه السلام how the *ghusl* of Friday became obligatory. So he said: 'Verily Allah completed the obligatory prayers with the supererogatory prayers, and completed obligatory fasting with supererogatory fasting, and completed the obligatory ablutions with the *ghusl* of Friday, in order to compensate

---

[285] *Wasāʾil al-shīʿa*, v. 2, p. 936, ḥ. 1

for mistakes, shortcomings, forgetfulness, and deficiencies [in the ablutions].'[286]

❖ Muḥammad b. Muslim has narrated from one of the two Imams (al-Bāqir or al-Ṣādiq) ﷺ: 'Perform the *ghusl* of Friday unless you are sick or fear for your life.'[287]

❖ Muḥammad b. Muslim has narrated from Imam al-Ṣādiq ﷺ: 'The *ghusl* of Friday is a purification, and expiation for whatever sins fell between that Friday and the last.'[288]

❖ Aḥmad b. Muḥammad b. Abī Nasr has narrated from al-Riḍā ﷺ: 'My father would perform the *ghusl* of Friday before the sun reached its zenith.'[289]

❖ ʿAbd Allah b. Ṭalḥa said: I asked Abū ʿAbd Allah [al-Ṣādiq] ﷺ about the lizard. He said: 'It is unclean and metamorphosed (i.e., it used to be a human that Allah punished by changing to a lower life form), every one of them. If you kill one, then perform *ghusl*.'[290]

❖ ʿAlī b. Mūsā b. Ṭāwūs has said in his book, *al-Iqbāl*: I found in the books of worship the following statement from the Prophet ﷺ: 'Whoever reaches the month of Rajab and performs *ghusl* on its first, fifteenth, and final days, will be free of sins like the day he was born from his mother.'[291]

❖ Yūsuf al-Kunāsī has narrated from Abū ʿAbd Allah [al-Ṣādiq] ﷺ: 'When you come to the grave of al-Ḥusayn ﷺ, go to the Euphrates and perform *ghusl*.'[292]

Subsidiary Issues

A. If someone does something to necessitate *wuḍū'* while performing *ghusl*, precaution requires him to repeat the washing of whatever limbs he has already washed, even if the stronger legal opinion is that he should continue with his *ghusl* then perform *wuḍū'* for prayer. And if someone does something to necessitate *ghusl* [before one's *ghusl* is complete], they must repeat the *ghusl* again [from the beginning].

B. If someone doubts whether he washed a particular limb after moving on to another, his doubt is ignored. If he doubts whether he washed the

---

[286] *Wasā'il al-shīʿa*, v. 2, p. 944, ḥ. 7
[287] *Wasā'il al-shīʿa*, v. 2, p. 945, ḥ. 11
[288] *Wasā'il al-shīʿa*, v. 2, p. 945, ḥ. 14
[289] *Wasā'il al-shīʿa*, v. 1, p. 947, ḥ. 22
[290] *Wasā'il al-shīʿa*, v. 2, p. 957, ḥ. 1
[291] *Wasā'il al-shīʿa*, v. 2, p. 959, ḥ. 1
[292] *Wasā'il al-shīʿa*, v. 2, p. 962, ḥ. 1

left side of his body after finishing *ghusl* (for example, by putting on clothes, beginning prayer, leaving the bathroom, or doing anything that signifies he has finished it), he should also ignore this doubt.

C. If someone knows with certainty that he forgot to wash a spot on his body, or he could not have done so because of some barrier to his skin, then he must wash it and this will suffice [without repeating the *ghusl*], God-willing.

Third: *Tayammum*

***A: Occasions for* tayammum**

The noble *sunna*:

- Muḥammad b. Ḥumrān and Jamīl have both narrated: We said to Abū ʿAbd Allah [al-Ṣādiq] ﷺ: The *imām* of a group of people enters a state of major ritual impurity while traveling, and he does not have enough water for *ghusl*. Should someone from his group perform *wuḍūʾ* and lead the prayer? He said: 'No, rather the *imām* should perform *tayammum* and lead the in prayer, for Allah Almighty has made the earth a [source of] purification.'[293]
- ʿUbayd Allah b. ʿAlī al-Ḥalabī has narrated that he asked Abū ʿAbd Allah ﷺ about a man who passes by a well but he does not have a bucket. He said: 'He does not need to go into the well, for the Lord of Water is the Lord of Earth. He should perform *tayammum*.'[294]
- Ṣafwān said: I asked Abū al-Ḥasan [al-Kāẓim] ﷺ about a man who needs to perform *wuḍūʾ* for prayer, but is unable to find any water. Then he found some water for *wuḍūʾ* but it costs a hundred or [even] a thousand dirhams, which he has available. Should he buy it for *wuḍūʾ* or should he perform *tayammum* instead? He said: 'No, rather he should buy it. A similar thing has happened to me before, so I bought [water] and performed *wuḍūʾ*, and by that I bought an abundant wealth.'[295]
- Muḥammad b. Muslim said: I asked Abū Jaʿfar [al-Bāqir] ﷺ about a man with a wound or injury, who is in a state of major ritual impurity. He said: 'It is no problem that he performs *tayammum* rather than *ghusl*.'[296]

---

[293] *Al-Kāfi*, v. 3, p. 66, ḥ. 3
[294] *Wasāʾil al-shīʿa*, v. 2, p. 965, ḥ. 1
[295] *Wasāʾil al-shīʿa*, v. 2, p. 997, ḥ. 1
[296] *Wasāʾil al-shīʿa*, v. 2, p. 967, ḥ. 5

❖ 'Abd Allah b. Sinān has narrated from Abū 'Abd Allah 🕮, concerning a man who enters a state of major ritual impurity while traveling, has only a little water with him, and fears for thirst if he performs *ghusl* with it. He said: 'If he fears thirst then he should not spill a single drop of water, and should perform purification with soil, for soil is more beloved to me.'[297]

Rulings:

1. If someone cannot find even the least amount of water sufficient for ritual self-purification (whether *wuḍū'* or *ghusl*), despite trying to find it, then he must use dust to purify himself. It is sufficient for a person to be convinced that there is not enough water, whether searching for it himself, someone else searching on his behalf, or because two just persons – or even one just person – have informed him to this effect. It is obligatory for him to obtain water for himself if there is water for sale, on condition that this does not cause him unbearable difficulty (*ḥaraj*).

2. Fear is another reason for purifying oneself with dust: if someone fears some harm will come to him by using water, for example that the skin on his hands will crack, then he can use dust as well. As for minor harm that is usually discounted, this is not sufficient as a reason for performing *tayammum*. Whoever fears contracting an illness or exacerbating an existing one is also allowed [to perform *tayammum*]. As for someone who uses water in spite of probable harm, then precaution requires him to use dust as well, whether washing with water is forbidden – as it would be if the harm is extreme – or not.

3. Someone who fears thirst, whether for himself or others, or even for animals – domesticated or otherwise – may perform *tayammum* and in place of *wuḍū'*. Even for a disbeliever who is at war with the Muslims, precaution requires that he should be given water and the Muslim should perform *tayammum* for prayer. The same applies to the apostate.

4. If there is not sufficient time to perform ritual purifications with water, *tayammum* will suffice. Howeer, if there is enough time left to pray even a single *rak'a* with *wuḍū'*, then the strongest opinion is that prayer with [*wuḍū'*] is valid. In fact, precaution requires one to choose it over *tayammum*, even if he can offer the entire prayer on time with *tayammum* but only part of it on time with *wuḍū'*.

5. If, in order to use water, someone must do something unlawful—for example, if the water is located on someone else's property, it is unlawful to trespass without the owner's permission—then one ought to perform

---

[297] *Wasā'il al-shī'a*, v. 2, p. 996, ḥ. 1

tayammum. The same applies if the water is in a gold or silver container, or if the water is located on a battlefield such that if one was to go and use it they would be killed, etc.

B: What can we use for tayammum?

The noble *sunna*:

❖ Imam al-Ṣādiq 🕮 said: 'If you come to a well while you are in a state of major ritual impurity, and you cannot find a bucket or anything else to bring out water, then perform *tayammum* with soil, for verily the Lord of Water is the Lord of Soil. And do not go down into the well or spoil the people's water.'[298]

❖ Al-Sukūnī has narrated from Imam al-Ṣādiq, from his father, from ʿAlī 🕮, who was asked about performing *tayammum* from gypsum. So he said: 'Yes (it is fine).' Then it was asked: And with [the mineral] lime? So he said: 'Yes.' Then it was asked: And with ash? So he said: 'No, for it is not taken from the earth, rather it only comes from trees.'[299]

❖ Muʿāwiya b. Shurīḥ said: A man asked Abū ʿAbd Allah 🕮, while I was with them: A snowstorm reaches us. We want to perform *wuḍūʾ* but we cannot find anything except ice (or snow). How do we perform *wuḍūʾ*? Do we rub our skin with it? He said: 'Yes.'[300]

Rulings:

1. Anything that can be called 'the face of the Earth' is sufficient for *tayammum*, whether this is dust (or soil), sand, stone, or clay.

2. Plaster, gypsum, millstones, marble, or any other things from the ground that have specific uses, can all be used for *tayammum*, so long as they have not ceased to be considered as being from the earth.

C: Wipings of tayammum

The noble *sunna*:

❖ Zurāra said: I asked Abū Jaʿfar 🕮 about *tayammum*, so he struck his hands upon the earth, raised them and shook them off, then wiped his brow and [the backs] of his hands, once each.[301]

---

[298] *Wasāʾil al-shīʿa*, v. 2, p. 965, ḥ. 2
[299] *Wasāʾil al-shīʿa*, v. 2, p. 971, ḥ. 1
[300] *Wasāʾil al-shīʿa*, v. 2, p. 975, ḥ. 2
[301] *Wasāʾil al-shīʿa*, v. 2, p. 976, ḥ. 3

- Al-Kāhilī said: I asked [the Imam ﷺ] about *tayammum*. So he struck his hands upon the carpet, then wiped his face with them, then wiped each of his hands, one over the back of the other.[302]
- Zurāra said: I said to Abū Jaʿfar ﷺ: How is *tayammum* performed? He said: 'One strikes his hands [on the earth] once [if it is a substitute] for *wuḍū'* and twice for *ghusl*. Then he shakes them off and [wipes] the face once and the [backs of his] hands once. When he reaches water, then he must perform *ghusl* if he was in a state of major ritual impurity, or *wuḍū'* if he was not.'[303]

Rulings:

1. *Tayammum* consists of two wipings. After striking both your palms on the ground, or placing them upon it, you wipe your face from your hairline to the bridge of your nose and the top of your eyebrows. It is more appropriate to wipe your eyebrows as well.
2. Precaution requires that you wipe both your hands together over your forehead and eyebrows. However, if you wiped with your fingers alone, then this suffices – God-willing.
3. Next, you wipe the palm of your left hand over the back of your right and then the palm of the right over the back of the left, beginning with the wrist and ending at the tips of the fingers, in whatever manner that would customarily be called 'wiping.' It is not necessary to wipe between one's fingers, or any folds of skin.
4. *Tayammum* requires the following conditions: (i) making one's intention (*niyya*) when striking one's hands on the ground; (ii) that the legal agent performs the actions himself if he is able; (iii) that he wipes his face after striking, then the back of his right hand, followed by the left; (iv) that these actions follow one after another such that they are considered a single act; (v) that he wipes from high to low; (vi) and that he wipes his skin without any barrier. And it is recommended precaution that both the wiping limb and the limb being wiped in *tayammum* are free of any impurity.
5. It is not necessary to remove hair from the back of the hand or the forehead; it is sufficient to wipe over it. If there is a medical dressing on either the part of the body that is wiping or being wiped, it suffices to wipe with it or over it.
6. If performing *tayammum* for oneself is unbearably difficult (*ḥaraj*), then another person can take his hand, strike the ground with it and then

---

[302] *Wasā'il al-shīʿa*, v. 2, p. 976, ḥ. 1
[303] *Wasā'il al-shīʿa*, v. 2, p. 978, ḥ. 4

wipe the requisite areas using it. But if that is also difficult, someone else can act in his place, striking his own hands on the ground and then wiping them over the person who is unable to do so.

D: Rules of tayammum

The noble sunna:

❖ Ḥammād b. ʿUthmān said: I asked Abū ʿAbd Allah 🕮 about a man who does not find water: must he perform *tayammum* for every [individual] prayer? So he said: 'No, it is like water.'[304]

❖ Zurāra said: I asked Abū Jaʿfar 🕮: Can a man pray all of his prayers of the night and day with a single *tayammum*? He said: 'Yes, so long as he does nothing to break his state of ritual purity, or so long as he does not encounter water.' I said: And if he encounters water while he has already entered a state of prayer? He said: 'He should abandon his prayer and perform *wuḍūʾ* if he has not yet bowed, and if he has already bowed [once] then he should remain in prayer, for verily *tayammum* is one of the two sources of ritual purification.'[305]

❖ Abū ʿUbayda said: I asked Abū ʿAbd Allah 🕮 about a menstruating woman who wants to ritually purify herself, but she is traveling and has no water with her. What suffices her for *ghusl* when the time of prayer has come? He said: 'If she has the ability to [at least] wash her vagina, then she should do so. Then she should perform *tayammum* and pray.' I said: And if her husband comes to her in that situation? He said: 'Yes, if she washed her vagina and performed *tayammum* then there is no problem.'[306]

❖ Zurāra has narrated: I said to Abū Jaʿfar 🕮: What if one encounters water and had already prayed with *tayammum*, and there is still time [to pray]? He said: 'His prayer is complete and he does not need to repeat it.'[307]

❖ Muḥammad b. Muslim has narrated that he heard Abū ʿAbd Allah 🕮 saying: 'If you did not find water and wanted [to pray with] *tayammum*, then delay performing *tayammum* until the end of the time [for prayer], for even if you missed water, you would not miss earth.'[308]

---

[304] *Wasāʾil al-shīʿa*, v. 2, p. 990, ḥ. 3
[305] *Wasāʾil al-shīʿa*, v. 2, p. 991, ḥ. 1
[306] *Wasāʾil al-shīʿa*, v. 2, p. 564, ḥ. 1
[307] *Wasāʾil al-shīʿa*, v. 2, p. 983, ḥ. 9
[308] *Wasāʾil al-shīʿa*, v. 2, p. 993, ḥ. 1

❖ Zurāra has narrated from one of the two Imams 🕮 that he said: 'If the traveler could not find water, and searched throughout the time for prayer, and he feared that he would miss the time for prayer [if he continued searching], then he should perform *tayammum* and pray at the end of the time for prayer. Then if he found water, he would not need to make up that prayer; and he should perform *wuḍū'* for the next prayer.'[309]

❖ It is narrated that 'Abd al-Raḥmān b. Abī Najrān asked Abū al-Ḥasan Mūsā b. Jaʿfar 🕮 about three individuals who were traveling. One of them was in a state of major ritual impurity, the second was a corpse, and the third did not have *wuḍū'*. The time of prayer had come, and they only had enough water for one of them. Which one should use the water, and what should they do? He said: 'The one in the state of major ritual impurity should perform *ghusl*. The corpse should be prepared by *tayammum*, as well as the one without *wuḍū'*, because *ghusl* for major ritual impurity is obligatory, *ghusl* of the dead is a *sunna*, and *tayammum* for the third is permissible.'[310]

Rulings:

1. Dust (or earth) is capable of ritual purification (*ṭahūr*) like water, but only if water cannot be used. So a believer can perform *tayammum* at any time he wishes, before the time of prayer or after it, in these circumstances (the unavailability of water). Precaution requires *tayammum* be delayed until someone is sure that these circumstances will not be alleviated before the time for prayer has elapsed.

2. It is permissible to offer a number of prayers with *tayammum* so long as the circumstances that require it (the unavailability of water) have not been alleviated and there is no likelihood of them being alleviated.

3. If someone performs *tayammum* believing that the circumstances requiring it will remain, but they are ultimately alleviated before the time for prayer has finished, he does not need to repeat his prayer.

4. Whoever purifies himself with dust in place of *ghusl*, it suffices him for both *wuḍū'* and *ghusl*, whether he was impure because of sexual intercourse or any other reason, and whether the *ghusl* was obligatory or supererogatory.

5. If the reason for *tayammum* is removed (for example, ritually pure water becomes avialble) before someone offers their prayers, their *tayammum* is voided. But if this happens during the prayer, then if he has already

---

[309] *Wasā'il al-shīʿa*, v. 2, p. 982, ḥ. 2
[310] *Wasā'il al-shīʿa*, v. 2, p. 987, ḥ. 1

performed *rukūʿ* he should continue with his prayer; otherwise, he must repeat his prayer with *wuḍūʾ*. Precaution requires that he complete his prayer with *tayammum* and then repeat it again with *wuḍūʾ*.

6. Whoever knows in advance that he will not be able to purify himself with water at the time of prayer, should perform *ghusl* or *wuḍūʾ* ahead of time. The same applies if he knows that he will not be able to purify himself with dust.

Section Four: Types of Bleeding in Women

First: Menstruation (*ḥayḍ*)

The noble *sunna*:

❖ Muḥammad b. Yaʿqūb has narrated from ʿAlī b. Ibrāhīm, from Muḥammad b. ʿĪsā, from Yūnus, from multiple people, that they asked Abū ʿAbd Allah ﷺ about menstruation and the *sunna* in his time. So he said: 'Verily the Messenger of Allah ﷺ introduced three traditions (*sunan*), and explained in them every problem for those who hear and understand, until none could claim anything about it based on personal opinion.'

So Imam al-Ṣādiq ﷺ went on to explain the *sunna* for a hypothetical menstruating woman in reference to her dates and days, establishing the appearance of the signs of the monthly cycle, and gave the example of a story that happened in the age of the Messenger of Allah ﷺ. He said: 'As for the first tradition, it pertains to the woman who has menses for a known number of days, without confusion, but experiences spotting and the blood continues, but she knows the dates and length of her cycle. There was a woman named Fāṭima b. Abī Ḥubaysh who experienced spotting (irregular bleeding) and the blood continued to appear. So came to Umm Salama, who asked the Messenger of Allah ﷺ about it. So he said: "She must leave her prayer for the number of days of purity or the length of her menses." And he said: "It is only some local bleeding [from a vein in the womb]." So he ordered that she perform *ghusl* [after those days], secure a cloth between her legs, and pray.'

Abū ʿAbd Allah ﷺ said: 'This is a tradition of the Prophet ﷺ for the one who knows the dates of her time free of menses without any confusion. Do you not see that he did not ask her how many days? And he did not say: "If it is more than such-and-such days then you are spotting." This tradition (*sunna*) is only or those who have a known number of days, whether more or fewer, after she comes to know it. Similarly, my father gave a verdict about this when he was asked about a woman who was spotting, and said: "It is only from a vein in the womb or Satan's kick, so she should leave her prayer for the number of days that she is normally free of menses, and then perform *ghusl* and *wuḍū'* for every prayer." It was asked: Even if the blood was still flowing? He said: "Even if it is still flowing like a channel.'" Abū 'Abd Allah 🕮 said: 'This is the explanation of the narration of the Messenger of Allah 🕮, and is in agreement with it. So this is the *sunna* for the woman who knows the length of her time without menses, and not its time but only its number of days, fewer or more.

And as for the *sunna* of she who bled for some preceding days, but confusion overcame her regarding the length of bleeding and whether it was more or fewer [days], until she forgets its number of days or dates of the month, so it is a different tradition.' And the Imam explained—in what follows—its ruling, which is to refer to the signs indicated by the blood, leading with an example from the story of the woman affected by that who sought the advice of the Messenger of Allah 🕮. So Imam al-Ṣādiq 🕮 said about her: 'When Fāṭima b. Abī Ḥubaysh came to the Prophet 🕮, she said to him: I menstruate continuously and do not experience any menses-free period. So the Prophet 🕮 said to her: "That is not menstruation, rather it is but [blood from] a vein, so when your period comes then refrain from your prayer, and when it subsides then perform *ghusl* washing off the blood, and pray." And she would perform *ghusl* at the time of every prayer, sitting in her sister's tub, and the yellowness of the blood would rise in the water.'

Abū 'Abd Allah 🕮 continued: 'Do you not hear how the Messenger of Allah commanded this woman differently than the other? Do you not see how he didn't say to her: "Cease your prayer during your period-free time"? Rather, he said to her: "If your time of menstruation comes then cease your prayer, and when it passes then wash and pray." So this is the explanation for a woman who is confused about her days, and did not know their number or its time (dates). Have you not heard how she said: I am always bleeding and never in a state of purity, and my father says: She has been bleeding for seven years continuously, and less than this is doubtful and confused. So for this reason it was necessary that she knew the beginning of the blood from its recession, and the changing of its colour from black to something else.

'And that is because the blood of menses is black, which is known, and if she had known her days then she would not have needed to be aware of the blood's colour, because the *sunna* concerning menstruation is yellowness and viscosity, etc., during her days of menstruation, then it is all understood to be menses. If there was black blood or something other than that, then this indicates for you that bless or more blood during the days of menstruation is menses—all of it—if the days [of her cycle] are known. When she is ignorant of her days and their number, then by then she must look at the ebb and flow of blood, and changes in its colour, and stop praying according to those factors. And I do not see that the Prophet ﷺ ever said to her: "Wait for such-and-such days, and whatever exceeds it is spotting (*istiḥāḍa*)." Similarly, he never ordered the first [case] to do this. And my father issued the same verdict as this when a woman from our family was spotting, and asked my father ؑ about it. So he said: "If you see a flood of blood then do not pray, and when you see a time free of bleeding—even an hour of the day—then perform *ghusl* and pray."'

Abū ʿAbd Allah ؑ continued: 'And I see the answer of my father ؑ here is different than his answer in the case of the first woman whose bleeding was irregular. Do you not see that he said: "Stop praying for the amount of your menses-free days" because of the number of days, whereas in this instance he said: "If you see that copious blood floods out (*lit.* 'a sea of blood'), then stop your prayer." Then he ordered her, in this instance, to observe the blood's ebb, flow, and changes [in its colour]. And his saying using the word "flood," resembling the meaning of the Prophet's ﷺ saying that the blood of menses is known to be black. And my father called it "flood-like" because of its quantity and colour. So this is the *sunna* of the Prophet ﷺ for she who is confused about her days until she knows them, and she knows them by the [qualities of] the blood, what of it was from fewer or more days.

'As for the third *sunna*, it concerns she who has not had any preceding days and had never seen blood, and she saw the first of what she knew, and it continued. So the *sunna* is different than the first and second.'

Then the Imam explained the *sunna* of this type of woman in observing the rules of menstruation according to Allah's knowledge, the known number of days, and told the story of what happed to the woman experiencing menstruation, and said: 'That is because a woman named Ḥamna b. Jaḥsh came to the Messenger of Allah ﷺ and said: I have been bleeding intensely. So he said: "Insert cotton." So she said: It is too severe for that; I am flowing copiously. So he said: "Harness [it in place], and observe [the rules of] menstruation monthly, according to Allah's knowledge, for six or seven days, then perform *ghusl*, and fast for twenty-three or twenty-four days. Perform *ghusl* before the dawn prayer. Delay the noon prayer and hasten the afternoon prayer, and perform *ghusl*. Delay the dusk prayer and hasten the evening prayer, and perform *ghusl*.'

Abū ʿAbd Allah ﷺ continued: 'I see that he (the Messenger of Allah) has established a different tradition in this instance as opposed to the first or the second, because its commandment is different from the commandment of these two. Do you not see that if her days were less than seven, or if they were five or less, what he has said to her about observing [the laws of] menstruation for seven days, so [in her case] the commandment is to leave the prayer for those days, and that she is experiencing irregular bleeding and not menses? And similarly, if she bled for more than seven days, and [for example] she bled for ten or more days, then he would not command her to pray, and she would be [considered] menstruating, then he added an explanation in his saying to her treat it as menses? And it is not [treated as] menses unless the woman wants to be responsible for what the observances of a menstruating woman. Do you not see that he did not say to her to observe [the rules of] menses for the specific number of days of your menses? And this explains his saying to her "according to Allah's knowledge," because he was saying to her that all of it was in the knowledge of Allah Almighty, and this is a clear explanation that it was she had not [experienced] a day before that ever, and this is the *sunna* for she who sees blood for the first time and it continues. She sees that the maximum time limit of her menses is seven [days], and the utmost limit of her menses-free period is twenty-three [days], until her days become known to her, and she adjusts accordingly. All instances of menstrual bleeding fall under these three traditions (*sunan*); it almost never waivers from one of them. If she knew her specific days, fewer or more, then she follows [the rules according to] her days, and there is no specific number other than her days. And if her days become confused, arriving earlier or later, or her blood changes colour, then the *sunna* established for her is to observe the ebb and flow of blood and changes in its conditions. And if she had not experienced menses before that, and it the first she has seen bleeding, then her time is seven [days] and her menses-free period is twenty-three [days]. If the blood continues monthly, then she performs in every month like what he said to her. If the blood ceases in fewer or more than seven [days], then she performs *ghusl* the moment she sees that she is free of menses, and prays. And she stays like that until she sees what is in the second month. If the blood stops at the same time as in the first month, whether they are the same length, or a third if it was now known that this would become her time and known habit. She acts upon this and ignores whatever else, and this is [now] her tradition (*sunna*) for the future if she has irregular bleeding. It has become a pattern because her menses-free period and the time was established that was followed by two or three cycles of menses, according to the saying of the Messenger of Allah ﷺ that she who knows her days: "stop praying for the [number of] days of your menses-free time." Thus we know that that a single menses-free period does not establish a *sunna* (habit) for her. Hence he says: "Cease praying for the [number of] days of your menses-free time," but established for her the menses-free period, and its minimum is two cycles of menses consecutively.

'And if she became confused about her days and they increase or decrease until there is no clear limit, not even in the blood's colour, she knows the ebb and flow of blood, and she follows no pattern other than this, according to the saying of the Messenger of Allah ﷺ: "If the bleeding increases than stop praying, and if it ebbs then perform *ghusl*," and according to his saying that the blood of menses is distinctively black. This is like the saying of my father ﷺ: "if she sees a flood of blood." So if this is not the issue, but bleeding continues, then it is still spotting (irregular bleeding), and the blood was of one colour and one situation (quality), then the *sunna* is seven days and twenty-three days, because the situation is like the story of Ḥamna when she said: Blood is flowing from me copiously.'[311]

What is menstruation?

Menstruation is defined as the emission of blood from the womb of a healthy woman or girl who has attained puberty, and which is not the result of childbirth or the breaking of the hymen. Menstruation is given different names such as the 'period' or 'monthly cycle' as well, and experiencing menstrual bleeding is one of the clearest indicators that a girl has reached puberty.

Facts about the monthly cycle

First, menstruation is something natural which women usually experience every month, and which affects their physical and mental states. Islam has legislated specific laws to take this into account.

Secondly, by considering menstruation a natural phenomenon, it is a sign of a woman's good health that she experiences such bleeding, unlike all other kinds such as spotting, puerperal bleeding, blood in her urine, or blood resulting from injury or disease. Hence, the bleeding women experience is

---

[311] *Wasā'il al-shī'a*, v. 2, p. 542, ḥ. 1

considered menstruation except in exceptional circumstances, for example if it cannot be considered such.

Thirdly, there are a number of signs by which a woman can recognize menstrual bleeding. They are as follows:

A. Because a woman experiences her monthly cycle every four weeks, it is a regular occurrence with a specific time and a specific quantity.

B. This monthly cycle is usually accompanied by a number of states by which a woman can sense that she is beginning to menstruate: for instance, emotional changes, discomfort in the abdominal region, fatigue, and even nausea. Each woman has her own experience in this regard, which allows her to recognize her monthly cycle with ease.

C. Because the blood of menstruation also has specific qualities, we will discuss them below, as menstrual bleeding can be recognized in this way as well.

The conditions of menstruation

The noble *sunna*:

❖ Ibn al-Ḥajjāj has narrated from Imam al-Ṣādiq 🕊: 'Three can be married in every instance: she who did not experience menses [yet], and like her one who does not experience menses.' The narrator said: What is her limit? He 🕊 said: When she is under nine [lunar] years of age, and she who has not been entered [in intercourse], and she who is postmenopausal or does not experience menses for any reason.' The narrator said: And what is its limit? He 🕊 said: 'If she was fifty [lunar] years old.'[312]

❖ Ibn al-Ḥajjāj asked Imam al-Ṣādiq 🕊 about of when a woman reaches menopause, so the Imam 🕊 answered: 'When she is fifty [lunar] years old.'[313]

❖ Shaykh al-Ṭūsī in *al-Mabsūṭ*: A woman's menopause is when she has reached fifty [lunar] years of age, unless she is a Qurayshī woman, for it is narrated that they can menstruate until they are sixty.[314]

❖ Muʿāwiya b. ʿAmmār has narrated from Abū ʿAbd Allah 🕊: 'The minimum of what constitutes menses is three days [of bleeding].'[315]

---

[312] *Wasāʾil al-shīʿa*, v. 15, p. 406, ḥ. 4

[313] *Wasāʾil al-shīʿa*, v. 15, p. 406, ḥ. 4

[314] *Wasāʾil al-shīʿa*, v. 2, p. 581, ḥ. 5

[315] *Wasāʾil al-shīʿa*, v. 2, p. 551, ḥ. 1

❖ Ṣafwān said: I asked Abū al-Ḥasan al-Riḍā 🕮 about the minimum that constitutes menses. So he 🕮 said: 'Its minimum is three days and its maximum is ten.'[316]

❖ In *Daʿāʾim al-Islām* it is narrated that Abū ʿAbd Allah 🕮 said: 'The minimum time that constitutes menses is three nights.'[317]

❖ ʿAlī b. Abī Ṭālib 🕮 said: 'There is no menses more than ten days.'[318]

❖ Imam Abū ʿAbd Allah 🕮 said: 'The minimum of menses-free time is ten nights.'[319]

❖ Muʿāwiya b. ʿAmmār has narrated from Imam al-Ṣādiq 🕮: 'Verily the blood of spotting and the blood of menses do not come from a single point of origin. The blood of spotting is cold, while the blood of menses is hot.'[320]

❖ Ḥafṣ b. al-Bakhtarī has narrated that a woman came to see Imam Abū ʿAbd Allah 🕮. She asked about a woman who bleeds continuously such that she cannot tell if it is menses or something else. So he told her: 'Menstrual blood is hot; it is black and it is expelled with force and heat. Blood of spotting (irregular bleeding) is yellowish and cool. So if the blood is hot and expelled with fore, and its colour is black, then cease prayer.' The narrator added: As the woman left, she said: By Allah, a woman could have added nothing more to this.[321]

❖ In response to a woman who asked about some of the details of menstruation, Imam al-Ṣādiq 🕮 said: 'Menstrual blood has no obscurity; it is hot and you will find it is accompanied by a burning sensation.'[322]

Rulings:

Menstruation does not normally occur unless the following conditions are fulfilled:

1. A girl is at least nine years old
2. A woman has not yet passed the age of menopause
3. The bleeding lasts for at least three days
4. The bleeding does not last for longer than ten days
5. The bleeding continues for three days

---

[316] *Wasāʾil al-shīʿa*, v. 2, p. 551, ḥ. 2

[317] *Mustadrak al-wasāʾil*, v. 2, p. 11, ḥ. 4

[318] *Mustadrak al-wasāʾil*, v. 2, p. 11, ḥ. 1

[319] *Mustadrak al-wasāʾil*, v. 2, p. 12, ḥ. 2

[320] *Wasāʾil al-shīʿa*, v. 2, p. 537, ḥ. 1

[321] *Wasāʾil al-shīʿa*, v. 2, p. 537, ḥ. 2

[322] *Wasāʾil al-shīʿa*, v. 2, p. 537, ḥ. 3

6. It has been at least ten days since any previous menstrual bleeding
7. The blood has the appearance of menstrual blood, or an appearance indicating that it could be menstrual blood

The appearance of menstrual blood

Menstrual blood is nothing secret – as has been mentioned in a tradition – and because it is something which only women experience, a woman can usually recognize when she is experiencing menstrual bleeding without needing to check for any of its indicators. But in situations where someone is confused or uncertain, they can recognize menstrual bleeding from other kinds by the description given to it in the noble *sunna*, namely:

A. Menstrual blood is usually dark red or black in colour
B. It is normally thick
C. It comes out with heat
D. It is usually accompanied by a burning sensation
E. It usually comes out forcefully

Differences in the regularity of women's cycles

With regards to menstruation, women are of two categories:

First are those who have a regular menstrual cycle, second are those who do not.

The first kind, who have a regular cycle, are of three types:

1. Those who have a regular time of the month and duration of bleeding
2. Those who have a regular duration of bleeding
3. Those who have a regular time of the month

As for the second kind, who do not have a regular cycle, they are also of three types:

1. Those who are experiencing their first menstrual cycles
2. Those whose cycle is irregular
3. Those who forget or are otherwise unaware of their cycle

Women with regular menstrual cycles

The noble *sunna*:

❖ Samāʿa said: I asked about a virgin servant who experiences menses for the first time, to which the Imam 🕮 responded: 'If two months agree on the number of days equally, then those are her days.'[323]

Rulings:

As we mentioned previously, women with regular menstrual cycles are of three types:

A. **Women with a regular time of the month:** Namely those women who have had at least two consecutive monthly cycles at specific intervals in time. For example, a woman whose period begins on the fifth of every lunar month at least twice in a row is said to have a regular time of the month. She acts according to this regularity so long as it remains so; but if she begins bleeding early and this bleeding continues into her regular time, while the total duration remains less than ten days, then the full duration is treated as menstruation so long as the blood is consistent in appearance and it was possible for her period to last this long.

B. **Women with a regular duration of bleeding:** These are women whose menstrual cycle is fixed with regards to its number of days but not the date on which it begins. So, a woman might see on at least two consecutive occasions that her bleeding lasts seven days, but each time [it begins] on a different date. For example, she might start bleeding on the first of one month and on the fifth of the next. In this case, she has a regular duration for her menstrual bleeding. Thus, when she experiences bleeding for the duration of her previous cycles, she treats this as menstruation, but if she experiences bleeding beyond this—so long as it does not exceed ten days—then this, too, is treated as menstruation.

But if a woman with regular duration experiences bleeding wherein the blood does not match the appearance of menstrual blood, then she treats it as menstruation if there is some other indication that it is such, like change in her physical and emotional states that would usually indicate that she was due to menstruate, or the fact that there is no other possible source for this bleeding other than menstruation – such as disease, injury, or spotting.

---

[323] *Wasāʾil al-shīʿa*, v. 2, p. 545, ḥ. 1

If, however, the blood bears no resemblance to menstrual blood, and it could be the result of spotting that has occurred for some reason, or some internal injury, then the most likely ruling is that she is still in a state of ritual purity.

C. **Women with a regular time of the month and a regular duration for their menstruation:** These are women whose bleeding is regular as to when it begins and how long it lasts (and this is known by its occurring as such on at least two consecutive occasions), such as a woman who experiences menstrual bleeding between the fifth and eleventh of every lunar month without fail. In this case, she has both a regular time of the month and a regular duration. And there are some subsidiary rulings that apply to this woman:

1. If a woman with a regular time of the month and duration experiences bleeding at the right time of the month but not for the regular duration—whether longer or shorter—and after bleeding stops, she begins bleeding again for the regular duration but at the wrong time of the month, then if the blood from the first instance resembled menstrual blood and there was a gap of at least ten days between the two instances, both are treated as menstruation. But if the gap between the two was less than ten days, then the regular time of the month is given precedence: the first instance is treated as menstruation so long as she is not certain that it was not because of other indicators.
2. If a woman with a regular time of the month and duration experiences bleeding for her regular duration but at a different time of the month, whether before or after her usual time, and experiences bleeding at the usual time and for the usual duration, then she is considered to be menstruating in the instance which occurs within her regular time. The other bleeding is treated as spotting (*istiḥāḍa*) unless she knows through other indications that her regular cycle has changed, such as if the bleeding at her usual time did not match the appearance of menstruation, while the other bleeding did; or if her state during her regular days was normal, while during the other bleeding she experienced physical and emotional states that would normally accompany menstruation; and any other indicators that would suggest her cycle has changed—whereat she would treat this bleeding as menstruation, and her bleeding during the normal time of the month as spotting. **To summarize:** Her regular cycle remains a distinctive indicator for determining the start and end of her menstruation, but it does

not overrule other indicators if they unanimously suggest that her cycle has changed.

3. In any conflict between time and duration for a woman who has a regular time of the month and duration for her menstruation, preference should be given to time in determining when she is menstruating. So if she experiences bleeding at the regular time but for more or fewer days that usual, while experiencing bleeding at another time but for the expected number of days, then she should assume that the bleeding at the regular time of the month is menstruation.

Two subsidiary rulings

First – The rulings for a woman with a regular monthly cycle, whether in timing or duration, cease to apply if she experiences two consecutive periods which are at variance with her regular cycle; she may experience two consecutive periods which are regular – whether with regards to timing or duration – in which case she has a new regular cycle, or she may experience two which are at variance with her regular cycle, in which case she must follow the ruling of a woman without a regular cycle.

Second – These rulings do not cease to apply because of a single irregular period.

Women without regular menstrual cycles

The noble *sunna*:

❖ Samāʿa b. Mahrān said: I asked about a virgin servant who experiences menses for the first time, and in the first month it was for two days a month, and then in the third the number of days was different from that; her period in this month was not alike in its number of days. The Imam 🕮 said: 'Then she should wait and refrain from prayer as long as she sees blood that does not exceed ten days, and if two months are the same in the number of days, then that is her cycle.'[324]

Rulings:

Women without regular cycles also fall into one of three categories:

A. Women who are experiencing menstruation for the first time.

---

[324] *Al-Kāfī*, v. 3, p. 79, ḥ. 1

B. Women with irregular cycles, namely those who have had several monthly cycles without any regularity with regards to timing or duration.

C. Women who have forgotten or are otherwise unaware of their regular cycle; these are women who had a regular cycle but have since forgotten it because their menstruation stopped for a period of time due to pregnancy, breastfeeding or illness.

Here we will discuss the rulings for these women in the following points:

1. Women without regular menstrual cycles forgo acts of worship as soon as they experience bleeding matching the description of menstruation and follow the rulings of menstruation.
2. If the bleeding does not match the description of menstruation and there are other indicators that this bleeding is not menstruation, such as if she is ill or has suffered an injury, then it is not considered menstruation.
3. But if a woman is otherwise healthy and experiences bleeding, it is most likely to be menstruation, as menstruation is a sign of health.
4. A woman without a regular menstrual cycle is said to have a regular menstrual cycle when she experiences two consecutive periods which are regular with regards to timing, duration or both, as we have already discussed.

Rulings for menstruating women

The noble *sunna*:

- Muḥammad b. ʿAlī al-Ḥalabī has narrated from Imam al-Ṣādiq ﷷ: '*Ghusl* for the state of major ritual impurity and *ghusl* for menstruation is one.' The narrator asked the Imam if a menstruating woman must perform *ghusl* like that of the one in a state of major ritual impurity. So the Imam said: 'Yes.'[325]
- Imam al-Bāqir ﷷ said: 'If a woman is menstruating, it is unlawful for her to pray, but she should perform the *wuḍū'* of prayer at the time of prayer, then sit in a ritually pure place and engage in the remembrance of Allah Almighty, glorify Him, proclaim His oneness and praise, for

---

[325] *Wasā'il al-shīʿa*, v. 2, p. 567, ḥ. 5

the amount of time it would take her to pray. Then she should ask for her needs.'[326]

❖ Imam al-Riḍā ☙ said: 'If a woman is menstruating, then she cannot fast or pray.'[327]

❖ Zurāra has narrated: I asked Imam al-Bāqir ☙ about the menstruating woman and the person who is in a state of major ritual impurity: can they recite anything of the Qur'ān? He said: Yes, whatever they wish, except verses of prostration, and they can engage in the remembrance of Allah in any circumstance.'[328]

❖ Mu'āwiya b. 'Ammār said: I asked Imam Abū 'Abd Allah al-Ṣādiq ☙ about a menstruating woman: is she lawful to her husband? He said: 'Apart from her vagina.'[329]

Rulings:

There are special rules which apply to a menstruating woman, as we shall discuss:

First: All acts of worship which require ritual purity, such as prayer, fasting, circumambulation, and seclusion in a mosque, are forbidden to her. Here are some relevant subsidiary rulings:

1. If a woman begins menstruating in the middle of prayer, her prayer is invalidated [and should be abandoned] even if she began bleeding just before *taslīm*.

2. The same applies to fasting (*ṣawm*), as a menstruating woman should not fast. Her fast is invalidated if she begins bleeding during the day, even if only a moment before *maghrib*.

3. A woman does not need to compensate (*qaḍā'*) for daily prayers missed while she is menstruating, but she must compensate for obligatory fasts missed in this way.

4. If the time for prayer sets in and a woman knows that if she delays the prayer she will begin bleeding before being able to perform it, she must pray immediately. If she deliberately delays her prayer until she bleeds, then she must compensate for the missed prayer.

5. If a menstruating woman has completed of her menses near the end of the time for prayer, and there remains enough time for her to

[326] *Wasā'il al-shī'a*, v. 2, p. 587, ḥ. 2
[327] *Wasā'il al-shī'a*, v. 2, p. 586, ḥ. 2
[328] *Wasā'il al-shī'a*, v. 1, p. 493, ḥ. 4
[329] *Wasā'il al-shī'a*, v. 1, p. 494, ḥ. 7

ritually purify herself, make ready for prayer, and perform at least a single *rakʿa* of it, she must hasten to prayer. Should she deliberately delay it until the time for prayer has passed, she must compensate for the missed prayer.

6. If a menstruating woman is unsure whether she has time for prayer when she has finished her menses, she must perform her prayer.
7. A menstruating woman is allowed to perform a prostration of thanksgiving and she is obliged to prostrate if she listens to a verse of the Qurʾān for which prostration is obligatory (*ayat al-sajda*).
8. It is recommended that a menstruating woman cleans herself of menstrual blood at the times of prayer, changes her sanitary dressings, performs *wuḍūʾ*, sits on her prayer mat facing the *qibla*, and occupies herself with remembrance (*dhikr*) of Allah and supplication for the usual duration of her prayer.

Second: It is forbidden for a menstruating woman to touch the text of the Qurʾān, to touch the names of Allah (so long as they are referring to Him), and also the names of the Prophets and Imams ﷺ according to precaution.

Third: She is forbidden from reciting those verses of the Qurʾān which require an obligatory prostration, or even their respective *sūra*s based on precaution.

Fourth: She is forbidden to loiter or remain in mosques, or to put anything in them. As for passing through mosques by entering through one door and leaving from another, there is no problem with this except in the Holy Sanctuary and the Prophet's Mosque, through which a menstruating woman should not pass.

Fifth: Her husband is forbidden from engaging in penetrative vaginal intercourse with her, even if he does not ejaculate inside of her. It is forbidden for him to insert any part of his penis into her based on precaution. However, both parties can enjoy any other kind of permitted sexual activity together. Some pertinent rulings are:

1. It is recommended that the husband pay expiation (*kaffāra*) if he penetrates his wife. It is said that it is obligatory, which accords with recommended precaution.

2. The expiation for penetrating her at the beginning of her menstruation is a single dinar[330], half a dinar in the middle of it, and a quarter of a dinar at the end of it. This should be paid to the poor [from among the Shīʿī community]. The beginning of her menstruation refers to the first third, the middle to the second third, and the end to the final third.
3. After a woman is cleansed of her menstrual blood, her husband may have intercourse with her before she performs *ghusl*, but it is strongly emphasized that she washes her vagina as a matter of precaution beforehand, and it is recommended precaution that they forgo intercourse until after she has performed *ghusl*.

Sixth: Menstruation, according to the criteria mentioned in the chapter on divorce, invalidates divorce (*ṭalāq*) and *ẓihār*.

Seventh: A woman must perform *ghusl* after her menstrual bleeding has stopped in order to perform any obligatory acts of worship that require ritual purity, such as prayer, circumambulation and fasting:

1. The *ghusl* for menstruation is identical to the *ghusl* after sexual intercourse.
2. *Ghusl* suffices for both post-coital impurity and menstrual impurity, so if there is a woman who is cleansed of her menstrual bleeding and is also impure from sexual activity, a single *ghusl* will suffice her for both of them.
3. The obligation for a menstruating woman to perform *ghusl* does not mean she herself is a ritually impure during her menstrual bleeding; her body is ritually pure so long as it has not been contaminated by menstrual blood or some other impurity. The same is true for her sweat, and she can go about her life as normal.

Second: Spotting (*istiḥāḍa*)

The noble *sunna*:

❖ Muʿāwiya b. ʿAmmār has narrated from Imam al-Ṣādiq ﷺ: 'Verily the blood of spotting and the blood of menses do not come from a single point of origin. The blood of spotting is cold, while the blood of menses is hot.'[331]

---

[330] From the perspective of the *sharīʿa*, a *dīnār* is 18 carats of gold, or 3.46 grams.

[331] *Wasāʾil al-shīʿa*, v. 2, p. 537, ḥ. 1

- Ḥafṣ b. al-Bakhtarī has narrated that a woman came to see Imam Abū ʿAbd Allah ﷺ. She asked about a woman who bleeds continuously such that she cannot tell if it is menses or something else. So he told her: 'Menstrual blood is hot; it is black and it is expelled with force and heat. Blood of spotting (irregular bleeding) is yellowish and cool.[332]
- From *Daʿāʾim al-Islām*: We have narrated from them ﷺ: 'If a woman bleeds continuously then she is experiencing irregular bleeding. Menstrual blood is viscous, thick, and malodorous, while the blood of irregular bleeding is thin.'[333]

What is spotting?

First: The Arabic term for spotting (*istiḥāḍa*) literally means 'a continuation of menstrual bleeding.'

Second: From those narrations which explain the rulings for spotting, we understand the same linguistic meaning, insofar as most of the discussions revolve around a woman whose bleeding continues beyond her usual period.

Hence we know that the basic idea of spotting is a continuation of menstrual bleeding, though another word could be used for that.

The nature of spotting blood differs from that of menstrual blood, and they do not necessarily emerge from the same source. Spotting is any blood, the cause or source of which is unknown to us, and which has not been shown to be the result of menstruation, injury, post-childbirth bleeding, or a torn hymen).

The appearance of blood in spotting

Although the blood that appears in spotting is not of a single variety, there are some attributes which distinguish it from menstrual blood:

1. It is usually yellow in colour
2. It is cool
3. It is thin
4. It emerges without force
5. It is not accompanied by a burning sensation
6. There is no lower or upper limit to its quantity

---

[332] *Wasāʾil al-shīʿa*, v. 2, p. 537, ḥ. 2
[333] *Mustadrak al-wasāʾil*, v. 2, p. 43, ḥ. 2

Subsidiary issues

1. The characteristics of spotting blood are often the opposite of the characteristics of menstrual blood.
2. However, spotting could take on the characteristics of menstrual bleeding, and that is in situations when we cannot say that a woman is experiencing menstruation; for example, if it lasts less than three days or more than ten, then whatever she experiences outside of this is treated as spotting, even if it has the traits of menstruation.
3. Spotting can happen to women and girls of any age, they do not necessarily have to have reached puberty.

Kinds of spotting

Spotting can be classified into three kinds according to the amount of blood:

1. It could be thin and slight to the extent that it does not run when a sanitary towel is removed, such as when a woman is changing her sanitary towel: the blood is there but it does not run. This is light spotting.
2. It could be of such a quantity that it will run when the towel is removed but, will stop again when the towel is put pack in place. This is medium spotting.
3. It could also be so intense that the blood soaks the sanitary towel. This is heavy spotting.

Each of these kinds of spotting has their own rulings, which we shall detail presently:

Light spotting

1. A woman experiencing light spotting must perform *wuḍū'* before every prayer, obligatory or recommended. She must perform *wuḍū'* before *fajr* prayer, *ẓuhr*, *'aṣr*, and so on. She cannot combine two prayers with a single *wuḍū'*.
2. There is no need for her to perform *ghusl* after her spotting has stopped.
3. A woman with light spotting must perform *wuḍū'* before every act of worship that requires ritual purity, such as circumambulation, touching the text of the Qur'ān, etc. She must repeat her *wuḍū'* every time she wants to repeat these deeds.
4. She does not need to repeat her *wuḍū'* for forgotten parts of the prayer, precautionary *rak'as*, or for *sahw* prostrations, if she performs them immediately after the prayer with no interruption.

Medium spotting

1. So long as a woman is experiencing medium spotting that can be contained with sanitary towels, she can pray by performing *wuḍūʾ* for each prayer, exactly like a woman with light spotting.
2. But if she uses a sanitary towel and the blood flows, she must perform *ghusl* for each pair of prayers: one *ghusl* for the prayers of *ẓuhr* and *ʿaṣr*, another for the prayers of *maghrib* and *ʿishāʾ*, and another for *fajr*, like a woman experiencing heavy spotting.
3. Precaution requires that she replace the sanitary towel at least once a day and wash herself, according to the widespread opinion of the scholars. It is most appropriate that she chooses the beginning of the day for *ghusl*, cleansing herself before the *fajr* prayer, washing and then applying a new sanitary towel to contain her bleeding until the end of her prayer.

Heavy spotting

1. It is obligatory for a woman experiencing heavy spotting to perform *ghusl* before every prayer, though it is permissible for her to suffice herself with a single *ghusl* for every pair of prayers (*ẓuhr* and *ʿaṣr*, *maghrib* and *ʿishāʾ*, and *fajr* by itself). This *ghusl* means that she need not perform *wuḍūʾ* for each prayer. But if she does not pray immediately after performing *ghusl,* then she must perform *wuḍūʾ* for each prayer, like a woman experiencing light spotting.
2. She must replace her sanitary towel whenever blood is visible through it, but it is not necessary to do so if it is not visible, though it would be more precautious.
3. She cannot combine more than two obligatory prayers with a single *ghusl*. She can rely on the *ghusl* of her obligatory prayers in order to offer supererogatory ones, but she must perform *wuḍūʾ* for every pair of *rakʿa*s she offers in this way.
4. She must go to pray straight after *ghusl*, although she can recite the *adhān* and *iqāma,* any narrated supplications beforehand. She need not restrict herself to the obligatory components of prayer only; she can also perform the supererogatory actions of it.
5. She must prevent blood from coming out by any means available to her, but in situations where the blood is in such large quantities that she cannot prevent its dicharge, there is no obligation for her to do so.

Rules for spotting

1. In order for the fast of a spotting woman to be valid, she must perform the aforementioned *ghusl*s during the day according to her duty (see

above). If she does not perform them then her fast is invalid and so is her prayer. As for *ghusl* for the *maghrib* and *ʿishāʾ* prayers, this has no bearing on the validity of her fast, even if it is more precautious to observe it as well.[334] As for the *wuḍūʾ*s, they have absolutely no relation to the validity of her fast.

2. If a spotting woman knows that her bleeding will cease before the time for prayer has lapsed, such that she will be able to pray on time and in a state of ritual purity, she should delay her prayers until that time.
3. A spotting woman must offer the prayer of signs (*ṣalāt al-āyāt*) if there is an occasion for it, and she must purify herself in the same manner that she purifies herself for her daily prayers.
4. *Tayammum* takes the place of *ghusl* and *wuḍūʾ* if a spotting woman is unable to perform either of these.
5. The strongest opinion is that a woman suffering from medium or heavy spotting can enter mosques and remain in them without needing to perform *ghusl*, although it is recommended precaution that she should perform *ghusl* for that too.
6. It is recommended precaution to avoid sexual intercourse without *ghusl*, and the strongest opinion is that it is disliked (*makrūh*). The same applies to reciting *sūra*s in which there is a verse of prostration.

Third: Puerperal (post-childbirth or postpartum) bleeding (*nifās*)

What is postpartum bleeding?

Nifās is bleeding experienced by a pregnant woman during childbirth when the first part of the baby emerges or during the first ten days thereafter, with the possibility that it is actually the blood of childbirth. There is no minimum quantity, so postpartum bleeding can be a single drop of blood, and it can continue for up to ten days. If it exceeds ten days, it is no longer treated as postpartum bleeding, but rather as spotting, according to the strongest opinion. The blood that comes out before the baby is not treated as postpartum bleeding.

---

[334] This is recommended precaution; if a spotting woman forgoes the *ghusl* for *maghrib* and *ʿishāʾ* for no valid reason, then she has sinned and her prayers are invalid. However, this does not affect either the fast of the day that has just finished or the fast of the day that is to come.

Rulings for postpartum bleeding

The noble *sunna*:

❖ Yūnus b. Yaʿqūb has narrated that he heard Abū ʿAbd Allah ﷺ saying: 'The woman with bleeding after childbirth refrains from prayer for the number of days as for she would for her menses, then examines herself, performs *ghusl* and prays.'[335]

❖ Abū Mūsā al-Bannāʾ has narrated that he heard Abū ʿAbd Allah ﷺ saying: 'The woman who dies as a result of bleeding after childbirth is resurrected from her grave without an accounting because she died in the pains of her delivery.'[336]

Rulings:

1. Bleeding experienced by a woman after a miscarriage is postpartum bleeding, and if there is any doubt about the miscarriage one must investigate according to common sense.
2. Bleeding experienced by a woman before the first part of the child emerges is not postpartum bleeding unless one knows with certainty that it is. This is true even if it only precedes the birth shortly, and Allah knows best.
3. There is no minimum duration for postpartum bleeding; it could last mere moments.
4. If a woman sees no blood at the time of birth, nor in the ten days thereafter, she is not experiencing postpartum bleeding.
5. If the bleeding continues past ten days, and if a woman has a period of regular duration, then she should treat the duration of her period as the duration of her puerperal bleeding, and the rest as spotting. But if she does not have a period of regular duration, then she should treat the first ten days of bleeding as *nifās* and the rest as spotting.
6. A woman who gives birth to twins and experiences bleeding with each birth, each case of bleeding is an independent case of postpartum bleeding, and any period between them without bleeding is considered one of ritual purity.
7. If a woman's postpartum bleeding stops for a few days and then she starts again before ten days have passed since the birth, and this bleeding does not exceed the tenth day, then both cases were postpartum bleeding unless she knows with certainty that one of them was not.

---

[335] *Wasāʾil al-shīʿa*, v. 2, p. 610, ḥ. 1
[336] *Mustadrak al-wasāʾil*, v. 2, p. 50, ḥ. 3

8. A woman with postpartum bleeding must perform *ghusl* once her bleeding stops; then she will be ritually pure and may perform her religious duties, even if the bleeding stops before the usual number of days for her period.
9. A woman with postpartum bleeding is forbidden to do all the things that are forbidden the menstruating woman.
10. The *ghusl* for puerperal bleeding is identical to the *ghusl* for post-coital impurity and also suffices for *wuḍūʾ*.

Section Five: Cleanliness and Adornment

1: Etiquettes of ritual purity and adornment

Allah says:

'O Children of Adam! Put on your adornment on every occasion of prayer...'[337]

'...Indeed Allah loves the penitent and He loves those who keep clean.'[338]

'Say, "Who has forbidden the adornment of Allah which He has brought forth for His servants...?"'[339]

Some insights from these verses

From the aforementioned verses of the Qurʾān, we deduce that cleanliness and adornment are two of the values endorsed by the revelation, and with which the believer must concern himself. A believer is clean person who maintains the purity of his body, his clothes, and his home just as he maintains the purity of his thoughts, words, and deeds.

A believer is a pleasant and attractive person who loves adornment by looking after his hair, beard, and clothes. He trims his hair, perfumes and anoints his body, and uses hair dye if needed. This is how cleanliness and adornment enter the life of the believer from every angle.

And insofar as people's customs have changed with regards to the methods of keeping clean and beautifying oneself, the believer must make use of them based on the general command of Allah when the Qurʾān encourages him to pursue adornment and purity. He should not wait for specific instructions

---

337 Sūrat al-Aʿrāf (7):31
338 Sūrat al-Baqara (2):222
339 Sūrat al-Aʿrāf (7):32

regarding each and every new tool or invention. For example, cleaning streets, homes, and cars; keeping the air, water, and nature in general free from pollution; moving factories and vehicles which cause pollution and noise far from residential areas – all of these are instances of purity that the religion of Islam endorses.

Similarly, adorning the streets with trees and flowers, and mosques with gardens and pleasant smelling herbs, and cities with green spaces and parks—all of this falls under the adornment which the revelation has bid the faithful to pursue.

Women making use of beauty products – within the framework of religious law – is yet another example of adornment.

The *sunna* of the Messenger ﷺ has opened a broad horizon so that we know the extent of the importance that Islam places on cleanliness and adornment. It is up to the reader to ponder on the traditions narrated from the Prophet and his Household to learn how we can live a pleasant life, and how we can concern ourselves with matters of cleanliness and adornment in our bodies and clothes, just as we concern ourselves with worship and repentance that purify our spirits, by Allah's grace. We have mentioned a selection of these traditions in our more detailed manual of Islamic laws.

The noble *sunna*:

- Muḥammad b. ʿAlī b. al-Ḥusayn has narrated that the Messenger of Allah ﷺ said: 'There are three kinds of disease and three kinds of cure. As for the diseases, they are of the blood, indigestion, and mucus. The cure for diseases of the blood is bloodletting, and the cure for mucus is the bathhouse, and the cure for indigestion is walking.'[340]
- Sulaymān al-Jaʿfarī has narrated from Abū al-Ḥasan: 'Visiting the bathhouse every other day and will not increase your weight, and using it every day will melt the fat around the kidneys.'[341]
- Muʿāwiya b. ʿAmmār has narrated from Abū ʿAbd Allah: 'Three things will help you gain weight and three things which will help you lose weight. As for the things that will help you gain weight, they are habitually using the bathhouse, smelling nice things, and wearing smooth clothes. As for those which will make you thin, they are regularly eating eggs, fish, and vegetables.' Al-Ṣadūq has said: Regularly

---

[340] *Wasāʾil al-shīʿa*, v. 1, p. 361, ḥ. 3
[341] *Wasāʾil al-shīʿa*, v. 1, p. 362, ḥ. 1

using the bathhouse every other day, no; and the one who uses it daily loses weight.[342]

- Al-Ḥasan b. ʿAlī b. Shuʿba has narrated in *Tuḥaf al-ʿUqūl* from the Prophet ﷺ: 'O ʿAlī, beware of entering the bathhouse without wearing a waistcloth; cursed—cursed—is the one who looks and the one who is looked at.'[343]
- Abū ʿAbd Allah ؑ has narrated from the Messenger of Allah ﷺ: 'Whoever believes in Allah and the Last Day will not enter a bathhouse unless he is wearing a waistcloth.'[344]
- ʿAbd Allah b. Muskān has said: We were together with our companions and entered the bathhouse. When we exited, we met Abū ʿAbd Allah ؑ, so he said to us: 'Where are you coming from?' We said: From the bathhouse. So he said: 'May Allah protect your washing.' We said to him: May we be your ransom. Then we came with him until he entered the bathhouse, so we sat with him until he left, whereupon we said to him: May Allah protect your washing. So he said: 'May Allah purify you.'[345]
- Imam al-Ṣādiq ؑ said: 'The one who washes his head with common mallow (the name of a medicinal plant, *Althaea officinalis*) will have poverty banished from him and his sustenance will be increased,' and he said: 'It is a charm.'[346]
- Manṣūr Buzurj said: I heard Abū al-Ḥasan ؑ saying: Washing the head with cedar (powder made from dried cedar leaves) attracts sustenance.'[347]
- Abū Baṣīr has narrated from Abū ʿAbd Allah ؑ the saying of the Commander of the Believers ؑ: 'Lime (a depilatory powder) is a charm and purification for the body.'[348]
- Ibn Abī ʿUmayr has narrated from some of our companions that Abū ʿAbd Allah ؑ said: 'The *sunna* of lime is every twenty-five days, so if twenty days have passed and you do not have any, then seek a loan from Allah.'[349]

---

[342] *Wasāʾil al-shīʿa*, v. 1, p. 363, ḥ. 4
[343] *Wasāʾil al-shīʿa*, v. 1, p. 364, ḥ. 5
[344] *Wasāʾil al-shīʿa*, v. 1, p. 367, ḥ. 5
[345] *Wasāʾil al-shīʿa*, v. 1, p. 382, ḥ. 1
[346] *Wasāʾil al-shīʿa*, v. 1, p. 384, ḥ. 5
[347] *Wasāʾil al-shīʿa*, v. 1, p. 385, ḥ. 1
[348] *Wasāʾil al-shīʿa*, v. 1, p. 387, ḥ. 3
[349] *Wasāʾil al-shīʿa*, v. 1, p. 391, ḥ. 1

- ʿAmmār al-Sābāṭī has narrated from Abū ʿAbd Allah ﷺ: 'Applying lime (to remove pubic hair) once in the summer is better than ten times in the winter.'[350]
- Ibrāhīm b. ʿAbd al-Ḥamīd has narrated that Abū al-Ḥasan said: 'One who applies dye to himself has three characteristics: he inspires awe in war, love in women, and his lovemaking is increased.'[351]
- Muʿāwiya b. ʿAmmār said: I saw Abū Jaʿfar applying blood-red henna.[352]
- Hammād b. ʿUthmān has narrated from Abū ʿAbd Allah: '*Kuḥl* causes hair to grow, dries tears, purifies the saliva, and improves eyesight.'[353]
- Zurāra has narrated from Abū ʿAbd Allah ﷺ: 'Verily the Messenger of Allah ﷺ would apply *kuḥl* before he slept; four times for the right eye and three for the left.'[354]

Rulings:

Here we will mention some of the etiquettes of cleanliness and adornment mentioned in those traditions:

1. Bathing once every two days.
2. Avoiding public bathing without covering oneself.
3. It is recommended [in public baths] to cover everything between the knees and the navel in addition to the obligatory covering of the private parts.
4. Recite some narrated supplications before entering the bath or bathing.
5. It is disliked to sleep, lie down, comb one's hair, or brush one's teeth in the bath, and it is disliked to wash one's head with clay—and that is the head and face with a covering or the like thereof—or to scrub the bottom of one's feet with a stone, or to use water already used in the bath.
6. It is disliked to go to the bath while hungry.
7. It is recommended to put on a turban (i.e. wrap a cloth or towel around one's head) when leaving the bath.
8. It is recommended to use hair removing agents or remove body hair every fifteen days.

---

[350] *Wasāʾil al-shīʿa*, v. 1, p. 392, ḥ. 1
[351] *Wasāʾil al-shīʿa*, v. 1, p. 400, ḥ. 3
[352] *Wasāʾil al-shīʿa*, v. 1, p. 408, ḥ. 1
[353] *Wasāʾil al-shīʿa*, v. 1, p. 411, ḥ. 4
[354] *Wasāʾil al-shīʿa*, v. 1, p. 413, ḥ. 1

9. And to scrub the body with a fine scrub or other suitable powder after hair removal.
10. It is recommended to use black dye.
11. It is recommended for a woman to dye her hand with henna.
12. It is disliked for a woman to neglect beautifying herself within the confines of religious law.
13. It is recommended to perfume oneself, comb one's hair, and tidy one's beard.
14. It is disliked to play with the beard.
15. It is disliked to allow the beard to grow longer than a fistful.
16. It is recommended to trim the moustache [short].
17. It is recommended to clip one's nails.
18. It is recommended to remove hair from one's underarms.
19. It is recommended to remove pubic hair.
20. It is recommended to anoint the body with violet-scented oil.
21. It is recommended to brush one's teeth, and this is a strongly recommended act in the law, not to mention a way of maintaining good health and hygiene. Everyone is aware of the benefits of good oral hygiene for the teeth, mouth, and gums.

2: Rulings and etiquettes of using the lavatory

Below we will discuss the rulings pertaining to using the lavatory, including the obligation to conceal one's private parts, respecting the *qibla* and choosing an appropriate place, and the method of cleaning oneself after using the lavatory.

A: Covering the private parts

1. A man's private parts are his penis, testicles, and rectum, though it appears that his rectum is concealed by his buttocks. A woman's private parts are her vagina and rectum with regards to other women like herself; she must cover them with any covering possible from every onlooker, even the insane, or minors capable of discerning the difference between right and wrong. Covering, here, means to conceal the skin, though precaution requires that she cover the shape as well. In addition to this, a woman must cover her entire body – aside from her hands and face – from non-*maḥram* men.
2. It is forbidden for a Muslim to look at the private parts of another Muslim, aside from women who are permitted to him either as wives or concubines, and obligatory precaution requires him not to look at the private parts of a disbeliever as well.

3. Everything aside from the front and back parts is not necessary to cover, and this ruling applies to a woman with regards to other women like her, and her *maḥram* male relatives. It also applies to a man with regards to other men, and his *maḥram* female relatives. However, it is recommended to cover everything between the navel and the knees, though is not obligatory even in the case of the buttocks or the thigh.
4. It is not permitted to look at another's private parts in the reflection of a mirror or clear water, or displayed on a video screen, or anything else that can be called 'looking.' Obligatory precaution requires one to look away from images and films that display people's private parts, and it is forbidden to look at these images or films with lust, or if it is likely to lead one to do something forbidden.

B: Respecting the qibla

1. Out of respect for the *qibla,* Islam forbids facing directly towards or away from it when urinating or defecating, even if only by turning one's private parts away from it. Obligatory precaution requires that one's private parts should not turn to it even if one is not facing it directly while sitting.
2. It makes no difference whether one is in a building or in the middle of the desert with regards to the aforementioned prohibition. However, if one does not know the direction of the *qibla*, then it is neither obligatory to observe this, nor is it obligatory to force a child or insane person to do so, even if it would be better.
3. One can avoid facing the *qibla* [while urinating or defecating] by turning away to the extent that common sense says you are no longer facing it. It is unnecessary to turn away from the *qibla* to the extent that you are facing away from it at a right angle.
4. In situations of substantial necessity (*ḍarūra*) this ruling no longer applies, such as when using the bathroom on an aeroplane, when one is ill, or when one is avoiding being seen by onlookers, etc. If one is forced to either face towards or away from the *qibla*, it is best to face away from it.

C: The place of defecation

It is forbidden to defecate on someone else's property without his permission; the same applies to private bathrooms or pay-toilets if the fee has not been paid. The same also applies to public thoroughfares and places of gathering, or lands that belong to someone. It further applies to graveyards, if defecating would be done in such a way that it was disrespectful to the dead, or any other place which would cause distress or harm to others.

D: How to cleanse oneself after defecation (istinjā')

One must purify the urethra and rectum before prayer or any other act that requires ritual purity of the body, such as circumambulation. This is known as *istinjā'* and the details of this act are as follows:

1. One must wash the [entrance of the] urethra twice, though three times is better, and it is not enough to remove the physical ritual impurity without water if one is able to use water. It suffices to wash the rectum until all faecal matter has disappeared; there is no need to check its odour or colour if no matter visibly remains. It is permissible to wipe it three times with stones, scraps of cloth or tissues, or different sides or parts of the same stone, scraps, etc. If three wipes are insufficient, then wipe as many times as necessary to clean it. Also, if one wipes it and then washes it, it is better. It is impermissible to use respected items for *istinjā'* such as papers with the name of Allah or His prophets written upon it, bones, or droppings, and whoever does this is sinful, though the rectum will still be considered clean.
2. If performing *istinjā'* of the rectum by wiping, the faeces must not have spread beyond the usual place, then it is obligatory to wash the rectum and any contaminated regions around it with water as a precaution. It is also required that anything used for wiping is ritually pure.

E: Expelling remaining urine (istibrā')

1. Islamic law recommends that a man perform *istibrā'* after urination to expel whatever drops of urine remain in his urethra. If he has done this, then any unknown moisture which may subsequently exit his urethra is deemed to be ritually pure, and there is no need for him to perform *wuḍū'*.
2. *Istibrā'* means to do whatever cleanses the urethra of drops of urine, by manually pushing out and squeezing beginning at the base of the penis and going to its head, once, twice, or thrice, because everyone is different. We do not find a specific method mentioned in the sources, but some jurists have said:
   It is best to perform *istibrā'* as follows: wait until urination has stopped, and then begin by purifying the rectum. Then, place the middle finger of the left hand on the rectum and wipe to the base of the penis three times. Then, placing one's thumb over the top side of the penis and

one's index finger under it, squeeze it from bottom to top three times, then squeeze its head three times.[355]

And perhaps it is more thorough if we add to this tensing the muscles at the base of the penis to squeeze out any urine that remains.

3. If a man performs *istibrā'* and then is unsure whether some moisture that emerges from his urethra is urine or not, he should assume it to be ritually pure.
4. A woman is not obligated to perform *istibrā'*; any unknown moisture which comes from her urethra is assumed to be ritually pure unless she knows it to be urine. But the best course of ation is that she performs *istibrā'* by any means that cleanses her urethra of any traces of urine, whether by tensing her muscles or applying pressure to it, etc.
5. If some moisture comes out [of the urethra] as the result of foreplay, or such a long time after urination that one knows his urethra was free from urine, then this moisture is not considered ritually impure, even if the person has not performed *istibrā'*.

Section six: The etiquettes of illness and rules pertaining to death

Death and us

Among the most beneficial things is being mindful of death while striving for life. Perhaps this best sums up the Islamic attitude towards death. You are forever labouring toward your Lord laboriously, and you will encounter Him. Your labour is a journey and your demise is a bridge; so prepare for your life so that tomorrow you will not be one of those who say: **'Alas, had I sent ahead for my life [in the Hereafter]!'**[356]

It is only by remembering death and our meeting with Allah, and by preparing for these, that you can – God-willing – be one of those about whom our Lord has said: **'O soul at peace! Return to your Lord, pleased, pleasing! Then enter among My servants! And enter My paradise!'**[357]

Death is but a journey; what follows is far greater than death. By constantly remembering death, the human being will strive for what follows it, and by being mindful of his death, a person will come to know the value of his life in this world. It is an opportunity that he will never have again, so he must seize it without wasting any time: so he prays most of the night, seeks forgiveness

---

[355] Ṭabatabā'ī (the jurist), *al-'Urwat al-wuthqā* vol. 1, chapter on *istibrā'*
[356] Sūrat al-Fajr (89):24
[357] Sūrat al-Fajr (89):27-30

in the early hours of the morning, gives food to the poor, and honours the orphan. As for he who forgets death, see what his Lord says about him: '**No indeed! Rather you do not honour the orphan, and do not urge the feeding of the needy, and you eat the inheritance rapaciously, and you love wealth with much fondness. No indeed! When the earth is levelled to a plain, and your Lord and the angels arrive in ranks, the day when hell is brought [near], on that day man will take admonition but what will the admonition avail him?**'[358]

Remembering death makes life easier for you; in fact, it makes you see it in its true light. It is only a single step of a long journey, so why do we grieve for what we lose in life, and why do we become happy to the point of delusion by what we are given in it? What is the source of this despair that grips those who seek this world, such that when they lose part of it they are distraught, and when they seize a part of it they become miserly?

All good qualities and the very pillars of goodness itself are found in a believer through death and its remembrance: he will neither fear death when he faces his enemy, nor soften when he suffers hardship, nor slacken in doing good, and he will be always on his guard against evil and transgression.

Repentance: How and when?

'[Acceptance of] repentance by Allah is only for those who commit evil out of ignorance, then repent promptly. It is such whose repentance Allah will accept, and Allah is All-knowing, All-wise. But [acceptance of] repentance is not for those who [knowingly] go on committing misdeeds: when death approaches any of them, he says, "I repent now." Nor is it for those who die while they are faithless. For such We have prepared a painful punishment.'[359]

The Prophet ﷺ says: 'If repentance leaves no trace on the one who repents, then he is not penitent; [rather, the penitent is he who seeks to] please whom he has wronged, returns to his prayers, is humble towards others, and protects himself from lust. His neck grows lean by fasting through the day and his skin yellow from praying by night. His stomach becomes hollow from lack of food, his back bent for fear of Hellfire, his bones melt out of desire for Paradise, his heart quivers in terror at the angel of death, and his skin trembles upon his body at the thought of the Hereafter. These are the effects of repentance; so if you see a servant with these qualities, then he is penitent and doing good to himself.'

---

[358] Sūrat al-Fajr (89):17-23
[359] Sūrat al-Nisā' (4):17-18

The noble *sunna*:

- Imam al-Ṣādiq ﷺ said: 'Religion is not protected but by rebelling against desire, and contentment is not achieved but by wariness and obedience.'[360]
- Imam al-Ṣādiq ﷺ said: 'Verily Allah loves the penitent confessor.' And he said: 'The Messenger of Allah would repent to Allah seventy times every day despite being sinless. He would say: "I seek forgivenss from Allah and I repent to him." And he would say: "I repent to Allah."'[361]
- Zurāra has narrated from one of the two Imams ﷺ: 'Spending a night in sickness or aching brings a greater and more magnificent reward than a year's worship.'[362]
- The Messenger of Allah ﷺ said: 'One night's fever is expiation for [the sins of] a year.'[363]
- Regarding a child's illness, ʿAlī ﷺ has said: 'It is expiation for its parents.'[364]
- Imam ʿAlī ﷺ said: 'Whoever conceals from others the aching [or illness] that afflicts him for three days, and complains [only] to Allah, it will be his right over Allah to free him from it.'[365]
- Imam al-Ṣādiq ﷺ said: 'Complaining (in a negative sense) is not when a man says: I was sick or unwell last night. Rather, complaining is to say: Woe is me for what nobody has noticed.'[366]
- It is narrated from Abū ʿAbd Allah ﷺ: 'Whichever believer visits a sick believer when he awakes in the morning, he will be followed by seventy thousand angels. When he sits, he will be engulfed in mercy and they will seek forgiveness for him until it becomes darkness falls. And if he visits him in the evening, then the same will happen until morning.'[367]
- Abū ʿUbayda al-Ḥadhdhāʾ has narrated: I said to Abū Jaʿfar ﷺ: Tell me something by which I might benefit. So he said: 'O Abū ʿUbayda! Increase your remembrance of death, for verily a man does not increase

---

360 *Mustadrak al-wasāʾil*, v. 12, p. 112, ḥ. 10
361 *Mustadrak al-wasāʾil*, v. 12, p. 119, ḥ. 2
362 *Wasāʾil al-shīʿa*, v. 2, p. 622, ḥ. 6
363 *Wasāʾil al-shīʿa*, v. 2, p. 635, ḥ. 22
364 *Wasāʾil al-shīʿa*, v. 2, p. 626, ḥ. 1
365 *Wasāʾil al-shīʿa*, v. 2, p. 628, ḥ. 9
366 *Wasāʾil al-shīʿa*, v. 2, p. 631, ḥ. 3
367 *Wasāʾil al-shīʿa*, v. 2, p. 636, ḥ. 1

his remembrance of death but that he subsequently restraints himself in worldly affairs.'[368]

Rulings:

1. A believer must always think of the Hereafter, forever preparing for a long journey which there is no avoiding. And when its time comes, it cannot be delayed or advanced by a single second.
2. Part of preparing for death is repentance; it is a religious duty to repent as soon as one sins. The conditions for fulfilling repentance are as follows: (a) [sincere] regret for the sin, (b) resolving never to do it again, (c) putting right whatever religious duties the sin has corrupted (such as prayer and *zakāt*), and (d) restoring the rights of others.
   Among the etiquettes of repentance are pleading to Allah for forgiveness and seeking intercession with him through the Prophet and his Household, seeking their protection, striving in the way of Allah through giving charity, doing righteous deeds with dedication, and praying for forgiveness in the early hours [of the morning].
3. One must return anything with which he has been entrusted, and restore any rights he has taken from others, when he realizes he will soon die. If there is someone he trusts to execute his last will, then it is sufficient for him to [generally] enjoin this person to do it in such a way that nothing is left out.
4. One must also will that someone fulfil any obligations he was unable to perform during his lifetime, such as pilgrimage (*ḥajj*). As for things such as missed prayers and fasts, which are obligatory for his executor to undertake, he must inform him of them as a matter of obligatory precaution.
5. It is impermissible to deprive any inheritors of their rights by, for example, falsely giving some property to others [to conceal its existence or prevent its being inherited]. And it is a matter of precaution that he should not conceal any property he has from them (such as private bank accounts in his name), or whatever is owed to him by others.
6. It is best to specify the inheritance of one's small children. In fact, it is obligatory if failure to do so will mean that they are deprived of their rights. It is also best to appoint someone appropriate to undertake this important task.

---

368 *Wasā'il al-shī'a*, v. 2, p. 648, ḥ. 1

Rules pertaining to the deathbed

The noble *sunna*:

❖ Abū Baṣīr has narrated: We were with Imam Abū Jaʿfar 🕮 when he was told: ʿIkrama is on his deathbed, while he accepts the views of the *khawārij* (a heretical sect). So Abū Jaʿfar 🕮 said to us: 'Wait or me until I return to you.' So we said: Yes. After a delay he returned, and said: 'If only I had reached ʿIkrama before his soul had [reached his throat], then I could have taught him some beneficial words. However, I reached him after [that].' So I said: May I be your ransom, what are those words? He said: 'I swear by Allah, it is what you are upon (i.e., your religion, Shīʿism). So you should prompt your dying ones, at the moment of death, to testify [to the fact that] "there is no god but Allah," and [to] the *walāya* [of the Imams 🕮].'[369]

❖ Imam al-Ṣādiq 🕮 said: 'Do not leave your dead alone, or verily Satan will play with their insides.'[370]

❖ ʿAlī b. Yaqṭīn has narrated: I asked al-ʿAbd al-Ṣāliḥ 🕮 about the case of a woman who dies while her [living] child is still inside her. He said: 'Cut open her abdomen and remove her child.'[371]

Rulings:

1. Some of the obligations that the living have towards the deceased are to look after them according to the dictates of the *sharīʿa* by facing them towards the *qibla* as they pass away, then washing, shrouding, praying over, and burying their body. If no one [from the deceased's community] fulfills these obligations, then everyone has sinned; but if a group of people fulfil these tasks, then the others are relieved of them.

2. The heir (*walī*) of the deceased is more entitled to look after these affairs than others, so anyone wishing to undertake any of these tasks must seek his permission. And if he neither performs these tasks, nor allows anyone else to do so, this entitlement is revoked, and precaution dictates that – at this time – permission must be sought from the next relative in descending order of proximity by relation to the deceased. It is best to seek permission from the Islamic legal authority as well.

3. A husband is most entitled to look after his wife, and thereafter the heirs follow [based upon] their priority in inheritance.

---

[369] *Wasāʾil al-shīʿa*, v. 2, p. 665, ḥ. 2
[370] *Wasāʾil al-shīʿa*, v. 2, p. 671, ḥ. 2
[371] *Wasāʾil al-shīʿa*, v. 2, p. 673, ḥ. 2

4. A son has priority over the mother of the deceased, though precaution requires that her permission be sought also.
5. Precaution requires that the deceased be turned to face the *qibla* in such a way that if he was sat up straight, his face will be towards it. If someone knows they are about to die, then precaution dictates that they should lie down in this fashion.
6. It is recommended to encourage the dying to recite the two testimonies of faith, affirm his belief in the *walāya* of the Infallible Imams, and any other true doctrines (for example, that the resurrection is true, the questioning in the grave is true, paradise and perdition are true, etc.). And it is recommended that the dying person repeat after the person reciting it to him with his tongue, or at least with his heart.
7. Once his spirit has departed, the deceased's eyes should be shut, his mouth closed, his jaws should be shut, his arms and legs laid straight, and then he should be covered with a robe. Furthermore, it is best to inform the believers of his death so that they can all share in the reward of attending his funeral procession.
8. If people are unsure whether someone is dead, they must wait until it has been conclusively established. And if there is a good reason for delaying his preparation for burial, then his burial should not be delayed more than that reason necessitates.
9. The best course of action is that no one should touch the dying person as they are in the pangs of death. Also, it is disliked for anyone who is in a state of post-coital or menstrual ritual impurity to be present at the deathbed. Finally, it is disliked to leave the body deceased alone [at any time] after he has passed away [until burial].

Washing the deceased

The noble *sunna*:

❖ Ṣāliḥ b. Kaysān has narrated that Muʿāwiya said to al-Ḥusayn ﷺ: Has news reached you of what we did to Ḥujr b. ʿAdī and his companions, the followers (*shīʿa*) of your father? So he ﷺ said: 'And what did you do with them?' He said: We killed the, enshrouded them, and prayed over them. So al-Ḥusayn ﷺ laughed, then said: 'The people will be your opponent [on Judgment Day], O Muʿāwiya; and if we kill your followers, then we do not enshroud them, pray over them, bury them, or inter them.'[372]

---

[372] *Wasāʾil al-shīʿa*, v. 2, p. 704, ḥ. 3

❖ Zurāra has narrated from Abū ʿAbd Allah 🕮: 'If the unborn child has completed four months, then it must be bathed.'[373]

❖ Abū Numayr, the servant of al-Ḥarth b. al-Mughīra al-Naṣrī, has narrated: I said to Abū ʿAbd Allah 🕮: Tell me, until what age can a [deceased] boy be bathed by women? He said: 'Up to three [lunar] years of age.'[374]

❖ ʿAmmār b. Mūsā has narrated that he said to Abū ʿAbd Allah 🕮: What should be done if a Muslim man dies, and there is no Muslim man or woman from his near relatives available, but there is a Christian man, or some Muslim women who are not relatives? He said: 'Out of necessity, the Christian man should perform *ghusl* and then bathe the deceased.' And what about a Muslim woman who dies while there are no Muslim women, or Muslim men from her near kinsfolk, but there are Christian women, and Muslim men who are not relatives? He said: 'The Christian women should perform *ghusl* and then bathe the deceased.'[375]

Rulings:

1. It is a duty upon all Muslims to wash their deceased, and this ruling applies to their [deceased] children and insane persons as well.

2. Regarding miscarried foetuses, if they were they fully-formed and reached four months in the womb, then their ruling is the same as that of a grown person with regards to washing, shrouding, and burial. However, it is not obligatory to pray over them. If the foetus was less than four months, it should be shrouded and buried [but not washed].

3. The one who washes the body of the deceased must do so intending to seek nearness to Allah, and if he makes this intention before washing, then this suffices him for the duration of the three washes, which we shall discuss in detail. However, if he renews his intention with each washing, then this is more precaution. If there is more than one person performing the washing, all of them must make this intention, unless some are washing and others are merely helping. It is unnecessary for those helping [but not washing] to make the intention of seeking nearness to Allah, though it is better if they do so.

4. The washer and the deceased must be of the same gender: a male must be washed by a male, and a female only by a female. Deceased children under five years of age are exempt from this, as are spouses when one washes another, and the same applies to *maḥārim* relatives.

---

[373] *Wasāʾil al-shīʿa*, v. 2, p. 696, ḥ. 4
[374] *Wasāʾil al-shīʿa*, v. 2, p. 712, ḥ. 1
[375] *Wasāʾil al-shīʿa*, v. 2, p. 704, ḥ. 1

5. If there is no one of the same gender to wash a corpse, then a person of the other gender can pour water on the body over a cloth, then wrap the body in a shroud and bury it.
6. In addition to being of the same gender, as we have discussed, jurists require that those washing a body be of legal maturity, sound mind, Muslim, and able to perform *ghusl* properly – and the requirement of legal maturity is in accordance with precaution.

Who is exempt from being washed?

1. A martyr who is slain in Allah's way and dies in battle; he is not washed but rather shrouded in his clothes, prayed over, and buried. And if the martyr has been stripped of his clothes, he is shrouded. However, the shoes and belt of a martyr should be removed if they are made of leather.
2. One sentenced to death according to the Islamic laws of punishment or retribution (*qiṣāṣ*). He is washed, shrouded, and camphor is applied [while he is still alive]; then, when he is slain, he is prayed over and buried.
3. Body parts; although if they contain the heart, they are treated as the deceased and therefore must be washed, shrouded, prayed over, and buried. In this case, a robe or cloth suffices as a shroud, but precaution requires that an outer covering be added.
4. If the body part in question was not the chest, but contains a bone, it is sufficient to wash it, wrap it, and bury it. But if it does not contain a bone, it should be wrapped in a scrap of cloth – based on precaution – and buried.

How is the deceased to be washed?

The noble *sunna*:

❖ Yūnus has narrated from one of the Imams عليهم السلام: 'When you want to bathe the dead, place him upon the washing surface facing the *qibla*. If he is wearing a shirt, then remove his arms from it and place it over his genitals, and pull it down to the top of his knees. If he was not wearing a shirt, then cover his genitals with some cloth. Proceed to the cedar leaf powder in a basin and pour water over it, stirring it with your hand until it foams up. Separate the foam in something and pour the rest into a pitcher of water. Then wash his hands three times, just as a man in a state of major ritual impurity, until the elbows. Then wash his private parts. Thoroughly wash his head with the foam, working hard not to let any water enter his nostrils or ears. Then, lay him on his left side and pour the water over half of his head down to his feet, three times. Rub [the water over] his body gently, and similarly his back and abdomen. Then, lay him on his right side, and do the same thing as with the other. Then empty the water from the pitcher and rinse it out with pure water. Then wash your hands until the elbows. Fill the pitcher with water and add pieces of camphor, and do with it what you did the first time [with the cedar]: begin with his hands, then his genitals, then wipe his abdomen gently, and if anything comes out of him then clean him. Then wash his head, turn him onto his left side, and wash his right side, back, and abdomen. Then turn him onto his right side, and wash his left side just as you did the first time. Then wash your hands until the elbows, empty the pitcher, and fill it with pure water. Wash him with pure water like you had washed him the first and second times, and dry him with a clean cloth. Take some cotton, sprinkle it with camphor, and place it over his genitals, front and back, filling his rear with the cotton lest anything come out from it. Take a long cloth, one *shibr* (hand span) wide, and stretch it from his groin, tightly tying it around his thighs and winding it around them. Then pass the end from under his legs up to the right side, and tuck it into the place where you had started winding it. And the cloth is long; tightly wind it around the thighs from the groin to the knees.'[376]

- ❖ Imam al-Ṣādiq ﷷ said, as part of a longer narration: 'When you turn the deceased (or dying) to the *qibla*, face it by its face (such that if it were sat up, it would be facing the *qibla*), and do not make contrary way like "the people" (i.e., the non-Shīʿa, inclining it on its side towards the *qibla*).'[377]
- ❖ Imam al-Ṣādiq ﷷ said: 'Whoever washes a deceased person and carries out the trust, Allah will forgive him.' The narrator asked: And how is the trust carried out? He said: 'He does not disclose what he saw.'[378]
- ❖ Zurāra has narrated that Abū Jaʿfar ﷷ said: The water for [washing] the deceased is not heated.'[379]
- ❖ Abū ʿAbd Allah ﷷ said: 'Do not remove any hair or nails from the corpse, and if anything falls off, then place it inside the shroud.'[380]

---

[376] *Wasāʾil al-shīʿa*, v. 2, p. 679, ḥ. 3
[377] *Wasāʾil al-shīʿa*, v. 2, p. 688, ḥ. 1
[378] *Wasāʾil al-shīʿa*, v. 2, p. 692, ḥ. 2
[379] *Wasāʾil al-shīʿa*, v. 2, p. 693, ḥ. 1
[380] *Wasāʾil al-shīʿa*, v. 2, p. 694, ḥ. 1

Rulings:

1. The deceased is washed with three kinds of water: water infused with cedar leaf powder, water with camphor, and then plain water, in that order.
2. The washing of the deceased is exactly like the *ghusl* for post-coital impurity. It begins with the head, then the right side of the body, followed by the left. However, washing it by immersion is nearest to precaution.
3. Cedar leaf powder or camphor must be added to the water in such a quantity that common sense would deem it to be water infused with these ingredients, while still a kind of water (i.e., 'cedar water,' 'camphor water').
4. If cedar leaf powder or camphor cannot be found, then precaution requires the body be washed with pure water in place of them, and if there is no water available for washing at all, then *tayammum* should be performed – once suffices, but three times is most cautious.
5. If one fears that the deceased will disintegrate as a result of washing because he was either burnt, drowned, etc., then one should pour water over him without any rubbing, if possible. Otherwise *tayammum* should be performed once, though it is recommended precaution to do it three times.
6. If someone dies while in a state of consecration (*iḥrām*), his body does not need to have camphor applied, as it is already in a pleasant state and there is no other goodness beyond this.
7. The way of performing *tayammum* for the deceased is for someone to strike their hands on the ground once or twice and then place them on the locations of *tayammum*; the face and hands of the deceased. It is best to strike one's own hands on the ground a second time before wiping them over the hands of the deceased.

Rulings pertaining to the washing of the deceased

1. It is a condition of washing the deceased that whoever is performing the act must have the intention of seeking nearness to Allah. On this basis, one is not allowed to ask for payment except for covering basic expenses or for agreeing to undertake it on short notice.
2. It is also a condition that the water be ritually pure, and that every hand that washes be ritually pure. In fact, it is a condition that the limbs of the deceased be free of physical ritual impurity before washing begins.
3. In the same manner, it is necessary to remove anything that prevents water from reaching the skin of the deceased wherever possible.

4. Scholars also require that anything being used to wash the deceased must be lawful for usage, such as the water, the place of washing, the jug used to pour the water, etc. Observing this accords with precaution, as we have discussed in the other acts of ritual purity.
5. The washer must avert his gaze from the deceased's private parts, but failing to do so does not invalidate the washing.
6. If the body of the deceased is tainted by ritual impurity, such as by some blood that comes out of it or a wound, it is unnecessary to repeat the washing except as a recommended precaution. Although it is necessary to purify his body, even after he has already been lowered into the grave, so long as this does not cause unbearable difficulty (*ḥaraj*).

Shrouding the deceased

1. Shrouding a Muslim is a collective obligation upon all Muslims (that is, if some of them do not shroud a decedent, the entire community will have sinned), and this must be done in three robes: a waistcloth, a shirt, and a shroud.
2. The waistcloth is wrapped around the deceased from his navel to his knees, and anything that can be called a waistcloth suffices. The shirt extends from the shoulders to middle of the calf, though it is better that it reaches the foot. The shroud must cover the entire body. And it is more cautious to wrap it in such a way that it is made to overlap itself horizontally, and so that both sides can be tightened vertically.
3. The deceased should not be wrapped in the hide of a carrion, nor in anything that has been usurped, nor in a ritually impure item of clothing (even if this is an impurity that may be lawfully overlooked in the case of prayer), nor in pure silk. It is more cautious to avoid a robe with golden thread in it, and anything made from an animal— whether hide, hair, or fur—whose flesh is not eaten. As for something made from the hide of an animal whose flesh is eaten, if the item cannot be called clothing, then it is more cautious to avoid using it for shrouding too.
4. If the burial shroud becomes ritually impure – after the deceased has been wrapped in it – then it must be purified, whether by washing, removing the contaminated part, or by changing it, be it before or after it has been lowered into the ground.
5. Each person's shroud should be paid for out of his own wealth. A wife's shroud should be purchased by her husband if he is able, otherwise someone should offer to pay for it, or she could have left a will for someone to do so. If the executor of the will acts upon it, then the husband is relieved of the duty. And it is most cautious to include all

the necessary expenses for the burial with the shroud, so the husband must bear this cost.

6. It is recommended that the shroud be well-made, that its material be cotton and its colour white, with no dye except ink—for it has been narrated that the shroud of Allah's Messenger had red ink upon it. The shroud should also be paid for with lawful wealth, and it is better if it was made from the *iḥrām* of the deceased and his prayer clothes. It is recommended to pour some camphor or fragrant powder made from grains of wheat on him, and it is also good to bury him with a piece of Imam al-Ḥusayn's soil (or clay).
7. It is recommended to inscribe on the fringes of the shroud the testimony of the deceased: that he believes in the oneness of Allah, the prophethood of Muhammad ﷺ, the Imamate of the infallible Imams عليهم السلام, mentioning their names. This is done by writing: 'so-and-so, the son of so-and-so, bears witness that...' It is recommended to inscribe the Qur'an in its entirety on the shroud, or on another piece of cloth to be included with the shroud.
8. It is recommended that a believer prepare his shroud before he dies so that he will not be recorded amongst the negligent (*ghāfilīn*).

Anointing the body and the etiquettes of the funeral procession

1. Camphor must be wiped over the deceased's seven points of prostration (the forehead, palms of the hands, the knees, and the two toes). The most cautious course of action is to include his nose as well.
2. Anointing comes after washing the body, either before wrapping it in the shroud, during it, or after it. It is best to anoint the body before shrouding it, and it is a matter of precaution that the camphor should be ritually pure, permitted for use, powdered, and fragrant.
3. If someone dies in a state of consecration (*iḥrām*) for *ḥajj* before having performed circumambulation, then they are exempt from being anointed.
4. It is recommended to inform the faithful of the death of their brother in faith so that they can obtain the reward of attending his funeral prayers, and walking in his funeral procession. It is recommended for those walking in the procession to supplicate with narrated invocations, and for them to follow the procession on foot, not riding anything, and to carry the coffin on their shoulders, not by some other means of transportation, except in cases of [practical] necessity. The one walking in the procession should be humble, pondering and taking a lesson from this experience. He should walk behind or to the side of the coffin, not

in front of it, nor should he put a decorous garment upon it. It is recommended that four persons to carry the coffin.

5. It is disliked to laugh, play, or engage in amusement when attending a funeral. It is also disliked for anyone who is not from among the bereaved to turn their cloak inside out [as a mark of mourning]. It is also disliked for anyone to speak anything other than the remembrance of Allah, or for those walking to hasten, or to strike their hands upon their thighs or their arms, or to follow the coffin with a censer.

Praying over the deceased

The noble *sunna*:

- ❖ An group from the Jews came to the Messenger of Allah ﷺ and asked him a question, to which he ﷺ responded: 'What believer prays over the deceased but that Allah makes Paradise obligatory for him—except [when the deceased] is a hypocrite or impious.'[381]
- ❖ ʿAlī b. Jaʿfar said: I asked [my brother] Mūsā b. Jaʿfar ﷺ about who is praying [over the deceased]: can he recite *takbīr* before the *imām*? He said: 'He cannot recite it but with the *imām*, so if he recited it before him, then he must repeat the *takbīr*.'[382]
- ❖ Al-Yasaʿ b. ʿAbd Allah al-Qummī said: I asked Abū ʿAbd Allah ﷺ if a man can perform the funeral prayer alone. He said: 'Yes.' I said: And if it is two people praying? He said: 'Yes, but one stands behind the other and not at his side.'[383]

Rulings:

1. It is obligatory to offer funeral prayers for all deceased Muslims, except those children who died before reaching six years of age, though it is permitted to do so for any child born alive.
2. For the funeral prayers to be valid, the following conditions must be observed:
    a. The one leading the prayer must be a believer (a Shīʿī Muslim).
    b. The prayer must be done with the permission of the heirs – according to obligatory precaution.
    c. The one praying must be legally mature; the prayer of a minor is insufficient, according to obligatory precaution.

---

[381] *Wasāʾil al-shīʿa*, v. 2, p. 762, ḥ. 1
[382] *Wasāʾil al-shīʿa*, v. 2, p. 792, ḥ. 1
[383] *Wasāʾil al-shīʿa*, v. 2, p. 805, ḥ. 1

3. The time for these prayers is after the body has been washed and shrouded, and if these cannot be performed, then after the private parts have been covered. If the body has been covered by dirt, they can pray over it while he is in his grave and there is no need to exhume him from it, according to the strongest legal opinion.
4. If a body part of the deceased contains his heart, then it must be prayed over.
5. If the deceased has a number of heirs, then it is obligatory to obtain the permission of all of them. It is permitted for a woman for a woman to perform the prayers over the person if she was his heir, but she cannot lead the prayers in congregation. She can also give permission to others to pray over him.
6. It is best to offer prayers in congregation over the deceased, and the apparent ruling is that the conditions for such a congregation are the same as those for other congregational prayers, except that the *imām* here does not bear anything on behalf of those who follow him aside from receiving the permission of the heirs.

How to pray over the deceased

The noble *sunna*:

❖ Muḥammad b. Muhājir has narrated from his mother, Umm Salama, that she said: I heard Abū ʿAbd Allah ﷺ saying: 'When the Messenger of Allah ﷺ prayed over the deceased, he would recite *takbīr* and *tashahhud*. Then he would recite *takbīr* and invoke blessings and supplications upon the prophets. Then he would recite *takbīr* and supplicate for the believers, seeking forgiveness for the faithful men and women. Then he would recite the fourth *takbīr* and supplicate for the deceased. Then he would recite the fifth *takbīr* and end the prayer. When Allah Almighty forbade him from praying for the hypocrites, he would perform *takbīr* and *tashahhud*, then he would recite *takbīr* and ask for blessings upon the prophets, then he would recite *takbīr* and supplicate for the believers, then he would recite a fourth *takbīr* and end the prayer without praying for the deceased.'[384]

❖ Imam Abū ʿAbd Allah [al-Ṣādiq] ﷺ said: 'Once, when a man from among the hypocrites died, al-Ḥusayn b. ʿAlī ﷺ came out walking and was met by one of his followers. The Imam said to him: "Where are you going?" So he said: I am escaping the funeral of this hypocrite and [avoiding] praying over him. So al-Ḥusayn said to him: "Stand next to

384 *Wasāʾil al-shīʿa*, v. 2, p. 793, ḥ. 1

me. Listen to what I say and repeat the same thing." Then he raised his hands and said: "O Lord, disgrace Your slave (the dead hypocrite) among the slaves of Your land. O Lord, roast him in the intensity of Your fire. O Lord, make him taste the heat of Your punishment, for verily he was loyal to Your enemies, and an enemy to Your friends, and hated the household of Your Prophet."'[385]

- ❖ It is narrated from Abū Baṣīr: I said to Abū ʿAbd Allah [al-Ṣādiq] ﷺ: What is the reason that we recite five *takbīrs* ('*allāhu akbar*') over the dead, while our opponents (i.e., the Sunnīs) recite only four? He said: 'It is because the pillars upon which Islam is built are five: prayer, the poor rate, fasting, pilgrimage, and the *walāya* (allegiance and divine guardianship) of us, the People of the House. Thus Allah assigned a *takbīr* for each pillar, and you attest to all five of them, where as your opponents (the non-Shīʿa) attest to four and reject one. That is why they recite four *takbīrs* over their dead, while you recite five.'[386]
- ❖ Ismāʿīl al-Ashʿarī has narrated that he asked Imam al-Riḍā ﷺ about the funerary prayer. He said: 'As for the believer (the Shīʿa), there are five *takbīrs*, and for the hypocrite, there are four and no *salām* in it.'[387]
- ❖ ʿAlī b. Jaʿfar has narrated that he asked his brother, Mūsā b. Jaʿfar ﷺ, about a man who was eaten by predatory beasts or birds, and only his bones remain, devoid of flesh. What is done with him? He said: 'Wash him, enshroud him, pray over him, and bury him.'[388]
- ❖ It is narrated that Abū ʿAbd Allah [al-Ṣādiq] ﷺ was asked: Can women pray over the deceased? So he said: 'Verily when Zaynab, the daughter of the Messenger of Allah, died, Fāṭima ﷺ came out with her women and prayed over her sister.'[389]

Rulings:

1. The common method of praying over the deceased is to pronounce five *takbīrs*. Following the first *takbīr*, one recites the two *shahādas*; then invokes blessings on Muḥammad ﷺ and his Household after the second; then prays for the believing men and women after the third; then prays for the deceased and asks for the forgiveness of his sins after the fourth; and then finishes with the fifth.

---

[385] *Wasāʾil al-shīʿa*, v. 2, p. 770, ḥ. 2
[386] *Wasāʾil al-shīʿa*, v. 2, p. 775, ḥ. 17
[387] *Wasāʾil al-shīʿa*, v. 2, p. 784, ḥ. 1
[388] *Wasāʾil al-shīʿa*, v. 2, p. 815, ḥ. 1
[389] *Wasāʾil al-shīʿa*, v. 2, p. 817, ḥ. 1

2. It is permissible to supplicate with languages other than Arabic during the prayers for the deceased, so long as the *adhkār* (the *takbīrs*) are recited in Arabic.
3. There is no *taslīm* in prayers for the deceased, nor is there any bowing or prostration, and it is forbidden to add anything to it with the intention of it being a (mandated) part of the law, because this is a forbidden innovation (*bid'a*).
4. The deceased must be placed lying on his back, perpendicular to the worshippers behind him, with his head pointing to the right of those praying. There should be no barrier between the worshipper and the deceased, such as a wall or curtain, nor should the funeral prayer be taking place at a distance from him except with a 'connection' through the ranks of worshippers. The worshipper must face the *qibla*, and the deceased must have been washed and shrouded, or [at least] have his privates covered if there is no shroud available.
5. The worshipper must stand stationary during prayer, not doing anything at odds with standing (i.e., such that the person could no longer be said to be 'standing'). Each part of the prayer must follow on from the one before it so that its outward appearance is maintained. The intention to pray must be made for a specific deceased person, and the prayer must be performed seeking nearness to Allah.
6. There is no need for the worshipper to be in a state of ritual purity, nor for his clothes and body to be ritually pure. However, the most cautious course of action is to ensure that there is nothing that would otherwise invalidate one's obligatory prayers, namely: speaking, laughing, or turning away from the *qibla*.
7. If no one prays over the deceased until he has been buried, then it is obligatory to pray over his grave. The same applies if it is discovered after burial that the prayer was invalid. It is impermissible to exhume the body for the purposes of prayer.
8. It is permitted to offer a single prayer for multiple decedents.
9. It is recommended to choose a location frequented by the faithful for funeral prayers so that the congregation will be larger. However, this does not include mosques (this applies exclusively to places of worship that are juristically designated as mosques, not generic Islamic centres) because it is disliked to perform funeral prayers in any mosque besides the Holy Sanctuary.
10. As for how to perform prayers for the deceased, it is as follows when joined to recommended *dhikrs* as well:
    a. After the first takbīr you say: *'ash-hadu allā ilāha ill allāh, waḥdahu lā sharīka lahu, wa ash-hadu anna muḥammadan*

ʿabduhu wa rasūluh, arsalahu bil-ḥaqq bashīran wa nadhīran bayna yaday as-sāʿa' (I bear witness that there is no deity save Allah, alone and without partner, and I bear witness that Muḥammad is His servant and messenger, whom He sent with the Truth, a bringer of glad tidings and a warner, on the eve of the Hour).

b. After the second takbīr you say: *'Allāhumma salli ʿalā muḥammad wa āli muḥammad wa bārak ʿalā muḥammad wa āli muḥammad, warḥam muḥammadan wa āli muḥammad ka afḍal mā ṣallayta w'abārakta wa taraḥḥamta ʿalā ibrāhīm wa āli ibrāhīm, innaka ḥamīdun majīd, wa sallī ʿalā jamīʿ al-anbiyāʾ wal-mursalīn wash-shuhadāʾ waṣ-ṣiddīqīn wa jamīʿ ʿibād allah iṣ-ṣāliḥīn'* (O Allah! Exalt Muḥammad and Muḥammad's Household, and bless Muḥammad and Muḥammad's Household, and grant mercy to Muḥammad and Muḥammad's Household, like the best exaltations, blessings, and mercy you bestowed on Abraham and the Household of Abraham. Verily you are Most-praiseworthy, Most-glorious, and [may You] exalt all the prophets, messengers, martyrs, the veracious, and all of Allah's righteous servants!)

c. And after the third takbīr you say: *'Allāhumm aghfir lil-mu'minīn wal-mu'mināt, wal-muslimīn wal-muslimāt, al-aḥyāʾ minhum wal-amwāt, tābiʿ baynanā wa baynahum bil-khayrāt, innaka mujīb al-daʿwāt, innaka ʿalā kulli shay'in qadīr.'* (O Allah! Forgive the believing men and women, and the Muslim men and women, and the living amongst them and the dead, and let us succeed them in good deeds, verily You are the answerer of supplications, verily You have power over all things!)

d. After the fourth takbīr you say: *'Allāhumma inna hadha ʿabduka wabn ʿabdika, wabn ammatika, nazala bika wa anta khayru manzūlin bih. Allāhumma inna lā naʿlamu minhu illā khayran, anta aʿlamu bihi minna. Allāhumma in kāna muḥsinan fa zid fī iḥsānihi, wa in kāna musī'an fa tajāwaz ʿanhu waghfir lahu. Allāhum ajʿalhu ʿindaka fī aʿlā ʿilliyīn wakhluf ʿalā ahlihi fil-ghābirīn, warḥamhu bi raḥmatika yā arḥam ar-rāḥimīn.'* (O Allah! Verily this is Your bondsman, the son of Your bondsman and the son of Your bondswoman, he has gone to You and You are the best destination. O Allah! We only know good from him, but You know him better than us. O Allah! If he was good then increase his goodness, and if he was a sinner, overlook his shortcomings and forgive him. O Allah! Lodge him with the highest of the high with You, look after those whom he has left behind, and grant him Your mercy, O Most-merciful of the merciful!)

e. After the fifth *takbīr* your prayer is complete.

f. If the deceased was female, then the supplication after the fourth takbīr is as follows: *'Allāhumma inna hadhihi amatuka wabnatu ʿabdika wabnatu amatika, nazalat bika wa anta khayru manzūlin bih. Allāhumma inna la naʿlam minhā illa khayran, wa anta aʿlamu biha minna. Allāhumma in kānat muḥsina fa zid fī iḥsānihā, wa in kānat musīʾa fa tajāwaz ʿanhā waghfir lahā. Allāhumm ajʿalhā ʿindaka fī ʿalā ʿilliyīn, wakhluf ʿalā ahlihā fī al-ghābirīn, warḥamuhā bi raḥmatika yā arḥam ar-rāḥimīn!'* (O Allah! Verily this is Your bondswoman, the daughter of Your bondsman and the daughter of Your bondswoman, she has gone to You and You are the best destination. O Allah! We only know good from her, but You know her better than us. O Allah! If she was good then increase her goodness, and if she was a sinner, overlook her shortcomings and forgive her. O Allah! Lodge her with the highest of the high with You, look after those whom she has left behind, and grant her Your mercy, O Most-merciful of the merciful!)

How to bury the deceased

The noble *sunna*:

- Yūnus has said: I heard a narration from Abū al-Ḥasan Mūsā [al-Kāẓim] ﷺ, and if I remember it while I am inside a house, then I can feel it closing in on me. He said: 'When you bring the deceased to his graveside, delay [lowering him into the grave] for an hour, for verily he is preparing himself for the questioning [by the two angels].'[390]
- Ibn ʿAbbās has narrated that when the Prophet ﷺ placed Fāṭima b. Asad, the mother of ʿAlī b. Abī Ṭālib ﷺ, into her grave, he went until he was next to her head, then said: 'O Fāṭima, verily [the angels] Munkir and Nakīr are coming to ask you about your Lord. Tell them: "Allah is my Lord, Muḥammad is my prophet, Islam is my religion, the Qurʾān is my book, and my brother (i.e., the Prophet's brother, ʿAlī ﷺ) is my *imām* and my *walī*."' Then he said: 'O Lord, make Fāṭima firm in these

---

[390] *Wasāʾil al-shīʿa*, v. 2, p. 836, ḥ. 1

three expressions.' Then he exited her grave, and scooped [some earth] upon her.'[391]

- Abū Jaʿfar [al-Bāqir] ؑ has narrated that the Prophet ﷺ said to ʿAlī ؑ: 'O ʿAlī, bury me in this place, and elevate my grave four fingers above the earth, and sprinkle water upon it.'[392]
- Abū ʿAbd Allah [al-Ṣādiq] ؑ was asked about a Christian man who was traveling with some Muslims and dies. He said: 'No Muslim can wash him, there is no honor [in it]; and he does not bury him or stand over his grave, even if it was his father.'[393]
- Ḥishām b. Sālim said: I heard Abū ʿAbd Allah [al-Ṣādiq] ؑ saying: 'Fāṭima lived for seventy-five days after [the martyrdom of] her father, and was never seen cheerful or laughing. She would visit the graves of the martyrs every Friday, and twice on Mondays and Thursdays, and would say: "Here was the Messenger of Allah ﷺ, here were the polytheists.'[394]
- Muḥammad b. Aḥmad b. Yaḥyā has narrated from Muḥammad b. Ismāʿīl b. Bazīʿ that he heard Abū Jaʿfar [al-Bāqir] ؑ saying: 'Whoever visits the grave of his believing brother, sits by his grave, faces the *qibla*, places his hand upon the grave, and recites *Sūrat al-Qadr* seven times, he will be secure from the great terror.'[395]

Rulings:

1. Burying the deceased is a collective obligation (thus, if some from the community fail to complete it, the entire community has sinned). It is obligatory to bury a Muslim's body in the ground. It is not sufficient to place the body in a coffin or mausoleum without burying him, except in situations of compelling necessity (*ḍurūra*).
2. The deceased should be placed in his grave laying on his right side such that his face is turned towards the *qibla*. Body parts should also be buried this way if possible.
3. The primary obligation of burial is that it actually takes place, even without the intention of seeking nearness to Allah. So if a machine is used to excavate the ground and place the deceased's body within, then this is sufficient so long as the deceased's heir authorized the burial. No one is allowed to hasten his burial without the heir's permission.

---

391 *Wasāʾil al-shīʿa*, v. 2, p. 844, ḥ. 9
392 *Wasāʾil al-shīʿa*, v. 2, p. 856, ḥ. 3
393 *Wasāʾil al-shīʿa*, v. 2, p. 865, ch. 39, ḥ. 1
394 *Wasāʾil al-shīʿa*, v. 2, p. 879, ḥ. 1
395 *Wasāʾil al-shīʿa*, v. 2, p. 881, ḥ. 3

4. The [non-legally-mature] child of a Muslim man or woman must be buried in the Islamic fashion according to the strongest opinion.
5. A believer cannot be buried in the graveyard of non-Muslims if that would constitute a disgrace to him.
6. A body cannot be buried in a usurped place, nor in the grave of another person if their body has not yet disintegrated completely, nor in an endowment (*waqf*) without the permission of its trustee, nor in an endowment not intended for this purpose, such as those for mosques or schools, nor in communal places of gathering, nor in roads where the burial will cause damage to them.
7. Body parts of the deceased that become detached from him, such as hair and teeth, must be buried with him by placing them in his shroud.

Rulings about graves

1. One may not disrespect the deceased, for example, by exhuming his body.
2. Exempt from this are cases where some right may be fulfilled by exhuming the body, such as if it was buried in usurped land, or in a usurped shroud, or the body must be exhumed in order to prove a crime, or if obtaining another person's rights depends on the body being examined.

   These rights and others like them make it permissible to exhume a body, so long as they outweigh the dignity of the deceased. On the other hand, if the value of the shroud, the ground, or the right that is under dispute is negligible, then the principle (*aṣl*) of justice, the principle of avoidance of harm (*lā ḍarar wa lā ḍirār*), and the ruling that prohibits exhuming the deceased – all of these call for the living person to obtain his right by some other means, even if he is not satisfied thereby, as his agreement is only a [valid] requirement if there is no harm or wrong done to the deceased by exhuming his body and disrespecting him. And Allah knows best.
3. It is fitting to include with the above the possibility of exhuming a body if some general good depends upon it, for example if there is a highway suffering from congestion and the only way to resolve this is to widen the road over the adjoining graveyard. So if the deceased persons are removed from there to another location after they have been exhumed, the harm is lifted. It is not unlikely that such an action would be permitted, if the general good outweighed the dignity of the deceased *and* no other option was available.

4. Scholars also allow the deceased to be exhumed if they have been buried without proper washing or shrouding, so long as this does not cause any harm to anyone.

Ghusl for touching a corpse

The noble *sunna*:

❖ Muḥammad b. Muslim said: I asked one of the two [Imams] ﷻ about a man who closes the eyes of the deceased: must he perform *ghusl*? He said 'If he touched the body while it still had warmth in it, then no; but if he touched it after it had become cold, then he must perform *ghusl*.' I said: What about the person who washed the corpse: does he perform *ghusl* [for himself]? He said: 'Yes.' I said: Does he perform *ghusl* before bathing, dressing, and enshrouding it? He said: 'He washes the corpse, then washes his hands from the shoulder, then dresses and enshrouds the corpse, and then performs *ghusl* himself.' I said: What of the one who carries the corpse [after it has been wrapped in its burial shroud]: must he perform *ghusl*? He said: 'No.' I said: And the one who enters his grave, must he perform *wuḍū'*? He said: 'No, unless he wishes to perform [dry] ablution with the grave's dirt.'[396]

❖ Al-Ḥasan b. ʿUbayd said: I wrote to al-Ṣādiq ﷺ, asking: Did the Commander of the Believers ﷺ perform *ghusl* after performing the funerary bath of the Messenger of Allah ﷺ after he died? So he answered: 'The Prophet ﷺ is pure and purifying, but the Commander of the Believers ﷺ did it to thereby establish a *sunna*.'[397]

❖ It has been narrated from Abū ʿAbd Allah [al-Ṣādiq] ﷺ: 'If part of a person is severed from him, it is dead. So if a person touches it, then it contained bone, then he is obliged to perform *ghusl* for touching it. If, however, the part contained no bone, then *ghusl* is not obligatory.'[398]

Rulings:

1. *Ghusl* is obligatory for anyone who touches the body of the deceased after it has grown cold and before it has been purified by the three washings. But once the deceased has been purified, only *tayammum* is necessary. It is a matter of obligatory precaution to perform *ghusl* after touching any corpse, whether the deceased is Muslim or non-Muslim,

---

[396] *Wasāʾil al-shīʿa*, v. 2, p. 927, ḥ. 1
[397] *Wasāʾil al-shīʿa*, v. 2, p. 928, ḥ. 7
[398] *Wasāʾil al-shīʿa*, v. 2, p. 929, ḥ. 11

young or old, or even a miscarried foetus, were it customarily considered a person.

2. If a living person's hair brushes against that of the deceased, or someone's hand touches the deceased's hair, then there is no need for *ghusl* unless that would typically be considered contact (*mass*) with the deceased. For example, common sense says that placing one's hand on the deceased's head, face or hand, upon which there is hair, counts as making contact with the corpse. Touching the deceased's bones, fingernails, teeth, or the like thereof, also requires *ghusl*, as these also involve making contact with the deceased – according to precaution.
3. Limbs severed from the deceased, if they contain a bone, require *ghusl* when touched. As for bones without flesh, if a year or more has passed since their burial, then there is a tradition which says there is no need for *ghusl* if one touches them.
4. Whoever needs to perform *ghusl* for touching a corpse cannot pray or perform any other act of worship that requires ritual purity, until he has performed *ghusl*. The strongest opinion is that he does not need to perform *wuḍū'* in addition to *ghusl*.
5. One who needs to perform *ghusl* for touching a corpse may enter mosques and recite *sūra*s containing a verse of prostration according to the strongest opinion, but it is the most cautious course of action is to avoid whatever someone in a state of post-coital or menstrual impurity must avoid.

Prayer

Prayer is a sign of faith

'Those who maintain the prayer and spend out of what We have provided them, it is they who are truly the faithful. They shall have ranks near their Lord, forgiveness and a noble provision.'[399]

Faith takes many forms; in the heart it manifests as awe, in the intellect as certainty, in deeds as reliance upon Allah, in behaviour as prayer, and in economics as spending for good causes. And when we ponder on these attributes mentioned at the beginning of *Sūrat al-Anfāl*, we see that there is a connection between faith and between realities that manifest in the material world. It is these realities that bring us out of utter darkness and into the light of truth (knowing Allah, remembering Him, His signs, and His laws). This is how faith appears in the form of relying upon Allah, praying to Allah, and spending on Allah's servants.

But what completes the realities of faith? Is it not prayer?

Let us heed the words of Allah's Messenger ﷺ when he said: 'Whoever completes his *wuḍū'*, beautifies his prayers, pays his *zakāt*, suppresses his anger, restrains his tongue, seeks forgiveness for his sins, and cares deeply for the Household of his Prophet, has surely completed the realities of faith, and the gates of Paradise are flung open for him.'

Prayer (*ṣalāt*) is a connection between a servant's heart and Allah's light; it is the believer's ascent (*miʿrāj*) to Allah's throne. As the Commander of the Faithful ؑ says: 'If the worshipper knew the extent to which Allah's majesty surrounded him, he would never raise his head from prostration.'

It is a symbol of man's servitude towards Allah and the complete submission of all his life's affairs to His command.

That is why prayer is the first deed about which a servant will be questioned. ʿAlī ؑ narrates from Allah's Messenger ﷺ: 'Verily the pillar of the religion is prayer, and it is the first of the Son of Adam's deeds that will be examined. If [his prayer] is correct, then the rest of his deeds will be considered. But if it is incorrect, then none of his remaining deeds will be considered.'[400]

---

[399] Sūrat al-Anfāl (8):3-4
[400] *Biḥār al-anwār* 79/227

[Prayer] is the framework of Allah's remembrance, which is surely greatest, and the language by which a servant can address Allah directly. In a word, it is the pillar of the religion, the axis of its laws, the moment of bearing witness to the truth, and the motto of establishing justice.

Abu Jaʿfar 🕮 says: 'Prayer is the pillar of the religion, and it is that of a pole in the middle of a tent. If the pole is firm, then the pegs and ropes are firm. But if it bends and breaks, then no peg or rope would be firm.'[401]

Maintaining the prayer is a symbol of faith's refinement and sophistication, as our Lord says: '**We revealed to Moses and his brother [saying], "Settle your people in the city, and let your houses face each other, and maintain the prayer, and give good news to the faithful."**'[402]

This is how Allah's gives glad tidings to the faithful for their prayer and worship. It is narrated that Imam al-Ṣādiq 🕮 said: 'The one who prays has three qualities: When he stands in prayer, blessings shower upon him from the depths of the heavens onto the top of his head, and the angels surround him from beneath his feet to the highest heavens, and an angel calls out: "O you in prayer! If you knew with whom you were intimately conversing, you would never cease!"'[403]

The mark of faith

Prayer is a mark of faith and a provision for the believer on the Day of Resurrection. Let us heed the words of the Creator when He addresses His messenger: '**Tell My servants who have faith to maintain the prayer and to spend out of what We have provided them with, secretly and openly, before there comes a day on which there will be neither any bargaining nor friendship.**'[404]

And in this vein it is narrated that Imam al-Ṣādiq 🕮 said: 'An old man will be brought on the Day of Judgement and given his book, and he will see that his bad deeds and good deeds are, whereat he will become distressed and call out: "O Lord! Will you consign me to Hellfire?" And the Almighty will

---

[401] Ibid., 218
[402] Sūrat Yūnus (10):87
[403] *Biḥār al-anwār* 79/215, tradition no. 30
[404] Sūrat Ibrāhīm (14):31

respond: "O old man! I am ashamed to punish you while you would pray in the abode of this world, so go with my servant to Paradise."'[405]

Prayer extinguishes the fires of sin, which a person ignites between one prayer and the next, as it has been mentioned in a tradition narrated from the Prophet ﷺ: 'There is no prayer whose time comes save that an angel calls out before the people: "O people! Go to your fires which you have ignited upon your backs and extinguish them with your prayers!"'[406]

Reverence in prayer

Reverence (*khushū'*) in prayer is a sign of true faith. It means – based on what we can understand from the following verses – that nothing distracts a worshipper from the remembrance of his Lord, whether business or trade; so that if someone stands to worship his Lord, he does not think of his own interests and amusements. This is one of the conditions for the houses of knowledge which Allah has allowed to be raised up, and which He has made a lantern of His light. Our Lord says, after the famous Light Verse: **'In houses Allah has allowed to be raised and wherein His Name is celebrated, He is glorified therein, morning and evening, by men whom neither trading nor bargaining distracts from the remembrance of Allah, and the maintenance of prayer and the giving of *zakāt*. They are fearful of a day wherein the heart and the sight will be transformed.'**[407]

Those who squander their prayers

As for those who squander or abandon their prayers, their recompense is to lose control over their lusts, as Allah says: **'But they were succeeded by an evil posterity who neglected the prayer, and followed [their base] appetites. So they will soon encounter [the reward of] perversity.'**[408]

Abandoning prayers gradually leads such a person to deny the right path and discourage the believers from prayer: **'He neither confirmed [the truth], nor prayed, but denied [it] and turned away.'**[409]

---

[405] *Biḥār al-anwār* 79/204, tradition no. 4
[406] Ibid., 209, tradition no. 21
[407] Sūrat al-Nūr (24):36-37
[408] Sūrat Maryam (19):59
[409] Sūrat al-Qiyāma (75):31-32

But will it really come to this? No, for someone who intentionally abandons prayer is a disbeliever. This is what has been narrated from Allah's Messenger ﷺ: 'Whoever intentionally abandons prayer has disbelieved.[410]

That is because the dividing line between true Islam and faithlessness is prayer, and 'all that stands between a servant and disbelief is abandoning prayers,' as Allah's Messenger ﷺ has said.[411]

The end result of all this is a blazing fire whence they woefully confess that they had abandoned their prayers, and thereby abandoned all goodness and virtue, and their destination was Hellfire. Our Lord says: **'Every soul is hostage to what it has earned. Except the People of the Right Hand. [They will be] in gardens, questioning concerning the guilty: "What drew you into Hell?" They will answer, "We were not among those who prayed. Nor did we feed the poor. We used to gossip along with the gossipers, and we used to deny the Day of Retribution, until death came to us."'**[412]

This is how the Imam ﷺ prayed

Ḥammād b. ʿĪsā narrates: One day, Abū ʿAbd Allah [al-Ṣādiq] ﷺ asked me: 'Do you pray well, O Ḥamād?' I said: 'My master! I have in my keeping a valuable book on prayer.' He said: 'No problem. Stand up and pray!'

So I got up in front of him, facing the *qibla*, and I began to pray, bowing and prostrating.

Then he said: 'O Ḥammād! You don't know how to pray well. It is a shame that a man should have spent sixty or seventy years in this world without offering a single perfect prayer!'

Feeling embarrassed, I said: 'May I be your ransom! Teach me how to pray.'

So Abū ʿAbd Allah ﷺ stood up straight, facing the *qibla*, and placed both his hands upon his thighs with his fingers closed, and brought his feet together until they were only the distance of three spread fingers apart. His feet pointed forward without turning aside from the *qibla*. He stood perfectly still in awe. Then he said: '*allāhu akbar*' and then recited *[Sūrat] al-Ḥamd* with clear

---

[410] *Muḥajjat al-bayḍā'* 1/301
[411] *Nahj al-faṣāḥa*, tradition no. 1098
[412] Sūrat al-Mudaththir 74/37-47

enunciation, then he recited *qul huwa allāhu aḥad* (*Sūrat al-Ikhlāṣ*), then he paused for a breath while standing before saying '*allāhu akbar*' while standing.

Then he bowed and cupped his palms over his knees with their fingers spread out, and he pushed his knees back until his back was level, such that if you were to pour a drop of water or oil upon him it would not roll off [because of how level his back was]. He stretched out his neck and closed his eyes, before repeating '*subḥānallāh*' three times with clarity and fluency, and then said: '*subḥāna rabbī 'l-ʿaẓīmi wa biḥamdih.*'

Then he rose, and when he was still, he said: '*samiʿ allāhu liman ḥamidah.*' Then he pronounced *takbīr* while standing and raising his hands to either side of his face.

Then he prostrated, placing his hands on the ground with the fingers together, while his elbows were aligned with either side of his face, and said: '*subḥāna rabbī 'l-aʿlā wa biḥamdih*' three times, and he did not put any part of his body on another part. He prostrated on eight points of his body: His forehead, his two palms, his knees, and the big toes of each foot. These seven are obligatory, but placing the nose on the ground is *sunna* and this is *irghām*.

Then he raised his head from prostration and when he was sitting up straight, he said: '*allāhu akbar*' and sat, resting his weight on his left side, placing the top of his right foot over the bottom of his left. Then he said: '*astaghfirullāh wa atūbu ilayh.*' Then he said a *takbīr* while sitting and prostrated again and repeated what he had said in the first prostration. And he did not rest on any part of his body on anything else while bowing or prostrating, and he allowed his elbows to point out sideways; he did not rest his arms on the ground.

He prayed two units (*rakʿas*) like this; then he sat in *tashahhud* with his fingers joined, and after he finished the *tashahhud* he said the *taslīm*.

Then he said: 'O Ḥammād! Pray like this; do not turn from side to side or play with your hands or fingers, and do not spit on your left or right, or in front of you.'[413]

---

[413] *Mustadrak wasāʾil al-shīʿa, kitāb al-ṣalāt, abwāb afʿāl al-ṣalāt, bāb* 1, tradition no. 1, and this tradition can be found in the same chapter and section of *Wasāʾil al-shīʿa* with minor differences in wording.

Section one: Preliminary rules for prayer

First: Obligatory and supererogatory prayers

1. Allah has made five sorts of prayer obligatory for the human being, namely:
   a. The five daily prayers
   b. The prayer of signs (*āyāt*)
   c. The prayer for obligatory circumambulation (*ṭawāf*)
   d. The prayer for the deceased
   e. Compensatory prayers for those prayers missed by parents, which fall to the eldest child when they are deceased.
2. The daily prayers are five obligatory prayers:
   a. *Ẓuhr*, which is four units (*rakʿa*s) and called 'the middle prayer' (*ṣalāt al-wusṭā*)
   b. *ʿAṣr*, which is four units
   c. *Maghrib*, which is three units
   d. *ʿIshāʾ*, which is four units
   e. *Fajr*, which is two units
3. When travelling – according to the conditions mentioned below – one must shorten his four-unit prayers by performing them as only two units.
4. On Friday, there is the Friday prayer, which consists of two units and two sermons, in place of *ẓuhr* prayers, according to the details and conditions mentioned below.
5. Because prayer is the offering of every god-fearing person, and it is the best means of obtaining nearness to Allah, it is innately recommended. This means that a servant can seek nearness to Allah as much as he wants by performing units of prayer, which will put tranquillity in his heart, prevent him from evil and indecent acts, and bring him closer to Allah.
6. In the *sunna*, we find much encouragement to perform the supererogatory prayers which are specifically set for certain times and places, such as the prayers on the nights of the month of Ramaḍān, the prayer for visiting the grave of the Prophet ﷺ and those of his Household, and also the prayer for entering a mosque, and so on.[414]
7. The best supererogatory prayers are the daily ones, consisting in total of thirty-four *rakʿāt* (units of prayer) on every day except Friday. They are divided as follows:

---

[414] For more details of such prayers, one can refer to a manual of supplications or an encyclopaedia of *ḥadīth*.

a. Eight units before the obligatory *ẓuhr* prayer.
b. Eight units before the *ʿaṣr* prayer.
c. Four units after the *maghrib* prayer.
d. Two units of *wutayra* after the *ʿishāʾ* prayer, offered while seated and counted as a single unit [standing].
e. Two units before *fajr* prayers.
f. Eleven units of night prayers (*ṣalāt al-layl*), arranged as follows:
    i. Eight units of night prayers.
    ii. Two units for the *shafʿ* prayer.
    iii. A single unit for *witr*.
g. The time for night prayers is from midnight[415] until daybreak (*fajr*), and it is proper for travellers to offer them before midnight, along with any others who have a valid excuse to do so.
h. As for Fridays, an additional four units are added to the sixteen units for *ẓuhr* and *ʿaṣr* prayers.
i. One should offer supererogatory prayers in unites of two at a time, except for *witr* prayer, which is only a single unit.

Second: The times for daily prayers

Maintaining one's prayers

Insofar as prayer is the pillar of the religion, then the most important thing affirmed by tens of narrations is to observe the times of prayer and maintain one's prayer therein. Whoever offers his daily prayers on time and looks after them, he will meet Allah with a promise that he will enter Paradise. Anyone who offers his prayers on time is not counted amongst the negligent (*ghāfilīn*).

Squandering one's prayers and trivializing them – even though they will be the first thing that someone is questioned about when he meets his Lord – means wasting one's life, because if a person's prayers are pure and accepted, all of his other deeds are pure and accepted as well!

And since there are narrations affirming that Satan is always terrified of a believer so long as the believer keeps praying his five daily prayers on time, why would any of us squander these prayers? Why wouldn't we pray them on time? Why wouldn't we slam shut the door through which Satan creeps, and allow major sins to enter by treating our prayers with disdain?

---

[415] Midnight is the time which evenly divides sunset and sunrise, and is usually close to 12:00AM.

Since praying punctually is the most beloved act of worship in Allah's eyes, even above kindness to one's parents or struggling (*jihād*) in Allah's way, then why wouldn't we endear ourselves to Allah and protect ourselves from His wrath?

And since we will be blessed with the intercession of Allah's Messenger ﷺ on the Day of Accounting, there is nothing for us to do except pray our prayers on time. Therefore:

1. A believer should never take his prayers lightly or treat them as trivial. He should hasten to offer his prayers at the beginning of their time or as soon as he is able. He must not give any non-essential tasks priority over prayer.
2. Just as it is impermissible to delay one's prayers until after their specified time, especially the dawn prayers, one should use any means necessary to wake up before sunrise and pray this prayer on time.
3. Whoever knows that staying up at night will prevent him from waking up for morning prayers should sleep early so that he can wake up for prayer.
4. Whoever suffers from a heavy sleep, such that he will not wake up by himself for prayer, must take whatever steps necessary to ensure that he will wake up on time, such as asking someone else to wake him, using an alarm clock, etc.

The times of obligatory prayers

The noble *sunna*:

❖ The Messenger of Allah ﷺ entered the mosque where some of his companions had gathered, and said to them: 'Do you know what your Lord has said?' They replied: Allah and His messenger know best. He said: 'Verily your Lord says: "Concerning the five obligatory prayers, whoever prays them in their appointed times, and preserves them, will meet me on Judgment Day with his entry to Paradise guaranteed. And as for the one who did not pray them in their proper times, and did not preserve them, then it is up to me if I want to either punish or forgive him."'[416]

---

[416] *Wasā'il al-shī'a*, v. 3, p. 80, ḥ. 1

❖ Imam al-Bāqir 🕮 said: 'Whichever believer preserves the obligatory prayers, and prays them in their appointed times, will not be counted among the neglectful.'[417]

❖ Imam Abū ʿAbd Allah al-Ṣādiq 🕮 said: 'Our Shīʿa are tested by the appointed times of the prayer and how well they preserve them.'[418]

The time for *ẓuhr* and *ʿaṣr*

The noble *sunna*:

❖ Zurāra has narrated from Imam al-Ṣādiq 🕮: 'When the sun begins to decline, then the time for the two prayers has begun, except that this (*ẓuhr*) is before that (*ʿaṣr*).'[419]

❖ It has been narrated that Imam Abū Jaʿfar al-Bāqir 🕮 said: 'The Messenger of Allah 🕮 would lead the people in congregational *ẓuhr* and *ʿaṣr* prayers (one following shortly after the other) when the sun begins its decline, without any particular excuse for doing so.'[420]

❖ Imam al-Ṣādiq 🕮 said: 'When you have completed the *ẓuhr* prayer, then the time for the *ʿaṣr* prayer has begun, unless you have some prayer beads, and it is up you whether you want to prolong or shorten it.'[421]

Rulings:

1. The shared time for *ẓuhr* and *ʿaṣr* begins after the sun has passed its zenith and ends when it sets.

2. The specific time for the *ẓuhr* prayer is from the beginning of this time (after the sun has passed its zenith) for the duration it normally takes to offer the *ẓuhr* prayer.

3. The specific time for the *ʿaṣr* prayer is the duration it normally takes to offer *ʿaṣr* prayers at the end of the shared time.

4. Everything between these two exclusive times is shared between these two prayers, although it is obligatory to pray *ẓuhr* before *ʿaṣr*.

5. If, during the shared time, a person accidentally offers the *ʿaṣr* prayer before that of *ẓuhr* and later realizes his error, his prayer is still valid and counted as *ẓuhr*, and he must now offer *ʿaṣr*. However, the most cautious course of action is for him to offer four units with the intention of discharging his duty, whatever it may be. But if someone offers the *ẓuhr* prayer – in such a state – at the exclusive time for *ʿaṣr*, then his prayer

---

[417] *Wasāʾil al-shīʿa*, v. 3, p. 79, ḥ. 3
[418] *Wasāʾil al-shīʿa*, v. 3, p. 83, ḥ. 22
[419] *Wasāʾil al-shīʿa*, v. 3, p. 95, ḥ. 21
[420] *Wasāʾil al-shīʿa*, v. 3, p. 92, ḥ. 6
[421] *Wasāʾil al-shīʿa*, v. 3, p. 96, ḥ. 4

is still valid and he must offer a compensatory prayer for *ʿaṣr*, though it the most cautious course of action is to compensate both prayers. However, precaution also requires that the person neither specify his intention to offer these prayers on-time or as compensatory prayers, nor as specifically *ẓuhr* or *ʿaṣr* prayers, but rather that he form an intention of 'seeking to discharge his duty, whatever it is.'

6. If someone prays *ʿaṣr* thinking that he has already offered the prayers for *ẓuhr*, and subsequently realizes he has not prayed *ẓuhr* before finishing his prayer, then he must switch his intention to offering the *ẓuhr* prayer, and complete it with this intention. He need not do anything else.
7. If someone prays *ʿishāʾ* thinking that he had already prayed *maghrib*, only to realize during his prayer that he had not in fact done so, then he must switch his intention to *maghrib* so long he has not yet gone into *rukūʿ* (bowing) a fourth time. But it is more precautious to finish the prayer and then offer both prayers together again.

The time for *maghrib* and *ʿishāʾ*

The noble *sunna*:

- It has been narrated that Imam al-Ṣādiq ﷺ said: 'The time of *maghrib* is when the sun has set and its disc has disappeared.'[422]
- And in another narration from Imam al-Ṣādiq ﷺ, he said: 'When the sun has set then it is lawful to break the fast and the prayer becomes obligatory. When *maghrib* has been prayed, then the time for *ʿishāʾ* has begun, and lasts until the middle of the night.'[423]
- Shihāb b. ʿAbd Rabbih has narrated that Imam Abū ʿAbd Allah al-Ṣādiq said to him: 'O Shihāb, surely I love to pray *magrhib* when I see stars in the sky.'[424]
- Imam al-Ṣādiq ﷺ said: 'The earliest time of *ʿishāʾ* is when the redness has left the sky, and its latest time is the darkest point of the night, meaning the middle of the night.'[425]
- Imam al-Riḍā ﷺ said: 'The earliest time for *magrhib* is sunset, and its sign is that the eastern horizon has become dark.' And in another place he said: 'The time for *maghrib* is from sunset until twilight ... and the

---

422 *Wasāʾil al-shīʿa*, v. 3, p. 130, ḥ. 16
423 *Wasāʾil al-shīʿa*, v. 3, p. 130, ḥ. 19
424 *Wasāʾil al-shīʿa*, v. 3, p. 128, ḥ. 9
425 *Wasāʾil al-shīʿa*, v. 3, p. 135, ḥ. 4

indicator of sunset is the disappearance of redness from the eastern side of the sky.[426]

Rulings:

1. The shared time for *maghrib* and *'ishā'* prayers begins when the disc of the sun disappears below the horizon and the sky reddens and continues until midnight.

2. The exclusive time for *maghrib* extends from the beginning of this time for as long as it would normally take to pray *maghrib*.

3. The exclusive time for *'ishā'* prayers is prior to the end of the shared time to the extent required to pray *'ishā'*.

4. Both *maghrib* and *'ishā'* can, in times of compelling necessity (*ḍarūra*), be offered up until the time of *fajr*.

   This applies to someone who falls asleep or forgets to pray until the middle of the night has passed, or to a menstruating woman whose bleeding ceases after midnight. And it is best for one in this situation to intend neither that he is praying 'on time' nor as a compensatory prayer.

5. Whoever deliberately delays praying either or both *maghrib* and *'ishā'* until after the middle of the night, the strongest opinion is that their time also extends until *fajr* as well, without specifying the intention of praying on-time or late, even though such a person is sinful for delaying his prayers deliberately.

The time for *fajr* prayers

The noble *sunna*:

❖ Zurāra has narrated from Imam al-Bāqir 🕮 : 'The time of the morning prayer is between the beginning of daybreak until sunrise.'[427]

❖ Imam al-Ṣādiq 🕮 said: 'The time of *fajr* is when day breaks until morning rises in the sky, and one should not delay [praying] it intentionally, but it is time for the one who was working, forgot, or was asleep.'[428]

---

[426] *Mustadrak al-wasā'il*, v. 3, p. 131, ḥ. 3
[427] *Wasā'il al-shī'a*, v. 3, p. 152, ḥ. 6
[428] *Wasā'il al-shī'a*, v. 3, p. 151, ḥ. 1

Rulings:

1. The time for the *fajr* prayer begins with daybreak[429] and lasts until sunrise.
2. It is highly recommended to hasten to pray *fajr* at the beginning of its time rather than delaying it until almost sunrise, except for one who is sleeping, who forgets or who is pre-occupied. But it is best to offer this prayer before the sky becomes entirely illuminated, while it is still dark and gloomy.

Rulings pertaining to prayer times

1. It is necessary to be certain or convinced that the time for prayer has set in before beginning to offer one's prayers; it is not permitted to pray ahead of time. If someone prays before the prayer time, his prayer is invalid and will not be counted.
2. Times for prayer can be known by the following means:
    a. By obtaining that knowledge personally (for example, by looking at the sky, or the length of shadows).
    b. Relying on the testimony of two just witnesses that the time for prayer has set in. In fact, the apparent ruling is that the testimony of a single just person will suffice.
    c. Relying on hearing the *adhān* of a trustworthy *mu'adhdhin*. Some jurists go further, stipulating that the *mu'adhdhin* must be just, but it is sufficient that he is reliable.
    d. Relying on accurate scientific calculations which have been produced by a trustworthy expert and yield a sense of conviction.
3. If someone prays sincerely believing that the time for prayer has begun, only to realize afterwards that the prayer in its entirety fell before its allotted time, his prayer is invalid and he must repeat it. But if even a part of the prayer fell within the correct time, his prayer is deemed valid.
4. If someone delays his prayer until the end of its time, for any reason, until there is only enough time for him to offer a single unit (*rak'a*) of it, he must pray the prayer with the intention of praying on time. Anyone who offers a prayer, of which at least one unit falls within the

---

[429] At pre-dawn, some whiteness appears at the edge of the eastern horizon like a column, and this is called 'false dawn.' This whiteness fades after some time and the sky returns to darkness. A short while later comes another whiteness (called lateral whiteness; second dawn) which spreads towards the right and left (full width) through the edge of the eastern sky. This second light is called 'true dawn' or 'morning twilight' and it signals the time for the *fajr* prayer.

time, has offered the prayer on time. However, it is impermissible to intentionally delay his prayer until this time.

5. If the time for prayer is so short that, if one were to perform all the supererogatory actions connected to it, time would run out, then it is obligatory to forgo the supererogatory acts and restrict oneself to the what is obligatory.
6. It is obligatory to delay prayers in the following situations:
    a. When there is an impediment to offering prayer properly, and it is expected or possible that this impediment will be removed before the time for prayer ends, such as an illness which prevents one from praying standing-up. However, it is still permitted to hasten to prayer with *tayammum* even if there is the possibility that the impediment to water ablutions will be removed.
    b. To make the necessary preparations for prayer where these are lacking, such as ritual ablutions, ensuring that one's clothes are ritually pure, that the place in which one is praying is permitted to use etc.
    c. To learn the rules pertaining to prayer as well as its various components and conditions.
    d. If prayer conflicts with another time-critical obligation, such as purifying a mosque of ritual impurity, saving an innocent's life, or repaying a loan to a debtor if one is able.

Sunan ***pertaining to the time for prayer***

1. It is highly recommended to hasten to prayer and offer one's prayers at the earliest moment possible, in the preferred time (*waqt al-faḍīla*), and to avoid delaying them unnecessarily. It is also recommended to pray as soon as possible, even after the preferred time has lapsed, as the closer a prayer is offered to the beginning of its time, the better that prayer is.
2. There is no problem with combining the prayers of *ẓuhr* and *ʿaṣr*, or *maghrib* and *ʿishāʾ*, with a single *adhān* and two *iqāmas*. However, it is recommended to leave a break between every two prayers that share a common time, even if this is only the duration required to perform supererogatory prayers (*nawāfil*) and post-prayer acts of worship (*taʿqībāt*).
3. It is recommended to occupy oneself with *tasbīḥ*, supplications, and righteous deeds at midday.
4. It is disliked to delay the *ʿaṣr* prayer beyond the time whereat one's shadow lengthens to six feet or more.

5.   It is recommended to compensate for missed prayers as soon as possible; missing obligatory prayers for any reason should not be taken lightly, nor should one be lazy in compensating it.

Third: Rules for the *qibla*

Allah says: **'We certainly see you turning your face about in the sky. We will surely turn you to a *qibla* of your liking: so turn your face towards the Holy Mosque, and wherever you may be, turn your faces towards it! Indeed those who were given the Book surely know that it is the truth from their Lord. And Allah is not oblivious of what they do.'**[430]

What is the qibla?

1.   The location of the Ka'ba is the *qibla* of the Muslims and worshipers all over the world must turn in its direction.

2.   The direction of the Sacred Mosque, which contains the Ka'ba, broadens the further away the one facing it is. It is only obligatory to face its general direction (such that one could be said to be facing it). Hence, it is correct for the scholars to say that people in Iraq should face the Iraqi corner of the Ka'ba, which contains the Black Stone, while people in Syria should face the Syrian corner, whereas those in the Maghrib (i.e., North Africa) should face the *maghribī* corner, and those in Yemen should face the Yemeni corner.

It is unnecessary to work out the precise direction of the Ka'ba; rather, it suffices to do whatever can be called turning towards it.

Determining the qibla

The noble *sunna*:

❖   Imam al-Bāqir 🙼 said: 'There is no [valid] prayer except by facing the *qibla*.' It was said to him: What is the boundary of the *qibla*? The Imam said: 'What is between the east and west is the *qibla*—all of it.' It was said to him: What about someone who prays in a direction other than the *qibla*, or who prays at the wrong time because the day is cloudy? The Imam said: 'He repeats that prayer.'[431]

❖   It is narrated that a man asked Imam al-Ṣādiq 🙼: I prayed *'aṣr* [on a mountain] above Abū Qubays; was it permissible, though I am above the Ka'ba? The Imam said: 'Yes, verily it is the *qibla* from its place [on the ground] up to the heavens.'[432]

---

[430] Sūrat al-Baqara (2):144
[431] *Wasā'il al-shī'a*, v. 3, p. 226, ḥ. 2
[432] *Wasā'il al-shī'a*, v. 3, p. 247, ḥ. 1

❖ It is narrated that Samāʿa b. Mahrān asked the infallible Imam 🕊 about prayers during the night or day when one cannot see the sun, moon, or stars. So he said: 'You should strive hard to arrive at your conclusion, as well as to confirm the *qibla*.'[433]

❖ Zurāra said: I asked Abū Jaʿfar 🕊 what to do if one is confused about the *qibla* [such that they absolutely cannot determine its direction]. So he said: 'He prays in whatever direction he wishes.' It is also narrated that he said: 'He prays [each prayer four times] in four directions.'[434]

❖ Imam al-Ṣādiq 🕊 was asked about prayer on a boat. So he said: 'Face the *qibla*, and when the boat shifts directions, if possible to turn again to face the *qibla* then one should do so. Otherwise, he should pray whatever direction he faces. If he is able to pray standing, then he should do so, and if he cannot, then he should sit and pray.'[435]

Rulings:

3. Muslims must work out their position in relation to the Kaʿba so that they can turn to face the Sacred Mosque. This can be accomplished using whatever available means that give them confidence. However, it is recommended precaution that they use a method that gives them definite knowledge, even though the strongest legal opinion is that [a reasonable degree of] confidence suffices.

4. Anyone who does not know the direction of the Sacred Mosque must try and find it using whatever indications rational persons would consider reliable. For example:

   a. Calculating its direction using the position of stars in relation to a person's geographic location, whether on land, sea, or in the air.

   b. Relying on the word of a just believer or any trustworthy person. In this manner one can rely upon the [commonly accepted] *qibla* of the people in a country he is visiting, so long as he does not know them to be mistaken.

   c. One can search for the *qibla* using any scientific means available, such as looking at the movement of the winds, or the location of the Sun and the Moon at different times in different lands, so long as this method is deemed reliable by rational persons.

5. Anyone who cannot determine the direction of the *qibla* can pray in whatever direction he likes, but there is a famous legal opinion that he

---

[433] *Wasāʾil al-shīʿa*, v. 3, p. 224, ḥ. 3
[434] *Wasāʾil al-shīʿa*, v. 3, p. 226, ḥ. 3, 4
[435] *Wasāʾil al-shīʿa*, v. 3, p. 235, ḥ. 13

should pray in four directions [at right-angles to one another], and this is recommended precaution.

6. A traveller must work out the direction of the *qibla*. He is not allowed to offer his obligatory prayers while riding on something, unless he can offer them without any defects, as when one is on a plane, train, or boat, and he will not be bothered by their movements. But if the vehicle is not steady, like a boat in turbulent waters or a plane during take-off or landing, etc., then precaution requires the traveller to delay his prayers until he can offer them while he is steady. And so he must always face towards the *qibla*; adjusting towards it whenever his means of transportation turns. However, if he cannot maintain his position facing the *qibla* and he fears that he will miss his prayers, he should face it to whatever extent possible in his prayers, even if this is only for the *takbīrat al-iḥrām*. Otherwise, he can offer his prayers without facing it; and the same applies to someone who is compelled to pray while walking.
7. One riding on a vehicle or walking can offer his supererogatory prayers without needing to face the *qibla*. However, when one is not moving, he must always face the *qibla* while praying.

Fourth: Rules for covering

The noble *sunna*:

- Imam al-Ṣādiq ﷺ said: 'It is impermissible for a Muslim woman to wear a headscarf or outer garment that does not conceal anything (e.g., the fabric is very sheer, or the garment is worn tightly so that her figure is plainly visible).'[436]
- It is narrated from Imam al-Ṣādiq ﷺ: 'If a [woman] has reached the age where she menstruates, then she cannot pray unless she wears a headscarf.'[437]
- It is narrated from Imam al-Bāqir ﷺ: 'Whoever has soaked his garment should not pray until he worries the time will run out. He should change his garment, but if he could find nothing else, then he prays naked while sitting, gesturing for prostration and bending slightly in place of bowing. And if they were in a congregation then they should separate from their area, then they pray as described, individually.'[438]

---

[436] *Wasā'il al-shī'a*, v. 3, p. 281, ḥ. 2
[437] *Wasā'il al-shī'a*, v. 3, p. 296, ḥ. 13
[438] *Wasā'il al-shī'a*, v. 3, p. 328, ḥ. 1

Rulings:

The duty to observe covering

1. It is obligatory for both men and women to cover themselves during prayer, whether there is anyone there to see them or not. It is also obligatory to cover for the subsidiary acts of prayer, such as making up for a forgotten prostration or a forgotten *tashahhud*, and also for the *sahw* prostrations, according to recommended precaution. It is not obligatory to cover for funeral prayers, though it is recommended. It is also not obligatory for prostrations performed due to reciting a verse of obligatory prostration, or for prostrations of thanksgiving. Aside from these exceptions, it makes no difference whether a prayer is obligatory or supererogatory: it is always obligatory to cover.
2. During prayer, a man must cover his private parts, and it is recommended that he cover everything between his navel and his knees too.
3. For a woman, she must cover her entire body, including her hair and head,[439] except for her face, her hands to the wrists, and the tops and bottoms of her feet.[440]
4. It is not obligatory for a woman, while praying, to have covered or removed any beauty products on her face, such as *kuḥl*, blush, or any other kind of make-up, nor does she need to cover any of her jewellery, even though we do say she must cover these things from any onlookers. And it is most precautious to cover any hair of hers that is connected to the hair on her head.
5. A girl who has not yet reached the age of legal maturity does not need to cover her hair, head, or shoulders, during prayer, even if we say that her prayers are correct and valid.

Requirements for the covering

The covering used in prayer must be:

1. Ritually pure
2. Permitted for use (e.g., something not stolen or used without permission)

---

[439] That is, things like the ears, or the area below the chin, and generally whatever is not the face should also be covered, not just the hair.

[440] Earlier, it was mentioned that a woman's covering around non-*maḥram* individuals necessitates covering the feet as well, in or outside of prayer. However, if no non-*maḥrams* are present during prayer, the tops and bottoms of feet can be left uncovered.

3. Not made from any part of an animal slaughtered in a non-*ḥalāl* fashion
4. Not made from any part of an animal whose flesh is forbidden
5. Not made from either gold or silk, in the case of men

The first condition: Ritual purity

The noble *sunna*:

❖ Khayrān al-Khādim said: I wrote to the Imam ﷺ asking him about a garment that has come into contact with wine or pork: can I pray in it or not? For our companions (i.e., the Shīʿa in our locale) differ about it, with some of them saying: Pray in it, for Allah has only made wine unlawful to drink—while others say: Do not pray in it. So he ﷺ wrote: 'Do not pray in it, for it is dirty.'[441]

❖ Imam al-Ṣādiq ﷺ was asked what to do if a speck of urine reaches someone's thigh: the person prays, and then remembers afterwards that he did not wash that spot. The Imam said: 'He washes it and repeats his prayer.'[442]

❖ It is narrated that Imam ʿAlī ﷺ said: 'If one does not know whether what they felt was urine or water, then they should pay it no mind.'[443]

❖ Safwān b. Yaḥyā wrote to Abū al-Ḥasan ﷺ, asking him about a man who has two garments. One of them came into contact with urine, but he does not know which. The time for prayer has come and he is worried he will miss it, and he has no water. What should he do? He said: 'He performs the prayer once in each of them.'[444]

Rulings:

1. The clothes and body of the worshipper must be ritually pure while in prayer, and were someone to intentionally pray with ritual impurity on their clothing or person, their prayer would be invalid.
2. Prayer is only invalidated if the worshipper is aware of the presence of ritual impurity on his clothes or body, and this ruling has several corollaries:
    a. If the worshipper discovers that his clothing or body was ritually impure *after* completing his prayer, his prayer is considered valid.

---

441 *Wasāʾil al-shīʿa*, v. 2, p. 1055, ḥ. 4
442 *Wasāʾil al-shīʿa*, v. 2, p. 1025, ḥ. 3
443 *Wasāʾil al-shīʿa*, v. 2, p. 1060, ḥ. 4
444 *Wasāʾil al-shīʿa*, v. 2, p. 1082, ḥ. 1

b. If the worshipper had prior knowledge that his clothing or body was ritually impure, but subsequently forgot and prayed while the ritual impurity was still present, then he must repeat his prayer if there is still time, or compensate for it if the time has already lapsed, as a matter of obligatory precaution.

c. If, during prayer, one discovers the prior presence of ritual impurity on his clothing or person, then his prayer is invalid if there is still time [for him to purify himself or his clothing, and repeat it]. But if there is insufficient time [for this], then if he is able to either cleanse the impurity or remove it immediately—in a way that would not lead to him interrupting his prayer—he should do so, and finish his prayer, which would be considered valid. If someone were unable to remove the impurity in this way, then he should finish the prayer, and it will be considered valid.

d. If someone realizes that his clothes or body have become ritually impure during prayer, or if he is aware of the ritual impurity and it is possible that it has just manifested, and there is time for him to cleanse it or change his clothes without interrupting his prayer, or he is able to remove the impure article of clothing from his person because he is wearing something under it, then he should do so, finish his prayer, and it will still be considered valid. But if he cannot do that, he should repeat his prayer after removing the impurity; although, if there is insufficient time [before the time of prayer lapses], then he should complete his prayer in spite of the ritual impurity, and he need not do anything else.

3. Based on the aforementioned ruling, ignorance of a ritual impurity's presence does not invalidate the prayer, even if the prayer was performed with the actual presence of that ritual impurity.

Exceptions in ritual purity

There are a number of scenarios which are exempt from concerns of ritual purity in prayer, and these have been mentioned in our religious texts as follows:

1. If the clothing or body of a worshipper has been contaminated by the blood of wounds or sores from which he currently suffers, until he has fully recovered: it is permissible to offer prayers with this blood [present] in situations where it is difficult to change one's clothes or remove the blood from his body and purify it. However,

this is with the condition that the wound is significant and will take a while to heal; as for small wounds that heal quickly, they are not included in this exemption.
As for blood from nosebleeds, and blood that comes from the mouth and gums, neither are exempted since they are not considered wounds.

2. If the clothes or body are contaminated by blood – be it that of the worshipper or any other person, or lawful food animal – but the area affected by blood is smaller than a *dirham*, which is – as is well-known – the size of the thenar (*ʿaqd al-ibhām*).[445] This ruling does not include the blood of menstruation or childbirth. As for blood from spotting, the blood of ritually impure animals, the blood of carrion, or the blood of something whose flesh is not eaten, obligatory precaution requires that these too are also excluded from this exception.
3. It is permissible to pray with ritual impurity on one's clothes or body in any extenuating circumstances. For example:
    a. Ritual purification or changing would be impossible due to the unavailability of water.
    b. The Absence of a spare garment into which one could change.
    c. The presence of any barrier to undressing, such as [extreme] cold, illness, or maintaining decency.
    d. The impossibility of purification or changing due to limited time [for the prayer].
    e. It is impossible due to [some sort of compelling] fear.
4. Small articles of clothing such as socks, hats, caps, shoes, handkerchiefs, belts, ties and the like with which it is not possible to cover one's private parts, are also exempt so long as these are not made from a) any part of an animal which has not been slaughtered in a *ḥalāl* fashion, or b) anything that is a source of impurity itself (*ʿayn al-najāsa*).

The second condition: Permitted for use

1. In order for one's prayers to be valid, according to the well-known legal opinion, the clothes of the worshipper must be permitted (*mubāḥ*) for him to use, as opposed to usurped (*maghṣūb*).
2. Prayer is invalidated by wearing usurped clothing if the following conditions are met:

---

[445] The muscle protrusion at the base of the thumb.

   a. The worshipper knowingly wears the usurped clothing without being compelled to do so by extenuating circumstances.
   b. The worshipper knows that the clothing is usurped.
3. Many jurists say that one example of usurped clothing is when a worshipper wears something that he has purchased with money on which he has not paid *khums*, *zakāt*, or the like thereof; and this is in accordance with precaution.

The third condition: Avoiding parts of animals not slaughtered in a ḥalāl *fashion*

1. The validity of prayer requires that the clothing of the worshipper does not contain even a tiny part, even if it is so small that it would not cover his private parts, from an animal not slaughtered in a *ḥalāl* fashion (*mayta*), such as its hide or fur.
2. If one receives an item of clothing made from animal by-products from a Muslim, or there is some indication that it has been used by a Muslim, it is treated as ritually pure. However, this is with the condition that there are some indications that provide a sense of confidence that the animal was properly slaughtered [according to Islamic law]. As for a Muslim market that receives most of its products from abroad without paying attention to religious criteria, or from a country whose inhabitants never pay any attention to Islam or its teachings, one cannot legitimately assume that items purchased from such a market are ritually pure or *ḥalāl*.
3. Carrying any part of an animal not slaughtered in a *ḥalāl* fashion in prayer causes the prayer to be invalidated, even if one does not actually wear it (for example, a non-*ḥalāl* leather wallet or phone case). This is according to precaution.

The fourth condition: Avoiding parts of animals whose flesh is not eaten

1. It is impermissible to offer prayers in clothes made from the hide or pelt of an animal whose flesh is not eaten, nor [clothes made] from its hair, wool, fur, feathers, or the like thereof.
2. A worshipper's prayer is invalidated if his clothing has been contaminated by the excrement of an animal whose flesh is not eaten.
3. Some scholars say that there is no difference with regards to an animal whose flesh is forbidden, whether it is of those whose blood gushes out when slaughtered or not, such as forbidden sea creatures, in response to ambiguity about the latter.

The fifth condition: Avoiding gold and silk (in the case of men)

1. A man may not prayer while wearing gold, just as he is generally forbidden from wearing gold or adorning himself with it, whether this is an item of clothing stitched or hemmed in gold,[446] or whose buttons are gold; or whether this is a golden chain around his neck, a gold ring on his finger, a gold watch, or gold rims on his spectacles,

2. A man must never wear pure silk, whether in prayer or at any other time. Wearing silk invalidates prayer, and its prohibition even includes such a small piece that it could not cover one's private parts.[447]

Fifth: The place of prayer

The noble *sunna*:

❖ It is narrated from Imam al-Mahdī 🕮 : 'It is unlawful to use the property of others without permission.'[448]

❖ It has been narrated from Sulaymān b. Ṣāliḥ that Imam al-Ṣādiq 🕮 said: 'None of you may establish prayer while waking, riding, or reclining unless he is sick. You should position yourself for the *iqāma* wherever you plan on praying, for it is when he takes to the *iqāma* that he is thus in prayer.'[449]

❖ Abū Baṣīr said: I asked Imam Abū 'Abd Allah al-Ṣādiq 🕮 about a man and woman who are praying together in a house, the woman to the right of the man and by his side. So he said: 'No, unless there is a hand span separating them, or an arm's length, or suchlike.'[450]

❖ It is also narrated from Imam al-Ṣādiq 🕮, as to whether a man can pray while a woman prays by his side, that he said: 'No problem.'[451]

❖ Imam 'Alī 🕮 said: 'There is no problem praying in a church or synagogue, whether the prayer is obligatory or supererogatory, but a mosque is better.'[452]

❖ Imam al-Ṣādiq 🕮 said: 'There are ten places where one should not pray: upon mud, water, in a lavatory, upon graves, in the middle of the

---

[446] This refers to actual gold, and not simply golden-coloured items like thread, buttons, chains, etc.

[447] This includes silk ties, which are very common in the west.

[448] *Wasā'il al-shī'a*, v. 3, p. 423, ḥ. 2

[449] *Mawsū'at al-fiqh* of al-Shīrāzī, v. 2, p. 268

[450] *Wasā'il al-shī'a*, v. 3, p. 427, ḥ. 4

[451] *Wasā'il al-shī'a*, v. 3, p. 329, ḥ. 1

[452] *Wasā'il al-shī'a*, v. 3, p. 439, ḥ. 6

road, upon an anthill, the resting place of camels, where water flows, upon wetlands, and upon ice (or snow).'[453]

- Imam al-Ṣādiq ﷺ said: 'Do not pray in the house of a Zoroastrian, but there is no problem to pray in the house of a Jew or Christian.'[454]
- Imam al-Ṣādiq ﷺ said: 'Do not pray in a house wherein wine or intoxicants are kept.'[455]

Rulings:

Where should we pray?

1. It is permissible to pray in every place, because Allah's Messenger ﷺ has said: 'The earth was made a place of prostration (*masjid*) for me, and its soil [made] pure. Wherever [I was when] the time of prayer caught me, that is where I prayed.'[456]
2. The place of prayer must be free from any impurity that could contaminate the body or clothing of the worshipper. As for dry [and hence non-transferrable] impurities, these are unproblematic, save in the place where the worshipper prostrates his forehead, as that location must be free from all ritual impurities.
3. It is incorrect to offer prayers in front or beside the grave of an Infallible unless there is some sort of barrier that common sense would say removes the disrespect of turning one's back to that Infallible.
4. It is impermissible to pray in an unsteady place, such as a moving vehicle, except in extenuating circumstances, or on something that is shaking to the extent that it would prevent one from observing the stillness required in prayer.
5. Scholars say that a woman must stand behind men when praying, and that the two should not be standing side-by-side,[457] or women in front of men, although the strongest legal opinion[458] is that this is actually disliked [and not unlawful]. However, if there was absolutely no separation between them, then obligatory precaution requires the prayer to be repeated.

---

[453] *Wasā'il al-shī'a*, v. 3, p. 441, ḥ. 6
[454] *Wasā'il al-shī'a*, v. 3, p. 336, ḥ. 1
[455] *Wasā'il al-shī'a*, v. 3, p. 449, ḥ. 1
[456] *Wasā'il al-shī'a* 3/323, *abwāb makān al-muṣallī*, ch. 1, tradition no. 5
[457] For the sake of clarity, this does not refer to standing in a mixed-gender prayer row, which is not allowed in congregational *ṣalāt*; rather it means the men on one side of a congregation and the women on the other with a separation between them.
[458] The term 'strongest legal opinion' refers to the *fatwā* of His Eminence.

Whether one accepts the opinion that it is disliked or that it is prohibited, both conditions are removed if there is a distance of at least ten cubits (about 500cm) separating them.

This [condition of] dislike is also removed in extenuating circumstances, or when there is a shortage of time. However, a man and woman should not stand directly side-by-side during prayer; it is obligatory to observe precaution by leaving some kind of gap between them, even if it is only a hand-span, except in Mecca.

The condition of permissibility

6. Usurping the property of others (*ghaṣb*) is forbidden, and the use of any usurped property, whether by the usurper himself or someone else, is also forbidden. Likewise, it is impermissible – under usual circumstances – to use the property of another without his permission. As for praying in a usurped place, or in a place where one has not been authorized to pray, does this invalidate the prayer? The well-known legal position is that it does invalidate the prayer, but there is a minority opinion that it does not. However, observing the well-known position accords with precaution.

Sixth: Rules and manners pertaining to mosques[459]

The noble *sunna*:

- The Messenger of Allah ﷺ said: 'There is no prayer for the neighbor of the mosque except inside the mosque.'[460]
- Zurayq has narrated that he heard Imam al-Ṣādiq (ع) saying: 'Whoever prays in congregation inside his house, eschewing the mosque, has no prayer. And the one who prays with him has no prayer unless he has an excuse preventing him from [praying in] the mosque.'[461]
- Zurāra has narrated from Imam al-Bāqir: 'If you enter a mosque wishing to sit, then do not enter it unless you are ritually pure. When you enter it, face the *qibla*; then supplicate and ask of him, and announce your entrance, and praise Allah and send blessings upon the Prophet ﷺ.'[462]

---

[459] As mentioned earlier, there is an important technical, legal difference between a mosque and a Ḥusayniyya or Islamic centre, even if many of the same etiquettes apply. This section applies to places of worship that are juristically designated as mosques.

[460] *Wasā'il al-shī'a*, v. 3, p. 487, ḥ. 1

[461] *Wasā'il al-shī'a*, v. 3, p. 420, ḥ. 1

[462] *Wasā'il al-shī'a*, v. 3, p. 516, ḥ. 2

- Abū Dharr said: I entered upon the Messenger of Allah ﷺ while he was sitting in the mosque. He said to me: 'Verily there is a greeting for the mosque.' I said: And what is that greeting? He said: 'To pray two units of prayer.'[463]
- In advising Abū Dharr, the Prophet ﷺ said: 'O Abū Dharr, a good word is charity, and every step one walks towards prayer is charity. O Abū Dharr, whoever answers the call of Allah, and gives charity for the construction of Allah's mosques, his reward from Allah will be Paradise.' So Abū Dharr said: How should one behave in Allah's mosques? He said: 'Do not raise your voices in them, or enter into falsehood in them, or buy and sell in them, and leave vain matters as long as you are in them. Surely the one who ignores these things has none but himself to blame on Judgment Day.'[464]

Rulings:

1. It is recommended to build and erect mosques, for they are houses of worship and seeking nearness to Allah. One should avoid excess in decorating them, as this would be contrary to the place's spirituality. It is nearest to precaution to avoid decorating them with images or figurines of anything that possesses a soul (i.e., living things).
2. It is strongly recommended to keep mosques alive by worshipping and supplicating in them, especially by offering one's daily prayers therein. Narrations state that there is no prayer for the neighbour of a mosque except in it.[465]
3. Mosques are Allah's houses, so they cannot be sold, treated as personal property, or taken as private holdings. It is also impermissible to take anything out of them, whether furnishings, carpets, tools, or equipment attached to them; or building materials, such as metal, bricks, pebbles, doors, windows, etc., unless this is for the sake of the mosque itself.
4. The ritual purity of the mosque must be maintained. This means that it is forbidden to contaminate them with ritual impurity in any way, shape, or form. And should it become ritually impure, it is obligatory to cleanse it of impurity straight away and purify its place (where the impurity was) immediately, whether it was part of the building that was contaminated, or some of its furnishings.

---

[463] *Wasā'il al-shī'a*, v. 3, p. 517, ḥ. 2

[464] *Wasā'il al-shī'a*, v. 3, p. 507, ḥ. 3

[465] Which is to say, that if one lives adjacent to a mosque, or within earshot of its call to prayer, then their prayer is of questionable validity should they fail to pray it inside of the mosque without good reason.

5. It is forbidden to bury the deceased in mosques if that would lead to the mosque being ritually contaminated, but it is nearest to precaution to avoid burying the deceased in them in any situation.

Section two: Acts of prayer

First: The *adhān* and *iqāma*

The noble *sunna*:

❖ Ismāʿīl al-Juʿfī has narrated from Imam al-Bāqir 🕮: 'The *adhān* and *iqāma* are [together] comprised of thirty-five expressions.' So he counted them on his hand, one by one: eighteen expressions for the *adhān* and seventeen for the *iqāma*.[466]

❖ Abū Bar a-Ḥaḍramī and Kulayb al-Asadī have narrated that Imam al-Ṣādiq 🕮 was speaking to them about the adhān: '*Allāhu akbar. Allāhu akbar. Allāhu akbar. Allāhu akbar. Ashhadu an lā ilāha illa allāh. Ashhadu an lā ilāha illa allāh. Ashhadu anna muḥammadan rasūl allāh. Ashhadu anna muḥammadan rasūl allāh. Ḥayya ʿalā al-ṣalāh. Ḥayya ʿalā al-ṣalāh. Ḥayya ʿalā al-falāḥ. Ḥayya ʿalā al-falāḥ. Ḥayya ʿalā khayri 'l-ʿamal. Ḥayya ʿalā khayri 'l-ʿamal. Allāhu akbar. Allāhu akbar. Lā ilāha illā allāh. Lā ilāha illā allāh.* And the *iqāma* is similar to that.'[467]

❖ In a narration from Imam al-Bāqir 🕮 in which he explained the *adhān* and *iqāma*, after mentioning the *adhān*, he said: 'And the *iqāma* is similar except that it contains "*qad qāmati 'l-ṣalā, qad qāmati 'l-ṣalāh*" between "*ḥayya ʿalā khayri 'l-ʿamal*" and "*allāhu akbar*."'[468]

❖ It is narrated from Imam al-Ṣādiq 🕮: 'If you recite the *adhān* and *iqāma*, two rows of angels pray behind you. If you recite [only] the *iqāma*, then one row of angels pray behind you.'[469]

❖ Imam al-Ṣādiq 🕮 said: 'Do not leave out the *adhān* in any of your prayers; but if you do [leave it out for some of them], then [at least] do not leave it out for *maghrib* and *fajr*, for neither of those can be shortened.'[470]

❖ Imam al-Ṣādiq 🕮 said: 'Do not speak when the *iqāma* of prayer is being recited, and if you do then repeat the *iqāma*.'[471]

---

[466] *Wasāʾil al-shīʿa*, v. 4, p. 642, ḥ. 1

[467] *Wasāʾil al-shīʿa*, v. 4, p. 644, ḥ. 9

[468] *Wasāʾil al-shīʿa*, v. 4, p. 644, ḥ. 8

[469] *Wasāʾil al-shīʿa*, v. 4, p. 620, ḥ. 3

[470] *Wasāʾil al-shīʿa*, v. 4, p. 623, ḥ. 3

[471] *Wasāʾil al-shīʿa*, v. 4, p. 629, ḥ. 3

- It was said to Imam al-Ṣādiq ﷺ: Can a person speak during the *adhān*? He said: 'No problem.' Then it was asked: What about during the *iqāma*? He said: 'No.'[472]
- Imam al-Bāqir ﷺ said: 'When you recite the *adhān*, then clearly pronounce *alif* and *hā'*, and recite blessings upon the Prophet ﷺ whenever you mention him, or whenever someone mentions him around you, be it in the *adhān* or otherwise.'[473]

Rulings:

1. Narrations differ about the number of clauses in the *adhān* and *iqāma*, but the famous (*mashhūr*) opinion given by our scholars, and that which the majority of the faithful act upon, is that it consists of eighteen parts, namely:

Allāhu akbar (Allah is greatest) – Four times

Ashhadu an lā ilāha ill allāh (I testify that there is no god but Allah) - Twice

Ashhadu anna muḥammadan rasūl allāh (I testify that Muḥammad is the Messenger of Allah) - Twice

Ḥayy 'alā al-ṣalāh (Hasten to prayer) - Twice

Ḥayy 'ala al-falāḥ (Hasten to success) - Twice

Ḥayy 'alā khayr il-'amal (Hasten to the best of deeds) - Twice

Allāhu akbar (Allah is greatest) - Twice

Lā ilāha ill allāh (There is no god but Allah) – Twice

2. The *iqāma* consists of seventeen parts, two *takbīrs* (*allāhu akbar*) at the beginning, one *tahlīl* (*lā ilāha ill allāh*) at the end, and the phrase '*qad qāmat al-ṣalāh*' (prayer has been established) twice after '*ḥayya 'alā khayr il-'amal*.' Other than these, it is the same as the *adhān*.
3. As for bearing witness to the *walāya* of 'Alī, and that he is the Commander of the Faithful ('*ashhadu anna 'aliyyan walī allāh*'), the jurists have said that this is not actually part of the *adhān* or the *iqāma*; rather it completes the testimony that Muḥammad ﷺ is Allah's

---

[472] *Wasā'il al-shī'a*, v. 4, p. 629, ḥ. 4
[473] *Wasā'il al-shī'a*, v. 4, p. 669, ḥ. 1

Messenger. Today, this has become an emblem of our sect, and therefore it is best to proclaim it in hope of divine reward.

Rules pertaining to the **adhān** *and* **iqāma**

1. It is recommended to perform the *adhān* to inform the faithful that the times for daily obligatory prayers have begun, and to encourage them to offer their prayers at the beginning of that time. And reciting the *adhān* [for this purpose] is only for the beginning of prayer times.
2. Just as it is highly recommended for the worshipper to recite the *adhān* and *iqāma* for his solo prayer – in fact it is nearest to precaution to avoid omitting the *iqāma* for any man who is not travelling or in a rush. If someone is praying in a congregation, then the *adhān* and *iqāma* of the congregation suffices him. Also, the *adhān* and *iqāma* are not only for the beginning of prayer times: they can be recited by the worshipper immediately before he prays, even if his prayer is delayed from the beginning of its time. In this recommendation there is neither distinction between men and women, nor between the traveller and non-traveller.
3. *Adhān* and *iqāma* are only for the daily obligatory prayers, whether these are offered on time or are being compensated for later.

Second: Intention

Allah says: '**Say, "Everyone acts according to his character. Your Lord knows best who is better guided with regard to the way."**'[474]

While everyone's actions may appear very similar from the outside, it is the intention underlying these actions that makes them distinct. So, for a devoted worshipper, prayer will be a spiritual journey toward Allah, while for the one who is simply paying lip-service, prayer will be a weight around his neck. Thus, everyone who acts only does so in accordance with his character, which narrations about the aforementioned verse explain to mean his intention. Because Allah knows people's intentions and goals best, He knows best who is better guided.

Rules pertaining to intention

The noble *sunna*:

❖ The Messenger of Allah ﷺ sad: 'The intention of the believer is conveyed in his deeds, just like the intention of the wrongdoer.'[475]

---

[474] Sūrat al-Isrāʾ (17):84

[475] *Wasāʾil al-shīʿa*, v. 1, p. 40, ḥ. 22

- Imam al-Ṣādiq ﷺ said: 'Worship is of three kinds: people who worship Allah Almighty out of fear—which is the worship of a slave, and people who worship Allah Almighty seeking reward—which makes worship a kind of transaction, and people who worship Allah Almighty out of love for him—which is the worship of freemen, and that is the best kind of worship.'[476]
- Imam ʿAlī b. al-Ḥusayn ﷺ said: 'There is no [counted] deed but with intention.'[477]
- It is narrated from Imam al-Ṣādiq ﷺ: 'Verily Allah Almighty has said: "I am the best associate, and whoever associates something else with me in his deeds, I shall not accept them unless they were sincerely [and solely] for me."'[478]

Rulings:

1. An intention is required for all acts of worship, including prayer. Without it, deeds are invalidated. Intention is one of the fundamental pillars (*arkān*) of prayer.
2. Intention (*niyya*) means one's aim when performing a deed. If you aim to obey Allah's command in order to seek nearness to him, then your intention is sincere and your deed is accepted – God-willing! On the other hand, if your aim is not obedience but something else, such as [keeping a] reputation or showing-off to people, then your deed is invalid.
3. An intention is materialized by having a motivation in one's heart, such that the impulse to perform an act of worship, like prayer, is for the sake of obeying Allah's command. It is unnecessary to pronounce one's intention, or formally articulate it in one's mind. Rather, it is enough to be aware of it.
4. In order to realize an intention, it is not necessary to specify each individual detail pertaining to the act of worship, such as whether a prayer is being offered on-time or late, shortened or full, or whether it is obligatory or recommended, unless obeying Allah's command depends on intending these details.
5. A prayer is valid based on the intention with which it was begun. Thus, if one begins a prayer with the intention of performing an obligatory prayer, but he forgets this during the prayer and imagines that he is performing a supererogatory one—or even completes it with this in

---

[476] *Wasāʾil al-shīʿa*, v. 1, p. 45, ḥ. 1
[477] *Wasāʾil al-shīʿa*, v. 1, p. 33, ḥ. 1
[478] *Wasāʾil al-shīʿa*, v. 1, p. 44, ḥ. 9

mind—his prayer is valid according to the intention with which he began it.[479]

6. If one performs an act of worship sincerely for the sake of Allah, and after, he intends that it would also serve to show-off, or he becomes conceited, this does not [legally] invalidate his prayers.[480]

Third: *Takbīrat al-iḥrām*

1. *'Allāhu akbar'* (Allah is greatest) is the expression with which prayer is opened, and this is called either the *takbīra* of consecration (*iḥrām*) or of opening (*iftitāḥ*).
2. It is obligatory to pronounce the *takbīr* in proper Arabic; it does not suffice to pronounce it in improper Arabic or to translate it into another language.
3. Obligatory precaution requires that the *takbīr* be pronounced independently. That is, it should not be attached to the *iqāma* or [a part of] any supplication that precedes it. It is recommended precaution that it should not be attached to anything that follows it either, such as a supplication or the *bismillāh*, either. If one joins it to what follows it, he must pronounce it *'allāhu akbaru̱'* with a *dhamma* ('u' sound) on the *rā'* (the final 'r' sound); wheras if he does not join it to what follows, then he should not put any vowel after the *rā'*.
4. *Takbīrat al-iḥrām* is one of the fundamentals of prayer. Omitting it intentionally or accidentally invalidates the prayer. As for adding another *takbīr*, the majority opinion of the jurists is that the same rule applies. And precaution requires – if one accidentally adds another *takbīr* – that one complete the prayer, then repeat it, even if the strongest opinion is that there is no need to repeat the prayer.[481]
5. It is recommended to raise both open hands, with fingers joined, to the ear when reciting this *takbīr*, with the palms facing the *qibla*, as a sign of humility and supplication towards Allah – as has been mentioned in narrations – and it is recommended to do this for all the *takbīrs* of prayer.

---

[479] I.e., the prayer is valid as an obligatory one.

[480] Although, it is possible such prayers may not be accepted by Allah on the grounds that the act was corrupted through the change in intention.

[481] This is only if the additional *takbīr* was done with the intention of it being *takbīrat al-iḥrām*. It is, however, *mustaḥabb* to recite up to seven *takbīrāt*, but only one would be done with the intention of *takbīrat al-iḥrām*.

Fourth: Standing (*qiyām*)

The obligation to stand

1. It is obligatory the worshipper to perform his prayers while standing, without supporting himself with anything else. This is under normal circumstances, as we shall detail below. As for one who is ill or otherwise unable to stand, he should pray however he is able, whether by supporting himself with something else, leaning on something, sitting or lying down, as we shall discuss.
2. Standing while reciting the *takbīrat al-iḥrām* is a fundamental (*rukn*) of prayer, just as standing before bowing in *rukūʿ* (what is called 'standing joined to bowing') is a fundamental. In other words, omitting either of these – whether intentionally or accidentally – will invalidate one's prayers.
3. Standing while reciting *Sūrat al-Fātiḥa* and another *sūra* of the Qurʾān, while reciting the four *tasbīḥ*s, and after bowing, are all obligatory, but they are not 'fundamentals', which is to say that they invalidate the prayer when omitted intentionally, but *not* when omitted accidentally.

How to stand when praying

4. Under normal circumstances, standing is achieved by standing upright in a manner that common sense would call 'standing', and being still to the extent that one is not moving either his body or his limbs. This is the popular opinion of our jurists and it accords with obligatory precaution. One must also be standing independently, meaning that he is not resting his weight or leaning on anything else; this is also according to the famous view and in accordance with recommended precaution.

In exceptional circumstances

5. In exceptional circumstances, such as illness, infirmity, or suchlike, the worshipper must try to stand to the extent he is able, on a sliding scale from standing independently, to supporting his weight on something, or leaning against a wall or another person; and if he cannot stand in any way, shape, or form, then he should switch to praying while seated. And if he is not able to sit, he can pray lying down on his right side. If he cannot lie on his right side, then on his left (facing the *qibla* with the front of his body), or else he should pray while lying on his back (as one would be on his death bed), facing the *qibla* with the bottom of his feet.

6. If someone is able to pray standing but cannot bow from a standing posture, he may bow from a sitting position. If he cannot bow or prostrate at all, he should pray standing and lower his head or eyes for bowing and prostration, placing a something suitable for prostration upon his forehead while he lowers his head for it.
7. If, at the start of the prayer time, a person is unable to stand, but thinks that he may regain strength enough to stand at the end of the time for prayer, then it is obligatory for him to delay his prayers until [near] the end of the time.
8. Whoever is able to stand, but fears that he will exacerbate his illness by standing for prayer, is allowed to sit in prayer. The same principle applies if one fears he will exacerbate it by praying seated: he can pray lying down.

Fifth: Recitation (*qirā᾿a*)

1. Recitation is one of the obligatory elements of prayer, and in technical terms this means whatever *sūra*s of the Qur᾿ān or *dhikr*s the worshipper recites before bowing in each unit (*rakʿa*) of prayer.
2. It is obligatory to recite *Sūrat al-Fātiḥa* in both units of *fajr* prayer, and in the first two units of all other daily prayers. The same applies to all other prayers of at least two units, whether obligatory or supererogatory.
3. The well-known view of the jurists is that a complete *sūra* must be recited in each of the first two units of prayer (following *al-Fātiḥa*) and that it is insufficient to recite just part of one. This opinion is in accordance with precaution.

The rules of recitation

The noble *sunna*:

❖ Al-Ḥasan b. Ziyād has narrated that he asked one of the two (Imam al-Bāqir or Imam al-Ṣādiq ﷺ): What do you say about a man who recites from a copy of the Qur᾿ān while he is praying, having placed a lamp nearby? He said: 'There is no problem with that.'[482]

❖ Muʿāwiya b. ʿAmmār said: I asked Abū ʿAbd Allah ﷺ about reciting behind the prayer leader in the latter two units of prayer. So he ﷺ said: 'He may recite *al-Fātiḥa* while whoever is behind him recites *tasbīḥ* (saying '*subḥān allāh*'), and if you were praying by yourself then you may

---

[482] *Wasā᾿il al-shīʿa*, v. 4, p. 780, ḥ. 1

recite either one of them (*al-Fātiḥa* or *tasbīḥ*); and if you wished to do so, then *tasbīḥ*.'[483]

- Imam al-Ṣādiq ﷺ said: 'If you are behind the prayer leader, and he has finished reciting *al-fātiḥa*, then you say: "All praise is for the Lord of the Worlds," and do not say: "Amen (*āmīn*)."'[484]
- Abū ʿAbd Allah al-Ṣādiq ﷺ said: 'It is detestable to recite [all of] *qul huwa allāhu aḥad* in a single breath.'[485]
- Al-Fuḍayl b. Yasār said: Abū Jaʿfar ﷺ commanded that if I recite *qul huwa allāhu aḥad*, then after it I should say '*kadhālik allāhu rabbī*' three times.[486]
- Imam al-Riḍā ﷺ has written, in his letter to al-Maʾmūn: 'Pronouncing *bismillāh al-raḥmān al-raḥīm* audibly (i.e., not in a whisper) before every prayer is a *sunna*.'[487]
- Abū Saʿīd al-Khudrī has narrated that before the recitation the Prophet ﷺ would say: '*Aʿūdhu billāhi min al-shayṭān al-rajīm* (I seek refuge with Allah from Satan, the condemned).'[488]

Rulings:

4. Recitation in prayer is not a fundamental (*rukn*), so whoever omits it accidentally has not invalidated his prayer.
5. If someone omits *Sūrat al-Fātiḥa* accidentally, only to remember whilst reciting the second *sūra*, he must go back and recite *al-Fātiḥa* and a second *sūra* again [In this way] his prayer will still be valid. The same applies if one forgets to recite anything at all, or forgets the second *sūra*, and then remembers while in *qunūt*: he must go back and recite again, and his prayer will be valid.
6. One must recite *al-Fātiḥa* and any other chapters of the Qurʾān he recites in prayer correctly with regards to syntax and pronunciation, according to the widely-available printed copies in our possession. As for what experts in recitation (*ahl al-tajwīd*) and linguists discuss, such as *hamzat al-qatʿ* and *hamzat al-waṣl*, the final-vowel on words, the elongation of vowels, etc., these are not obligatory to observe unless failing to do so will somehow alter the meaning of the recitation.

---

[483] *Wasāʾil al-shīʿa*, v. 4, p. 781, ḥ. 2
[484] *Wasāʾil al-shīʿa*, v. 4, p. 756, ḥ. 1
[485] *Wasāʾil al-shīʿa*, v. 4, p. 754, ḥ. 1
[486] *Wasāʾil al-shīʿa*, v. 4, p. 756, ḥ. 9
[487] *Wasāʾil al-shīʿa*, v. 4, p. 758, ḥ. 6
[488] *Wasāʾil al-shīʿa*, v. 4, p. 801, ḥ. 6

7. It is obligatory for one who cannot recite well to learn how, and the same applies to learning any other parts of prayer.
8. One must perform the recitation while in a state of stillness, and whilst avoiding any movements that would be contrary to the outward form of prayer.

***Reciting* ʿazāʾim**[489]

9. As a matter of obligatory precaution, one must avoid reciting the *ʿazāʾim* in obligatory prayers. If someone recites one of these, he must either switch to reciting another *sūra* or stop at the verse of prostration, not recite it, and his prayer is valid. If he recites the verse of prostration, he must [pause to] prostrate while praying, before standing and reciting *Sūrat al-Fātiḥa* and what follows it again, before bowing. In this case, obligatory precaution requires him to repeat his prayer.

In the latter two units of prayer

10. In the third unit of *maghrib* prayers, and the third and fourth units of *ẓuhr*, *ʿaṣr*, and *ʿishāʾ* prayers, the worshipper may choose between reciting *Sūrat al-Fātiḥa* by itself, or reciting the four *tasbīḥ*s (namely: *'subḥān allāh, wa 'l-ḥamdu lillāh, wa lā ilāha ill allāhu, wallāhu akbar'*). This is in accordance with recommended precaution. The strongest opinion, however, is that any kind of supplication, *dhikr*, or *tasbīḥ* will suffice, and there is no need to use a specific formula.
11. It is sufficient to recite the four *tasbīḥ*s just once – according to the strongest opinion – but it is recommended precaution to repeat it three times. There is no problem with reciting it more than three times if it is done with the general intention of reciting *dhikr*, and not of it being a required part of the prayer.

Loud and quiet recitation

12. When reciting *Sūrat al-Fātiḥa* and another *sūra* from the Qurʾān in *fajr* prayers. and the first two units of *maghrib* and *ʿishāʾ* prayers, a man must recite them aloud (meaning at least above a whisper).
13. And in the first two units of *ẓuhr* and *ʿaṣr* prayers, both men and women must recite them quietly (meaning at a whisper). The same applies to the last unit of the *maghrib* prayer, and the last two units of all others.
14. As for a female worshipper, it is not obligatory for her to recite aloud in the above loudly-recited prayers; she can choose whether to recite quietly or aloud, so long as there is no non-*maḥram* man present who

---

[489] See footnote no. 1.

can hear her voice. If there is, then obligatory precaution requires that she recite quietly, especially if there is a risk of reciting loudly leading to something sinful. She must recite the quiet prayers quietly, the same as a man.

15. If a man intentionally recites a prayer quietly when it is obligatory to recite it aloud, or a man or woman intentionally recites a prayer loudly when it should be recited quietly, their prayer is invalid. But if this happens out of forgetfulness or ignorance of the ruling, then the prayer is valid.

Sixth: Bowing (*rukūʿ*)

1. Bowing is one of the five fundamentals of prayer; it is obligatory to bow exactly once in each unit of all obligatory and supererogatory prayers (except for the funeral prayers, which contain no bowings or prostrations, and the prayer of signs – *ṣalāt al-āyāt* – which contains five bows in each unit).
2. Because bowing is a fundamental component of prayer, adding to or omitting it, whether done intentionally or otherwise, will invalidate the prayer, except in some situations when praying in congregation, which we shall discuss in a moment.
3. What is required for bowing is to bend one's back, recite *dhikr,* and remain still during the *dhikr* and after rising from the bowing posture, and raising one's head and standing up straight again after bowing.

Bowing

4. It is obligatory when bowing to bend one's back, as is well-known amongst all Muslims, but it suffices as a definition for bowing to say that all or some of the fingers must touch one's knees.

Dhikr

5. It is obligatory to recite *dhikr* of Allah when bowing, and precaution requires the worshipper to say '*subḥān allāh*' three times, or '*subḥāna rabbī 'l-ʿaẓīmi wa biḥamdih.*' However, the strongest opinion is that all kinds of *dhikr*, whether saying '*subḥān allāh*', '*alḥamdu lillāh*', '*lā ilāha ill allāh*', '*allāhu akbar*', or any other kind of *dhikr* is acceptable, so long as it is repeated three times.
6. It is obligatory to recite *dhikr* after reaching the full bowing position and becoming motionless, just as it is obligatory to complete the *dhikr* before rising from bowing.
7. It is obligatory for the *dhikr* recited in bowing to be recited in succession and in proper Arabic, such that the letters are pronounced properly to

the extent that the worshipper is able, and that the words are properly formed with regards to grammar (*iʿrāb*).

Stillness

8. It is obligatory for the worshipper to remain still and steady; obligatory precaution requires that this stillness must last for the duration of the obligatory *dhikr*. In fact, this precaution even extends to any recommended *dhikr* which the worshipper recites intending it to be a supererogatory *dhikr* recited when bowing.[490]

Rising from bowing

9. A worshipper may not go down into prostration directly from a bowing posture; first he must raise himself completely from bowing and stand still, before lowering himself into prostration from a standing posture. If he intentionally fails to do this, then precaution requires him to repeat his prayer, according to the what is the famous view among the jurists.

Bowing in exceptional circumstances

10. If the worshipper cannot bow completely according to the description above, then he should bow to the extent he is able, even if this means resting his weight on a walking stick, or leaning against a wall or another person. He should only bow from a sitting posture if he is completely unable to bow while standing.

Sunan *of bowing*

When bowing there are many recommended (*mustaḥabb*) acts mentioned in the *sunna*, of which we shall mention the most important:

1. To say a *takbīr* before bowing, while still standing, and raising one's hands as described for *takbīrat al-iḥrām*.
2. While bowing, to to lock one's knees straight and place the palms of one's hands on them.
3. To make one's back level while bowing, and to stretch out one's neck level with one's back.

---

[490] The worshipper might recite a supererogatory *dhikr* as a generally recommended *dhikr* with no connection to the actions of prayer. In this case, he does not need to remain still and steady while reciting this *dhikr*. As for *dhikr* recited as one of the supererogatory actions of prayer, obligatory precaution requires him to be still and steady during this *dhikr* as well.

4. To say, after rising from bowing: '*samiʿ allāhu liman ḥamidah*,' and to add: '*al-ḥamdu lillahi rabb il-ʿālamīn, ahl al-jabarūti wal-kibriyāʾ, wal-ʿaẓama lillāhi rabb il-ʿālamīn.*'

Seventh: Prostration (*sujūd*)

Prostration is a fundamental of prayer

1. It is obligatory to prostrate twice in every unit of obligatory and supererogatory prayer (with the exception of the funeral prayers, which have neither bowing nor prostration).
2. Prostration is achieved, according to what is well known among the jurists, by placing one's forehead upon the ground with the intention of glorifying Allah.
3. These two prostrations are, together, an essential component of prayer:
    a. A prayer – whether obligatory or supererogatory – will be invalidated if the worshipper omits the two prostrations, intentionally or otherwise.
    b. An obligatory prayer will be invalidated if the worshipper adds two additional prostrations, whether intentionally or otherwise.
    c. Prayer is invalidated if the worshipper *intentionally* omits one of them or adds another.
    d. Prayer is not invalidated, according to the strongest opinion, if a single prostration is omitted or added *unintentionally*.

Obligations of prostration

4. In prostration, the following things are obligatory:

First: Placing seven points of the body on the ground, namely: the forehead, the two palms, the two knees, and the two big toes. These are called the seven points of prostration (*al-masājid al-sabʿa*).

Second: Reciting remembrance (*dhikr*), just as it is obligatory to do so when bowing. Any kind of remembrance of Allah suffices, whether saying '*al-ḥamdu lillāh*', '*lā ilāha ill allāh*', '*allāhu akbar*' or reciting *tasbīḥ*. However, precaution is to opt for *tasbīḥ* (glorification) which either consists of saying '*subḥān allāh*' three times, or saying '*subḥāna rabbī l-aʿlā wa biḥamdih*' [at least] once.

It is best to repeat the latter *tasbīḥ* ('*subḥāna rabbī 'l-aʿlā wa biḥamdih*') three times and repeat any other *dhikr*s (in lieu of *tasbīḥ*), should the worshipper choose them, three times as well.

Third: Remaining still in prostration; and it is nearest to precaution to remain so for the duration of the obligatory *dhikr*, and – in fact – for the supererogatory *dhikr* as well, if it is recited as a recommended part of the prayer.

Fourth: Lifting one's head from prostration and sitting still for a moment before going into the second prostration.

Fifth: It is nearest to precaution to ensure that the seven points of prostration remain still in their respective places, and that none of them are lifted until the *dhikr* is complete. If one lifts one of his points of prostration during *dhikr*, intentionally or otherwise, he must repeat the *dhikr* as a matter of precaution, but his prayer is still valid, God-willing.

Sixth: The place of prostration must be level, [such that] the place of one's forehead should not be higher or lower than that of the knees by more than four closed fingers (approximately 8cm). It is nearest to precaution to observe this between all other points of prostration as well, especially relative to the knees.

Seventh: *Dhikr* must be recited continuously, in proper Arabic, and with correct pronunciation to the extent one is able to do so, and with correct declension.

Eighth: The forehead must be placed on something suitable for prostration (see below), and the surface upon which prostration occurs must be ritually pure.

Rules for prostration

5. It is obligatory, as a matter of precaution, to prostrate in the manner that is well-known amongst the Muslims. It is incorrect, for example, to lie on the floor so that one's stomach presses against it and one's legs are outstretched, because this is not considered a form of prostration as practiced by the religious community (*mutasharri'a*), even if the seven points of prostration are touching the ground.
6. With regards to the two big toes, the strongest opinion says that it suffices for any part of them to be in contact with the ground, whether their top, or their bottom, even if it is nearest to precaution to place their tips upon the ground.
7. If, during prayer, one loses that which is suitable for prostration upon, then precaution requires that he finish his prayer prostrating on whatever is available, then repeat the prayer so long as there is ample time [before the time for prayer ends]. On the other hand, if time is short, he should prostrate on his garment, something made from

minerals [such as agate, if one wears a ring set with it], or the back of his hand.

8. If someone involuntarily lifts their head from the ground, there is no problem with putting it back down and finishing the prostration, and there is no need to do anything else, as it will be counted as a single prostration.
9. If the worshipper is unable to bend himself fully to prostration, he should bend to the extent he is able, and raise the object upon which he prostrates to his forehead. If he is not able to do that either, he should incline his head in place of prostration. If even this is [unbearably] difficult for him, then he should indicate prostration with his eyes and, failing that, he should intend it with his heart.
10. Prayer is not valid when performed upon something unstable, such as a piece of soft sponge, an inflatable object, a mattress stuffed with feathers, soft soil into which his hands and feet can sink, piles of wheat or barley, or suchlike.

The place of the forehead

11. During prostration, one's forehead must be placed on the earth, or some vegetation of the earth which is neither eaten nor used for clothing.
12. To determine whether a kind of earth or vegetation is eaten or worn, one should see what it is commonly considered: if it is called a plant or earth, then one can prostrate upon it, but if it is commonly treated as something that can be eaten or worn as clothing, then one cannot.
13. Prostrating on the ground or on dust is better than prostrating on plants or paper, and better than all other surfaces is prostration upon the earth (clay) of Karbalā᾿, according to narrated traditions.

Etiquettes of prostration

14. In prostration, the following actions are recommended:
    a. To recite *takbīr* after one has risen from bowing and is standing straight [prior to prostration], though one can recite a *takbīr* while inclining to bow.
    b. To raise both hands while reciting *takbīr*, as we have discussed.
    c. To say '*astaghfirullāha rabbī wa atūbu ilayh*' ('forgive me, my Lord; I repent to You') while sitting between prostrations
    d. To recite a *takbīr* after lifting one's head from the first prostration and sitting still for a moment, a second for the second prostration before bending down again, and a third after raising one's head from the second prostration. It is also

recommended to lift one's hands [to the side of the head] while reciting these *takbīrs*.

Prostrations while reciting the Qur'ān

15. It is obligatory for anyone who recites a verse of obligatory prostration[491] in the Qur'ān to prostrate. These verses occur in four *sūras* known as the *'azā'im*[492]. It is also recommended to prostrate at other verses of prostration in the Qur'ān, occurring in eleven places[493].

Eighth: *Tashahhud*

1. It is obligatory to sit for the *tashahhud* (testimony) after completing the two prostrations in the second *rak'a* (unit) of all prayers, as well as the third unit in the *maghrib* prayer, and the fourth units in *ẓuhr*, *'aṣr*, and *'ishā'* prayers.
2. *Tashahhud* is obligatory, but not an essential element (*rukn*) of prayer, its exclusion only invalidates the prayer if the worshipper leaves it out intentionally, not accidentally.
3. The act of tashahhud is to sit after raising one's head from the second prostration and to say, once one is sitting still: '*ashhadu an lā ilāha ill allāh waḥdahu lā sharīka lah, wa ashhadu anna muḥammadan 'abduhu wa rasūluh, allāhumma ṣalli 'alā muḥammadin wa āli muḥammad*' ('I testify that there is no god but Allah, One and without partner, and I testify that Muḥammad is His servant and messenger. O Allah, send your blessings upon Muḥammad and the family of Muḥammad').
4. It is obligatory to ensure that the sentences, words, and letters of the *tashahhud* are recited uninterruptedly, and in proper Arabic to the extent one is able.
5. In *tashahhud*, it is recommended:
    a. For a man to sit on his haunches and for a woman to keep her thighs together while sitting.
    b. For the worshipper to say '*al-ḥamdu lillāh*' before the two testimonies of faith above, or '*bismillāhi wa billāhi wa'l-ḥamdu lillāhi wa khayr ul-asmā'i lillāh*.'

---

[1] There are four *sūras* which contain obligatory prostrations in the Qur'ān, collectively known as *'azā'im*. These are: al-Sajda (32):15, Fuṣṣilat (41):37, al-Najm (53):62, and al-'Alaq (96):19.

[2] These are 7:206, 13:15, 16:50, 17:109, 19:58, 22:18, 22:77, 25:60, 27:25-26, 38:24, 84:21.

c. To say, when rising to stand for the third rakʿa from *tashahhud*: '*bi ḥawl lillāhi wa quwwatihi aqūmu wa aqʿud*.'

Ninth: *Taslīm*

1. *Taslīm* is the last part of prayer, and it is obligatory though not an essential part, so omitting it intentionally invalidates the prayer, but not accidentally.
2. The time of *taslīm* is after *tashahhud* in the final unitof every prayer, while sitting still – as in *tashahhud*.
3. *Taslīm* consists of two expressions: '*as-salāmu ʿalayna wa ʿalā ʿibād illāh il-ṣāliḥīn*' and '*as-salāmu ʿalaykum wa raḥmat ullāhi wa barakātuh*' ('peace be upon us, and upon Allah's righteous servants,' and 'peace be upon you [all], with Allah's mercy and blessings,' respectively). It is only obligatory to recite one of them, so if one recites the first expression first, the second is recommended. But if one recites the second expression first, this suffices and there is no need for the first. However, it is precaution to recite the second expression in all circumstances, as there is the possibility that both it and the first constitute a single obligatory act.
4. As for the expression: '*as-salāmu ʿalayka ayyuhā 'n-nabī wa raḥmatullāhi wa barakātuh*' ('peace be upon you, O Prophet, with Allah's mercy and blessings'), it is not one of the expressions of *taslīm*, but actually one of the subsidiaries of *tashahhud*. It is recommended, but not obligatory.
5. The expressions of the *taslīm* must be recited in proper Arabic with proper observance of continuity between the words and letters.

Tenth: Order of actions

1. Because prayer (*ṣalāt*) is an act of worship consisting of a specified set of actions, details, and a specific form, one must observe the specific form, order, and arrangement laid down for it in the *sharīʿa*. It is impermissible to re-arrange the order of actions as one pleases; instead, one must follow the order found in our religious texts, which are narrated according to the acts of Allah's Messenger ﷺ and the Imams of Guidance عليهم السلام.
2. If the worshipper intentionally breaks the specified order of actions, then his prayer is invalidated, whether this break took place in the actions themselves or the words he was supposed to recite. We shall discuss this further below under the heading 'Deficiencies in Prayer,' God-willing.

Eleventh: Continuity

1. It is obligatory for the worshipper to maintain the proper form of prayer which is well-known amongst religious persons. Part of this is maintaining a continuity of actions and ensuring that there is no gap between them that would break the prayer's form.
2. Just as among the actions of prayer, so too must the worshipper observe continuity in his recitation of the Qur'ān and *adhkār*, not leaving [significant] gaps between them, or between expressions, words, or letters, to the extent that he no longer appears to be reciting a single, continuous text.
3. If the worshipper intentionally fails to maintain this continuity and fluency in his recitation of the Qur'ān and *adhkār*, such that the form of recitation or *dhikr* is lost, his prayer is invalidated.

Twelfth: *Qunūt*

1. *Qunūt* is a supplication, offered by raising one's hands in front of his face, with their palms facing upwards towards the heavens, and their backs towards the ground. This takes place after reciting from the Qur'ān, but before bowing, in the second unit of most prayers.
2. *Qunūt* is a recommended act in all prayers, whether obligatory or supererogatory.
3. It is only recommended – as we pointed out earlier – to perform this once, before bowing in the second unit of every prayer, except in the following situations:
    a. In the prayers for the two *ʿīd*s, wherein it is recommended to perform *qunūt* five times in the first unit and four times in the second.
    b. In the prayer of signs (*ṣalāt al-āyāt*) there are two or five *qunūt*s.
    c. The Friday prayer contains two *qunūt*s.
4. It is unnecessary to recite a specific supplication while in *qunūt*. Rather, it suffices for the worshipper to recite any supplication he pleases, and he is allowed to supplicate in languages other than Arabic, even though it is more cautious to avoid doing so.

Thirteenth: *Taʿqīb*

A large number of traditions stress the importance of spending one's time after prayer reciting some supplications, *dhikr*s, and verses of the Qur'ān, rather than getting up and leaving straight away. After all, in facing the pressures of Satan, his own desires, and material life, the servant desperately needs to entreat his Lord in the morning, noon, and night to seek His assistance, plead for His forgiveness, and place his trust in Him.

Traditions narrated from Allah's Messenger 🕮 and his Household 🕮 in this regard abound, all of which strongly recommend engaging in acts of post-prayer worship (*ta'qīb*). These narrations guide us to the supplications and *dhikrs* most suited for these moments. Details of these can be found in our more comprehensive practical legal manual under the rules pertaining to acts of worship.

Section three: Rules for deficiencies in prayer (*khilal fī al-ṣalāt*)

First: Things which invalidate prayer

The noble *sunna*:

* ❖ 'Alī b. Ja'far asked his brother, Imam Mūsā b. Ja'far 🕮, about a man who is praying. During his prayer, his head is injured and some blood trickles from the injury. Does that invalidate his *wuḍū*? So he said: 'It does not break his *wuḍū*', but it breaks his prayer.'[494]

* ❖ Imam al-Ṣādiq 🕮 said: 'Whoever prays during the incorrect time, his prayer is invalid.'[495]

* ❖ Imam al-Ṣādiq has narrated from his father that 'Alī 🕮 said: 'Whoever experiences something that would void his *wuḍū'* during prayer, his prayer is void and he should [renew his *wuḍū'* and] begin again.'[496]

* ❖ In the book *al-Khiṣāl*, it is narrated from the Commander of the Believers 🕮: 'The Muslim does not join his hands during his prayer, while he stands before Allah Almighty, resembling the people of disbelief—meaning the Zoroastrians.'[497]

* ❖ Zurāra has narrated that he heard Imam al-Bāqir 🕮 saying: 'Turning around (away from the *qibla*) breaks the prayer if it was done with the entire body.'[498]

* ❖ It is narrated from the Messenger of Allah 🕮: 'The prayer is not correct if there is anything in it of the words of man (*kalām al-ādamiyīn*).'[499]

* ❖ Imam al-Ṣādiq 🕮 said: 'Smiling does not break the prayer, but guffawing does, although it does not break *wuḍū'*.'[500]

---

[494] *Wasā'il al-shī'a*, v. 4, p. 1247, ḥ. 17

[495] *Wasā'il al-shī'a*, v. 3, p. 79, ḥ. 6

[496] *Mawsū'at al-fiqh* of al-Shīrāzī, v. 4, p. 343

[497] *Mawsū'at al-fiqh* of al-Shīrāzī, v. 4, p. 345

[498] *Wasā'il al-shī'a*, v. 4, p. 1248, ḥ. 3

[499] *Mawsū'at al-fiqh* of al-Shīrāzī, v. 4, p. 362

[500] *Wasā'il al-shī'a*, v. 4, p. 1253, ḥ. 4

❖ Imam al-Ṣādiq ﷺ was asked if weeping violates the prayer. So he said: 'Surely weeping at the remembrance of Paradise or the Fire is among the best actions in prayer, but crying over his dead [friends or relatives] corrupts his prayer.'[501]

Rulings:

There are twelve things which invalidate prayer:

1. Being deprived of one of the act's conditional requirements during prayer
2. Experiencing a loss of ritual purity during prayer
3. Joining one's hands together (*takattuf*)
4. Turning away from the *qibla*
5. Speaking
6. Guffawing
7. Crying for worldly matters
8. Doing something which effaces the outward form of prayer
9. Eating or drinking
10. Saying '*āmīn*' after reciting *Sūrat al-Fātiḥa*
11. Adding or omitting something
12. Experiencing doubts which invalidate the prayer

First: Being deprived of one of the requirements of prayer

1. If the worshipper realizes during his prayer that he has been deprived of one of the conditional requirements for prayer, his prayer is invalidated unless he can somehow rectify the situation (as we have discussed above in the preliminaries to prayer).
2. The conditional requirements of prayer are those things related to timing and the *qibla*, as well as dress, location, their ritual purity and permitted usage, etc.

Second: Experiencing a loss of ritual purity

1. The emission of urine, faeces, or flatulence (leading to a state of minor ritual impurity), or semen or menstrual blood (leading to a state of major ritual impurity) during prayer invalidates it because it breaks [its requisite] ritual purity.
2. It makes no difference whether this happens intentionally, accidentally, or as a matter of necessity – except for one afflicted with incontinence

---

[501] *Wasā'il al-shī'a*, v. 4, p. 1251, ḥ. 4

or unexpected bleeding, insofar as these persons have their own special rulings.

Third: Joining one's hands together

Joining one's hands together (*takattuf*) means placing one hand over another while standing in prayer, as is the common practice of some Islamic sects. It invalidates the prayer, and the most cautious course of action is that one refrains from it in all other states of prayer.

Fourth: Turning away from the qibla

1. Turning away from the *qibla* with the whole body and facing the opposite direction, or ninety-degrees to the right or left invalidates the prayer, whether this is done intentionally or otherwise.
2. As for turning the entire body away from the *qibla* less than ninety degrees to the left or right: it invalidates the prayer if it is done intentionally, or if it causes the worshipper to be facing away from the *qibla* according to what is customarily understood.

Fifth: Speaking intentionally

Prayer is interrupted by intentionally uttering something other than the Qur'ān, *dhikr*s, or giving an obligatory response to a greeting of peace. The details of this are as follows:

1. Intentionally uttering a word made up of two or more syllables invalidates prayer.
2. Intentionally uttering a word made up of a single syllable with its own meaning (e.g., 'no!') invalidates the prayer as well, so long as one is aware of the meaning and intends this meaning.
3. Intentionally uttering two syllables without any meaning, if done with the intention of communicating something thereby, according to the strongest opinion, invalidates the prayer. But if they are uttered without intending any meaning, then it is [still] precaution to repeat the prayer.
4. As for uttering unintentionally uttering a meaningless syllable, there is no problem with it.
5. If the worshipper uses a single syllable denoting a commonly understood meaning, such as the sound of the *'ayn* for *'alayhi al-salām* (peace be upon him), or 'te' for 'telephone' or any other sort of reference, then obligatory precaution requires him to repeat the prayer.

Sixth: Guffawing

Guffawing means to laugh loudly, at length, and to tremble from laughter. This invalidates the prayer, even if it was involuntary. As for smiling, there is no problem with it.

Seventh: Weeping intentionally

Weeping intentionally in prayer *for worldly reasons* invalidates the prayer, even if it is done without sound (based on precaution). But there is no problem with weeping out of fear of Allah, or in awe or humility before Him, or for affairs of the Hereafter in general. In fact, this kind of weeping is among the best deeds.

Eighth: Doing something to break the form of prayer

Prayer is invalidated by performing any action which deprives it of its outward form as dictated by the practice of religious persons who are aware of its rules and limits. For example, jumping, dancing, or clapping a lot, all break the form of the prayer, whether done intentionally or not. Remaining silent for a long time, which deprives the prayer of its form, such that an observer could not say that the person is still engaged in prayer, also invalidates it.

Ninth: Eating and drinking

1. Prayer is invalidated by eating and drinking in such a way as deprives prayer of its form, whether intentionally or accidentally.
2. Precaution requires the worshipper to avoid all food and drink which would disrupt the common-sense continuity and fluency of his prayer.
3. There is no problem with swallowing the small pieces of food that remain in the mouth or between the teeth, nor is there any problem with swallowing a hard candy kept in the mouth that dissolves gradually.

***Tenth: Saying* 'āmīn'**

Uttering the word *āmīn* after reciting *Sūrat al-Fātiḥa* causes the prayer to be invalidated except in cases of necessity (such as compulsion or *taqiyya*), irrespective of whether it is said loudly or quietly, or whether one is leading a congregation, praying in one, or praying individually.

Eleventh: Adding to or omitting from the prayer

1. Adding or omitting an essential element of the prayer, whether intentionally or otherwise, invalidates the prayer.
2. Adding or omitting an obligatory component which is non-essential to the prayer invalidates it if done intentionally, but not if it is accidental.

Twelfth: Experiencing doubts

Prayer is invalidated by doubting how many units one has offered throughout prayers consisting of two or three units, or during the first two units of those which consist of four. We shall discuss these details in the section on doubts, below.

If, after completing the prayer, one doubts whether he has done something to invalidate the prayer, he should assume that he has not, and his prayer is valid, God-willing.

If there emanates from the worshipper excessive movement or a lengthy silence but he is not sure whether or not this has broken the outward form of the prayer, it is not unlikely that he can assume his prayer is still valid. However, the most cautious course of action is to repeat the prayer after finishing it.

Responding to greetings while in prayer

1. It is obligatory for the worshipper to respond to the Islamic greeting of peace (*salām*). If he does not do so, he is sinful, but his prayer is not invalidated. As for greeting someone who is praying, it is disliked.
2. When praying, one must respond to greetings in kind. In other words, the response must be the same expression as the one which was offered first. So if the greeter says '*as-salāmu 'alaykum*' it is obligatory to respond with exactly the same sentence. If someone gives a response in improper Arabic, he must still give a proper response.

Interrupting prayers

1. It is impermissible to interrupt obligatory prayers except when some necessity demands it. It is permissible in the following cases:

   First: If one must interrupt the prayer in order to ward off [imminent] harm from his self or another.

   Second: If some harm will come to his own property or that of another if he does not interrupt his prayer.

   Third: If the worshipper forgets the *adhān* and *iqāma* and remembers before bowing.

   Fourth: If the worshipper has a debt and someone comes to collect it while he is prayer, and he is both able to pray and pay the debt, then he should do so. But, if he can only pay it if he interrupts his prayers and there remains ample time to pray but he cannot pay the debt afterwards, he is permitted to interrupt his prayer. On the other hand, if there is not enough time to repeat his prayer after paying the debt, then he is not allowed to so interrupt it.
2. If it is obligatory for someone to interrupt his prayer but, in spite of this, he continues and finishes his prayer, then the apparent ruling is that his prayer is valid, even if he is sinful for failing to do what was obligatory for him.

Second: Rules pertaining to doubts and deficiencies in prayer

Preliminaries

First: Saying that a prayer is invalidated by something for which we do not have explicit textual evidence (*naṣṣ*) is problematic. For this reason, when doubt rises, caution requires that we try to correct our prayers if possible and then repeat them as well.

Second: Certainty (*yaqīn*) is to know something without hesitation, such as when the worshipper knows he is in the first unit of prayer, or the third, etc. Doubt (*shakk*) is when one hesitates between two or more possibilities equally, without inclining more towards any one of them than the others.

Probability (*ẓann*) is hesitation between one option which is more likely and one which is less; so we say that the more likely option is 'probable.'

Naturally, [definite] knowledge and certainty are not affected in the least by possibilities or doubts: certainty is not broken by doubt. In this case, probable knowledge (*ẓann*) occupies the same position as knowledge, meaning that the same rules apply to it as certainty. Thus, if probability overcomes doubt and one possibility seems more likely, then the worshipper should act on that probability exactly as though it was certain knowledge. But in cases where the doubt and hesitation cannot be removed, there are specific rules in place.

The noble *sunna*:

- Zurāra has narrated form one of the two Imams, al-Bāqir or al-Ṣādiq عليهما السلام: 'If someone did not know whether he had performed three or four units of prayer but his view settles on three, then he stands at performs one additional unit, and he is not required to do anything else. Certainty cannot be violated by doubt, and doubt cannot enter into certainty—one cannot mix with the other. Rather it is doubt which is broken by certainty; so he completes [the prayer] with that certainty, and based upon it, and pays no mind to doubt, whatever the circumstance.'[502]
- Imam al-Ṣādiq عليه السلام said: 'If one doubts during *maghrib*, then repeat it, and if one doubts during *fajr*, then repeat it.'[503]
- It is narrated from Abū al-Ḥasan al-Riḍā عليه السلام: 'If you do not know how many units you have prayed, and your mind cannot settle on anything, then repeat the prayer.'[504]

---

[502] *Wasā'il al-shī'a*, v. 5, p. 321, ḥ. 3
[503] *Wasā'il al-shī'a*, v. 5, p. 304, ḥ. 1
[504] *Wasā'il al-shī'a*, v. 5, p. 327, ḥ. 1

- Imam al-Ṣādiq ﷺ, speaking to one of his companions, said: 'O ʿAmmār, I can summarize for you all doubts in two sentences: when you doubt [the number of units] then go by the greater number. If you have already recited the *taslīm*, then complete whatever you suspect that you left out.'[505]

Rulings:

Types of doubt

Doubts in prayer fall into one of three categories:

1. Doubts which cause the prayer to become invalid, of which there are eight.
2. Doubts which should be ignored, of which there are six.
3. Doubts which are valid and should be addressed in prayer according to specific rules which we will outline, and of which there are nine.

First: Doubts which invalidate the prayer

Those doubts which cause the prayer to become invalid should they persist are eight in number:

1. Doubting the number of units offered in a two-unit prayer.
2. Doubting the number of units offered in the *maghrib* prayer.
3. Doubting whether one unit has been offered or more than one.
4. Doubting whether two or more units have been offered in four-unit prayers (*ẓuhr*, *ʿaṣr* and *ʿishāʾ*) *before* completing the two prostrations of the second unit. The famous view of the jurists is that this doubt invalidates the prayer, but obligatory precaution requires the worshipper to complete the prayer and follow the rules for one whose doubt came *after* the two prostrations of the second unit, and then repeat the prayer thereafter.
5. Doubting whether one has offered two units or five, or more than five. This doubt invalidates the prayer according to the well-known view of the jurists. However, obligatory precaution requires the worshipper to assume he has offered two units, complete the prayer, and then repeat it.
6. Doubting whether one has offered three units or six, or between three and more than six, according to the well-known view. Obligatory precaution requires that the worshipper assumes he has

---

[505] *Wasāʾil al-shīʿa*, v. 5, p. 317, ḥ. 1

offered three units, complete his prayer with a fourth, and then repeat it.

7. Doubting whether one has offered four units or six, or between four and more than six, according to the well-known view. Obligatory precaution requires the worshipper to assume he has offered four units, complete his prayer, perform two prostrations for error (*sahw*), and then repeat his prayer.
8. If one doubts how many units he has prayed generally, such that he has no idea how many he has prayed.

If someone experiences one of the aforementioned doubts that would cause his prayer to be invalidated, he is not allowed to interrupt his prayer straight away. Instead, he must remain still for a moment and think until he attains certain—or at least probable—knowledge of which of the two possibilities is correct, and then act accordingly. However, if his doubt persists, then he is allowed to abort his prayer.

Second: Doubts which should be ignored

As for those doubts which should be ignored during prayer, they are as follows.

First are those doubts which occur after one has passed their relevant point in prayer.

1. If, while praying, someone doubts whether or not he has performed some parts of the prayer, and this doubt arose before he has moved onto the part that comes after it, he should perform the part which he has doubt about. For example, if he doubts whether he has recited *takbīrat al-iḥrām* but has not yet begun what comes after it, he must recite a *takbīr*.
2. However, if the doubt arises only after he has passed the relevant point in prayer (meaning he has begun performing a part of the prayer that comes after the part about which he has doubt), then he should ignore his doubt. He should assume that he has performed the suspect part and continue his prayer without any worry. For example, if someone doubts whether he has recited *takbīrat al-iḥrām* while he is reciting *Sūrat al-Fātiḥa*.
3. It makes no difference whether the part of prayer started after the component affected doubt is obligatory or supererogatory. Thus, if someone doubts having performed *takbīrat al-iḥrām* while he is engaged with reciting *isti'ādha* ('seeking refuge,' which is a

recommended act), or if he doubts having performed recitation while he is in *qunūt*, etc., then he should ignore his doubts.

4. The exception to this rule of passed parts in prayer is if someone doubts whether he prostrated while he is in the processing of standing up [for the next unit of prayer]. In this specific situation, it is obligatory for him to go back and perform the prostration, because we have a clear text (*naṣṣ*) [from an Infallible] stating this. Obligatory precaution requires that we include the *tashahhud* with this ruling; so if someone doubts having recited it it while he is standing up, then he must – as a matter of precaution – return to the sitting position and recite the *tashahhud* with the intention of seeking divine reward.

Second are those doubts that arise after concluding the prayer with *taslīm*:

1. If someone doubts the validity of their prayer in a general sense after reciting the obligatory *taslīm*, then he should ignore it.
2. If someone doubts having fulfilled some of the conditions of prayer or having performed some parts of it (whether words, deeds, essentials or non-essentials) after reciting the obligatory *taslīm*, then he should ignore his doubt.
3. If someone doubts the number of units of prayer he has offered after the obligatory *taslīm*, then he should also ignore his doubts, so long as one of the possibilities he hesitates between is correct for the prayer he has offered. So, for example, if someone doubts his *fajr* or *maghrib* prayers after *taslīm* and hesitates between having offered two or three units.

Third are those doubts which occur after the time for prayer has lapsed.

If, after the time for prayer has lapsed, someone is uncertain whether or not he has prayed (e.g. he is unsure whether or not he has prayed *fajr* after the sun has risen), he should ignore his doubts and assume that he did pray. The same applies if he thinks it probable that he did not pray or doubts the validity of his prayer.

Fourth are those doubts experienced by someone who doubts obsessively.

1. Anyone who frequently doubts in his prayer is called an 'obsessive doubter' (*kathīr al-shakk*) and he must ignore his doubts.

2. The criterion which determines whether someone is obsessive in their doubting is common sense (*ʿurf*).
3. If an obsessive doubter is uncertain about something to do with his prayer (whether the number of units, the performance of actions, or the fulfilment of conditions) he should assume that he has done whatever was required of him, even if he has not yet passed its point in prayer (e.g., if he is uncertain whether he has performed a bowing while he is standing, then he should assume he has bowed).
4. If a persistent doubter is uncertain whether he has done something to ruin his prayer, then he should assume that he has not (e.g., if he thinks he might have bowed twice, he should assume that he has not).
5. If someone is unsure of how many units he has offered, he should assume the higher number so long as this does not lead to his prayer becoming invalid (e.g,. someone who hesitates between three and four units in a four-unit prayer should assume he has offered four). But if the higher number would invalidate the prayer, then he must assume the lesser number (e.g., someone who hesitates between three and five units should assume he has offered three).

Fifth are those doubts experienced by a congregation's leader or its constituents.

If the *imām* of a congregational prayer is unsure of how many units he has offered – or, according to the strongest opinion, even if he is unsure about whether he has performed an action of prayer – but someone following him in prayer is able to inform the *imām* of the correct number by some means, then the *imām* should ignore his doubts, refer to the follower, and act on that follower's memory. The reverse is also true: if the follower is unsure but the *imām* remembers, the follower should disregard his own doubts and follow the *imām*. So if the *imām* hesitates between three or four units but the follower remembers that it is three, the *imām* should refer to him, and the same applies if he is unsure whether he has performed a second prostration or not but the follower remembers: the *imām* must refer to the follower. The reverse also applies. And there is no need here for precautionary prayers (*salāt al-iḥtiyāṭ*).

Sixth are those doubts pertaining to the number of units in supererogatory prayers.

If someone is unsure how many units he has offered in a recommended prayer, then if one of the possibilities renders the prayer valid and the other invalid, then he should assume that the valid possibility is correct (e.g., if someone doubts whether he has offered two or three units in the supererogatory prayers for *fajr*, he should assume that he has offered two). And if both possibilities render the prayer valid (e.g., doubting between oneor two units), then he can assume whichever he prefers, though it is always better to assume the lower number.

Third: Valid doubts

The nine forms of valid doubts are as follows:

1. Hesitating between two or three units after finishing the two prostrations, in which case one should assume he has offered three units and begin the fourth. Then, immediately upon completing the prayer, he should offer a single unit of precautionary prayer from a [normal] standing position, or two from a sitting position, but obligatory precaution requires him to perform a single unit while standing.
2. Hesitating between two or four units after finishing the two prostrations, in which case one should assume he has offered four and then straight after his prayer perform a precautionary prayer of two units from a normal standing position.
3. Hesitating between two, three, or four units after finishing the two prostrations, in which case one should assume he has offered four. Then, straight after his prayer, he should offer two units of precautionary prayer while standing and two more while seated. The apparent ruling is that he must offer the two units while standing before offering the two while seated.
4. Hesitating between performed four or five units after finishing the two prostrations, in which case one should assume he has offered four, recite *tashahhud* and *taslīm*, and then perform two prostrations of error (*sahw*) for possibly having added something to the prayer.
5. Hesitating between three and four units at any point in prayer, in which case one should assume he has offered four, complete the prayer, and then perform a precautionary prayer of either one unit while standing, or two units while seated. But [in this case] it is precaution to opt for two units while seated.
6. Hesitating, while standing at the beginning of a *rakʿa* (unit), between four and five units. In this situation, the worshipper must return to a seated position and conclude the prayer with *tashahhud* and *taslīm*, before offering a precautionary prayer consisting of either two units while seated or a single unit standing.

7. Hesitating, while standing at the beginning of a unit, between three and five units. In this situation, the worshipper must return to a seated position and conclude the prayer with *tashahhud* and *taslīm*, before offering a precautionary prayer consisting of two units offered while standing.
8. Hesitating, while standing at the beginning of a unit, between three, four, or five units. In this situation, the worshipper must return to a seated position and conclude his prayer with *tashahhud* and *taslīm*, before offering two precautionary prayers: one of two units standing and another of two units sitting, and the apparent ruling is that he must offer the standing prayer before the seated one.
9. Hesitating, while standing at the beginning of a unit of prayer, between five and six units. In this situation, the worshipper should return to a seated position and conclude his prayer with *tashahhud* and *taslīm*, and then perform two prostrations for inattention (*sahw*).

***Precautionary prayer* (ṣalāt al-iḥtiyāṭ)**

For anyone who needs to perform precautionary prayers because of some of the aforementioned doubts, it is obligatory to do so *immediately* after his prayers. He should stand and make the intention of precautionary prayer, recite a *takbīr*, recite *Sūrat al-Fātiḥa* by itself, then bow, rise, and perform two prostrations before concluding his prayer with *tashahhud* and *taslīm*. This is if he needed to perform a single unit of precautionary prayer. If he needs to perform two units, then he offers the second after the first, before concluding the prayer with *tashahhud* and *taslīm*. And if the precautionary prayer is to be offered while seated, then he should offer two units while sitting.

Precautionary prayers have all the same requirements and conditions as other prayers, such as ritual purity, permitted use, facing the *qibla*, etc.

***Prostration for mistakes* (ṣujūd al-sahw)**

It is obligatory to perform two prostrations for mistakes (known as *sajdatay al-sahw*) after prayer for the following reasons:

1. Speaking accidentally (as previously defined).
2. Reciting *taslīm* at the wrong moment in prayer, like in the first unit.
3. Forgetting a single prostration – according to precaution.
4. Forgetting to recite *tashahhud*.
5. Doubting whether one has offered four or five units after finishing the two prostrations, as we have just discussed.

6. Standing when one should be sitting, or the reverse – according to recommended precaution.
7. For any accidental addition to, or omission from, parts of the prayer – according to recommended precaution.

How to prostrate for mistakes

To perform a prostration for mistakes, one should intend – immediately after his prayer – to prostrate for mistakes, then prostrate and place his forehead on something suitable for prostration. And it is precaution – if one wishes to recite a *dhikr* – to say either:

- *'Bismillāhi wa billāhi, as-salāmu 'alayka ayuh al-nabī wa raḥmatullāhi wa barakātuh.'*
- *'Bismillāhi wa billāhi wa ṣall allāhu 'alā muḥammad wa ālih.'*
- *'Bismillāhi wa billāhi allāhumma ṣalli 'alā muḥammad wa ālih.'*

Then he should lift his head from prostration and perform another prostration like the first. According to the strongest opinion he should then sit and recite *tashahhud* if this prostration was on account of forgetting the *tashahhud* in his prayer; and according to precaution, he should do this even if the prostration was for another reason. Then, also based on precaution, he should recite *taslīm*, sufficing himself with one of the formulas thereof.

Compensating for forgotten parts of prayer

If someone forgets to perform a single prostration (as opposed to both prostrations in a single unit) and does not realize this until the bowing of the next unit or later, he must compensate for it after finishing his prayer, and then perform two prostrations for mistakes (*sahw*) as a matter of precaution.

If someone forgets the *tashahhud* completely, or just some parts of it, the rules are as follows:

1. If the first *tashahhud* was forgotten, then the worshipper must perform two prostrations for mistakes after the prayer, and the *tashahhud* he recites as part of that will suffice him. The same applies to forgotten parts of this *tashahhud*. However, it is recommended precaution [in case of forgetting] all or part of the first *tashahhud* to compensate for it *in addition* to the above.
2. If the second *tashahhud* was forgotten and the worshipper realizes this after *taslīm*, then he should recite the *tashahhud* and then recite the *taslīm* again, before performing two prostrations for mistakes on account of reciting the *taslīm* in the wrong place (see above).

3. When compensating for forgotten parts of the prayer, all the prerequisites of prayer itself apply, such as ritual purity, proper covering, facing the *qibla*, etc. (see above).
4. One must recite the obligatory *dhikr* when making up for a forgotten prostration, and the two testimonies of faith, and invocations of blessings upon the Prophet and his Household, when making up for a forgotten *tashahhud*.

Additions and omissions in prayer

1. If someone intentionally adds obligatory actions to the prayer or omits them, his prayer is invalidated.
2. If someone errs in the obligatory components of prayer by addition or omission – other than the fundamental (*arkān*) components – because he was unaware of the ruling, then obligatory precaution requires that the rules of deliberate addition or omission be applied. This is in cases where he was wilfully ignorant of the rules.[506] But if he was ignorant of these rulings through no fault of his own, then the strongest opinion is that these be treated as accidental (*sahw*).
3. If someone errs in reciting loudly or quietly – such as by reciting *al-Fātiḥa* and another *sūra* quietly in *fajr* prayers, or in the first two units of *maghrib* or *ʿishāʾ*, or by reciting these aloud in the first two units of *ẓuhr* or *ʿaṣr* – then the strongest opinion is that [his prayer is valid and] he need not do anything.
4. If, whilst engaged in prayer, one realizes that his ritual purity was invalid, or that he had begun the prayer without proper ritual purity, his prayer is invalidated [and should be aborted].
5. If someone accidentally prays before the time for the prayer has begun, his prayer is invalid [and must be repeated in its proper time].
6. If someone prays facing a direction that is completely away from the *qibla* or with his back towards it, then obligatory precaution requires him to either repeat or compensate the prayer if he was ignorant of the ruling. In other cases, it is recommended precaution to do so.[507]

---

[506] This means that he could have readily known the rules but did not seek to do so.

[507] Meaning in cases where he was not ignorant of the ruling, but did not face the *qibla* because he was not aware of the proper direction and he was unable to discern it before the time for prayer lapsed, or because he erred in his locating of the *qibla* and prayed facing the opposite direction, in which case it is recommended precaution for him to repeat the prayer.

Section four: Rules for other prayers

First: Prayers for the traveller

The noble *sunna*:

- The Messenger of Allah ﷺ said: 'Whoever prays four units while traveling, I am innocent of him before Allah.'[508]
- Abū al-Ḥasan the First [al-Kāẓim] ؑ said: 'All of your dwellings [when traveling] in which you do not take up residence, in them you must shorten your prayers.'[509]
- Imam al-Ṣādiq ؑ said: 'You may pray the full prayer [when traveling] in four places: the Sacred Mosque, the Mosque of the Messenger ﷺ, the Mosque of Kūfa, and the sanctuary of al-Ḥusayn b. ʿAlī ؑ.'[510]
- And in another narration, Imam al-Ṣādiq ؑ said: 'From the storehouses of Allah's knowledge is the completion [of the prayer] in four places: the sanctuary of Allah, the sanctuary of His Messenger ﷺ, the sanctuary of the Commander of the Believers ؑ, and the sanctuary of al-Ḥusayn b. ʿAlī ؑ.'[511]
- Abū Saʿīd al-Khurāsānī has narrated: Two men [who were traveling] entered upon Abū al-Ḥasan al-Riḍā ؑ in Khorasan, and asked him about shortening the prayer. So he said to one of them: 'You must shorten your prayer because you came here intending to see me.' And to the other he said: 'You must pray in full, because you came here intending to see the Sultan (i.e., the ruler).'[512]
- It is narrated from Imam al-Ṣādiq ؑ: 'If a man resolves that he will stay for ten days, then he must offer his prayers in full. But if he is unsure whether he will reside [in one place for ten days]—maybe just for today or tomorrow—then he shortens his prayers until he reaches one month. If he has remained in that city for more than a month, then he must pray his prayers in full [even if he is still unsure about how long he will stay].'[513]

---

[508] *Wasāʾil al-shīʿa*, v. 5, p. 538, ḥ. 3

[509] *Wasāʾil al-shīʿa*, v. 5, p. 520, ḥ. 1

[510] *Wasāʾil al-shīʿa*, v. 5, p. 546, ḥ 14

[511] *Wasāʾil al-shīʿa*, v. 5, p. 543, v. 1. Here 'completion of the prayer' means that in these four locations, one who is travelling may pray the complete prayer rather than shortening. See the rulings below for details.

[512] *Wasāʾil al-shīʿa*, v. 5, p. 510, ḥ. 6

[513] *Wasāʾil al-shīʿa*, v. 5, p. 527, ḥ. 13

- Imam al-Ṣādiq ﷺ was asked about a man who prayed in full while he was traveling. The Imam said: 'If there is time left then he should repeat the prayer, but if the time has passed, then no.'[514]

Rulings:

It is obligatory for a traveller (*musāfir*) to perform his *ẓuhr*, *ʿaṣr,* and *ʿishāʾ* prayers in a shortened form when the following eight conditions are met:

No. 1: Travelling the required distance

1. The distance covered by the traveller must be no less than eight parasangs[515] (approximately 28 miles), whether one-way (i.e., eight parasangs in one direction, whether departing or returning) or as a round trip (i.e., four parasangs outbound plus four returning).
2. By a round trip we mean that the combined distance of a single outbound journey and single return adds up to eight parasangs. As for someone who makes multiple journeys back and forth over a shorter distance (such as a single parasang, for example), and the total of these journeys adds up to eight parasangs, this is not classed as travelling, and he is not allowed to shorten his prayers.
3. If the town in which he lives has walls – as they did in olden days – then the traveller begins counting the distance he travels from the walls of the town. If there are no walls, then his distance is counted from the last houses or buildings which are customarily deemed to be part of that town. This applies to small and medium cities. As for very large cities and metropolises, then his distance is counted from wherever he would customarily be considered a traveller and outside of his home region. For example, if he began his journey at the airport, train station, or entered a highway, etc.
4. As for the end point of his journey for calculating its distance, this is the place he to which he intends to travel, and not the city walls or the beginning of its buildings. So if his destination was a particular marketplace in the middle of the city, the distance of his journey is counted until he reaches that marketplace.

No. 2: Intending to travel the required distance

1. For the rules of travelling apply to the traveller, he must intend to traverse the required distance from the beginning of his journey.

---

514 *Wasāʾil al-shīʿa*, v. 5, p. 530, ḥ. 1

515 A parasang (*farsakh*) is an old unit of distance, equivalent to roughly 3.5 miles or 5.6 kilometres.

2. Anyone who does not know how far he has travelled, such as someone who has lost his way, whose goal is not fixed, or who is hunting game, etc., should not shorten his prayers on his outbound journey. However, on his return journey, he must shorten his prayers if his course is eight parasangs or more.

No. 3: Continuity of intention

Just as the traveller must intend to cover the required distance from the beginning of his journey, he must also continue to intend this during his journey. So if the traveller changes his destination en route but before he has reached four parasangs, or becomes uncertain of his destination within that distance, then must offer his prayers fully, because this change in destination is treated as an interruption in his journey.

That having been said, if someone has shortened his prayers en route before he changed his destination, then he does not need to repeat them afterwards.

No. 4: Not passing through his place of residence

The traveller must not, at the beginning of his journey or while en route, intend to pass through his usual place of residence, or spend ten days or more in a specific place, until he has traversed eight parasangs. Whoever does this must offer full prayers, because [intentionally] spending ten days or more somewhere interrupts his journey, and if he passes through his place of residence the ruling also ceases to apply.

No. 5 The permissibility of his journey

1. The traveller's journey should not be prohibited or with the goal of doing something prohibited, in which case he must offer full prayers. Here are some examples of prohibited or sinful journeys:
   a. If the journey in of itself is forbidden, such as a journey which will cause severe harm to a person; or the journey of a son which his parents have forbidden, if contravening them will cause them distress; or a journey with the intention of deserting the army (for details of this, see the chapter on *jihād*).
   b. If the goal of the journey was forbidden; such as someone who travels to murder an innocent, to steal something, to wrongfully seize the property of others, to cause people distress, or to support a tyrant.
   c. Someone on a journey to hunt for sport must offer full prayers. But if his goal is to seek sustenance and obtain provisions for himself or

his dependents, or for the purposes of trade, he should shorten his prayers. The same ruling applies to fishing.

2. Anyone whose journey is not prohibited in of itself, nor for the purposes of doing something prohibited, but who does something prohibited while travelling—such as backbiting a believer, usurping some property, concluding a forbidden transaction, drinking wine, gambling, attending immoral gatherings, viewing immoral films, etc.—so long as this was not the *intended goal* of his journey, then he should still shorten his prayers, even though he is sinful and should repent for his behaviour.

No. 6: He should not be a nomad

To qualify as travelling, a person should not be a nomad – i.e., someone who has no specific place of residence – such as Bedouins, who do not settle in a particular place, but travel from place to place in search of pasture and water, and carry their homes with them. Such people should always offer full prayers when travelling, no matter how far the journey, as they cannot properly be called 'travelling' [in a legal sense]. The same is true of someone who has been itinerant his whole life and has not taken a permanent residence for himself.

No. 7: Travelling should not be his occupation

1. Anyone whose journey is part of his occupation should offer full prayers and obligatory fasts while journeying for work, even if he sometimes uses his work for personal benefit—for example, if a taxi driver takes his provisions and family to another country. Here are some instances where travelling may be said to be part of a person's job:
   a. A taxi, bus, or lorry driver and anyone who assists them in their work.[516]
   b. A train conductor and anyone who assists him.
   c. An aeroplane pilot, their assistants, and the crew, whether engineers, stewards and stewardesses, or security personnel, who are always on-board for flights.
   d. The captain and crew of a ship, and anyone else whose work means they continuously travel aboard a ship.
   e. Tour and pilgrimage guides who accompany tourists and pilgrims on their journeys, if this is their regular employment.

---

[516] Note that this only applies to taxi, bus, or ferry drivers or train conductors who meet the travel conditions outlined above—i.e., a cab or bus driver who travels around within a single city all day does not meet this criteria, and still needs to pray full prayers. The same may also apply to those working on ships if they are, for instance, coast guard officers who simply cover a small amount of water.

f. Shepherds, donkey drivers, camel drivers, lumberjacks, and the like.
g. Employees of government offices and ministries whose work involves travelling [by its legal definition] constantly, such as tax collectors, assessors, engineers, and workers who maintain highways.

2. If someone whose occupation is travelling undertakes a journey that has no connection to his occupation, such as going to *ḥajj*, pilgrimage to shrines, or on holiday, he should shorten his prayers, unless he goes on these journeys as part of his work, such as a taxi driver who hires out his taxi for travelling to *ḥajj* and performs *ḥajj* at the same time himself—he must offer full prayers.
3. Offering full prayers on journeys related to his work requires that he not spend ten or more days in his place of residence or anywhere else. Residing somewhere interrupts the above ruling and he must shorten his prayers on the first journey thereafter, and then offer full prayers from the next journey onwards. However, it is precaution to offer both full and shortened prayers in the first journey, and it makes no difference here whether his period of residence was intentional or not.

No. 8: Reaching the permitted threshold (*ḥadd al-tarakhkhuṣ*)

1. The permitted threshold (*ḥadd al-tarakhkhuṣ*) is the point at which the traveller begins shortening his prayers on his outbound journey and resumes offering full prayers on his return journey.
2. Most likely, this threshold is where the traveller leaves behind the houses and enters the countryside, such that he can no longer hear the *adhān* [from his hometown] and he is no longer visible from the houses and their owners cannot see him. Today, most cities have road signs which inform you when you are leaving the city limits and these are close to what we mean here. The same applies when returning from a journey: prayers cease to be shortened as soon as the traveller reaches this threshold for his homeland or place of residence, i.e. when he enters a built up area and can hear the *adhān* of the city.
   As for in large cities, such as Mecca, and Kufa in the past, it is obligatory precaution – when returning from a journey – for the worshipper to delay the prayer until he has reached his own house.
3. In unusual circumstances, such as if a person's home town is in an elevated position, such that its landmarks are visible from at a great distance, or if it is in a deep valley such that as soon as you leave it you can no longer see any trace of it, or its buildings are very tall and can been seen from a long way away, or if the starting point of the journey is somewhere without houses or an *adhān*: in all of these and similar

circumstances, the criterion for determining the threshold is to imagine a city sitting normally on flat land, and work out where the threshold would be for it.

Rules for residency

1. Whoever knows that he will stay somewhere other than his homeland (whether this is another city, a village, a tent, or the wilderness) for ten days or more, or intends to stay ten days or more, follows the same rules as someone in his homeland with regards to offering full prayers and fasting. It makes no difference whether this decision was his own choice, a matter of necessity, or if he was compelled to make it.
2. To count as staying somewhere for ten days, it is sufficient to remain there for ten days and nine nights. It is not necessary to count the tenth night as part of it. If someone intended to stay somewhere from the morning of the first day of the month until sunset on the tenth day, this is sufficient to be considered as residence. It also suffices to make up a day from part of another day: like if a person decides to reside somewhere from midday on the first day of a month until midday on the eleventh day, then this is also sufficient [as residence] and he must offer full prayers. However, it is precaution to offer both shortened and full prayers in this situation.
3. To count as residing, a person must spend the entire ten days in a single town or village, not between two distinct locations (e.g., intending to spend ten days divided between Najaf and Karbalā'), or else this is not counted as residing and the person must shorten his prayers. However, this is not affected if, for example, a river divides a city into two parts but both sides are customarily treated as a single city (e.g., the two halves of Baghdad).
4. If a city is very big, such that it is not customarily thought of as a single location, even if it is given a single name, then one must intend to stay in a particular region of that city. For example, in a city like New York, the region of Brooklyn is considered distinct from that of Long Island, or New Jersey, or the other boroughs of NYC, On the other hand, if a city is like Tehran or Cairo, such that a resident there – whether in its north or south – is customarily thought of to be living in a single city, then it suffices to reside in any part of it. And this can be defined based on whether one thinks travelling from one region to another is considered a journey or not. If it is not considered a journey, then it is a single city.
5. Intending to reside somewhere does not mean you cannot leave that place at all during those ten days. In fact, if someone intends – whether

from the beginning or during his stay – to visit the outskirts of the city, such as its parks and countryside, so long as this is not more than four parasangs away, does not invalidate his residency there. In this case, he must continue to offer full prayers so long as he is said to be residing there according to common sense, so long as he returns to the city on the same day – like setting out in the morning and returning in the afternoon.

6. If someone intends to reside somewhere for ten days, and upon completing these ten days intends to add more days to his stay, he should continue offering full prayers without any need to intend another ten days. Residency here means staying in a single place for ten *or more* days, not that every ten days requires a new intention. The rulings for residency remain effective so long as he has not interrupted his residency by travelling afresh from its locale.
7. When someone intends to reside somewhere, all the rules for someone who is in his homeland apply to him, whether this be offering full prayers, fasting as normal, the recommendation to perform the daytime supererogatory prayers (which no longer applies when travelling), and the obligation of attending Friday and *ʿīd* prayers (so long as all of their prerequisites are met).

If someone is uncertain about the length of his stay

1. If a person travels and his journey meets the distance requirement to shorten his prayer, but he does not know whether he will stay for at least ten days at his destination or not, then he must shorten his prayers so long as he is uncertain, for up to thirty days. After thirty days, he must offer full prayers, even if he does not intend to stay for ten [more] days, and even if he plans to travel before ten days have elapsed.
2. The above ruling is for someone who remains in this state of uncertainty for thirty days somewhere that is customarily treated as single location. If he spends this amount of time in a number of different locations, or during a continuous journey, he should continue to shorten his prayers even after thirty days.

Rules for mistakes in the traveller's prayer

1. If a traveller offers full prayers while he should have offered shortened ones, the ruling is as follows:
   a. If a traveller was aware of the ruling to shorten his prayers and he intentionally prays a complete four-unit prayer, then his prayer is invalidated.

b. If he offers a complete prayer because he was unaware of the obligation to shorten it, then he does not need to repeat his prayer.
c. If he knew the ruling for shortening his prayers on a journey, but was unaware of some of its details pertaining to rulings for a traveller and offered full prayers, then he must either repeat the prayer if its time has not lapsed, or compensate for it if it has.
d. If he knew the ruling for shortening his prayers on a journey, but he was unaware that this particular journey required him to shorten his prayers (e.g., he thought that the route he was taking did not meet the distance requirement, while actually it did) and so offered full prayers, he must either repeat or compensate for his prayers.
e. If he forgot that he was travelling, or he forgot the ruling for shortening his prayers, and remembers while the time for the prayer has not lapsed, then he must repeat the prayer shortened. If he remembers after the time for prayer has lapsed, then it is obligatory precaution to compensate for the prayer if he had forgotten the ruling, but not if he had forgotten he was travelling.
f. If he was aware of the ruling and aware that he was travelling, but he offered full prayers because of inattentiveness, then his prayer is also invalid, and he must either repeat or compensate it.

2. In the case of someone begins a four-unit prayer with the intention of offering it fully, forgetting that he is travelling or [forgetting] the ruling itself, only to remember during the prayer: if he remembers before bowing in the third unit, then he should complete the prayer in its shortened form and this suffices him. But if he remembers after bowing in the third unit, his prayer is invalid and he must repeat it shortened.
3. If someone must offer full prayers – such as one who resides somewhere for ten days – but begins a four-unit prayer with the intention of shortening it, unaware of his duty, and then realizes this during the prayer, then he must change his intention to offering the full prayer, and his prayer will still be valid.

Second: Prayers in conditions of fear and danger (*ṣalāt al-khawf wa al-muṭārada*)

1. In conditions of fear or danger, four-unit prayers can be offered shortened like the traveller's prayer, irrespective of whether the worshipper is travelling, praying in congregation, or praying individually.
2. By 'fear' (*khawf*), we mean any fear that requires him to shorten his prayer. In other words, shortening his prayer helps assuage his fears and gives him a greater opportunity to deal with the situation. This fear

could be the result of a war or military confrontation, being pursued by an oppressive enemy, by security forces, by criminals or by predatory animals, and anything like this. If shortening the prayers helps the worshipper better deal with the enemy, escape or hide in these circumstances, then it is obligatory to offer the prayer of fear.

3. As for situations where a person is overcome by fear, but it does not require him to shorten or otherwise hurry his prayers—for example, if he is afraid of an enemy, or on the battlefield, but he is staying somewhere for long enough to offer his prayers fully and in the normal manner—then he should offer them fully, so long as he is not travelling.

Danger prayers

4. By 'danger' (*muṭārada*) we mean a situation where battle with an enemy has been joined or one is actually engaged in fighting [or evading] criminals, wild animals, or any other dangerous situation which does not allow him to offer his prayers in the normal fashion, whether fully or shortened.
5. Because prayers can never be abandoned under any circumstances, a Muslim who finds himself in these situations must pray in any manner possible: sitting, standing, lying down, walking or riding, facing the *qibla* or not; and he must fulfil whatever parts of the conditions of prayer possible. Anything he cannot perform, he must do something else in its place: if he cannot bow or prostrate, he should incline his head; and if he cannot do that, then he should indicate [bowing or prostration] with his eyes; and if he cannot do any of these, then he must recite *tasbīḥ*, saying in place of each *rakʿa* (unit): '*subḥān allāh wa'l-ḥamdu lillāh wa lā ilāha ill allāhu wallāhu akbar*.' He should try to open his prayer by reciting *takbīrat al-iḥrām* while facing the *qibla*, if possible. If he offers his prayers in this fashion, they are still valid and – God-willing – there is no need to repeat them or compensate for them later.
6. Those in dangerous situations, such that prevent them from prayer in its conventional fashion, should reduce their prayers in length and in fashion as they would in situations of fear and travelling. But, when they are neither travelling, nor in fear of attack, they should only reduce the physical form in which they pray (i.e., not the number of units). For example:
    a. Someone who is being thrown about by waves in the middle of the ocean, waiting to be rescued.
    b. A mountain climber who fell and is now hanging by his rope waiting for someone to help him.

c. A parachutist whose canopy gets caught on something tall and leaves him suspended in mid-air.

   d. A prisoner in a tiny cell which only has enough space for him to stand, sit or lie down, or someone who is held restrained to a chair or pillar for long periods of time.

Third: Compensating for missed prayers

The noble *sunna*:

❖ Zurāra said to the Imam 🕮: a man misses a prayer while traveling and remembers it when he is no longer traveling. So he said: 'He compensates for whatever he missed, so if it was the prayer of the traveler, then he performs it the same way even if he is no longer traveling. Alternatively, if he is traveling and wishes to compensate for a prayer missed while he was not traveling, he prays it in full, just as it was missed.'[517]

❖ Imam al-Ṣādiq 🕮 was asked about a man who forgot a prayer but cannot remember which one. So he said: 'He prays three, four, and two units. Thus, if it was *ẓuhr*, *ʿaṣr*, or *ʿishāʾ*, then he has prayed four, and if it was *maghrib* or *fajr*, then he prayed those too.'[518]

Rulings:

1. If someone misses a daily prayer in its allotted time, he must compensate for it outside of its time. It does not matter whether he missed it intentionally, accidentally, or due to ignorance, illness, or sleeping through the entire time of prayer.

2. A person must also compensate for a prayer if he realizes that it was invalid for any of the aforementioned reasons.

3. Someone who was unconscious (e.g., in a coma) for the duration of the time for obligatory prayers does not need to compensate for them. Someone who was intoxicated by alcohol or other mind-altering substances must make up for prayers he missed while in this state, whether he knew these substances were intoxicating or not, and whether he took them voluntarily and sinfully, or out of necessity or by force.

4. One can make up for obligatory prayers at any time of the day or night, whether travelling or at home. Any prayers missed while travelling must be shortened, and any prayers missed while at home must be offered in

---

[517] *Wasāʾil al-shīʿa*, v. 5, p. 359, ḥ. 1
[518] *Wasāʾil al-shīʿa*, v. 5, p. 365, ḥ. 2

full, irrespective of whether the worshipper is at home or travelling when he wishes to make up for them.

5. If someone misses a prayer while at the beginning of its time he was at home but by the end he was travelling, or the opposite, then the strongest opinion is that he must opt to perform whatever was obligatory upon him when the time for prayer lapsed. But it is precaution to offer both full and shortened compensatory prayers in this situation.
6. A worshipper does not need to offer compensatory prayers before offering those prayers whose time is currently in effect; so someone who owes compensatory prayers can occupy himself [first] with his current prayers even when there is ample time.
7. It is impermissible to appoint someone else to offer make up prayers on your behalf while you are still alive, even if you know that you will never be able to offer them all.

Making up for the missed prayers of parents

The noble *sunna*:

❖ Imam al-Ṣādiq ﷺ said: 'Prayer, fasting, pilgrimage, charity, piety, and supplication meet the deceased in his grave, and his reward their reward will be written for the one who performs them [on his behalf] as well as for the deceased.'[519]

Rulings:

8. It is the duty of the eldest son to make up for the missed [obligatory] prayers and fasts of his parents after their death, so long as these were not missed sinfully but because of a valid reason, and they had to compensate for them but were unable. However, it is obligatory precaution to make up for everything that they owed in prayers and fasts.
9. In the absence of a son, then it is precaution that the closest people—among the males—to the deceased should make up for his prayers and fasts as a collective obligation, and it is nearest to precaution that this duty proceeds in order of seniority.
10. If the deceased has left a will to employ someone to make up for the prayers and fasts he owes, this duty is lifted from the eldest son so long as the person hired performs it properly. This duty is also lifted if someone else volunteers to perform it.

---

[519] *Wasāʾil al-shīʿa*, v. 2, p. 655, ḥ. 3

11. It is unnecessary for the eldest son to personally make up for the deceased's prayers; he can also hire another person to compensate in place of the deceased, whereat the person he hires must intend to make up for the prayers and fasts of the deceased, not the son.

Fourth: Hired prayers

1. It is permitted to hire a person to make up for missed prayers and fasts, as well as any other acts of worship, on behalf of the deceased. It is also permitted for another to volunteer to do this for free.
2. Some jurists say that it is not permissible to hire those with impediments to prayer, especially those whose prayers must be offered by inclining their head for bowing and prostration, or who are unable to stand. There is a problem with this opinion, however, insofar as the essence of prayer is to remember Allah and the prayer of every person is according to their own individual duty. So the apparent ruling is that there is no problem in hiring people with impediments to prayer, though the path of precaution is obvious (namely, to observe the former view).
3. It is unnecessary for the hired individual to match the gender of the deceased. A man can be hired to perform a woman's worship, just as a woman can be hired to perform a man's, and the person hired always follows the rulings pertaining to their own gender with regards to issues such as loud or quiet recitation.

Fifth: Congregational prayer

Its definition

Congregational prayer is when one person imitates another in prayer – according to specific conditions that we shall mention – and follows him in the acts of prayer without going ahead of him. The one being led is called a 'follower' (*ma'mūm*), while the one leading is called a 'leader' (*imām*). And we will discuss the details, conditions, rules and etiquettes pertaining to this.

Its recommendation

The noble *sunna*:

- The Messenger of Allah ﷺ said: 'Whoever prays the five daily prayers in congregation, the best will be thought of him.'[520]
- It is narrated that Zurāra and al-Fuḍayl asked the Imam ؑ if prayer in congregation is obligatory. So he said: 'Prayer is obligatory, but not

---

[520] *Wasā'il al-shī'a*, v. 5, p. 371, ḥ. 4

gathering for all of the obligatory prayers. However, it is a *sunna*, and whoever abandons it—renouncing it and the congregation of believers—without reason has no prayer.'[521]

- Abū Saʿīd al-Khudrī has narrated that the Messenger of Allah ﷺ said: 'Congregational prayer is better than individual prayer by 25 degrees.'[522]

Rulings:

1. It is very highly recommended to pray all the obligatory prayers in congregation,[523] particularly the daily prayers. And this is strongly emphasized for the *fajr*, *maghrib*, and *ʿishāʾ* prayers, and for anyone who hears the call to congregational prayer.
   The exception to the obligatory prayers is that of circumambulation, as there is a question as to its validity when performed in congregation.
   Many narrations have been transmitted affirming the importance of congregational prayers, speaking of their reward and superiority, and criticizing those who abandon them.
2. Whoever avoids attending a congregation because he dislikes it, narrations state that he has no prayer (meaning his prayer is not accepted).
3. It also does not befit a believer to avoid attending a congregation at the slightest of excuses. Wherever you are when the time for prayer sets in, whether it is the shops, the office, the library, school or university, or even in the street, you should hasten to attend congregational prayers whenever possible, so long as you are not prevented by a genuine reason. A believer must take care to ensure that avoiding mosques and congregations does not become a habit for him, as this is the sign of a hypocrite according to the narrations.
4. Because the merit of congregational prayers and their highly recommended status are so indispensable in Islamic law, there is no room to deny them. Satan whispers to the believer about details of the branches of Islam to dissuade him from practicing them, such as making him doubt the justness of the *imām*, or his lack of knowledge about the *imām*, etc. Thus, the believer must always beware of these Satanic insinuations.

---

[521] *Wasāʾil al-shīʿa*, v. 5, p. 371, ḥ. 2

[522] *Wasāʾil al-shīʿa*, v. 5, p. 374, ḥ. 14

[523] And praying in congregation could even be obligatory for some prayers, as we will discuss.

Forming a congregation

The noble *sunna*:

❖ Zurāra has narrated that he asked Imam al-Ṣādiq 🕮: Can two men constitute a congregation? So the Imam said: 'Yes, and the follower stands to the right of the prayer leader.'[524]

❖ Al-Qāsim b. al-Walīd said: I asked the Imam 🕮 about a man who prays with another man, while there are women with them. He said: 'One man stands to the side of the other, and the women stand behind them.'[525]

Rulings:

5. On occasions other than the Friday and *ʿīd* prayers, a congregation needs only two people: an *imām* and a follower, whereat the follower stands to the right of the *imām*. However, the more members there are in a congregation, the more reward and merit it carries. As for Friday and *ʿīd* prayers, these congregations require at least five worshippers, one of whom is the *imām*.

6. For a congregation, it is necessary to specify the *imām* (in the intention of the follower), whether by name, description, or nomination, whether in one's mind or verbally. For example, intending to follow 'this *imām* at the front of the congregation' even if the follower does not know his name or any other details about him. It is invalid to follow another follower, so if someone is praying as a follower someone else cannot come and [intend] to follow him as if he were an *imām*.

Reaching the congregation

The noble *sunna*:

❖ It is narrated from Imam al-Riḍā 🕮: 'If you enter the mosque and find the first row is complete, then there is no problem if you stand in a second row by yourself, or wherever you like—and the best is near the prayer leader.'[526]

Rulings:

7. One can join the congregation by joining the *imām* at the beginning of the prayer, or at the beginning of each unit (*rakʿa*), during the recitation of the Qurʾān or – at the very latest – when the *imām* is bowing and

---

[524] *Wasāʾil al-shīʿa*, v. 5, p. 379, ḥ. 1
[525] *Wasāʾil al-shīʿa*, v. 5, p. 405, ḥ. 3
[526] *Mustadrak al-wasāʾil*, v. 6, p. 498, ḥ. 4 / Ḥ. 7302

before he begins to raise his head, even if he has already finished the *dhikr*.

8. If a worshipper pronounces *takbīrat al-iḥrām* intending to join the congregation while the *imām* is bowing, but the *imām* raises his head before the worshipper can bow, then the worshipper should act in one of three ways:
9. Switching his intention to pray individually and continuing with his prayer.
10. Remaining standing for as long as it takes for the *imām* to rise for the following *rakʿa* and then joining him.
11. Following the *imām* into prostration and all the other acts of prayer until he stands for his next *rakʿa*, but not counting those acts as constituting a *rakʿa*.
12. If someone is offering supererogatory prayers and a congregational begins, and the worshipper fears that he will miss the congregation if he continues with his own prayers, he is permitted – rather, it is recommended – to abort his prayers and join the congregation at its beginning.

Rows of congregation

The rows of congregation must be arranged according to the following four conditions:

First: Connection

The rows of the congregation must be straight and unified, without people scattered here and there. For this reason, the follower should stand behind the *imām* or to one side of him without there being a large gap, and individual followers – if they are abundant in number – should be connected to the *imām*, whether directly or through their proximal connections with others, either in front or to either side of them.

Any delay in pronouncing *takbīrat al-iḥrām* by the row in front does not affect the prayer of those behind them, so long as they are in a condition of being ready and prepared to pray. So it is valid for rows further back to pronounce *takbīrat al-iḥrām* before those rows in front of them, though it is recommended precaution that they wait.

Second: The absence of any barrier

There should not be any barrier between the *imām* and his followers that would prevent them from seeing him, or between one follower and another connected to the *imām*. This is the case if the followers are men, or women praying behind another woman. As for a barrier between a male *imām* and female followers, there is no problem with this so long as they are still able to follow the *imām* in his actions.

Third: Followers must not stand in front of the imām

It is a condition of congregation that a follower should not stand in front of the place of the *imām*; in fact, the follower should stand a little back and to the right of him if there is only one follower. If there is more than one follower, they should form a line standing behind the *imām*. If a person stands in front of the *imām* from the beginning of prayer, or moves in front of him during it, his congregational prayer is invalidated. Although the follower is allowed to stand level (in the same 'row') with the *imām*, it is precaution to stand at least a little back from him.

Fourth: The imām *must not stand in an elevated position*

The place where the *imām* stands must not be even a step higher than the place where his followers are standing, as in buildings, though this does not apply if the difference in elevation is slight (less than twenty centimetres, for example).

There is no problem with the follower standing at a higher elevation than the *imām*, such as on the roof of a house or shop, so long as this does not invalidate the unity of the congregation.

Rules of congregational prayer

The noble *sunna*:

❖ Imam al-Ṣādiq ﷺ was asked about reciting behind the prayer leader. So he said: 'No, for the prayer leader is responsible for recitation [of the two chapters], and not for the prayer of those who are behind him. He is only tasked with the recitation.'[527]

❖ ʿAbd al-Raḥmān b. al-Ḥajjāj said: I asked Abū ʿAbd Allah ﷺ about praying behind a prayer leader: do I recite [the two chapters] behind him? So he said: 'As for prayers which are not recited aloud (i.e., those recited at a whisper), those are made for him, so do not recite behind him. And as for prayers which are recited aloud (i.e., above a whisper), only he has been commanded to recite aloud in order to be heard behind

---

[527] *Wasāʾil al-shīʿa*, v. 4, p. 421, ḥ. 1

him. So if you heard, then listen, and if you heard nothing, then recite.'[528]

❖ 'Alī b. Ja'far asked his brother, Imam Mūsā b. Ja'far 🕮, about a man who prays behind the prayer leader, following him in the two afternoon prayers: should he recite [the two chapters]? He said: 'No, but he glorifies and praises his Lord (i.e., he recites *subḥān allāh* or *al-ḥamdu lillāh*), and sends blessings upon his Prophet 🕮.'[529]

❖ It is narrated that the Imam 🕮 was asked about a man who comes to prayer and prays one unit of *maghrib* with the *imām*, and it is his first unit while he knows the peopl are in their second unit: does he recite *tashahhud* with them? He said: 'Yes.' It was asked: And the second as well? He said: 'Yes.' It was asked: All of them? He said: 'Yes; it is but a blessing.'[530]

❖ Jamīl b. Ṣāliḥ has reported that he asked Imam al-Ṣādiq 🕮: Which is better: for a man to pray by himself at the outset of the time for prayer, or for him to delay a little and pray with the people of the mosque, if he was their prayer leader? He said: 'Delaying and praying with the people of the mosque [is better], if he was the prayer leader.'[531]

Rulings:
First: Recitation

The follower in a congregation must perform all the parts of the prayer, whether these are words or actions, except for reciting *al-Fātiḥa* and another *sūra* in the first two units, since the *imām* recites these on behalf of the follower. This is assuming that the follower is performing the first and second *rak'ats* at the same time as those of the *imām*. However, if he is performing his first or second units while the *imām* is in his third and fourth units (such as if the follower joined the congregation late), then the follower must also recite for himself. Some details of this are as follows:

1.   The follower in congregational prayers must forgo the Qur'ānic recitation in the first two *rak'ats* of prayers which are offered aloud (*fajr*, *maghrib*, and *'ishā'*) if he can hear the sound of the *imām*, even if he cannot hear it clearly. If he cannot hear the sound of the *imām*

---

[528] *Wasā'il al-shī'a*, v. 5, p. 422, ḥ. 5
[529] *Wasā'il al-shī'a*, v. 5, p. 426, ḥ. 3
[530] *Wasā'il al-shī'a*, v. 5, p. 467, ḥ. 1
[531] *Wasā'il al-shī'a*, v. 5, p. 388, ḥ. 1

– not even a murmur – then it is recommended that he recite *al-Fātiḥa* and another *sūra* quietly.
2. In those prayers which are offered quietly (*ẓuhr* and *ʿaṣr*), it is recommended precaution to forgo recitation, whereat it is also recommended to occupy oneself with *dhikr* of Allah and sending blessings on Muḥammad and his Household.
3. In the third and fourth units, however, the obligation to recite the Qurʾān [on the part of the follower] or *tasbīḥ* remains.

Second: Following the *imām*'s actions

1. It is impermissible for a follower in congregation to precede the *imām* in the acts of prayer, or to delay following them, to such an extent that it violates the outward form of the congregation. It is obligatory to follow the *imām*, either by performing the act at the same time as him, or [only] slightly afterwards.
2. If the follower accidentally raises his head from bowing or prostration before the *imām*, or thinking that the *imām* had already raised his head, he must go back and follow the *imām* if the latter is still bowing or in prostration, and his prayer is still valid.

Third: Following the *imām*'s words

It is unnecessary to copy the *imām*'s words, whether in recitation, *tasbīḥ*, or *dhikr*, whether these are obligatory or supererogatory, and whether the follower can hear the *imām*'s words or not. It is unnecessary for the follower to recite his own words at the same time or after the *imām*, although, if he does, it is recommended precaution to recite them a little after him, especially in *taslīm*.

The exception to this rule is *takbīrat al-iḥrām*; the follower is not allowed to precede the *imām* in this, and it is precaution to delay pronouncing that *takbīr* until after the *imām*.

Fourth: Being late for a congregation

If someone is late for a congregation and only reaches it while the *imām* is in his second, third or fourth units of prayer, they should pronounce *takbīrat al-iḥrām* and join the congregation, treating this as their first unit. Then they should follow the congregation until the *imām* recites *taslīm*, and afterwards they should complete whatever unit remain of their prayer individually [although it would still be counted as a congregational prayer]. This ruling has the following corollaries:

1. If the worshipper offers the first or second unit of his prayer at the same time as the third or fourth of the *imām*, he must recite *al-Fātiḥa* and another *sūra*. If the *imām* does not leave him sufficient time to do so[532], he can restrict himself to reciting just *al-Fātiḥa*.
2. If the worshipper joins a congregation before the *imām* bows in the third or fourth unit, then he must recite *al-Fātiḥa* and another *sūra*, and if there is not enough time for both, he can suffice himself with *al-Fātiḥa*. And if, when he reaches the congregation, he knows that the *imām* will not leave him enough time to recite even *al-Fātiḥa*, then he should wait until the *imām* bows and then join him in bowing without needing to recite.
3. If the *imām* sits for *tashahhud* in the second unit while the follower is in his first unit, then it is precaution for him to squat (*tajāfī*)[533] rather than sitting completely, but also to follow the *imām* in reciting the *dhikr* of *tashahhud*.
4. A follower who is one unit behind the *imām* must recite *tashahhud* in the second unit of his own prayer (which will be the third of the *imām*). In this case, he must fall behind the *imām*, recite *tashahhud*, and then join the *imām* standing, or bowing while having recited the formula of *tasbīḥ* at least once.

The imām *of the congregation*

The noble *sunna*:

- Abū ʿAlī b. al-Rāshid said: I asked Abū Jaʿfar ﷺ: Verily your followers differ among each other; should I pray behind all of them? So he said: 'Do not pray except behind one whose religion you trust.'[534]
- It is narrated from Imam Jaʿfar b. Muḥammad ﷺ as part of a longer narration: 'It is preferable to pray the prayer at the outset of its time, and the merit of congregational prayer over individual prayer is twenty-four [degrees]. But prayer behind someone who knowingly sins in his actions (a *fājir*) is invalid; and [one must] pray only behind the people of *walāya* (i.e., the prayer leader must be a Twlever Shīʿa).'[535]

---

[532] Meaning that reciting the additional *sūra* would delay him such that the form of congregational prayer would be lost.

[533] Squatting (*tajāfī*) here means a state between sitting and getting up, such that the worshipper lifts his knees of the earth, sitting on his haunches and supporting himself with his fingers.

[534] *Wasāʾil al-shīʿa*, v. 5, p. 388, ḥ. 2

[535] *Wasāʾil al-shīʿa*, v. 5, p. 392, ḥ. 6

- Abū Jaʿfar has narrated from the Commander of the Believers ﷺ: 'None should pray behind the insane or the son of adultery.'[536]

Rulings:

1. To be an *imām* of a congregational prayer, one must have the following qualities:
   a. Legal maturity (*bulūgh*) according to precaution, although some traditions state that a boy who has not yet matured can still lead prayers.
   b. Sanity.
   c. Faith (that is, he must be a Twelver Shīʿa).
   d. Justness.
   e. Legitimate birth.
   f. Male (if some or all of the followers are men); a woman can only lead other women.

Justness

2. What does it mean to be just (*ʿādil*)? It means for someone to have the spirit of piety and a characteristic deeply rooted in the soul (a habit or *malaka*), which prevents him from committing major sins or persisting in minor sins, and from any act which is contrary to honourable behaviour and would suggest a lack of concern for his religion.
   It is not necessary to investigate whether someone is just, rather it is sufficient that his good public persona demonstrates his justness, or at least gives one grounds for believing in it.
3. In establishing the justness of an *imām* whom the worshipper does not know personally, anything that gives him a feeling of confidence or trust suffices. For example: the testimony of two just witnesses or even one, being informed by a group of people, seeing two just persons following him [in prayer] or any individual [following him] who gives him confidence in the *imām*, or seeing a group of the faithful following him. All of these things [are sufficient to] yield confidence.

Sixth: Friday prayers

Allah says: **'O you who have faith! When the call is made for prayer on Friday, hurry toward the remembrance of Allah, and leave all business.**

---

[536] *Wasāʾil al-shīʿa*, v. 5, p. 397, ḥ. 2

That is better for you, should you know. And when the prayer is finished disperse through the land and seek Allah's grace, and remember Allah greatly so that you may be felicitous. When they sight a deal or a diversion, they scatter off towards it and leave you standing! Say, "What is with Allah is better than diversion and dealing, and Allah is the best of providers.'"[537]

The Qur'ān considers Friday to be a holiday (*ʿīd*) for the *umma* (community, or nation), and emphasizes that Islam is unique not only in its message as compared to previous religious communities, but in its rituals as well. Jews and Christians, for example, have their own messages – the Torah and the Bible – and their own sacred days (Saturday and Sunday), but in *Sūrat al-Jumuʿa* the Qur'ān gives Friday prayers and the day of Friday itself their true significance in the Islamic way of life. From the outside, this is a symbol of Islam's independence as a religious tradition, while from the inside it is a symbol of unity and harmony.

And it is from these considerations and others that the divine call emanates to hasten to the Friday prayer and leave behind whatever it is you are doing, be it amusement, trade, or the other worldly affairs. Hence, the Friday prayer, for some Muslim sects and scholars, is an obligatory practice when its conditions are met.

However, many Muslim scholars consider the presence of an Islamic government and the Just Imam [from the Prophetic Household] as prerequisites for establishing the Friday prayer. Perhaps this centres on the fact that the Friday prayer serves both a religious and political function, and oppressors should not be allowed to use it to misguide the people and strengthen their own grip on power. It is one of the clearest and most important occasions for which Muslims gather, which the tyrants can take as a popular platform to misguide society. When we study history, we see how the sermons of Friday prayers were used to wage war against Allah's *awliyā'*, just as the Umayyad dynasty used them to preach against Imam ʿAlī ﷺ and the Prophet's Household ﷺ in general. Today, we see corrupt scholars turning the Friday sermons into a mouthpiece for the oppressors to the extent that they receive their sermons pre-written from the government itself and take a salary for this!

In this vein, a tradition has been narrated from Imam ʿAlī ﷺ in the book *Daʿā'im al-Islām*: 'There is no government, no corporal or capital punishment, and no Friday prayer except with an *imām*.'

---

[537] Sūrat al-Jumuʿa (62):9-11

Friday is a holiday for the Muslims, and it is the foremost day of the week. Its eve[538] is a night of worship and prayer, in which it is recommended to increase one's supplication to Allah, occupy oneself with recommended acts of worship, visit graves in remembrance of death, invoke Allah's mercy upon their occupants, and learn from their fate. This is especially true for the graves of the Imams of Guidance عليهم السلام, and the shrine of the Master of Martyrs, Abū ʿAbd Allah al-Ḥusayn عليه السلام. It is also a time to renew one's pledge with Allah's Messenger, his Household, and Imam al-Ḥujja عليه السلام, to remain steadfast on the path of the message of Islam.

One should also keep in touch with relatives, attend to the poor, and exchange visits with one's brethren on this noble day.

It is also fitting to hold oneself to account on this day and renew one's resolve to regularly perform righteous deeds and resist deviation and misguidance.

Generally speaking, Friday is not a day for play and diversion, or a day to be occupied with trivial things. Rather, it is an opportunity for the faithful to dedicate their time to worshipping and remembering Allah with the best of deeds, in that the Friday prayer is distinguished by its duties, sermons and social significance.

Thus, every believer is tasked with obeying this divine command so long as he does not have a religiously valid reason for not doing so; and as Allah calls every week for the Friday prayer, this duty remains a measure of the unity of the *umma* and the strength of their faith, in relation to their undertaking this important religious duty.

The noble *sunna*:

- Imam al-Bāqir عليه السلام said: 'The Friday prayer is obligatory, and gathering for it is mandatory with the Imam. Whoever abandons it for three consecutive Fridays without a valid excuse has abandoned three obligatory acts, and no one leaves three obligatory acts except a hypocrite.'[539]
- The Prophet ﷺ said: 'Verily Allah has made the Friday prayer obligatory upon you [all] until Judgment Day.'[540]

---

[538] Meaning the night that comes before it, as the Islamic day begins at sunset. Thus, the Islamic day of Friday begins on Thursday following sunset.

[539] *Wasāʾil al-shīʿa*, v. 5, p. 4, ḥ. 8

[540] *Wasāʾil al-shīʿa*, v. 5, p. 6, ḥ. 22

- In one of his sermons, the Commander of the Believers ﷺ said: 'The Friday prayer is obligatory upon every believer, except children, the sick, the insane, the elderly, the blind, the traveler, the woman, the slave, and whoever is two *farsakhs* away (approximately 6 miles).'[541]
- Muḥammad b. Muslim said: I asked the Imam ﷺ about the Friday prayer. So he said: 'It is [established] with *adhān* and *iqāma*. The prayer leader comes out after the *adhān*, ascends the *minbar* (pulpit), and delivers a sermon. The people do not pray so long as the prayer leader is on the *minbar*. Then the prayer leader sits on the *minbar* for as long as it takes him to recite *qul huwa allāhu aḥad* (i.e., *Sūrat al-Ikhlāṣ*), and stands to deliver the [second] sermon. Then he descends and leads the people in prayer. He leads them in the first unit with the chapter *al-Jumuʿa*, and in the second with *al-Munāfiqūn*.'[542]
- And in another narration it is mentioned: 'And the prayer leader must perform two *qunūts* in it: one in the first unit before bowing, and again in the second unit after bowing.'[543]

Rulings:

How to offer the Friday prayer

1. The Friday prayer takes the place of *ẓuhr* prayers on this day, and whoever prays it on time does not need to offer *ẓuhr*.
2. The Friday prayer consists of two units like *fajr* prayers, and it is precaution [for the leader of the congregation] to recite them aloud, in addition to the the necessary sermons.
3. The two sermons read before the prayer are considered a part of it.
4. It is permitted to recite any *sūra* in addition to *al-Fātiḥa* in the two units, although it is recommended to recite *al-Jumuʿa* in the first *rakʿa* and *al-Munāfiqūn* in the second.
5. It is also recommended to perform two *qunūts* during it; the first one before bowing in the first unit, and the second after bowing in the second unit.

The time of the Friday prayer

6. The time for the Friday prayer begins as the sun moves past its zenith – like *ẓuhr* prayers – and its time ends, as a matter of precaution, when a thing's shadow becomes equal to it in length.

---

[541] *Wasāʾil al-shīʿa*, v. 5, p. 3, ḥ. 6
[542] *Wasāʾil al-shīʿa*, v. 5 p. 15, ḥ. 7
[543] *Wasāʾil al-shīʿa*, v. 5, p. 2, ḥ. 2

7. According to precaution, when this time comes to an end, the Friday prayer lapses and it will not suffice the worshipper to perform it outside of its time, nor can he make up for it. Instead, it is obligatory for him to perform *ẓuhr* in this situation, and it is precaution to delay offering *ẓuhr* prayers until one is certain that the time for the Friday prayer has lapsed.
8. If the time for the Friday prayer ends while one is praying [it], he should finish his prayer and it will be considered valid, whether he is leading the congregation or following.
9. Whoever is obliged to perform Friday prayers must hasten to them and not suffice himself with *ẓuhr* prayer, unless the time for the Friday prayer ends and he cannot reach it.

Conditions for Friday prayers

10. Friday prayers are offered in place of *ẓuhr* as an obligation under the following conditions:
    a. The presence of the Imam or one appointed by him.[544]
    b. A sufficient number of people in the congregation; at least five persons, one of whom is the *imām* (prayer leader).
    c. Reading the two sermons before the prayer.
    d. Performing Friday prayers in congregation; they cannot be performed individually.
    e. Ensuring that the distance between one Friday prayer and another is not less than a single parasang (about 3.5 miles or 5.7km).

The two sermons

11. According to precaution, each of the two sermons must contain praise of Allah and invocations of blessings upon the Prophet Muḥammad ﷺ and his Household عليهم السلام, admonitions, calling people to piety and reciting a brief *sūra* of the Qurʾān. [At least these components of the two sermons should be in Arabic.]
12. It is precaution, aside from Arabic components [mentioned above], that the rest of the sermons be spoken in the language of the worshippers.

---

[544] From the available legal indicators, it is apparent that the position of the Friday prayer leader is an appointment made by the position of General Authority (*al-walāyat al-ʿāmma*), which belongs to the Just Imam. The order of priority for one who leads the prayer is as follows: The Infallible Imam, his specifically appointed deputy, his general deputy, and in their absence it is permissible to establish Friday prayers with their general permission for one who does not fear doing so, and who is capable of delivering a sermon to the people. And Allah knows best.

13. The sermons must be read out before the prayer and not after it.
14. The preacher must deliver the sermons standing, so long as he is able to do so.
15. The preacher must leave a gap between the two sermons by sitting down briefly.
16. The sermon must be delivered with a voice raised loud enough for at least the minimum number of people in the congregation to hear it (four persons). In fact, all the worshippers should be able to hear it, even if this requires a loudspeaker.
17. It is recommended precaution to remain still while the sermons are being delivered and for the preacher to be in a state of ritual purity.
18. It is obligatory precaution for the members of the congregation to remain silent and hear the sermon, though it is best that they actively pay attention to its content as well.
19. The first sermon can be delivered before the sun has moved from its zenith so long as it lasts until that time, and afterwards it must include the obligatory parts of the sermon mentioned above.
20. It is precaution that the preacher and the *imām* be the same person whenever possible.
21. The preacher should be articulate, eloquent, and aware of the needs his day and age and the interests of the Muslims. He must act upon what he admonishes people to do, so that his admonitions will have an effect on their hearts.

    The preacher must also deal with the contemporary social and political issues affecting the Muslims in his sermon, address their spiritual and material problems, and direct them to hold fast to the bonds of faith.
22. It is recommended that the preacher wears a turban and leans upon a staff or a weapon [such as a sword], that he sit upon the *minbar* during the noontime *adhān*, beginning his sermon after it, and that he gives a greeting of peace to all of the congregation before beginning his sermon.

Who must attend?

23. Friday prayers are obligatory – in times when they can be obligatory – on anyone who is:
    a. Legally mature and of sound mind.
    b. Male (women are not counted for the number of required participants, even though their prayers are valid should they attend the congregation).
    c. Free (i.e., not a slave).

d. Residing in the land [where the Friday prayer is held] (i.e., not travelling)
e. Not suffering from blindness, disability, or illness.
f. Not an elderly man for whom it is difficult to attend the prayers.
g. Not more than two parasangs (approximately 11.4 km or 7 miles) from the place where Friday prayers are held.

Rules for the Friday prayer

24. Anyone who does not possess all of the above qualities (e.g., a woman, elderly man, slave, or traveller) can still pray in the Friday congregation and his prayers will be valid in place of *ẓuhr*.
25. If Friday prayers are obligatory and their time begins, it is not permissible for a man to miss them even by travelling, unless there is something so important that his individual duty to attend the Friday prayer is suspended, and failing to attend to it immediately will cause him legally-recognized unbearable hardship.

    It is also unlawful for him to miss any part of the prayer (including the sermons), even if he is busy with other things such as business.
26. The *imām* of the Friday prayer must meet all the conditions that apply to the *imām* of any congregational prayer, just as all of the rulings pertaining to congregational prayer also apply here.
27. If the congregation disperses before the prayer begins – whether during the sermons or after them – and there are less than four followers left, the obligation for the Friday prayer is suspended, and offering *ẓuhr* prayers becomes obligatory. But if the worshippers disperse *during the prayer* such that there are less than four followers in the congregation, then it is precaution to complete the Friday prayer, and then perform the *ẓuhr* prayer as well.
28. If someone reaches the Friday congregation after the sermons have been read, his prayer is still valid. And if the *imām* is already in his second unit of prayer, that person may still join the congregation, completing his prayers after the *imām* has recited *taslīm* (the greeting of peace).
29. Doubting the number of units offered in the Friday prayer invalidates it.

Seventh: *ʿĪd* prayers

The noble *sunna*:

- Imam al-Ṣādiq ﷺ said: 'The prayers of the two *ʿīds* are mandatory.'[545]
- Imam al-Bāqir ﷺ said: 'There is no prayer for the day of *fiṭr* or *aḍḥā* except with a just prayer leader.'[546]
- It is narrated from Imam al-Ṣādiq ﷺ: 'Whoever could not attend the congregation of the people for the two *ʿīds* should perform *ghusl*, spruce himself up with whatever he can find, and pray alone in his house as he would pray in the congregation.'[547]
- In a tradition from Imam al-Ṣādiq ﷺ it is narrated: 'The sermon [for the prayers] of the two *ʿīds* is after the prayer.'[548]
- Imam al-Ṣādiq ﷺ said: 'One should not perform the prayers for the two *ʿīds* in a covered mosque or house. It should only be prayed in a desert or an open field.'[549]

Rulings:

1. Prayers on the two *ʿīds* – *Fiṭr* and *Aḍḥā* – are obligatory in congregation in the presence of an Infallible Imam ﷺ when the necessary conditions for the performance of Friday prayers are met. As for during the Occultation of the Imam, it is recommended to offer them in congregation or individually, except if there is a righteous leader, as represented by a jurist with authority over the *umma* (the global community of believers).
2. In the state of recommendation (i.e., during the Occultation and in the absence of a righteous leader [such that the prayer becomes recommended rather than imperative]), it is unnecessary for the conditions of Friday prayers to be met.
3. The time for *ʿīd* prayers are between sunrise on the day of *ʿīd* until the sun passes its zenith on the same day.
4. *ʿĪd* prayers consist of two units performed as follows:
    a. Takbīrat al-iḥrām.
    b. In the first unit, one recites *al-Fātiḥa* and another *sūra*.
    c. Five *takbīrs*, with a *qunūt* after each *takbīr*.
    d. Then a *takbīr* followed by bowing.

---

[545] *Wasāʾil al-shīʿa*, v. 5, p. 94, ḥ. 1
[546] *Wasāʾil al-shīʿa*, v. 5, p. 95, ḥ. 1
[547] *Wasāʾil al-shīʿa*, v. 5, p. 98, ḥ. 1
[548] *Wasāʾil al-shīʿa*, v. 5, p. 112, ḥ. 11
[549] *Wasāʾil al-shīʿa*, v. 5, p. 117, ḥ. 2

   e. Then two prostrations, followed by standing for the second unit.
   f. In the second unit, one recites *al-Fātiḥa* and another *sūra*, then performs four *takbīrs* with a *qunūt* after each one.
   g. Then a *takbīr*, followed by bowing, followed by two prostrations, *tashahhud* and *taslīm*.
5. It is obligatory to read out two sermons after prayer whenever the prayer is obligatory (i.e., during the age of an Infallible Imam or during the Occultation in the presence of a righteous leader). As for in situations where *ʿīd* prayers are recommended, it is precaution to give two sermons when these prayers are performed in congregation.
6. As in all other prayers, the *imām* of the congregation recites *al-Fātiḥa* and another *sūra* on behalf of his followers. As for *takbīrs*, *dhikrs*, supplications, etc., each follower must recite them himself.

Eighth: The prayer of signs (*ṣalāt al-āyāt*)

Occasions

1. It is obligatory to perform the prayer of signs on the following occasions:
   a. A solar eclipse.
   b. A lunar eclipse.
   c. An earthquake, even if it does not cause fear.
   d. Any natural phenomenon (in the heavens or on the earth) which causes fear, such as dust storms, intense darkness, thunder and lightning, volcanic eruptions, landslides, avalanches, etc., so long as these events frighten the majority of people in the area.

Timing

2. The prayer of signs for solar and lunar eclipses is from their beginning until their end.
3. For earthquakes and all other terrifying natural phenomena which do not last a long time, they have no specific time for the prayer of signs. Instead, it is obligatory to pray as soon as the sign has appeared. And if one delays the prayer, whether sinfully or out of necessity, the obligation remains in effect for the rest of his or her life [until he prays it], and they must pray it with the intention of praying on-time at whatever time they choose to offer it.

Method

4. The prayer of signs is two units and each unit has five bows and two prostrations. It is offered as follows:

a. Takbīrat al-iḥrām
b. Recite *al-Fātiḥa* and another *sūra*, then bow
c. Rise from bowing and recite *al-Fātiḥa* and another *sūra*, then bow
d. Repeat a total of five bows in this manner
e. After rising from the fifth bow, go down into two prostrations, before standing up for the second unit
f. The second unit is identical to the first, and the prayer is concluded with *tashahhud* and *taslīm*.

It is permissible for the worshipper to restrict himself to reciting *al-Fātiḥa* and another *sūra*, which he then divides into five parts, bowing after each. This functions as a substitute for repeating *al-Fātiḥa* and another *sūra* five times.

5. Everything that is obligatory or recommended in daily prayers, whether preliminaries, conditions, parts of prayer or *dhikr*s, is also obligatory and recommended (respectively) in the prayer of signs, except for the *adhān* and *iqāma*; they are not valid for the prayer of signs, instead it is recommended to say before the prayer: 'The prayer! The prayer! The prayer!'

Rules

6. Someone who knew that a solar or lunar eclipse would take place, but ignores it and does not pray, is sinful and he must compensate for the prayer. He must also compensate for it if he knew about them but forgot before the time for the prayer passed.
7. If someone did not know about the eclipse except after its time has passed, and the eclipse was total (whether solar or lunar), then he must compensate for the missed prayer. But if the eclipse was partial, he does not need to.
8. The obligation to perform the prayer of signs is only for the people of the geographic region where the natural phenomenon occurs.
9. If a woman is experiencing menstruation or puerperal bleeding (*nifās*) when the natural phenomenon occurs, then she does not need to perform the prayer of signs.

Ninth: Supererogatory prayers

It is narrated from Imam al-Ṣādiq and Imam al-Riḍā عليهما السلام: 'Prayer is the offering of every pious individual.'

A man came to Allah's Messenger ﷺ and said to him: 'Ask Allah to let me into Paradise!' to which the Messenger responded: 'Occupy yourself with abundant prostration.'

The Infallibles 🕮 have forbidden us from laziness and lassitude towards the worship of Allah. So whoever wishes to attain Paradise and the satisfaction of his Lord must strive for that, and the clearest way into Paradise is through offering voluntary prayers abundantly. Abū ʿAbd Allah al-Ṣādiq 🕮 said: 'Beware of laziness! Your Lord is most-merciful; He is grateful for even a little. Verily a man who prays two units of payer voluntarily, seeking Allah's countenance thereby, Allah shall admit him to Paradise!'

Imam al-Ṣādiq 🕮 would encourage his followers to increase their number of prayers because, as he says: 'The most beloved of deeds to Allah is prayer, which is the final testament of the prophets. How good it is that a man should bathe or perform ablutions, and have performed *wuḍū'* properly, then withdraw to a place no one else can see him, whereat Allah honours him while he bows and prostrates. Verily when a servant prostrates and prolongs his prostration, Iblīs calls out: 'Woe is me! They obey while I sinned; they bow while I refused.'

It befits a believer to seek nearness to Allah whenever he has the opportunity by performing voluntary prayers, for these prevent him from indecencies and wrongs, cleanse him of the impurity of vices and bad manners, elevate him to the highest levels of servitude to Allah, and release him from the bonds of matter and the shackles of desire.

Many narrations have come in this regard, encouraging people to offer supererogatory prayers at auspicious times and places, and at special times when they are seeking to strengthen their bonds with Allah. And we have highlighted some of these prayers in our detailed manual of law.

Fasting (*Ṣiyām*)

Fasting in the Qur'ān and *Sunna*

Allah Almighty has said: **'O you who have faith! Prescribed for you is fasting as it was prescribed for those who were before you, so that you may be pious.'**[550]

Fasting is an act of worship made obligatory on the faithful in this age, just as it was made obligatory for those who lived in previous ages. It is one of the pillars of the religion and marks of faith.

The purpose behind the act of fasting is to nurture the spirit of piety (*taqwa*); not just to practice restraining the self from its lawful desires, but to enable it to better resist unlawful ones. This is only because worship is, for the human being, to seek nearness to Allah and increase his piety, which is why our Exalted Lord says: **'O mankind! Worship your Lord, who created you and those who were before you, so that you may be pious.'**[551]

Elsewhere He says: **'The month of Ramaḍān is one in which the Qur'an was sent down as guidance to mankind, with manifest proofs of guidance and the Criterion. So let those of you who witness it fast [in] it, and as for someone who is sick or on a journey, let it be a [similar] number of other days. Allah desires ease for you, and He does not desire hardship for you, and so that you may complete the number, and magnify Allah for guiding you, and that you may give thanks.'**[552]

Why is the fast during the month of Ramaḍān? Because it is the month of the Qur'ān, and because the Qur'ān is Allah's book, with which He guides mankind towards the absolute truths and a straight path. As such, it is a book of manifest proofs which gives the final and decisive word on those truths needed by mankind. Hence it is the criterion by which truth can be separated from falsehood.

When a believer fasts in the month of Ramaḍān, he prepares his soul to receive the guidance of the Qur'ān, its manifest proofs, and its criterion separating truth from falsehood. Is it not the case, after all, that fasting nurtures piety, increases humility, and bestows tranquillity upon one's heart?

---

[550] Sūrat al-Baqara (2):183
[551] Sūrat al-Baqara (2):21
[552] Sūrat al-Baqara (2):185

Fasting – especially in the month of Ramaḍān – is one of Allah's sacred rituals, by which the Muslims honour their Lord, who has guided them to the truth. And is this truth not proclaimed within these acts of worship, full of manifold benefits?

The great benefits brought about by fasting require that a servant thank his Beneficent Lord, Who prescribed fasting for him, and blessed him with those benefits in this world and the next!

It has been narrated from Imam al-Riḍā 🖼 : 'They were only enjoined to fast that they might know the pain of hunger and thirst, and thereby realize their neediness of the Hereafter. [It was enjoined] so that the one who fasts might be humble, lowly, needy, employed [in the service of Allah], expecting recompense in the Hereafter, aware [of his Lord], patient in the face of the hunger and thirst which afflicts him; so that he might earn divine reward thereby as well as restrain his desires; and that this might be an admonition for them in this world, an exercise in discharging the duties He has imposed upon them, and a guide for them in the next.'

What is fasting?

The noble *sunna*:

❖ It is narrated from Imam al-Ṣādiq 🖼 : 'There is a *zakāt* (charitable tax) for everything, and the *zakāt* of the body is fasting.'[553]

❖ Imam al-Ṣādiq 🖼 said: 'Whoever [intentionally and prematurely] breaks his fast [even] one day during the month of Ramaḍān, the spirit of faith leaves him.'[554]

❖ Al-Ḥalabī said: I asked Abū 'Abd Allah (Imam al-Ṣādiq) 🖼 about [distinguishing] the white thread [of dawn] from the black thread. He said: 'The white thread of day from the black thread of night.' And he said: 'Bilāl and Ibn Umm Makhtūm would call the *adhān* for the Prophet 🖼. The latter was blind, and he would call the *adhān* while it was still night, whereas Bilāl would call the *adhān* when *fajr* was rising. So the Prophet 🖼 said: "If you hear the voice of Bilāl then refrain from food and drink, for morning has come to you."'[555]

❖ It is narrated form Imam al-Ṣādiq 🖼 : 'It is obligatory to break the fast at the time the sun sets. One should stand opposite the *qibla* and check to see if the redness has vanished from the east. When it has passed

---

[553] *Wasā'il al-shīʿa*, v. 4, p. 3, ḥ. 2
[554] *Wasā'il al-shīʿa*, v. 4, p. 176, ḥ. 12
[555] *Wasā'il al-shīʿa*, v. 4, p. 79, ḥ. 1

from overhead to the direction of the west, then breaking the fast becomes obligatory and the sun has set.'[556]

Fasting (*ṣawm*) literally means to refrain, give up, or restrain oneself from something. In religious terminology it means giving up certain things forbidden [during fasting] by the religion – such as eating, drinking, and sexual intercourse – during a specific time and under specific conditions. The intention behind fasting must be to seek nearness to Allah and to obey His command. The time of fasting is from true dawn (the white line on the horizon) until the legal sunset.

Fasting in the month of Ramaḍān is one of the most important acts of worship and a pillar of the religion. Its obligatory nature is known with certainty and the jurists have said that anyone who denies that has left the fold of Islam, insofar as to deny the duty to fast is tantamount to denying the prophetic message. Anyone who believes in its obligatory nature but does not practice it because he deems it unimportant is sinful.

Conditions for fasting

The noble *sunna*:

- Imam al-Ṣādiq ﷺ said: 'If a man dies and he is fasting while traveling, do not pray over him.'[557]
- ʿAbd al-Raḥmān has narrated that he asked Imam al-Ṣādiq ﷺ about a man who fasts during the month of Ramaḍān while he is traveling. He said: 'If it had not reached him that the Messenger of Allah forbid that, then he does not need to make up for it and his fast suffices him.'[558]
- Ayyūb b. Nūḥ said: I wrote to Abū al-Ḥasan the Third (al-Hādī) ﷺ, asking about someone who is unconscious for a day or more: does he need to compensate for what he has missed? So he ﷺ wrote: 'He does not need to make up for fasting or prayer.'[559]
- Al-Ḥalabī asked Imam al-Ṣādiq ﷺ about a woman who begins her morning fasting, and when the day or evening arrives she begins her period. Does she break her fast? He said: 'Yes, even if it was the time of *maghrib* she must break her fast.' [The narrator] said: And I asked him about a woman who is free of menses at the beginning of the day (i.e., after *fajr*) during the month of Ramaḍān, who performs *ghusl*, and has

---

[556] *Wasāʾil al-shīʿa*, v. 4, p. 9, ḥ. 1
[557] *Wasāʾil al-shīʿa*, v. 4, p. 124, ḥ. 9
[558] *Wasāʾil al-shīʿa*, v. 4, p. 121, ḥ. 2
[559] *Wasāʾil al-shīʿa*, v. 4, p. 161, ḥ. 1

not eaten: what should she do? He said: 'She breaks her fast that day because it was [already] broken by blood.'[560]

❖ Al-Ḥalabī said: Abū ʿAbd Allah al-Ṣādiq ﷺ was asked about a man who was in a state of major ritual impurity (*janāba*) during the month of Ramaḍān and forgot to perform *ghusl* until the month of Ramaḍān ended. He ﷺ said: 'He must make up for his prayers and fasts.'[561]

Rulings:

1. Islam is a condition for the acceptance of fasting, so when a non-believer embraces Islam, he does not need to compensate for those days of fasting he missed before this.
2. Legal maturity (*bulūgh*): fasting is not obligatory on a child until he or she reaches the age they can marry, although their fasts are still accepted.
3. A sound mind: fasting is not obligatory for someone who is insane and does not understand fasting.
4. Freedom from major ritual impurity during all hours of the day. Fasting is not obligatory for women experiencing menstrual or puerperal (post-childbirth) bleeding, and if a woman experiences bleeding before sunset, she must break her fast. If her bleeding continues even for a little after daybreak, her fast is invalid and she must make it up later.
   As for a woman who is spotting, she must perform whatever ablutions she needs to and her fast is valid so long as she observes her ablutions during the day.
5. Residency: someone who is travelling must break his fast, and compensate for it on other days of the year. The remainder of the traveller's rulings, which we have mentioned regarding prayer, also apply to fasting.
   a. An exception to fasting while on a journey are the three days one fasts during *ḥajj* if he cannot find a sacrificial animal.
   b. Also exempt from this rule is one who leaves ʿArafāt before sunset and cannot find a head of cattle; he must fast eighteen days in place of it.
   c. If someone travels after midday, he does not break his fast.
   d. If someone becomes a resident before midday and he has not already broken his fast, he should fast for that day.
6. Wellness: whoever fears serious harm to himself, his family, or his property as a result of fasting, he is allowed to break his fast, in fact he

---

560 *Wasāʾil al-shīʿa*, v. 4, p. 162, ḥ. 1
561 *Wasāʾil al-shīʿa*, v. 4, p. 170, ḥ. 4

is obliged to break his fast at this point because protecting himself from harm is a religious obligation.

The criterion for harm is that something might cause [legally valid] unbearable difficulty for him, or that repelling this harm is more important in the eyes of the Lawgiver than fasting, such as saving a life from loss, a woman's dignity from violation, a secret of the *umma* being disclosed, etc.

7. Health: someone who is ill must break his fast in the month of Ramaḍān, and then fast for an equivalent number of other days.
   Included in this ruling is someone who is healthy but fears illness as a result of fasting, or for whom fasting will cause unbearable difficulty (*ḥaraj*).

Rules for those unable to fast

1. Anyone too weak to fast due to old age or illness (like one suffering unbearable thirst, diabetes, kidney problems, etc.) must offer a redemption (*fidya*) for each day they do not fast by feeding a poor person with one measure (*mudd*) of foodstuff.
2. A woman who is too weak to fast because she is pregnant or breastfeeding, or who fears causing harm to her child, should break her fast, and give charity (*ṣadaqa*) for every day she does not fast by feeding a poor person one measure of foodstuff. It is precaution for her to make up for any fasts she has missed, if she is able, between now and the following Ramaḍān.
   If a breast-feeding woman finds someone who can wet-nurse her child, or can use formula for her child, then so long as this does not cause her distress (*ḥaraj*) or harm to the child, then she can fast, if Allah wills.
3. Whoever is afflicted with thirst and fears for himself may [break their fast and] drink the minimum needed to hold back it back, and should not quench it with water, according to one transmitted report.

Rules for the intention to fast

1. Because fasting is an act of worship, intention (*niyya*) is a precondition for its validity. This is because the essence of fasting is to avoid anything that would break your fast, and to resolve to deny yourself these things, so intention is a part of its essence. A Muslim must fast as an act of worshipping Allah, sincerely seeking His countenance; his act must not be contaminated by a desire to show off (*riyāʾ*), win reputation, or pursue anything besides his Lord.
2. If a person forms his intention to fast from the night before the fast, this is sufficient. There is no need for him to renew his intention at

daybreak or during the day; if he forgets he is fasting or falls asleep, this has no effect on the fast itself.

3. If someone intends to fast 'tomorrow', this will suffice him even if he does not specify that it is for the month of Ramaḍān, or was ignorant of the fact that it was.
4. It is not required to know all the things that will break your fast in detail; it suffices to fast by avoiding whatever things the *sharīʿa* bids him to avoid.
5. It is permitted to make the intention to fast after *fajr* prayers for a supererogatory fast. If someone does not intend to fast and then changes his mind to do so, then so long as he has not done anything that would have invalidated his fast, it is permissible. Likewise, it is permissible to do this for compensatory fasting for missed fasts in Ramaḍān until midday.
6. If someone intends to break his fast but then changes his mind before he does anything to break it, this does not affect his fast.

Fasting on a day of doubt (*yawm al-shakk*)

1. It is recommended to fast on a day when there is doubt about whether it is the first of Ramaḍān or not. This is done with the intention of fasting the last day of Shaʿbān, and a person can also intend to fast for a missed day of fasting. If he fasts in this manner, then learns that it is the first day of Ramaḍān, it suffices.
2. If someone does not intend to fast but learns during the day that it is Ramaḍān, and so long as it is before midday and he has not done anything that would have invalidated his fast, he must form the intention to fast, and his fast is valid. As for after midday, he must make the intention and fast, but it is precaution to make up for it as well.

Things which break the fast (*mufṭirāt*)

The noble *sunna*:

❖ Muḥammad b. Muslim said: I heard Abū Jaʿfar (al-Bāqir) ﷺ saying: 'The one who fasts is not harmed by whatever he does if he avoids three things: eating and drinking, women, and submerging himself in water.'[562]

[562] *Wasā'il al-shīʿa*, v. 4, p. 19, ḥ. 1

❖ Abū Baṣīr has narrated from Imam al-Ṣādiq 🕮: 'Fasting is [refraining] from food and drink, and [the one who fasts] should guard his tongue from nonsense and falsehood in Ramaḍān and any other time.'[563]

❖ It is narrated that Imam al-Riḍā 🕮 was asked about a person who, while he is fasting, encounters a cloud of smoke from incense, and the smoke reaches his throat. He said: 'It is permissible; there is no problem with it.' And he was asked about someone who is fasting and dust gets in his throat. He said: 'No problem.'[564]

❖ Samāʿa said: I asked the Imam 🕮 about a man who gargles water due to thirst, and some of it reaches his throat. He said: 'He must repeat his fast, although if it was from [gargling during] wuḍūʾ then there is no problem with that.'[565]

❖ Muḥammad b. Muslim has narrated from Abū Jaʿfar (Imam al-Bāqir) 🕮: 'O Muḥammad, beware of chewing gum, for I was doing so today and I was fasting, and I discovered something of it in myself.'[566]

❖ Al-Ḥalabī said: Abū ʿAbd Allah 🕮 was asked about a woman who is cooking while she fasts, and she tastes [but does not consume] the broth to check it. So he said: 'No problem.'[567]

❖ ʿAbd Allah b. Sinān has narrated from Abū ʿAbd Allah al-Ṣādiq 🕮, concerning a man who is thirsty during the month of Ramaḍān: 'It is no problem if he sucks on his ring.'[568]

Rulings:

Fasting means avoiding sexual intercourse, food, and drink, and each of these categories contains a number of sub-categories such as masturbation, foreplay for one who suffers premature ejaculation, and intentionally remaining in a state of major ritual impurity until daybreak.

The same applies to submerging oneself fully in water (according to one opinion), inhaling thick dust, taking an enema, or vomiting (as shall be detailed below).

We shall discuss each of these categories in detail by Allah's leave, beginning with the rules about the three major ones:

---

[563] *Wasāʾil al-shīʿa*, v. 4, p. 19, ḥ. 2

[564] *Wasāʾil al-shīʿa*, v. 4, p. 48. ḥ. 2

[565] *Wasāʾil al-shīʿa*, v. 4, p. 50, ḥ. 4

[566] *Wasāʾil al-shīʿa*, v. 3, p. 74, ch. 36, ḥ. 1

[567] *Wasāʾil al-shīʿa*, v. 4, p. 74, ch. 37, ḥ. 1

[568] *Wasāʾil al-shīʿa*, v. 4, p. 77, ḥ. 2

A – Rules for food and drink

One who is fasting must not consume any food or drink for as long as he is fasting. Here are some of the pertinent details and rules for this:

1. One who is fasting should clean his teeth before *fajr* so that no pieces of food remain between them; if any pieces remain, then it is most cautious that he avoids swallowing them.
2. There is no problem with swallowing saliva, even if it collects in the mouth and has a taste or viscosity. It is permissible to suck on a ring (typically the stone, to generate saliva) just as there is no problem with any saliva produced by thinking of food.
3. Mucus from the nasal cavity or from the chest does not invalidate the fast if swallowed, though it is recommended precaution to spit it out if it reaches the vicinity of the mouth.
4. One who is fasting must prevent anything that would lead to food or drink reaching his insides, such as drinking liquids through his nose via a tube, etc. As for putting medicine in his ears or eyes, there is no problem with this even if its taste reaches his throat.
5. One who is fasting must refrain from sustenance and fluid delivered through a needle. If he receives nutrition in this way, it is precaution to avoid all other things that could break his fast, and then make up for this day of fasting as well.

B – Sexual intercourse

1. Sexual intercourse is forbidden to men and women who are fasting, whether this leads to ejaculation or not.
2. Rectal intercourse is also forbidden and invalidates the fast of both parties.
3. Intercourse with eunuchs or animals is also forbidden as a matter of precaution (and both of them are major sins whether one is fasting or not).
4. Masturbation is also forbidden, and whoever seeks to climax whether by touching, kissing or even looking the other gender, images of them, or pornographic films, or even someone who attempts to ejaculate by imagining things, has invalidated his fast.
5. But if anyone does the above without intending to ejaculate, but then does so accidentally, there is nothing upon him.
6. It is precaution to avoid anything that might lead to ejaculation; so he should not touch his wife or even kiss her if he fears he might ejaculate. But someone who does not worry about this, yet it happens to him unexpectedly, there is nothing upon him.

7. Involuntary ejaculation while sleeping does not invalidate the fast, even if the one fasting knows that if he sleeps he will experience an emission, though it is best to avoid this so long as it does not cause him any difficulty.

Other things which invalidate the fast

1. Thick dust which is like food, or heavy vapour which is like drink, both invalidate the fast, hence the one fasting must avoid them. Normal dust and vapour do not invalidate the fast, though it is better to avoid them, and the same applies to smoke.
2. If someone enters a state of major ritual impurity the night before he is due to fast, he must purify himself before *fajr*. If he puts this off until daybreak comes, then he must make up for the fast of that day.
3. If someone puts off purifying himself [of major ritual impurity] and sleeps, or wakes up once and then goes back to sleep until morning, then he must make up for the fast of that day as well.
4. If someone experiences an emission or involuntary ejaculation during the day, he does not need to rush and perform *ghusl* straight away.
5. If someone experiences a night omission, or has intercourse with his wife, and then sleeps intending to perform *ghusl* before *fajr*, but sleeps until morning, then his fast remains valid.
6. Anyone who wakes up in the morning outside of the month of Ramaḍān in a state of major impurity, but performs *ghusl* and intends to perform a voluntary fast, he is permitted to do so. However, if he is compensating for a Ramaḍān fast, he must choose another day to do so, if he awakes in a state of major impurity.
7. If a woman finishes her menses, she must purify herself before *fajr*, and the same applies to a woman with puerperal bleeding, otherwise they must make up for their fasts if they had put off *ghusl* until morning.
8. According to precaution, a woman experiencing spotting must perform whatever daytime *ghusl*s are obligatory upon her in order for her fast to be valid. As for the *ghusl*s for *maghrib* and *ʿishāʾ*, these are not required for her fast to be valid, even though it is more appropriate that she does whatever her duty is while spotting, that her fast be complete.
9. The rulings for enemas are as follows:
    a. There is no problem with someone who is fasting inserting a suppository into his rectum.
    b. A liquid enema is forbidden according to precaution, and if someone who is fasting has one then he should make up for his fast as a matter of precaution.

10. Vomiting intentionally means that the fast must be made up for; vomiting unintentionally does not.

11. One of the greatest sins is to invent a lie about Allah, His Messenger ﷺ, or the Imams ؏, and this prohibition is strongly emphasized when one is fasting in the month of Ramaḍān. There is some hesitation as to whether this invalidates the fast or not, but it is recommended precaution that anyone who commits this sin must make up for his fast. In fact, he should renew his *wuḍū'* as well.

12. It is disliked to submerge oneself in water and it is recommended precaution to avoid this. It is best that anyone who does this also makes up for his fast.

Rulings regarding ignorance, error, and compulsion

1. Anyone who was wilfully ignorant of one of the things that would invalidate his fast and then does this while fasting, then if this was something that his fast does not depend on – such as waking up in a state of major ritual impurity, submerging himself in water (according to the opinion that this is prohibited), or vomiting – then his fast is valid, although it is recommended precaution to make up for his fast.
   If it was something which directly affects his fast, such as sexual intercourse, eating, or drinking, then he must make up for his fast but he need not offer expiation (*kaffāra*).

2. Whoever does something forbidden because he was ignorant of the ruling, but he is blameworthy for his ignorance, it is obligatory precaution that he make up for the fast, though there is hesitation about whether he must offer expiation.

3. Whoever eats or drinks forgetfully, there is nothing upon him (he should continue that fast), no need to make up the fast, and no expiation either.

4. If someone is physically forced to break his fast against his will, for example if he is force-fed, this does not invalidate his fast. If he is coerced into breaking his fast and does so [himself], then he need not offer any expiation, but there is hesitation about whether he must make up for the fast, and it is obligatory precaution that he makes up for it.

5. Whoever is compelled by necessity to break his fast does not need to offer expiation, but he must make up for the fast on another day.

6. Whoever is coerced into breaking his fast before the proper time of *maghrib* because of *taqiyya* (concealment of the true faith in order to protect one's life), he does not need to offer an expiation. There is hesitation about whether he must make up for the fast, although making up for it is in accordance with precaution.

7. If someone accidentally swallows water while rinsing his mouth, or food while tasting, or an insect flies down his throat, then his fast remains valid.

The ruling for someone who intentionally breaks his fast

1. The expiation for breaking one's fast [before the correct time] is one of three things, [for each day the fast is broken]: either freeing a slave, fasting for two consecutive months, or providing sixty poor persons with 750 grams of foodstuff such as bread, wheat, barley or any kind of food that will sustain them – and whoever cannot do this should give whatever charity he is able. It is best to follow the order given for these expiations beginning with freeing a slave, or if one is unable then fasting for two consecutive months, or if one is unable to do that, then feeding sixty poor persons.
2. Expiation is obligatory upon anyone who intentionally and knowingly breaks his fast without any [legally] valid excuse; eating, drinking, engaging in sexual intercourse, or failing to avoid ejaculation. As for someone who remains in a state of major ritual impurity until *fajr*, then it is obligatory precaution for him to offer expiation as well. As for someone who sleeps and does not awake to perform *ghusl* until *fajr*, he does not need to offer expiation.
3. If someone breaks his fast with something inherently unlawful, such as someone who fornicates during daylight hours in the month of Ramaḍān – we seek refuge in Allah! – then according to precaution, he must offer all three expiations together. And insofar as there are [usually] no slaves to free in this day and age, he must fast two consecutive months and feed sixty persons, and if he is unable to do either or both of these then let him seek Allah's forgiveness!

When is it obligatory to only make up for a fast?

1. If someone does not know that it is *fajr* and continues to do things that would invalidate his fast, only to realize that it is *fajr*, he must make up for that fast. It does not matter if this happened because he relied on the unsubstantiated word of someone else, presumed continuity (*istiṣḥāb*) of the night, or thought (*ẓann*) that it was not yet *fajr*. Of course, if he had checked the sky and did not see the signs of *fajr*, took the word of someone trustworthy, or was waiting for the *adhān*, only to later realize his mistake, then there is nothing upon him.
2. It is not permitted to break the fast until one knows that the disc of the sun has fully declined beneath the horizon (sunset), which is known by the absence of redness in the eastern sky. So if someone believes this to

be the case because he has relied on the word of someone trustworthy, or after checking himself, only to realize he has made a mistake, there is nothing upon him. Of course, if someone is hasty to break his fast before being certain, he must make up for that fast; for example, if the sky is filled with clouds and he believes it to be night [but did not investigate thoroughly].

3. Whoever makes himself vomit intentionally must make up for the fast of that day, but if someone burps and food comes out unintentionally, then there is nothing upon him.
4. Whoever rinses his mouth with water and swallows some accidentally, and if he was rinsing his mouth for no reason or to cool himself down, then he must make up for the fast. If he was rinsing his mouth for obligatory prayers, then there is nothing upon him. If it was for supererogatory prayers, then there are two opinions [in this regard] and it is obligatory precaution to make up for it.
5. Anyone who takes a liquid enema should make up for his fast, based on precaution.
6. Anyone in a state of ritual impurity who goes back to sleep until morning, though he had intended to perform *ghusl* before *fajr*, should fast for the rest of the day, but also make up for that day as a matter of precaution.
7. Whoever forgets to perform *ghusl* for major ritual impurity for some days of the month of Ramaḍān and does not make any other *ghusl* during them, whether obligatory or supererogatory, must make up for his fasts, just as he must make up for his prayers [from that period] according to the strongest opinion. And based on precaution he should also make up for fasts at times other than Ramaḍān, so if someone fasts the month of Rajab to make up for missed fasts or as expiation, then realizes he was in a state of major ritual impurity, he should repeat whatever was upon him.

   In the same way, this is precaution for a female who is fasting and forgets to perform *ghusl* after her menstruation, puerperal bleeding, or spotting.

Rules for making up missed fasts

The noble *sunna*:

❖ Al-Kulaynī has narrated—through a sound chain of transmitters—from Muḥammad b. Muslim, from one of the two Imams عليهما السلام, saying: I asked about a man who knew that it was Ramaḍān, and he was ill, and he died before he could become well. He عليه السلام said: 'He owes nothing. But compensation is due for the one who first becomes well again, and then dies before he can make up [his fasts missed due to illness].'[569]

❖ Al-Kulaynī has narrated—through a sound chain of transmitters—that al-Ṣaffār said: I wrote to [Imam al-ʿAskarī] 🕮, [asking him]: A man dies while owing ten days' worth of compensatory fasts for the month of Ramaḍān, and he has two executors. Is it permissible for each to perform five days of compensatory fasting for him? So his 🕮 missive read: 'The eldest executor performs ten days of compensatory fasting for him, God willing.' And al-Ṣadūq has reported this as well, and said: I possess this missive in his 🕮 handwriting.[570]

❖ Al-Kulaynī has narrated—through a sound route—from al-Ḥalabī, who said: I asked Abū ʿAbd Allah 🕮 about a man who still owes compensatory fasts for the month of Ramaḍān: can he perform supererogatory fasting? He said: 'Not until he compensates for what he owes from the month of Ramaḍān.'[571]

Rulings:

1. A Muslim must make up whatever fasts he has missed during the month of Ramaḍān after fasting became obligatory for him. As for any days he did not fast because he was a child, or a disbeliever, or insane, then he does not need to. The same applies to elderly men and women for whom fasting is too difficult; they should offer a redemption (*fidya*) for their fasts, and do not need to make up for them.

2. If someone misses a fast due to illness, and this illness persists until the following Ramaḍān, then he must offer a redemption of one measure (*mudd*) for each day he missed.

   The same applies to a woman who experiences bleeding and then is afflicted by an illness until the next Ramaḍān.

   The same applies to someone who travels for the duration of the year. It is precaution to make up for missed fasts.

3. It is precaution that a person not delay making up for missed fasts from one Ramaḍān until the following Ramaḍān, and it is best to start making up for them straight away.

4. Anyone who must make up for missed Ramaḍān fasts cannot offer supererogatory fasts until he makes up for them.

5. Someone who is making up for missed Ramaḍān fasts can break his fast before midday. After midday, he must continue fasting, and if he

---

[569] *Wasāʾil al-shīʿa*, v. 10, p. 330, ḥ. 2

[570] *Wasāʾil al-shīʿa*, v. 10, p. 330, ḥ. 3

[571] *Wasāʾil al-shīʿa*, v. 10, p. 346, ḥ. 5

intentionally breaks his fast thereafter he must offer expiation by feeding ten poor persons or fasting for three days, in addition to making up for that day [again].

6. Whoever intentionally misses fasts during the month of Ramaḍān, or [intentionally] travels in that time [absent a legally valid reason], and then dies, his heir must make up for these missed fasts on his behalf.

Etiquettes of fasting

The noble *sunna*:

❖ Al-Kulaynī, in a reliable report, has narrated from Abū ʿAbd Allah 🕮: 'Whoever completes his fast, Allah Almighty says to his angels: "My servant has sought succor from My punishment, so give him it." And Allah delegates His angels to supplicate for the fasting people, and He does not order them to supplicate for anyone but that He answers them.'[572]

❖ Shaykh al-Mufīd has recorded that the Messenger of Allah 🕮 said: 'The one who fasts is engaged in worship even when he sleeps on his bed, so long as he does not backbite another Muslim.'[573]

❖ Shaykh al-Mufīd has recorded that Imam al-Ṣādiq said: 'Giving your brother [in faith] something to break his fast and cheering his spirits is greater than the reward of your fast.'[574]

❖ Al-Ṣadūq has recorded, via his chain of transmitters, from al-Ḥalabī, that Abū ʿAbd Allah 🕮 was asked about breaking the fast before or after the prayer. He said: 'If there was a group of people with you who fear that they will be prevented from dinner, then one should break their fast with them, and if not, then one should pray first and then break the fast.'[575]

Rulings:

A. Avoiding sins

1. While one is fasting, the prohibition on lying is strongly emphasised, especially in matters relating to Allah, his Messenger, and the Imams.

2. There is also special emphasis placed on the prohibition of backbiting, slandering, name-calling, arrogance, and stirring up prejudices, and as a

---

[572] *Wasāʾil al-shīʿa*, v. 4, p. 97, ḥ. 1
[573] *Wasāʾil al-shīʿa*, v. 4, p. 98. ḥ. 2
[574] *Wasāʾil al-shīʿa*, v. 4, p. 101, ḥ. 7
[575] *Wasāʾil al-shīʿa*, v. 4, p. 108, ḥ. 1

consequence anything which leads to infringing upon the rights of others or causes distress to them.

3. It is also obligatory to avoid treacherous glances, looking at things which are forbidden to look at, and listening to things which are forbidden to listen to; in this way someone will also be fasting with his hearing, sight, and speech.

4. If the one who is fasting is able to observe a religious silence like that of Mary 🙶, not speaking except when necessary, or for the purposes of *dhikr*, then he should do so. This is part of the perfection of one's fast, God-willing.

5. Fasting purifies the believer's heart of envy, resentment, and malice, and a person must try to achieve this if he is to attain the highest levels of piety, God-willing.

B. Abstinence in fasting

1. A person must keep his fast safe from anything that will arouse his lusts; he should neither engage in foreplay or touch his wife erotically, nor kiss her, nor look at her [lustfully], nor listen to lustful speech; all of which applies if he fears he will be unable to restrain himself. But if he does not fear this, then there is no problem [with these things]. And the same applies to a woman with regards to her husband.

2. A person should avoid wearing make-up containing musk or anything whose taste will reach the throat.

3. It is disliked to snort anything up the nose while fasting, but there is no problem with putting medicine into the ear, and it is disliked to use suppositories.

4. It is disliked to [intentionally] smell any plant with a pleasant scent, such as roses, but it is recommended to perfume oneself with pleasant smelling perfume, as it is an ornament for one who fasts. However, it is disliked to use musk, perhaps because of its heavy scent.

5. A man is permitted to sit in water without that being disliked, just as it is permitted for him to cool himself with a fan, or to cool himself with his garment. But it is disliked for a woman to sit in water [however, cooling herself with a fan or her garment is not a problem].

C. Looking after one's health

1. Someone who is fasting musk look after their health and avoid anything that will cause harm to it while fasting, whether cupping, bleeding, pulling out teeth, blood-letting, or loitering in the bathroom, if this is harmful to his health or causes weakness.

2. Similarly, it is disliked for him to tear (damage) the clothing on his body.

How is the crescent established?

The noble *sunna*:

❖ It is narrated that Imam al-Ṣādiq 🕮 was asked about the crescent moons [mentioned in the verses of the Qur'ān). He said: 'It is the new moons of the months. When you see the new moon then fast, and when you see the new moon [signaling the end of the month of Ramaḍān] then break the fast.'[576]

❖ 'Alī b. Ja'far asked his brother, Imam Mūsā b. Ja'far 🕮, about a man who sees the new moon in the month of Ramaḍān [signaling its end], but only he sees it and no one else. Should he [continue to] fast? He said: 'If he has no doubt [about what he saw], then he must break his fast. Otherwise, he should [continue to] fast with the people.'[577]

❖ Imam al-Ṣādiq 🕮 said: 'If the new moon disappears before the redness in the eastern sky, then it is the first night, and if it disappears after that redness then it is the second night.'[578]

Rulings:

The criterion for establishing the new crescent for the months of Ramaḍān and Shawwāl is sighting it. When it appears clearly on the horizon, there is no problem; someone who sees it must start fasting [the following morning] for the beginning of Ramaḍān or break his fast for the beginning of Shawwal, whether other people have seen it or not, and whether the religious authorities accept his testimony of having seen the moon or not.

As for someone who has not seen the crescent himself, the following are valid methods for establishing that the crescent has been sighted:

First: The verdict of the authoritative jurist. It is unnecessary for the Muslims to investigate the viewpoint of his ruling so long as they still trust his competency as a jurist and his just character.

---

[576] *Wasā'il al-shī'a*, v. 4, p. 186, ḥ. 21
[577] *Wasā'il al-shī'a*, v. 4, p. 188, ḥ. 1
[578] *Wasā'il al-shī'a*, v. 4, p. 204, ḥ. 3

Second: An authoritative testimony. If two just men testify that they have seen the crescent with their own eyes, you must accept their testimony whether the people accept it or not.

This is the case unless there is a valid reason to doubt their testimony; for instance, if there are discrepancies between their respective descriptions of the crescent, or if the sky is clear and it is easy for the people to see the crescent but they cannot; these are some examples of factors which can introduce doubts about the validity of their testimony.

Third: Widespread knowledge that gives one certainty. So if a group of people claim to have seen the moon such that it makes us confident that the crescent exists in the skies, this is sufficient. This is not conditional upon their being just, legally mature, male, or anything else.

Fourth: Astronomical calculations that yield certainty. If the sky is overcast and these calculations yield absolute certainty that the crescent would be visible [to the naked eye] were the skies clear, then this establishes the appearance of the crescent.

The same is true if certainty is obtained by advanced technologies, and by certainty we mean such a level of confidence that rational persons would disregard any option to the contrary.

Rules for seclusion (*iʿtikāf*)

What is seclusion?

Seclusion (*iʿtikāf*) is to remain an extended time in a house of Allah for the purpose of worshipping Him. The same [general] conditions apply to it as do to all other acts of worship, such as the worshipper being a Muslim, of sound mind, and acting out of pure intention.

It is also a condition that this act of worship not be mixed with anything forbidden, such as causing harm or detriment to oneself or others, etc. So if seclusion will harm the person because of an illness, an enemy, or if doing it will infringe upon the rights of others, then it is not valid as an act of worship according to what the jurists have said.

Its conditions

Seclusion has its own conditions as well, namely:

First: Fasting – seclusion is not valid unless the worshipper is fasting, nor is it valid in situations where one cannot fast, such as illness, travelling, *ʿīd* days, or *tashrīq* for one who desires to perform seclusion in Mina.

Second: Seclusion must last for three days; it is neither valid for two days, nor for five. It is only valid for three or six days, though it is precaution to treat it as two sets of three days. So one cannot perform seclusion for ten days; they must either make it nine days or twelve.

Third: Seclusion must be performed in the congregational mosque in which Friday prayers are led by a just *imām*, or at least congregational prayers. Seclusion is not permitted in places other than mosques,[579] nor in small mosques which no congregation attends, and not even in local mosques in the cities. Instead, seclusion must be performed in one of the main mosques of the region.

It is best to perform seclusion in one of four mosques: the Holy Sanctuary, the Prophet's Mosque, the Mosque of Kufa, or the Mosque of Basra.

Seclusion is a recommended act and it only becomes obligatory through making a vow (*nadhr*). The rules pertaining to making a vow to perform seclusion and to do anything else are the same. See the section on vows for more details.

Rules for seclusion

The noble *sunna*:

- Al-Ṣadūq has recorded—via a sound chain of transmitters—from al-Ḥalabī that Abū ʿAbd Allah ﷺ said: 'There is no seclusion (*iʿtikāf*) but with fasting in the [area's] central mosque.'[580]
- Al-Ṣadūq has recorded—via a sound chain of transmitters—from Samāʿa: I asked Abū ʿAbd Allah ﷺ about someone performing the rite of seclusion and has sex with his wife. He said: 'He is like one who broke his fast during a day of the month of Ramaḍān.'[581]
- Al-Ṣadūq has recorded—via a sound chain of transmitters—from Dāwud b. Sirḥān: I was in Madina during the month of Ramaḍān, so I told Abū ʿAbd Allah ﷺ that I wanted to perform the rite of seclusion. So what should I say and what do I oblige myself? So he said: 'Do not

---

[579] This refers to places of worship designated as *masājid* according to the strict Islamic legal definition, as opposed to general Islamic centers.

[580] *Wasāʾil al-shīʿa*, v. 10, p. 538, ḥ. 1 / Ḥ. 14062

[581] *Wasāʾil al-shīʿa*, v. 10, p. 547, ḥ. 2 / Ḥ. 14084

exit the mosque except for unavoidable necessities, and do not sit in the shade until you return your seat [in the mosque].'[582]

Rulings:

1. One must remain in the mosque as an act of worship. This is the essence of seclusion. This means that if someone leaves the mosque unnecessarily, his act of worship is invalidated, and the same applies if he leaves the mosque for an extended period of time due to some necessity or emergency such that the form of seclusion is lost. As for leaving the mosque for some necessity which common sense does not deem to conflict with a state of remaining in the mosque, there is no problem. For example, if someone goes out for food or drink, to use the bathroom, take a bath, visit someone who is ill, attend a funeral, attend to the need of a fellow believer or the like thereof, so long as he leaves for the shortest time possible and then returns.[583]
2. Certain things are forbidden for someone in a state of seclusion, and failing to abide by some of the conditions or seclusion or committing some sins can potentially void it. For example:
    a. Sexual activity, whether intercourse, touching, or kissing with lust, for both men and women.
    b. Masturbation, because it invalidates the fast and it is forbidden at all times.
    c. Smelling pleasant fragrances for enjoyment.
    d. Unnecessary buying, selling, or other transactions.
    e. Arguing about religious or worldly affairs with the intention of overcoming the other party or demonstrating one's own superiority. However, there is no problem with arguing to establish the truth and repel the other party from error.
3. It makes no difference whether these five aforementioned acts are done by day or night, even though some things which are forbidden by day because of the fast are permitted by night, such as eating and drinking.
4. Anything that invalidates fasting also invalidates seclusion if done intentionally, but it does not invalidate it if done unintentionally.
5. If someone invalidates their seclusion, they must make up for it if it was an obligatory seclusion, or if they were on the third day of a recommended seclusion. As for invalidating it on the first or second day of a recommended seclusion, it is not necessary to make up for it.

---

[582] *Wasāʾil al-shīʿa*, v. 10, p. 550, ḥ. 3 / Ḥ. 14091

[583] As described above, even such necessary breaks must not conflict with the state of *iʿtikāf* and, thus, common sense would not deem him to have broken his act.

6. Seclusion is invalid when performed by someone for whom fasting is invalid, such as a traveller or a sick person. It is also invalid for a slave without the permission of his master, or for a wife without her husband's permission if her seclusion would interfere with his conjugal rights.

The Fifth (*Khums*)

Why do we pay *khums*?

When the Qur'ān explains the obligation to pay *khums*, the thread of its discussion draws a connection between it, belief in Allah, and striving in His way: '**Know that whatever thing you may come by, a fifth (*khums*) of it is for Allah and the Messenger, for the relatives and the orphans, for the needy and the traveller, if you have faith in Allah and what We sent down to Our servant on the Day of Separation, the day when the two hosts met; and Allah has power over all things.**'[584]

Khums and *jihād*, then, are like twins; both of them are realities of faith. Is not faith submitting to Allah and whatever He has commanded? So whoever chooses to believe must also affirm his belief in *khums*.

In the verses of *zakāt* (almsgiving), we also find it connected to prayer, just as we find in those verses connected to *jihād* an explicit command to spend [in the way of Allah]. All of this demonstrates that the religion is founded upon prayer, expenditure, and *jihād*.

But why? Because the essence of religion is to leave behind one's own desires in favour of guidance, to ascend above worldly attractions to the highest degrees of the Hereafter. This reality manifests itself in a believer when he resists his love of wealth, and purifies himself from attraction to worldly things. Allah says: '**Take charity from their possessions to cleanse them and purify them thereby, and bless them. Indeed your blessing is a comfort to them, and Allah is All-hearing, All-knowing.**'[585]

Allah calls it charity (*ṣadaqa*) when He says: '**Allah brings usury to naught, but He makes charities flourish. Allah does not like any sinful ingrate.**'[586] This is because whoever gives his wealth seeking Allah's countenance affirms his faith in the religion, and in the reward promised to those who give charity, as it was revealed to Allah's Messenger.

---

[584] Sūrat al-Anfāl (8):41
[585] Sūrat al-Tawba (9):103
[586] Sūrat al-Baqara (2):276

Spending in Allah's way is also called *jihād* when He says: **'Go forth, whether [armed] lightly or heavily, and wage *jihād* with your possessions and persons in the way of Allah. That is better for you, should you know.'**[587]

This is because sincerely giving your wealth for Allah reflects the *jihād* against the [base] self, its lusts, and its natural inclination to live forever on this earth. At the same time, religion is freeing oneself from desires and going to Allah's guidance. Without this liberation, man will be tied down to this world and its lusts, forced to live in the prison of his ego and endure the poverty of his greed. On the other hand, the one who spends his wealth in Allah's way is liberated from that, and he will be one of the successful: **'And those who are saved from their own greed - it is they who are the felicitous.'**[588]

The role of *khums* in religious life

By studying the history of Shīʿī religious life over the last fourteen centuries, we become more convinced of the wisdom behind the legislation of *khums*, as it plays a fundamental role in laying the foundations of religious life, such that *khums* becomes its basis; whereas without it, religious life is threatened with collapse.

Religious seminaries, which remain a candle of guidance, a symbol of independence, and the first line of defence for spiritual values – these seminaries can only exist through a system of religious tithing.

Those who pay *khums* must know that it is through their donations that the flag of the Prophet's Household ﷺ remains aloft, the religious seminaries with their countless benefits remain active, and those who pay the *khums* themselves remain independent and dignified.

Contrariwise, those who avoid paying *khums* should know that what they are not merely sinning by withholding what is due to Allah and the descendants of His Messenger, but they are clearly undermining the very values which they claim to believe in, and helping – whether they realize it or not – to erase the symbols of the religion and spread corruption in the *umma* (the community of believers).

That is because today we are facing a deliberate cultural assault to destroy the symbols of our religion, corrupt the values of our society and alienate our youth from them. Do you not see how our enemies began to enter our

---

[587] Sūrat al-Tawba (9):41
[588] Sūrat al-Ḥashr (59):9

society through satellite channels, the internet, and movies? More dangerous than all of that are the networks distributing drugs contributing to the delinquency of our young people. If we cannot find the will to strive our utmost to spread the culture of our religion, back the efforts of our activists, and support our religious institutions and preachers, then the stench of corruption and the storm of immorality will engulf our religion, our children, and everything we have – heaven forbid!

This is why people must take extra care to ensure that they have paid Allah's dues and observed His commands. And Allah is the granter of success and assistance.

Upon what must *khums* be paid?

The noble *sunna*:

❖ It is narrated from al-ʿAbd al-Ṣāliḥ (Mūsā b. Jaʿfar) ﷺ: '*Khums* is owed on five things: the spoils of war, diving (e.g., pearls), treasures, mines, and salt marshes.'[589]

Rulings:

Khums must be paid on seven things:

1. War booty
2. Mineral wealth
3. Buried treasures
4. [Wealth from] diving
5. Licit wealth mixed with illicit wealth
6. Land purchased by a non-Muslim citizen (*dhimmī*) from a Muslim
7. Surplus income

First: War booty

The noble *sunna*:

❖ Abū Baṣīr has narrated from Abū Jaʿfar (Imam al-Bāqir) ﷺ: 'Everything [gained from fighting] upon the testimony that there is no god but Allah, and Muḥammad is the Messenger of Allah, a fifth of it belongs to us, and it is unlawful for anyone to buy anything from *khums* until he has given us our right.'[590]

---

[589] *Wasāʾil al-shīʿa*, v. 4, p. 339, ḥ. 4
[590] *Wasāʾil al-shīʿa*, v. 4, p. 339, ḥ. 5

❖ Al-Ḥalabī has narrated from Abū ʿAbd Allah (Imam al-Ṣādiq) ﷺ concerning a man from among his companions who is in a brigade, and while he is with them, some spoils of war are gained. He said: 'He gives one fifth [to us] and [the rest of his share] is made good (i.e., lawful) for him.'[591]

Rulings:

War booty is that which is captured by the victor in warfare, such as weapons and supplies, military encampments and perhaps even fortresses, such as the fort at Khaybar. *Khums* is due on all of these. As for lands which fall into the possession of the Muslims after the conquest, which are called 'conquered by force' (*al-maftūha bil-ʿunwa*), the most likely ruling is that there is no need to pay *khums* on them as they are not customarily treated as booty.

Second: Mineral wealth

The noble *sunna*:

❖ Muḥammad b. Muslim has narrated that he asked Abū Jaʿfar (Imam al-Bāqir) ﷺ about gold, silver, brass, iron, and lead mines. So he said: 'There is *khums* [due] on all of them.'[592]

❖ Muḥammad b. Muslims has narrated that he asked Abū Jaʿfar ﷺ about *milāha*. So he said: 'And do you mean by *milāha*?' I said: Salty marshland from which the water is gathered and it becomes salt. So he said: 'This [is a kind of] mine for which *khums* [is due].' I said: And sulfur, and petroleum, which are extracted from the earth? So he said: 'There is *khums* [due] on this and whatever resembles it.'[593]

Rulings:

1. Mineral wealth refers to sources of precious substances such as gold and others, and customarily included under this heading is anything brought out of the ground which has a specific use, whether gold, silver, lead, brass, iron, rubies, peridot, and all other precious stones. The same applies to coal, oil, and gas; and to arsenic, antimony, salt, gypsum, millstones, semi-precious stones, and anything like this that is taken from the earth but which has qualities that make it useful.
2. If something is not customarily considered a mineral, then there is no *khums* due on it.

---

[591] *Wasāʾil al-shīʿa*, v. 4, p. 340, ḥ. 8
[592] *Wasāʾil al-shīʿa*, v. 4, p. 342, ḥ. 2
[593] *Wasāʾil al-shīʿa*, v. 4, p. 343, ḥ. 4

3. In order for *khums* to be due on minerals, their price must be at least twenty *shar'ī* dinars[594] after taking into account the cost of extracting and refining them.

Third: Treasure

The noble *sunna*:

❖ Al-Riḍā ☷ was asked about the amount of treasure at which *khums* becomes obligatory. So he said: 'Whatever [reaches the level at which] *zakāt* becomes obligatory on its wealth, then there is *khums* due, and whatever does not reach that limit such that *zakāt* is owed, then there is no *khums* due from it.'[595]

Rulings:

Treasure (*kanz*) refers to remnants from the life of ancient peoples which has value in the eyes of rational persons. It makes no difference whether this value is intrinsic such as precious metals and stones, or archaeological, such as ancient pottery, books, etc. And it makes no difference whether this was buried underground, in the middle of a wall, the hollow of a tree, or in the depths of the ocean. It also makes no difference whether the one who buried it did so intentionally, or if it was buried as the result of natural forces. It also makes no difference whether its origin lies in the pre-Islamic or Islamic eras. Ultimately, the criterion is whether or not a thing is customarily be counted as treasure.

It is a condition that the value of the treasure should be equal to the minimum value required for the payment of *zakāt* on gold, namely twenty dinars. Others say that it is sufficient if its value is equal to two hundred dirhams,[596] and this is according to precaution.

Fourth: Diving

The noble *sunna*:

❖ In a report from al-Ḥalabī, he said: I asked Abū 'Abd Allah (Imam al-Ṣādiq) ☷ about ambergris and diving for pearls. So he said: 'There is *khums* on it.'[597]

---

[594] Which is equivalent to the value of 69.6 grams of gold.
[595] *Wasā'il al-shī'a*, v. 4, p. 345, ḥ. 3
[596] Equivalent to 483 grams of silver.
[597] *Wasā'il al-shī'a*, v. 4, p. 347, ḥ. 1

- Imam Abū al-Ḥasan Mūsā b. Jaʿfar عليه السلام was asked about what was taken from the sea—of pearls, ruby, and peridot—and gold and silver mines: is there *zakāt* on them? So he said: 'If its value reaches one dinar, then there is *khums* due on it.'[598]

Rulings:

1. Allah has placed precious riches in the ocean in the form of rare stones and archaeological treasures. And when someone searches for these treasures beneath the waves, it is called 'diving' and *khums* is owed on his findings. This includes ambergris (a waxy substance discharged by the sperm whale which is used for producing perfumes and musks), which a person does not need to dive under water to retrieve, but is able to rise from the ocean [on its own].
2. Exempt from this is fishing, manufacturing sea salt, or sea plants, etc., none of which are customarily considered diving.
3. The minimum value on which *khums* is payable is a single *sharʿī* dinar, even if someone obtains a number of deposits close to one another; this is after he has deducted his provision from the sum and the cost of the equipment he uses for diving, which is treated as part of his provision. If there is a team of divers, then each individual diver's share must reach the minimum value; their shares are not counted collectively.

Fifth: Licit wealth mixed with illicit wealth

The noble *sunna*:

- Ḥasan b. Ziyād has narrated from Abū ʿAbd Allah (Imam al-Ṣādiq) عليه السلام: 'A man came to the Commander of the Believers, and said: O Commander of the Believers, I have received some wealth and I do not know if its source was lawful or unlawful. So he said to him: "Pay the *khums* on that wealth, for verily Allah Almighty will be pleased with that wealth once *khums* is paid; and avoid whatever the source of which is unknown.'[599]
- ʿAmmār has narrated that Abū ʿAbd Allah (Imam al-Ṣādiq) عليه السلام was asked about work a man does for the Sultan and profits thereby. He said: 'No, unless he cannot afford food, drink, or means [of survival]. So if he did that and acquired something by it, he must send its *khums* to the People of the House.'[600]

---

598 *Wasāʾil al-shīʿa*, v. 4, p. 347, ḥ. 2
599 *Wasāʾil al-shīʿa*, v. 4, p. 352, ḥ. 1
600 *Wasāʾil al-shīʿa*, v. 4, p. 353, ḥ. 2

Rulings:

1. Whoever earns money without observing the bounds of the *sharīʿa*, or works in a company or institution in which licit and illicit wealth is mixed, must – if he wishes to purify his earnings – pay *khums*. This applies if he does not know the amount of illicit earnings mixed in with his wealth so that he can be free of [those illicit earnings] by giving them as charity, or if he does not know its proper owner so that he could obtain his pardon by any means possible.
2. As for someone who knows the quantity of illicit wealth, even approximately (e.g., 'more than half'), then he must give away [in charity] whatever quantity would discharge his moral responsibility (i.e., the amount he is certain of).
3. If he knows the property's rightful owner, then he should seek his pardon [in whatever way that pleases the rightful owner].

Sixth: A non-Muslim citizen when purchasing land from a Muslim

The noble *sunna*:

❖ Abū ʿUbayda al-Ḥadhdhāʾ said: I heard Abū Jaʿfar (Imam al-Bāqir) ﷺ saying: 'Whichever *dhimmī* buys land from a Muslim, he owes *khums* on it.'[601]

Rulings:

The strongest opinion is that a non-Muslim citizen (*dhimmī*) must pay *khums* on any land he purchases from a Muslim; it makes no difference whether this land was in use or left vacant. But *khums* is only payable on the land, not any buildings or vegetation it contains. And in the same way, it is permissible for those responsible for the collection of *khums* to seek restitution for this.

Seventh: Surplus income

The noble *sunna*:

❖ Muḥammad b. al-Ḥasan al-Ashʿarī said: Some of our companions wrote to Abū Jaʿfar the Second (Imam Muḥammad b. ʿAlī al-Jawād) ﷺ: Inform us about *khums*. Is it due upon everything a man profits, little or great, on every kind of item and ware? And how is that? The response in his handwriting read: '*Khums* is after provisions [are accounted for].'[602]

---

[601] *Wasāʾil al-shīʿa*, v. 4, p. 352, ḥ. 1
[602] *Wasāʾil al-shīʿa*, v. 4, p. 348, ḥ. 1

- Samāʿa said: I asked Abū al-Ḥasan ﷺ about *khums*. So he said: 'It is on whatever people profit from, little or great.'[603]

Rulings:

What is income?

1. Income (*fā'ida*) is any profit a person obtains, whether by his labour, such as a farmer, artisan or merchant, or without his labour, such as someone who inherits unexpectedly, or receives a gift from the ruler. The criterion here is obtaining the thing in question, as accords with Allah's saying: '**Know that whatever thing you may obtain, a fifth of it is for Allah…**'[604]
2. Hence the criterion for *khums* is not merely earning (*iktisāb*). If it so happens that someone obtains some land and makes a great profit when he sells it, then he must pay *khums* on it, even if he did not take this as a source of earnings for himself.
3. In the same way, gifts, presents, unexpected inheritance, and whatever is obtained from the enemy through treaties, are also subject to *khums*.
4. Yes, expected inheritance – like that received from a father – is not included in *khums* due to an explicit textual evidence (*naṣṣ*) in that regard. And perhaps this is because it is not something 'obtained' (*ghanīma*).
5. As for dowry payments (*mahr*) and divorce settlements (*khalʿ*), it is precaution and, in fact, the strongest legal opinion, that *khums* should be paid on them. The same applies to compensation payments (*diyyāt*).
6. Someone who sells his blood, kidneys, or any other organ, and thereby has wealth in surplus to his needs, must pay *khums* on the excess.
7. Whoever's livelihood is derived from *khums*, and finds himself with an excess, he must pay *khums* on it.
8. Orchards, farms, smallholdings, etc., could be for personal use only, in which case there is no *khums* owed on their produce, surplus, or the amount one benefits from their fruit and meat. On the other hand, if they are owned as a business, then any profit is treated as something obtained, and *khums* it is owed. The same applies to anyone who sells the excess produce of his own personal orchard, or even the produce of his own garden; *khums* must be paid on these.

---

[603] *Wasā'il al-shīʿa*, v. 4, p. 350, ḥ. 6

[604] Sūrat al-Anfāl (8):41

9. Whoever engages in a number of businesses, such as farming, manufacture, or different kinds of trade, must calculate his profits from them collectively and not individually.
10. Capital (*ra'smāl*) is not counted as provision, so *khums* must be paid upon it unless a person needs it for his livelihood—such as an estate on which to grow produce, a car which he goes to work with, or a shop in which he conducts business—such that if he lost it, his livelihood would be ruined. In this case, the apparent ruling is that he does not need to pay *khums* on that.

What is provision?

1. Provision (*mu'ūna*) is that which is exempt from *khums*, namely:
    a. Whatever people spend in their day-to-day lives, whether on necessities, luxuries, good causes, or charitable donations.
    b. Government-imposed taxes, expiations, compensation payments, and all unexpected expenses.
    c. Also included are things which a person needs, like a house to live in, a garden to rest in, and a car, or any other means of transportation.
    d. Also included are a person's expenditures on their partner and children, on their studies, and any other affairs in their life, even if they are wealthy.
    e. Also included is the cost of *ḥajj*, whether obligatory or supererogatory.
    f. And if someone has any earnings surplus to his provision, *khums* must be paid on it.
2. If someone is unable to secure a deposit for a home, the funds of obligatory *ḥajj*, the cost of a car if he has need of one, the gift for his daughter to marry, etc., except by saving money over many years, then the most likely ruling is that this is counted as part of his provision, and so there is no *khums* due upon these savings.
3. Anyone who borrows money for his expenses can count the repayment of this loan as part of his provision.
4. If someone purchases more supplies than he needs for a given year, and these purchases were ordinary, such that someone would say that this was part of his provision, then it is counted as such. Otherwise, *khums* must be paid on the excess as a matter of obligatory precaution.

Annual provisions

Khums is only obligatory on earnings and income that are in excess of one's provision, and because most people organize their finances on a yearly basis

– especially farmers in lands like ours – then one can calculate his provision on an annual basis, too.

Dividing the shares of *khums*

The noble *sunna*:

❖ Ḥammād b. ʿĪsā has narrated from some of our companions that al-ʿAbd al-Ṣāliḥ [al-Kāẓim] 🕮 said: '*Khums* is due on five things: spoils of war, diving, treasure [in the earth], mines, and salt marshes. One fifth is taken from all of these kinds of produce, for it belongs to the one to whom Allah designated it (i.e., the Imam). Four fifths of it is divided between those who have fought or those who supported that. The [remaining] one fifth is divided in six shares: Allah's share, the share of the Messenger of Allah, the share of the near relatives, the share of the orphans, the share of the needy, and the share of the wayfarers (e.g., someone stranded in a journey). The share of the Messenger of Allah belongs to "those vested with authority" after him as inheritance. For [the Imam] are three shares: two from inheritance, and one apportioned to him by Allah. Half of the one fifth is entirely his, and the remaining half is [divided] between his household. So [there is] a portion for their orphans, a portion for their needy, a portion for their wayfarers, divided between them according to the Book and the *sunna*.'

Then he 🕮 said: 'These are the people for whom Allah has designated *khums*; they are the relatives of the Prophet, whom Allah has mentioned when He said: "And warn your tribe and relatives." And they are from the House of ʿAbd a-Muṭṭalib themselves, male and female. Not a single one of them is from the households of the Quraysh or the Arabs. None of their servants among or from them has [a share] of this *khums*. Rather the people's charity is lawful for [the servant], and nothing from *khums* is for him, because Allah Almighty says: "Call them by their fathers."'[605]

Rulings:

1. *Khums* is divided into two shares. One share is for the Imam 🕮, and during his Occultation this is given to whichever righteous jurists look after the affairs of the faithful in his stead. The other share is given to needy *sayyids*, whether orphans, poor persons, or travellers.

2. A jurist can dispose of the Imam's share as he sees most consistent with Allah's commandments, the *sunna* of His Messenger 🕮, and to spread the message of Islam and manage the affairs of the faithful, including

---

[605] *Wasāʾil al-shīʿa*, v. 4, p. 358, ḥ. 8

observing the conditions of the *sayyid*s. If any of them is needy, and the share of the *sayyid*s is insufficient for them, then their needs must be met from the share of the Imam.

3. *Sayyid*s are descendants of ʿAbd al-Muṭṭallib, whether they are from the line of Imam ʿAlī 📿, ʿAqīl, ʿAbbās, or anyone else. However, priority should be given to the descendants of Fāṭima 📿 because of their direct relation to the Prophet 📿.

The alms tax (*zakāt*)

Zakāt on wealth

The noble *sunna*:

❖ Imam Mūsā b. Jaʿfar 📿 said: 'Protect your wealth by [paying] *zakāt*.'[606]

❖ Imam Abū Jaʿfar al-Bāqir 📿 said: 'Surely Allah Almighty coupled *zakāt* with prayer; thus He said: "Establish the prayer and give *zakāt*." So whoever establishes the prayer but did not give *zakāt*, it is as if he did not establish the prayer.'[607]

❖ And he (al-Bāqir) 📿 also said: 'There is no worshipper who withholds anything from the *zakāt* on his wealth but that Allah makes that, on Judgment Day, a serpent of fire encircling his neck, biting his flesh, until the accounting is complete. And it is as Allah Almighty says: "They will be collared with what they were miserly with on Judgment Day," meaning what they were stingy with of *zakāt*.'[608]

❖ It is narrated from Imam al-Bāqir 📿: 'Once, when the Messenger of Allah 📿 was in the mosque, he suddenly said: "Stand, O so-and-so; stand, O so-and-so; stand, O so-and-so," until he five individuals stood. Then he said: "Get out of our mosque and do not pray in it, for you did not pay *zakāt*."'[609]

❖ Imam al-Bāqir 📿 said: 'We have found in the Book of ʿAlī 📿 that the Messenger of Allah 📿 said: "If you have withheld the *zakāt* then the earth withholds [from you] its blessings.'[610]

---

[606] *Wasāʾil al-shīʿa*, v. 6, p. 4, ḥ 5
[607] *Wasāʾil al-shīʿa*, v. 6, p. 11, ḥ. 2
[608] *Wasāʾil al-shīʿa*, v. 6, p. 11, ḥ. 3
[609] *Wasāʾil al-shīʿa*, v. 6, p. 12, ḥ. 7
[610] *Wasāʾil al-shīʿa*, v. 6, p. 13, ḥ. 12

❖ It is narrated from Imam al-Ṣādiq عليه السلام that the Messenger of Allah ﷺ said: 'Prayer (*ṣalāt*) is not accepted from eight people; among them is he who withholds the *zakāt*.'[611]

Rulings:

1. *Zakāt*, like prayer, is one of the essentials of faith, namely one of those obligations about which there is no disagreement amongst Muslims. Numerous verses of the Qurʾān explicitly affirm it as such, twenty-six of which mention it alongside prayer, and the number of traditions about it in the noble *sunna* reach the level of *tawātur*.[612] Whoever denies that this is a religious duty while knowing this has surely left the fold of Islam. In the Prophet's ﷺ final advice (*waṣiyya*) to ʿAlī عليه السلام, he says: 'O ʿAlī! Ten kinds of people from this *umma* have disbelieved in Allah, the Exalted...!' Amongst them he mentioned those who do not pay *zakāt*. Then he said: 'O ʿAlī! Eight kinds of people from them will not have their prayers accepted by Allah...!' Again, he mentioned those who do not pay *zakāt*. Then he said: 'O ʿAlī! Whoever withholds a carat (*qīrāṭ*) of *zakāt* due upon his property, then he is neither a believer, nor a Muslim, nor worthy of respect. O ʿAlī! He who forgoes paying the *zakāt* will ask Allah to return to this world [so that he can have the opportunity to pay it]. That is Allah's saying: **'When death comes to one of them, he says, "My Lord! Take me back!"'**[613]
2. Here we must point out that the *zakāt* mentioned in the Qurʾān does not only mean *zakāt* in the specific legal sense of the term; it includes all of a Muslim's monetary duties, whether *khums*, *zakāt*, *fiṭra*, charities (*ṣadaqa*), spending on the deprived, righteous deeds, etc.
3. This spending of wealth is called *zakāt*, which literally means 'purification' and 'growth,' because the human soul is purified and cleansed thereby. Allah says: **'Take charity from their possessions to cleanse them and purify them thereby...'**[614] And spending wealth in this way also cleanses and grows the wealth itself.

---

[611] *Wasāʾil al-shīʿa*, v. 6, p. 16, ḥ. 22

[612] Meaning that there are so many traditions narrated by so many people, identical in words or meaning, that there can be no question that they are an authentic representation of the words and deeds of the Prophet ﷺ.

[613] Sūrat al-Muʾminūn (23):99

[614] Sūrat al-Tawba (9):103

Who must pay *zakāt*?

The noble *sunna*:

❖ Yūnus b. Yaʿqūb said: I sent a message to Abū ʿAbd Allah 🕮 saying: I have a younger brother. When does he have to pay *zakāt* on his wealth? He said: 'When prayer becomes obligatory upon him, then *zakāt* has become obligatory upon him...'[615]

❖ ʿAbd al-Raḥmān b. al-Ḥajjāj said: I said to Abū ʿAbd Allah 🕮: A woman from my family is mentally ill. Is she obliged to pay *zakāt*? So he said: 'If she is able to work in spite of it, then there is *zakāt* due for her; and if she is unable to work in spite of it, then there is none.'[616]

❖ It is reported that a man asked Imam al-Ṣādiq 🕮 about the wealth of a slave. Is *zakāt* due on it? So he said: 'No, whether he had thousands of dirhams or was needy, there would be nothing of *zakāt* owed for him.'[617]

Rulings:

Zakāt must be paid by anyone who meets the following criteria:

First: Legal maturity (*bulūgh*). *Zakāt* is not obligatory on someone beneath the age of legal maturity, even in the year he will mature.

Second: Soundness of mind (*ʿaql*). There is no *zakāt* levied upon someone who is legally insane (*majnūn*) for the duration of the year, nor upon one who suffers temporary bouts of insanity, so long as he is customarily treated as insane.

Three: Freedom (*ḥurriyya*). There is no *zakāt* levied on the possessions of slaves, even if they are allowed to own property.

Fourth: Ownership (*tamalluk*). There is no *zakāt* levied on property before one owns it completely. For example: property that is to be gifted to someone before he takes possession of it, property which is bequeathed to someone but which that person has not yet received, or a loan insofar as the loaned property or money does not properly belong to the creditor until he takes possession of it from the debtor.

---

[615] *Wasāʾil al-shīʿa*, v. 6, p. 55, ḥ. 5
[616] *Wasāʾil al-shīʿa*, v. 6, p. 59, ḥ. 1
[617] *Wasāʾil al-shīʿa*, v. 6, p. 60, ḥ. 3

Fifth: Freedom of disposal (*tamakkun min al-taṣarruf*). If someone owns property upon which he must ordinarily pay *zakāt* but he is not currently able to dispose of it freely for any reason, then there is no *zakāt* due upon it. Whether he is able to dispose of it or not is determined by common sense.

Sixth: Meeting the threshold (*niṣāb*). It is only obligatory to pay *zakāt* on property when it reaches a specific minimum value, called the threshold. We shall discuss the exact thresholds for *zakāt* below, God-willing.

Upon what must *zakāt* be paid?

The noble *sunna*:

- ❖ It has been narrated from one of the two Imams, al-Bāqir or al-Ṣādiq عليهما السلام : 'Alongside the prayer, Allah Almighty has obligated the *zakāt* on [various kinds of] wealth, and the Messenger of Allah صلى الله عليه وآله established a *sunna* for nine things, and pardoned from that their by-products: on gold, silver, cattle, sheep, wheat, barley, dates, and raisins, and he exempted what is made from those.'[618]
- ❖ Al-Ḥarth asked Imam al-Ṣādiq عليه السلام upon what *zakāt* is owed. So he said: 'Wheat, barley, corn, rice, *sult* (a type of barley), and lentils—*zakāt* is owed on all of these.' Then he said: 'Whatever is measured by dry measure (*ṣāʿ*) and reaches *awsāq* (a unit of dry measure), *zakāt* is owed upon it.'[619]

Rulings:
Zakāt must be paid on nine things:

1. Camels
2. Cows
3. Sheep (camels, cows, and sheep are collectively called 'livestock.')
4. Gold
5. Silver (collectively known along with gold as 'monies')
6. Wheat
7. Barley
8. Dates
9. Raisins (wheat, barley, dates, and raisins are collectively regarded as 'crops')

---

[618] *Wasāʾil al-shīʿa*, v. 6, p. 34, ḥ. 4
[619] *Wasāʾil al-shīʿa*, v. 6, p. 39, ḥ. 2

Cattle

Four conditions must be met for these three kinds of livestock before *zakāt* is due upon them, namely:

First: Threshold

1. There are twelve thresholds for camels:
    a. Five camels, whose *zakāt* is a single sheep. There is no *zakāt* on less than five camels.
    b. Ten camels, whose *zakāt* is two sheep.
    c. Fifteen camels, whose *zakāt* is three sheep.
    d. Twenty camels, whose *zakāt* is four sheep.
    e. Twenty-five camels, whose *zakāt* is five sheep.
    f. Twenty-six camels, whose *zakāt* is a she-camel who has entered her second year of her life.
    g. Thirty-six camels, whose *zakāt* is a she-camel who has entered the third year of her life.
    h. Forty-six camels, whose *zakāt* is a she-camel who has entered the fourth year of her life.
    i. Sixty-one camels, whose *zakāt* is a she-camel who has entered the fifth year of her life.
    j. Seventy-six camels, whose *zakāt* is two she-camels in their third year.
    k. Ninety-one camels, whose *zakāt* is two she-camels in their fourth year.
    l. One hundred and twenty-one camels and above, their *zakāt* is one she-camel in her fourth year for every fifty camels, and one she-camel in her third year for every forty camels.
2. As for the thresholds of cows, they are two:
    a. Thirty cows, whose *zakāt* is a cow in her second year of life.
    b. Forty cows, whose *zakāt* is a cow in her third year of life.
    c. Above this, one can count the cattle in groups of thirty or forty, or alternate between the two.
3. As for sheep, they have five thresholds:
    a. Forty sheep, whose *zakāt* is a single sheep, and there is no *zakāt* on less than this number.
    b. One hundred and twenty-one sheep, whose *zakāt* is two sheep.
    c. Two hundred and one sheep, whose *zakāt* is three sheep.
    d. Three hundred and one sheep, whose *zakāt* is four sheep.
    e. Four hundred and above, whose *zakāt* is one sheep for every hundred.

4. And anything between two thresholds is excused (that is, one rounds down); it is only obligatory to pay *zakāt* on the threshold that has been met.

Second: A year of ownership

In order for *zakāt* to be levied upon livestock whose quantity reaches the minimum threshold, their owner must have had them for at least a whole year, in addition to all the other conditions.

Once livestock of a sufficient quantity reach their twelfth month, *zakāt* is due on them and this liability remains even if some of the criteria later lapse. So, if during the twelfth month of their ownership, one or more criteria for the payment of *zakāt* lapse, this does not affect the *zakāt* which is already due, under any circumstances. However, the accounting for the next year only begins at the end of the twelfth month.

Third: Pasturage

The livestock must have been pastured for the year, meaning that they must have been grazed naturally [and not fed by hand].

Fourth: Not being used as labour

The final criterion is that the livestock should not have been used as labour, whether for irrigating crops, tilling fields or carrying loads, etc. If livestock was used in this fashion, then no *zakāt* is due for it. This is determined by custom, so if some livestock are customarily considered to be beasts of burden, they are exempt, otherwise they are not.

Gold and silver

The noble *sunna*:

- It has been narrated from Imams al-Bāqir and al-Ṣādiq عليهما السلام: 'There is nothing owed on gold which is under 20 *mithqāl* (1 *mithqāl* = 4.25 grams). When 20 *mithqāl* have been reached, then a half *mithqāl* is due up to twenty-four *mithqāl*. Once twenty-four *mithqāl* have been reached, then three fifths of a dinar are owed up to twenty-eight *mithqāl*. And according to this scale it increases by amounts of four.'[620]
- Imam al-Bāqir عليه السلام said: 'For silver, when it reaches two hundred dirhams then five dirhams are owed, and nothing is owed for silver between multiples of two hundred. So if two hundred dirhams are increased by thirty-nine dirhams then there is nothing [additional]

[620] *Wasā'il al-shī'a*, v. 6, p. 93, ḥ. 5

owed until it reaches four hundred dirhams; nothing [additional] will be owed from a fraction until it reaches four hundred. And the same applies to dinars according to this scale.'[621]

❖ It has been narrated from Imams al-Ṣādiq and al-Kāẓim ﷺ: 'There is no *zakāt* on raw metals; it is only due on dinars and dirhams.'[622]
❖ Imam al-Ṣādiq ﷺ said: 'There is no *zakāt* on jewels.'[623]

Rulings:

Zakāt must be paid on gold and silver according to the following conditions:

First: Threshold

1. Gold has two thresholds:
   a. Twenty *sharʿī* dinars, whose *zakāt* is 2.5% or half a *sharʿī* dinar.
   b. Forty *sharʿī* dinars, whose *zakāt* is also 2.5%. Thereafter, every four dinars is counted for the purposes of *zakāt*.
   c. If there are fewer than twenty dinars, no *zakāt* is due on them, and if there are more than twenty dinars but less than the next increment of four, there is also no *zakāt* due on this excess, and so on.
2. Silver also has two thresholds:
   a. Two hundred dirhams, whose *zakāt* is five dirhams.
   b. Every forty dirhams thereafter, whose *zakāt* is a single dirham.
   c. Just as there is no *zakāt* due on gold beneath the lower threshold, so too is the case for silver. Thus, there is no *zakāt* on less than two hundred dirhams, nor is there any [additional] *zakāt* on quantities of silver between the forty-dirham increments.

Second: Struck (minted) coins

According to the well-known [legal opinion], *zakāt* is only due on gold and silver that have been struck as coins and are actually used as a medium of exchange. It makes no difference whether these coins were struck in the Islamic period or pre-Islamic period, or whether there is any writing on them, or whether the markings of the authority which struck them are still visible as a result of usage.

---

621 *Wasāʾil al-shīʿa*, v. 6, p. 97, ḥ. 6
622 *Wasāʾil al-shīʿa*, v. 6, p. 106, ḥ. 5
623 *Wasāʾil al-shīʿa*, v. 6, p. 106, ḥ. 2

Third: A year of ownership

As was the case with livestock, gold and silver must have been in the possession of a single owner for a complete year, as well as meeting all the other criteria outlined, in order for *zakāt* to be due on them.

By reaching the twelfth month of ownership, *zakāt* is due on gold and silver, and this obligation remains thereafter; and is not affected if some of these criteria later lapse in the twelfth month.

Crops

Conditions for zakāt being due

1. *Zakāt* becomes due on the four kinds of crops when the following criteria are met:
    a. Threshold: 847.66kg.
    b. Ownership: The source crops must be owned by someone before *zakāt* becomes due on their yields. Ownership is achieved either as a result of growing the crops (in the case of wheat and barley), through purchase or being given them, etc. For example, someone must have purchased the date palms or vines before their dates or grapes ripen in order to owe *zakāt* on them. Ownership is also achieved by purchasing the fruits themselves while they are still on the trees before the time that *zakāt* is due on them.

When is it obligatory to pay the zakāt?

2. The *zakāt* becomes due on the crops when it is time to harvest them. It is recommended precaution to consider their *zakāt* due when the grains of wheat and barley appear, when the dates turn yellow or red, and when the unripe grapes appear on the vine.

When is the threshold determined?

3. The threshold of the crops is determined and they are weighed once they have dried out. So if the weight of the fresh dates (*raṭab*) meets the threshold, but once they have dried out their weight is less than that of the threshold, then no *zakāt* is owed.
4. If the owner of the produce disposes of it, whether by eating, giving it away, or donating to charity some of it before the time of harvest, there is nothing due upon him. But if this is after the harvest and *zakāt* has become due on it, he must pay *zakāt* on whatever he has disposed of, if it is a significant quantity.

When must the zakāt be paid?

5. The *zakāt* must be paid when the wheat and barley are threshed, the dates are cut, and the grapes are picked. If payment is delayed until after this time and some of the produce is lost, then the *zakāt* of this lost portion must be guaranteed and compensated for. The one who is appointed to collect the taxes by the religious authorities can also seek payment of *zakāt* from the owners of agricultural produce at this time.

Amount of zakāt

6. The amount of *zakāt* due on the crops differs according to the kind of irrigation used to grow them.
    a. If the irrigation of the crops is natural, such as flowing water (whether through rivers or irrigation channels), rainwater, springs, or the natural moisture of the ground—as is the case with date palms and vines in valleys with moist soil – then the amount of *zakāt* due is 10% of the produce.
    b. If the irrigation is done through artificial means, such as buckets, drawing water from wells, water pumps, sprinklers, water wheels, etc., then the amount of *zakāt* due is 5% of the produce.
    c. If the crops are irrigated by a combination of both methods, and the relative importance of each is equal, then the *zakāt* is 7.5% of the produce. But if one method is more important, or customary usage determines that one predominates, then the *zakāt* rate for that method is levied.

Deductibles

7. *Zakāt* is calculated after government taxes and rates have been deducted from the produce, and after government agents or anyone else have taken a share of it – rightfully or wrongfully – if the owner cannot avoid this in some way. It is only after these deductions that the threshold of the produce is calculated.
8. The strongest legal opinion is that expenses and provisions are also deducted from the produce before *zakāt* is calculated. This includes the wages of farm workers and guards— if these are paid from the fruits of date palms, grape vines, or crops— or who is given their fruits [in exchange] for the use of an animal, etc. As for other monetary expenses, such as the cost of fertilizer, seeds and preparing the ground for planting, it is precaution that these are not deducted from the produce value before *zakāt* is calculated.

How can *zakāt* can be spent?

The noble *sunna*:

❖ Concerning a man who gives *zakāt* on his wealth to a man he believes to be poor, but later finds to be wealthy, Imam al-Ṣādiq 🕮 said: 'It does not suffice him for it [as *zakāt*].'[624]

❖ Saʿīd b. Ghazwān said: I asked Abū ʿAbd Allah 🕮: How much does one man receive from the *zakāt*? He said: 'Give to him of *zakāt* until he reaches sufficiency thereby.'[625]

❖ Abū Baṣīr has narrated that he said to Imam Abū Jaʿfar 🕮: There is a man from our companions who is embarrassed about taking *zakāt*, so I give him *zakāt* without calling it that to him. So he said: 'Give it to him and do not call it [*zakāt*], and do not humiliate the believer.'[626]

Rulings:

Zakāt can be spent on the following:

1. The poor (*fuqarāʾ*)
2. The needy (*masākīn*)
3. Those who collect the *zakāt*
4. Those whose hearts are to be reconciled (*al-muʾallifa qulūbuhum*)
5. For the freeing of slaves (*taḥrīr al-raqīq*)
6. For debtors (*ghārimīn*)
7. In Allah's way (*fī sabīl allāh*)
8. On the wayfarer (*ibn al-sabīl*)

And the details of this are as follows:

First & second: The poor and needy

1. A poor person (*faqīr*) is someone who cannot secure his own livelihood or that of his dependents according to his social position and his needs. Someone who can meet his daily living expenses but who cannot provide a home for his family to live in, or cannot afford a car and this is a necessity for him, is counted as poor. The same is true with regards to all other needs of life, which differ from one person to another, from one country to another, and from one time to another.

---

[624] *Wasāʾil al-shīʿa*, v. 6, p. 148, ḥ. 5
[625] *Wasāʾil al-shīʿa*, v. 6, p. 179, ḥ. 5
[626] *Wasāʾil al-shīʿa*, v. 6, p. 219, ḥ. 1

Because *zakāt* is paid on an annual basis, a poor person defined as someone who cannot secure his livelihood for a complete year. As for a needy (*miskīn*) person, he is in a worse state than the poor one.

2. Whoever has a source of livelihood, such as some land that he can cultivate, or livestock, or real estate, which provides a continuous source of income, or a salaried job, a business, or capital for investment, etc., and the income of this suffices his yearly needs, it is impermissible for him to receive *zakāt*. However, if the revenue from this source is insufficient for his needs, he is allowed to make up the difference with *zakāt*.
3. No one is disqualified from receiving *zakāt* on the basis of their having a home, a housekeeper, a means of transportation, furnishings, and other household necessities, clothes, or the like thereof, commensurate with their social standing; the only criterion is that their revenues are not sufficient for their annual provisions. In fact, if the poor person does not possess these things, it is permissible to pay him a quantity of *zakāt* that covers his annual provision and allows him to purchase his necessities of life according to the living standards of his country.
4. A poor person who is able to learn a profession that will guarantee his provisions, he must – as a matter of precaution – learn it and not rely on *zakāt*. However, he is still allowed to receive *zakāt* while he is learning this profession if he is still customarily considered poor, even if he is unable to obtain a loan.

Third: Those who collect *zakāt*

Collectors are those who have been appointed by the Imam عليه السلام or his representative, whether specific or general (i.e., the religious authorities), to collect the *zakāt*, gather it, look after it, keep accounts of it, and then convey it to him or to its worthy recipients. Someone who works in this job is entitled to a portion of the *zakāt* proportional to his work, even if he is wealthy.

Fourth: Those whose hearts are to be reconciled

And they are of two kinds:

1. Disbelievers who are given *zakāt* to secure their allegiance, cement their friendship with the Muslims, and attract them to Islam; and to repel their evil, or to make use of them in specific areas such as *jihād*.
2. Those Muslims whose faith is weak, who are given *zakāt* with the goal of cementing their connection to Islamic society.

Fifth: Freeing slaves

A share of the *zakāt* can be spent on purchasing slaves – while a system of slave ownership exists – and freeing them, and this was Islam's practical program for ending slavery.

Sixth: Debtors

Debtors are those who are overwhelmed with debts and unable to repay them. They are given the *zakāt*, even if they are able to otherwise secure their yearly provisions, on the condition that they had not spent their loan in disobedience to their Creator.

Seventh: In the way of Allah

This includes all good and righteous deeds, such as striving in Allah's ways and developing countries, such as excavating canals, or building bridges, roads, schools, libraries, cultural institutions, educational centres and mosques; saving the faithful from the clutches of the oppressors, supporting those striving in Allah's way, printing useful books, supporting religious scholars and students, and any other work or project that yields a public benefit to the *umma*.

Eighth: The wayfarer

A wayfarer is a traveller whose wealth and provisions have been used up while travelling, or whose means of transportation has been lost and he has no means of replacing it, even if he is wealthy in his homeland. And the conditions for paying *zakāt* to the traveller are as follows:

1. His journey should not have been for sinful purposes.
2. He should not be able to obtain what he needs [some other way], even by taking a loan or selling some of his unnecessary possessions.

Conditions for those who receive *zakāt*

The noble *sunna*:

- The Messenger of Allah ﷺ said: 'The one who gives charity to our enemies is like a thief in the Sanctuary of Allah.'[627]
- In the *tafsīr* (exegesis) of Imam al-ʿAskarī (ع), concerning the words of Allah Almighty, 'Establish the prayer and give the *zakāt*,' he said: 'Establish the prayer completely, and its *wuḍūʾ*, *takbīr*s, standing, recitation, bowing, prostration, and [observing] its limits. And give

---

[627] *Wasāʾil al-shīʿa*, v. 6, p. 155, ḥ. 14

zakāt to the rightful—do not give it to disbelievers, hypocrites, or the *nāṣib* (someone who opposes the Holy Household or their Shīʿa).'[628]

- Imam al-Ṣādiq ﷺ said: 'Do not give even a little *zakāt* to anyone who alleges Allah compels His servants to disobey Him, or tasks them with what they are unable to bear.'[629]
- Imam al-Ṣādiq ﷺ said: 'Five are ineligible for *zakāt*: the father, mother, child, slave, and woman (i.e., wife), and that is because they are his family members, who already depend on him.'[630]

Rulings:

Those entitled to receive *zakāt* must meet four conditions:

First: Belief. *Zakāt* is not given to disbelievers, nor is it given to those Muslims who do not believe in correct doctrines (e.g., rejection of the Imamate of any of the Twelve Imams, or heretical doctrines even if the proposed recipient is ostensibly a Twelver), unless they fall under the category of 'those whose hearts are to be reconciled' or 'in the way of Allah.'

Second: They should not be supporting immorality. It is impermissible to give *zakāt* to those who will spend it sinfully, especially if withholding payment to them will work to discourage them from sinning.

Third: That the one receiving the *zakāt* should not be entitled to the maintenance (*nafaqa*) of the one giving it. It is not permissible for someone to give the *zakāt* taken from his own wealth to his parents, grandparents, children, or grandchildren, nor to his spouse to whom he must pay maintenance. This is if someone is paying them from the share of the poor and needy, but if he is giving them the *zakāt* on another basis, such as their being burdened with debt, or they are those whose hearts are to be reconciled, or it is in Allah's way (so long as these categories apply to them), then there is no problem with this. As for the wayfarer, he is given enough money to return to his homeland, not for his annual provision.

Fourth: The person receiving the *zakāt* cannot be a Hashemite. The Hashemite cannot receive *zakāt* from a non-Hashemite. However, he can still use those philanthropic institutions funded by *zakāt*, such as schools, hospitals, bridges, etc.

---

628 *Wasāʾil al-shīʿa*, v. 6, p. 154, ḥ. 13
629 *Wasāʾil al-shīʿa*, v. 6, p. 156, ḥ. 1
630 *Wasāʾil al-shīʿa*, v. 6, p. 165, ḥ. 1

Zakāt al-fiṭra

The noble *sunna*:

- Imam al-Ṣādiq ﷺ said: '*Al-fiṭra* is obligated by whatever obligates *zakāt*.'[631]
- Concerning one born on the eve of *fiṭr*, or the Jew or Christian who accepts Islam on the eve of *fiṭr*, Imam al-Ṣādiq ﷺ said: 'They do not owe *fiṭra*. There is no *fiṭra* until a person reaches one month [after birth or Islam].'[632]
- Imam al-Kāẓim ﷺ was asked about a man who is needy of charity: does he have to pay *al-fiṭra*? So he said: 'He does not owe *fiṭra*.'[633]
- Isḥāq b. ʿAmmār said: I asked Abū ʿAbd Allah ﷺ about the *fiṭra*: can we gather it and give its monetary value to a single Muslim man? He said: 'There is no problem with that.'[634]
- Al-ʿĪṣ b. al-Qāsim said: I asked Abū ʿAbd Allah ﷺ about when *al-fiṭra* should be paid. So he said: 'Before the prayer on the Day of *Fiṭr*.'[635]
- Ibrāhīm b. ʿUqba wrote to the Imam ﷺ, asking him about *al-fiṭra*: is it lawful to give it to someone other than a believer (a Shīʿa)? So he wrote back to him: 'You should not give your *zakāt* but to a believer.'[636]

Rulings:

The obligation to pay *fiṭra*

1. The *zakāt al-fiṭrā* is obligatory each year by the consensus of the Muslims, and is after the month of fasting has ended, according to the details below.
2. Because *zakāt al-fiṭra* is an act of worship, it must be paid with the intention of seeking nearness to Allah, as is the case with the *zakāt* on wealth.
3. *Zakāt al-fiṭra* must be paid by everyone who is mature, of sound mind, free, wealthy, and conscious – according to the majority opinion of later scholars – at sunset on the eve of *ʿĪd*. An individual must pay his own *fiṭra* and that of his dependents, as we shall outline below.

---

631 *Wasāʾil al-shīʿa*, v. 6, p. 226, ḥ. 1
632 *Wasāʾil al-shīʿa*, v. 6, p. 245, ḥ. 1
633 *Wasāʾil al-shīʿa*, v. 6, p. 223, ḥ. 6
634 *Wasāʾil al-shīʿa*, v. 6, p. 238, ḥ. 2
635 *Wasāʾil al-shīʿa*, v. 6, p. 240, ḥ. 4
636 *Wasāʾil al-shīʿa*, v. 6, p. 249, ḥ. 2

Its quantity and kind

4. The quantity of *fiṭra* is a single measure (*ṣāʿ*), which is roughly equivalent to three kilograms, of wheat, barley, rice, dates, raisins, corn, or a similar foodstuff.
   It is obligatory precaution to choose whichever food is the staple crop for people in the land in which the legal agent (the person tasked with carrying out the obligation) lives. It is recommended precaution to choose one of the four *zakāt* crops (wheat, barley, dates, and raisins), if any of these are the staple for the land.
5. The legal agent can provide the food itself or its equivalent monetary value.

Its time

6. *Fiṭra* is due from the eve of *ʿĪd*, when the aforementioned conditions are fulfilled, until midday on the day of *ʿĪd* for anyone who has not prayed the *ʿĪd* prayer. If someone wishes to pray the *ʿĪd* prayer, it is precaution that he should pay the *zakāt* before prayer time. If he delays payment until later, he should set the *zakāt* aside [with intention] in advance. Otherwise, it is precaution that he pays it without the intention of paying it on time or making up for its late payment.

Setting it aside and transporting it

7. The legal agent can set aside the *fiṭra* (whether in the form of foodstuffs or their equivalent monetary value) at the time it is due, then pay it to a poor person later if he could not pay it sooner.
8. It is obligatory precaution not to send the *fiṭra* from the country he is living in to another country unless there is no one entitled to receive it where he lives, or if he is sending it to a jurist (*faqīh*).

***Fiṭra* for dependents and guests**

9. The legal agent must pay *fiṭra* for himself and for anyone who is considered his dependent when the eve of *ʿĪd al-Fiṭr* sets in, whether these are young or old, Muslim or non-Muslim, entitled to maintenance from him or not, close relatives or not, free or slaves, whether they live with the legal agent or not (such as a son who is studying in another country but is still the legal agent's dependent).
10. The host must pay *fiṭra* on behalf of his guests who were staying with him from before the eve of *ʿĪd*, with their consent, and so long as they intend to remain after the crescent for Shawwāl is sighted. This is on the condition that they are dependent upon their host during their stay,

meaning that they are staying with him for a sufficient length of time before and after *ʿĪd*.

How *fiṭra* should be spent

11. *Zakāt al-fiṭra* can be spent in the eight ways already mentioned for the *zakāt* of wealth. But it is precaution to only spend it on poor and needy believers, and it is permitted to spend it on the children of poor believers or give it to them.
12. A non-Hashemite's *fiṭra* should not be given to a Hashemite, but a Hashemite's *fiṭra* can be given to anyone.

Expenditure and charity (*ṣadaqa*) in the noble *sunna*

The effects of charity:

- The Messenger of Allah ﷺ said: 'Charity repels an evil death.'[637]
- And he ﷺ said: 'Give charity, for surely [giving] charity increases wealth substantially; so give charity, [and] may Allah have mercy upon you.'[638]
- Zurāra has narrated from Imam al-Ṣādiq عليه السلام: 'Sustenance descends because of [giving] charity. Whoever is certain that [sustenance] follows is lavish in giving. Surely Allah sends down aid in proportion to provision.'[639]

The perfection of faith:

- Al-Mufaḍḍal b. ʿUmar said: I heard Abū ʿAbd Allah Jaʿfar b. Muḥammad عليه السلام saying: 'A servant does not perfect his faith until he possesses four qualities: his manners are beautified, his spirit is generous, he holds to the best in his words, and gives the best from his wealth.'[640]

The Shīʿa and the poor:

- Muḥammad b. ʿAjlān said: I was with Abū ʿAbd Allah عليه السلام when a man entered and gave the greeting of peace. So [the Imam] asked him: 'How are those you left behind, of your brothers?' So he beautified their praised, commended, and extoled them. So the Imam said to him: 'And how do their wealthy visit their poor?' So he said: 'Very little.' The Imam said: 'So how do their wealthy see [to the needs] of their poor?'

---

[637] *Wasāʾil al-shīʿa*, v. 6, p. 255, ḥ. 2
[638] *Wasāʾil al-shīʿa*, v. 6, p. 257, ḥ. 8
[639] *Wasāʾil al-shīʿa*, v. 6, p. 257, ḥ. 11
[640] *Wasāʾil al-shīʿa*, v. 6, p. 259, ḥ. 21

He said: 'Very little.' The Imam said: 'So how is the connection of their rich to their poor concerning what they possess?' He said: You are describing manners rarely found among us. So the Imam said: 'Then how do these people claim to be Shīʿa?'[641]

They do good works

❖ The Messenger of Allah ﷺ said: 'All of good (*maʿrūf*) is charity.'[642]

[641] *Wasāʾil al-shīʿa*, v. 6, p. 298, ḥ. 3
[642] *Wasāʾil al-shīʿa*, v. 6, p. 321, ḥ. 1

Pilgrimage (*Ḥajj*)

The noble *sunna*:

- Imam al-Riḍā said: 'The reason for making the pilgrimage obligatory at least one time is that Allah Almighty set the obligations according to the strength of the least of the people. So from these obligations, the obligatory pilgrimage (*ḥajj*) is once, then He wished the stronger people [perform it more] according to their level of endurance.'[643]
- It is narrated from Abū ʿAbd Allah al-Ṣādiq ﷺ: 'If a man is financially capable of performing the pilgrimage, but puts it off without having some business that legitimately excuses him, then he has abandoned a law from the laws of Islam (*sharīʿa min sharāʾiʿ al-islām*).'[644]
- It is narrated from Imam al-Ṣādiq ﷺ: 'Whoever dies and did not perform the pilgrimage, which is the proof of Islam, with nothing having prevented him from it—being needy or ill—such that he cannot endure the pilgrimage, or the Sultan (i.e., the government) prevents him, then he dies as a Jew or a Christian.'[645]

Definition of *ḥajj*

1. Ḥajj is one of the prescriptions of Allah's law, and in Islamic parlance it means to travel to Allah's House, the Holy Sanctuary and sacred sites, while performing specific rites there in a particular period of time.

The rulings of *ḥajj*

The noble *sunna*:

- It is narrated from Abū ʿAbd Allah ﷺ: 'Even if a boy performed the pilgrimage ten times, as soon as he attains puberty he is obliged to fulfill the obligations of Islam (i.e., he must perform the pilgrimage again).'[646]
- Abū al-Ḥasan Mūsā ﷺ said: 'The slave is not obliged to perform the greater or lesser pilgrimages until he is freed.'[647]
- Abū Baṣīr said: I heard Abū ʿAbd Allah ﷺ saying: 'Whoever was offered the pilgrimage, even upon a lame donkey that is missing its tail, which

---

[643] *Wasāʾil al-shīʿa*, v. 8, p. 13, ḥ. 3
[644] *Wasāʾil al-shīʿa*, v. 8, p. 17, ḥ. 3
[645] *Wasāʾil al-shīʿa*, v. 8, p. 19, ḥ. 1
[646] *Wasāʾil al-shīʿa*, v. 8, p. 20, ḥ. 2
[647] *Wasāʾil al-shīʿa*, v. 8, p. 22, ḥ. 2

resists [traveling], he is [still considered] capable of performing the pilgrimage.'[648]

Rulings:

2. *Ḥajj* is divided into obligatory and recommended categories; obligatory *ḥajj* is sub-divided into three further categories:

   First: *Ḥijjat al-islām*, which is obligatory just once in a person's lifetime, so long as they fulfil the criteria for it being obligatory.

   Second: That which a person makes obligatory upon himself by way of a vow, pledge, or oath.

   Third: That which becomes obligatory for a person when he hires himself out to perform *ḥajj* on behalf of someone else. All other types of *ḥajj* are recommended.

3. *Ḥijjat al-islām* is obligatory once in the life of anyone who fulfils the following criteria:

   First: Legal maturity

   Second: Soundness of mind

   Third: Freedom

   Fourth: Ability (*istiṭāʿa*), herein defined as the following conditions being met at a single time:

   a. Having funds for the journey
   b. Ability to meet the physical requirements [of the pilgrimage]
   c. The absence of any obstructions to the route
   d. Having sufficient time to perform the pilgrimage
   e. Going to *ḥajj* will not cause serious problems for his livelihood or that of his dependents.

The *mawāqīt*

The noble *sunna*:

❖ Imam al-Ṣādiq ﵇ said: 'The are five locations for entering a state of consecration (*iḥrām*), which were designated by the Messenger of Allah ﷺ. The pilgrim of the greater or lesser pilgrimages (*ḥajj* and *ʿumra*) should not enter a state of consecration before or after them. He designated Dha al-Ḥulayfa for the people of Medina, and it is the Mosque of the Tree (*masjid al-shajara*) where they pray and the pilgrimage is obligated. For the people of Greater Syria (*al-shām*), he designated al-Juḥfa. For the people of Yemen, he designated Yalalam.

[648] Wasāʾil al-shīʿa, v. 8, p. 27

None should turn from the appointed places of the Messenger of Allah ﷺ.’[649]

- Isḥāq b. ʿAmmār said: I asked Abū Ibrāhīm ؑ about a man who comes intending to perform lesser pilgrimage (*ʿumra*) in Rajab, but the new moon (of Shaʿbān) appears before he reaches al-ʿAqīq (his *mīqāt*). Should he assume the state of consecration before the appointed place and make it [*ʿumra*] for Rajab, or should he delay assuming the state of consecration until al-ʿAqīq and make it for Shaʿbān? He said: ‘Assume the state of consecration for Rajab, before the designated location, because Rajab is virtuous and that was what he had [originally] intended.’[650]

Rulings:

4. The *mawāqīt* (sing. *mīqāt*) are places the Lawgiver has designated as the stations whereat the *ḥajj* and *ʿumra* pilgrims can enter a state of consecration (*iḥrām*). They number ten in total:
    a. **First:** Dhū al-Halīfa, whence is situated the Shajara Mosque.
    b. **Second:** Wādī al-ʿAqīq
    c. **Third:** Juḥfa
    d. **Fourth:** Qarn al-Manāzil
    e. **Fifth:** Yalamlam
    f. **Sixth:** Duwayrat al-Ahl, meaning the home of a *ḥajj* pilgrim that lies beyond the *mīqāt*.
    g. **Seventh:** Mecca, which is the *mīqāt* for the *ḥajj* of *tamattuʿ*
    h. **Eighth:** Adnā al-Ḥill, the *mīqāt* for consecrating for *ʿumra mufrada*.
    i. **Ninth:** Fakhkh
    j. **Tenth:** Parallel to one of the five *mawāqīt* mentioned above.

Acts of *ʿumrat al-tamattuʿ*

The noble *sunna*:

- Imam al-Ṣādiq ؑ said: ‘Whosoever completes [recitation] of the Qur’ān in Mecca will not die without first seeing the Messenger of Allah ﷺ and his (the reciter’s) place in Paradise.’[651]
- In his will to ʿAlī ؑ, the Prophet ﷺ said: ‘O ʿAlī, verily ʿAbd al-Muṭṭalib established five traditions (*sunan*) during the pre-Islamic Age

---

[649] *Wasāʾil al-shīʿa*, v. 8, p. 222, ḥ. 3
[650] *Wasāʾil al-shīʿa*, v. 8, p. 326, ḥ. 2
[651] *Wasāʾil al-shīʿa*, v. 9, p. 383, ḥ. 7

of Ignorance, which Allah Almighty included for him in Islam: he forbid the wives of fathers to their sons...' until he ﷺ said: 'And there was no established number of circumambulations for the Quraysh, so ʿAbd al-Muṭṭalib established seven circumabulations, and Allah carried that into Islam.'[652]

❖ It has been narrated from Abū ʿAbd Allah ؑ in a longer narration: 'The rite of walking hurriedly between Ṣafā and Marwa is obligatory.'[653]

Rulings:

5. The acts of *ʿumrat al-tamattuʿ* are five:
    a. Consecration (*iḥrām*) at one of the *mawāqīt.*
    b. Circumambulation around Allah's House.
    c. Two *rakʿats* of *ṣalāt al-ṭawwāf* at the Station of Abraham.
    d. Running between Ṣafā and Marwa.
    e. Cutting one's hair.
6. The obligatory components of consecration are:
    a. Intention
    b. Putting on the clothes of consecration
    c. To call out *labbayk* ('I am at your service')

Violations of consecration

7. Things that will invalidate a person's state of consecration, which are forbidden to someone in a state of consecration, and which require expiation to be paid if performed are:
    1. Hunting.
    2. Sexual activities and anything related to them.
    3. Smelling pleasant odours or scenting oneself with them.
    4. A man wearing clothes [other than what is obligated for the rite].
    5. Applying *kuḥl.*
    6. Looking at oneself in a mirror.
    7. Wearing shoes and socks.
    8. Sinning.
    9. Disputation.
    10. Killing insects that feed on the body (e.g., mosquitos).
    11. Wearing a ring for decoration.
    12. A woman wearing a bracelet for decoration.
    13. Using makeup.

---

[652] *Wasāʾil al-shīʿa*, v. 9, p. 414, ḥ. 1
[653] *Wasāʾil al-shīʿa*, v. 9, p. 510, ḥ. 1

14. Removing hair.
15. A man covering his head or a woman covering her face.
16. A man travelling under shade.
17. Causing oneself to bleed.
18. Trimming one's fingernails.
19. Cutting down trees or plants.
20. Bearing arms.

Acts in *ḥajj al-tamattuʿ*

8. As for the acts of *ḥajj al-tamattuʿ*, they are:
   a. Consecration
   b. Staying at ʿArafāt
   c. Staying at Muzdalifa
   d. Stoning the rearmost devil
   e. Sacrifice
   f. Shaving and cutting the hair
   g. Circumambulation of *ziyāra* (visitation)
   h. Prayers for the circumambulation of *ziyāra*
   i. Running between Ṣafā and Marwa
   j. The 'circumambulation of women' (*ṭawwāf al-nisāʾ*)
   k. Prayers for the 'circumambulation of women'
   l. Spending the night in Minā
   m. Stoning the three devils

Ḥajj and *ʿumra* have many detailed rulings connected to them. For more details of these, one can refer to *Aḥkām al-ʿIbādāt* or *Manāsik al-Ḥajj* by the same author.

Jihād[654]

The noble *sunna*:

- Imam ʿAlī ﷺ said: 'Verily the Messenger of Allah ﷺ sent out a detachment of soldiers. When they returned, he said: "Welcome to the people who have accomplished the lesser combat (*jihād*)—the greater combat still remains for them." So it was said: O Messenger of Allah, what is the greater combat? He said: "Combat against the self."'[655]
- It is narrated from the Commander of the Believers: 'Combat against the self (*jihād al-nafs*) is the dowry for Paradise.'[656]
- In a narration from Abū ʿAbd Allah ﷺ, he said: 'There is no faith without deeds, and deeds are from it; and faith is not established but by deeds.'[657]
- Abū ʿAbd Allah ﷺ said that the Messenger of Allah ﷺ said: 'Islam is bare, so its dress is modesty, its adornment is fidelity, its chivalry is righteous deeds, and its support is piety (*waraʿ*)! For everything there is a foundation, and the foundation of Islam is love of us, the People of the House.'[658]
- A man came to al-Ṣādiq ﷺ and said: O Son of the Messenger of Allah, inform me about the noblest manners. So he said: 'Pardoning the one who has wronged you, maintaining a relationship with one who tries to cut their relationship with you, giving to one who refuses to aid you, and speaking the truth even if it is against yourself.'[659]
- Imam Abū ʿAbd Allah ﷺ: 'Surely we do not consider any man a believer until he is submissive and obedient to our command. If you follow our command and exercise restraint from sins, then you will be adorned by it—may Allah bless you—and you will be an affliction to our enemies and Allah will strengthen you.'[660]
- Abū Jaʿfar ﷺ said: 'The best of worship is abstinence of the stomach and privates.'[661]

---

[654] The concept of *jihād* has been the subject of severe distortion and manipulation at the hands of imposters and extremists. In this section, His Eminence briefly outlines the true Islamic definition of the term, and provides some of the broad rulings that govern its application.

[655] *Mustadrak al-wasāʾil*, v. 2, p. 270, ḥ. 1

[656] *Mustadrak al-wasāʾil*, v. 2, p. 270, ḥ. 10

[657] *Wasāʾil al-shīʿa*, v. 11, p. 127, ḥ. 3

[658] *Wasāʾil al-shīʿa*, v. 11, p. 141, ḥ. 6

[659] *Wasāʾil al-shīʿa*, v. 11, p. 156, ḥ. 6

[660] *Wasāʾil al-shīʿa*, v. 11, p. 192, ḥ. 1

[661] *Wasāʾil al-shīʿa*, v. 11, p. 198, ḥ. 2

- It is narrated from Abū ʿAbd Allah ﷺ: 'The Commander of the Believers ﷺ was asked: what is restraint (*zuhd*) as concerns this world? He said: "Steering clear of what is unlawful in it."'[662]
- Abū ʿAbd Allah ﷺ said: 'Exercising restraint towards this world is not achieved through ridding oneself of wealth, nor through forbidding oneself what is lawful; rather, exercising restraint in this world consists of not treating what you possess as more reliable than what Allah Almighty possesses.'[663]
- The Commander of the Believers ﷺ said: 'Verily the Messenger of Allah ﷺ said: "Surely the dinar and dirham ruined those who came before you, and they are a source of ruin for you [as well]."'[664]
- The Commander of the Believers ﷺ said: 'Perfume yourselves by seeking forgiveness, and do not dishonor yourselves with the stench of sins.'[665]

Introduction

The term '*jihād*' encompasses numerous kinds of struggle, beginning at struggling with the self (*jihād al-nafs*) and its desires, and ending with dedicating one's life entirely to Allah and volunteering to fight in an effort to raise the banner of truth, enjoin good, forbid evil and resist tyranny is perpetuated.

Jihād is one of the best means of seeking recourse to Allah, as He says: **'O you who have faith! Be wary of Allah, and seek the means of recourse to Him, and wage *jihād* in His way, so that you may be felicitous.'**[666]

From this verse, we deduce that *jihād* is a divine means [of seeking recourse to Allah], which could become an individual obligation; such as defending Muslims and the religion of Islam against danger. It could also be a strongly emphasized recommendation, such as struggling to convey the message of Islam and [peacefully] spread the true religion.

---

662 *Wasāʾil al-shīʿa*, v. 11, p. 314, ḥ. 11
663 *Wasāʾil al-shīʿa*, v. 11, p. 314, ḥ. 13
664 *Wasāʾil al-shīʿa*, v. 11, p. 319, ḥ. 3
665 *Wasāʾil al-shīʿa*, v. 11, p. 356, ḥ. 17
666 Sūrat al-Māʾida (5):35

Section one: Struggle against challenges

Against whom should we struggle?

The noble *sunna*:

❖ Aṣbagh b. Nubāta has narrated, as part of a longer report from the Commander of the Believers ﷺ: '*Jihād* has four aspects: commanding virtue, forbidding vice, to be honest among the citizenry, and to fight against *al-fāsiqīn* (those who openly commit acts of disobedience to Allah). Whoever commands virtue has strengthened the back of the believer. Whoever forbids vice has forced Satan's abasement. Whoever is honest among the people accomplishes that with which he is tasked. Whoever is angered on behalf of Allah Almighty, Allah will be angered on his behalf.'[667]

❖ Imam ʿAlī ﷺ said: 'The tax of valor (*zakāt al-shajāʿa*) is fighting in the way of Allah.'[668]

❖ Imam ʿAlī said: 'Fight in the way of Allah with your hands; and if you cannot do that, then with fight with your tongues, and if you cannot do that, then fight with your hearts.'[669]

❖ Fuḍayl b. ʿIyāḍ said: I asked Abū ʿAbd Allah ﷺ about *jihād*: is it a *sunna* or is it obligatory? So he said: '*Jihād* is of four kinds: two of them are obligatory, one is a *sunna* that cannot be established but with [one of] the obligatory [kinds], and one is a *sunna*. As for one of the obligatory forms, it is the struggle of man against his soul from disobeying Allah, and it is the greatest *jihād*. And struggling against **"the disbelievers in your vicinity"**[670] is obligatory. As for the *jihād* which is a *sunna* that cannot be established except with an obligatory form, it is when fighting against the enemy is obligatory upon the entire *umma*, and if it were abandoned then torment would come to them, which is from the torment of the *umma*. And this is a *sunna* for the Imam alone that he goes against the enemy with the *umma* and fights them. As for the *jihād* which is a *sunna*, so [it is] every *sunna* a man fights to establish, attain, and enliven. Working and striving to this end is among the best of deeds, because it gives life to a tradition (*sunna*), and the Messenger of Allah ﷺ said: "Whoever establishes a good *sunna* will be given its

---

[667] *Tafsīr nūr al-thaqalayn*, v. 3, p. 523, ḥ. 229
[668] *Mīzān al-ḥikma*, v. 2, p. 125
[669] *Biḥār al-anwār*, v. 97, p. 49
[670] Sūrat al-Tawba (9):123

reward, and the reward of everyone who acts upon it until Judgment Day, without reducing their rewards at all.'"[671]

❖ Imam ʿAlī said: 'Allah has obligated the purification of faith from polytheism (*shirk*), the exclusion of arrogance from prayer, that *zakāt* brings about sustenance, fasting as a trial of creation's sincerity, pilgrimage is a means of [seeking] proximity to the religion, and [obligated upon] *jihād* glory for Islam...'[672]

❖ Imam al-Ṣādiq 🕊 said: '*Jihād* is the greatest of things after the obligatory [prayers].'[673]

❖ Abū ʿAbd Allah 🕊 said: 'All of goodness is in the sword and under the shadow of the sword. No people rise but by the sword, and the sword is the key of Paradise and the Fire.'[674]

❖ It has also been narrated by Abū ʿAbd Allah 🕊 from the Messenger of Allah 🕊: 'Paradise has a gate called the Gate of the Fighters (*bāb al-mujāhidīn*). They pass through it when it is open with their swords tied to them. They pass through a way station and the angels welcome them.' He said: 'Whoever abandons *jihād* will be dressed with humiliation and poverty by Allah in his livelihood and his religion will be annihilated. May Allah honor my nation by its horse hooves and spear tips.'[675]

❖ The narrator said to Imam Abū ʿAbd Allah 🕊: I saw in a dream that I said to you that fighting without an Imam to whom obedience is obligatory is unlawful, like a corpse, or blood, or the flesh of swine. So I said to myself: Yes, it is just like that. So Abū ʿAbd Allah 🕊 said: 'It is like that; it is like that.'[676]

❖ Abū ʿAbd Allah 🕊 said: 'When the Messenger of Allah wanted to send a detachment he would call them, tell them to sit with him, and would say: "Advance in the name of Allah, and by Allah, and in the way of Allah, and upon the religion of the Messenger of Allah. Do not go to extremes, do not maim, do not betray, do not kill the elderly, children, or women. Do not cut down trees unless you have no choice. Whichever man from among the least of the Muslims or the highest is sympathetic to the polytheists then he is safe until he hears the words of Allah. If

---

[671] *Wasāʾil al-shīʿa*, v. 11, p. 16, ḥ. 1
[672] *Nahj al-balāgha*, saying 252
[673] *Mīzān al-ḥikma*, v. 2, p. 125, from *Wasāʾil al-shīʿa*, v. 11, p. 7
[674] *Wasāʾil al-shīʿa*, v. 11, p. 5, ḥ. 1
[675] *Wasāʾil al-shīʿa*, v. 11, p. 5, ḥ. 2
[676] *Wasāʾil al-shīʿa*, v. 11, p. 32, ḥ. 1

he follows you, then he is your brother in faith, and if he refuses you, then get him to safety and seek the help of Allah.'"[677]

- ʿAbbād b. Ṣuhayb said: I heard Abū ʿAbd Allah ﷺ saying: 'The Messenger of Allah ﷺ would never attack the enemy at night.'[678]
- The Commander of the Believers ﷺ said: 'The Messenger of Allah ﷺ forbade dumping poison into the cities of the polytheists.'[679]

Man must maintain the rules of the religion with the strength he has been granted, and struggle against anyone who impedes him in this way, even his own parents, children, brothers, spouse, tribe, or people. And we shall detail each of these below:

A: Parents, between resistance and kindness

A child is raised in the embrace of a family, wherein it finds fertile ground to develop its abilities, learn its customs and receive, from its environment, its language, culture, and much experience. But when it matures and Allah grants it wisdom and intellect, it enters a new phase of life. And perhaps a call to reformation reaches it that is foreign to the family in which it was raised. Here begins the first step in her struggle for change and reform, and a difficult balance is set in motion. From one side, it feels that it must honour its family, but on the other it has its own aspirations. The Qurʾān addresses this balance, when it enjoins children to be kind to their parents, show the utmost respect to them, never be rude to them, and not even utter the word 'uff' (a syllable of reproach). However, it also forbids children from worshiping them, submitting absolutely to their whims, associating them with Allah, or obeying them in disobedience to the religion. That is because true human movement comes from knowledge, not blind following.

And Allah strikes a parable for this with his prophet, Abraham ﷺ, when he stood before his paternal uncle saying:

'Father! Indeed a knowledge has already come to me which has not come to you. So follow me that I may guide you to a right path.'[680]

And Abraham challenged his uncle and his people, and struggled against them with all his might, when he told them:

---

[677] *Wasāʾil al-shīʿa*, v. 11, p. 43, ḥ. 2
[678] *Wasāʾil al-shīʿa*, v. 11, p. 46, ḥ. 1
[679] *Wasāʾil al-shīʿa*, v. 15, p. 62, ḥ. 1 / Ḥ. 19989
[680] Sūrat Maryam (19):43

'When Abraham said to Azar, his father,[681] "Do you take idols for gods? Indeed I see you and your people in manifest error."'[682]

From this insight, we can glean the following rules:

First: Every human being must look afresh at their culture, thoughts and opinions in life as soon as they reach maturity. If a person finds that the heritage and culture of their forefathers is irrational, they must set out in search of the truth themselves.

Second: Parents must educate their children from their youngest age on how to think properly, nurture the gifts of intellect and wisdom in them, and encourage them to study and investigate things for themselves.

Third: If your parents call you to submit to idols and falsehood, and surrender yourself completely to tyranny, then you must be kind to them without obeying them, as they will not avail you against Allah on the Day of Resurrection.

Fourth: Every generation desires to continue following its own ways, and to bestow upon these ways a sense of sacred legitimacy, but this is impermissible since it is making up the law, and an innovation. The only legitimate governance is that of Allah, and no opinion, custom, or experience can be given sanctity or divine legitimacy. Neither should children submit to any governance except that of Allah with regards to religious laws.

Fifth: To become learned in religion, perceive its realities, and be acquainted with its rules, we must follow the approach endorsed by the texts of the religion itself. We do not always have to follow the way that our forefathers demand; perhaps that way is neither right nor divine. Perhaps it was the specific circumstances in which our fathers lived that gave rise to that way of doing things.

B: Struggling with children

Our children may admire the life of this world, perhaps to the extent that they are willing to transgress the limits of the *sharīʿa* because of it, and even try to lure their parents towards it. In this situation, parents must struggle to defend the boundaries of the religion, for the sake of themselves and their

---

[681] Note that in Imāmī interpretation, "father" in this instance is not literal, rather we believe it refers to his uncle.

[682] Sūrat al-Anʿām (6):74

children. Allah says: 'O you who have faith! Do not let your possessions and children distract you from the remembrance of Allah, and whoever does that - it is they who are the losers.'[683]

And elsewhere He says: 'O you who have faith! Indeed among your spouses and children you have enemies; so beware of them. And if you excuse, forbear and forgive, then Allah is indeed all-forgiving, all-merciful.'[684]

And in the story of Noah, he tries to save his son from drowning, but his son refuses to come with him. This is a lesson to every believing father: he must always do his utmost to reform his son, but when the latter refuses to change, he must leave him to his fate without causing himself to perish with him.

Today, as our people face successive waves of false ideologies and faithless cultures, we must equip ourselves to struggle, lest we see our own children swept away in their currents. And Allah the Supporter.

C: Struggling with brothers

The human being grows up in a family, surrounded by parents, children, and siblings. Often, one feels pressure from one's siblings, especially the elder siblings insofar as they exercise a degree of authority over him, and might try to curb his intellectual freedom, and force him in the direction of misguidance. In this situation, one must struggle against them to remain true to his faith. In the story of Joseph 🕮 and his brothers, there are lessons for anyone who would take heed: they were jealous of him and threw him into the depths of the well, but Allah helped him. In the same way, we see that Moses 🕮 grew angry with his brother, Aaron, when their people went astray. And the Commander of the Faithful 🕮 held a hot iron close to the hand of his brother, 'Aqīl, when the latter asked him for money from the public treasury that he was not entitled to take.

D: Struggling with husband and wife

A believing man or woman may find themselves under pressure from their spouse when struggling for the sake of Allah. This is something that will sap their will to continue their struggle, but in this situation they must resist this pressure and surmount it, seeking Allah's satisfaction.

---

[683] Sūrat al-Munāfiqūn (63):9
[684] Sūrat al-Taghābun (64):14

Despite the importance of harmony between a husband and wife, this should not overrule the importance of religion and its boundaries in the eyes of a believer. This is why a husband and a wife must prioritize their faithfulness to the religion above any other family affairs.

E: Struggling with a community (or tribe)

A person's community exerts a kind of authority over them and a person may feel, as a result, that they must submit to its authority. Such authority is acceptable so long as it exists within the boundaries of religious teachings and laws, but not if it transgresses them. This is why Allah told his Prophet ﷺ to warn his near relatives, by saying: '**Warn the nearest of your kinsfolk.**'[685] And it is well-known that warning (*indhār*) someone is a kind of *jihād*, insofar as warning someone implies a danger and makes the continuance of the relationship dependent upon that person accepting the warning. Allah strikes a parable for us using the prophet Abraham ﷺ and the believers who were with him, and how they disassociated from their people: '**There is certainly a good exemplar for you in Abraham and those who were with him, when they said to their own people, "Indeed we repudiate you and whatever you worship besides Allah. We disavow you, and between you and us there has appeared enmity and hate for ever, unless you come to have faith in Allah alone," except for Abraham's saying to his father, "I will surely plead forgiveness for you, though I cannot avail you anything against Allah." "Our Lord! In You do we put our trust, and to You do we turn penitently, and toward You is the destination."**'[686]

This verse shows us that a person's struggle against his disbelieving community begins from the moment he forsakes their authority for the authority of Allah.

The connection between a person and his family and community should not be one of blind following, such that they can pressure him to do whatever they want.

F: Struggling against a people

Struggling with one's people is exemplified by disassociating from the faithless and avoiding their company, disassociating from the hypocrites and challenging them, and confronting illegitimate or tyrannical leadership (*ṭāghūt*) and rejecting its authority. This is the most public form of struggle and that

---

685 Sūrat al-Shuʿarāʾ (26):214

686 Sūrat al-Mumtaḥana (60):4

which is discussed by the religious texts. In other words: It is this scope of struggle that one immediately understands from the verses of the Qurʾān, that the messengers practiced with their nations, and that Allah's *awliyāʾ* practiced with all un-Islamic societies.[687]

Rules for enjoining good and forbidding evil

Introduction

1. Enjoining good and forbidding evil is one of the qualities of the Muslim *umma*, one of the reasons for its superiority and the cause of it attaining the level of '**the best nation [ever] brought forth for mankind**';[688] and it is one of the qualities of the righteous believers amongst the People of the Book.
   Amongst this *umma* is a group of people for whom enjoining good and forbidding evil is a greater obligation than others, such as the scholars, the pious, those who fight in the way of Allah, and those are supporters of Allah. Allah has purchased from them their lives and property, and it is they whom Allah has established upon the earth.
2. Enjoining good and forbidding evil is evidence of Allah's authority (*walāya*) which He has placed amongst the faithful, and which is a means for obtaining His mercy. It is the right of a believer over his brother that the latter should enjoin him to good and forbid him from evil, and it is obligatory for a believer to respond to his brother when the latter does this.
3. Enjoining good and forbidding evil is the steadiest of courses; just like in maintaining the prayer and enduring hardship, we must resolve ourselves to undertake them and rely on Allah, and not allow any feeling of weakness, grief, or hesitation to enter our hearts.
4. The apparent ruling is that enjoining the good and forbidding the evil can be expressed in words, whether verbally or in writing, or by changing one's facial expression, or through an action which displays enjoining good or forbidding evil, such as pointing with one's hand, or avoiding the company of one who commits evil, etc.
5. Some jurists say that 'enjoining' means encouraging another person to do an action, while 'forbidding', means dissuading them from it. By token of this, enjoining the good includes arranging good projects, and forbidding evil means destroying the foundations of sinfulness. And

---

[687] Refer to the expanded legal work of His Eminence for more on the rules of warfare.

[688] Sūrat Āl ʿImrān (3):110

what this jurist mentions is recommended precaution, but the strongest opinion is that enjoining good and forbidding evil are restricted to what we have mentioned above about signalling one's approval or condemnation by action, and avoiding enjoining good and forbidding evil by speech [alone] or something resembling speech.

The obligation of enjoining good and forbidding evil

The noble *sunna*:

- It is narrated that a man came to the Messenger of Allah ﷺ, and said to him: Tell me, what is the best of deeds? So he said: 'Faith in Allah.' The man said: Then what? He said: '[Maintaining] the bonds of kinship (*ṣilat al-raḥm*).' The man said: Then what? He said: 'Commanding good and forbidding evil.'
  It is narrated from him ﷺ: 'Two boys were leaping on a rooster and plucked out its feathers, not leaving a single one on it. Nearby, an old man was standing in prayer, and did nothing to order or forbid them, so Allah commanded the earth to swallow him up.'[689]
- It is narrated from the Imam ؑ: 'Woe upon those who obtain the world by their religion, and woe upon those who kill the ones commanding [them] fairness among the people.'[690]
- Jābir has narrated from Abū Jaʿfar ؑ: 'Whoever walks to the tyrant ruler and commands him to fear Allah, and admonishes and instills fear in him, he will have the like of the reward of the two weighty things from jinn and mankind, and the like of their [collective] rewards.'[691]
- It is narrated from the Prophet ﷺ: 'Whoever commands good and forbids evil is the *khalīfa* of Allah and His Messenger on earth.'[692]

Rulings:

1. Good (*maʿrūf*) is whatever Allah has commanded, and evil (*munkar*) is whatever he has forbidden, whether the doer of the deed knows this or not. If he knows the moral status of an act, he must be enjoined and forbidden [regarding it], and if he does not, then he should be taught.
2. If the good is recommended (*mandūb*) and evil is disliked (*makrūh*), enjoining good and forbidding evil becomes a recommended act.

---

689 *Biḥār al-anwār*, v. 97, p. 82
690 *Mustadrak al-wasāʾil*, v. 12, p. 184, ḥ. 23
691 *Mustadrak al-wasāʾil*, v. 12, p. 178, ḥ. 5
692 *Wasāʾil al-shīʿa*, v. 12, p. 179, ḥ. 7

3. Enjoining good and forbidding evil are duties for every believing man and woman, and they are collective obligations: if someone undertakes them, others are released from the duty, but if no one undertakes them, then all have sinned.
4. If enjoining good and forbidding evil requires a group of Muslims to be formed, and it is possible to do so, then it becomes obligatory so long as it does not cause undue distress. In this case, if someone's participation is essential but he refrains from joining them, then he is sinful and there is no obligation for anyone else.
5. It is obligatory to prepare the means of enjoining good and forbidding evil as a matter of collective obligation to the extent that one is able; so if someone must travel a certain distance to undertake a duty, then he must do that even if it involves spending money. The same is true if enjoining good and forbidding evil depends upon him having a telephone, for example, or a loudspeaker, a placard, or anything else which the immediate performance of this duty depends upon – it becomes a collective obligation to obtain these things.
6. As for the more fundamental preliminaries for enjoining good and forbidding evil, which someone would not be accused of dereliction by forgoing—for instance, setting up a television or radio station, a newspaper, or educational, cultural and media institutions – there is some hesitation as to whether it is obligatory to undertake these. According to precaution, it is obligatory.
7. According to religious texts on this subject, it appears that the goal behind enjoining good and forbidding evil is to establish good and remove evil. Therefore, so long as evil exists and good is inoperative, the obligation to enjoin good and forbid evil remains in force, for as long as the conditions, which we shall mention shortly, are met. So if my friend enjoins someone to good but they do no obey him, but I think that person might obey me, it is obligatory for me to enjoin him to good as well, and the same applies to forbidding evil.
8. Part of enjoining good and forbidding evil is educating those people who are unaware of what you are calling them to, even if they are wilfully ignorant of this.
9. This obligation is most strongly emphasized in relation to one's relatives, as Allah says: **'O you who have faith! Save yourselves and your**

families from a Fire.'[693] And He says: **'Warn the nearest of your kinsfolk.'**[694]

And elsewhere, He says: **'And those who believed afterwards and migrated, and waged *jihād* along with you, they belong to you; but the blood relatives are more entitled to one another…'**[695]

Thus, the more influence someone has over another person, the greater their obligation to enjoin them to good and forbid them from evil; for example, towards one's spouse, children, and community. And if someone is an employer, manager, or teacher with authority, then they must use their position to undertake these two duties.

Conditions for enjoining good and forbidding evil

The noble *sunna*:

- Masʿada b. Sadaqa has narrated that Imam Abū ʿAbd Allah ﷷ was asked about commanding good and forbidding evil: is it obligatory upon the entire *umma*? So he said: 'No.' So it was said to him: And why not? He said: 'It is only [obligatory] upon the strong who are obeyed and know good from evil, not upon the weak who are not guided on the way—to this from this—going from speaking truth to falsehood. And that is indicated in the Book of Allah Almighty when He says: **"There has to be a nation among you summoning to the good, bidding what is right, and forbidding what is wrong."**[696] This [verse] is particular, not general, as Allah Almighty has said: "Among the people of Mūsā is a nation who guide [the people] by the truth and do justice thereby"[697]—and He did not say: "[obligatory] upon the nation (*umma*) of Mūsā and not upon his people," who in that day were various nations, and a nation can be an individual, like Allah Almighty said: **"Indeed Ibrāhīm was a nation [all by himself], obedient to Allah."**[698] He is saying "obedient to Allah Almighty," and it is not [obligatory] upon whoever knows that in this [time of] peace from hardship, when he has no strength or numbers, and none would obey him.'

  Masʿada said: And I heard Abū ʿAbd Allah ﷷ saying, in response to a question about a narration reported from the Prophet ﷺ: '"Surely the

---

[693] Sūrat al-Taḥrīm (66):6
[694] Sūrat al-Shuʿarā' (26):214
[695] Sūrat al-Anfāl (8):75
[696] Sūrat Āl ʿImrān (3):104
[697] Sūrat al-Aʿrāf (7):159
[698] Sūrat al-Nahl (16):120

best *jihād* is a just word [said] to a tyrant." What does it mean?' The Imam said: 'This is on [the condition] that he commands it after he himself knows it (i.e., practices it), and that the tyrant will accept the command from him—if not, then it is not obligatory.'[699]

Rulings:

Jurists say that enjoining good and forbidding evil depends upon four conditions:

First: That the one undertaking them knows how to enjoin and forbid, in addition to what constitutes good and evil.

Second: They think that their enjoining and forbidding will have an effect. If they know that it will not help, they are released from the obligation [in that particular circumstance].

Third: The one who is committing evil or forgoing good must be persistent in this behaviour. If there is any sign of reform in him, then the obligation is lifted.

Fourth: Enjoining good and forbidding evil must not be harmful. If someone thinks that he, his property, or any other Muslim will come to harm which will cause unbearable difficulty as a result of enjoining good or forbidding evil, then he is released from the obligation.

Here are the details for these conditions:

1. The first condition has the following subsidiaries:
    a. One can know good and evil either by learning them oneself or following a scholar. And if the jurists disagree as to whether something is forbidden, then one should forbid those who believe it to be forbidden but not those who do not.
    b. If someone who commits an evil deed was unaware of its prohibition, one must guide him. Even if he was [aware of the law but] ignorant its situational applicability (e.g., he knows that blood is ritually impure, but he did not know that there was blood on his garment), then the apparent ruling is that there is no obligation to inform him–unless, of course, the evil deed was of a kind which is necessarily known to be prohibited in every form, such as in cases of protecting life and chastity.

---

[699] *Wasāʾil al-shīʿa*, v. 11, p. 400, ḥ. 1

2. The second condition, namely the possibility that their admonitions will have an effect, is unanimously accepted by the jurists and most of the texts state:
    a. Obligatory precaution requires one to admonish someone even if it is unlikely to be accepted, and perhaps the wisdom behind this is to cause discomfort to those who sin.
    b. The apparent ruling is that it is obligatory to observe the different levels of admonition, even if it has no effect; such as forbidding evil with one's heart and avoiding the company of sinners.
3. As for the third condition, namely that the perpetrator of the sin persists in it:
    a. To be released from your obligation, you must be certain that the sinner has desisted from sinning. Simply presuming this to be the case is insufficient to release you from the obligation to enjoin good and forbid evil.
    b. It is sufficient to see a religiously valid expression of desisting; for example, a display of regret and repentance, or anything else that would customarily give one confidence of the fact [that the subject has reformed].
4. As for the fourth condition, namely that enjoining good and forbidding evil should not cause harm:
    a. The kind of harm which releases one from a religious duty is harm to the extent that it causes unbearable difficulty, such as fear for the life, property, or family of oneself or others. As for minor harm which people normally endure in order to attain their day-to-day goals, this does not release them from their religious duties.
    b. Unbearable difficulty, such that rational persons would not endure for the sake of attaining their own person goals, releases someone from religious obligations as well. It must be something hard to bear, and each person is aware of their own state; everyone differs in their coping abilities. The criterion for difficulty is personal and subjective.
    c. It suffices to have a reasonable fear of coming to harm. Although one should ignore Satanic insinuations (*waswasa*), it is unnecessary for a person to be [absolutely] certain that they will come to harm in order to be released from their religious duties.
    d. When there is a danger posed to Islam and Muslims, such as the appearance of innovations and the spread of corruption,

which threatens the very existence of the faith or the lives of Muslims, or anything as serious as this, then forbidding this kind of evil becomes *jihād* in Allah's way. In this case, the aforementioned conditions for enjoining good and forbidding evil no longer apply; the rules for *jihād* apply instead.

Levels of admonition

The noble *sunna*:

- The Commander of the Believers ﷺ said: 'Whoever abandons forbidding evil by his heart, tongue, and hand, is a corpse among the living.'[700]
- The Commander of the Believers said: 'The Messenger of Allah has ordered us to meet the people of disobedience (i.e., those who disobey Allah) with downcast faces.'[701]
- It has been narrated from the Prophet ﷺ: 'Whosoever among you sees something wrong should change it by his hand; and if he cannot, then by his tongue; and if he cannot, then by his heart, and there is nothing of faith beyond that.' And in another narration: '[and] that is the weakest [level] of faith.'[702]
- It has been narrated from al-Ṣādiq ﷺ: 'It suffices the believer that he sees something wrong, for verily Allah knows from his intention that it is hateful to him.'[703]

Rulings:

1. There are three levels to admonition: the heart, the tongue, and the hand. Each of these has its proper place, so the believer must choose wisely which is appropriate for his situation.
2. Admonition with the heart begins through disassociation from the sinner and disapproval of his action. Its next level is displaying anger in one's face or body language, as the Messenger bid us to show sinners our disapproval through our facial expressions, and by leaving sinful gatherings, and shunning their people.
   Disassociation from evil is one of the realities of faith and it is absolutely obligatory in all situations. As for making a show of this disassociation through one's facial expressions and withdrawing from the sinners, this

---

[700] *Wasāʾil al-shīʿa*, v. 11, p. 404, ḥ. 4
[701] *Wasāʾil al-shīʿa*, v. 11, p. 413, ḥ. 1
[702] *Mustadrak al-wasāʾil*, v. 12, p. 192, ḥ. 7
[703] *Mustadrak al-wasāʾil*, v. 12, p. 193, ḥ. 1

is subject to the conditions which we discussed above, for a reason that we shall discuss below, God-willing.

3. Turning away from the oppressors and not trying to curry favour with them, and avoiding sinners and their gatherings, is obligatory if this will dissuade them from whatever it is they are doing. On the other hand, if turning away from them will only increase them in blindness and wrongdoing, while interacting and spending time with them might lead to their reformation, then it is better to do the latter. But all of this depends on doing whatever is wisest according to the demands of the situation.
4. The second level is to admonish someone with a clear demand that they stop sinning. Although we say this is by the tongue, it can be spoken, written, a signal, or anything else which can be construed as a command or prohibition.
5. The jurists have mentioned that one should always suffice with the gentlest form of admonition that will [still] convey one's meaning. So if a signal is sufficient, there is no need to speak; if speaking kind words suffices, there is no need for harshness; and if reproaching someone suffices, there is no need to physically prevent them, and so on.

   It is precaution to use wisdom to determine what is best in a given situation, but it is generally permissible to use any kind of enjoinments or prohibitions so long as these do not lead to something forbidden, like belittling a fellow believer unnecessarily, or causing corruption and harm.
6. If the sinner is not dissuaded by a verbal admonition, jurists say it is permissible to physically prevent him from sinning – again, by using the gentlest form of admonition that will be effective. This begins by standing between him and the sin he wants to commit, such as restraining his hand from taking a glass of wine, or from striking someone unjustly. If this does not work, then destroying the means of sinning (e.g., throwing wine down the sink or breaking the items of gambling). And if this does not work, then striking the sinner himself may be necessary. However, it is a matter of obligatory precaution that one must refer to a jurist to determine what is obligatory in all times and places; *a believer should not resort to physical force of his own accord.* This restriction is to ward off problems in society and protect the social fabric.
7. If the sin is an indecency (*fāḥisha*), such as killing an innocent, raping a woman, or aggressing against the faithful, the apparent ruling is that every Muslim must immediately use force to prevent this, even if this involves doing things that would ordinarily be prohibited. For example:

forcing entry into the aggressor's home, spying on him, etc., so long as it is likely that a crime will be committed if someone does not intervene.

8. If the sinner is not dissuaded even when physical force is used, and the only means of stopping him is to harm or kill him, then the case must be referred to the religious authorities, according to details which we will lay out below. In fact, if a serious crime is being perpetrated and it is not possible to seek permission from the religious authorities, it is obligatory to intervene at once, giving priority to whatever is most important, as we discussed above with regards to killing an innocent and aggression.
9. A just jurist may undertake enjoining good and forbidding evil at all of its levels, andthe implementation of religious law, if the necessary obective conditions are met. These include, for example, having the attention and assistance of the faithful around him, and safety from oppressive rulers and the tribulations of the age. One who has permission from a jurist may also undertake it, within the bounds of the permission he has been given [by that jurist].
10. Anyone who works for an unjust ruler may not implement Islamic criminal punishments without the permission of a just jurist; and if he is compelled to do so, then he must restrict himself to the lowest level possible. If a tyrant wants to coerce him into killing righteous persons, he must not obey him, even if his refusal to do so will lead to his own death. There is no *taqiyya* in matters where the lives of others are at stake.

The etiquettes of enjoining good and forbidding evil

The noble *sunna*:

❖ It is narrated from Abū ʿAbd Allah ﷺ: 'One should only command good and forbid evil who has three characteristics: he acts by what he commands and has abandoned what he forbids, he is just in what he commands and forbids, and that he is gentle in what he commands and forbids.'[704]

❖ Jābir has narrated, as part of a longer report, from Abū Jaʿfar ﷺ: 'Oppose evil in your hearts, and reject it with your tongues, and hit their foreheads with it. And concerning Allah, do not fear the rebuke of the censurer. If you preached and they returned to the truth [then there is no problem], and there is no ground for action against them: **"The ground for action is only against those who oppress the people and**

---

[704] *Wasāʾil al-shīʿa*, v. 11, p. 419, ḥ. 3

commit tyranny in the land in violation of justice. For such there will be a painful punishment."[705] [However in that case] you should fight them with your bodies and hate them with your hearts—without seeking power, desiring wealth, or willing oppression in victory—until they adhere to the command of Allah and pass into His strict obedience.'[706]

Rulings:

1. When it comes to inviting others towards Allah, one of the clearest realities is that the caller must himself possess the qualities of the pious. He must follow the example of the messengers and prophets in obeying Allah before bidding others to do so, and by avoiding sins before forbidding others from them.
2. Because Allah has bid us to cooperate in good deeds and piety, and because enjoining good and forbidding evil is one of the highest examples of good deeds and piety, then if a believer cooperates with his brethren in undertaking this duty, he will have a greater effect. This is especially so at this time, when the enemies of Islam have arrayed themselves in parties and institutions, and collaborate with one another in sinfulness and enmity.
3. Spreading goodness in society and effacing evil might call for the creation of religious foundations, such as educational institutions, and Islamic and cultural centres. The believers must concern themselves with this so that they can protect their brethren from falling into falsehood.
4. The media through which the message of Islam is conveyed must develop in step with social conditions. Today, there are television and radio stations, news networks, information agencies, and new forms of media (computers and the internet); all of these forms of communication are being used to spread misguidance. How wonderful it would be if the faithful worked together to create a superior kind of media, through which virtue could be promoted and Allah's message could be spread.
5. Because the faithless and the sinful use highly developed scientific tools, such as sociological, psychological, and pedagogical studies, and employ these to spread their ways of thinking, so too must religious seminaries develop programs of study in these subjects to keep up with the times, and to be able to resist falsehood, by Allah's leave. In this way, the

---

[705] Sūrat al-Shūrā (42):42

[706] *Wasāʾil al-shīʿa*, v. 11, p. 403, ḥ. 1

leading scholars and those with insight must strive to educate a new generation of preachers, and furnish them with whatever they need to undertake the duty of enjoining good and forbidding evil in the best way possible, according to Allah's saying: **'Invite to the way of your Lord with wisdom and beautiful preaching.'**[707] And there is no doubting that proper educational programs are the best way to inculcate a student with wisdom and give him knowledge of what his environment requires.

6. The best guidance is Allah's guidance, and the *sunna* of the Messenger and his Household ﷺ. Preachers must seek illumination from the light of the Qur'ān and traditions with the utmost care and seriousness, so that they will memorize the texts of revelation, ponder upon them, make them the centre of their discussions, and interpret current affairs in their light. And Allah is the Supporter.

---

[707] Sūrat al-Naḥl (16):125

Part Three: Selected Rulings for Transactions and Contracts

Chapter One: Jurisprudence for a Good Life

First: Security in Islamic living

Allah says in the Qur'ān: **'Allah has promised those of you who have faith and do righteous deeds that He will surely make them successors in the earth, just as He made those who were before them successors, and He will surely establish for them their religion which He has approved for them, and that He will surely change their state to security after their fear, while they worship Me, not ascribing any partners to Me. And whoever is ungrateful after that - it is they who are the transgressors.'**[708]

Security is the primary need and utmost necessity for which every living thing feels the need, in order to protect its own life and its earnings. This manifests itself on a number of levels:

1. It is a psychological necessity which, in its highest forms, manifests as peace and tranquillity, and the freedom of the heart from distress, fear, and grief, and the absence of evil, enmity, and malice.
2. It is a moral trait, based on moderation, and avoiding sins and indecencies.
3. It is a good social practice, in which every individual respects the rights of others in all dimensions.
4. It is a civilizational aspiration which will lead people to a society based upon *tawḥīd* (divine unity), such that people will not take one another as lords.
5. It is a cultural purity, in which there is neither falsehood nor fabrications against Allah, nor any barring of the way to the truth.

Security in this sense is the manifest dimension of faith, and this is the reason that the Arabic words for faith (*īmān*) and security (*aman*) are used in a similar sense; a believer (*mu'min*) is someone who gives safety (*amān*) and acknowledges every right and truth.

---

[708] Sūrat al-Nūr (24):55

1: Security as tranquillity in the heart

The noble *sunna*:

- Imam al-Ṣādiq ﷺ said: 'From a Muslim man's health of certainty, he does not seek to please people by displeasing Allah, and does not blame them for what Allah has not given him. For surely sustenance is neither given due to the greed of the stingy, nor deflected by the antipathy of the averse. Even if one of you fled from his sustenance like he flees death, [nevertheless] his sustenance will reach him like death will reach him.'
  Then he said: 'Surely Allah, in His justice and equity, made the spirit and comfort [to be] in certainty and contentment, and made worry and sorrow [to be] in doubt and discontent.'[709]
- It is narrated that the Commander of the Believers ﷺ said: 'No servant will find the taste of faith until he realizes that has reached him could not have missed him, and whatever has missed him could not have reached him, and that the one who dispenses harm or benefit is Allah Almighty.'[710]
- It is narrated that Imam al-Ṣādiq ﷺ said: 'There is nothing without a limit.' The narrator said to him: May I be your ransom, what is the limit of reliance (*tawakkul*) upon Allah? He said: 'Certainty.' The narrator said: Then what is the limit of certainty (*yaqīn*)? He said: 'To fear nothing (because Allah is with you).'[711]

Rulings:

Believing in Allah, trusting in Him, relying upon Him, being wary of disobeying Him, avoiding His punishment, and observing His bounds: all of these work to produce a sense of security, tranquillity, and satisfaction. When the heart is at peace with faith, devoid of lusts, built upon love and contentment, free from the inner indecencies (such as envy, pride, and enmity), peace and security will predominate over all aspects of a person's life.

For this reason, we must strive to grow affection and peace in our hearts, and nurture trust and humility in our spirits, and cleanse our souls of impurities and lusts.

---

709 *Biḥār al-anwār*, v. 67, p. 143
710 *Biḥār al-anwār*, v. 67, p. 154
711 *Biḥār al-anwār*, v. 67, p. 180

2: Security and the way of balance

The noble *sunna*:

❖ The Commander of the Believers ﷺ said: 'The right and left are delusory, and the middle way requires hard work, [while] the Book and the Prophetic narrations remain upon it.'[712]

Rulings:

The believer has only been commanded to observe balance in his life, while one who is negligent is forever going to extremes; do you not see how he is thrown about by his passions? While he forever goes from one extreme to another, the believer is upon the straight path. While others swerve left and right, the believer remains safe from the demons of extremism.

As such, a believer should not set out on any course without first pondering and reflecting on its consequences, so that his thoughts will always precede his actions, his perception will always precede his direction, his planning will always precede his affairs, and his preparations will always precede his journey, because going at a steady pace (i.e., a balanced approach to life), by which the behaviour of a believer is distinguished, is a means of keeping him safe from the perils of extremism.

3: Security and caution

The noble *sunna*:

❖ Concerning the attributes of the pious, Imam ʿAlī ﷺ said: 'He spends the night vigilant, and begins his day happy—avigilant for what he was warned about concerning negligence, and happy for what has reached him of grace and mercy.'[713]

Rulings:

A person who fears nothing is wary of nothing, and a person who is wary of nothing enjoys no security. One of the believer's most prominent qualities is fear and precaution, and hence one of his most visible achievements is safety from danger. A believer must always beware of Allah's stratagem, by avoiding sinning and being wary of neglecting any area of his life.

---

712 *Nahj al-balāgha*, sermon 213

713 *Nahj al-balāgha*, sermon 193

4: Societal security and respecting the rights of others

The noble *sunna*:

❖ The Messenger of Allah ﷺ said: 'The Muslims are brothers. They recompense one another with their blood, they strive to protect the least of them, and they are one hand against the [non-Musims].'[714]

❖ The Commander of the Believers ؏ said: 'The believer neither cheats his brother, nor betrays him, nor forsakes him, nor denounces him.'[715]

Rulings:

We can sum up the rule of peace between people (societal security) in two words: acknowledgement and respect. If everyone acknowledges everyone else and respects their rights, then peace rules and security is established for all. Only systems of government whose laws and rights are respected can attain this kind of security.

That is why it is impermissible to seize power in the land, or unjustly interfere in the affairs of other people, just as a Muslim must always avoiding wronging others, and protect their rights, both material and spiritual.

5: Tawḥīd and the government of peace and security

The noble *sunna*:

❖ The Messenger of Allah ﷺ said: 'Beware of mingling with the ruler for it banishes religion, and beware of his assistance, for surely you should not praise his command.'[716]

❖ Imam ʿAlī ؏ said: 'Distance yourself from the ruler to protect yourself from the wiles of Satan.'[717]

❖ ʿUmar b. Ḥanẓala said: I asked Abū ʿAbd Allah ؏ about two men who had a dispute concerning a debt or inheritance, so they sought the verdict of the ruler or his judges. Is this lawful? So he said: 'Whoever seeks the verdict of an unjust ruler (*ṭāghūt*) and thereby receives a judgment in his favor, then what he receives thereby is ill-gotten property (unlawful gains), even if it was his clearly established right,

---

[714] *Biḥār al-anwār*, v. 97, p. 42

[715] *Mīzān al-ḥikma*, v. 7, p. 222, ḥ. 14659

[716] *Mīzān al-ḥikma*, v. 4, p. 510, ḥ. 8729

[717] *Mīzān al-ḥikma*, v. 4, p. 511, ḥ. 8733

because he obtained it by the verdict of an unjust ruler even though Allah has commanded him to disbelieve in him (*al-ṭāghūt*)...'[718]

Rulings:

Although tyrants and dictators claim that they are maintaining security in their countries, nevertheless it is they who are the most dangerous source of tension and fear, because they divide people into different groups. They weaken some (the majority) for the benefit of others (the minority), interfere with people's rights to independence, respect, freedom and prosperity, stand in the way of progress, forcing backwardness on society while living lives of opulence themselves. They are the kings who, when they enter a town, devastate it, and reduce the mightiest of its people to the most abased[719]; they are those who, were they to wield authority, would try to cause corruption in the land, and to ruin the crop and the stock.[720]

That is why one must avoid tyrants, oppose their rule, and remain steadfast upon the path of *tawḥīd*, all the while striving to implement the teachings of the religion and respect Allah's rites.

6: Cultural and intellectual security

The noble *sunna*:

- The Messenger of Allah ﷺ said: 'Shall I inform you of the best of manners of the people of this world and the next?' So the people said: Of course, O Messenger of Allah. So he said: 'Spreading peace in the world.'[721]
- The Messenger of Allah ﷺ said: 'Whoever bears false witness against a Muslim man or *dhimmī* or anyone from the people, will be strung up by his tongue on Judgment Day, and [placed] with the hypocrites in the absolute lowest level of the Fire.'[722]
- The Messenger of Allah ﷺ said: 'Whoever conceals testimony when called to give it is like the one who bears false witness.'[723]

---

[718] *Mīzān al-ḥikma*, v. 8, p. 185, ḥ. 16500
[719] An allusion to Sūrat al-Naml (27):34
[720] An allusion to Sūrat al-Baqara (2):205
[721] *Biḥār a-anwār*, v. 76, p. 12
[722] *Mīzān al-ḥikma*, v. 5, p. 178, ḥ. 9718
[723] *Mīzān al-ḥikma*, v. 5, p. 177, ḥ. 9713

❖ The Messenger of Allah ﷺ said: 'Whichever man Allah has given knowledge, but he keeps it secret while he is aware of it, will meet Allah Almighty on Judgment Day bridled with a bridle of fire.'[724]

Rulings:

Peace and security will not reign over a nation for whom words have no value. Words are something with which man has been entrusted. If they express his thoughts and are not used for false testimony, foolish speech, deceitful oaths, or to conceal the truth, then Man has used them properly and they have become a means of obtaining security; otherwise, they are a tool for corruption and discord.

Consequently, we must spread peace with our words, avoid foolish talk, testify for the sake of Allah, turn away from false oaths, and speak only the truth.

Justice in Islamic society

Allah says: **'Certainly We sent Our Messengers with manifest proofs, and We sent down with them the Book and the Balance, so that mankind may maintain justice; and We sent down iron, in which there is great might and uses for mankind, and so that Allah may know those who help Him and His Messengers in [their] absence. Indeed Allah is All-strong, All-mighty.'**[725]

Justice is one of the most visible values to emanate from believing in the truth: if you believe in everything that is true and right, then you will enact it as a result, by acting according to your belief in it, and its demands.

Justice means to live a life of balance; neither being immoderate nor going to extremes in any situation; neither being wasteful nor stingy, monastic nor profligate. Wrongdoing and aggression are contrary to justice, because wrongdoing violates Allah's right, and aggression violates the rights of the people.

Justice means establishing the truth as it is, without inclining away from it; while the truth is the balance by which we must judge between people if we want justice to reign.

---

[724] *Mīzān al-ḥikma*, v. 6, p. 472, ḥ. 13510
[725] Sūrat al-Ḥadīd (57):25

The means of implementing justice (*'adl*), establishing truth and fairness (*qisṭ*)[726] are as follows:

1. Sending messengers.
2. Revealing scriptures with laws.
3. Sending down and setting up the scale [of justice], the most important manifestation of which is an Imam who judges between people with fairness.
4. Sending down iron (weapons), containing great might to confront those who wrong others.
5. Encouraging those who [legitimately] fight (*mujāhidīn*) to assist Allah and His messengers with iron (weapons).

1: Maintaining justice

The noble *sunna*:

❖ The Messenger of Allah ﷺ said: 'Justice is a protective shelter and an enduring paradise.'[727]
❖ The Commander of the Believers said: 'Justice is the lifeblood of the law (*ḥayāt al-aḥkām*).'[728]

Fairness is the divine wisdom underlying Allah's sending of messengers. Scripture is its vehicle, the scale [of justice] is that which implements it, iron is its weapon, and those who struggle [in its way] are its maintainers.

Every nation has a messenger, and their messenger judges between them with fairness.

Allah has ordered people to observe justice and do good, and forbidden them from indecency and wrongdoing. He has commanded those who believe to be maintainers of justice for Allah, and to bear witness with fairness, just as He has bid them to be maintainers of fairness and witnesses for Allah. By rights, justice is implemented; so if every person is given his right, then justice has been achieved.

---

[726] What do the words *'adl* and *qisṭ* mean? *'Adl* means to be balanced, whether in one's individual life or one's social relations; *qisṭ*, on the other hand, is an important aspect of *'adl*. It means to respect the rights of others, especially their monetary rights. To do *qisṭ* means to give others their fair share (*qisṭ*), which is their right. So *'adl* includes *qisṭ*, which itself is a kind of *'adl*.

[727] *Mīzān al-ḥikma*, v. 6, p. 79, ḥ. 11667

[728] *Mīzān al-ḥikma*, v. 6, p. 81, ḥ. 11685

Justice is the content of Allah's messages. Allah bids people to justice as He bids them to fairness; therefore, we must realize them by any [legitimate] means available.

2: Justice in politics

The noble *sunna*:

- The Messenger of Allah ﷺ said: 'The first people to enter the Fire will be the unjust autocrat, and the one who possesses enormous fortune but did not give the wealth its right, and the prideful pauper.'[729]
- In his explanation of the verse: 'Know that Allah revives the earth after it is dead,' Imam al-Kāẓim ؑ said: 'He does not revive it by raindrops, rather Allah sends men who revive justice. So the earth is revived by the revival of justice; and justice is established in it, [which is] more beneficial than forty mornings of rain.'[730]

Islamic governance rests on the foundations of truth, which is exemplified by justice and the balance, which lies between anarchy and tyranny. To rise above anarchy, there must be government by divine authority, and to rise above tyranny, there must be consultation.

Allah's justice is manifested in politics too, by ensuring that every group of people has its legitimate rights. Even in warfare it is impermissible for one to usurp the rights of the other.

The relation of Muslims to others is the same: in times of peace a Muslim must be good to them and fulfil their rights, and in warfare a Muslim must not overstep the prescribed bounds against them unless the enemy does so first; and even then he may not go to greater extremes than them.

3: Justice in recompense and responsibility

The noble *sunna*:

- Imam ʿAlī ؑ said: 'Reward is in proportion to tribulations.'[731]

Divine justice is made manifest in the practice of responsibility and recompense. The human being is responsible for his own actions and recompensed for them. If he does good, then he receives good, and if he does

---

[729] *Mīzān al-ḥikma*, v. 6, p. 90, ḥ. 11724
[730] *Mīzān al-ḥikma*, v. 6, p. 81, ḥ. 11686
[731] *Mīzān al-ḥikma*, v. 2, p. 37, ḥ. 2340

evil, then he receives evil. Conversely, he is not responsible for the actions of others, unless he has played a role in bringing them about.

That is why no one will be held responsible for the actions of anyone else who persists in straying, nor for that over which he is powerless, nor for what he is coerced into doing, or compelled to do by necessity. The limits of human responsibility are those of his efforts and deeds connected to his own free will, volition, and actions, whether positive or negative.

4: Economic justice

The noble *sunna*:

- Imam ʿAlī ﷺ said: 'By justice, blessings are doubled.'[732]
- Imam al-Ṣādiq ﷺ said: 'The wealth of a Muslim individual is unlawful unless he gladly parts with it.'[733]
- Imam al-Ṣādiq ﷺ said: 'Whoever damages anything of the roadways of the Muslims is liable [for any resultant harm].'[734]
- Zurāra has narrated from Imam Abū Jaʿfar ﷺ: Samura b. Jundub had a date palm on land owned by a man from the Anṣār, and the home of the Anṣārī was by the gate to the garden. [Samura] would pass by the gate on his way to his date palm without seeking permission [to enter the Anṣārī's land]. So the Anṣārī told him to seek permission [to enter] when he came, but Samura refused. When he refused, the Anṣārī went to the Messenger of Allah ﷺ, complaining and informing him about the situation. So the Messenger of Allah ﷺ sent for [Samura] and informed him about what the Anṣārī had said, and his complaints. He said: 'When you wish to enter then seek permission [first],' but [Samura] refused. So when he refused, [the Prophet] attempted to bargain with hum until he arrived at a price [for the Anṣārī to simply buy the tree from Samura], as Allah willed, but [Samura] refused to sell it. [The Prophet] said: 'In exchange for it you will receive a date palm prepared for you in Paradise.' So [Samura again] refused the offer. So the Messenger of Allah ﷺ said to the Anṣārī: 'Go and tear up [the tree] and cast it before him, for verily there is no harm and no injury [in Islam].[735]

---

732 *Mīzān al-ḥikma*, v. 6, p. 79, ḥ. 11671
733 *Al-Fuṣūl al-muhimma*, v. 2, p. 454, ḥ. 2264
734 *Wasāʾil al-shīʿa*, v. 19, p. 179, ḥ. 2
735 *Wasāʾil al-shīʿa*, v. 17, p. 341, ḥ. 3

Rulings:

Fairness is the ideal value for economics in all of its dimensions. When economics becomes divorced from fairness, it must be returned to it – even if this means creating new laws—so that no one will be deprived of his rights, or wronged even to the extent of a date fibre, or suffer harm. Warding off injustice and maintaining fairness are the fundamental principles upon which rest many of the religious rulings concerning economic activity. It is because of them that:

1. Money must pass between people rightfully.
2. No one else may enrich himself from other people or dispose of their property without their consent.
3. It is impermissibe to enrich oneself from an illegitimate source, or consume wealth falsely (i.e., without right).
4. Whoever harms another person must compensate them for that harm.
5. A person's use of their rights and free disposal of their property should not lead to other people being deprived of their rights.

5: Justice in the family

The noble *sunna*:

- The Messenger of Allah ﷺ said: 'The person with the greatest right over a woman is her husband, and the person with a greatest right over a man is his mother.'[736]
- The Messenger of Allah ﷺ said: 'Jibraʾīl continued to advise me about women to the extent that I thought they should not be divorced except for an [act of] open indecency.'[737]
- The Messenger of Allah ﷺ said: 'There is no milk better for a child than that of its mother.'[738]

Rulings:

Justice permeates a believer's communal life, his relationship with his parents, his wife, and his children. The Qurʾān commands that children be ascribed to their parents, as that is fairer in the sight of Allah. It commands that a person must do justice between his wives, and that if he cannot, then he must not take more than one. It forbids him from distressing his parents. Based on all of this:

---

[736] *Mīzān al-ḥikma*, v. 4, p. 283, ḥ. 7863
[737] *Mīzān al-ḥikma*, v. 4, p. 283, ḥ. 7869
[738] *Mīzān al-ḥikma*, v. 4, p. 138, ḥ. 7268

1. Family ancestry must be preserved.
2. A believer must give everyone their rights.
3. A man must treat his wife well, and a wife must fulfil her duties towards her husband.
4. The criterion in marital relations is a just balance between a wife's duties and her wealth.
5. Islamic laws concerning children, especially with regards to breastfeeding, nursing, spending, upbringing, and education, must always be observed.

6: Justice in legal judgement

The noble *sunna*:

- It is narrated that Imam al-Ṣādiq ﷷ one day said to his companions: 'Beware of bringing legal grievances against one another to the people of tyranny, and instead look to a man from among you who knows something of our judgments, and appoint him [as an arbitrator] between you, for I have made him a judge [over you], so seek his verdict.'[739]
- Imam ʿAlī ﷷ has narrated that when he went to Yemen, the Messenger of Allah ﷺ told him: 'When a verdict is sought from you, do not give a judgment to either litigant until you have heard from the other.' The Imam said: 'I did not experience doubt in issuing a judgment after that.'[740]

Rulings:

Justice is most clearly manifested in the lives of nations on two occasions: once when the law is promulgated, and once when it is applied to disputes (i.e., when judgements are passed on the law's basis). Insofar as the origin of Islamic Law is the Divine Lawgiver, then it is legal judgement that is the most visible manifestation of justice. Therefore, the law must be implemented as Allah has bid if justice is to be realized through legal judgement. This is achieved by turning aside from people's desires when governing, because most people incline to their own opinions (which could be false); so a judge must not incline whichever way the people incline, nor should he issue a judgement based on his own preferences and desires, or because he prefers one group, or supports one faction or people, and judge according their wishes.

---

[739] *Mustadrak al-wasāʾil*, v. 3, p. 172, ḥ. 3

[740] *Biḥār al-anwār*, v. 101, p. 275, ḥ. 2

By the same token, a judge must beware popular pressure and discontent which might be to encourage him to do something, dissuade him from something else, or otherwise persuade him to deviate from the proper ruling.

Peace is the goal of every believer

Allah Almighty says:

'O you who have faith! When you issue forth in the way of Allah, try to ascertain: do not say to someone who offers you peace, 'You are not a believer,' seeking the transitory wares of the life of this world. Yet with Allah are plenteous gains. You too were such earlier, but Allah did you a favour. Therefore, do ascertain. Allah is indeed well aware of what you do.'[741]

A believer's heart is filled with the tranquillity of peace. Is not a believer someone who acknowledges others and respects their rights? Is not peace (or complete security) the manifestation of this acknowledgement of other people's rights?

A believer's tongue is a truthful messenger of his heart, and so the greeting of peace (*salām*) is a truthful expression of its contents, which the believer utters when he enters a house, meets a fellow believer, with regards to Allah's messengers and chosen servants, when he bids farewell, and even when he faces the ignorant.

In fact, fighting and *jihād* only exist with the aim of achieving peace and spreading it throughout the land.

1: Peace before warfare

The noble *sunna*:

❖ In his letter to Mālik al-Ashtar, when he appointed him, Imam ʿAlī ﷺ said: 'Do not reject the peace [treaties] to which your enemy calls you, and Allah will be pleased with that. Surely in peace there is a rest for your military, comfort from worries, and security for your homeland.'[742]

Rulings:

The ultimate goal of fighting is not to achieve material objectives, but to please Allah. Therefore, spreading peace must be the fundamental objective of fighting, and nothing else.

---

[741] Sūrat al-Nisāʾ (4):94

[742] *Nahj al-balāgha*, letter 53, p. 442

2: The security of houses

The noble *sunna*:

❖ Abū al-Jārūd has narrated from Abū Jaʿfar 🕮: 'When a man from among you enters his house, and there is anyone in it, then give them the greeting of peace. And if there was no one there, then say: Peace be upon us from our Lord; and Allah will say: "Greetings and goodly blessings from Allah."'[743]

❖ Imam al-Ṣādiq 🕮 said: '"Peace" is the greeting of our religion and the protection of those under our care.'[744]

❖ Imam al-Ṣādiq 🕮 said: 'When a man enters upon his family he sends the greeting of peace, and makes his footsteps audible, and clears his throat. He does these things until they hear that he has arrived, so that he does not see anything that is detestable [to see].'[745]

Rulings:

Homes have a special sanctity and their inhabitants have a right to feel safe. Because of the importance of this right, it is impermissible to intrude into them, or climb over their walls. One must make known their presence before entry, so that their inhabitants know who is entering their home, and seek the latter's permission. This is one example of giving greetings of peace. It is proper etiquette to ask permission before entering the private rooms of the house (such as a bedroom), especially at times when people are usually resting.

3: Peace is the greeting of the faithful

The noble *sunna*:

❖ It is narrated that the great Prophet 🕮 said: 'O Anas! Give the greeting of peace to whomever you meet. Allah will increase your rewards (*ḥasanāt*). And when you give the greeting of peace in your house, Allah will increase your blessings (*baraka*).'[746]

❖ Imam al-Ṣādiq 🕮 has narrated from the Messenger of Allah 🕮: 'When you meet then meet with the greeting of peace and shake hands, and when you part, then part by seeking [each other's] forgiveness.'[747]

---

[743] *Biḥār al-anwār*, v. 73, p. 3, ḥ. 3
[744] *Mīzān al-ḥikma*, v. 5, p. 534, ḥ. 8834
[745] *Biḥār al-anwār*, v. 73, p. 11
[746] *Biḥār al-anwār*, v. 73, p. 3, ḥ. 5
[747] *Biḥār al-anwār*, v. 73, p. 5, ḥ. 13

- Imam al-Ṣādiq ﷺ said: 'Surely of the things that obligate [Allah's] forgiveness are offering the greeting of peace and [speaking] lovely words.'[748]
- It is narrated from the two Imams, al-Bāqir and al-Ṣādiq ﷺ: 'The heaviest thing that will be placed in the scale on Judgment Day is sending blessings (*ṣalāt*) upon Muḥammad and upon the people of his house.'[749]
- The Messenger of Allah ﷺ was asked: How do we send blessings upon you? So he said: 'By saying: "O Allah, send blessings upon Muḥammad and the family of Muḥammad, as You sent blessings upon Ibrāhīm and the family of Ibrāhīm; verily You are praiseworthy and glorious...'[750]
- Imam al-Kāẓim ﷺ was asked: What are the meanings of the blessings (*ṣalāt*) of Allah, and the angels, and the believers? So he said: 'The blessings of Allah are a mercy from Allah, the blessings of the angels are a purification from them for and individual, and the blessings of the believers are a supplication from them on his behalf.'

Rulings:

Believers live with the tranquillity of peace between themselves (there is no enmity, spite, or anger between them), so when they meet they exchange greetings of peace, and when they part company, they bid farewell with peace also. In fact, you will see that a believer disassociates himself from an ignorant person with peace – peace, here, meaning separation – and without intending him any harm.

Governing by truth

Allah says:

'"Shall I seek a judge other than Allah, while it is He who has sent down to you the Book, well-elaborated?" Those whom We have given the Book know that it has been sent down from your Lord with the truth; so do not be one of the sceptics.'[751]

Arranging social relations around the axis of truth is the basis upon which a just community is founded, and the wisdom contained in the Book of

---

[748] *Biḥār al-anwār*, v. 73, p. 11, ḥ. 46
[749] *Mīzān al-ḥikma*, v. 5, p. 431, ḥ. 10497
[750] *Mīzān al-ḥikma*, v. 5, p. 431, ḥ. 10500
[751] Sūrat al-Anʿām (6):114

Allah deals with this form of social arrangement. Usually governing (*ḥukm*) means to pass judgement (*qaḍāʾ*), though it can also mean legislation.

So truth is the goal, and the means of a society reaching it is the Messenger who judges by the revealed scripture from Allah.

And it appears that Allah's rulings fall into three categories:

1. That which relates to a core precept of the religion (such as divine authority and political association), and whoever does not judge by it is a disbeliever.
2. That which relates to judging between people (such as *qiṣāṣ* punishments),[752] and whoever does not implement it is a wrongdoer.
3. That which relates to behaviour and morality, and whoever does not judge by this is a sinner.

And because our exalted Lord relates the truth to us and He is the best of judges, so there is no rule except His and we cannot submit to anyone except Him.

1: Allah's rule

The glorious Qurʾān:

- **'All the response of the faithful, when they are summoned to Allah and His Apostle that He may judge between them, is to say, "We hear and obey." It is they who are the felicitous.'**[753]
- **'Whatever thing you may differ about, its judgement is with Allah. That is Allah, my Lord. In Him, I have put my trust, and to Him do I turn penitently.'**[754]

Rulings:

Rule, whether in legislation or implementation, belongs only to Allah and is sent down from Him. Man receives this just rule through the divine messengers. Even though the human intellect might understand the bases of this rule, human beings cannot derive Allah's rulings independently without recourse to messengers who recite Allah's purified scripture. This makes it obligatory for the believer to seek out Allah's ruling in every issue and to submit

---

[752] *Qiṣāṣ* are those punishments relating to wounding and murder, whereby a punishment equivalent to the crime is inflicted upon the perpetrator.

[753] Sūrat al-Nūr (24):51

[754] Sūrat al-Shūrā (42):10

himself, psychologically and practically, to all the rules of the *sharīʿa*. Both extremism and negligence are impermissible regarding Allah's laws.

2: Who is the ruler?

The glorious Qurʾān:

❖ **'We sent down the Torah containing guidance and light. The prophets, who had submitted, judged by it for the Jews, and so did the rabbis and the scribes, as they were charged to preserve the Book of Allah and were witnesses to it. So do not fear the people, but fear Me, and do not sell My signs for a paltry gain. Those who do not judge by what Allah has sent down—it is they who are the faithless.'**[755]

Rulings:

Rule belongs to Allah, but who is Allah's vicegerent (*khalīfa*) who implements this rule on earth? Allah's vicegerent is none other than he whom Allah has appointed – it cannot be just anyone – and Allah has appointed the prophets and the righteous as His vicegerents upon the earth, and the scholars who judge by Allah's scripture.

3: Inclusivity of the law

The glorious Qurʾān:

❖ **'We sent down the Torah containing guidance and light. The prophets, who had submitted, judged by it for the Jews, and so did the rabbis and the scribes, as they were charged to preserve the Book of Allah and were witnesses to it. So do not fear the people, but fear Me, and do not sell My signs for a paltry gain. Those who do not judge by what Allah has sent down—it is they who are the faithless. In it We prescribed for them: a life for a life, an eye for an eye, a nose for a nose, and an ear for an ear, a tooth for a tooth, and retaliation for wounds. Yet whoever remits it out of charity, that shall be an atonement for him. Those who do not judge by what Allah has sent down—it is they who are the wrongdoers. We followed them with Jesus son of Mary, to confirm that which was before him of the Torah, and We gave him the Evangel (Gospel) containing guidance and light, confirming what was before it of the Torah, and as guidance and advice for the Godwary. Let the people of the Evangel judge by what**

---

755 Sūrat al-Māʾida (5):44

Allah has sent down in it. Those who do not judge by what Allah has sent down—it is they who are the transgressors.'[756]

Rulings:

It appears that contravening Allah's law in the rights of others is oppression (*ẓulm*), in behaviour it is sinfulness (*fisq*), and in the fundamentals (expressing loyalty and disassociation) it is disbelief (*kufr*). For this reason, it is obligatory to implement Allah's laws completely with regards to the rights of people, and to strive to build a healthy society that is free from immorality, deviance, and corruption, by holding fast to the religion's laws in government, which stipulate loyalty to Allah's friends (*awliyāʾ*) and disassociation from His enemies.

4: The impartial ruler

The glorious Qurʾān:

- **'O David! Indeed, We have made you a vicegerent on the earth. So judge between people with justice, and do not follow your desires, or they will lead you astray from the way of Allah. Indeed there is a severe punishment for those who stray from the way of Allah, because of their forgetting the Day of Reckoning.'**[757]
- **'And he said, "My sons, do not enter by one gate, but enter by separate gates, though I cannot avail you anything against Allah. Sovereignty (judgement) belongs only to Allah. In Him I have put my trust; and in Him let all the trusting put their trust."'**[758]

Rulings:

Following people's desires, especially [those of the] the wealthy and powerful among them, is what threatens the health of the Islamic system, and shows that we must make the Qurʾān the criterion for judgement.

For this reason, an Islamic ruler must be wary of following people's desires, and rely only upon Allah. He must strive to purify his policies from ignorance, emotions, and self-interest, and sort the truth from among them, and to resist the forces of various pressures. The faithful must turn towards Allah's rulings with the entirety of their consciousness and free will, rather than waiting for practical guarantees of money and power, because these usually rest in the

---

[756] Sūrat al-Māʾida (5):44-47
[757] Sūrat Ṣād (38):26
[758] Sūrat Yūsuf (12):67

hands of the same wealthy and powerful people we mentioned above, who introduce erroneous directions into government.

The rule of the righteous jurists

The glorious Qur'ān:

- **'Indeed We have sent down to you the Book with the truth, so that you may judge between the people by what Allah has shown you; do not be an advocate for the traitors.'[759]**
- **'Eavesdroppers with the aim of [telling] lies, eaters of the unlawful—if they come to you, judge between them, or disregard them. If you disregard them, they will not harm you in any way. But if you judge, judge between them with justice. Indeed Allah loves the just.'[760]**

Rulings:

The most important qualities of an Islamic ruler are two:

1. Deep understanding of Allah's ruling that he might judge between the people by it.
2. Judging according to the truth and not be meek before the treacherous; and truth is represented by fairness, which means giving everyone their due.

Applying these and other conditions found in the Qur'ān and *sunna* to the real world brings us nearer to the governance of the righteous jurists, but we must not make this government – in turn – into an innovated form of rule by adding things which have no religious basis. The most important attributes of someone who rules by Allah's command are as follows:

1. Being free of influence from personal desires.
2. Not calling people to follow him.
3. Avoiding all kinds of self-interest, selfishness, and partisanship.
4. Not behaving haughtily in the earth in Allah's name, nor violating Allah's laws or the people's rights, for that will turn his rule into an idol who is worshipped apart from Allah.

The faithful must distinguish between a just ruler and an unjust one; they should obey someone who calls them to Allah's servitude, and reject anyone

---

[759] Sūrat al-Nisā' (4):105
[760] Sūrat al-Mā'ida (5):42

who calls them to his own servitude, for Allah has commanded us to reject the rule of tyrants.

The sanctity of life

Allah says:

'That is why We decreed for the Children of Israel that whoever kills a soul, without [its being guilty of] manslaughter or corruption on the earth, is as though he had killed all mankind, and whoever saves a life is as though he had saved all mankind. Our Messengers certainly brought them manifest signs, yet even after that many of them commit excesses on the earth.'[761]

Life is one of humanity's most fundamental rights; it is a religious value which springs from respecting others and acknowledging their rights. This is why the sanctity of a person's life is one of the greatest sanctities [mentioned] in the Qur'ān.

Murder is not an ordinary crime, insofar as it goes against human nature and is a grave act of wrongdoing, because it deprives someone else of their right to life.

And in order to preserve the sanctity of blood and respect for the value of human life, Allah gave a power to the heirs of someone slain unjustly, and based the social contract on the prohibition of murder, just as He made retribution a source of life for the society.

1: The value of life

The noble *sunna*:

- It is narrated from Imam al-Bāqir ﷺ: 'Whoever intentionally kills a believer, Allah Almighty places all of the sins of the victim upon the killer and relieves the victim of them. And concerning this Allah Almighty has said: **"I desire that you earn [the burden of] my sin and your sin, to become one of the inmates of the Fire."**'[762]
- It is narrated from Imam al-Ṣādiq ﷺ: 'Allah Almighty revealed to Mūsā b. ʿImrān: "O Mūsā, tell the Israelites [that I have said]: Beware of killing an inviolable life without right; for verily the one from among

---

[761] Sūrat al-Mā'ida (5):32

[762] *Biḥār al-anwār*, v. 101, p. 377, ḥ. 42; the verse referenced is Sūrat al-Mā'ida (5):29

you who kills a person in this world, I will kill him in the Fire one hundred thousand times in the way that his companion was killed.'"[763]

- It is narrated that Imam al-Bāqir ﵇, concerning the words of Allah Almighty: 'Whoever saves a life, it is as if he has saved all mankind,' said: 'He did not kill it [though he was able], or he saved someone from drowning or burning. But greater than all of these is [to save a life by] bringing it from misguidance to guidance.'[764]

Rulings:

Evil attributes, especially those such as looking down at some people and envying others, could reach a point where they pose an actual danger to a person's life. A believer must try his utmost to purify himself of these [negative] qualities, just as a believing society must work to cleanse people's heart of prejudice and egotism, that it might tear out the very roots of corruption and criminality and maintain people's respect for human life.

Hence a culture of respecting life must be spread throughout society by any means possible, and any ignorant cultures which treat human life with contempt must be confronted and shown to be devoid of wisdom.

2: To prevent the crime of murder

The noble *sunna*:

- It is narrated from Imam al-Ṣādiq ﵇: 'Taking a life is among the major sins, because Allah Almighty says: "Should anyone kill a believer intentionally, his requital shall be hell, to remain in it [forever]; Allah shall be wrathful at him and curse him and He shall prepare for him a great punishment."'[765]
- Imam al-Ṣādiq ﵇ was asked about a believer who intentionally kills another believer: is there forgiveness for him? So he said: 'If he had killed him for his faith, then there is no forgiveness for him. If he had killed him out of hatred or for some worldly reason, then his penance is that he is executed for it. If nobody was aware of it, then he must hasten to the victim's guardians (or relatives) and admit to them that he killed their companion. Then, if they forgive him rather than having him killed, he pays them blood money (*diyya*), frees a person (i.e., a

---

[763] *Biḥār al-anwār*, v. 101, p. 377, ḥ. 40
[764] *Biḥār al-anwār*, v. 101, p. 380
[765] *Biḥār al-anwār*, v. 101, p. 371

slave), fasts for two consecutive months, and feeds sixty paupers in repentance to Allah.'[766]

- Imam al-Ṣādiq ﷺ said: 'A believer is still within the bounds of his religion as long as inviolable blood does not stain him.' And he said: 'One who intentionally kills a believer is not graced with forgiveness [from Allah].'[767]

Rulings:

To protect life and prevent the crime of murder, it must be made clear that extinguishing someone's life is a terrible sin, and that the recompense for killing a believer intentionally is an eternity of punishment in Hellfire. One of the fundamental articles of the *umma*'s constitution must be a prohibition on murder. A just retribution must be wrought on the perpetrator, and people must not harbour a murderer.

3: Killing a child

The glorious Qur'ān:

1. **'That is how to most of the polytheists the slaying of their children is presented as decorous by those whom they ascribe as partners [to Allah], that they may ruin them and confound their religion for them. Had Allah wished, they would not have done it. So leave them with what they fabricate.'**[768]
2. **'They are certainly losers who slay their children foolishly without knowledge, and forbid what Allah has provided them, fabricating a lie against Allah. Certainly, they have gone astray and are not guided.'**[769]
3. **'When the girl buried alive will be asked for what sin she was killed.'**[770]

Rulings:

Killing a child is a truly reprehensible kind of murder, firstly because the killer is supposed to protect the victim and keep them safe; secondly, because the victim is weak and unable to protect his or herself. For this reason:

1. The terrible culture of child killing, which used to be widespread in pre-Islamic Age of Ignorance, but was obliterated by the bearers of revelation, must be confronted.

---

[766] *Biḥār al-anwār*, v. 101, p. 378
[767] *Biḥār al-anwār*, v. 101, p. 378
[768] Sūrat al-An'ām (6):137
[769] Sūrat al-An'ām (6):140
[770] Sūrat al-Takwīr (81):8-9

2. It appears that the [primary] form of child killing today is abortion, when the child is in its earliest stage of life in the womb. The crime of abortion is widespread in many lands; it has even become legal in some. We must confront this crime by any means available to us.

Guilt and innocence

Allah says: **'Your Lord would not destroy the towns until He had raised a Messenger in their mother city to recite to them Our signs. We would never destroy the towns except when their people were wrongdoers.'**[771]

To spread security in all quarters of a faithful city, the human being must be protected wherever he is, and he should not be convicted of a crime without irrefutable evidence to that effect. This is a right given to all human beings. One of the divine conducts (*sunan ilāhiyya*) is to treat people as innocent and not hold them responsible for the crimes of others, not to punish them without having exhausted every means to guide them (*itmām al-ḥujja*), and not to punish the innocent for the crimes of another. This is a manifestation of Divine Justice.

So Allah would never destroy a town until He had exhausted every means to guide them; **'This is because your Lord would never destroy the towns unjustly while their people were unaware.'**[772] This ensures that a person cannot be made to bear the sin of another, and the innovation of 'preemptive justice' – which requires punishment *before* any crime has been committed – is rendered invalid.

1. Knowledge is a precondition for guilt

Divine law is marked by mercy and adorned by wisdom. Allah does not punish a people without first sending messengers to warn them, nor does He seize one who is unaware until He has informed him. This is why the ignorant person is excused until he knows, even if he was wilfully ignorant, because knowledge is a condition for liability.

Consequently, religious scholars must warn people and teach them the religious laws. No ignorant person will be excused after they have been warned.

2. Human innocence

When we speak about responsibility and its exceptions, we must also speak about the principle of 'innocent until proven guilty,' and that each person

---

[771] Sūrat al-Qaṣaṣ (28):59

[772] Sūrat al-Anʿām (6):131

only bears responsibility for his own action or inaction. No one will be wronged by making them bear the burdens of another, unless they did something to make them culpable in that, in which case they will bear their own burden to the extent of their culpability. This is why family members cannot be punished for a crime of which their relative is accused.

Security and protection[773]

Allah says: '**[The faithful are] penitent, devout, celebrators of Allah's praise, wayfarers, who bow [and] prostrate [in prayer], bid what is right and forbid what is wrong, and keep Allah's bounds - and give good news to the faithful.**'[774]

The human being must protect that which is sacred to him, guard his soul against lusts and enmity, and keep safe his wealth from foolishness and waste. Perhaps the first thing that must be protected is chastity, especially that of women – because it is the thing nearest to danger – then life, and then wealth.

In this way, protecting the sanctity of the human being in its various forms is a responsibility shared between the individual and those around him. Just as other people are not allowed to violate your sanctity, likewise you must prevent them from doing so.

The human being must also maintain Allah's bounds and laws, and protect his faith and [any] trusts he has been given.

1: Legitimate defence

The noble *sunna*:

- Imam al-Ṣādiq has narrated from his father, Imam al-Bāqir ﷺ: 'Surely Allah abhors the [believer] who, when his home is entered [in aggression or unlawfully] does not fight back.' And he also said: 'If a man enters upon you, seeking to cause harm to you or your property, then hasten to strike him if you can, for surely a thief is one who wages

---

773 Pondering on the word 'security' (*iḥṣān*), its derivatives and the places in which it is used will lead us to understand three dimensions to its meanings: First, there is something valuable which we want to watch over; second, surrounding this thing with something to safeguard it; third, that this safeguard must be fixed and continuous such that its owner can rely on it and feel at ease.

This is where the words 'security' (*ḥiṣn*) and 'protection' (*ḥifẓ*) differ in meaning: protection means to guard something when it is in danger, while security means to place it in a safe situation where it will not be exposed to danger.

774 Sūrat al-Tawba (9):112

war against Allah and His Messenger; and I take responsibility for whatever follows you from it (i.e., whatever happens as a result).'[775]

❖ Abū Ayyūb said: I heard Abū ʿAbd Allah ﷺ saying: 'Whoever enters a believer's house [unlawfully] has waged war against him, so in that situation his blood is lawful to the believer, and I take responsibility for it.'[776]

❖ Imam al-Ṣādiq ﷺ said: 'If a man climbs up [somewhere to spy] over a group of people, or he looks at them through something (e.g., a window or a hole in the wall), and they fired [an arrow] at him—which struck and killed him, or gouged his eye—then they owe no penalty.' And he said: 'Once a man spied through the room of the Messenger of Allah ﷺ, so the Messenger of Allah came with an arrowhead to gouge his eye. When he found him, he ran off. So the Messenger of Allah ﷺ said: 'O filth, I swear by Allah, if you had stayed there I would have gouged your eye.'[777]

❖ Concerning a man who is killed for his money (or property), it is reported that the Messenger of Allah ﷺ said: 'Whoever was killed for his money has died a martyr, even if I, personally, would have abandoned the money to [the assailant] and not fought him.'[778]

Rulings:

Life is precious and protecting it is a duty, whether it is your own life or the life of another innocent. One method of achieving this is through the legitimate defence of life and its honour, which is why Islamic jurisprudence permits – or, in fact, obliges – you to protect life, chastity, honour, and any other sacred thing.

2: Defending the sanctity of others

The noble *sunna*:

❖ Imam al-Ṣādiq has reported from his father, from the Commander of the Believers ﷺ, that the Messenger of Allah ﷺ said: 'Whoever hears a man call out [in distress], "O, [help!]" to the Muslims, and does not respond to him, is not a Muslim.'[779]

❖ The Messenger of Allah ﷺ said: 'Do not hesitate when a man is being wrongfully killed (and in another narration: wrongfully struck), for

---

[775] *Wasāʾil al-shīʿa*, v. 11, p. 91, ḥ. 2, 3
[776] *Wasāʾil al-shīʿa*, v. 18, p. 543, ḥ. 3
[777] *Wasāʾil al-shīʿa*, v. 19, p. 49, ḥ. 6
[778] *Mustadrak al-wasāʾil*, v. 2, p. 243, ḥ. 1, 2
[779] *Wasāʾil al-shīʿa*, v. 18, p. 590, ḥ. 1

surely the curse [of Allah] descends upon whomever is present and does not come to his defense.'[780]

- The Messenger of Allah ﷺ said: 'Your aiding the weak is among the best [forms] of charity.'[781]
- The Commander of the Believers ؑ said: 'O Believers, he who sees our enemies doing wrong and calling him to it, and he rejects it in his heart, is saved and acquitted [from it]. And whoever rejects it with his tongue is rewarded, and is better than the other. And whoever rejects it by the sword so that the word of Allah will be made high, and the word of the wrongdoer will be made low, so he is the one who has reached the way of guidance, and stood upon the path, and certainty illuminates his heart.'[782]

Rulings:

Defending the sanctity of other persons – whether their life, chastity, or wealth – is just like defending the sanctity of oneself: it is not only permissible, it is obligatory! The verses of the Qur'ān command that fairness be maintained in society, and justice defended, just as they stress the importance of assisting the oppressed against their oppressor by any means possible.

3: Impregnable fortresses

The noble *sunna*:

- It has been narrated from the Messenger of Allah ﷺ: 'A man is not left alone with a [non-*maḥram*] woman but that the third one present is Satan.'[783]
- Imam al-Sajjād ؑ said: 'Putting wealth to good use is the completion of magnanimity.'[784]
- Imam ʿAlī ؑ said: 'Among the [qualities of] magnanimity is seeking to improve one's property.'[785]
- The Messenger of Allah ﷺ said: 'Being economical in one's expenditures is half of sustenance.'[786]

---

780 *Tajāwaz al-difāʿ al-sharʿī*, p. 160
781 *Wasā'il al-shīʿa*, v. 11, p. 108, ḥ. 2
782 *Nahj al-balāgha*, maxim 373
783 *Mīzān al-ḥikma*, v. 9, p. 108, ḥ. 18363
784 *Mīzān al-ḥikma*, v. 9, p. 281, ḥ. 19038
785 *Mīzān al-ḥikma*, v. 9, p. 281, ḥ. 19039
786 *Mīzān al-ḥikma*, v. 8, p. 138, ḥ. 16418

Rulings:

Legitimate defence is an important aspect of protection's existence as a social value conducive to security and peace, but it is not everything; so to ensure that life, chastity, and property are kept safe and sound, there must be institutions – like fortresses – set up to guard peace and security, and grant people peace of mind.

It is a citizen's duty to be ready to defend the value of security by protecting themselves, their chastity, their wealth, their rights, and Allah's bounds in a variety of ways.

Chastity is preserved through abstinence: by women not showing off their beauty, observing the laws and etiquettes of modesty, behaving appropriately with men, and following the rules and manners of married life. This, in its entirety, is one such fortress which protects society from corruption.

The code of practice for women in Islamic law is broad indeed, and we must learn it, strive to implement it, and persist in it, especially with regard to the new issues that have arisen in the modern age.

Life is protected through the natural duties which the divine law has laid down in the hundreds of laws and etiquettes promulgated to this end. We cannot enumerate all of them here, so we will suffice ourselves with mentioning the most important:

The human being must keep his mind and body healthy, and undertake to do everything he can for the sake of his own health and wellbeing, and that of his family. He must also protect the health of nature from pollution, and governments must strive to promote public health.

To protect wealth from theft, fraud, and embezzlement, one must pay attention to organizing his life's affairs. In Islamic jurisprudence there are tens of pieces of advice and rulings whose goal is to maintain fairness and ensure that no person wrongs another openly (e.g., by theft or robbery) or secretly (e.g., by embezzlement and usury).

The Qur'ān is a treasure trove of spiritual, ethical, cultural, and legal teachings for the *umma*, and it contains Allah's bounds, which our Lord has commanded us not to transgress. One of these bounds is people's faith, which our Lord has commanded us not to squander. Yet the question is: how can we protect these sacred values?

The answer is that we should act according to the following:

First, we must make the Qurʾān the axis of our learning, the centre of our culture, and the cornerstone of our legislation. Nothing else must be treated as equal to the Qurʾān, for the Qurʾān is superior to all other forms of speech, just as Allah is superior to His creation.

Second, our religious seminaries must show a greater interest in the Qurʾān; make the memorization of the Qurʾān and mastery of its language a prerequisite for further study; make Qurʾānic commentary a subject of study for the duration of the seminary program; and make the verses of the Qurʾān the centrepiece for all legal and doctrinal studies. Students should not be distracted from this by secondary subjects which do not yield much benefit in the current times.

Third, we must acquaint people with their Lord's revelation, so that they can ponder on its verses and see their lives through its vision; and this can only be accomplished by further efforts in the fields of education and media. And success is from Allah.

Second: The jurisprudence of provision and livelihood

Food and drink

Allah says: 'It is He who made the earth tractable for you; so walk on its flanks and eat of His provision, and to Him is the resurrection.'[787]

And Allah says: 'Eat the lawful and good things Allah has provided you, and be wary of Allah in Whom you have faith.'[788]

Peace is one of the highest goals of an Islamic society, and obtaining provision is one of its primary pillars, and depends on food, drink, shelter, health, and education.

Food is considered the primary need of a person, hence feeding others is the fundamental responsibility man has towards his fellow human beings. All food is permitted for man save that which Allah has forbidden (which is very little). But a person must look to his food and choose that which is purest. Food, in turn, gives him energy, which he must use for piety and good works. The human being must look after his food and not be immoderate or wasteful with it.

---

[787] Sūrat al-Mulk (67):15
[788] Sūrat al-Māʾida (5):88

1: Food and the value of life

The noble *sunna*:

- The Messenger of Allah ﷺ said: 'The one who goes to bed with a full stomach while his neighbor is hungry has not believed in me.' And he said: 'Whoever from the people of a town sleeps at night while among them are people going hungry, Allah will look to them [about it] on Judgment Day.'[789]
- It has been narrated from the Commander of the Believers عليه السلام: 'The believer does not satisfy [his appetite] while his brother [in faith] goes hungry.'[790]
- Imam al-Ṣādiq عليه السلام said: 'Whoever is compelled to eat a carcass (i.e., an animal that died rather than being slaughtered), or blood, or pork, but does not eat it and dies, is a disbeliever.'[791]

Rulings:

Food is a primary need for all human beings. It is obligatory to search for food, obtain and consume it, just as it is obligatory for people to feed those unable to find food for themselves, and just as storing it for days of scarcity is important. Allah has commanded us to go out in search of sustenance, and the verses of the Qurʾān very clearly indicate that it is obligatory to eat and drink in order to preserve one's life, just as reason dictates. The [religious] texts also indicate that it is necessary to feed the poor and needy, and spend from that which Allah has provided us.

2: The general permissibility of foodstuffs

The noble *sunna*:

- Concerning the consumption of the domesticated mule's meat, Muḥammad b. Muslim and Zurāra have narrated from Imam al-Bāqir عليه السلام: 'The Messenger of Allah ﷺ forbade its consumption on the day of Khaybar, but only in that instance, because [mules] were a [means of] carriage for the people. Unlawful only is that which Allah has prohibited in the Qur'ān.'[792]
- Imam al-Ṣādiq عليه السلام said: 'My father was asked about the meat of domesticated mules. So he said: "The Messenger of Allah ﷺ forbade its consumption because it was a carriage of the people that day.

---

[789] *Wasāʾil al-shīʿa*, v. 8, p. 490, ḥ. 1
[790] Wasāʾil al-shīʿa, v. 3, p. 90
[791] *Wasāʾil al-shīʿa*, v. 11, p. 479, ḥ. 3
[792] *Wasāʾil al-shīʿa*, v. 16, p. 322, ḥ. 1

Unlawful only is that which Allah has prohibited in the Qurʾān, and if not, the no.'"[793]

Rulings:

Islam is a lenient religion with which Allah broke the shackles placed on mankind's intellect and the bonds placed around its neck; by which He gave them back the state of freedom in which they were created. One dimension of Islam's leniency is the principle that everything is permitted until its illicitness is confirmed by a definitive stipulation, and the principle that everything is ritually pure until it becomes evident, by a clear indicator, that it is impure. Likewise, the general principle that the foodstuffs provided by Allah are lawful [for consumption] unless explicitly prohibited; it is a very useful principle.

3: Making use of whatever is in the earth

The noble *sunna*:

- Muḥammad b. Sinān has narrated he asked Abū al-Ḥasan ﷺ about river water. So he said: 'Surely the Muslims are partners in water, fire, and pasturage.'[794]
- It has been narrated from Imam ʿAlī ﷺ: 'It is unlawful to deny [someone] salt and water.'[795]

Rulings:

Every human being has the right to make use of the earth, which Allah spread out for mankind, and travel along its routes, which He marked for them with no distinction between one person and another. Every human being has the freedom to use whatever minerals the depths of the earth contain, and from the sustenance it contains, just as energy produced by fire is everybody's right.

4: Permissible and good sustenance

The glorious Qurʾān:

- **'O you who have faith! Eat of the good things We have provided you, and thank Allah, if it is Him that you worship.'**[796]
- **'They ask you as to what is lawful to them. Say, "All the good things are lawful to you." As for what you have taught hunting dogs [to catch], teaching them out of what Allah has taught you, eat of what**

---

[793] *Wasāʾil al-shīʿa*, v. 16, p. 324, ḥ. 7
[794] *Wasāʾil al-shīʿa*, v. 17, p. 331, ḥ. 1
[795] *Wasāʾil al-shīʿa*, v. 17, p. 331, ḥ. 2
[796] Sūrat al-Baqara (2):172

they catch for you and mention Allah's Name over it, and be wary of Allah. Indeed Allah is swift at reckoning.'[797]

Rulings:

The verses of the Qur'ān bid us to eat from Allah's good and permissible sustenance, and to avoid filth:

1. Allah has only permitted us good things as sustenance, not filth.
2. There are some good things and some kinds of filth which the divine revelation has specified for mankind, and others known to all mankind (such as the foulness of human excrement), and some about which people differ:
    a. We must refer to the revelation to understand those things which the religion specifies as good or foul.
    b. We must refer to our shared human culture to discern those things that people generally agree to be good or foul.
    c. In everything else, each people must refer to their own culture; so if they believe something to be good, they should eat it, and if they think it foul, they should avoid it.

House and home

Allah says:

'Remember when He made you successors after [the people of] ʿĀd, and settled you in the land: you build palaces in its plains, and hew houses out of the mountains. So remember Allah's bounties, and do not act wickedly on the earth, causing corruption.'[798]

From the Qur'ān, we understand that the ultimate purpose of a home is as follows:

1. To protect lives, property, and chastity from aggression.
2. To conceal oneself from the eyes of others, hide one's faults, keep one's secrets, and be alone with oneself and one's nearest and dearest.
3. To create a healthy atmosphere for cooperation, mutual assistance, and living together, usually amongst members of a single family.

---

[797] Sūrat al-Māʾida (5):88
[798] Sūrat al-Aʿrāf (7):74

4. To keep oneself free from immorality and indecency, and to occupy oneself with the private remembrance and worship of Allah, far from the eyes and distractions of other people.

Verily the house in which a believer lives (and the area surrounding it from town and country) is actually a place where many religious rulings can be applied, such as security (*amn*), protection (*ḥiṣāna*), piety, cooperation, kindness, purity, remembrance [of Allah], and the like thereof.

And from various verses of the Qurʾān and traditions, we understand that the best way to build a house is that which grants the following:

1: Firmness and protection

The noble *sunna*:

- It has been narrated from Imam al-Ṣādiq ﷺ: 'Whoever builds [a home] but and skimps [in construction materials] in his construction would not be rewarded.'[799]
- Islam has forbade staying in a ruined house, as has been narrated from the Prophet ﷺ: 'Three people Allah will not give protection: a man staying in a ruined house, a man who prays in the middle of the road, and a man who dispatches his leaves his riding animal without securing it.[800]
- Imam al-Ṣādiq ﷺ disliked [people] sleeping on an unwalled roof, and said: 'Whoever sleeps upon a roof without a wall, I am absolved of responsibility for him.'[801]

Rulings:

Insofar as protecting one's life is a religious and rational duty, as we discussed under the rules for protection, it is necessary to pay attention to things such as firmness, stability, and safety regulations when building a house. And this necessity can be either recommended or obligatory depending on the level of [potential] danger; so if there is a high level of danger, such that ignoring these matters might put people's lives at risk, then it is obligatory to observe them and forbidden to ignore them. An example of this is if the house is in a region prone to earthquakes and someone builds it too weak to withstand them, such that common sense says that he is putting his own life in danger. On the

---

[799] *Biḥār al-anwār*, v. 73, p. 150, ḥ. 12

[800] *Biḥār al-anwār*, v. 73, p. 157, ḥ. 2

[801] Which means that if something happens to him, then he has none to blame but himself. *Biḥār al-anwār*, v. 73, p. 178, ḥ. 2

other hand, if the danger is limited or slight, then protecting oneself from it is recommended and failing to do so is disliked.

2: Space, sunlight, and cleanliness

The glorious Qur'ān:

- **'You may see the sun, when it rises, slanting toward the right of their cave, and, when it sets, cut across them towards the left, and they are in a cavern within it. That is one of Allah's signs. Whomever Allah guides is rightly guided, and whomever He leads astray, you will never find for him any guardian or guide.'[802]**

The noble *sunna*:

- Abū al-Ḥasan ﷺ was asked: What is the best way to live in this world? So he said: 'A spacious home and many loved ones.'[803]
- It has been narrated from Imam al-Bāqir ﷺ: 'Among the miseries of living is tight living quarters.'[804]
- Regarding the cleanliness of the home and prohibiting its pollution, many narrations have been transmitted. Among them, it has been narrated from Imam ʿAlī ﷺ: 'Clean your homes of spiderwebs, for leaving them in the house brings about poverty.'[805]
- And from among the prohibited things, the Messenger of Allah ﷺ said: 'Do not leave trash overnight in your homes, but throw it out daily, for it is the seat of Satan.'[806]

Rulings:

1. From the verse – *Sūrat al-Kahf*, verse 17 – we understand the importance of clean air and sunlight for a home, such that the verse says that the People of the Cave lived on the side of a mountain – a place known for its clean air – and that the sun would shine on them at the beginning and the end of the day (such that it gave them enough warmth to keep their bodies healthy).
2. Narrations call for the house to be spacious, clean, and ritually pure, and for it to be a place for maintaining and restoring good health. Likewise, from these values and principles we can derive a number of new rulings about pollution of the natural world and congestion in our modern

---

[802] Sūrat al-Kahf (18):17
[803] *Mustadrak al-wasāʾil*, v. 1, p. 243, ḥ. 3
[804] *Biḥār al-anwār*, v. 73, p. 153, ḥ. 31
[805] *Biḥār al-anwār*, v. 73, p. 175, ḥ. 3
[806] *Biḥār al-anwār*, v. 73, p. 175, ḥ. 4

cities, and the necessity of separating residential homes from tall buildings.

2: Privacy and peace

The noble *sunna*:

- Imam al-Ṣādiq ﷤ said: 'There are three things in which there is comfort for the believer: A spacious home that conceals his privacy and bad situation from the people, a righteous woman who supports him in the affair of this life and the next, and a daughter or sister who is taken from his home [only] by death or marriage.'[807]
- The Messenger of Allah ﷺ said: 'Three things extinguish the light of the worshipper'—until he said: 'or directing one's vision into [private] rooms for which he has not been permitted.'[808]

Rulings:

In the verses of the Qurʾān we find many verses which teach us about the sanctity of houses and forbid us from entering them without the permission of their inhabitants, or climbing over their walls rather than coming through their doors. Islam even commands those inside the houses to seek permission from their inhabitants before entering some of their private rooms at times of rest and privacy, just as other verses say that it is necessary for there to be a curtain present when asking questions from the wives of the Prophet. From all of this we glean the following:

1. Houses should be built in a way to maintain privacy.
2. Windows and entrances for light should be in the middle of the house, and far from the sight of neighbours and passers-by.
3. Bedrooms should be as far as possible from the living space to maintain privacy, even from other inhabitants of the same house, such as children and servants.
4. It is impermissible to look into houses or eavesdrop, whether by normal means, through binoculars, by monitoring phone lines, or using electronic surveillance equipment.

---

[807] *Biḥār al-anwār*, v. 73, p. 149, ḥ. 2

[808] *Mustadrak al-wasāʾil*, v. 1, p. 245, ḥ. 2

4: Decorating a house

The noble *sunna*:

- It is narrated from Imam al-Ṣādiq ﷺ: 'Verily Allah Almighty loves beauty and beautification, and hates misery and whatever creates it. Surely Allah Almighty, if He bestows grace upon a servant, then I love that he looks after it.' It was said: And how is that? He said: 'One who cleans his garment, perfumes his scent, improves his home, and sweeps its courtyard. Even [lighting] the lamp before the setting of the sun banishes poverty and increases sustenance.'[809]
- Imam ʿAlī ﷺ said: 'Beautification is from among the manners of the believers.'[810]
- Imam al-Bāqir ﷺ said: 'Increase the amount of birds in your homes. They keep Satan busy and away from your sons.'[811]
- Imam al-Riḍā ﷺ said: 'Sweeping your patio will bring sustenance.'[812]
- It is narrated that Abū Khadīja said: I saw *āyat al-kursī* written (displayed) in the house of Abū ʿAbd Allah ﷺ. I was passing by the house and saw it in the *qibla* of its prayer space.[813]

Rulings:

Allah has not forbidden the faithful from enjoying the adornments of worldly life; in fact, He has commanded it when visiting a mosque, insofar as adornment brings about affection between people. Even women are not forbidden from adorning themselves in private settings and in front of their *maḥārim*[814] relatives – she is only forbidden from displaying her adornments to others. And Allah has counted houses with doors, furniture, and decoration as amongst the ornaments of this world; and many narrations affirm that Allah loves beauty and beautification, so there is no doubt that a house – as a place in which the human being lives – is one of the most obvious situations where this applies.

---

[809] *Biḥār al-anwār*, v. 73, p. 141, ḥ. 5
[810] *Mīzān al-ḥikma*, v. 2, p. 81, ḥ. 2509
[811] *Wasāʾil al-shīʿa*, v. 8, p. 381, ḥ. 5
[812] *Biḥār al-anwār*, v. 73, p. 172, ḥ. 10
[813] *Biḥār al-anwār*, v. 73, p. 151, ḥ. 20
[814] *Maḥārim* are those relatives to whom a woman's marriage is forbidden (e.g., father, brother, son) and who are allowed to see her without the covering she wears in front of other people.

5: Simplicity and avoiding immoderation (waste)

The noble *sunna*:

❖ It has been narrated from Imam ʿAlī ﷺ: 'Five things go to waste (and among them he mentioned): a lamp to guide in the daylight, oil when it spoils, and illumination by which none benefit.'[815]

❖ It has been narrated from Imam al-Ṣādiq ﷺ: 'Everything built [beyond what is necessary for] subsistence is unhealthy for its owner on Resurrection Day.'[816]

Rulings:

Immoderation (*isrāf*) means to exceed what is commonly needed in the affairs of life, and it is something disliked and criticized in anything in which it leads to the following negative consequences:

1. Wasting money with no reasonable benefit, such as [needlessly] switching a light on during the day.
2. Exceeding one's normal needs, such as a house with tens of rooms for a small family that need only three or four.
3. If something became a cause of corruption in one's general outlook and causing one to feel superior to others.

6: An appropriate location

The noble *sunna*:

❖ Abū Dharr said: The Messenger of Allah ﷺ said to me: 'O Abū Dharr, I advise you, so remember that Allah might benefit you thereby: [live] adjacent to the graveyard so that it will remind you of the hereafter.'[817]

❖ It is narrated from the Commander of the Believers ﷺ that he wrote to Ḥarith al-Hamdānī: 'Live in the best locale, for it is the gathering place of the Muslims, and beware of places of negligence and repugnance.'[818]

Rulings:

The ideal home, in terms of location, is one in which the purpose of a home can be achieved with the greatest ease, namely: security and safety,

---

815 *Biḥār al-anwār*, v. 73, p. 164, ḥ. 4
816 *Biḥār al-anwār*, v. 73, p. 150, ḥ. 10
817 *Mustadrak al-wasāʾil*, v. 1, p. 246, ḥ. 3
818 *Biḥār al-anwār*, v. 73, p. 156, ḥ. 2

cleanliness and light, privacy and beauty, earnings and benefits, and remembrance [of Allah] and purity.

7: Remembrance and purity

The noble *sunna*:

❖ In a tradition narrated from Imam al-Ṣādiq ☝, he said: 'Surely the houses in which prayers are offered and the Qur'ān is recited are illuminated for the people of the heaven like the stars of the sky shine for the people of the earth.'[819]

Rulings:

The idea house is one from which the remembrance of Allah rises and from which shines the light of purity and faith. It is for this reason that:

1. It is recommended to set aside a specific place in the house for prayer and remembrance.
2. It is recommended to offer some prayers – even recommended ones – in the house to spread the spirit of worship throughout the home, and to contribute to the moral upbringing of the children.
3. It is recommended to recite the Qur'ān in the house.
4. It is generally recommended for the people living in the house to engage in the remembrance of Allah at different times (before eating and afterwards, before sleeping and when waking up, when performing *wuḍū'*, *ghusl*, and so on) so that the house will be blessed and built upon the continuous remembrance of Allah.

8: Benefits and blessings

The noble *sunna*:

❖ The Messenger of Allah ☝ said: 'Whoever eats from the hard work of his labor, Allah will look to him with mercy, and he will never be punished.'

Rulings:

Islam instructs us to seek lawful provisions, and to arrange our livelihood and economics. Some instances of this are: Islam encourages us to be economically productive, meaning that we can turn our home into a unit of

---

[819] *Wasā'il al-shī'a*, v. 3, p. 554, ḥ. 1

production in the national economy, rather than merely a place of consumption, whether this production takes the form of agriculture or light industry.

9: Cooperation and mercy

The noble *sunna*:

❖ Imam al-Ṣādiq has narrated from his father عليه السلام: "ʿAlī and Fāṭima sought the decree of the Messenger of Allah ﷺ concerning household responsibilities. So the Prophet ﷺ decreed that Fāṭima is tasked with what is inside the door, and decreed ʿAlī عليه السلام responsible for what was beyond it.'[820]

❖ Imam ʿAlī عليه السلام said: 'The Messenger of Allah ﷺ visited us while Fāṭima was sitting with the cooking pot, and I was cleaning the lentils. He said: "O Abū al-Ḥasan!" I said: "I am at your service, O Messenger of Allah." He said: "Listen, for my speeh is naught but the command of my Lord: No man helps his wife in her house but that for every hair on his body a year's worship [registered], fasting all its days and standing in prayer all its nights, and He rewards him like the that of the patient ones, [who were] the Prophet Dāwud, Yaʿqūb, and ʿĪsā عليهم السلام. O ʿAlī! The one who serves his family in the house without disdain [for it], Allah writes his name in the record of martyrs."'[821]

Rulings:

The family is the social unit responsible for preserving the values of Muslim society, the most important of which are the spirits of mutual cooperation and kindness. The ideal home furnishes these values – in the form of a family – with ease.

10: A place for teaching and upbringing

The noble *sunna*:

❖ It has been narrated from Imam al-Ḥasan عليه السلام: 'I saw my mother, Fāṭima, standing [in prayer] to welcome the eve of Friday. She remained in bowing and prostration until the [white] pillar [of light signaling] morning appeared. I heard her supplicating for the believing men and women by name and increasing her supplication for them, while she asked nothing for herself. I said: "O mother, why don't you supplicate

---

[820] *Mustadrak al-wasāʾil*, v. 2, p. 422, ḥ. 6

[821] *Mustadrak al-wasāʾil*, v. 2, p. 423, ḥ. 2

for yourself like you do for others?" She said: "O son, [first] the neighbor, then [one's] home.'"[822]

Rulings:

A religious house is a niche for the Lord's light, a place for teaching and providing a righteous upbringing. If the atmosphere of the house reverberates with the sound of divine remembrance and shines with the glow of learning, then the children of the house will have a childhood thus illuminated by the people of remembrance and knowledge.

The first school children attend for religious education is their mother's womb, her embrace, and then the shadow of the father and his teachings.

The home should have a collective program for the whole family, through which the parents strive to nurture the spirit and intellects of their children.

Health and wellbeing

Allah says:

'Whoever acts righteously, [whether] male or female, should he be faithful, - We shall revive him with a good life and pay them their reward by the best of what they used to do.'[823]

'...those who follow the Messenger, the uninstructed prophet, whose mention they find written with them in the Torah and the Gospel, who bids them to do what is right and forbids them from what is wrong, makes lawful to them all the good things and forbids them from all vicious things, and relieves them of their burdens and the shackles that were upon them - those who believe in him, honour him, and help him and follow the light that has been sent down with him, they are the felicitous.'[824]

A good life is one of the values promoted by faith; the cornerstone of a good life is good health; and good health is achieved by protecting one's health, convalescence, and psychological wellbeing.

---

[822] *Fāṭimat al-zahrāʾ bahjat qalb al-muṣtafā* of Aḥmad al-Raḥmānī al-Hamdānī, p. 79

[823] Sūrat al-Naḥl (16):97

[824] Sūrat al-Aʿrāf (7):157

Protecting one's health means keeping clean, eating and drinking in moderation, and choosing good things over bad ones.

Convalescence includes fasting, prayer, pilgrimage, and seeking the health benefits of honey.

Psychological wellbeing protects the human being from many illnesses and helps him recover from many others.

1: Looking after one's life and limb

The true religion calls people to lead a good life, and our Lord bids us to respond to His Messenger when he summons us to that which gives us life. The call of the righteous is a good life in this world and the Hereafter, and the means of achieving this is righteous deeds. Good health is one of the necessary conditions for a good life.

2: Health and severe harm

The noble *sunna*:

- It has been narrated from Imam al-Ṣādiq ﷺ: 'Everything from grains and fruits that causes harm to a person's body is thus unlawful to consume, except in situations of dire necessity.'[825]
- The Messenger of Allah ﷺ said: '[There is] no harm and no injury [in Islam].'[826]

Rulings:

1. There are kinds of illness that might not lead to death, loss of limb, or loss of strength, but they could still cause severe harm, such as diabetes. This might not mean that someone will die; in fact, people can live with it for many long years, but it is common sense that this is very harmful for the person thus afflicted. The apparent ruling in illnesses such as these is that it is obligatory to take measures to avoid contracting them wherever possible.
2. The strongest opinion is that it is obligatory to hasten to repel severe harm from a person if neglecting that would mean their death; so when afflicted with such a disease, the person must seek treatment and medicine.

---

[825] *Tuḥaf al-ʿuqūl*, p. 251

[826] *Man lā yaḥḍuruh al-faqīh*, v. 3, p. 59, ḥ. 9

Public health and corruption

Allah has forbidden people from spreading corruption upon the earth in the strongest possible terms. Avoiding major corruption is the wisdom behind the prohibition of taking the disbelievers as guardians. For this reason, it is obligatory to work to prevent the spread of corruption in all of its forms. This includes having a concern for public health, in order to protect the public from being exposed to danger and corruption themselves. For this reason:

1. Harmful foodstuffs must be removed from circulation by regulating food producers and distributors.
2. By the same token, water sources must be managed, whether springs, rivers, reservoirs, pumps, channels, and pipes, to protect them from being contaminated by disease, chemicals, or other harmful substances.
3. Fatal epidemics must be managed through inoculation programs, and through preventing people from infected areas moving to uninfected ones.
4. A system of health monitoring must be set up in schools, public places, factories and all other places of gathering, to prevent the spread of epidemics.
5. Marriage must also be monitored to prevent the spread of sexually transmitted diseases, and also to protect any resulting children from genetic disorders.

4: Public health and the good life

Our Lord has forbidden uncleanliness as this causes illness; so carrion, swine flesh, and any other kinds of harmful food and drink are forbidden, because all of these are enemies to your health.

Teaching and learning

Allah says:

'It is He who sent to the unlettered [people] a Messenger from among themselves, to recite to them His signs, to purify them, and to teach them the Book and wisdom, and earlier they had indeed been in manifest error.'[827]

Cooperating in good deeds and piety is an important Islamic principle and a value from which we can derive tens of other values, such as cooperating to promote public health, education, and wellbeing.

---

[827] Sūrat al-Jumuʿa (62):2

Education is a right held by the ignorant person over all other persons, but some are more responsible for this than others, namely: the prophets, scholars, near relatives, and those who manage the affairs of the Muslims.

The noble *sunna*:

- Imam al-Ṣādiq ﵇ said: 'I read in the book of ʿAlī: "Surely Allah did not take a covenant from the ignorant to seek knowledge until he took a covenant from the scholars to be generous in giving knowledge to the ignorant, because knowledge was before ignorance."'[828]
- Imam al-Bāqir ﵇ has narrated from the Messenger of Allah ﷺ: 'Surely all that walks on the earth and swims in the sea, and everything in the air that possesses a spirit, and all of the people of heaven and earth, seek forgiveness for the teacher of good. The scholar and the student are alike in reward, and on Resurrection Day they will come like a throng of racehorses.'[829]
- Imam ʿAlī ﵇ said: 'Teach your children swimming and archery.'[830] And this narration is advising us to teach our children what they will need to know in life.
- Imam al-Ṣādiq ﵇ said: 'Hasten to impart narrations (i.e., religious knowledge) [to your children], before the [corrupt schools of religious thought] beat you to it.'[831]
- In an address to the people, Imam ʿAlī ﵇ said: 'O people, I have a right over you, and you have a right over me. As for your right over me, it is that I give you advice, and disburse your spoils of war to you, and teach you so that you will not be ignorant, and that I educate you so that you will know.'[832]
- When the Prophet ﷺ sent Muʿādh b. Jabal to Yemen, he advised him concerning the responsibilities obligated upon him. So he said: 'O Muʿādh! Teach them the Book of Allah, and reform their etiquette upon righteous manners.'[833]

Rulings:

1. It is obligatory to spend money on one's family, and one of the affairs of the family according to our current customs is education; so taking

---

[828] *Biḥār al-anwār*, v. 2, p. 67
[829] *Biḥār al-anwār*, v. 2, p. 17
[830] *Wasāʾil al-shīʿa*, v. 15, p. 194, ḥ. 2
[831] *Wasāʾil al-shīʿa*, v. 15, p. 196, ḥ. 1
[832] *Nahj al-balāgha*, sermon 34
[833] *Tuḥaf al-ʿuqūl*, p. 219

care of a child's education is the duty of his or her parents, and failing to do so is a failure to discharge one's duty to one's dependents.

2. By the same token, it is obligatory for a father to teach his children whatever they need in life – whatever custom would be deemed a matter of upkeep depending on the time, place, and household. There are many traditions encouraging the faithful to teach their children correct beliefs, good manners, and whatever else they need to learn, such as reading, writing, and swimming.
3. It is the Islamic government that guards people's rights, implements the general values of society, and that must spread knowledge, especially knowledge upon which people's religious knowledge or life's affairs depend.
4. For this reason, the state must devote its attention to providing the necessary means and methods, and make education compulsory for all, striving against illiteracy and combating ignorance.

Third: The jurisprudence of offspring and family ties

Affection

Allah says: '**That is the good news Allah gives to His servants who have faith and do righteous deeds! Say, "I do not ask you any reward for it except love of [my] near relatives." Whoever performs a good deed, We shall enhance for him its goodness. Indeed Allah is All-forgiving, All-appreciative.**'[834]

People's relations to one another must be on the basis of spiritual affection, of which love of Allah, His Messenger, and his near relatives is the foundation. By the same token, loving one's own family and community – so long as it does not conflict with this divine love – is too. As for affection that rests on the basis of idols worshipped besides Allah, such as un-Islamic prejudices and material attachments, these are not virtuous. And from this fact, we can glean the following rulings:

1. A believer must be kind and affectionate towards the people.
2. You must like for your believing brother what you like for yourself.
3. A sound marriage rests on the foundation of affection.

Relations between the faithful

Allah says: '**[They are as well] for those who were settled in the land and [abided] in faith before them, who love those who migrate toward them,**

[834] Sūrat al-Shūrā (42):23

and do not find in their breasts any need for that which is given to them, but prefer [the Immigrants] to themselves, though poverty be their own lot. And those who are saved from their own greed - it is they who are the felicitous.'[835]

In the environment of a believing society, the values of Islam are realized, as is truth, justice, security, and a noble provision. In order to achieve this environment, relations between the faithful must be strengthened to the level of brotherhood.

This brotherhood is achieved by holding fasting to Allah's rope, as embodied in His Book and His Messenger, defending one another and cooperating together in good deeds and piety, and by avoiding negative behaviour such as ridicule, assuming the worst of others, spying (fault-finding), and backbiting; and by [the believers] adorning themselves with virtues such as altruism, reform, and defending the oppressed.

1: Between love and material values

The noble *sunna*:

- The Messenger of Allah ﷺ said to his companions: 'What is the firmest handle of faith?' So they said: Allah and His messenger know better, while some of them said the prayer, and others said the alms tax, while others said fasting, and still others said the greater and lesser pilgrimages, and yet others said fighting [in the way of Allah]. So the Messenger of Allah ﷺ said: 'There is merit in what each of you mentioned, yet that is not it. Rather, the firmest handle of faith is love for the sake of Allah and hatred for the sake of Allah, [which is] seeking nearness to Allah's [appointed] guardians (*awliyāʾ*), and being far away (*al-tabarrī*) from the enemies of Allah Almighty.'[836]
- The Messenger of Allah ﷺ said: 'The love of a believer for a believer, for the sake of Allah, is among the greatest branches of the faith.'[837]

Rulings:

A nation will only overcome efforts to divide it when it follows its leader, holds fast to the value of truth, and lives together with love, affection, and brotherhood. And our Lord has recorded the nature of the bond between the

---

835 Sūrat al-Ḥashr (59):9
836 *Al-Maḥāsin*, v. 1, p. 264
837 *Al-Maḥāsin*, v. 1, p. 263

first Muslims, honouring the Helpers (*anṣār*).[838] This is an example of what Islam does to people's hearts, to show generation after generation of mankind, and in particular the Muslim *umma*, the secret of success in history. The first generation of the righteous were only able to lead the world because they had this high spiritual position.

2: The connection between different generations

One aspect of the bond of brotherhood is that it transcends the limitations of time and place, in that the believer has a positive bond with those believers who came before him, and in that we see him asking forgiveness for their sins. In fact, it transcends all such limitations (whether cultural or natural), so the Muslim asks His Lord not to put dislike towards other believers in his heart (even if these believers differ from him in their opinions, race, language, etc.)

3: Brotherhood and reconciliation

The noble *sunna*:

- The Commander of the Believers ﵇, upon his death advised his two sons, al-Ḥasan and al-Ḥusayn ﵉: 'I advise the two of you, and all of my sons, and my family, and whomever my message reaches, to fear Allah, settle your affair, and reconciliation between each other. For surely I heard your grandfather, the Messenger of Allah ﷺ, saying: "Reconciling discord [between people] is better than all of prayer and fasting."'[839]
- It is narrated from Imam al-Ṣādiq ﵇: 'A charity beloved by Allah is bringing about reconciliation between the people when there is strife, and creating nearness between them when they were distant.'[840]
- Imam al-Ṣādiq ﵇ said: 'Causing reconciliation between two people is more beloved to me than giving charity of two dinars.'[841]

Rulings:

The bond between the faithful reaches such a high level that it makes them brothers to one another, and this requires them to seek reconciliation between themselves. Just as one part of a river cleanses another part of impurity,

---

[838] The Helpers (*anṣār*) are the Muslims of the Aws and Khazraj tribes in Medina who pledged to protect the Prophet with their lives before he and the Emigrants (*muhājirīn*) emigrated there from Mecca, where they were suffering persecution.
[839] *Biḥār al-anwār*, v. 72, p. 24, ḥ. 3
[840] *Nūr al-thaqalayn*, v. 5, p. 88
[841] *Nūr al-thaqalayn*, v. 5, p. 88

so too must the faithful continuously seek to set right whatever will spoil their relations with one another, so that the bonds of brotherhood are strengthened in their lives.

4: Mutual respect

For Islam to establish a firm social edifice, it enjoins us to hold our brethren in sufficient esteem so that one group of men does not deride another, or one group of women another. The Qur'ān forbids us from name-calling, exchanging unpleasant nicknames, assuming the worst of others, fault-finding or backbiting about them, in order that we receive mercy and forgiveness.

Family ties

The glorious Qur'ān:

❖ Allah says: **'And those who join what Allah has commanded to be joined, and fear their Lord, and are afraid of an adverse reckoning.'**[842]

Rulings:

Insofar as the goal of the faithful is to create a civilized society for mankind, the way in which they achieve this is by joining together the limbs of society; which is in turn accomplished through two interrelated frameworks, the first of which watches over the second. The first is the divine framework which is watched over by the lofty values of revelation stemming from divine authority, a branch of which is the authority of the Prophet and Imams, and then the authority of the faithful over one another. As for the second, it is the human framework, whose first circle is formed by the family, which then expands until it encompasses all human culture, including one's community, homeland, people, and nation; and the divine framework watches over the human framework.

1: The bond of walāya

The noble *sunna*:

❖ Al-Jahm b. Ḥumayd said: I said to Abū 'Abd Allah 🕮: There are relatives of mine who are upon another affair (i.e., they are not Shī'a). Do they have a right upon me? He said: 'Yes, the right of kinship, which nothing severs. Yet if they were upon your affair (i.e., the *walāya* of the

---

[842] Sūrat al-Ra'd (13):21

holy household), then they would have two rights [upon you]: the right of kinship and the right of Islam.'[843]

Rulings:

Perhaps the largest single division of divine teachings are those whose goal it is to arrange human relations. The framework of culture or natural law for these relations is greatly influenced by the divine religions, indicating that these relations themselves are given great importance in religion. Organizing these relations on firm foundations is one way in which this importance is shown. The verse above describes the faithful in an absolute sense as those who join what Allah has commanded to be joined, whether this is a divine bond (such as loyalty – *walāya* – to Allah's Messenger and his Household) or a human one endorsed by religion, such as family ties, and even the tie between believers, the bond of neighbours, of a single land, or a single people.

2: The pillar of civilization

The noble *sunna*:

- It is narrated from Imam al-Bāqir ﷺ: '[Maintaining] the bond of kinship purifies one's deeds, causes wealth to grow, repels misfortune, makes easy the reckoning, and delays death.'[844]
- It is narrated from Imam al-Ṣādiq ﷺ: '[Maintaining] the bond of kinship and [filial] piety ease the reckoning and protect against sins, so maintain your family ties and be respectful to your brothers, even if by offering *salām* and returning its reply.'[845]

Rulings:

There are two subcategories of human relation; one is chosen by us, the other imposed upon us. It is you who chooses your religion, sect, and political affiliation, but it is Allah who determines where you are born, and who your parents, relatives, and community are.

A strong culture rests upon these two pillars of choice and imposition, so it is up to its members to uphold their pledge to Allah and His covenant. If they choose a religion and do not retreat from their choice under pressure and hardship, just as they respect the determination of their Lord, then they will treat their relatives well and cooperate with them. On the other hand, those who

---

[843] *Al-Kāfi*, v. 2, p. 157, ḥ. 30
[844] *Biḥār al-anwār*, v. 71, p. 111, ḥ. 71
[845] *Biḥār al-anwār*, v. 71, p. 131, ḥ. 98

violate the divine covenant and break their family ties, their path is towards corruption, which will lead to wrongdoing, division, and regression.

Children and offspring

The glorious Qur'ān:

- Allah says: **'Wealth and children are an adornment of the life of the world, but lasting righteous deeds are better with your Lord in reward and better in hope.'**[846]

Rulings:

Children are an adornment of the life of this world, but what are truly of fundamental value in this life are lasting righteous deeds. So whoever uses this adornment to seek that which is with Allah, and does not let himself be led astray by it – avoiding pride, conceit and aggression with it – while bearing his duty to spend for it, treat it well, and bring it up, then this will be made a lasting righteous deed that will benefit him on a day when no wealth or children will avail him. But whoever takes children as goods of vanity and disbelief, then he has been led astray from his faith by them, and they will be no good to him.

Allah has blessed mankind with children, and made love of their children decorous to them. He has placed benefit in them for their parents, protected them from being killed, and demonstrated the foolishness of the idol-worshippers who perpetrated this crime. He also warned against going to extremes in the love of one's children at the expense of one's faith, mentioned that they are a test (*fitna*) and amongst them are enemies, and said that they will not avail their parents anything against Allah. He warned too against Satan, who operates amongst them, and declared that a child of unrighteous conduct is not part of one's household.

1: Marriage and increasing offspring

The noble *sunna*:

- The Messenger of Allah ﷺ said: 'Whoever loves to emulate my character should act according to my *sunna*, and marriage is from my *sunna*.'[847]

---

[846] Sūrat al-Kahf (18):46

[847] *Biḥār al-anwār*, v. 100, p. 222, ḥ. 36

- Imam al-Ṣādiq ﷺ said: 'The inheritance of Allah for his believing servant is a righteous child who will seek forgiveness for him [after his passing].'

Rulings:

Children are an adornment of this life, and its tillage, and they are Allah's bequest from His righteous servants. Islam strongly encourages people to marry and have children. Many Islamic teachings and legal rulings turn on this encouragement, which traces a balanced path between the extremes of monasticism – which forsakes this adornment for the sake of the Hereafter – and worldliness, which forsakes the Hereafter for the sake of this adornment.

The Qurʾān intimates that our children are lofty goals. A single child brings contentment to the family, and an abundance of children brings strength to society: for they are its soldiers and defenders, and they will become an economic treasure for the *umma* as well.

2: Protecting one's children

A person must respond to the blessing of a child by giving thanks to Allah, and to him falls the responsibility of protecting and guarding this child. For this reason, one of the greatest sins is killing one's children. Islam forbade the barbaric practice of burying one's daughters, and killing one's sons out of fear of poverty.

3: An adornment of this life

The noble *sunna*:

- The Messenger of Allah ﷺ said: 'A righteous child is a sweet basil from the sweet basils of Paradise.'[848]
- Imam al-Ṣādiq ﷺ said: 'Daughters are goodnesses and sons are blessings (*niʿma*). [On Judgment Day] good deeds will be rewarded, but one will be questioned about the blessings.'[849]
- Imam al-Ṣādiq ﷺ said: 'Verily Allah Almighty will have mercy upon a man by the strength of his love for his son.'[850]
- It has been narrated from Imam al-Ṣādiq ﷺ that 'Mūsā b. ʿImrān said: 'O Lord, which deeds are best in Your sight?' So He said: 'Love of children, for it is their nature to affirm My divine unity, so when they

[848] *Biḥār al-anwār*, v. 101, p. 90, ḥ. 1
[849] *Biḥār al-anwār*, v. 101, p. 90, ḥ. 3
[850] *Biḥār al-anwār*, v. 101, p. 91, ḥ. 9

die [while they are still children] I enter them into My Paradise through My mercy.'[851]

Rulings:

Because children are an adornment for this life, we must enjoy them as much as we can, and not let this be tempered by any negative feelings, such as those that motivated the idol-worshippers to kill their children out of fear of poverty, or that caused their faces to darken if they were given news of a female child. Every child – whether a boy or a girl – is an adornment for this life; we should not hold back our affection towards them unless they become a tribulation for us – and in Allah we seek refuge! It is for this reason that:

1. We must be wary of family breakdowns and always remember the role of the family in raising an intelligent and caring child.
2. Parents must care for their children, as this is a guarantee for their own future comfort.
3. A father must provide food, drink, clothes, shelter, medicine, and any other means of preservation to his children, and nurture their physical development.
4. Parents must do their utmost to educate their children in the aspects of religion that will benefit them, and in those things that will prepare them for their worldly life.
5. The main focus of educating our children must be on matters of belief, morality, laws, and social etiquettes.

4: Children are a trial

Because desires have been made to appear decorous to people, and because the intellect is shrouded by following desires, and obscured by their gloom, children are a test – one of them could even be an unexpected adversary.

The trial posed by children has three branches: the lightest of these is going in search of sustenance from unlawful sources for their sake; the second is following a corrupt way of life out of love for them; the most serious, however, is arrogance towards the truth because one feels conceited because of them.

Loving one's children is a good and natural thing, but sometimes it could lead to forbidden things if someone wants to provide for them through illicit gains, not realizing that to feed your children with forbidden earnings is a

[851] *Biḥār al-anwār*, v. 101, p. 105, ḥ. 103

grave violation of their rights, in that their flesh and blood will grow from the unlawful, and that will lead them astray and corrupt them in future.

In being a member of his family, a believer must make his God-wariness the ultimate criterion. His love for his spouse or children should never take him away from obeying Allah. For this reason, he must disassociate from whomever his Lord disassociates, even if it is his own father or son.

In man's heart there is a buried pride and a hidden rebelliousness, connected sometimes to wealth and others to power; when man becomes wealthy, he becomes rebellious, as he does if given power. If we do not wish to become conceited or rebellious because of our children, we must closely observe ourselves and remember always that wealth and power do not endure, and if they endure that is only because we do not; on the Day of Judgement, wealth and sons will be of no use to us.

Chapter Two: Transaction Law – General Principles

First: General rules for earning (*makāsib*)

1: General rules for earning sustenance

The noble *sunna*:

❖ Allah's Messenger ﷺ says: 'Worship is seventy parts; the best of them is seeking the lawful [sustenance.]'

❖ Imam al-Ṣādiq ؏ says: 'There is no good in anyone who does not enjoy gathering wealth from a lawful source to meet his needs, support his religion, and maintain ties with his relatives.'

Rulings:

1. Economic activity and earning a living to be self-sufficient is strongly recommended in Islamic teachings, especially to be generous to one's family and undertake one's social responsibilities such as good deeds and spending in Allah's way.

2. A person should not give up economic activity under the cloak of asceticism in worldly matters, for balance in life between material and otherworldly concerns is encouraged by the religion of Islam.

3. Earning a living could become obligatory if one's own life or the life of those for whose provision he is religiously responsible – or if any other religious duties – depend upon this.

4. By the same token, economic activity could become religiously prohibited if it uses illicit means or has illicit goals.

5. Everyone who undertakes economic activity – whether trade, craft, or a profession of any sort – should focus his efforts on seeking sustenance by licit and permitted means.

6. It is recommended to seek sustenance and earn a living nobly. This is accomplished by concerning oneself with seeking the lawful and not the unlawful, avoiding harming oneself by exposure to difficulties and hardships standing in the way of sustenance, and not forgoing anything else that Allah desires from the human being – whether obligatory or recommended actions – in favour of seeking this world.

7. Narrations emphasize the precept of being lenient and easy-going in economic activities, especially when dealing with others. In a general sense, no one should prioritize earning a living over their moral development.

8. It is disliked to use any means which might expose the human being, in the course of his business interactions, to the risk of falling into

dishonesty, fraud, or any other thing forbidden when buying, selling, or engaging in any other kind of transaction.

9. It is disliked to pursue crooked economic practices that will cause harm to others indirectly, such as interfering with transactions of buying or selling that about to be completed between other parties, or trying to take over the transaction for oneself.

2: The lawful and unlawful in economic activities

The glorious Qur'ān:

❖ Allah says: **'Woe to the defrauders who use short measures; who, when they measure [a commodity bought] from the people, take the full measure, but diminish when they measure or weigh for them.'**[852]

Rulings:

1. The basis for all economic transactions is the absolute freedom of the human being therein, so long as both parties consent to it and it falls within the framework of religious law.
2. One of the most important goals of licit business is to ensure that everyone receives their due by maintaining fairness, which is one of the manifestations of justice our Lord has enjoined upon us. This is as opposed to wrongdoing, which our Lord has condemned in the strongest possible terms.
3. All business and financial transactions must be done on the basis of mutual agreement; the very foundation of consuming lawful money is that its owner is pleased to give it to you.
4. Embezzling people's money is forbidden, unless there is some legitimate excuse for this, and it makes no difference whether this money belongs to Muslims or non-Muslims.
5. It is obligatory for the individual to avoid any business dealings or financial transactions which fall within the remit of wrongdoing and sinfulness. For example:
    a. Someone using his centre to obtain money illegitimately.
    b. Short measuring, which means shortening the measure or lightening the weight, or dishonesty when selling or during any other deal.
    c. Wrongly consuming the property of orphans.
    d. Wronging one's wife financially.

---

[852] Sūrat al-Muṭaffifīn (83):1-3

e. Deceitfulness in transactions.

Trade on the basis of mutual consent

The glorious Qur'ān:

- Allah says: **'O you who have faith! Do not eat up your wealth among yourselves unrightfully, but it should be trade by mutual consent. And do not kill yourselves. Indeed Allah is most merciful to you.'**[853]

Rulings:

This verse affirms that all financial transactions rest on the principle of mutual consent by both parties, which itself rests on three realities:

1. The agreement of will and resolution: one of the pillars of mutual consent is the existence of a firm resolve in both parties to adhere to the stipulations of the contract they are agreeing upon. If one side's will is lacking for some reason or another, then there is no mutual consent or contract. For example, if a marriage is contracted with a woman who does not desire this contract, and has therefore not resolved to adhere to its stipulations, then this contract is problematic so long as both sides do not share the same resolve.
2. The agreement of each party's respective will is another pillar of mutual consent. If their respective wills are not in agreement, then the contract loses its very essence. For example, if the buyer is purchasing a shop, while the seller is selling a residential property, then the contract is ineffective because their wills are not in agreement.
3. The motivation of each party, or their intention (*niyya*), is one of the hidden aspects of their two wills. It is insufficient for their two wills to be in agreement for the contract to be effective; these two wills must also be sound. This means that if both parties agree, or even one of them agrees, based on a corrupt intention – such that they would not have agreed to the contract in its absence, meaning that their will was corrupted from its foundation – then the contract itself is corrupted and rendered void. So if someone hires a van to carry wine, for example, then the very contract of rental is invalidated because his intention was improper.

---

[853] Sūrat al-Nisā' (4):29

Second: General rules for contracts

Introduction

The glorious Qur'ān:

❖ Allah says: **'O you who have faith! Keep your agreements. You are permitted animals of grazing livestock, except what is [now] announced to you, disallowing game while you are in pilgrim sanctity. Indeed Allah decrees whatever He desires.'**[854]

Rulings:

1. The basis of all contracts is the obligation to fulfil them according to what both parties agreed upon. It is impermissible to default on them because Allah has commanded us to fulfil them, just as he has commanded us to fulfil all pledges.
2. There is no difference between contracts that were common in the time of Allah's Messenger ﷺ and the Imams ﷺ, and those which have come into being since then (such as contracts for insurance, imports, exports, and international economic and business agreements), or will come into being in the future.
3. There are boundaries and general rules laid down by the religion for contracts in a general sense, the most important of which we shall highlight below:

1: Conditions for the formula used in contracts

The noble *sunna*:

❖ Imam al-Ṣādiq ﷺ has said: 'Only words permit and only words prohibit.'

Rulings:

1. Contracts and transactions, in form, are composed of an offer (*ījāb*) and acceptance (*qabūl*) which express the mutual consent between two parties.
   For offer and acceptance, anything that signifies the contract – whether words, deeds, writing or a signal – is sufficient, verbal or non-verbal. So it is valid to conclude a contract of sale, rental, marriage[855], guarantee,

---

[854] Sūrat al-Mā'ida (5):1

[855] The rules pertaining to offer and acceptance in marriage and divorce are distinguished from other contracts and declarations by a higher standard of solemnity

exchange, security, or any other kind of contract, or legal declarations, such as divorce, bequests, etc., via telephone, fax, internet or e-mail, or by any medium of communication that both parties agree to rely upon.

2. The offer of a contract should precede its acceptance, but that is not obligatory so long as the contract (whether verbal or written) yields the desired meaning. For example: if the buyer signs the contract of purchase for a house before the vendor, the contract is still valid.
3. The acceptance must be linked to the offer in such a way that the two would customarily be treated as a single contract. If there is a lengthy gap between the two such that common sense sees it as breaking the state of forming a contract, then the contract is ineffective.
4. Accord between offer and acceptance is a fundamental condition for the validity of a contract. If the offer from one party is for a certain commodity or comes with a particular condition, while the acceptance from the other party is given for a different commodity or for another condition, then the contract is incomplete.
5. It is possible to conclude a contract absent verbal acceptance if there is something else which functions in its place, such as silence, or a particular action, or some other indication. The criterion for all of this is the existence of some non-verbal indication that the other party intends to adhere to the contract and mutual consent from both parties.

2: The limits of a contract

The glorious Qur'ān:

❖ Allah says: **'Those who exact usury will not stand but like one deranged by the Devil's touch. That is because they say, "Trade is just like usury." While Allah has allowed trade and forbidden usury. Whoever, on receiving advice from his Lord, relinquishes [usury], shall keep [the gains of] what is past, and his matter shall rest with Allah. As for those who resume, they shall be the inmates of the Fire and they shall remain in it [forever].'**[856]

The noble *sunna*:

❖ The Messenger of Allah ﷺ said: 'Evil earnings are those earned by usury.'[857]

---

because of the weighty consequences that result from them. An interested reader should refer to the special rulings for this in the appropriate place.

[856] Sūrat al-Baqara (2):275

[857] *Wasā'il al-shī'a*, v. 12, p. 426, ḥ. 13

❖ Imam al-Bāqir ⸛ said: 'The most wicked of earnings are those earned by usury.'[858]

❖ If usury were lawful then people would abandon commerce and that of which they are needful. So Allah made usury unlawful so that the people might incline from the unlawful towards the lawful, and to [lawful] commerce of buying and selling.'[859]

❖ The Messenger of Allah ⸛ said: 'He is not from us who cheats, harms, or tricks a Muslim.'[860]

Rulings:

Usury is one of the most egregious examples of something that contravenes the boundaries intended by the Divine Lawgiver for contracts, namely the boundary of fairness and the prohibition of consuming the wealth of others illegitimately.

It is one of the most strongly emphasized prohibitions. The Qur'ān has explicitly forbidden it numerous times and the number of traditions forbidding it achieves the level of *tawātur* (certainty achieved by multiple successive chains of transmitters). Taking usury is a major sin.

Taking usury is unlawful, as is paying it, bearing witness to a contract that includes it, or writing such a contract. Yes, there could be exceptional circumstances (emergency or compulsion) where necessity makes it permissible, but this does not change the ruling of prohibition to one of overall permissibility. Therefore, it is necessary to limit ourselves to only those situations where it is absolutely necessary. And there will be a detailed discussion of usury in the chapters on purchase and loans.

3: Eligibility of the contracting parties

The glorious Qur'ān:

❖ Allah says: '**Do not give the feeble-minded your property which Allah has assigned you to manage: provide for them out of it, and clothe them, and speak to them honourable words.**'[861]

---

[858] *Wasā'il al-shī'a*, v. 12, p. 423, ḥ. 2

[859] *Wasā'il al-shī'a*, v. 12, p. 424, ḥ. 8

[860] *Biḥār al-anwār*, v. 100, p. 146, ḥ. 51

[861] Sūrat al-Nisā' (4):5

Rulings:

There are conditions which both parties to a contract or transaction must possess without exception, namely:

1: Legal maturity

This applies as a condition to all contracts. However, even though a child is not free to dispose of his property as he wishes, there is no evidence that his dealings are automatically valueless and ineffective. So long as they are done with the permission of his legal guardian and under the former's supervision, they are effective (binding). Therefore, we see that it is the practice of Muslims to send their children to buy and sell things under the supervision of their legal guardians and with the latter's permission.

2: Sound mind

There is no value to a contract effected by someone who is either insane, intoxicated to the point where he lacks discernment, sleeping, inattentive, joking, or anyone else who does not seriously intend to conclude the contract, even if both parties consent to the contract after his impediment is lifted.

3: Freedom of choice

By freedom of choice we mean that neither party should be coerced into the contract, insofar as one under coercion has no freedom to choose. As such, he is unqualified to conclude a contract, and there is no value to any contract he concludes [in such a condition], unless he consents to it later [when coercion is no longer a factor].

A state of coercion is whenever the individual's freedom to choose as he desires is removed, for example: if his life, property, or family are threatened in an unbearable manner. In other words, minor disturbance and simple annoyance do not constitute coercion.

4: The right to dispose of property

One of the most obvious conditions for contracts is that the parties are both owners of the property in question and have the right to dispose of it per the contract they are signing (e.g., the commodity and price in sale and rental). Any contract is a kind of disposal (use), and as such it is only effective if the parties to the contract are qualified to dispose of it, such as the owner himself, his agent, or his legal guardian.

4: The object of a contract (or, the conditions of compensation)

The glorious Qur'ān:

- Allah says: **'O you who have faith! Indeed wine, gambling, idols and the divining arrows are abominations of Satan's doing, so avoid them, so that you may be felicitous.'**[862]

Rulings:

The object of a contract (meaning the things to which the contract applies, such as the price and the commodity) is subject to particular conditions, namely:

1: That it can be legally owned

If something cannot be legally owned then it cannot be part of a contract, whether as payment or commodity, and to do so is treated as consuming wealth illegitimately. For example, making contracts for sources of ritual impurity (*aʿyān al-najāsa*) which have no licit uses with which rational persons would concern themselves, or making contracts for tools of gambling, books of misguidance, and the like.

2: Lawfulness

A contract cannot apply to something forbidden, such as usurped or stolen property, or property obtained via legal recourse to illegitimate courts of law. Likewise, it is impermissible to contract for intoxicants, drugs, idols, counterfeiting, etc., because these are instances of unlawful wealth. The same applies to anything a person obtains through legal recourse to oppressors.

3: Disposal

There should not be any impediments to a contracting party freely disposing of his wealth, such that would make him unable to deliver it to the other (whether payment or commodity). So one cannot conduct transactions with an endowment (*waqf*) or deposit (*rahn*) because his authority to dispose of them is not absolute; it is limited by the framework of religious law.

4: Ownership

It is not valid to make a contract for an object that one does not own, such as a bird in the sky, a fish in the sea, a mineral in the depths of the earth or the bottom of the ocean, or water in the clouds, before any of these have been

---

[862] Sūrat al-Māʾida (5):90

obtained and taken possession of. These four conditions encompass all forms of contracts and transactions without exception.

Third: Forbidden sources of income

1: General rules

The noble *sunna*:

❖ Allah's Messenger has said: 'The things I fear most for this *umma* (community) of mine are illicit gains, hidden lusts, and usury.'

Rulings:

1. In principle, the religion deems permissible every action in which a person can engage, and every activity through which he can strive to earn a living, apart from those exceptions that the religion makes in transactions and forbidden sources of income.
2. As a general rule, Islam has forbidden any kind of contract for something inherently unlawful and forbidden, because when Allah forbids a thing or its consumption, it is unlawful to assign it a monetary value.
   In this way, Allah has forbidden contracting for any deed whose prohibition has been established in Islamic Law, such as the forbidden forms of astrology, magic and soothsaying, or convening and attending gatherings of immoral amusements, music, and entertainment, or frequenting bars, nightclubs, brothels, casinos, or cinemas where pornographic films are shown, or producing and displaying forbidden erotic books and magazines, or companies for the production, sale, and rental of forbidden audio and video materials, or producing forbidden films, etc.
3. When we say that it is forbidden to contract for such things, we do not mean only for buying and selling, rather this includes any way in any kind of contracting (whether sale, purchase, rental, exchange, settlement, loan, dowry, deposit, investment, etc.).

2: Contracts involving sources of ritual impurity

The glorious Qur'ān:

❖ Allah says: **'You are prohibited carrion, blood, the flesh of swine, and what has been offered to other than Allah, and the animal strangled or beaten to death, and that which dies by falling or is gored to death, and that which is mangled by a beast of prey - barring that which you**

may purify - and what is sacrificed on stone altars [to idols], and that you should divide by raffling with arrows...'[863]

Rulings:

It is forbidden to conduct transactions involving ritually impure substances, and any transaction conducted is invalidated. Some rules pertaining to this are as follows:

1: Intoxicants

It is impermissibe to work in the field of intoxicants in any way, shape, or form, and the same applies to illicit drugs: one may not produce, transport, sell, purchase, store, or advertise them. Anything [even peripherally] connected to the activities of producing, trading, and otherwise servicing them is forbidden.

2: Carrion

It is impermissible to trade carrion of animals whose blood spirts, and those parts of them in which life is said to have inhered.[864]

3: Dogs

It is impermissible to form contracts concerning dogs without use (i.e., dogs not used for things like protection or hunting) whether living or dead. As for dogs who have a permissible and reasonable purpose, such as hunting dogs, guide dogs, or guard dogs, or trained police dogs, then the strongest opinion is that it is valid to form contracts concerning them and it is permissible to acquire them.

4: Pigs

It is impermissible to conduct transactions involving pigs, whether living or dead, or for their flesh, hide, or any other part of them.

5: Other sources of ritual impurity

It is impermissible to conduct transactions for other sources of ritual impurity unless they have a permitted use, in which case it is permissible to conduct transactions for them, such as the sale of urine for tanning, or blood for transfusions or use in scientific laboratories for a legitimate purpose.

---

[863] Sūrat al-Māʾida (5):3

[864] This is generally said to refer to limbs and parts of the body with blood vessels. Thus, hair and the like are excluded.

3: Fraud and deception

The noble *sunna*:

❖ It has been narrated from Allah's Messenger in a tradition detailing forbidden things: 'Whoever defrauds a Muslim in buying or selling is not from us, and he will be raised on the Day of Resurrection with the Jews, for they are the ones who defraud the Muslims most!'

Rulings:

It is forbidden to commit fraud (cheating) in transactions and contracts, and one example of fraud is deception (*tadlīs*), which means to conceal the faults of a commodity and presenting an unrealistic picture of it.

4: Gambling and wagers

The glorious Qur'ān:

❖ Allah says: **'O you who have faith! Indeed wine, gambling, idols and the divining arrows are abominations of Satan's doing, so avoid them, so that you may be felicitous.'**[865]

Rulings:

Games are divided into the following categories:

1. Games using tools of gambling with bets, which are forbidden.
2. Games using tools of gambling[866] but without betting; it is obligatory precaution to avoid these, especially in the cases of backgammon and chess, about which we have many traditions.
3. Games not using tools of gambling but involving bets are also forbidden.
4. Games devoid of tools of gambling, and not involving bets and returns, are fine so long as there is no other reason for them to be prohibited.
5. An exception to the prohibition on betting is placing bets on horse racing and archery; these are permissible (and they shall be explained in their proper place, God-willing).

---

[865] Sūrat al-Mā'ida (5):90

[866] This typically includes games that use cards or dice.

5: Singing and music[867]

The glorious Qur'ān:

❖ Allah says: **'Among the people is he who buys diversionary talk that he may lead [people] astray from Allah's way without any knowledge, and he takes it in derision. For such there is a humiliating punishment.'**[868]

Rulings:

1. Singing and things connected to music, and using any kind of forbidden instruments of entertainment, is prohibited, even if the singing is done with words from the Qur'ān, supplications, or poetry about things that would be lawful in and of itself.
2. It is forbidden to earn a living by singing in any way, shape, or form, whether being paid to perform, or crafting and selling its instruments, or renting them out, and any other contract that involves music and singing.
3. Also forbidden are audio and video cassettes, CDs, etc., which contain singing. It is forbidden to share, produce, buy, sell, or rent them, or form any sort of contract concerning them.

6: Earning from other forbidden sources

The noble *sunna*:

❖ Allah's Messenger ﷺ has said: 'If Allah has forbidden a thing, He has forbidden profiting from it.'[869]

❖ And in the Prophet's ﷺ advice to ʿAlī ؑ, he said: 'O ʿAli! Illicit is profit from carrion, dogs, pigs, the dowry of a fornicatress, the bribe of a judge, and the payment of a soothsayer!'[870]

Rulings:

In a general sense, it is forbidden to conclude contracts of any kind for any sort of prohibited thing. Whatever thing Allah has prohibited, He has also prohibited profiting from it and conducting transactions with it. Here we will point out a few examples of this:

---

[867] The definition of these terms depends on common sense; so the average person can interpret what constitutes music and singing.

[868] Sūrat Luqmān (31):6

[869] Ibid. p55, tradition no. 29

[870] Wasāʾil al-shīʿa 12/63, abwāb mā yuktasab bih, ch5, tradition no. 9

1. It is forbidden to conclude contracts for tools, devices, and instruments used for forbidden things if they do not [also] have a permitted use, such as items for illicit music and the instruments of gambling.
2. It is forbidden to earn a living by what would be customarily understood as helping others to commit forbidden acts.
3. It is impermissible to deal in fraudulent bank notes.
4. It is impermissible to earn a living from or trade things which have no reasonable permissible benefit.
5. It is forbidden to deal in books of falsehood and misguidance, or any other cultural or intellectual materials that lead people astray, be they newspapers, magazines, digital files, films, CDs, etc.[871]
6. It is forbidden to produce statues of living creatures, such as humans and animals, and it is forbidden to conclude any kind of contract involving them. It makes no difference whether these are made from wood, metal, stone, clay, or anything else, if the statues are complete and include all the visible limbs of the body. As for crafting some parts of an animal or a human being, such as busts, there is no problem with this.
7. It is forbidden to practice magic, teach it, learn it, or earn a living by it.
8. It is forbidden to give or receive a bribe, and this is [here defined as] something paid in legal courts in order to attain something which is not your right, or prevent someone else from obtaining theirs.

Fourth: Addenda

1: Hoarding

The noble *sunna*:

❖ The Commander of the Faithful ﷺ wrote in his letter to Mālik al-Ashtar: 'Prevent hoarding, for Allah's Messenger ﷺ prevented it. Selling should be easy and done with fair scales, and a price such that neither the vendor nor the buyer are wronged. So whoever is tempted to hoard after your prohibition, then penalize and punish him without being excessive.'

---

[871] It is generally permitted to purchase books of misguidance if it is for the sole purpose of refuting them, by one who is qualified to do so.

Rulings:

1. It is forbidden to hoard staple crops, and narrations have specified these as wheat, barley, dates, raisins, and oil.
2. Forbidden hoarding, according to the narrations, consists of hoarding the aforementioned commodities for forty days in times of fertility and under normal conditions, and for three days under exceptional conditions such as times of high prices, scarcity of a particular commodity, or drought. This definition is based on the most common situations, so a shorter or longer time could be classified as hoarding according to differing circumstances, and according to what the jurist in authority determines.
3. The religious authority (*al-ḥākim al-sharʿī*) can compel a hoarder to sell his hoarded commodities, without setting a price for it, unless he attempts to sell it at an inflated price, in which case he can be forced to lower the price but without inflicting a loss upon him.

2. Withdrawals, or the right of annulment

What is a right of withdrawal?

The right of withdrawal (*khiyār*) means the right to annul a contract afforded to one or both parties, or to a third party. There are many situations in which this right is given, of which we shall mention the most important:

First: Withdrawal from the meeting (which is particular to sale): so long as the two parties have not departed the meeting in which the buying and selling has taken place, each of them has the right to annul the transaction. If they separate, this right is forgone and the sale must take place.

Second: Withdrawal of the animal (again, particular to sale), meaning that whoever purchases a living animal has the right to withdraw from the sale within three days of the contract.

Third: The withdrawal condition, whereby both parties agree that one or both of them have the right to void the contract within a pre-agreed time. Within this time, the party granted this right may void the transaction, even without any reason.

Fourth: Withdrawal as a result of being wronged, and here being wronged means being deceived or tricked. So whoever has been deceived into transferring his wealth [to someone else], and the amount he was cheated would typically considered intolerable, then he has the option of cancelling the transaction.

Five: Withdrawal as a result of delay: if someone purchases a commodity without paying the price or taking possession of the goods, the vendor must wait three days from when the contract was made. Then, if the buyer pays the price, he is most entitled to the goods; otherwise the vendor has the right to void the transaction. It appears that this right applies to all contracts save that of marriage.

Sixth: Withdrawal as a result of viewing: when two parties agree on a contract for goods described to but not seen by the buyer, and when these goods are delivered the buyer sees that they are not as described; or, when two parties agree on a contract for goods seen by the buyer, but once these goods are delivered these goods are not as the buyer saw them – in both cases, the buyer has the right to void the contract.

This right applies not only to contracts of sale, but also rental and compensation.

Seventh: Withdrawal due to swindling. This right applies if either party falsely represents any object of the contract to deceive the other party thereby, which is called swindling. In this situation, the deceived party has the right to void the transaction as soon as he discovers the deception.

Eighth: Withdrawal due to failure to deliver: if either party is unable to live up to their side of the agreement, the other party has the right to dissolve the contract.

Ninth: Withdrawal due to faults. This right belongs to anyone who finds a fault in the object of a contract, whereby the possessor of this right may choose between voiding the transaction and fulfilling it while receiving the difference in price for the faulty goods.

Chapter Three: Rules for Contracts and Agreements

Rules for sale

1. Like all contracts, sale requires an offer from the vendor and an acceptance from the buyer.
2. Sale by exchange is valid, meaning that each party – both the vendor and the buyer – give what they have to the other with the intention of buying and selling, without pronouncing a specific verbal formula to conclude the contract. This is because mutual agreement is the essence of a contract, and this can be expressed by words and deeds (that is, exchange).
3. We have already discussed the conditions for both parties in a contract, namely: legal maturity, soundness of mind, intention, free choice, and the right of disposal.
4. We also mentioned the conditions for the items being exchanged, namely: that they have value, are permissible to own, are actually owned by the parties, and that the parties have free reign to dispose of them. To this we add two further conditions to the commodity and its price:
    a. That the quantity of both the commodity and its price are known by a customary measure, such as weight, scale, number, length, time (such as the age of an animal or plants), or the like thereof (such as watts for electricity, or bytes in the case of some items of computer equipment).
    b. That they are known to both parties in kind and description in those areas whereby prices, demand, or usage would vary with any differences in these. This can be achieved either by inspection or description.

Kinds of sale

5. Two parties can agree on a contract of sale on the principle of the commodity being exchanged for immediate payment (cash purchase), or they could agree to the commodity being delivered immediately and the payment deferred (credit purchase), or they could agree it on the opposite, namely that payment is given at once and the commodity is delivered later (advance purchase). Each of these three kinds of sale has rules which we have mentioned at length in the second part of our more detailed legal manual of transactions, *Aḥkām al-Muʿāmilāt*.

Resale with the specification of gain

6. With regards to price and profit, sale is divided into four kinds:
    a. **First:** A specifically defined commodity could be sold for a specifically defined price by mutual agreement between the

parties, without any reference to the original price of the commodity, or the amount or percentage of profit that the vendor is making, or any loss he is incurring in the transaction. This kind of sale is called 'bargaining' (*musāwama*).

b. **Second:** A commodity could be sold at the price at which it was purchased, or with a set mark-up. For example, if someone buys a commodity for ten dinars, then informs the buyer that its original price is ten dinars, but he is seeking to make two dinars of profit (or twenty percent) with this sale. And this kind of sale is called 'sale with specification of gain' (*murābaḥa*).

c. **Third:** A commodity could be sold at less than its purchase value, informing the buyer of its price and of the loss incurred. And this kind of sale is called 'sale with specification of loss' (*muwāḍaʿa*).

d. **Fourth:** A commodity could be sold at the same price as it was purchased, without profit of loss, and this is called 'resale at cost' (*tawliya*).

Money changing

9. Money changing is of two kinds; (i) selling currency, and (ii) selling gold and silver.

First: Selling currency

The apparent ruling is that the criterion used by jurists for selling gold and silver currency is considering these to be a commonly-used currency and medium of exchange, rather than purely gold or silver.

Hence the validity of such a transaction depends on the immediate exchange of monies when selling gold or silver currency, and it is a matter of obligatory precaution that all currency transactions involve an immediate exchange of monies, even when these do not use gold and silver currency. So if someone sells a thousand Kuwaiti dinars for ten thousand Saudi riyals, then the transaction is only valid if these are exchanged in the same sitting.

As for the sale of currencies with a deferred exchange – even if only an hour later – such transactions are invalid.

Second: Selling gold and silver

a. When selling gold for gold or silver for silver, whether fashioned or unfashioned, such transactions are only valid so long as there is no difference in weight. So ten grams of gold cannot be sold for eleven grams, or for ten grams plus a fee. The same applies to selling silver for silver, insofar as any addition here is usurious.

However, for gold and silver which have not been made into currency, there is no need to exchange them immediately.

b. It is impermissible to sell fashioned gold or silver like for like with an increase, with the increase representing the fee for fashioning jewellery from them. But this is permissible via two separate transactions, such that the goldsmith sells a gold necklace for a mutually agreed-upon price (including the cost of his labour) and the payment is made in common currency. Then, afterwards, he purchases gold offered by the buyer for a separate mutually agreed-upon price, which he must also pay with common currency.

Selling agricultural produce

10. One form of prohibited transaction is speculative purchases (namely those which contain risk). This rule plays an important role in the issue of selling agricultural produce, such as fruits and crops, insofar as selling these before they have ripened and become ready for harvest is usually speculative and will cause strife between the two parties, and insofar as the produce will – in the intervening period – be exposed to potential harms and losses. And this is something that will cause a dispute between the vendor and buyer. But if this speculative element is removed by any means possible then it is permissible to sell.

Equivalent interest

11. Usury – in addition to its appearance in loans, which is most important form – can also appear in other transactions of purchase and sale under certain conditions. This is called transaction interest or equivalent interest.
12. Equivalent interest means selling a commodity in exchange for the like thereof with an addition (e.g., selling a thousand litres of milk in exchange for one thousand one hundred litres of milk). Because both commodities are of a single type, a thousand units of one is worth a thousand units of the other, and the hundred units that remain have no equivalent. This is a form of illegitimately consuming wealth, which is explicitly prohibited in the Qur'ān and *sunna*.
13. Equivalent interest only occurs if the following two conditions are met in the transaction:
    a. First: That the two commodities are of a single kind, such as selling wheat for wheat or rice for rice.

b. Second: That the two commodities are quantifiable by measure or weight.

14. By 'being of a single kind' (*waḥdat al-jins*) means having a single source, so wheat and its [derivative] flour are both treated as a single source, as are dates and their syrup, milk and its butter and any other dairy product made from it, grapes and vinegar, apples and juice, and so on.
15. Distinctions between commodities of a single kind with regards to their attributes or quality do not exempt them from this rule.
16. The criterion which determines a commodity to be quantifiable is the customary practice of the land and its people; if different lands have different customs, then each land has its own ruling.

Preemption (*shuf'a*)

The noble *sunna*:

❖ Imam al-Ṣādiq ﵇ was asked about who has the right of preemption. What things does it apply to? For whom is it vaid? Is there preemption in [contracts concerning] animals? How does it work? So he said: 'The right of preemption is permissible in everything from animals, earth, or commodities. So if only two people are partners in something, and one of them wants to sell his share, his partner has a greater right to it than others; and if there are more than two [partners] then there is no right of preemption for any of them.'[872]

❖ Imam al-Ṣādiq ﵇ said: 'Concerning the right of preemption among partners in the joint ownership of two lands and residences, the Messenger of Allah ﷺ decreed, "No harm and no injury [in Islam] (*lā ḍarar wa lā ḍirār*)..."'[873]

❖ Imam al-Ṣādiq ﵇ has reported from the Messenger of Allah ﷺ: 'There is no right of preemption in boats, rivers, and roadways.'[874]

❖ Imam al-Ṣādiq ﵇ said: 'There is no right of preemption except between two partners who have not [yet] divided [shares].'[875]

---

[872] *Wasā'il al-shī'a*, v. 17, p. 321, ḥ. 2
[873] *Wasā'il al-shī'a*, v. 17, p. 319, ḥ. 1
[874] *Wasā'il al-shī'a*, v. 17, p. 322, ḥ. 1
[875] *Wasā'il al-shī'a*, v. 17, p. 316, ḥ. 1

Rulings:

1. The right of preemption (*shufʿa*) means that one partner is entitled to obtain the share of the other should the latter wish to sell it to a third party under certain conditions.
   For example: Two persons jointly own an orchard; if one of them sells his share to a third-party, his partner has the right to obtain it by preemption – namely, he can obtain that share his partner sold from the buyer without the latter's consent.'
2. The right of preemption requires:
   a. That the joint ownership is between only two persons.
   b. That the shared property is real estate that can be divided – according to the majority opinion of the jurists – such as a land, an orchard, a home, a shop, or any other building which can be divided.
   c. That the share is being transferred to the third party by means of sale.
3. The partner is entitled to demand preemption under the following conditions:
   a. That he is a Muslim, if the preempted buyer is also a Muslim.
   b. That he is aware of the details of the price, according to obligatory precaution.
   c. That he is able to pay the price.
4. Preemption must be immediate; when one partner learns of the sale of the other's share, he must preempt the sale immediately. If he delays in doing so without any valid religious or customary reason, then he has forgone his right to pre-empt, and preemption becomes invalid forthwith.

Investment (*muḍāraba*)

The noble *sunna*:

❖ Imam al-Ṣādiq ﷺ was asked: I sell some goods for you, and the return is [divided] between you and me. [Would that be permissible?] So the Imam said: 'No problem.'[876]

❖ Al-Ḥalabī has narrated that he asked Imam al-Ṣādiq ﷺ about a man who is given wealth, and told: Go to such-and-such land—do not travel any farther—and buy [goods] from there. So the Imam said: 'So if he traversed beyond [that place] and the wealth was spoiled, then he is liable; and if he buys some commodities and he loses them, then he is

---

[876] *Wasāʾil al-shīʿa*, v. 13, p. 185, ḥ. 1

liable. But if he made a profit then it is shared between the two of them.'[877]

Rulings:

1. Investment (*muḍāraba*) means a combination of wealth and work to produce goods and profit; it is a form of financial partnership between two parties to gain wealth. It works by one party providing capital (the investor) to the other (the agent), for the latter to work with it, and the profits are shared between them. So it is an agreement between one party who has capital and other party who is able to invest that capital in some permissible economic activity.
2. A contract of investment – like all contracts – must consist of an offer and acceptance, and any word or deed to that effect suffices; so the act of handing over wealth suffices.
3. Both parties in this contract must meet the usual qualifications for a contract, namely legal maturity, soundness of mind, freedom of choice, lack of foolishness [with financial matters], and the right of disposal. For the agent, in addition to the aforementioned qualifications, he must also be able to carry out the economic activity specified in the contract of partnership.
4. For the partnership to be valid, the capital must meet the following conditions:
    a. It must be immediately available property, not a loan.
    b. It must be known in quantity and quality.
    c. It must be specified by the parties involved.
    d. The quantity of the capital must not be greater than the agent's capacity to use it in economic activity, such that he is unable to fulfil his responsibilities with regard to it.
5. Regarding any profits that result from this partnership, the following conditions apply:
    a. They must be divided in a universal manner, whether by fractions (such one-third and two-thirds) or percentages (such as sixty-forty).
    b. The division of profits must be agreed upon by both parties in the contract, whether by fractions or percentages.
    c. The profits must only be divided between the silent partner and the agent. As for stipulating that a share of the profits must be paid to a third-party, it is precaution to avoid this.

---

[877] *Wasāʾil al-shīʿa*, v. 13, p. 181, ḥ. 2

6. The apparent ruling is that there is no need to stipulate that the profits in silent partnership derive from trade alone; it is permissible to obtain profits in any permitted economic activity, whether trade, manufacture, agriculture, livestock, fishing, and the like.
7. Unless otherwise specified, investment is a contract that can be voided at any time by either party.
8. A contract of investment is automatically invalidated by the death of either party, but it can be continued in the form of a new contract between the deceased's heir and the other party.

Rules of partnership (*sharika*)

The noble *sunna*:

- Dāwud al-Abzārī said: I asked Imam al-Ṣādiq ﷷ about a man who wishes to buy some commodity, but he does not have the available funds. So a companion comes to him and says: Take funds from me, and we will divide the profits between us. So the Imam said: 'If there are profits then they are [shared] between them, and if there is a loss then it is upon both of them.'[878]
- It has been narrated from Imam al-Ṣādiq ﷷ: 'Verily the Messenger of Allah ﷺ permitted partnership in residences and lands.'[879]

Rulings:

1. A contract of partnership (*sharika*) is the association of two or more people in an economic or financial endeavour in which each of the partners provides a specific share of the capital (whether currency or commodities), and profits and losses are divided in a manner agreed upon in the contract.
2. The validity of a contract of partnership is conditioned upon the following:
    a. The mutual agreement of all parties, which is the most important condition of a contract of partnership.
    b. Offer and acceptance, whether by word or deed.
    c. The eligibility of all parties to participate in the partnership, namely by being endowed with the usual conditions for contracts (legal maturity, soundness of mind, freedom of choice, right of disposal, etc.).

---

[878] *Wasā'il al-shī'a*, v. 13, p. 174, ḥ. 3
[879] *Mustadrak al-wasā'il*, v. 13, p. 451, Ḥ. 15871

   d. That the capital of the partnership and its efforts are licit and religiously permissible.

3. A partnership is formalized – as we mentioned above – when two or more parties share in providing the capital for a company; there is no minimum or maximum amount for each partner, unless the contract of partnership itself specifies this.

Managing a partnership and working in one

4. If a contract of partnership is drawn up specifying the responsibilities of some or all of the partners, whether on an individual or collective basis, then it must be observed and it is impermissible to contravene it. The same applies with regards to the manner in which the partnership is to be run.

   But if this is not specified, then none of the partners, or anyone else, has the right to access or dispose of the capital without the permission of the rest of the partners.

5. The actions of the agents and management of a partnership are protected [from liability], hence if the company faces losses, or costs which are not due to any person's fault or contravening of some bounds, then there is no compensation due.

6. If the contract of partnership does not specify how profits and losses are to be shared, then they are shared equally when all the partner's shares in the company's capital are equal, or proportionally when these shares are different.

7. Unless otherwise specified, a contract of partnership can be revoked at any time (i.e., so long as nothing is mentioned in the text of the contract of partnership which specifies a particular duration or task to be completed). So any of the partners is free to withdraw from the partnership at any time he wishes, under two conditions:
   a. That this withdrawal does not harm the remaining partners.
   b. That this withdrawal is not an act of treachery or betrayal, as this is prevented by the principle of 'no harm and no injury' (*lā ḍarar wa lā ḍirār*).

   In cases where the partnership has a duration specified by the text of the contract, the apparent ruling is that common sense deems it necessary to remain in the partnership until that duration has elapsed; so no partner can withdraw before that, in order to adhere to the contract and the stipulation imposed therein.

8. A contract of partnership is automatically invalidated if one of the partners ceases to be qualified to participate in contracts, namely in one of the following situations:

a. One of the partners dies.
b. One of the partners becomes insane; though there is some hesitation as to whether temporary insanity invalidates the contract.
c. When one of the partners is prevented from disposing of his wealth because of insolvency or idiocy.

Rules for settlement (*ṣulḥ*)

The noble *sunna*:

❖ Allah's Messenger ﷺ has said: 'The proof is upon the plaintiff, the oath upon the defendant, and settlements (*ṣulḥ*) are permissible amongst Muslims, save for those which permit a forbidden thing, or forbid a permitted thing.'

Rulings:

1. A settlement (*ṣulḥ*) is a contract legislated for the purposes of resolving an ongoing dispute, or preventing a potential one. In other words, it is a contract whose purpose is to end conflict and prevent disagreement.
2. Even though a settlement yields benefits for many other kinds of contract, it is not subordinate to them but an independent contract in its own right; hence the rules of other contracts do not apply to it.
3. Settlements are one of the most useful kinds of contract for society because it is compatible with all other kinds of contract, and is the broadest of them in scope. Even though settlements were originally legislated in Islamic Law to resolve disputes and prevent conflict, it is not necessary for there to be any dispute, whether actual or potential, for a settlement contract to be valid. In fact, it is permissible to conclude such a contract under any circumstances.
4. The fundamental condition for the validity of a settlement is that it should not result in something prohibited becoming permissible, or vice versa. So one cannot get around the prohibition on interest by a settlement, whereby the creditor and the debtor agree on a settlement whereby the latter receives a thousand dinars now, in return for one thousand one hundred dinars a year later. Such a settlement is not valid because it involves the permission of something prohibited.
   As for a settlement which prohibits something permissible, an example would be a settlement between a husband and wife whereby he agrees never to have intercourse with another permanent plural wife, or whereby the unilateral power of divorce is placed in her hand.
5. It is permissible to conclude a settlement concerning part of a loan. For example, if one party has agreed to repay the other a thousand dinars

after a specified amount of time, but makes a settlement with him to pay eight hundred immediately, then this settlement is permitted insofar as this involves returning a portion of the loan and the writing-off of the remainder.

6. Like all contracts, a settlement consists of an offer and its acceptance, even if the settlement involves someone forgoing their right, or releasing another person from the responsibility of a loan; this depends on acceptance [of the other party] in order for this to constitute a settlement.
7. It is a condition that the object of an agreement must never be something whose acquisition is forbidden, such as sources of impurity (e.g., wine and pork), or illicit actions and gains (e.g., singing, gambling, etc.).
8. All of the usual conditions apply to both parties in a settlement: legal maturity, soundness of mind, absence of foolishness, freedom of choice, in addition to freedom from insolvency if the settlement is financial in nature.
9. A settlement is a binding contract on both parties; once its conditions are met, neither party has the right to abolish it except by rescinding it [mutually], or unless one of the rights to withdraw from a contract (see above) apply to it.

Rules for hire, lease, and rental (*ijāra*)

The noble *sunna*:

❖ Allah's Messenger ﷺ has said: 'Whoever denies a laborer his wage, Allah will cause his works to fail and deny him the scent of Paradise, and verily its scent can be smelled from five hundred years distance...!'

Rulings:

1. Hire or leasing (*ijāra*) is a contract for a service or work in return for a wage.
2. The fundamental bases of leasing are:
   a. Mutual agreement (i.e., a contract)
   b. The contracting parties
   c. The object of the lease
   d. The wage or fee
   e. The duration
   f. The service
3. Mutual agreement is the essence of all contracts, including leasing. This is accomplished through offer and acceptance. There is no need for this to be pronounced in a specific formula, rather it suffices to express this

in any formula which indicates leasing, and the physical act of exchange suffices as a signifier of this as in all other contracts.

4. Both parties must be endowed with all the necessary legal qualifications to conclude a contract: legal maturity, soundness of mind, freedom of choice, and freedom from impediments [to fulfilling the contract].
5. As for the object of the lease, the following conditions apply:
    a. It must be possible to own.
    b. It must be permissible.
    c. It must be free from restrictions on how it is to be disposed.
    d. It must be actually owned by one of the parties.
    e. It must be clearly known and identifiable to both parties so that there is no ignorance or risk involved in its being leased.
    f. It must be a specific thing; not one of several.
    g. It must not be something that will be completely consumed by usage, such as foodstuffs, whose usage means their total consumption.
    h. The object of the lease must be usable in the manner intended in the contract of hire.
6. With regards to duration – when this is one of the fundamental components of leasing, such as real-estate rental – it must be set down in a precise and known manner, such as for certain days, weeks, months, or years.
7. The wage is the compensation (or price) offered in return for the benefits the renter will accrue from his use of the object of the lease. To the wage apply all the general criteria, such as it being legal to own, permissible, free from restrictions, actually owned – as we have already mentioned – in addition to its being clearly known by description or inspection, or through the detailing of its necessary quantifiers such as weight, measure, number, etc.
8. The benefit accrued from the lease must be permissible, and far from risk or ignorance.
9. According to the contract of the lease, the lessor must adhere to the following:
    a. He must pay the wage of hire in the agreed time.
    b. He must use the object of the lease in an appropriate manner, or according to one specified by the lease contract.
    c. He must look after the object of the lease and not be neglectful towards it, or exceed the proper parameters for its use.
    d. He must return the object of the lease in good condition, and within the specified time, to the lessee or the lessee's agent.

10. The lessor is secure [from liability], meaning that he is not held responsible for loss or damage to the object of the lease so long as this was not caused by his own transgression (such as intentionally demolishing one side of a house) or negligence (such as lighting a fire in an inappropriate place inside a house, with the ultimate result that the building burns down).
11. A contract for lease is a contract binding on both parties; neither has the right to void it without the agreement of the other, or without stipulating a right of withdrawal for one or both of them in the contract itself.

Hiring persons

12. Just as it is possible to hire (or lease) real estate, objects, and means of transportation, it is also possible to hire people for work such that one person agrees to perform a particular task for another in return for a specific wage.
13. A labourer (*ajīr*) is someone who hires himself out for work in return for a wage, and he must be endowed with all the necessary qualifications for concluding a contract, such as legal maturity, soundness of mind, competency, and freedom of choice.
14. The labourer (or worker, employee, etc.) who agrees with an employer to perform an agreed-upon task for a specific period of the day (e.g., from nine o'clock in the morning until five o'clock in the evening) is not allowed to do anything during that time that would conflict with the right of the employer to the labourer's work without the employer's permission.
15. The labourer is protected against liability, meaning he is not held accountable for loss, damage, or defectiveness of things (such as tools, equipment, materials, etc.) placed at his disposal for him to work with, so long as this loss, damage, or defectiveness is not as a direct or indirect result of his own actions, such as transgression or negligence.

Rules for rewards (*juʿāla*)

The noble *sunna*:

❖ Imam al-Ṣādiq عليه السلام was asked: 'Suppose we appointed someone to purchase some land, a house, a manservant and a maid for us and set a reward (wage) for him?' The Imam عليه السلام replied: 'There is no problem with this.'

Rulings:

1. A reward (*juʿāla*) means to pay a fixed price to someone for some work. The one who pays is called a designator (*jāʿil*), the one who carries out the work is a worker (*ʿāmil*) and the payment is called a 'reward' (*juʿl*).
2. There are many practical examples of rewards, for example:
   a. A reward offered to anyone who returns something lost or stolen.
   b. A gift set aside for someone who undertakes a labour, or an artistic or literary commission.
   c. A prize set aside for the best students or employees.
   d. A reward for someone who carries out specific tasks above and beyond the call of duty.
   e. A reward offered by a military leader to those who carry out an important operation.
   f. Rewards offered for carrying out personal or private tasks.
3. In order for such a reward to become a contract, this requires some sort of commitment by the designator, whether verbal, written (such as a newspaper advertisement), or practical. There is no need for an acceptance from another party.
4. The designator must be endowed with all the necessary qualifications to conclude a contract, such as legal maturity, soundness of mind, competence, freedom of choice, and freedom from impediments (such as insolvency).
5. The worker must be able to undertake the specified task, without any other conditions. Even a child or legally insane person can carry out the task if they are capable.
6. As for the task for which the reward is offered, it must be:
   a. Permissible
   b. Reasonable
7. As for the compensation offered for this task, it must be clearly known, whether by description or by inspection.
8. If a number of people undertake the task, they all deserve a reward; if they all contributed equally then the reward is divided amongst them equally, otherwise it is divided according to their relative contributions.
9. A reward is not a legally binding contract before the specified task has been accomplished, so both the designator and worker can withdraw at any time before this point.

Rules for sharecropping

The noble *sunna*:

❖ Imam al-Ṣādiq عليه السلام was asked about a man who cultivates another man's land and, in return, must set aside a third [of the yield] for sowing, and a third for feeding livestock. The Imam عليه السلام said: 'This should not be called "sowing" or "livestock", rather he should say to the landlord: 'I will cultivate your land and you shall have such-and-such from it, whether half, a third, or whatever he specifies...'[880]

Rulings:

1. Sharecropping (*muzāraʿa*) means an agreement between a landlord and a tenant for the latter to cultivate agricultural land, and for the yields of this land to be divided between them in a manner agreed upon.
2. For a sharecropping contract to be valid, the following matters must be observed:
    a. Offer and acceptance displaying the mutual agreement between the two parties.
    b. The endowment of both parties with all the necessary qualifications to conclude a contract: legal maturity, soundness of mind, freedom of choice, freedom from impediments.
    c. For the yields of the land to be shared between them; the yields cannot belong in their entirety to just one of the parties.
    d. They must share all the yields of the land.
    e. The land must be suitable for agriculture, even if this is only through irrigation or other methods of preparation.
    f. The contract in all of its details must be clear such that there is no ambiguity that could cause strife. This is accomplished by specifying the duration of the contract, the share of each party, the kind of agriculture to be practiced, as well as the area of land, etc.
3. Sharecropping is a binding contract which cannot be voided save for in the following circumstances:
    a. When both parties mutually agree to void it.
    b. When one of the rights to withdraw from a contract is exercised.
    c. When the land becomes unsuited to agriculture because of the absence of water, for example, or because it is flooded.

---

[880] *Wasāʾil al-shīʿa*, 13/201, *aḥkām al-mazāriʿ wa al-masāqā*, ch. 8, tradition no. 10.

   d. When the tenant dies, if the contract specified that he should personally undertake the work.

4. It is not necessary for a contract of sharecropping to be between only two persons; the strongest opinion is that it can be between more than that. For example, one person can provide the land, a second the labour, a third the seeds and a fourth the tools and fertilizer. Sharecropping can also be contracted between different institutions and companies, or between them and individuals.
5. Government taxes and levies on land, or the rent payable for leasing land are – unless otherwise specified – the responsibility of the landlord initially, but if the contract specifies that all or part of these are the responsibility of the tenant and the latter agrees, the contract is valid.

Rules for plantation sharecropping (*masāqā*)

The noble *sunna*:

❖ Imam al-Ṣādiq ﷺ was asked about a man who gives another his land containing pomegranate, date, and fruit trees, saying: 'Irrigate it with this water, cultivate it, and you shall have half of its produce.' The Imam ﷺ replied: 'There is no problem with this.'

Rulings:

1. Plantation sharecropping is a contract between the owner of a fruit plantation and a tenant, who must water, prune, and fertilize them, and the produce is share between them however they have agreed.
2. Plantation sharecropping is a binding contract, so neither party can withdraw from it without a religiously valid excuse, and it cannot be voided except by one of the reasons mentioned above in the section on sharecropping.
3. The validity of a plantation sharecropping agreement depends upon the following:
   a. Mutual agreement, as embodied in an offer and acceptance, as we mentioned above in sharecropping.
   b. Both parties being endowed with the necessary legal qualifications, as mentioned above in sharecropping as well.
   c. That the plantation owner has the full right of disposal over his plantation, whether by ownership, lease, or agency.
   d. That the plantation sharecropping agreement is made at a time when the plantation requires irrigation or other tasks connected to the production and ripening of fruits to be performed. This must be before the appearance of the fruit, or after the appearance of the fruit but before it has completely ripened.

> e. Its essentials are set (e.g., fruit trees, grape vines, or date palms) and actually planted.
>
> f. The contract must be clear in its details so that there are no uncertain points which would lead to risk.

4. It is not a requirement for the validity of this kind of contract that the second party, namely the tenant, must undertake the work himself or directly; he can hire workers to help him in some tasks, or he have a team of workers under his supervision and management. In this case, he is the one who must pay their wages.

5. The majority opinion of the jurists is that a contract of planting is invalid. This is when one person gives his land to another to plant trees therein, and the planted trees are shared between them, whether or not a portion of the land is given to the worker.

Rules for agency (*wikāla*)

The noble *sunna*:

❖ Imam al-Ṣādiq 🕮 has said: 'Whoever appoints a man to carry out a task on his behalf, this appointment continues until he is divested of it just as he was appointed to it...'

Rulings:

1. Agency (*wikāla*) is a contract by which one person bestows some right of his upon another, for the latter to undertake work on behalf of the former. So if one person makes another an agent to sell his house, purchase a car, contract a marriage, or execute a divorce on his behalf, or anything like this, this is an agency contract.

2. Agency – as should be clear – is established by the mutual agreement of both parties, and this must be expressed in the form of an offer and acceptance, whether verbal written, by indication or deed.

3. Both parties (i.e., the appointer and the appointee) must possess all the usual qualifications for a legal contract (i.e., legal maturity, soundness of mind, freedom from impediments, and freedom of choice).

4. In addition to this, the appointer of an agent must have the right of disposal in the object of the agency contract. If, for example, he is legally prevented from disposing of it as he pleases, he cannot appoint someone else an agent over it.

5. It is also a requirement of the appointed agent – in addition to the general qualifications we mentioned – to be religiously and intellectually able to undertake the task he has been appointed to; so it is invalid to appoint someone in a state of consecration (*iḥrām*) to conclude a marriage contract, because he is religiously forbidden from doing so.

6. As for the object of an agency agreement, it is subject to the following conditions:
    a. It must be religiously permissible.
    b. It must be within the scope of authority of the appointer.
    c. The work for which an agent is being appointed must be possible to carry out by someone other than the appointer himself.
    d. The object of the agency agreement must be specified.
7. It is valid to appoint an agent in various standard contracts such as those of sale, hire/lease, gift, deposits, securities, settlements, sharecropping, and plantation sharecropping, as well as marriage, divorce, endowments, bequests, and the like.
8. Agency can either be general or particular in nature. Particular agency is the appointment of one person by another to carry out a specific task in a specific regard. As for general agency, it is the appointment of one person by another to manage all of their estate and carry out transactions on their behalf as they see fit.
9. An agent is obliged to abide by the limits of his agency as expressed in the contract, or those indicated by the context of the agreement and the regional custom.
10. It is permitted to appoint two or more persons as agents for the same subject.
11. It is permissible for an agent to appoint an agent of his own to carry out his tasks on his behalf, so long as he is permitted to do so by the one who appointed him.
12. Agency is a not a binding contract upon either party, but it is automatically voided in the following situations:
    a. If the agent or his appointer dies.
    b. If either the agent or his appointer becomes legally disqualified from conducting his own affairs, such as through being afflicted by madness.
    c. If the subject (*mawḍūʿ*) of the agency agreement ceases to exist.
13. It is permitted for both the plaintiff and the defendant in legal disputes and proceedings to appoint another person – most commonly, a lawyer – to oversee the court proceedings on their behalf.
14. It is impermissible for an agent in legal proceedings to resort to illegal methods on behalf of his client, just as it is impermissible for him to present as false that which he knows to be true, or present as true that which he knows to be false.
15. The agent is trusted with regards to the property, goods, real estate, and the like, which the appointer has placed at his disposal. He is not liable

for any loss or damage to them unless this was as a result of his own transgression or negligence.

16. Agency is established by the following:
    a. Knowledge [of his appointment].
    b. Religiously-admissible evidence.
    c. The declaration of the appointer.
    d. Any means which yields common-sense confidence and trust in his claim to be an agent, such as an official written appointment, as is common today.

Rules for bail (*kafāla*)

1. A security (or bail) is a contract whereby one party pledges to another that he will ensure the presence of an accused third party.
2. There are two kinds of security:
    a. Security for bringing the debtor to his creditor, or promising to discharge his dues if he cannot.
    b. Bail to ensure the presence of someone summoned to court, whether because of a complaint brought against him or because he is accused of a crime against the public good.
3. Security is a binding contract, and it requires the consent of both the sponsor (*kafīl*) and the person guaranteed by him (*makfūl*), as well as the display of this consent through offer and acceptance.
4. Both the sponsor and the guaranteed individual must be generally qualified to conduct legal contracts by being mature, of sound mind, free to choose, and without impediments. In addition to these general criteria, the sponsor must also actually be able to either bring the guaranteed person, or discharge his agreed-upon dues should he fail to do so.
5. Someone sentenced to corporal or capital punishment (*ḥadd*), or discretionary punishment (*taʿzīr*), is ineligible for bail, since it would prevent or delay the application of such a punishment.
6. If the security was given with the consent of the guaranteed person, then he is fully liable for any customary loss or harm that comes to the sponsor as a result of this security. On the other hand, if the security was contracted without his permission, then he has no obligation towards either the sponsor or the party to whom the guarantee was made.
7. The contract of security ends with the presence of the guaranteed person, whether by bringing him or by him appearing of his own volition. Therefore, if the creditor (to whom the security has been

given) forgives the debt, or if the guaranteed person discharges it, the contract also ends.

Rules for guarantees (*ḍimān*)

The noble *sunna*:

❖ It has been narrated from Imam al-Ṣādiq ﷺ that Allah's Messenger ﷺ said: 'Whoever guarantees [to fulfil] his brother's need, Allah will not look to his needs until he discharges it.'

Rulings:

1. A guarantee (*ḍimān*) is a pledge by one person (the guarantor) to fulfil an obligation or commitment of another individual.
2. The mutual consent of both parties is an essential element of a contract of guarantee, as in all other contracts. The two parties to this contract are the guarantor and the person to whom the guarantee is given (i.e., the creditor). As for the person who is being guaranteed (i.e., the debtor), his consent is not required. If the creditor and the guarantor reach an agreement, the guarantee is effective. This agreement is represented by an offer and acceptance between the two parties.
3. A guarantee is a binding contract, so if it is entered into validly and with the consent of both concerned parties, neither is permitted to withdraw from it.
4. The validity of a contract of guarantee depends upon the following:
    a. That both parties are endowed with the necessary legal qualifications of maturity, soundness of mind, freedom of choice, and freedom from impediments [to executing the contract]. As for not being insolvent, this is only a condition for person being guaranteed, not the guarantor himself.
    b. That the guarantee is effective, meaning that it is not dependent upon a condition (*sharṭ*) that means the guarantor can avoid adhering to the contract.
    c. That the loan being guaranteed is actually fixed, as when the debtor has borrowed money or purchased something on credit for which the guarantor then guarantees payment; or the loan should be as good as fixed, for example when two persons have agreed upon all the details of the loan and all that remains is a third-party guarantee for the debtor. In this situation the most likely ruling is that such a guarantee would be valid.
    d. That the guarantee is known in detail, as to avoid risk.

Rules for transference of debts (*ḥawāla*)

The noble *sunna*:

❖ Imam al-Ṣādiq 🕮 was asked about a man who transfers his debt to a third party: could that debt be transferred back to the original debtor again? He replied: 'It can never be transferred back to him, unless the third party had already become insolvent [and hence would not have been able to pay the creditor in the first place].'

Rulings:

1. A transference of debt (*ḥawāla*) means that a debtor transfers the liability of his debt to another person.
2. If a valid contract for the transference of debt is concluded, then the responsibility of repayment transfers from the debtor to the third party, and the original debtor is no longer responsible it.
3. The transference of debt is a binding contract and neither party has the right to void it without a legally valid reason. However, one or both parties have the right to stipulate a clause for voiding the contract. In that case, it is valid to void the contract if the stipulated condition is met.
4. For the transference of debt to be valid, there are conditions which we will outline below:
    a. All three parties (the creditor, the debtor, and the third party) must be endowed with the necessary legal qualifications to enter into contracts: maturity, soundness of mind, have freedom of choice, and not be *safīh* (foolish with money). The person to whom the debt is transferred must not be impeded because of insolvency, insofar as transference of debt involves the disposal of property which he would be impeded from using.
    b. All three parties must agree [to the contract and its stipulations].
    c. Offer and acceptance demonstrating this agreement.
    d. The debt being transferred must be known to both the person transferring the debt and the person to whom it is being transferred with regards to its type and quantity, such that there is no element of risk or ambiguity that might lead to disagreements or harm.
    e. That the two debts are equivalent in type, quality, and description.
    f. The lender does not have to accept the transference of debt (in which case the contract of transference cannot be validly

formed), even if the person to whom it is being transferred is wealthy and able to repay it.

Rules for gifts (*hiba*)

The noble *sunna*:

❖ In a tradition from Imam al-Bāqir ﷺ, we read: 'A gift or donation[881] can be reclaimed if one wishes, whether the recipient has been taken possession of it or not, unless it was given to a relative, in which case it cannot be reclaimed.'

Rulings:

1. A gift (*hiba*) is something given to another person without anything in return, and it is a contract that requires offer and acceptance.
2. Both parties must be endowed with the necessary legal qualities of maturity, soundness of mind, intent, and freedom of choice. In addition to this, the one giving the gift must not be impeded from the free disposal of his property because of foolishness in financial matters or insolvency, and he must also be the owner of the thing he is gifting.
3. In order for the contract of gift to be valid and for the property to be transferred, the recipient must take possession of it, even if this is not in the same sitting in which the contract is formalized.
4. A contract of gifting is non-binding, so the giver can void it and request the return of his gift except in the following circumstances:
    a. If it was given to a near relative of the first degree, or even lower degrees,[882] according to precaution.
    b. If the gift was given to a wife or husband (according to precaution).
    c. If all or part of the gift has been lost.
    d. If the gift was reciprocated.
    e. If the giver gave it in order to seek nearness to Allah.
    f. If the recipient utilizes the gift in such a way that its ownership is [irrevocably] transferred.
    g. If the recipient utilizes the gift in such a way that it is changed as a result.

---

[881] Gifts and donations are categories distinct from charity, as charity cannot be taken back, regardless of who has received it.

[882] Relatives are classed in three 'degrees', as outlined in laws of inheritance. Thus, one's parents and descendants are considered first degree relatives, while aunts and uncles are third degree relatives.

h. If either the giver or the recipient die after the contract is formalized, and possession is taken of the gift.

Rules pertaining to loans (*qarḍ*) and debts (*dayn*)

Loans are one of the clearest manifestations of the mutual trust that should exist between members of society, and one of the most visible examples of cooperation in good deeds. By giving loans, the wealthy discharge some of their responsibilities towards the less fortunate; giving a loan is one of the most highly recommended religious acts, especially when given to someone in need. There is an abundance of sources which encourage people in a believing society to support one another socially by giving loans.

The noble *sunna*:

❖ It has been narrated from Imam al-Ṣādiq ﷺ that Allah's Messenger ﷺ said: 'Whoever gives a loan to a believer with the intention of making that believer's affairs easy, the wealth he loaned is in *zakāt*,[883] and the angels pray for him until the loan is repaid.'

Rules for debts

1. A debt is some wealth or right due to one person from another
2. There are a number of causes for the existence of a debt, and generally they fall into two categories:

First: Voluntary causes, which a person chooses himself. The most obvious of these is to take a loan, or to purchase a commodity in advance with money (in which case the commodity is a debt), or to purchase something on credit (in which case the payment is a debt), or to lease something on the condition of delayed payment, or to delay a bridal dowry, and so on.

Second: Involuntary causes, such that some wealth or right becomes the responsibility of a person according to the Divine Law, for example: compensation owed if something is lost or damage as the result of a person's transgression or negligence, the maintenance costs of a permanent wife when a marriage contract is concluded, whether the husband likes it or not, etc.

3. A debt is either due on demand or deferred; for an on-demand debt (a debt with an unspecified repayment schedule), the creditor has the right to demand payment from the debtor at any time, and it is obligatory for the debtor to pay the debt on demand assuming he is able. As for a

---

[883] That is, if the recipient dies before repaying the loan, then it will count as *zakāt* for the lender.

deferred debt, the creditor does not have the right to demand its repayment before the specified period of time has elapsed, nor is the debtor expected to pay it before that time.

Rules for loans (*qarḍ*)

1. A loan (*qarḍ*) is a contract which entails the possessor of some kind of wealth giving possession of it to another person until a specified time, on the condition that the recipient of the loan returns it to him thereafter.
2. A loan is a binding contract, so the lender cannot – after all the conditions of a loan have been met – invalidate it and demand the return of the loan.
3. The validity of a loan depends upon the mutual agreement of the lender and the borrower. And, because a loan is a contract, it requires an offer and acceptance to demonstrate the mutual agreement of both parties.
4. Both parties to a loan contract must be endowed with the necessary legal qualifications to enter into a contract (i.e., maturity, soundness of mind, free will, and they must not be fiscally irresponsible), as well as no legal reason why the lender cannot dispose of the property in question (freedom from impediments).
5. The property being loaned must be verified and known, and it must be a specific, ownable item.
6. It is permissible to specify the duration of the loan, at the conclusion of which the loan must be settled. If a duration is specified, it must be observed, and the loan becomes like any other deferred debt, in that the lender does not have the right to demand repayment before this duration is concluded. In this case, the duration must be specified in such a way as to remove ambiguity and risk.
7. If someone borrows money in the form prevalent today (i.e., paper currency), then its value depreciates greatly as a result of war, sanctions, economic downturn or the like, then the *real value* of the loan must be repaid, and not merely the number of notes loaned. However, the most cautious course of action is to come to a mutually-agreed settlement.
8. If one person dupes another by taking some wealth from him in the form of a loan, without any initial intention of repaying it – meaning that the loan was simply pretence to obtain the said property – then this property does not become his to own, and utilizing it is forbidden.
9. The borrower must discharge his loan when the lender demands, if the loan was 'on demand' (that is, no payment timeframe was specified at the time of the loan), or when the duration has elapsed, if the debt was deferred.

10. If the borrower is in financial difficulty and cannot repay the loan, the lender does not have the right to pressure him or cause him difficulty by demanding the repayment of the loan; rather it is obligatory to put off the repayment until the borrower is able.
11. If the borrower is able to repay the loan and the time to repay it has come, it is forbidden for him to procrastinate or avoid paying it. In fact, this is a major sin.
12. It is obligatory for the borrower, when the lender demands repayment or when the time for the loan has expired, to do his utmost to repay the loan by any means possible, even if this means selling something he owns. The exceptions to this are as follows:
    a. The house in which he and his legal dependants dwell.
    b. Necessary articles of clothing, and even those he uses to embellish himself or for luxury needs.
    c. Any necessary means of transportation, whether a bike, car, boat, etc.
    d. Necessities of life, such as furnishings and household goods, kitchen goods and equipment, and other such things.
    e. Any space, furnishings, or necessities necessary for entertaining guests.
    f. Books of learning which he requires for his studies and education if he is engaged in such pursuits.

Usurious loans

13. A usurious loan is a loan given on the condition that more than the principle is repaid. This is forbidden in Islamic Law, whether this condition is explicitly stated in the contract, hidden, or implied. The criterion for determining that a loan is usurious rests on more than the principle being repaid, such that were it not for this addition, the lender would not issue the loan.
14. There are many kinds of forbidden addition, whether this takes the form of wealth, labour, usufruct, or features.[884] The same applies if someone issues a loan to another in one country on the condition that he repays it in another, when the cost of exchanging this money is so high that it would customarily be considered usury.
15. Repayment above the principle of the loan is only forbidden if it is the result of a contractual stipulation, such that if there were no addition (interest), then no loan would be forthcoming. As for the borrower

---

[884] Such as lending a worn book and demanding it would be returned brand new, or a low spec. computer to be returned as a high spec. version.

voluntarily giving an addition in the form of a gift, without any prior agreement (or implication), there is no problem. In fact, this is something recommended in Islamic Law.

Usurious wealth

16. If an interest-based loan is contracted, then the loan itself is valid, and the borrower takes possession of the loaned wealth and he may dispose of it, just as the lender owns whatever property the borrower repays to him from the loan itself. The only thing which is forbidden is to give and take the excess, in that this does not become the property of the lender; in fact, he must return it to its rightful owner.
17. Taking usury is a major sin for which a person must repent to Allah, and in order for his repentance to be accepted, he must return whatever usury he has taken. If he does not know the number of usurious contracts, or the amount of usury he has taken from people, he must pay whatever amount he is certain of being usurious. But it is precaution to reach a settlement with all the parties with whom he entered into such contracts if they are known to him, or with the religious authority (the *marja*ʿ) otherwise.
18. As for anyone who deals with interest: if all of his property is illicit, then it is forbidden to eat with him (i.e., food he has purchased with his illicit wealth), take gifts from him, and other such interactions. But if his property consists of licit gains mixed with illicit, then there is no problem with this.

Rules for collateral (*rahn*)

The noble *sunna*:

❖ Imam al-Bāqir ﷺ was asked about collateral and securities for purchases on credit. He said: 'There is no problem with it.'

Rulings:

1. Collateral (*rahn*) is when the debtor places something with the creditor as a guarantee of debt repayment, so that if he refuses or is otherwise unable to pay his dues, the creditor can take his due from the collateral.
2. Collateral can only be contracted with the mutual agreement of both parties, and this must be demonstrated through offer and acceptance.
3. Collateral is a binding contract for the one paying it, but non-binding on the one receiving it. In other words, the debtor cannot void the collateral and seek its return after the contract has been validly concluded unless his creditor forgoes his rights to the collateral, or if the collateral is released because the debt has been paid or cancelled. On

the other hand, the creditor can forgo the collateral because he is its legal beneficiary.

4. Both parties (the one providing collateral and the one receiving it) must be endowed with the basic legal qualifications for a contract (such as legal maturity, soundness of mind, intent, and freedom of choice), and the one providing the collateral must not be barred from disposing of the property because of insolvency.

5. The following are requirements for the wealth being used a collateral:

   a. It must be something that can be owned and whose ownership can be transferred (both practically and legally), so wine, pork, or the property of others cannot be used as collateral.

   b. It cannot be something which will spoil before the duration of the contract is concluded, if the deposit was for a deferred loan; so fruits cannot be given as collateral for a loan whose payment is deferred until the following year, because they will spoil.

   c. The collateral must be [clearly] specified.

   d. The person providing the collateral must be entitled to dispose of it freely; so usurped property cannot be used.

6. The one with whom the collateral is entrusted is not entitled to dispose of it in manners such as sale, rental, or the demolition of real estate, without the agreement of the borrower. As for simply making use of the collateral, such as driving a car, living in a house, then if this does not breach the trust of the borrower, it is most likely permissible. By the same token, however, the borrower may not sell or rent out the collateral without the agreement of the one to whom he has entrusted it.

7. The one who entrusted with the collateral can sell it in cases where the borrower has failed to pay the loan, even if it is one of those items which should not be sold [by a borrower] to pay off a loan, such as a family home or a personal means of transportation.

Rules for borrowing (*'āriya*)

The noble *sunna*:

❖ Imam al-Bāqir 🙵 was asked about a person who borrowed something which was then lost or stolen. He said: 'If he was trustworthy (*amīn*), then there is no penalty for him.'

Rulings:

1. Borrowing is when one person lends something to another without receiving anything in return, on the condition that the latter returns the item to him after he has used it.

2. A contract of borrowing is not binding upon either party, so the lender can void the contract and demand the return of the borrowed item whenever he wishes, just as the borrower can return it whenever he wants.
3. The most important element of borrowing is mutual agreement, as expressed by offer and acceptance. Sufficient for this is the act of handing over the item without anything being said by either party.
4. The lender must be endowed with all the necessary legal qualifications for disposal, such as maturity and soundness of mind, and that there are no impediments (which would prevent use or disposal of the property) because of foolishness in financial matters or insolvency.
5. Because borrowing is a usufructuary contract rather than a contract for transference of ownership, there are no conditions for the borrower save that he is able to utilize the thing being borrowed. Thus, it is valid to lend something to a discerning child or madman who is able to make use of it, and the same applies to someone who normally suffers from legal impediments [to contracts].
6. The borrowed item must not be something that will be consumed entirely through use, and the purpose of its use must be religiously lawful.
7. There are three fundamental issues which the borrower must observe:
    a. He must use the borrowed item in the correct manner and for its intended purpose.
    b. He must not lend the borrowed item or rent it out to a third party without the [prior] agreement of the lender.
    c. He must return the borrowed item to the lender after the term of borrowing (if that was specified) has concluded, or after he has made use of it – if it is of specific usage – or when the lender demands its return.
8. The borrower is responsible for loss or damage to the borrowed item, even if this is not the result of any transgression or neglect, in two situations:
    a. If the lender makes the borrowing conditional on the borrower being responsible for the item in all circumstances.
    b. If the borrowed item was made of gold or silver.
9. If the borrower uses the borrowed item in a manner other than that specified by the owner, such as building on land intended for agriculture, or uses it improperly, such as using a truck capable of carrying five tonnes to carry more than this weight, then this property is considered usurped and the borrower is responsible for any resulting

loss or damage. In addition to this, he must pay a fee for whatever benefits he has accrued from this improper usage.

Rules for deposits (*wadīʿa*)

The noble *sunna*:

❖ Allah's Messenger ﷺ said: 'Fulfilling trusts (*amāna*) attracts sustenance, treachery (*khiyāna*) attracts poverty.' And Imam al-Ṣādiq عليه السلام said: 'The caretaker of a deposit or commodity has been entrusted with them.'

Rulings:

1. A contract of deposit (*wadīʿa*) means to place something with another person for them to look after it. Or, to put it more succinctly: entrusting it to a caretaker.
2. A deposit is a trust for which its caretaker is responsible; no one may violate this trust, even if its owner is a profligate sinner. Agreeing to hold a deposit carries great reward if it falls under the general heading of cooperating in good deeds and piety, or looking after the needs of a fellow believer.
3. A deposit is not a binding contract on either party, so either of them may void it at will.
4. A deposit may only be concluded by mutual consent, and it depends upon offer and acceptance, verbal or otherwise.
5. Both parties to a deposit agreement must be endowed with the general qualifications of legal maturity and a sound mind, and the holder of the deposit must actually be able to safeguard it.
6. Agreeing to hold a deposit is not obligatory, but if someone does so then it is obligatory to safeguard it, protect it from harm, and return it to its rightful owner upon demand.
7. The liability of the deposit's caretaker is limited, meaning he does not bear any responsibility for loss or damage to the deposit, so long as this is not a result of his own transgression or negligence. Transgression (*taʿaddī*) means to use the deposit without the permission of the depositor, or in a way that custom does not consider appropriate. Negligence (*tafrīṭ*) means failing to take appropriate action to safeguard the deposit according to the demands of custom and common sense with regards to each individual thing, such that a person would be customarily considered to have squandered the deposit and neglected it.
8. A contract of deposit is invalidated by one of the following reasons:
    a. The death of either the depositor or the deposit holder.

b. The loss of either one of them of their legal qualification to enter into contracts, whether this is by being afflicted by madness, or no longer being able to safeguard the deposit [for some other practical reason].

c. By either party cancelling the contract, whether by the request of the owner that the deposit be returned, or by the deposit holder returning it to him.

Rules for admission (*iqrār*)

The noble *sunna*:

❖ Allah's Messenger ﷺ said: 'The admission of rational persons against themselves is permissible.'

❖ Imam al-Ṣādiq ؑ said: 'A faithful person is more honest about himself than seventy other faithful persons are about him.'

Rulings:

1. In Islamic law, an admission (*iqrār*) is when a person voluntarily testifies that another person has some right over him, or disavows a right over another person.

An example of the first is: 'I owe so-and-so a thousand dinars' or any other expression affirming that the other person has a right over him.

An example of the second is: 'I have no right over so-and-so', or 'So-and-so does not owe me anything', or any other expression that negates his right over another person.

2. For an admission to be valid and effective, it must:
   a. Be firm and certain, without doubt or hesitation.
   b. Consist of words that explicitly or apparently indicate a testimony in favour of the other party.
   c. To be effective and carry weight, it must be against the admitting person's own interests, such as acknowledging his debt to another person or relinquishing the debt of another towards him.
   d. The object of his testimony must be, when the testimony concerns property rights, something which can be legitimately owned by the person giving testimony; so one cannot make an admission about pork, wine, or any sort of devices or implements which are forbidden for a Muslim to own, because a Muslim cannot own these things.

3. The one making an admission must be endowed with all the general qualifications for contracts, including legal maturity, soundness of mind, intent, and freedom of choice. As for a minor, madman, someone who

is intoxicated, someone who is inattentive, unaware, joking, or under duress, his admission cannot be accepted. And the admission of someone who is fiscally foolish cannot be accepted in property matters.

4. The admission of someone on their deathbed, if they are accused of being untruthful in their testimony, is accepted only as regards the one third of their wealth [over which they have free disposal], and nothing above this amount.

5. If someone admits to something and then denies it, his denial is not accepted and his admission remains effective.

Rules pertaining to legal impediments (*ḥajr*)

The noble *sunna*:

❖ Imam al-Ṣādiq 🕮 said: 'The orphanhood of an orphan cease when he experiences a night emission while mature; if he experiences a night emission while he is not known as mature, and he is either simpleminded or weak, then his guardian should withhold his property from him...'

❖ And it is narrated that 'Ali 🕮 declared a man insolvent when he defaulted on his creditors. The Imam ordered that his property should be divided up between them, and that if the debtor refused, then he must sell that property and divide the proceeds between his creditors.

What is a legal impediment?

The word *ḥajr* means to prevent someone from something, and in Islamic legal parlance it means legally preventing someone from freely disposing of his property because of one of the following reasons: (i) not being legally mature, (ii) madness, (iii) foolishness with financial concerns, (iv) insolvency. And the one who is prevented from freely disposing of his property is called a 'ward' (*maḥjūr 'alayh*).

1. A minor who is not legally mature is legally a ward, meaning that he cannot dispose freely of his property (*māl*), responsibilities (*dhimma*), or self (*nafs*).

2. The legal ineffectuality of a minor in the aforementioned areas has nothing to do with the existence of a good reason or lack thereof; even if there is a good reason of the highest order for his actions, they are still not legally valid.

3. Guardianship (*walāya*) with the authority to manage the wealth and possessions of a child, as well as to look after his interests and affairs, devolves in the following order:

First to his father, then his paternal grandfather, then to the executor appointed by either of them, then to the religious authority (the *marjaʿ*). And in the absence of any religious authority, then the apparent ruling is that it devolves to any righteous believer. As for his mother, maternal grandfather, brother, or maternal or paternal uncles, they have no automatic authority over a minor in any way, shape or form.

4. The guardian (*walī*) must always look after the interests of the child when managing his property and other affairs.
5. A child's guardian may send him to safe institutions to learn appropriate industries, crafts, or arts, just as he is allowed to send him to schools to learn to read and write, and study other useful subjects; but he must always be concerned with protecting him from anything that will have a negative effect on his [religious] beliefs, corrupt his morals, or otherwise put him at risk of deviation.
6. The ruling for the insane (*majnūn*) is like that of a child in everything we have mentioned; he is legally ineligible to manage of his wealth, responsibilities, or self.
7. There is no disputing that guardianship over the insane, whose affliction with severe or debilitating mental illness began in childhood, is rightfully his father's and paternal grandfather's, and those who come after them according to the order mentioned for a child.
8. As for someone who is afflicted by debilitating mental illness after he has matured, and left the guardianship of his father and grandfather, then it is obligatory precaution that the father and the religious authority come to a mutual agreement on appointing his legal guardian.
9. A fool (*safīh*) is someone who is not sensible (*rashīd*), namely someone whose management of property does not fall within a rational framework, and whose behaviour would customarily be considered abnormal by sensible and rational persons in their management of property, whether in the acquisition or spending of wealth.
10. A fool (by the aforementioned definition) is legally unable to dispose of his own property, so his management of his wealth and property carry no weight, as we mentioned regarding with regards to the minor and the insane, and he is incapable of discharging his responsibilities (*dhimma*).
11. As for those matters concerning individual behaviour, no one who knows that this person is fiscally foolish is permitted to enter into

monetary transactions with him. As concerns social transactions, no one can judge another person to be legally foolish except by the verdict of the religious authority (a *marjaʿ*).

12. The property of a fool must not be placed at his disposal unless one is certain that he has come to his senses.
13. Insolvency (*iflās*) means that a person has insufficient wealth to discharge his debts; and if the religious authority issue a verdict that such a person cannot dispose of his own property as he pleases, then he becomes insolvent (since his assets have been effectively frozen). So the insolvent person (*muflis*) is one who is prevented from disposing of his wealth because he is unable to discharge his debts.
14. A person only becomes insolvent by the accumulation of debts under the following conditions:
    a. That the debts are legally established.
    b. That his possessions (namely: currency, moveable property, immovable property, debts owed to him by people) – aside from those of the above exempted from being used as loan repayment – are insufficient to cover the repayment of his debts.
    c. That the debts are due immediately ('on demand' as opposed to deferred); no person can be declared insolvent because of deferred debts whose payment is not yet due.
    d. That all or some of his creditors raise the matter with the religious authority, requesting that he be legally declared insolvent.
15. After the ruling of the religious authority has been issued, and a person has been legally declared insolvent and hence unable to dispose of his income, the authority (a *marjaʿ*) can begin selling his property and paying the dividends to his creditors, proportional to the debts owed to each.

Rules pertaining to the usurpation (*ghaṣb*) and destruction of property (*itlāf*)

The noble *sunna*:

❖ Allah's Messenger ﷺ said, in the tradition of prohibitions (*ḥadīth al-manāhī*): 'Whoever betrays his neighbour for so much as a hand-span of the earth, Allah shall place a collar around his neck that encompasses the seven earths, until he meets Allah on the Day of Resurrection dragging this collar, unless he repents and returns what he took.'

❖ The Commander of the Faithful ﷺ said: 'A stolen brick in a house is a deposit for its ruin.'

Rules concerning usurpation (*ghaṣb*)

1. Usurpation (*ghaṣb*) means unjustly taking ownership of another person's property (*māl*) or rights (*ḥaqq*).
2. It makes no difference whether the victim of usurpation is a Muslim or from the disbelievers whose property is honoured: so long as his rights are valid, it is forbidden and the usurper is responsible for it. It also makes no difference whether the victim or a person, an institution, or a company, or whether it is owned privately or by the government.
3. Three fundamental issues apply to usurpation:
    a. All forms of usurpation are a sin for which a person should repent to Allah, not only to avoid punishment in the Hereafter, but to avoid the negative financial consequences in this world – see below.
    b. It is obligatory to immediately relinquish control of the usurped thing (whether it is wealth, property, a right, or usufruct), so long as it still exists, and return it to its rightful owner, his guardian, or his inheritor.
    c. The usurper is liable for the usurped item.
4. The usurped item must be returned to its owner so long as it exists, even if returning it to him requires the usurper to spend money or undergo difficulty.
5. In addition to the above, the usurper must compensate the owner for any benefits he has been deprived of as a result of the usurpation.
6. If the usurped property was public property and not the property of a particular person, such as endowments (*waqf*), it must be handed over to the appointed trustee if there is one, otherwise it must be handed over to the religious authority.
7. If the usurped item is diminished or a usurped injured, the usurper is liable for it and he must return not only the item or the right to its rightful owner, he must also provide compensation for the loss in value.
8. If a usurper cultivates usurped land or plants in it, then the cultivation, plantation, and its yields belong to the usurper, and he must pay rental to the owner for as long as it is cultivated or planted. And if the owner demands that the cultivation or plantation be removed from the land, the usurper must abide by this even if this harms his interests, unless this would lead to wastage or ruin the ground.

It is also obligatory for him to level the ground and repair any damage done by planting, cultivating, and tearing-up the soil, unless the rightful owner is satisfied with another solution.

9. If something is usurped several times, meaning that person A usurps it from its rightful owner, then person B usurps it from person A, then person C usurps it from person B, and so on, and the usurped item is lost or damaged, then the person in whose possession the loss or damage was incurred is liable for it.
10. If some property comes into a person's possession and control through false or corrupt means, then it is in the same position – with regards to liability – as usurped property, even if it was not taken unjustly; so the person who receives this property is required to protect it and return it to its rightful owner.
11. If one person takes ownership of another free person unjustly, detaining him, preventing him from living his natural life, and forcing him to perform certain labours, and custom treats this behaviour as depriving the man thus imprisoned of certain benefits, then the person who has imprisoned him is liable for those benefits and must return them to him. It does not matter whether this is during his imprisonment or after his release.

Rules concerning loss or damage to property (*itlāf*)

12. Loss or damage to property (*itlāf*) is deemed another reason for liability (*ḍimān*). It falls into two categories: direct loss or damage (*bi'l-mubāshara*) and indirect (*bi'l-tasbīb*).
    a. A person might do something which directly causes loss or damage to property, without any intermediary, in which case he is definitely liable without a doubt. For example, if someone sets fire to some goods and incinerates them; pushes an animal into a ravine, resulting in its death; strikes a glass with a hammer and breaks it; throws a stone at a vase and smashes it; or drives his car into as wall and knocks it over; and so on, and so forth. In all of these and similar situations, the person responsible for the loss or damage is responsible for his actions; he is held liable and must provide compensation.
    b. A person might not inflict loss or damage by his actions directly. Rather, he may only contribute to it by doing or producing something which – indirectly – causes loss or damage, but still in a way whereby that person is considered its cause, and not simply the intermediary. For example:

- Someone digs a whole on a public highway without putting up any signs to warn passers-by. An animal or vehicle then falls into it, in which case the person who dug the whole is liable for any loss or damage caused. The same applies to excavations which various national agencies undertake if these are not accompanied by warning signs for passers-by.
- Throwing nails onto a main road, causing damage to tyres.
- Cutting the rope that ties an animal, releasing it.
- Building a wall without proper attention to the foundations, which later collapses on a passer-by.
- Opening a locked door and releasing animals.
- Putting a sharp object on a public footpath which someone falls upon, injuring themselves.

In all of the above examples and countless situations like them, it is the person responsible for the cause of the damage who is liable for compensating those affected. The ultimate criterion for this is custom, so whatever custom considers a cause for loss or damage, liability is thereby established.

Rules for oaths (*yamīn*)

The noble *sunna*:

❖ Imam al-Ṣādiq narrates that the Prophet ﷺ said: 'For whomever Allah is too magnificent to swear an oath by, Allah will give him something better than whatever he has lost as a result [of refusing to swear said oath].' The Imam ؑ said: 'Do not swear by Allah truthfully or falsely, for He says: **"Do not make Allah an obstacle through your oaths."**'[885]

Rulings:

1. Swearing oaths by Allah is something common amongst all kinds of people at all times and places, and the *sharīʿa* contains particular rules for it. Oaths (*yamīn* or *ḥilf*) are divided into four varieties:
   a. Oaths for emphasis (*ta'kīd*).
   b. Oaths for imploring (*munāshada*).
   c. Oaths for fulfilling contracts and commitments (*al-ʿaqd wa al-iltizām*), which are the variety discussed in books of jurisprudence.
   d. Vain oaths (*laghw*).

---

[885] Sūrat al-Baqara (2):224

Generally speaking, all oaths, whether truthful or vain, and whether connected to the past, present, or future, are discouraged (*makrūh*). The only exception is when an oath is sworn to prevent injustice against oneself or another.

2. An oath is a covenant between a person and his Lord in which the person swears by Allah that he will do or refrain from something in the future, according to the conditions which we will lay out; and to this apply the Arabic terms *yamīn, ḥilf,* and *qasam*.
3. If a person swears an oath according to the conditions below, then it is obligatory for him to adhere to his oath and fulfil its content. Should he willingly violate his oath, he must offer expiation (*kaffāra*). The Arabic term for breaking an oath is *ḥanth*, and the oath breaker is called *ḥānith*.
4. The expiation for breaking an oath is to release a slave, or feed ten poor persons, or clothe ten poor persons; and if one cannot do any of these three, he must fast for three days.
5. A binding oath – namely, one that must be fulfilled and for whose violation expiation is due – is only concluded if the following conditions are met:
   a. The one swearing the oath must be endowed with the general legal qualifications to enter into a contract, namely: legal maturity, soundness of mind, freedom of choice, and intent.
   b. The oath must be sworn by Allah; an oath is only binding when sworn by Allah and not when sworn by anyone else. The criterion is that custom considers a person to have sworn by Allah.
   c. The oath must be uttered by one who is able to speak, or expressed in a manner similar to speech, such as sign-language by someone who is mute or rendered incapable of speech by an illness.

      As for making an oath in writing, it is problematic.

      It is unnecessary that one make an oath in the Arabic language, rather one may establish an oath by any language one knows, or [in a way] that he at least knows the meaning of the oath.
   d. The oath must not contravene the *sharīʿa*. Any oath whose content contravenes the *sharīʿa*, such as one to stop performing an obligatory act, or to commit a forbidden one, is invalid. The same applies if it contravenes the preferences of the *sharīʿa*, such as vowing not to do something that is recommended (*mustaḥabb*), or to do something that is disliked (*makrūh*).

Furthermore, it has been established that an oath can be made to perform something obligatory (such as being kind to one's parents) or recommended (such as praying at the earliest possible time), or to avoid something forbidden (such as vexing the faithful) or disliked (such as sleeping with a full stomach).

e. The person who swears the oath must have the ability (*qudra*) to fulfil it, so an oath is only valid if the one swearing it has the ability to enact it.

6. When swearing an oath, it is not necessary to use one of the particles for oaths commonly used in the Arabic language, such as *wallāhi*, *billāhi*, or *tillāhi*. It suffices to swear an oath using words such as 'I swear by Allah...' ('*aqsamtu billāh*' or '*ḥaliftu billāh*').
7. An oath is not established through swearing by other than Allah, such as swearing by the Prophet ﷺ or Imams ؑ, the angels, the Qurʾān, the Kaʿba, or any other sacred things.
8. If a father forbids his child, or a husband forbids his wife, from swearing an oath, then this invalidates said oath. But if no prior forbiddance is issued by the father or husband against the oath, then the oath is valid, and its validity does not depend upon seeking their permission.
   However, should a child or wife swear an oath without the prior consent of their father or husband, then the father and husband have the right to release them from the oath, whereat the oath becomes vain and the aforementioned rules do not apply to it.
9. If all the conditions for swearing an oath are met, it is effective, becomes obligatory to fulfil, and it is forbidden for the one swearing it to break or contravene it. If he does, then he must offer expiation, but expiation is only due if he broke it intentionally. As for breaking an oath out of ignorance, forgetfulness, necessity, or compulsion, this is not considered oath breaking, and no expiation is due as a result.

Rules for vows (*nadhr*) and covenants (*ʿahd*)

The noble *sunna*:

❖ Imam al-Ṣādiq ؑ was asked about a man who says: 'A vow is upon me.' The Imam replied: 'A vow is nothing unless one dedicates [for its sake] some fasting, charity, offering, or pilgrimage to Allah.'

Rulings:

1. A vow (*nadhr*) means pledging to perform or avoid a specific action for the sake of Allah. For example, saying: 'For Allah, I must fast for five days.' Or: 'For Allah, I must give up smoking.'

2. A vow is not effective by only making the intention in one's heart; it must be uttered with an expression that indicates one is pledging to perform or avoid a specific act for sake of Allah.
3. A vow need not use the name 'Allah' – the apparent ruling is that it can use any of the Beautiful Names.
4. It is unlikely that a vow is conditional on being uttered in Arabic. Rather, a vow is effective using any expression that conveys the aforementioned meaning in any language.
5. In order for a vow to be effective, the person uttering it must be endowed with all the basic legal qualifications we mentioned for an oath.
6. A wife cannot make a vow when her husband forbids her from doing so, and if she makes a vow without his permission, he can annul her vow. But if he allows her to make a vow, he does not have the right to prevent her from fulfilling it afterwards.
7. As for a child, if custom dictates that a father's forbiddance renders a vow undesirable (*ghayr rājiḥ*), then it is a condition of the vow's validity that the father does not forbid it. Even if custom does not dictate this, then the most likely ruling is still the same; the best way to avoid such problems is for children to seek permission from their father before making a vow.

Kinds of vows

8. There are three kinds of vows (*nadhr*):
    a. First: A vow of thanksgiving (*nadhr al-shukr*); a vow made by someone to give thanks to Allah for a blessing He has bestowed upon them.
    b. Second: A vow of contrition (*nadhr al-zajr*); a vow made by someone to dissuade themselves from committing a forbidden or disliked act, or from forgoing an obligatory or recommended one.
    c. Third: A voluntary vow (*nadhr al-taṭawwuʿ*); a vow voluntarily made by someone independent of any conditions, such as by saying: 'For Allah, I must fast the first day of every month.'
9. Jurists are in agreement that the vows of thanksgiving and contrition are effective, but they disagree concerning the validity of voluntary vows. In our opinion, the strongest position is that this kind of vow is both valid and effective.

The object of a vow (*mandhūr*)

10. The object of a vow – i.e., the act which someone has vowed to perform or avoid – must be within the ability of the one making the vow. It must

also be an act of obedience to Allah (such as acts of worship by which a person seeks nearness to Allah, or manners and morals which are encouraged by the religion). As for legally neutral (*mubāḥ*) acts, there is no weight given to them as the objects of vows (such as vowing to eat a particular permissible item of food, or vowing not to) and the apparent ruling is that such a vow is meaningless.

11. It is obligatory to fulfil a vow in all of its details: if someone vows to perform an action connected to a certain time, place, or other context, then they are obliged to adhere to this when fulfilling the vow accordingly. For example, if someone vows to perform two units of prayer on the Day of *Tarwiya* in the Sacred Mosque, he must do as he vowed. If he prays anywhere except the Sacred Mosque, or on a day other than that of *Tarwiya*[886], then he has not fulfilled his vow.
12. If someone vows to fast on a particular day of each week (e.g., Thursday), and one of the two *ʿĪd*s fall on this day, or they experience menstruation, such that they are not allowed to fast, then they must break their fast and make up for it later.
13. If someone vows some wealth to one of the holy shrines without intending any specific use for it, then he should spend it for the sake of the shrine or for its pilgrims.
14. If someone vows some wealth to the Prophet ﷺ, one of the Imams (ʿa), or one of the *awliyāʾ* or righteous persons, then he should spend it on good causes and righteous deeds with the intention that its reward should return to the person for whom he made the vow.
15. If one or both parents vow to marry their daughter to a particular person, or category of people (e.g., a descendent of Allah's Messenger ﷺ), then when their daughter reaches the age of maturity the matter is entirely up to her, and no consideration is given to this vow. She must not be coerced into accepting it, nor is any expiation due from the one who made the vow, as such a vow is fundamentally problematic.
16. If someone breaks their vow, the expiation they must offer is identical to that of an oath breaker – according to the apparent ruling – although it is recommended precaution that they offer the expiation for intentionally breaking one's fast in the month of Ramaḍān.

Rules for covenants (*ʿahd*)

17. A covenant (*ʿahd*) means adhering to something, and a mere intention in one's heart is insufficient to undertake a covenant; it must be pronounced in the form of words that express its content. The form of

---

[886] That is the 8th of Dhūl-Ḥijja.

a covenant is: 'I make a covenant with Allah that I will do this...' or 'Upon me is a covenant with Allah to do this...'

18. The rules pertaining to covenants are identical to those of vows, save for a single issue, namely the object of a covenant. The object of a covenant does not need to be an act of obedience or a preferred deed; in fact, it can even be for legally neutral actions for which the religion has expressed no opinion, whether of approval or disapproval, as is the case with vows (*yamīn*).

19. Breaking a covenant after solemnizing it according to the proper conditions requires expiation. The apparent ruling is that the expiation for a broken covenant is the same as one offered for intentionally breaking one's fast during the month of Ramaḍān.

Rules for competitions (*musābiqāt*)

The noble *sunna*:

❖ Imam al-Ṣādiq 🕮 said: 'There is no competition save in feet, hooves, or arrowheads – meaning combat.'

❖ And he also said: 'Allah's Messenger raced horses, and he would say: "Verily the Angels bring the winnings for feet, hooves, and feathers (i.e., camels, horses, and arrows); everything besides that is forbidden gambling."'

Rulings:

1. Racing and target shooting are competitions in which it is legitimate to give a prize; and the goal of these [sports] is to train people to fight in Allah's way, and to prepare forces to face the enemy.

2. The religion of Islam allows races to be run with camels and horses.

3. Likewise, it has allowed competitions with arrows, called archery (*rimāya*).

4. The *sharīʿa* permits setting a prize (*ʿiwaḍ*) for competitions such as these.

5. The many other kinds of competition that exist today are also permitted, such as running races, weightlifting, football, swimming, motorsports, and similar competitions that might happen in the future. All are permitted so long as there is nothing prohibited involved, and as it is precaution to make any compensation offered as part of this a legal prize (*juʿāla* – see above).

6. Legal competitions are considered commutative contracts (*ʿaqd muʿāwiḍī*), which become effective through a verbal offer and acceptance, as in contracts of exchange.

7. Both parties must be endowed with all the necessary legal qualifications; legal maturity, soundness of mind, intent, and freedom of choice.

8. All legitimate forms of competition must abide by the following conditions:
    a. That the competitors must be able to participate in the announced competition.
    b. That the prize (*ʿiwaḍ*) must be specific and quantified, so that there is no ambiguity about it, if the competition has a prize. It is permissible to have archery competitions without any prize. As regards the permissibility of setting a prize, it makes no difference whether it is provided by one or more of the participants, a third party, or the public treasury.
    c. The distance, starting and finishing points in racing, as well as the number of shots, the target, and the number of points in archery, are visibly marked or known in such a way that removes any ambiguity or risk.
    d. Violent competitions such as freestyle wrestling, boxing, bullfighting, etc., are forbidden if they involve fatal harm to one's life. If they do not involve fatal harm and do not offer a prize, then they are permitted.
    e. There is no problem in giving the competitors cups, medals, and monetary or non-monetary prizes in the form of awards and encouragement, rather than being solely based on who won.

Rules for the final will and testament (*waṣiyya*)

The noble *sunna*:

❖ Imam al-Bāqir عليه السلام said: 'Wills are a right (*ḥaqq*); Allah's Messenger ﷺ made a will, and so should every Muslim.'

❖ Imam al-Ṣādiq عليه السلام said: 'Whoever does not make a proper will when he is dying, this represents a deficiency in his magnanimity and good sense...'

Wills (*waṣiyya*)

1. A will (*waṣiyya*) is:
    a. When one person takes a pledge from another to undertake certain acts and responsibilities – whether obligatory or recommended – after his death.
    b. Or, when one person orders that something (whether an item or usufruct) be given to another person. That thing is called a 'bequest' (*mūṣan bih*), and the person who receives it is called a 'beneficiary' (*mūṣan lah*).

c. To appoint a person to manage the affairs of his young children, called a 'custodian' (*qayyim*).

2. A will should be made via an explicit statement indicating its content, or by a signal which conveys the meaning in a clear or apparent way. The latter suffices, even in cases where the testator is still able to speak.
3. It is also valid to record a will in writing. If a person's written will is found after their death, and there are some contextual indicators that give confidence that it is the product of the decedent (such as bearing his signature, or the testimony of witnesses, or having been authenticated by a notary, etc.) then it is effective and must be executed within the bounds of Islamic law.
4. The strongest opinion is that the executor (*waṣī*) and beneficiary (*muwṣan lah*) need not formally accept the will (*waṣiyya*) in order for it to be valid. Yes, the other party in a testament (the beneficiary) has the right to reject it, and if he does so then it becomes meaningless, but if he does not reject it then it is effective.
5. A person's property remains his so long as he is alive and he has the right to dispose of it in its entirety as he pleases, within the framework of the *sharīʿa*. As for after his death, he has the right to dispose of only one third of his property as he sees fit, outside of obligatory dues.
6. A person's management of his property while ill on his death bed is effective without any dispute, whether this concerns a third or more of his property, and whether his management of the property included making donations or giving gifts, or commercial exchanges.
7. If a person makes a financial testament which is obligatory upon him, like a will to perform the *ḥajj*, then the costs must be extracted from the original estate, even if he does not specify it elsewhere in the will. This is unless he makes a testament to have it extracted from the third [of which he can freely dispose], in which case his testament should be enacted as written.
8. And as for non-obligatory financial testaments, such as a testament to do good and righteous deeds, or make a gift of some property to certain people or institutions: so long as the costs of all these testaments are equal to or less than a third of his estate, then they are valid and effective. On the other hand, if they are more than one third of his estate, and his inheritors permit the excess to be subtracted from the remainder, then all of his testaments are likewise valid. But if the inheritors refuse this, then his testaments are effective for anything up to one third of his estate, and invalid for anything in excess.
9. Testaments that contravene Islamic law are automatically invalid. If one leaves a testament that his inheritance must be divided up as he sees fit

(as opposed to the Islamically correct method of division), or he leaves all of it to a single inheritor while disowning all others from their legitimate shares, then the testament is null and void.

The testator (*mūṣī*)

10. In order for his testament to be valid, the testator must be endowed with the following qualifications:
    a. The general legal qualifications for entering into a contract, such as legal maturity, soundness of mind, intent, and freedom of choice.
    b. The testament of a child under ten years of age is not legally effective. As for a child who has attained ten years, then the strongest ruling – according to the well-known juristic opinion – is that his testament is valid if he was of sound mind, but this is only to the extent of testaments to do good and righteous deeds.
    c. A madman's will is not valid while he is insane. If, however, someone was of sound mind when they made their will only to be afflicted with madness later, then their will is not invalidated. The same applies to someone who is intoxicated: his will is not valid while he is intoxicated.
    d. As for a fiscally foolish person (*safīh*), his testaments regarding property are valid and effective so long as they accord with good sense. As for any other testament he makes, if his foolishness does not customarily render his day-to-day transactions ineffective, then these too are effective.
    e. The person must not be committing suicide. If someone tries to take their own life sinfully, and then makes a will before their die, their will is legally ineffective. However, martyrdom operations do not fall under this category.
11. And the executor (*waṣī*) must be endowed with the following qualities:
    a. Legal maturity.
    b. Sanity.
    c. Islam.
    d. Trustworthiness.
12. If the executor ceases to be qualified after the death of the testator, then the matter must be referred to the religious authority (*marja'*), who will appoint another in his place to execute the will.
13. If the executor is unable to execute the will by himself, the religious authority may appoint another person to help him.

14. If the executor betrays his responsibilities, then the religious authority is the arbitrator in this matter. He may remove the executor and appoint another in his place, or may appoint a trusted individual to supervise him, according to what the religious authority deems in the best interest of all parties.
15. The executor is protected by limited liability: he is not liable for any damage or loss that may befall the property under his control unless it was because he exceeded the bounds of his duties, neglected his responsibilities, or acted contrary to the will.
16. If the deceased has issued testaments without specifying their executor, then the matter must be referred to the religious authority, who will undertake their execution or appoint someone to do so.
17. The testator can, if he wishes, appoint an overseer to supervise the executor in carrying out his last will and testament.
18. The legal guardians of a minor are his father and paternal grandfather. If the father dies and the grandfather is alive, then he becomes the legal guardian of the minor. If a minor has no living father and or paternal grandfather, and there is no extant will from either designating guardianship of the minors, then the religious authority becomes responsible for them.
19. A father may appoint a custodian for his young children, in the case that the paternal grandfather is not present. In fact, he is obliged to do so if failing to appoint a custodian would cause their deaths or harm their future lives. Custodians of minors must be endowed with all the same prerequisites as an executor of monetary testaments.
20. If the executor appoints a custodian to perform a specific function in looking after the minors, then the latter should restrict himself to that, and in all other affairs refer to the religious authority. On the other hand, if the executor appoints him categorically without specifying any particular responsibilities, then the custodian becomes the child's legal guardian in all affairs that the deceased has left behind.
21. It is permissible to appoint multiple custodians for minors, and to appoint an overseer to supervise the care they provide.
22. A testament is not binding upon the testator, meaning he can withdraw it entirely or alter some of its details so long as he lives. He also is entitled to change the executor, overseer, custodians, and beneficiaries of his testament.

Chapter Four: Rules for Marriage and Family Life

Rules for marriage (*zawāj*)

Qur'ānic insights into the Islamic household

Anyone who ponders on the verses of the Qur'ān, especially those contained in *Sūrat al-Nūr*, will become aware (by Allah's leave) that all of the laws of the *sharīʿa* concerning the relationship between men and women are intended to lay firm foundations for a believing household (i.e., the family).

1. This lofty verse lays down the legal punishment for fornicators, in that they should be each subject to a hundred lashes without pity, as Allah says: '**As for the fornicatress and the fornicator, strike each of them a hundred lashes, and let not pity for them overcome you in Allah's law, if you believe in Allah and the Last Day, and let their punishment be witnessed by a group of the faithful.**'[887]
2. This is how the religion maintains the dignity of the family by protecting it with strong fortifications, as embodied by the prohibition on extramarital sexual relations between men and women. It could even be said that this is the foundation for all the other laws pertaining to the relation between men and women, including the prohibition on slander (*qadhf*), by which the family home is secured against wagging tongues, and given a social sanctity.
   Allah says: '**As for those who accuse honourable women and do not bring four witnesses, strike them eighty lashes, and never accept any testimony from them after that, and they are transgressors.**'[888]
3. In order to enshrine the sanctity of the family and protect it from rumourmongers, Allah forbade a husband accusing his wife of fornication, and required him to submit to the proceedings of a *liʿān* divorce (see below) instead. Equally, this purified society from using sexuality by immoral persons for political gain, and taught the Muslims the highest morality when it exposed those who spread tales of infidelity. Allah says: '**Indeed those who want indecency to spread among the faithful - there is a painful punishment for them**

[887] Sūrat al-Nūr (24):2
[888] Sūrat al-Nūr (24):4

in the world and the Hereafter, and Allah knows and you do not know.'[889]

4. And He enjoined people to respect other's homes by forbidding entry to them without first seeking permission of those within, mentioning that the wisdom behind this was that it is 'more decent' for the Muslims: **'O you who have faith! Do not enter houses other than your own until you have announced [your arrival] and greeted their occupants. That is better for you. Maybe you will take admonition. But if you do not find anyone in them, do not enter them until you are given permission, and if you are told: "Turn back," then do turn back. That is more decent for you. And Allah knows best what you do.'**[890]
5. And He commands the believing men and women to avert their gaze from what is forbidden from them to see, for that is also more decent for them: **'Tell the faithful men to cast down their looks and to guard their private parts. That is more decent for them. Allah is indeed well aware of what they do. And tell the faithful women to cast down their looks and to guard their private parts…'**[891]
From this verse, we glean that the purpose of these rulings is to protect one's private parts from fornication and cleanse its seduction from one's heart. Looking is the eye's own fornication and a snare of Satan, so averting one's gaze prevents anything more serious from happening. And perhaps this is why Allah orders the faithful to avert their gaze, which indicates – according to the apparent meaning – lowering it, and not allowing it to linger by averting it immediately.
6. Allah purified social life from sexualisation by forbidding women from making a display of themselves, and by prohibiting them from displaying their charms (save that which is apparent of them). He provides an example of this by prohibiting them from displaying their bosoms or necks, and instructing them to draw down their head coverings over their chests, while exempting them from covering up in front of their near relatives, servants, and male dependents lacking sexual desire; the wisdom behind this exception being that there is no need for covering in such instances. Children are also exempt so long as they are [at the psychological stage of

---

[889] Sūrat al-Nūr (24):19
[890] Sūrat al-Nūr (24):27-28
[891] Sūrat al-Nūr (24):30-31

development wherein they are] unaware of women's parts. Postmenopausal women are also exempt from covering so long as they do not forgo it as a way to display their beauty, and the wisdom behind this exception is that they do not expect to marry.

Allah says: '**and not to display their charms, except for what is outward, and let them draw their scarfs over their bosoms, and not display their charms except to their husbands, or their fathers, or their husband's fathers, or their sons, or their husband's sons, or their brothers, or their brothers' sons, or their sisters' sons, or their women, or their slave girls, or male dependants lacking [sexual] desire, or children uninitiated to women's parts. And let them not thump their feet to make known their hidden ornaments. Rally to Allah in repentance, O faithful, so that you may be felicitous.**'[892]

7. And He forbade men from secretly promising women that they would marry them, and only permitted men to say 'honourable words' (and honourable words means to propose marriage through the proper channels).

   Allah says: '**There is no sin upon you in what you may hint in proposing to [recently widowed] women, or what you may secretly cherish within your hearts. Allah knows that you will be thinking of them, but do not make troth with them secretly, unless you say honourable words, and do not resolve on a marriage tie until the prescribed term is complete.**'[893]

Marriage is a divine *sunna*

Islam has promoted marriage as a fundamental component of human life and classifies it as an action that is so highly recommended that it could even reach the level of an obligation. The Creator has encouraged it in many verses of the Qur'ān, discussed the wisdom behind it, and detailed some of its laws. By the same token, the Prophet ﷺ and the infallible Imams عليهم السلام have also encouraged it in many narrations.

The Qur'ān has highlighted marriage as a divine *sunna* in human existence and made it incumbent upon man to follow the path of this *sunna*, as it exists in response to the needs of the innate nature (*fiṭra*) with which man has been endowed.

---

[892] Sūrat al-Nūr (24):31

[893] Sūrat al-Baqara (2):235

Some of the positive social effects of marriage are an increase in Muslim children across the world; so in this way a married person has shared in increasing the proportion of believers in *tawḥīd* upon the earth.

It is in this vein that Imam al-Bāqir 🕮 narrates from the Prophet 🕮: 'A believer should not refrain from starting a family, for Allah will enrich him with a child that will make the earth heavy with *la ilāha ill allāh* ("there is no god but Allah").'

The scriptures affirm that marriage is a means to increase a Muslim's level of faith. Young people are constantly beset by sexual urges – powerful urges which, if left unchecked, play a harmful role in a person's life, use up his energy and talents, and lead him into immoral and destructive sexual relations. Marriage provides these young people with a moral and healthy means of satisfying and sating these urges. Not only that, but it also protects him from immorality and encourages him to direct his efforts into more positive pursuits.

In addition to the sexual needs it satisfies, marriage also fulfils the psychological need that the Qur'ān alludes to in the following verse: '**And of His signs is that He created for you mates from your own selves that you may take comfort in them, and He ordained affection and mercy between you. There are indeed signs in that for a people who reflect.**'[894]

In marriage, a person meets his emotional and spiritual need for a partner through affection, love, and familiarity.

Affection and mercy complete the edifice of the family home in that they provide bonds of stability, especially if a marriage provides righteous and blessed children who fill the house with warmth and happiness, and make both the man and woman feel a shared sense of responsibility to the family unit they both helped to build.

Rules pertaining to the gaze (*naẓr*)

The noble *sunna*:

❖ Concerning Allah Almighty's words, 'except what is apparent thereof,' Zurāra has narrated from Abū 'Abd Allah 🕮: 'The apparent adornments are *kuḥl* and rings.'[895]

---

[894] Sūrat al-Rūm (30):21
[895] *Wasā'il al-shī'a*, v. 14, p. 145, ḥ. 3

- Imam al-Ṣādiq ﷺ said: 'The first glance is for you, the second is against you and not for you, and in the third is your ruin.'[896]
- Imam al-Ṣādiq ﷺ said: 'A [Muslim] woman should not uncover herself among Jewish or Christian women, for they may describe her [hair or physique] to their husbands.'[897]
- The Commander of the Believers ﷺ said: 'Do not initiate the greeting of peace with [non-*maḥram*] women, and do not invite them to eat [with you].'[898]
- Samāʿa said: I asked Abū ʿAbd Allah ﷺ about men and women shaking hands. So he ﷺ said: 'It is unlawful for a man to shake a woman's hand unless she is unlawful for marriage: a sister, daughter, paternal aunt, maternal aunt, niece, etc. As for a woman whom it would be lawful for him to marry, he must shake her hand except from behind a garment, and he must not squeeze her hand.'[899]

Rulings:

1. It is not permitted for a man to look at a non-*maḥram* woman unless there is a necessity (*ḍarūra*), except within the well-known limits of the face and hands, and so long as he intends nothing furtive or lustful thereby.
2. It is permissible to look at *kitābī* women[900] and, in fact, all disbelieving women, Bedouin women and women from villages, so long as it is not lustful and there is no risk of something forbidden occurring. It is precaution to restrict one's gaze to what they customarily leave uncovered.
3. It is permissible for every man and woman to look at other members of the same gender so long as it is not furtive, lustful, or intended to be seductive, excluding the private parts (*ʿawra*), as only a spouse may see these and they must be covered from all others.
4. It is permissible to look and touch a member of the opposite sex in situations of necessity (*ḍarūra*), such as looking and touching for medical treatment, as long as the option to be treated by a member of the same sex is unavailable. This is permitted within the bounds of necessity only.

---

[896] *Wasāʾil al-shīʿa*, v. 14, p. 104, ḥ. 8
[897] *Wasāʾil al-shīʿa*, v. 14, p. 133, ḥ. 1
[898] *Wasāʾil al-shīʿa*, v. 14, p. 173
[899] *Wasāʾil al-shīʿa*, v. 20, p. 208, ḥ. 2 / Ḥ. 25446
[900] That is women belonging to the People of Book (*ahl al-kitāb*).

5. The religion permits looking at elderly women (*qawāʿid*)[901] to the extent that it is usual for them to reveal some of their hair, arms, etc. As for the breasts, stomach, and parts usually covered [even in front of *maḥram* relatives or in private], then they should not uncover these, nor should a man look at them. They must also not display their beauty; though, of course, beauty differs according to time and place, and custom is criterion for this.
6. One need not cover before immature children and infants, and they too can be looked at and touched. In fact, the apparent ruling is that before legal maturity they can be looked at, so long as this is not done with desire or in a way that leads to falling into something forbidden.
7. A man is allowed to hear the voice of a non-*maḥram* woman so long as he does not listen with lust or furtively, though it is recommended precaution that he does not do so anyway, save in situations of need or necessity as dictated by custom.
8. It is forbidden for a woman to cause a man (apart from her husband) to hear her voice when she makes it alluring by making it sound pleasant and soft.
9. It is impermissible to shake hands with a woman except from behind clothing, without applying pressure to her hand.
10. There is no problem with touching *maḥram*s so long as it is done without desire or potential to fall into something forbidden.
11. A man may look at a woman to whom he is proposing marriage, as he will be taking her as his partner in life, and contracting a permanent marriage with her. The same applies to a woman, in that it is not unlikely that she is allowed look at the man who is proposing to her, as she needs to know him. This accords with the prevailing wisdom recorded in the narrations of the Infallibles.
12. A man may look at a woman's face, hands, hair, and pleasant features, so long as he is likely to take her as a wife. It is obligatory precaution that he restricts himself to looking at only those women he already intends to marry. As for looking at women in order to *choose* one of them to marry, then it is obligatory precaution to refrain from this. It is also a condition that the man should not already know her, or have had her described to him in such a way that he has absolutely no need of seeing her.

---

[901] Meaning those women who are advanced in years and have no need of marriage.

13. It is unlikely that a man is allowed to look at the rest of her body save for her pleasant features, and in sheer clothing in order to know her figure. It is obligatory precaution to seek her permission before doing this, and avoid looking at her charms without her knowing. This is especially so if looking involves invading her personal modesty or peeking at her, as her pleasant features belong to her alone, and interfering with the property of others is not allowed without their permission.
14. Looking at a woman in this situation must not be done lustfully.

Women whom it is forbidden to marry

On grounds of religious differences

The noble *sunna*:

❖ Muʿāwiya b. Wahhab has narrated: I asked Abū ʿAbd Allah ﷺ whether a believing man can marry a Jewess or Christian woman? So he said: 'If he can find a Muslim woman, then what business does he have with a Jewish or Christian woman?' So I said: It may be that he has a desire for her. He said: 'If he did that, then he must forbid her from drinking wine or eating pork; and you should know that he has brought disgrace upon himself concerning his religion.'[902]

❖ Zurāra has narrated from Imam al-Bāqir ﷺ: 'There is no problem if a man wants to have a temporary marriage with a Jewish or Christian woman while he already has a wife.'[903]

Rulings:

1. A Muslim man cannot marry a polytheist woman; as for marrying *kitābī* women, such as Jews and Christians, the strongest opinion is its permissibility, though it is severely discouraged, and they must be educated in the Islamic practices of ritual purity, cleanliness, and abstains from wine, pork, etc. As for Zoroastrian women, it is obligatory precaution to avoid contracting permanent marriage with them.
2. It is not permissible to marry a *nāṣibi*[904] man or woman, but there is no problem with marrying a woman of a different Islamic legal school (*madhhab*). As for a marrying a man of an opposing legal school (i.e., a non-Twelver Shīʿa), it is a matter of precaution to abstain from it under

---

[902] *Wasāʾil al-shīʿa*, v. 14, p. 412, ḥ. 1
[903] *Wasāʾil al-shīʿa*, v. 14, p. 415, ḥ. 2
[904] Meaning someone who hates the Prophet's Household ﷺ or their followers.

ordinary circumstances, as a woman is typically influenced by her husband's religious beliefs.

On the grounds of consanguinity (*nasab*)

3. The following categories are forbidden for a man to marry on the grounds of consanguinity (kinship):
   a. Mother,
   b. Grandmother, whether paternal or maternal, and their ancestors,
   c. Daughters, granddaughters, great granddaughters, great-great granddaughters, and their descendants,
   d. Sisters, nieces and grand nieces, and their descendants,
   e. Maternal and paternal aunts, great aunts, and their ancestors.

And the male equivalents of these are forbidden for women to marry, so they cannot marry their father, maternal or paternal uncle, or sons, grandsons, brothers, nephews, and so on.

On the grounds of suckling (*riḍāʿ*)

The noble *sunna*:

❖ Imam al-Bāqir ﵇ has narrated that the Messenger of Allah ﷺ said: 'Whatever is forbidden by kinship is forbidden by suckling.'[905]

Rulings:

4. Breastfeeding (*riḍāʿ*) creates a connection between a child and his or her wet nurse, and between the child and the wet nurse's husband (the 'milk father' – *ṣāḥib al-labn*). It is like a consanguineous connection; hence the child becomes exactly like one of their own. Consequently, this connection spreads to include their relatives, according to the conditions and rules that we shall mention below. Here we will mention the most important relations which are created for the child – whether male or female – by breastfeeding, which prohibit marriage:
   a. The wet nurse and her husband (the milk father).
   b. The wet nurse's parents, her grandparents, and any of their ancestors.
   c. The wet nurse's children – whether she bore them before or after the breastfeeding – her grandchildren, and any of their descendants.

---

[905] *Wasāʾil al-shīʿa*, v. 14, p. 280, ḥ. 1

d. The wet nurse's brothers, sisters, uncles, and aunts, from both sides.
e. The wet nurse's husband's (the milk father) children from another wife, and any of their descendants.
f. The uncles and aunts of the wet nurse's husband (the milk father) and their ancestors.

On grounds of relation by marriage (*muṣāhara*)

5. A wife is forbidden from marrying her husband's father, sons, or any of the father's ancestors, or the son's descendants, whether by blood or suckling, whether she is a permanent or temporary wife, and merely by virtue of *contracting* a marriage with him, even if he has not consummated it.
6. A husband is forbidden from marrying his wife's mother and any of her ancestors by mere virtue of *contracting* a marriage with her. The same applies to any of the mother's other daughters – with the added condition that he has *consummated* his marriage – whether this daughter has grown up under his care or not; rather, even if she was born after they separated and divorced.
7. It is forbidden to marry a wife's nieces or aunts without the permission of the eldest of the two, or the satisfaction of both.

On the grounds of fornication (*zinā*)

8. Fornication which occurs after a marriage has been solemnized and consummated has no effect on the marriage's validity. If a man marries a woman and then fornicates with her mother or daughter, his wife is not forbidden to him. But if this occurs before consummation, then it is precaution for him to leave her.
9. However, if fornication occurred prior to marriage, for example with an aunt or uncle, then marriage to their daughters is forbidden; and if it occurred with anyone else, then such marriage is forbidden as a matter of precaution.

Marrying two sisters simultaneously

The noble *sunna*:

❖ It has been transmitted in *Qurb al-Isnād* from Imam al-Riḍā عليه السلام, that he was asked about a man who had a wife: is it lawful for him to engage in temporary marriage with her sister? So he عليه السلام said: 'No.'[906]

---

[906] *Wasāʾil al-shīʿa*, v. 14, p. 367, ḥ. 4

Rulings:

10. A man may not be married to two sisters at the same time, whether in a permanent or a temporary contract, and whether these are two sisters by blood or by suckling.

Marrying a woman during her waiting period (*ʿidda*)

The noble *sunna*:

❖ Al-Ḥalabī has narrated from Imam Abū ʿAbd Allah al-Ṣādiq ﷺ: 'If a man marries a woman during her waiting period and enters her then she would be forever unlawful to him, whether he knew [she was in her waiting period] or not. If he did not enter her, then she would become lawful for him [to properly wed after her waiting period] if he was ignorant [that she had been in her waiting period the first time], but not for the other [who knew that she was in her waiting period the first time but married her anyway].'[907]

Rulings:

11. A man cannot marry a woman who is in her waiting period following her previous husband, whether the marriage was permanent or temporary, and whether this waiting period is the result of divorce, death, or the end of the duration of their marriage (if it was a fixed-time marriage).
    If a man marries a woman while she is in this state, she is forever forbidden to him if they knew that this marriage was prohibited and that the woman was in her waiting period, or if even one of them was aware of this, whether he had intercourse with her or not.
    The same is true if they were both unaware of this, on the condition that the man has had intercourse with the woman.

Marrying a woman who already has a husband

12. As with marrying a woman during her waiting period, if a man marries a woman who already has a husband, she is also forever forbidden to him. If a man marries such a woman while aware that she is already married, then she is forever and categorically forbidden to him, whether he has had intercourse with her or not. As for marrying her while unaware of this fact, she is only forbidden to him (should she become single in the future) if he had intercourse with her.

---

[907] *Wasāʾil al-shīʿa*, v. 14, p. 345, ḥ. 3

Marrying while in a state of consecration (*iḥrām*)

The noble *sunna*:

❖ It has been reported from Abū ʿAbd Allah ﷺ as part of a longer narration: 'If the one in a state of consecration marries while he is aware that it is unlawful, then she will never [thereafter] be lawful to him [for marriage].'[908]

Rulings:

13. Someone in a state of consecration (*iḥrām*) cannot marry a woman, whether she is in a state of consecration or not, under any circumstances. If such a marriage is conducted with the knowledge that it is forbidden, then the woman is forever forbidden to the man, whether he had intercourse with her or not. But if the marriage is conducted while the parties are unaware of this fact, then she is not forbidden to him even if he has intercourse with her, but the contract is invalid in any case.

Marrying a fornicatress

The noble *sunna*:

❖ Zurāra said: I asked Abū ʿAbd Allah ﷺ about the words of Allah Almighty: 'The fornicator will not marry anyone but a fornicatress or an idolatress...' He ﷺ said: 'They are the women who are famous for their fornication, and the men who are famous for their fornication. They were infamous and well known for it. The people [like that] today are in that position. So if someone has had the legal punishment of fornication carried out upon them, or is infamous among [the people] for fornication, noebody should marry them until it is known that they have repented.'[909]

Rulings:

14. There is no problem in marrying a fornicatress after she has repented, whether by her partner or another person, but it is best, according to precaution, to wait until she has experienced a menstrual cycle to ensure that her womb is free from his or any other seed. As for a woman who is pregnant, there is no need for this; she can be married and intercourse may be had without delay.

---

[908] *Wasāʾil al-shīʿa*, v. 14, p. 378, ḥ. 1
[909] *Wasāʾil al-shīʿa*, v. 14, p. 335, ḥ. 2

15. If a man fornicates with a married woman, whether she is married permanently or temporarily, then she is forbidden to him forever as a matter of precaution, although the strongest opinion is that there is no such prohibition. The same ruling applies to fornication with a woman during the waiting period after a divorce, during which she can return to her husband. In this situation, precaution demands that he cannot marry her after she is separated from her husband, whether by divorce, death or the expiration of their marriage contract.

On the grounds of sodomy

The noble *sunna*:

❖ Imam al-Ṣādiq 🕮 said, concerning a man who molests boys: 'If he penetrated him then his daughter and sister become unlawful to him.'[910]

Rulings:

16. If one man sodomizes another, even if entry was only partial, he is forbidden from marrying the latter's mother or any of her ancestors, his daughter and any of her descendants, or his sister. It makes no difference whether the passive party is an adult or child, and the same applies – as a matter of precaution – even if the active party is a child, even though the strongest opinion is that he is not forbidden.

17. It is a matter of precaution that the mother, daughter, and sister of the passive party are forbidden to the active one, even if the sodomy took place after he has married one of them, especially if he divorces her and wants to remarry her afresh.

The marriage contract

The noble *sunna*:

❖ It is narrated from Imam al-Bāqir 🕮: 'A woman came to the Prophet 🕮, and said: Marry me [to someone]. So he said: "Who will have this woman?" So a man stood up and said: I will, O Messenger of Allah. He said: "What will you give her [for the dowry]?" He said: I own nothing... So he said: "Are you good at reciting anything from the Qur'ān?" He said: Yes. He 🕮 said: "The two of you are married upon [the dowry] that he recites something from the Qur'ān and he teaches it to her."'[911]

---

[910] *Wasā'il al-shīʿa*, v. 14, p. 339, ḥ. 1

[911] *Wasā'il al-shīʿa*, v. 14, p. 195, ḥ. 3

The essence of a marriage contract (*ʿaqd al-nikāḥ*)

1. The essence of a marriage contract is an agreement by two persons to live together in a shared existence, by which the woman becomes lawful to the man. This agreement consists of an offer from the woman or her representative and the acceptance of the man or his representative.
2. It is always the bride or her representative who initiates the offer of marriage, and this offer must include the word marriage (*nikāḥ*) wedlock (*tazwīj*), although the word *mutʿa* also suffices [even for a permanent marriage] so long as something is mentioned which indicates the intention of the marriage's permanence.
3. A marriage should always be solemnized in Arabic whenever possible, even if this means appointing someone to recite the words, as a matter of recommended precaution. Otherwise, any language will suffice so long as the meaning of marriage and wedlock is conveyed.
4. If the bride and groom are reciting the contract themselves, the woman says: 'I wed myself to you for the specified dowry' (*zawwajtuka nafsī ʿalā aṣ-ṣadāq al-maʿlūm*), or 'I marry myself to you...' (*ankaḥtuka nafsī...*), or 'I give myself to you...' (*mattaʿtuka nafsī...*) to which the man responds immediately: 'I accept the wedding/marriage/giving' (*qabiltu al-tazwīj/an-nikāh/al-mutʿa*).
5. If it is the representatives of the bride and groom are reciting the contract, then the bride's representative says to the husband's: 'I marry/wed/give my patron, [bride's name], to your patron, [groom's name], for the specified dowry.' (*zawwajtu/ankahtu/mattaʿtu muwakkilatī* [bride's name] *muwakkilaka* [groom's name] *ʿalā aṣ-ṣadāq al-maʿlūm*), to which the husband's representative replies immediately: 'I accept, on behalf of my patron, [groom's name], the marriage/wedding/giving' (*qabiltu li muwakkilī* [groom's name] *al-tazwīj/an-nikāḥ/al-tamattuʿ*).
6. It suffices for someone who is mute to communicate the offer and acceptance through making signs, or through any means that indicates an agreement, such as writing or using a stamp, so long as that would customarily be seen as demonstrating the solemnization of a contract.
7. Whoever recites the marriage contract must be endowed with the basic legal qualifications to enter into a contract, such as legal maturity and soundness of mind, whether he is reciting it for himself or another, whether as a representative (*wakīl*) or a legal guardian (*walī*).

Legal guardians for a marriage contract

The noble *sunna*:

❖ It has been narrated from Abū Jaʿfar al-Bāqir 🕮: 'The woman who is financially independent and not [fiscally] foolish, who has no master over her, can be married without the permission of a guardian.'[912]

❖ Imam Abū ʿAbd Allah al-Ṣādiq 🕮 said: 'The virgin [girl] who has a father cannot marry without his permission.'[913]

❖ It has been narrated from Abū al-Ḥasan 🕮: 'Concerning the virgin woman, her consent [to marry] is her silence (i.e., she does not object to the partner); for the non-virgin, her affair is her own.'[914]

Rulings:

8. The legal guardians for a marriage contract (*awliyāʾ al-ʿaqd*) are the father and paternal grandfather, and so on up the patrilineal line, meaning that the father's maternal grandfather is never included.

9. Legal guardianship is established for the father and grandfather in the case of minors, or a madman whose madness began at the age of legal maturity, or even one whose madness did not, according to the strongest opinion. But they have no guardianship over a mature adult male, or a mature adult woman who is no longer a virgin and has been previously married.

10. As for an adult virgin woman, precaution should not be abandoned by failing to seek her guardian's permission before marrying, even though the strongest opinion is that she can contract her own marriage if she is independent and practically no longer under his guardianship. His permission is not needed if he is absent such that his permission cannot be sought, if she needs to get married.

11. If a guardian's refusal to allow a virgin to marry will cause her serious harm, or contribute to social corruption, or cause her unbearable hardship, then his guardianship is nullified and she can marry immediately without his permission. But if she is not intellectually mature, then she becomes a ward of the religious authority (the *marjaʿ*).

---

[912] *Wasāʾil al-shīʿa*, v. 14, p. 201, ḥ. 1
[913] *Wasāʾil al-shīʿa*, v. 14, p. 205, ḥ. 2
[914] *Wasāʾil al-shīʿa*, v. 14, p. 206, ḥ. 1

Rules for the dowry (*mahr*)

The noble *sunna*:

❖ Al-Fuḍayl b. Yasār has narrated from Imam al-Bāqir 🕊: 'The dowry is whatever they (the bride and groom) are both pleased with whether it is little or much.'[915]

❖ Ibn 'Awwāḍ has narrated from Abū 'Abd Allah 🕊, concerning a man who marries a woman but does not have the specified dowry with him: can he have intercourse with her? He said: 'No problem; it is only a debt that he owes her.'[916]

❖ It has been narrated that Ibn Abī Naṣr asked Abū al-Ḥasan the First, al-Kāẓim 🕊, about a man who marries off his daughter: it it for him to spend her dowry? He said: 'No, it is not his.'[917]

❖ Al-Fuḍayl b. Yāsir has narrated from Imam al-Ṣādiq 🕊 that if a man marries a woman, but does not truly intend in his heart to give her dowry to her, it is fornication (*zinā*).[918]

❖ Ḥammāda b. al-Ḥasan said: I asked Abū 'Abd Allah al-Ṣādiq 🕊 about a man who marries a woman, and one of her conditions is that he does not marry another woman alongside her, and she is satisfied with that. So Abū 'Abd Allah said: 'This is a corrupt condition (i.e., it is invalid). There is no marriage except upon [the condition] of one or two dirhams.'[919]

❖ It has been narrated from the Messenger of Allah 🕊: 'Any woman who gives [her dowry as] charity to her husband before he has intercourse with her [for the first time], so Allah writes for her, for every dinar, [the reward of] freeing a slave.' It was said: O Messenger of Allah, what if [she gives it to him] after intercourse? He said: 'That is only [counted as] love and intimacy (*al-muwadda wa al-ulfa*).'[920]

❖ Al-Ḥalabī has narrated from Imam al-Ṣādiq 🕊, concerning a man who divorces a woman prior to [first] intercourse: 'He must pay her half of the dowry if he had specified anything [material] for her, and if he had not specified anything for her, then he must give her some benefit, similar to what the women from her family would receive.'[921]

---

[915] *Wasā'il al-shī'a*, v. 15, p. 1, ḥ. 3
[916] *Wasā'il al-shī'a*, v. 15, p. 14, ḥ. 2
[917] *Wasā'il al-shī'a*, v. 15, p. 26, ḥ. 1
[918] *Wasā'il al-shī'a*, v. 15, p. 21, ḥ. 1
[919] *Wasā'il al-shī'a*, v. 15, p. 29, ḥ. 1
[920] *Wasā'il al-shī'a*, v. 15, p. 36, ḥ. 1
[921] *Wasā'il al-shī'a*, v. 15, p. 55, ḥ. 7

Rulings:

12. Anything that both partners agree upon can be a dowry for the marriage contract. The dowry can be an item (*ʿayn*), a usufruct (*manfaʿa*), or a right (*ḥaqq*)... so were someone to conclude a marriage contract and specify teaching his wife the Qurʾān or Islamic law as a dowry, it is permissible.
    There is no lower or upper limit for the dowry, though it is best that it be the dowry specified in the *sunna*, which is five hundred silver dirhams.[922] If the husband wishes to augment this, then it is best that he gives it as a gift.
13. The wife becomes entitled to her dowry at the time of the marriage contract, so if it suffers loss or damage while still in her husband's possession, then he is liable. And if she finds fault with it, she can either return it or take the difference in value. Moreover, she has the right to deny herself to him until she receives the dowry in full, whether her husband is wealthy or poor. But if payment of the dowry has been deferred in the contract itself, the matter is different, and she is not allowed to do this.
14. Any conditions stipulated concerning the dowry must be observed by the consent of both parties, so if the woman is required – as a condition of the dowry – to use it to purchase furnishings for the house, then she must. But if there is no such stipulation, and this is a customary practice which both have consented to [simply] by participating in the marriage contract on the basis of custom, then she must also do this because it is an implicit stipulation. Of course, if the couple stipulate something that contravenes the Book of Allah or the *sunna* of His Messenger, like stipulating that he can never marry a second wife, or that he will not treat her equally with her co-wives, then that condition is void but the marriage contract and its dowry are still valid.

Rules for defects in the spouses

The noble *sunna*:

❖ Imam al-Kāẓim ﷺ was asked about a woman who has a husband, and his sanity is afflicted following marriage, or it becomes apparent that he is insane. He said: 'She may separate herself from him if she so wishes.'[923]

---

[922] One silver dirham is 4 grams of silver, so 500 = 2,000 grams of silver.
[923] *Wasāʾil al-shīʿa*, v. 14, p. 607, ḥ. 1

❖ Al-Ḥalabī has narrated in a report from the Imam 🕮, concerning a man who marries a woman, and he says that he is from such-and-such family but it is not so: 'She can dissolve their marriage,' or he said: 'She can return [to her family].'[924]

Rulings:

15. Any defect in the man which renders marital life impossible or causes unbearable hardship, confers upon his wife the right to separate from him and annul their marriage. For example:

    a. Madness (*junūn*) which reaches the level that he loses his discernment, whether it is permanent or cyclical, on the condition that it falls within the common-sense definition of madness. The same ruling applies to nervous disorders which render their sufferer unable to control his actions and make his company unbearable for his wife.

    b. Castration, impotence, or anything else that completely deprives the man of the ability to perform sexually, is grounds for his wife to annul the marriage. And included with this – according to the strongest legal opinion – is affliction with any illness that means he is categorically unable to have sexual intercourse, such as HIV/AIDS.

    c. Being sentenced to death, life imprisonment, or suffering from drug addiction and refusing to quit, all make married life unbearable for the woman, and she has the right to leave him.

    d. If she learns that her husband is sterile or that their genetics do not match (as pertains to having healthy children), is she allowed to leave him? The strongest opinion is yes, if this defect causes her unbearable difficulty.

    e. If she learns he is addicted to indecencies, or that he is afflicted with dangerous infectious diseases which she cannot avoid contracting if she lives with him, or anything that causes her genuine unbearable hardship by living with him, gives her the right to leave him.

16. It is best that any such separation is concluded after the matter has been raised with the religious authority and he has issued an explicit verdict.

---

[924] *Wasāʾil al-shīʿa*, v. 14, p. 614, ḥ. 1

Matters of deception and defects in the wife

The noble *sunna*:

- It has been narrated from Imam al-Ṣādiq ﷺ: 'A woman may be returned [to her family] for four things: vitiligo, leprosy, isanity, and *al-qarn*, which is *al-ʿafal* (an outgrowth or kind of swelling in the vagina which prevents or hinders intercourse and pregnancy)—if he did not [yet] have intercourse with her; if he did, then no [she is not returned].'[925]
- Abū ʿUbayda has narrated from Abū Jaʿfar al-Bāqir ﷺ: 'If there was deception because of *ʿafal*, vitiligo, madness, or [a particular kind of ailment which affects the bowels], the one with the apparent disability is returned to her family without [pronouncing] divorce.'[926]
- Muḥammad b. Muslim has narrated from Abū Jaʿfar al-Bāqir ﷺ: 'Returned are those [afflicted with] blindness, vitiligo, leprosy, and lameness.'[927]

Rulings:

17. If a man marries a woman on the basis of her being healthy, only for him to her discover that she is insane, suffers from leprosy, physical disability or deformity, or a chronic illness (whether it is visible or not), then he has the right to annul the contract if he does not accept her with her condition; but if he accepts her [after learning of it], then he loses this option.
18. If the two parties consent to the marriage contract based on stipulations, whether explicitly or implicitly known, and the man or woman changes what they agreed upon, the other party has the right to void the contract.
19. If it is stipulated that the woman is a virgin while she is not, or that she is young while she is actually old, or that she is a *sayyida* (from the lineage of the prophetic household) while she is not, or any other attributes that matter to a person, then the husband has the right to annul the contract.
20. If a man claims he is an engineer or a businessman, when he is actually a labourer or an employee, or he claims that he is unmarried while he already has a wife, or that he is from a certain country or tribe while he

---

[925] *Wasāʾil al-shīʿa*, v. 14, p. 592, ḥ. 1
[926] *Wasāʾil al-shīʿa*, v. 14, p. 593, ḥ. 5
[927] *Wasāʾil al-shīʿa*, v. 14, p. 594, ḥ. 7

is not, then his wife has the right to annul the marriage if she had consented to it on the basis of these attributes being disclosed to her.

21. The husband only has the right to annul the marriage on the basis of defects in his wife that we mentioned above if they existed before it was solemnized. As for defects that appear after the marriage has been consummated, or after it has been solemnized but before it is consummated, this does not give him the right to annul the marriage, but his right to divorce remains.

Maintenance (*nafaqa*)

The noble *sunna*:

❖ Abū Baṣīr has narrated from Imam al-Bāqir عليه السلام: 'Whoever has a wife and does not clothe her with what conceals her private parts, and feed her so that she keeps up her strength, it is a right upon the Imam that he separates them.'[928]

❖ Imam al-Ṣādiq عليه السلام has narrated from the Messenger of Allah ﷺ: 'Whichever woman leaves her house without the permission of her husband is owed no maintenance until she returns.'[929]

❖ Ibn Sinān has narrate from Imam al-Ṣādiq عليه السلام, concerning a man who divorces his wife while she is pregnant: 'Her waiting period is until she gives birth, and he owes her maintenance until then.'[930]

❖ Zurāra has narrated from Imam al-Bāqir عليه السلام: 'The woman who has been divorced for the third time is not owed maintenance by her husband; that is only for the woman whose husband can return to her.'[931]

Rulings:

22. It is obligatory to provide maintenance (*nafaqa*) for a wife who is not disobedient, and for divorcees still within their waiting period and able to return to their husbands, and for divorcees who are pregnant by their husband. The amount of maintenance a wife is entitled is determined by her social position (i.e., the living standard to which she is accustomed), so a woman of a wealthy background differs from a woman from a poor one, and the daughter of an important person differs from others. The criterion in all of this is custom (*ʿurf*).

---

[928] *Wasāʾil al-shīʿa*, v. 15, p. 223, ḥ. 2

[929] *Wasāʾil al-shīʿa*, v. 15, p. 220, ch. 6, ḥ. 1

[930] *Wasāʾil al-shīʿa*, v. 15, p. 220, ch. 7, ḥ. 1

[931] *Wasāʾil al-shīʿa*, v. 15, p. 232, ḥ. 2

23. A man is the maintainer of the household; he is the one who determines its maintenance based on the interests of the family, such as their place of residence, the nature of the residence, the kind of food, clothes, times of travel, etc. But it is best that he consults his wife and children in these matters, and he is not allowed to treat his family improperly.
24. The duty to pay maintenance is contingent upon acknowledging the husband's authority, so if a wife is disobedient, she is not entitled to maintenance (e.g., if she travels without his permission on an unnecessary journey).

The manners of spending according to the *sunna*

The manners of expenditure as detailed in the *sunna* give man the wisdom to help him manage the economics of his household, and we shall consider a few of these for our benefit:

1. It is recommended to be satisfied with a little and suffice oneself with it.
2. It is recommended for a person's life to be frugal.
3. It is recommended to have an intention when spending on one's family and avoid stinginess and waste.
4. It is recommended to be generous with one's dependents.
5. It is obligatory for a person to spend money on his dependents until their needs are met; this is why spending on one's family comes before voluntary acts of charity until their needs are met.
6. A person must not, fearing poverty, become afflicted by stinginess.
7. It is recommended that a person spend money every day, even if it is only a single dirham!
8. It is recommended for a Muslim to keep ties with his relatives by spending money on them.

Rules for temporary marriage (*mutʿa*)

The noble *sunna*:

❖ Bakr b. Muḥammad has narrated that he asked Imam al-Ṣādiq ﷺ about temporary marriage, so he said: 'I hate for a Muslim man to depart this world while there remains some characteristic from among those of the Messenger of Allah that he did not practice.'[932]

[932] *Wasāʾil al-shīʿa*, v. 14, p. 442, ḥ. 1

- It is narrated that Imam al-Bāqir ﷺ said: 'The pleasure of the believer is in three things: temporary marriage with women, spreading joy to his brothers, and praying at night.'[933]
- It is narrated that Imam al-Ṣādiq ﷺ said: 'Temporary marriage is a recommended act for men, and I dislike it for a man to depart from this world until he performs temporary marriage even if only once.'[934]

Introduction

Allah says: '**and married women excepting your slave-women. This is Allah's ordinance for you. As to others than these, it is lawful for you to seek [union with them] with your wealth, in wedlock, not in license. For the enjoyment you have had from them thereby, give them their dowries, by way of settlement, and there is no sin upon you in what you may agree upon after the settlement. Indeed Allah is All-knowing, All-wise.**'[935]

Allah's religion is a religion of human nature, and the enjoyment of desires is a part of human nature. Sexual desire is a human instinct like any other, and the religion of Islam has provided the proper means of satisfying it – including permanent and temporary marriage – while, at the same time, forbidding indecency, taking paramours, homosexuality, and any other illegitimate means of satisfying this desire. Allah says: '**but whoever seeks beyond that - it is they who are the transgressors.**'[936]

Contracting a temporary marriage is an arrangement to satisfy sexual desire within the framework of the Islam, under the supervision of the society and law, and through a solemn agreement, in which both parties must observe specific legal provisions, as well as whatever additional stipulations they might agree upon.

In this sense, it differs completely from indecency, which is merely a sexual act without any obligation to observe any duties that devolve from it, the most important of which is the responsibility for any resulting offspring.

By the same token, taking paramours (relationships between young boys and girls which usually take place in private and secretly) differs fundamentally from temporary marriage, because a paramour is not under the same legal protections that society confers upon a temporary wife, nor do both parties agree

---

[933] *Wasā'il al-shīʿa*, v. 14, p. 442, ḥ. 6
[934] *Wasā'il al-shīʿa*, v. 14, p. 443, ḥ. 10
[935] Sūrat al-Nisā' (4):24
[936] Sūrat al-Maʿārij (70):31

to abide by certain rules, like any other kind of friendship. And this is why such a relationship is rejected in matters of sexuality, as this leads to serious corruption in society.

Sexual desire is one of the strongest human instincts, and Allah has made it like this to strengthen the bonds of commitment between a man and a woman, and to guarantee their continued cooperation in building a family and facing the challenges of life, in order to be the fundamental building block in the edifice of society. If this desire is allowed to run amok, free from any legal restrictions or any social obligations, then it will not help strengthen these essential bonds; instead it will have the opposite effect, and cause the foundation of the family to crack and crumble.

Having a girlfriend – like indecency – is not a legally recognized relationship, while marriage – whether temporary or permanent – is an agreement between two persons that is recognized by both the [divine] law and the society.

The contract of temporary marriage

The noble *sunna*:

- Abān b. Taghlib said: I said to Abū ʿAbd Allah Imam al-Ṣādiq ﷺ: What expression is said to her [for temporary marriage]? He said: 'You say: I marry you temporarily according to the Book of Allah and the *sunna* of His Prophet, [and] there is no inheritance and nothing inherited, [for] such-and-such [number of] days, [or] if you wished, for such-and-such [number of] years, by such-and-such dirhams, and you specify the renumeration by which you are both satisfied, whether it is little or much. So when she says yes, I am satisfied [with that], then she is your wife, and you are the closest of people to her.'[937]

Rulings:

1. The essence of temporary marriage (*nikāḥ al-mutʿa*) is an agreement between a man and a woman to marry for a fixed period of time and for a specified dowry. The jurists have stated the proviso that this agreement must be expressed in clear words, such as the woman saying: 'I marry/give/wed myself to you...'
   Likewise, the man's acceptance must be given with a clear, unequivocal statement which expresses his consent to what the woman has said regarding the agreement, the duration, and the dowry.

---

[937] *Wasāʾil al-shīʿa*, v. 14, p. 466, ḥ. 1

The most correct legal opinion is that it is sufficient to demonstrate the agreement (which, in reality, is a solemn pledge by both parties) through any clear expression, whether it uses a particular form (such as the past tense, which is best, or the future tense), whether it is in Arabic or another language, and whether the Arabic is pronounced properly or not, so long as the agreement is expressed. Even writing and signing a document or something similar to this is sufficient, even if the most cautious course of action is to use speech to convey its meaning.

2. If the words are uttered unintentionally (as a slip of the tongue, for example), or the speaker is joking, or unaware of what they are saying, or compelled to say it, then their words have no effect, because the basis of marriage is a decision in one's heart and a sincere desire to fulfil the agreement.

    If either party knows that the other is insincere in the agreement, and is only searching for pleasure or money with no intention of adhering to the spirit of the contract, then this is not an agreement of temporary marriage.

    So if a man encounters a sinful woman and asks her for temporary marriage, and she accepts only to move things along, without actually believing in the marriage, and the man is aware of this fact, then this is not considered a contract of temporary marriage, because the spirit of a contract is the intention of both parties to adhere to it.

    The same applies if a woman knows that the man's only intention is not to adhere to the provisos of the agreement or its corollaries, but only to satisfy his sexual appetites, then there is a question about the validity of such an agreement.

3. If this agreement loses its customary usage, then its validity is cast into doubt. For example, if someone makes this agreement with a young woman for a single hour so that he may look at her mother. However, if it would ordinarily be possible for him to marry her, then there is no problem.

4. The same applies if the woman knows about the temporary marriage agreement but does not believe in it because she is from a different Islamic legal school (which does not consider temporary marriage valid), but does it seeking money or enjoyment without intending to abide by it: contracting such a marriage is problematic. It has been mentioned in a tradition from Imam al-Riḍā 🕮: '*Mut'a* is only allowed for someone who acknowledges it; it is forbidden for someone who is ignorant of it.'

The place of temporary marriage

The noble *sunna*:

❖ In a narration from Imam al-Riḍā 🕮 concerning temporary marriage, he said: 'You should not marry but a believer or a Muslim.'[938]

❖ 'Alī b. Faḍḍāl has narrated from Imam al-Ṣādiq 🕮: 'It is not a problem for a man to enter into a temporary marriage with a Jewish or Christian woman so long as he is a freeman.'[939]

❖ And he narrated from him 🕮: 'It is not a problem for a man to enter into a temporary marriage with a Zoroastrian woman.'[940]

❖ Al-Ḥasan al-Taflīsī said: I asked Imam al-Riḍā 🕮 about contracting temporary marriage with a Jewish or Christian woman. So he said: 'That you should perform temporary marriage with a free believing woman is dearer to me, and she is of greater sanctity than them.'[941]

❖ 'Abd Allah b. Abī Ya'fūr said: I asked Imam al-Ṣādiq 🕮 about a woman, and the man does not know her situation (i.e., if she is chaste or not). Can a man perform temporary marriage with her? So he said: 'He can test her [by suggesting that they commit fornication], and if she responds [positively] to [his suggestion of committing] immorality, then he [knows that he] should not do it (i.e., he should not contract temporary marriage with her).'[942]

❖ Al-Bazanṭī has narrated from Imam al-Riḍā 🕮: 'The virgin may not contract a temporary marriage without the permission of her father.'[943]

Rulings:

5. Temporary marriage is permitted amongst the faithful, and a believing man can contract temporary marriage with a Muslim woman from a different Islamic sect, so long as she acknowledges temporary marriage as a valid contract.

6. It is impermissible to enter into temporary marriage with a polytheist woman, nor with a *nāṣibī* woman who displays enmity towards the Prophet's Household 🕮. As for Jewish, Christian, and Zoroastrian women, it is permissible to enter into temporary marriage with them,

---

[938] *Wasā'il al-shī'a*, v. 14, p. 452, ḥ. 2

[939] *Wasā'il al-shī'a*, v. 14, p. 462, ḥ. 2

[940] *Wasā'il al-shī'a*, v. 14, p. 462, ḥ. 5

[941] *Wasā'il al-shī'a*, v. 14, p. 452, ḥ. 3

[942] *Wasā'il al-shī'a*, v. 14, p. 453, ḥ. 2

[943] *Wasā'il al-shī'a*, v. 14, p. 456, ch. 11, ḥ. 5

but the man must prevent them from drinking wine or violating other Islamic precepts.

It is impermissible to enter into a temporary marriage with anyone to whom permanent marriage is forbidden, such as women forbidden due to consanguinity, suckling, or marital bonds. Moreover, it is impermissible to marry two sisters temporarily, nor an existing wife's niece without her consent.

7. It is disliked to marry a woman who will not adhere to the stipulations of temporary marriage, and it could be forbidden if she does not acknowledge it as a valid contract. If, on the other hand, a man marries a sinful woman with the goal of protecting her from indecencies, he shall have a divine reward for that.

8. As for entering temporary marriage with a virgin, then if she is in charge of her own affairs (that is, she is living independently) the apparent ruling is that it is permitted, just as marrying her permanently. However, it is best avoided according to precaution.

9. But if a virgin's father consents, then it is permissible to enter into temporary marriage with her without any problem. However, if he has not given his consent, then it is impermissible for the man to penetrate her, according to precaution.

The dowry (*mahr*) and duration (*ajal*)

The noble *sunna*:

❖ It has been narrated from Imam al-Ṣādiq 🖤: 'There is no temporary marriage but with two things: a specified duration and a specified dowry.'[944]

❖ Imam al-Ṣādiq 🖤 said: 'If the duration is specified then it is a temporary marriage, and if the duration is not specified then it is a permanent marriage.'[945]

Rulings:

10. Both the dowry (*mahr*) and duration (*ajal*) are fundamental elements of a temporary marriage contract; a temporary marriage cannot be solemnized without both of these. The dowry must be known (specified). And if the woman diminishes the duration of the marriage, the man may request the return of a proportional sum of the dowry.

---

[944] *Wasā'il al-shī'a*, v. 14, p. 465, ḥ. 1
[945] *Wasā'il al-shī'a*, v. 14, p. 469, ḥ. 1

11. The duration must be specified such that there is no possibility of an increase or decrease therein, so if it is set in days, weeks, or years, it is valid.
    If no duration is mentioned, and the intention behind the contract was merely marriage, then this marriage becomes permanent, and if the intent was specifically temporary marriage, then the apparent ruling is that the contract [of temporary marriage] is invalid.

Rules pertaining to children and issues of separation

The noble *sunna*:

- ❖ In a narration concerning temporary marriage, Muḥammad b. Muslim said that he asked Imam al-Ṣādiq ﷵ: What if it is seen that she has become pregnant? He said: 'It is his child.'[946]
- ❖ Zurāra has narrated from Imam al-Bāqir ﷵ: 'When the duration has lapsed then there is separation without divorce.'[947]
- ❖ ʿAbd Allah b. ʿAmrū has narrated that he asked Abū ʿAbd Allah al-Ṣādiq ﷵ, in a report about temporary marriage: How [long] is the waiting period [of the woman after separation]? So he said: 'It is forty-five days or the next menses.'[948]

Rulings:

12. A man may withdraw from his temporary spouse during intercourse [prior to ejaculation]; in fact, it is recommended that he do so if he fears any resulting children will be without support, but he should specify this at the time of the contract.
13. If a temporary wife becomes pregnant, the child is attributed to him and he is not allowed to disown the child unless he is absolutely certain that it is not his, even if he has been practising withdrawal, for it is possible that his seed still reached her womb without his knowledge.
14. There is no divorce in temporary marriage, and if the man wishes to separate for her, he need only grant her the remainder of the duration [of the marriage], and she is separated from him. Should he wait until the duration expires, then she is separated from him automatically, without any need for a specific legal formula.
15. When the duration of a temporary marriage expires, or the man forgoes the remainder of the duration, and intercourse has not occurred, or the

---

[946] *Wasāʾil al-shīʿa*, v. 14, p. 488, ḥ. 1
[947] *Wasāʾil al-shīʿa*, v. 14, p. 473, ḥ. 3
[948] *Wasāʾil al-shīʿa*, v. 14, p. 474, ḥ. 4

wife is not legally mature (and hence incapable of conception), or infertile, then there is no waiting period (*ʿidda*) for her.

16. And if the wife is a fertile and legally mature, and the separation takes place after intercourse has occurred, then:
17. The waiting period of a pregnant woman is the duration of her pregnancy, just like a permanent wife.
18. The waiting period of a woman who is not pregnant and has monthly cycles is two monthly cycles, according to precaution.
19. The waiting period of a woman who is not pregnant but does not experience monthly cycles, despite being at the proper age for them, is forty-five days.
20. If the husband dies before separation (i.e., before the duration of the marriage expires or before forgoing it to his wife), then the temporary wife – so long as she is not pregnant – must observe a waiting period of four [lunar] months and ten days, like a permanent wife, and there is no difference here between a minor and an adult, or a fertile woman and an infertile one.
21. As for a woman whose husband dies while she is pregnant, then her waiting period is whichever is longer: her pregnancy or four months and ten days.

Rules for suckling (*riḍāʿ*)

Previously, we mentioned that suckling is one of the impediments for marriage between men and women. So what is the suckling that causes this, and what are its conditions?

Jurists have mentioned a number of conditions for suckling that would be classified as an impediment to the marriage of a man and a woman. These are:

Condition one: That the breast milk must follow marriage

1. The milk must come from a woman who has been married; so if an unmarried girl produces milk and suckles an infant, then this is not an impediment, nor does any relationship result from this according to the contents of the *sunna*. But it is a matter of precaution that marriage should be avoided with anyone who is a milk mother or a milk sister from this situation.
2. If a pregnant woman is divorced, then gives birth and suckles, an impediment results because this milk is from after a valid marriage.
3. If a pregnant woman is divorced, gives birth, remarries someone else, and suckles a child, then an impediment results, though the milk father is the first husband, not the second.

Condition two: The amount of suckling

1. For an impediment to result from suckling and a relationship to be produced, suckling must continue to the extent that it causes the child's flesh and blood to grow, or his bones to strengthen. This is known through an increase in his body weight, the continuation of his bone growth, the vigour of his complexion, and any of the other indicators known to wet nurses.
2. This growth must primarily result from suckling. If the child is fed other milks, then this condition is not met.
3. The Lawgiver has set two customary limits for this condition to be met, in order to make things easy for people; namely that the wet nurse must feed the child a day and a night, or fifteen consecutive feedings.
4. The following conditions also apply to suckling:
    a. It must be a complete suckling, as defined by customary usage, and this is demonstrated by the child becoming relaxed, leaving the breast, and perhaps sleeping.
    b. The breast feedings must be consecutive, so if two separate wet nurses look after him, this is insufficient even if they are both wives of the same husband.
    c. The feedings must be given directly from the breast. If the milk is removed from the breast first (for example, by a pump) and then given to the child, then the majority of jurists say that this does not produce an impediment as this is not considered a suckling.
    As for sucking the breast through a tube or the like thereof, this does not prevent an impediment from resulting, because it is considered suckling.
    d. Some have also added the proviso that the suckling must be while the wet nurse is still alive; so if the child finishes its final suckling after she passes away, this does not suffice as this is not called suckling. However, precaution should still be observed in this situation.[949]

Condition three: Suckling must take place before weaning

The suckling must be completed before the child finishes its second year. If the child is suckled after this point, then no relation or impediment results because he has already been weaned.

---

[949] Meaning that it must be assumed that (a) an impediment to marriage has been produced, but (b) no relationship of *maḥramiyya* results.

Condition four: Milk of a single husband

The husband (*faḥl*) of the woman who is breastfeeding is the crux of the rulings about suckling; the milk is considered as being his, and an impediment arises so long as there is a single husband, even if it is from several different wives. But no impediment results if there are numerous husbands, even if there is but a single woman.

The impediment arising from suckling

1. Suckling produces a relationship between the child and his wet nurse, and between him and the husband of his wet nurse (i.e. his 'milk father'), which is identical to that of consanguinity; he is like their own child. By the same token, this relation extends to their near relatives: the wet nurse's mother is his grandmother, her sister is his maternal aunt, her husband's sister is his paternal aunt, and if the child is female then she cannot marry the sons of the wet nurse or her husband, whether these are blood relations or sucking relations (as we laid out above), nor to the wet nurse's brother or her husband's brother.
2. Suckling relations cause marriage to be forbidden and looking to be permitted, but they do not produce a right to inherit, though sucking relatives should be treated kindly. If the suckled infant is an orphan without a mother, then suckling makes him a part of the family.
3. At this time, surrogate pregnancy – by which a husband's sperm and a wife's egg are implanted in the womb of another woman – has come into existence; so the child grows in the womb of a woman other than his mother. The question is: does the ruling of suckling apply to him insofar as he has been nurtured for many long months by this woman, to the extent that she is his birth mother, or is she just another woman? Precaution, and the strongest ruling, is that she is the same as a suckling mother, in which case the same rules apply. And Allah knows best.

Rules for divorce (*ṭalāq*)

Introduction

Divorce (*ṭalāq*) is the parting and separation of two spouses according to the conditions and rules of the *sharīʿa*.

Divorce, in a general sense, is permissible, but it is severely discouraged (*makrūh kirāhat^{an} shadīdat^{an}*). It has been narrated from Imam al-Ṣādiq ﵇ that Allah's Messenger ﷺ said: 'There is nothing Allah loves more than a home built by marriage, and nothing Allah despises more than a home destroyed in Islam by separation, meaning divorce.' And it has also been narrated from Imam al-Ṣādiq ﵇: 'There is nothing which Allah has permitted which He detests more than divorce, verily "Allah hates those who divorce very often and in big haste (like an epicure who keeps tasting this and that food).'"

Islam wants the bonds of marriage to remain strong between two spouses and to preserve the integrity of family.

A husband must see himself as the one responsible for looking after his family and solving any problems that may occur between himself and his wife in the best way possible, doing whatever is necessary to preserve their marital relationship.

But if relations become irreparably strained such that the problems cannot be solved between the spouses by themselves, and there is a risk of them separating, they should – according to the Qurʾān's directions – resort to the intervention of both party's relatives before thinking about divorce; so the husband's relatives send a representative and the wife's relatives send a representative, to examine together the reasons for the disagreement and the way to resolve it harmoniously. If these two reach a solution for both parties, they should try to implement it, and of course if both partners want to remain together as a family and avoid separation, they shall accept the solution and things will return to their proper course. Allah says: **'And if you fear a split between the two of them, then appoint an arbiter from his relatives and an arbiter from her relatives. If they desire reconcilement, Allah shall reconcile them. Indeed Allah is All-knowing, All-aware.'**[950]

The *sharīʿa* does not approve of divorce as a first resort, without initially exploring other options to avoid what numerous traditions call 'the most detestable of permitted things.'

If the sacred bond of marriage is tied between a man and a woman according to the rules of the *sharīʿa,* in the section on marriage, then it cannot be severed or untied except according to the specific laws and conditions laid down therein. It appears that these laws and conditions are intended to protect this bond from being severed as much as possible, and close off the routes to manipulating this sacred bond because of lusts and selfish desires.

---

[950] Sūrat al-Nisāʾ (4):35

Conditions for divorce

The noble *sunna*:

- It has been narrated from the two Imams, al-Bāqir and al-Ṣādiq ﷺ: 'There is nothing (no divorce) until the man says to the woman clearly and before two [male] just witnesses: "You are divorced;" or he says to her, "Begin your waiting period (*ʿidda*)," wishing [to indicate] divorce by that.'[951]
- Zurāra said: I asked Abū ʿAbd Allah ﷺ about a man who sends a divorce in writing to his wife, or writes to free his slave, but does not pronounce these by his tongue. He said: 'There is nothing until he speaks it by his tongue.'[952]
- Abū Baṣīr has narrated from Imam al-Ṣādiq ﷺ: 'The mute divorces by taking her headscarf, placing it upon her head, and then removing it.'[953]
- It has been narrated from Imam al-Bāqir ﷺ that he said: '... If he divorces her with a waiting period more than once, then there is nothing in addition to the one, and if he divorces her with a waiting period absent two just witnesses, then his divorce is not a divorce; and the witness of women is impermissible.'[954]
- Zurāra said: I asked one of the two (al-Bāqir or al-Ṣādiq) ﷺ about pronouncing divorce three times in one sitting. He said: 'It [only counts as] one [divorce].'[955]
- It has been narrated that Imam al-Ṣādiq ﷺ said: 'Every divorce is lawful except the divorce [pronounced by] the feebleminded, the child, the one afflicted by delirium, the insane, or the coerced.'[956]
- It has been narrated in a report from Imam al-Bāqir ﷺ: '... Even if a man pronounces divorce upon the *sunna*, and while she is not menstruating and without [having had] intercourse [since her last menses], and it is witnessed [by the requisite number of witnesses], but did not intended divorce, then that divorce is not a divorce.'[957]
- Imam ʿAlī ﷺ said: 'There is no divorce except after marriage, and no freeing [of the slave] but after possession.'[958]

---

[951] *Mustadrak al-wasāʾil*, v. 15, p. 295, Ḥ. 18292
[952] *Wasāʾil al-shīʿa*, v. 16, p. 51, ḥ. 1
[953] *Wasāʾil al-shīʿa*, v. 15, p. 301, ḥ. 5
[954] *Wasāʾil al-shīʿa*, v. 16, p. 282, ḥ. 2
[955] *Wasāʾil al-shīʿa*, v. 16, p. 311, ḥ. 2
[956] *Wasāʾil al-shīʿa*, v. 15, p. 327, ḥ. 3
[957] *Wasāʾil al-shīʿa*, v. 15, p. 285, ḥ.1 1
[958] *Wasāʾil al-shīʿa*, v. 15, p. 288, ḥ. 8

- Imam al-Ṣādiq ﷺ was asked about a man who divorces his wife while she is menstruating, so he said: 'Divorce not in accordance with the *sunna* is void.'[959]
- Imam al-Ṣādiq ﷺ said: 'If the absent husband wishes to divorce [his wife] he would leave her for a month.'[960]

Rulings:

1. The one pronouncing the divorce must be endowed with the basic legal qualities of maturity, soundness of mind, freedom of choice, and intent. Hence, divorce pronounced by a minor or a madman has no effect, nor by one who is coerced into doing so, nor by one who utters the words without really intending it, like one who is joking, not paying attention, or asleep.
   The same applies to one who is intoxicated by alcohol or hallucinating because of drug use; a divorce pronounced by such persons is invalid, nor is a divorce pronounced by anyone whose mental faculties and good judgement are impaired for any reason.
2. The wife who is being divorced must be:
   a. A permanent wife, for there is no divorce in temporary marriage.
   b. She must not be menstruating or experiencing puerperal bleeding, and her husband must be in the same region as her (this condition is for a wife with whom the marriage has been consummated but is not pregnant).
   c. That she should be free from menses and her husband should not have had intercourse with her since her last period (this condition applies to women who are not barren, legally immature, or pregnant).
3. For the divorce to be valid, the following conditions apply:

First, the divorce must be pronounced as an established expression, and not as a declarative or implicit statement. The proper formula is the word: *Ṭāliq*, in addition to something to specify the wife, whether a pronoun ('you'), a determining pronoun ('this') or a name. So for example, you might say: '*anti ṭāliq*' (you are divorced), or '*hadhihi ṭāliq*' (this [woman] is divorced), or '*fulāna ṭāliq*' (so-and-so is divorced), mentioning her name.

---

[959] *Wasāʾil al-shīʿa*, v. 15, p. 277, ḥ. 2
[960] *Wasāʾil al-shīʿa*, v. 15, p. 307, ḥ. 3

Second, the famous view among the modern jurists is that the formula must be uttered in Arabic with the aforementioned form, so long as the person is able to do that. However, this condition is not supported by available legal indicators with regards to non-Arabs. Nevertheless, it is obligatory precaution to act in accordance with the famous opinion here because of the great importance that Islam places on family affairs.

Third, the words of divorce must actually be uttered by one who is able to do so; a signal or written notice does not suffice. This is the famous view among the jurists and in accordance with obligatory precaution. However, there is a narration permitting a written divorce if it is written with intent, in the presence of witnesses, and meets all the other necessary conditions for a husband who is far from his wife.

As for someone who is unable to speak – for example, a mute – there is no problem in accepting his divorce in writing or through signals.

Fourth, the divorce must not be made contingent upon a condition being fulfilled, for example: 'If my son returns from travelling, you are divorced!' Or: 'If you leave the house without my permission, you are divorced!' Any such divorce is void.

Fifth, two persons must witness the divorce, with the proviso that they hear or see it, that they are both morally upstanding (*ʿādil*), and that they are together when they hear the formula of divorce or visually witness it. Moreover, they must both be men; women's testimony cannot be accepted in divorce, whether as sole witnesses, or witnessing alongside men.

Types of divorce

The noble *sunna*:

❖ Concerning a girl who has not experienced menses and a woman who has experienced menopause, Imam al-Ṣādiq 🕮 said: 'There is no waiting period for either of them, even if penetration occurred.'[961]

❖ And he 🕮 said: 'The *khulʿ* and *mubāraʾ* are a complete divorce and he (the ex-husband) is like any potential suitor [after it].'[962]

---

[961] *Wasāʾil al-shīʿa*, v. 15, p. 401, ḥ. 3
[962] *Wasāʾil al-shīʿa*, v. 15, p. 417, ḥ. 1

- Imam al-Ṣādiq ﷺ was asked about a man who divorces his wife before penetration occurs, and it was witnessed and known. So the Imam ﷺ said: 'She is estranged from him the instant the divorce is pronounced, and he is like any other potential suitor.'[963]
- And he ﷺ said regarding the third divorce (by the same husband): 'She will be unlawful to him [as a marriage prospect] until she [first] marries another husband other than him, and he sleeps with her.'[964]

Rulings:

4. A valid divorce, namely one which is legally effective, falls into two categories:

First: an irrevocable divorce, meaning the husband cannot return to his wife thereafter. This applies in the following situations:

i. Divorce before consummation.
ii. Divorce of a minor who has not attained legal maturity.
iii. Divorce of a barren woman.
iv. A *khulʿ* or *mubāra'a* divorce (see below).
v. The third divorce after two previous divorces and reconciliations.

Second: a revocable divorce, in which the religion gives the husband the opportunity to return to his wife during her waiting period (*ʿidda*), and this applies to every kind of divorce aside from those mentioned above as irrevocable.

5. A wife does not separate completely from her husband during a revocable divorce so long as she remains in her waiting period. She is still technically his wife and all of the rights associated with that are still in effect; she deserves full maintenance for her accommodation, clothing, and other needs. Full inheritance rights also remain should either of them die during the waiting period. The husband also cannot marry her sister, nor take a 'fifth' wife before her waiting period is finished.
6. A man who has issued his wife with a revocable divorce has no right to evict his wife from the marital home before her waiting period is finished, nor can she move out of the house – during the waiting period

---

[963] *Wasā'il al-shīʿa*, v. 15, p. 350, ḥ. 2
[964] *Wasā'il al-shīʿa*, v. 15, p. 353, ḥ. 10

– without his permission, except in cases of necessity or to discharge an urgent duty, as was the case before she was issued with a divorce.

7. 'Returning' (*rujūʿ*) means the wife returning to her husband during her waiting period. As for an irrevocable divorce, there is no option of return, nor is there any option of return after the waiting period has elapsed in a revocable divorce.
   Returning can take place either verbally, such that the husband announces his intention to remain married to his wife with any words that convey this meaning, or practically, meaning that the husband does something for his wife which indicates that he has revoked the divorce and intends to remain married to her, for example lifting her headscarf from her.

Rules pertaining to the waiting period (*ʿidda*)

8. The waiting period is the delay which must be observed by the wife in cases of divorce, death, or some other kind of legal separation. During this time, she cannot marry a new husband. As for someone who has no waiting period, she can marry as soon as she separates from her husband, whether by divorce or annulment.
9. There is no waiting for some kinds of women: a woman divorced before the marriage is consummated, and a woman who is barren due to menopause.
10. The waiting period (*ʿidda*) is divided into a number of categories, which we shall detail presently.

First: the waiting period for an ordinary divorcee

An ordinary divorcee, namely one who is not pregnant but experiences menses (i.e., she is neither a *sharʿī* minor nor postmenopausal), has a waiting period of three periods of purity from her menses: she is divorced in a condition of purity (first), then she has her first menses and becomes free of them (second), then she has her second menses and becomes free of them (third). As soon as she begins her third menses, this means she has finished her waiting period.

If a woman is at the age of menses but does not experience them for some reason, her waiting period is three [lunar] months from her divorce.

Second: The waiting period of a pregnant woman

If a pregnant woman is divorced, her waiting period is the duration of her pregnancy; if she either gives birth or miscarries, her waiting period is over. This is irrespective of whether either of these occurs shortly after the divorce – even by a matter of minutes – or after many months.

Third: The waiting period for temporary marriage

When the duration of a temporary marriage elapses, or the husband forgoes its remainder, and this is before the marriage has been consummated or postmenopausal, there is no waiting period. On the other hand, if the marriage was consummated:

Then the waiting period for a pregnant woman is like that of a permanent wife who is pregnant.

The waiting period of a woman who has menses and is not pregnant is the passage of two menses according to obligatory precaution.

The waiting period of a woman who has no menses but is at the right age for them is forty-five days.

Fourth: A widow's waiting period

If a free woman's husband dies, then she must observe a widow's waiting period (*ʿiddat al-wafāt*), whose length is four [lunar] months and ten days, if she is not pregnant. It makes no difference whether the widow is an adult or a minor, of childbearing age or not, whether she experiences menses or not, and whether she was a permanent or temporary wife.

And if she was pregnant, then her waiting period is whichever of the two durations is longer: her pregnancy or her widow's waiting period. If she gives birth before four months and ten days after her husband's death, then she must continue observing the waiting period until four months and ten days. But if her pregnancy lasts longer than this, then her waiting period lasts until she gives birth.

11. There are a number of rulings pertaining to a widow:

First, if she was in a revocable divorce, and her husband died while she was in her divorcee's waiting period, then she must begin the widow's waiting period afresh, and no consideration is given to her prior divorcee's waiting period.

Second, a widow must mourn for the duration of the waiting period, meaning that she should forgo anything that custom or tradition would deem to be beautification (*zīna*), whether on her body or clothing. However, mourning does not necessarily mean wearing black, only to forgo clothing deemed to be decorous. Wearing ordinary clothes is not considered decorous and there is no problem with it, even if they are coloured.

Moreover, personal hygiene and cleanliness is *not* considered decorous, whether keeping clean one's clothes, one's body, combing one's hair, trimming one's nails, bathing, using nice furnishings and furniture, or living in a nicely decorated home.

Third, a widow may leave her home during her waiting period to look after her affairs, especially if there is a necessity to do so, or to perform some recommended deeds, such as *ḥajj*, *ʿumra*, *ziyāra*, visiting relatives, looking after the needs of the faithful, or the like.

However, it is recommended precaution that she spend her nights in the marital home.

Fourth, the waiting period of a widow begins as soon as she is informed that her spouse has passed away and not at the moment he dies; so if she only learns of his death after months or even years have passed, she must begin her period of mourning from the moment the news reaches her.

Triple divorces

12. If a man divorces his wife three times, between which he has returned to her twice (meaning he returned to her after the first and second divorces), his wife is forbidden to him after the third divorce. But if she then marries another husband and he either divorces her or dies, the first husband is able to marry her once again, according to the conditions laid down in the detailed manual of Islamic law.

Khulʿ and *mubāraʾa* divorces

1. Divorce can be categorized according to which of a couple dislikes the other, into three types:
    a. When the husband dislikes the wife. This is a standard divorce in which the wife is entitled to half of her dowry if the marriage has not been consummated, or her entire dowry if it has. And we have mentioned its rules above.
    b. When the wife dislikes the husband and she seeks a divorce, but because the husband does not dislike her, and naturally does not wish to divorce her, she attempts to win his agreement to

divorce. She does this by forgoing some of her dowry or offering any other incentive in return for his agreement. This is called a 'taking off' (*khul'*) divorce because the wife moves to 'take off' the dress of marriage from herself by offering money to her husband.

c. When both the wife and the husband dislike each other, but the husband does not want a divorce, so the wife seeks to win a divorce by offering her husband wealth – at most forgoing her dowry – and this is a 'mutual parting' (*mubāra'a*) divorce, because the husband and the wife mutually separate from one another.

2. *Khul'* and *mubāra'a* divorces are irrevocable, and the husband cannot take his wife back during her waiting period, unless the wife takes back the property she offered her husband. If she returns to him and asks to return her property, then this divorce becomes a revocable one – if there is no other reason preventing it from being such – and the husband can return to her.
3. Both *khul'* and *mubāra'a* are a kind of divorce given in return for wealth that the wife offers her husband – as we said – but there are three differences between them:
   a. The dislike in *khul'* is only from the wife towards the husband, while in *mubāra'a* it is mutual.
   b. There is no upper limit to how much the wife can offer the husband in *khul'* to win her divorce; it is whatever both parties agree upon, whether equal to her dowry, or more or less than it. On the other hand, in *mubāra'a*, the amount offered must not exceed the dowry. In fact, it is recommended precaution for it to be less than that.
   c. For *khul'* to be valid, it is sufficient to use the word 'divorce' (*ṭalāq*) or *khul'* by itself. The husband need only say – after the offer has been made – 'I do *khul'* of you on this basis' (*khala'tuki 'alā kadhā*), or 'You are subject to *khul'* on this basis' (*anti mukhtala'a 'alā kadhā*), or even: 'You are divorced on this basis' (*anti tāliq 'alā kadhā*).

On the other hand, the matter is completely different with *mubāra'a*, as the word '*mubāra'a*' (lit. 'parting') does not unequivocally signify divorce in customary usage, so it is insufficient to use this word by itself for the divorce. In fact, it must be followed by the word *ṭalāq*, for example: 'I part from you on this basis and so you are divorced' (*bāra'tuki 'alā kadhā fa antī ṭāliq*), or using the word *ṭalāq* in some way: 'You are divorced in return for the property you have offered.' (*antī ṭāliq ʿalā mā badhaltī min al-māli*).

4. All of the rules pertaining to divorce mentioned above apply to *khulʿ* and *mubāra'a* too.
5. If the wife's dislike of the husband emanates from his abuse of her to the point where she cannot bear to live with him because of the physical, verbal, or emotional abuse she suffers at his hands, and then she gives him property to free herself from him and he divorces her, this divorce is not *khulʿ*; it is actually a revocable divorce and it is **forbidden** for him to take her money.

Rules for *ẓihār* divorces, foreswearing (*īlā'*), and mutual imprecation (*liʿān*)

First: *Ẓihār*

The noble *sunna*:

❖ Imam al-Ṣādiq ﷺ was asked about a man who says to his wife: You are to me like the back of my mother, or like her hand, or like her genitals, or like her soul, or like her ankle, would that be *ẓihār*? And would it necessitate upon him what is necessitated by one who pronounces *ẓihār*? So the Imam ﷺ said: 'The one who pronounces *ẓihār* to his wife, so he says: She is to him like the back of his mother, or like her hand, or like her leg, or like her hair, or anything from her, inteneding by that to make her unlawful for himself, he owes the expiation in all that is more or less than this. Similarly if he said: [she is to him] like some relatives, he would owe expiation.'[965]

❖ Imam al-Ṣādiq ﷺ said: 'There is no divorce unless it is intended as such, and no *ẓihār* unless it is intended as such.'[966]

Rulings:

Ẓihār was a kind of divorce in the pre-Islamic Age of Ignorance, which led to a wife forever being forbidden to her husband. It occurred when a man said to his wife: 'You are to me like my mother's rear,' whereby the husband compares his wife to his mother, who is forever forbidden to him. But the *sharīʿa* forbids *ẓihār* and instituted laws against it, as we shall explain:

1. The strongest opinion is that *ẓihār* is any expression by which a husband compares his wife to any of his female relatives, whom he

---

[965] *Wasā'il al-shīʿa*, v. 15, p. 512, ḥ. 4
[966] *Wasā'il al-shīʿa*, v. 15, p. 510, ḥ. 1

is forever forbidden from marrying, such as his mother, sister, or aunts, by saying: 'You are to me like my mother's/sister's rear/front.'

2. When *ẓihār* takes place – if it occurs in the conditions we shall mention – a man is forbidden from intercourse with his wife upon whom he has pronounced *ẓihār*, and if he wants to return to her he must offer expiation (*kaffāra*) first. The forbiddance on intercourse will not be removed except by paying expiation, and so it is most appropriate to avoid all forms of sexual enjoyment with a wife before paying this *kaffāra*.
3. *Ẓihār* does not take place merely by pronouncing the aforementioned formula; there are specific conditions that must be met:
    a. The husband must be legally mature, sane, possessing intent, and freedom of choice.
    b. Second, the husband must have consummated his marriage with the wife, and she must neither be experiencing menstruation nor puerperal bleeding; she must be in a period of purity [from both of these], in which her husband has not had intercourse with her – as we mentioned for divorce.
    c. The *ẓihār* must be pronounced in the presence of two just witnesses who actually hear its words, like in a divorce.
4. If the wife agrees to take her husband back after *ẓihār* and endures the absence of intercourse with him, then that is her choice. But if she will not endure this and wants this forbiddance brought to an end, she can raise the issue with the religious authority or his representative, such that the authority will summon her husband and present him with two choices: he must either offer expiation and return to intercourse with his wife, or he must divorce her. And if the husband does not choose one of these options, he is given three months to decide. But if the man remains unmoved after three months, the judge may have him arrested and restricted in his food and water until he chooses one of the options. The judge may not, however, put pressure on him to choose one option over the other; he must let the husband decide by himself.
5. The expiation for *ẓihār* is one of the three expiations, in their usual order of priority: the first is freeing a slave, then if he cannot do that – as one cannot today – fasting for two consecutive months, then if he cannot do that, feeding sixty poor persons. And only if he cannot do any of the above, even by borrowing money, then repentance is sufficient.

Second: Forswearing (*īlā*ʾ)

The noble *sunna*:

- Imams al-Bāqir and al-Ṣādiq ﷺ said: 'If a man vows that he will not approach his wife then he has no say and no right for four months, and there is no wrongdoing in his desisting from her during those four months. If the four months pass before he touches her, and she remains silent or is pleased [when he does once again], then he is within the law and it is permissible; while if she raises the case [with an Islamic court], then it will be said to him: either touch her or grant her divorce, and [in the latter] he has the right to return to her so long as three periods of mesnes-free time have passed. Thus, this is the *īlā*ʾ that Allah Almighty revealed in His Book and the *sunna* of His Messenger ﷺ.[967]

Rulings:

1. In Arabic, *īlā*ʾ literally means an oath or vow. What is meant here is the husband swearing an oath that he will not have sexual intercourse with his wife. Forswearing is effected in this way under the following conditions:
   a. The wife must be a permanent wife.
   b. The marriage must have been consummated.
   c. The oath must be to forgo sexual intercourse with his wife forever, or for more than four months.
   d. The intention of the husband in swearing this oath must be to distress his wife.
2. If the husband forswears sexual intercourse with his wife without fulfilling the above criteria, then it is still an oath and subject to all the usual laws pertaining to oaths, so long as it meets the criteria for being one.
3. As an oath, forswearing (*īlā*ʾ) is ineffective unless it is sworn using one of Allah's names, or any name which is usually used for Him.
4. If the husband forswears sexual intercourse with his wife, he must offer expiation in any situation, even if he has intercourse with her after the duration of the oath has lapsed. So if he forswears intercourse with her for five months – for example – and adheres to this until five months have passed, the expiation is due from him, exactly as if he had intercourse with her before the duration lapsed.
5. If a husband pronounces such an oath and his wife decides to remain with him regardless, this is her choice. But if she refuses to accept this,

---

[967] *Wasāʾil al-shīʿa*, v. 15, p. 536, ḥ. 1

she can raise the issue with the religious authorities who will summon the husband and give him four months from the date of the complaint to have intercourse with his wife and offer expiation. And if the husband does not comply with this, the judge can compel him to choose between two options: returning to his wife and offering expiation, or divorcing her. If he refuses to comply, he must be imprisoned and restricted in his food and drink until he chooses one of them.

6. The expiation due for *īlā'* is the same as the one due for violating an oath.

Third: Mutual imprecation (*li'ān*)

The noble *sunna*:

❖ Zurāra has reported: Abū 'Abd Allah 🕮 was asked about the words of Allah Almighty, 'As for those who accuse their wives [of adultery], but have no witnesses except themselves.' So he said: 'It is the slanderer who defames his wife. If he accused her and then admits that he lied against her then he is lashed with a lashing, and his wife is returned to him. If he refuses and persists he must testify against her four times, by Allah, that he is the truthful one, and on the fifth he curses himself if he is among the liars. If she wishes to avoid punishment—and the punishment [in this case] is stoning—then she testifies four times that he is the liar, and the fifth she calls down the wrath of Allah upon herself if he is truthful. If she did not do so, then she would be stoned, but if she did it (the mutual swearing) then she has avoided capital punishment and she will never be lawful for him [in marriage again] unto Resurrection Day.'[968]

Rulings:

1. Mutual imprecation (*li'ān*) is when a husband and wife invoke *mubāhala*[969] with regards to certain matters and according to specific rules.

2. There are two situations in which mutual imprecation is used:
   a. When the husband accuses his wife of fornication.
   b. When he denies that a child born in his home belongs to him.

---

[968] *Wasā'il al-shī'a*, v. 15, p. 588, ḥ. 7

[969] *Mubāhala* occurs when two parties have competing claims and there is insufficient evidence to resolve them; each swears by Allah to be telling the truth and invokes His curse on the liar.

3. It is impermissible for a husband to accuse his wife of fornication on the basis of suspicion, doubt, hearsay, or other such things which occasion his doubt.

   On the other hand, if the husband knows with certainty that his wife has been unfaithful and accuses her, his claim cannot be accepted on the basis of his word alone. Instead, he must either present his evidence – namely, four witnesses – or the wife must confess and accept the accusation – according to the conditions mentioned in their proper place.

   If, however, there is insufficient evidence to support his claim and she does not confess to fornication, then he can be whipped for defamation should his wife wish.
4. The only option left to the husband at this point to protect himself from punishment is by initiating proceedings of mutual imprecation: if he curses his wife – according to the details we shall outline below – then this establishes his case against her, but she too can curse him, thereby warding off any punishment by denying the charges.

Denying paternity

5. A husband may not deny the paternity of a child born to him in his bed (i.e., the marital home) so long as there is the possibility of it being his child. This possibility is established by his having vaginal intercourse with his wife and within at least six months prior to the birth, and no more than the maximum duration of a pregnancy.

   And he cannot deny the paternity of a child so long as there is any chance of it belonging to him, even if his wife had fornicated in this period; in fact, he must acknowledge the child and accept it as his own.
6. But, by the same token, he cannot acknowledge the child as his own if he is absolutely certain that it is not his.
7. If a man denies his paternity without having previously acknowledged it, and it is unknown whether the child can be legally ascribed to him, then his paternity is only voided if he initiates proceedings for mutual imprecation.

Method of mutual imprecation

8. Mutual imprecation must be performed in the presence of the religious authorities or their deputy appointed for this matter.
9. The process of mutual imprecation is as follows:
   a. The man begins – after accusing his wife of fornication or denying paternity – saying: 'I bear witness by Allah that I am truthful in what I said against her character' (*ashhadu billāhi innī*

lamin aṣ-ṣādiqīn fi mā qultu min qadhfihā) or '...in denying my paternity of her child' (*...min nafi waladihā*). And he must repeat this four times. Then he says: 'May Allah's curse be upon me if I am a liar' (*la'nat ullāh 'alayya in kuntu min al-kādhibīn*).

b. Then comes the wife's turn, in which she says: 'I bear witness by Allah that he is lying in accusing me of fornication' (*ashhadu billāhi innahu lamin al-kādhibīn fi maqālatihi min ar-ramī biz-zinā*) or '...in denying his paternity of my child' (*...min nafi al-walad*). She must repeat this four times and then say: 'May Allah's wrath be upon me if he is truthful' (*ghaḍab ullāh 'alayya in kāna min as-sādiqīn*).

What follows mutual imprecation?

10. Performing mutual imprecation according to the aforementioned conditions has the following effects:
    a. The husband and wife are separated.
    b. They are forever forbidden from one another. The husband may never return to a wife whom he has cursed, even with a new marriage contract.
    These two rules apply to both kinds of mutual imprecation; whether accusing the wife of fornication or denying paternity of a child.
    c. Specifically, in cases of mutual imprecation concerning accusations of fornication, the husband is spared the punishment for defamation because of his curse, and the wife is spared the punishment for fornication because of her curse.
    d. Specifically, in cases of mutual imprecation when the father denies his paternity of a child, the relation between the man and the child is severed and the child is not attributed to him, but is still attributed to the mother if she insists that the child is his. This means that any ruling based on blood relations cease to apply, so there is no prohibited degree of marriage (*maḥramiyya*) between the child and the husband's relatives, nor do the child and the husband inherit from one another in this fashion.

Appendix I: Glossary of Selected Terms

Adhān: The call to prayer. The one who makes the call to prayer is known as the *mu'adhdhin*.

Ajal: Duration, time period.

Akhlāq: Etiquette, behavior, manners.

***ʿAdl* (or *ʿadāla*)**: Justice; one who possesses this quality is known as *ʿādil*.

ʿAqd: A contract.

***ʿAqīda* (pl. *ʿaqā'id*)**: Doctrine; particularly religious creed.

***ʿAql* (pl. *ʿuqūl*)**: In general, and particularly in a more modern context, this refers to the intellect. However, in a more traditional sense (especially in relation to our *aḥādīth* and *riwāyāt*), it is the faculty that allows us to perceive and act upon the truth of the words of the Infallibles عليهم السلام.

ʿĀriya: Borrowing.

ʿAṣr: Time, age, era, epoch; in the case of this legal manual it mainly refers to the second obligatory prayer of the afternoon.

ʿAwra: One's privacy or private parts.

ʿAzā'im: The four chapters of the Qur'ān which contain verses the recitation of which necessitates prostration. These are: *Sūrat al-Sajda* (32), *Sūra Fuṣṣilat* (41), *Sūrat al-Najm* (53), and *Sūrat al-ʿAlaq* (96).

Bāṭil: False or invalid, esp. when pertaining to the voiding of acts of worship and social contracts.

Bulūgh: Legal maturity in Islam. The one who has reached the legal age of maturity is known as being *bāligh* (m.) or *bāligha* (f.).

Dayn: Debt.

***Dhikr* (pl. *adhkār*)**: Literally 'remembrance,' in most cases it means reciting certain invocations of Allah Almighty, such as *tasbīḥ*, *tahlīl*, *taḥmīd*, etc.

Dhimmī: A legally protected non-Muslim living under an Islamic government.

Ḍimān: A pledge or guarantee to fulfill the obligation or commitment of another individual.

Ḍurūra: A situation of compulsion or dire necessity, in which certain codes of Islamic law may be temporarily suspended.

Fajr / ṣubḥ: Morning; in the context of prayer, it is the morning prayer (known as *ṣalāt al-ṣubḥ* or *ṣalāt al-fajr*).

Farsakh/parsang: A unit of distance equivalent to roughly 3.5 miles or 5.6 kilometres.

Fatwā: An Islamic legal verdict arrived at by a qualified jurist derived from his interpretation of the most compelling evidence.

Fidya: This refers to the redemption one offers who is legally excused from fasting.

Fiqh: Literally meaning 'understanding,' this nearly always refers to Islamic law and jurisprudence.

Fiṭra: Something's original nature or state. May also be used to refer to the *zakāt* that is paid on ʿĪd al-Fiṭr.

Ghusl: A ritual bath that is required under certain conditions and is on other occasions recommended.

***Ḥadīth* (pl. *aḥādīth*)**: In its most technical sense, this means the recorded speech, actions, or lack thereof, of the Messenger of Allah ﷺ, while *riwāya* is used to refer to the same kind of reports concerning his Holy Household عليهم السلام. However, in general usage *ḥadīth* typically covers both meanings.

Ḥajj: The annual pilgrimage to Mecca.

Al-Ḥākim al-sharʿī: The Islamic judge, referring in this case to the *marjaʿ al-taqlīd*.

Ḥalāl: Lawful. In this case of meat in particularly, it means that the animal has been slaughtered by a Muslim according to the requirements of Islamic law.

Ḥaqq: May mean 'right' (both in the sense of something being correct, or in something being an entitlement), 'truth,' 'reality,' etc.

Ḥaraj: Unbearable difficulty.

Ḥarām: Unlawful, forbidden.

Ḥawāla: The transference of a debt's liability.

Ḥayāt: Life, the quality of being alive.

Ḥayḍ: Menstruation.

Hiba: A gift.

***Ḥujja* (pl. *ḥujaj*)**: An irrefutable, conclusive proof, evidence, or authority.

***Ḥukm* (pl. *aḥkām*)**: A legal ruling. In technical terminology there is a slight difference between a *ḥukm* and a *fatwa*, but in general they both refer to the legal verdict of a qualified Islamic jurist.

ʿIbāda: Worship, servitude.

ʿĪd: A holiday. There are four major *ʿīds* in the Imāmī Shīʿī faith:

al-aḍḥā, *al-fiṭr*, *al-ghadīr*, and Fridays, as well as a number of minor *ʿīd*s.

ʿIdda: The woman's waiting period following divorce, expiration of *mutʿa*, or being widowed.

Iḥrām: Consecration, a state of sanctity.

Iḥtiyāṭ: Caution or precaution, which may be either obligatory or recommended in certain circumstances. The related term *al-aḥwaṭ* refers to the most cautious course of action one could take in a given situation.

Ījāb: Offering, which is one of the fundamental components of contracts and transactions.

Ijāra: Hire or leasing, which is a contract for a service or work in return for remuneration.

Ijmāʿ: Consensus; most often this refers to *scholarly* consensus. Although there has been an historic debate over its particulars, *uṣūlī* Shīʿī scholars have largely considered this to be one of four valid and binding forms of evidence taken into consideration when attempting to arrive at a verdict.

Ijtihād: Exerting all possible and valid resources to arrive at a verdict for a given legal inquiry.

Īlāʾ: Foreswearing one's wife; a kind of marital separation.

***Imām* (pl. *aʾimma*)**: In its most general sense, *imām* means 'a leader.' Thus, one who is *imām al-ṣalāt* is 'the leader of the prayer.' In a more specific sense, it refers to *the Imam*, who is the divinely appointed successor to the Messenger of Allah ﷺ.

Īmān: Faith; in a legal sense, 'to possess *īmān*' means that an individual is specifically a Twelver Shīʿa.

Iqāma: In its most common usage here, this refers to the series of statements uttered between the call to prayer and the obligatory prayer itself, which is nearly the same in contents as the *adhān*.

Iqrār: Admission, confession.

ʿIshāʾ: Twilight; in the context of this legal manual, it mainly refers to *ṣalāt al-ʿishāʾ*, which is the second evening prayer after *ṣalāt al-maghrib*.

Isrāf: Excess, extravagance, waste.

Istibrāʾ: Expelling the remaining urine in the urethra after urination.

Istiḥāḍa: Spotting.

Istiḥāla: A change of state, such as water into steam.

Istinjāʾ: Purifying the urethra and rectum after using the restroom.

Itlāf: Destruction of property.

Iṭmi'nān: Confidence, calm assurance.

I'tikāf: A ritual form of spiritual retreat and isolation.

Janāba: A state of major ritual impurity necessitating *ghusl*.

Jihād: Struggle, combat, in a number of different senses.

***Ju'āla* (or *ju'l*)**: A reward, wage, or payment.

Kafāla: Bail, in a legal sense.

Kaffāra: Expiation; a kind of legal penalty.

Kāfir (pl. kuffār)

Ka'ba: The house of Allah in Holy Mecca, which is the *qibla* of the Muslims.

Khiyār: In contracts, this refers to the element of free will and lack of compulsion.

Khul': A form of divorce in which the wife seeks to reach a mutual agreement with the husband who is reluctant to grant the divorce.

Khums: The one-fifth tax.

***Kitābī* (or *ahl al-kitāb*)**: According to most jurists this refers to someone who is either a Jew, Christian, or Zoroastrian.

Kurr: A certain volume of water that is protected, to an extent, from being rendered ritually impure. Its opposite is known as *qalīl* or 'little' water.

Li'ān: A form of mutual imprecation between a married couple that results in divorce, also known as [a form of] *mubāhala*.

Maghrib: Literally meaning 'west,' it is typically used to refer to the time for the dusk prayer (which occurs when the sun has set in the west).

Maghṣūb: Usurped; *ghaṣb* meaning 'usurpation.'

Mahr: Dowry.

Maḥram: An individual who is either one's spouse, or forbidden to an individual for marriage (by factors like kinship or suckling), such as a sibling or a parent.

Makrūh: One of the five legal categories for actions, *makrūh* means that something is lawful but discouraged.

***Marja'* (pl. *marāja'*)**: A qualified jurist who is a valid source of emulation in matters of Islamic law.

Masāqā: Plantation sharecropping.

***Masjid* (pl. *masājid*)**: A mosque; by its legal definition this is a distinct entity from an Islamic center or prayer space, with a different set obligations and prohibitions.

Mubāḥ: One of the five legal categories for actions, *mubāḥ* means that something is merely lawful, and neither encouraged nor discouraged.

Mubāhala: A formalized rite of mutual cursing in which two disputing parties each stake their claim and call for the curse of Allah to be upon the liar.

Mubāra': Mutual parting; a kind of divorce.

Muḍāraba: Investment; a combination of wealth and labor to produce goods and profit.

Mudd: A measurement equaling about 750 grams.

Mufṭirāt: Things or actions that break one's fast.

Murtadd: An apostate; further subdivided into *millī* and *fiṭrī* (one who apostatizes after having converted to the religion of Islam and one who was born into the religion and then apostatizes).

Musābiqāt: Competitions sanctioned under Islamic law (e.g., horse racing, archery, etc.).

Mustaḥabb (or mandūb): One of the five legal categories for actions, *mustaḥabb* means that something is encouraged or recommended.

Mut'a: Temporary marriage.

Muzāra'a: Sharecropping.

Nadhr (or 'ahd): A vow to perform or avoid a specific action for the sake of Allah.

Nafaqa: Maintenance owed a spouse or a woman who is still in her waiting period (*'idda*) during a divorce.

Najāsa: Ritual impurity. Something which is ritually impure is said to be *najis*, and a physical source of ritual impurity is known as *'ayn al-najāsa*.

Nasab: Consanguinity.

Nāṣib (or nāṣibī): One who opposes or bears enmity toward the Shī'a of the Holy Household 📿.

Nawāfil (or nāfila): Supererogatory (recommended) prayers performed in addition to the five daily obligatory prayers.

Naẓr: One's gaze.

Nikāḥ ('aqd al-nikāḥ): Marriage (the marriage contract).

Niyya: Intention, awareness of purpose.

Qabūl: Acceptance, particularly as it concerns legal contracts.

Qaḍā': Typically referring to compensatory prayers.

Qarḍ: A loan.

Qibla: The direction of the holy Kaʿba in Mecca.

Qirāʾa: Reading, recitation; especially as it applies to reciting the Qurʾān.

Qisṭ: Respecting the rights of others, particularly their monetary rights; to give others their fair share.

Qiyām: Standing (in prayer).

Rahn: A deposit.

***Rakʿa* (or *rukʿa*)**: A unit or cycle (of prayer).

Riḍāʿ: Suckling.

***Rukn* (pl. *arkān*)**: A pillar, such as the pillars of prayer.

Rukūʿ: Bowing (in prayer).

Ṣadaqa: Charity.

Safīh: One who is foolish with money or finances.

Sahw: Error, mistake.

***Sajda* (or *sujūd*)**: Prostration (particularly in prayer).

Sajdatay al-sahw: The two prostrations for error in the obligatory prayer.

Ṣalāt: Islamically, this refers to the prayer (i.e., in the form of the daily prayers).

***Sayyid* (f. *sayyida*)**: One who is a descendent of the Holy Prophet صلى الله عليه وآله, a Hāshimī.

Shakk: Doubt. One who suffers from persistent doubts about religious acts is known as a 'persistent doubter,' or *kathīr al-shakk*.

Sharika: Partnership (in business).

Sharīʿa: The legal code of Islam.

***Sharṭ* (pl. *shurūṭ*)**: A condition (for fulfilling something).

Shirk: Attributing partners to Allah Almighty. One who commits *shirk* is known as a *mushrik*.

Shufʿa: Preemption (in contractual arrangements).

Ṣilat al-raḥm: Family ties, which one must strive to maintain.

***Ṣiyām* (or *ṣawm*)**: Fasting.

Ṣulḥ: Settlement (in a legal or contractual sense).

***Sunna* (pl. *sunan*)**: The habits, behaviors, and manners of the Messenger of Allah and his Holy Household عليهم السلام.

Ṭāghūt: A tyrant or oppressor; a false idol.

Ṭahāra: Ritual purity. Those things that bring about a state of ritual purity are known as *muṭahhirāt*.

Tahlīl: The formula, 'There is no god but Allah' (*lā ilāha illa allāh*).

Takbīr: The formula, 'Allah is greater' (*allāhu akbar*).

Taklīf: Legal responsibility. The legal agent bearing said responsibility is known as the *mukallaf*.

Ṭalāq: Divorce.

Taqiyya: Dissimulation or concealment of the true faith; a license available to the believer under certain circumstances such as threat to life or property.

Taqlīd: The process of following the legal verdict of a particular qualified jurist. The one in *taqlīd* is known as a *muqallid*.

Taqwa: Piety, the quality of being God-fearing and in reverence and awe of the Lord.

Tasbīḥ: The formula, 'Glory be to Allah' (*subḥān allāh*).

Tashahhud: The declaration of faith; especially as it is recited in *ṣalāt*, in which one declares his or her belief in the oneness of Allah and the prophethood of His messenger, Muḥammad ﷺ.

Taslīm: 1. The sending of the greeting of peace, such as at the end of *ṣalāt*; 2. Strict and absolute submission to the will of the Messenger of Allah and the divinely-appointed Imams عليهم السلام.

Tawakkul: Reliance; particularly the quality of complete reliance upon Allah.

Tawḥīd: The doctrine of Allah's divine unity.

Tayammum: Ritual purification by earth, sand, or dust, in the absence or unavailability of ritually pure water.

Taʿqībāt: Typically referring to the optional supplications that may be recited after the obligatory daily prayers.

Umma: Nation; the Islamic global community.

ʿUmra: The lesser pilgrimage to Mecca.

ʿUrf: Customary consideration. For instance, the expression 'whatever may be called water' really means 'whatever would be *customarily considered* to be water' by most people in a given place or era. It may also be thought of (to some extent) as meaning the prevailing wisdom or common sense consideration about a thing.

Wadīʿa: A deposit (of wealth or property) for another to look after.

***Wājib* (or *farḍ*)**: One of the five legal categories for actions, *wājib* means that something is obligatory, and that the punishment of Allah is warranted for its wilful neglect.

Walāya: This is a difficult concept to easily explain, but most simply we may say that it means adherence, loyalty, proximity in relation to the Holy Household ﷺ as the divinely-appointed representatives of Allah on earth. *Walāya* is the essence of faith, for it contains all matters within it.

***Walī* (pl. *awliyā'*)**: In general, it refers to one in a position of mastership or authority; it can also refer specifically to the Holy Household (e.g., *awliyā' allāh*) ﷺ or Imam ʿAlī (e.g., *'Aliyyun walī allāh*).

Waṣiyya: In the context of this manual, executorship over a final will and testament. The executor is known as the *waṣī*.

Wikāla: Deputyship, to be a representative (*wakīl*).

Wuḍū': Minor ritual purification by water; a prerequisite for *ṣalāt*.

***Yamīn* (or *ḥilf*, *qasam*)**: Swearing an oath (by Allah).

Yaqīn: Certainty, definite knowledge.

Zakāt: A form of alms or charitable taxation.

Ẓann: Speculation, probability. Knowledge which is *ẓannī* is speculative in nature and lacks certainty.

Zawāj: Marriage; the husband is the *zawj*, the wife the *zawja*.

Ẓihār: A pre-Islamic kind of divorce that leads to the wife being forever forbidden to her husband unless he pays *kaffāra*.

Zinā: Fornication, adultery.

Zīna: Adornment, such as with cosmetics, gold, or flashy clothing.

Ẓuhr: Noontime; in the context of this manual it refers to the obligatory noontime prayer.

Appendix II: Menstruation (*ḥayḍ*) flowcharts

Ḥayḍ flowchart A:

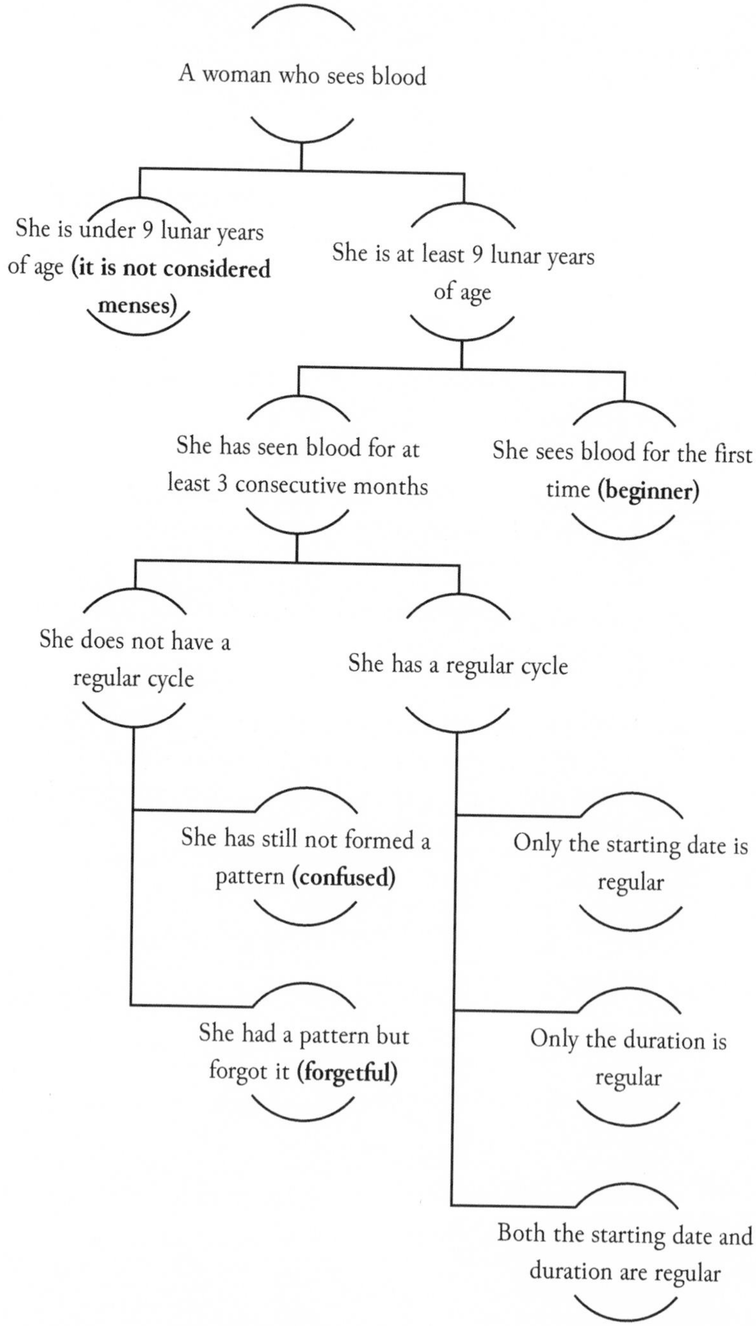

A woman who sees blood
She is under 9 lunar years of age **(it is not considered menses)**
She is at least 9 lunar years of age
She has seen blood for at least 3 consecutive months
She sees blood for the first time **(beginner)**
She does not have a regular cycle
She has a regular cycle
She has still not formed a pattern **(confused)**
She had a pattern but forgot it **(forgetful)**
Only the starting date is regular
Only the duration is regular
Both the starting date and duration are regular

Ḥayḍ flowchart B:

Other classifications of cycles

- The bleeding is irregular either in timing or duration for 2 consecutive months, while previously she had an established cycle
  - The irregularity affects both timing and duration **(confused)**
  - The irregularity affects only the duration **(the length of her cycle has changed)**
  - The irregularity affects only the timing **(the timing of her cycle has changed)**
  - The irregularity affects both the timing and duration, but the irregular start date and duration repeats itself for 2 consecutive months **(she has a new cycle both in timing and duration)**
- The bleeding is irregular either in timing or duration for 1 month and returns to normal **(her cycle is unchaged)**

Ḥayḍ flowchart C:

Situations of uncertainty

- She knows that something has come out but she does not know if the discharge is blood or not **(she must investigate)**
- She is uncertain that anything has come out of her **(she is not required to do anything)**
- She knows that she has discharged blood
  - She cannot tell if it is menses or spotting **(she must refer to what she knows about her cycle)**
  - She cannot tell if it is from an injury or menses **(she must investigate to see the blood's characteristics)**
  - She does not know if it is from menses or the hymen breaking **(she should refer to rulings regarding this in the detailed legal manual)**
  - She cannot tell if it is from the uterus or somewhere else **(the blood is still ritually impure, but there is no *ghusl* required)**

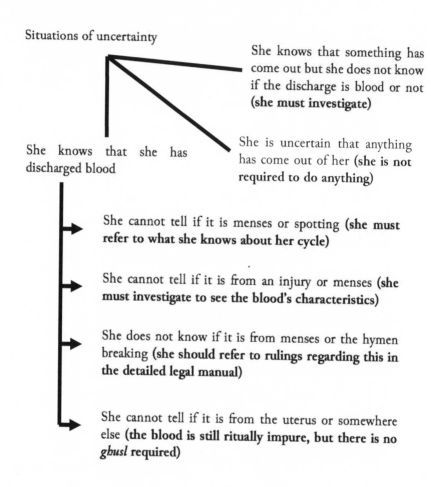

Made in the USA
Middletown, DE
29 December 2020

30255588R00286